Intermediate Financial Management

University of Wisconsin - Eau Claire
MBA 711
Select Chapters

11th Edition

Eugene F. Brigham | Phillip R. Daves

CENGAGE
Learning·

Australia • Brazil • Japan • Korea • Mexico • Singapore • Spain • United Kingdom • United States

CENGAGE
Learning

**Intermediate Financial Management:
University of Wisconsin - Eau Claire, MBA
711, Select Chapters, 11th Edition**

Senior Manager, Student Engagement:
Linda deStefano
Janey Moeller

Manager, Student Engagement:
Julie Dierig

Marketing Manager:
Rachael Kloos

Manager, Production Editorial:
Kim Fry

Manager, Intellectual Property Project Manager:
Brian Methe

Senior Manager, Production and Manufacturing:
Donna M. Brown

Manager, Production:
Terri Daley

Intermediate Financial Management, 11th Edition
Eugene F. Brigham and Phillip R. Daves

For product information and technology assistance, contact us at
Cengage Learning Customer & Sales Support, 1-800-354-9706

For permission to use material from this text or product,
submit all requests online at **cengage.com/permissions**
Further permissions questions can be emailed to
permissionrequest@cengage.com

This book contains select works from existing Cengage Learning resources and
was produced by Cengage Learning Custom Solutions for collegiate use. As such,
those adopting and/or contributing to this work are responsible for editorial
content accuracy, continuity and completeness.

Compilation © 2014Cengage Learning

ISBN-13: 978-1-305-00006-3
ISBN-10: 1-305-00006-4

WCN: 01-100-101

Cengage Learning
5191 Natorp Boulevard
Mason, Ohio 45040
USA

Cengage Learning is a leading provider of customized learning solutions with
office locations around the globe, including Singapore, the United Kingdom,
Australia, Mexico, Brazil, and Japan. Locate your local office at:
international.cengage.com/region.

Cengage Learning products are represented in Canada by Nelson Education, Ltd.
For your lifelong learning solutions, visit **www.cengage.com/custom.**
Visit our corporate website at **www.cengage.com.**

Printed in the United States of America

Brief Contents

Preface

Much has happened in finance recently. Years ago, when the body of knowledge was smaller, the fundamental principles could be covered in a one-term lecture course and then reinforced in a subsequent case course. This approach is no longer feasible. There is simply too much material to cover in one lecture course.

As the body of knowledge expanded, we and other instructors experienced increasing difficulties. Eventually, we reached these conclusions:

- The introductory course should be designed for all business students, not just for finance majors, and it should provide a broad overview of finance. Therefore, a text designed for the first course should cover key concepts but avoid confusing students by going beyond basic principles.
- Finance majors need a second course that provides not only greater depth on the core issues of valuation, capital budgeting, capital structure, cost of capital, and working capital management but also covers such special topics as mergers, multinational finance, leasing, risk management, and bankruptcy.
- This second course should also utilize cases that show how finance theory is used in practice to help make better financial decisions.

When we began teaching under the two-course structure, we tried two types of existing books, but neither worked well. First, there were books that emphasized theory, but they were unsatisfactory because students had difficulty seeing the usefulness of the theory and consequently were not motivated to learn it. Moreover, these books were of limited value in helping students deal with cases. Second, there were books designed primarily for the introductory MBA course that contained the required material, but they also contained too much introductory material. We eventually concluded that a new text was needed, one designed specifically for the second financial management course, and that led to the creation of *Intermediate Financial Management*, or *IFM* for short.

The Next Level: *Intermediate Financial Management*

In your introductory finance course you learned a number of terms and concepts. However, an intro course cannot make you "operational" in the sense of actually "doing" financial management. For one thing, introductory courses necessarily focus on individual chapters and even sections of chapters, and first-course exams generally consist of relatively simple problems plus short-answer questions. As a result, it is hard to get a good sense of how the various parts of financial management interact with one another. Second, there is not enough time in the intro course to allow students to set up and work out realistic problems, nor is there time to delve into actual cases that illustrate how finance theory is applied in practice.

Now it is time to move on. In *Intermediate Financial Management,* we first review materials that were covered in the introductory course, then take up new material. The review is absolutely essential, because no one can remember everything that was covered in the first course, yet all of the introductory material is essential for a good understanding of the more advanced material. Accordingly, we revisit topics such as the net present value (NPV) and internal rate of return (IRR) methods, but now we delve into them more deeply, considering how to streamline and automate the calculations, how to obtain the necessary data, and how errors in the data might affect the outcome. We also relate the topics covered in different chapters to one another, showing, for example, how cost of capital, capital structure, dividend policy, and capital budgeting combine forces to affect the firm's value.

Also, because spreadsheets such as *Excel,* not financial calculators, are used for most real-world calculations, students need to be proficient with spreadsheets so that they will be more marketable after graduation. Therefore, we explain how to do various types of financial analysis with *Excel.* Working with *Excel* actually has two important benefits: (1) a knowledge of *Excel* is important in the workplace and the job market, and (2) setting up spreadsheet models and analyzing the results also provide useful insights into the implications of financial decisions.

Corporate Valuation as a Unifying Theme

Management's goal is to maximize firm value. Job candidates who understand the theoretical underpinning for value maximization and have the practical skills to analyze business decisions within this context make better, more valuable employees. Our goal is to provide you with both this theoretical underpinning and a practical skill set. To this end we have developed several integrating features that will help you to keep the big picture of value maximization in mind while you are honing your analytical skills:

- Every chapter starts off with a series of integrating *Beginning of Chapter Questions* that will help you to place the material in the broader context of financial management.
- Most chapters have a valuation graphic and description that show exactly how the material relates to corporate valuation.
- Each chapter has a *Mini Case* that provides a business context for the material.
- Each chapter has an *Excel* spreadsheet *Tool Kit* that steps through all of the calculations in the chapter.
- Each chapter has a spreadsheet *Build-a-Model* that steps you through constructing an *Excel* model to work problems. We've designed these features and tools so that you'll finish your course with the skills to analyze business decisions and the understanding of how these decisions impact corporate value.

Design of the Book

Based on more than 30 years working on *Intermediate Financial Management* and teaching the advanced undergraduate financial management course, we have concluded that the book should include the following features:

- *Completeness.* Because *IFM* is designed for finance majors, it should be self-contained and suitable for reference purposes. Therefore, we specifically and purposely included (a) some material that overlaps with introductory finance texts and (b) more material than can realistically be covered in a single course. We included in Chapters 2 through 5 some fundamental materials borrowed directly from other Cengage Learning texts. If an instructor chooses to cover this material, or if an individual student feels a need to cover it on his or her own, it is available. In other chapters, we included relatively brief reviews of first-course topics. This was necessary both to put *IFM* on a stand-alone basis and to help students who have a delay between their introductory and second financial management courses get up to speed before tackling new material. This review is particularly important for working capital management and such "special topics" as mergers, lease analysis, and convertibles—all of which are often either touched on only lightly or skipped in the introductory course. Thus, the variety of topics covered in the text provides adopters with a choice of materials for the second course, and students can use materials that were not covered for reference purposes. We note, though, that instructors must be careful not to bite off more than their students can chew.

- *Theory and applications.* Financial theory is useful to financial decision makers, both for the insights it provides and for direct application in several important decision areas. However, theory can seem sterile and pointless unless its usefulness is made clear. Therefore, in *IFM*, we present theory in a decision-making context, which motivates students by showing them how theory can lead to better decisions. The combination of theory and applications also makes the text more usable as a reference for case courses as well as for real-world decision making.

- *Computer orientation.* Today, a business that does not use computers in its financial planning is about as competitive as a student who tries to take a finance exam without a financial calculator. Throughout the text we provide computer spreadsheet examples for the calculations and spreadsheet problems for the students to work. This emphasis on spreadsheets both orients students to the business environment they will face upon graduation and helps them understand key financial concepts better.

- *Global perspective.* Successful businesses know that the world's economies are rapidly converging, that business is becoming globalized, and that it is difficult to remain competitive without being a global player. Even purely domestic firms cannot escape the influence of the global economy, because international events have a significant effect on domestic interest rates and economic activity. All of this means that today's finance students—who are tomorrow's financial executives—must develop a global perspective. To this end, *IFM* also contains an entire chapter on multinational financial management. In addition, to help students "think global," we provide examples throughout the text that focus on the types of global problems companies face. Of course, we cannot make multinational finance experts out of students in a conventional corporate finance course, but we can help them recognize that insular decision making is insufficient in today's world.

Beginning of Chapter Questions

We start each chapter with several Beginning of Chapter (BOC) questions. You will be able to answer some of the questions before you even read the chapter, and you will be able to give better answers after you have read it. Other questions are harder, and you won't feel truly comfortable answering them until after they have been discussed in class. We considered putting the questions at the ends of the chapters, but we concluded that they would best serve our purposes if placed at the beginning. Here is a summary of our thinking as we wrote the questions:

- The questions indicate to you the key issues covered in the chapter and the things you should know when you complete the chapter.
- Some of the questions were designed to help you remember terms and concepts that were covered in the introductory course. Others indicate where we will be going beyond the intro course.
- You need to be able to relate different parts of financial management to one another, so some of the BOC questions were designed to get you to think about how the various chapters are related to one another. These questions tend to be harder, and they can be answered more completely after a classroom discussion.
- You also need to think about how financial concepts are applied in the real world, so some of the BOC questions focus on the application of theories to the decision process. Again, complete answers to these questions require a good bit of thought and discussion.
- Some of the BOC questions are designed to help you see how *Excel* can be used to make better financial decisions. These questions have accompanying models that provide tutorials on *Excel* functions and commands. The completed models are available on the textbook's website. Going through them will help you learn how to use *Excel* as well as give you valuable insights into the financial issues covered in the chapter. We have also provided an "*Excel* Tool Locater," which is an index of all of the *Excel* skills that the BOC models go over. This index is in the *Excel* file, *Excel Locations.xls*. Because recruiters like students who are good with *Excel*, this will also help you as you look for a good job. It will also help you succeed once you are in the workplace.

We personally have used the BOC questions in several different ways:

- In some classes we simply told students to use the BOC questions or not, as they wished. Some students did study them and retrieve the *Excel* models from the Web, but many just ignored them.
- We have also assigned selected BOC questions and then used them, along with the related *Excel* models, as the basis for some of our lectures.
- Most recently, we literally built our course around the BOC questions.[1] Here we informed students on day one that we would start each class by calling on them randomly and grading them on their answers.[2] We also informed them that our exams would be taken verbatim from the BOC questions. They complained a bit about the quizzes, but the students' course evaluations stated that the quizzes should be continued because without them they would have come to class less well prepared and hence would have learned much less than they did.
- The best way to prepare for the course as we taught it was by first reading the questions, then reading the chapter, and then writing out notes outlining answers to the questions in preparation for the oral quiz. We expected students to give complete answers to "easy" questions, but we gave them good grades if

[1]Actually, we broke our course into two segments, one where we covered selected text chapters and another where we covered cases that were related to and illustrated the text chapters. For the case portion of the course, students made presentations and discussed the cases. All of the cases required them to use *Excel*.
[2]Most of our students were graduating seniors who were interviewing for jobs. We excused them from class (and the quizzes) if they informed us by e-mail before class that they were interviewing.

they could say enough about the harder questions to demonstrate that they had thought about how to answer them. We would then discuss the harder questions in lieu of a straight lecture, going into the related *Excel* models both to explain *Excel* features and to provide insights into different issues.

- Our midterm and final exams consisted of five of the harder BOC questions, of which three had to be answered in two hours in an essay format. It took a much more complete answer to earn a good grade than would have been required on the oral quizzes. We also allowed students to use a four-page "cheat sheet" on the exams.[3] That reduced time spent trying to memorize things as opposed to understanding them. Also, students told us that making up the cheat sheets was a great way to study.

Major Changes in the Eleventh Edition

As in every revision, we updated and clarified sections throughout the text. Specifically, we also made the following changes in content:

References to, implications of, and explanations for the global economic crisis.
The text has been updated in almost every chapter to include real-world examples of the impact of the global economic crisis on financial markets and financial management. Many chapters have focused "Global Economic Crisis" boxes that discuss particularly important issues.

Updated big-picture graphics at the start of each chapter.
One of the major challenges students face in this second corporate finance course is seeing how all of the topics fit together. To aid the students' integration of the material from chapter-to-chapter and across their finance curriculum, we've included a graphic at the beginning of each chapter and in each PowerPoint show that clearly illustrates where the chapter's topics fit into the big picture.

Additional integration of the textbook and the accompanying *Excel Tool Kit* spreadsheet models for each chapter.
Many figures in the textbook are actually screen shots from the chapter's *Excel Tool Kit* model. This serves two purposes. First, it makes the analysis more transparent to the student; the student or instructor can go to the *Tool Kit* and see exactly how all of the numbers in a figure were calculated. Second, it provides an additional resource for students and instructors to use in learning *Excel*.

Significant Changes in Selected Chapters

We made many small improvements within each chapter; some of the more notable ones are discussed below.

Chapter 1: An Overview of Financial Management and the Financial Environment
We added a new box on globalization, "Columbus Was Wrong—the World Is Flat! And Hot, And Crowded," and a new box on the global economic crisis, "Say Hello to the Global Economic Crisis!" We completely rewrote the section on financial securities, including a discussion of securitization, and added a new section on the global crisis. New figures showing the national debt, trade balances, federal budget

---

[3]We did require that students make up their own "cheat sheets," and we required them to turn their sheets in with their exams so we could check for independence.

deficits, and the Case-Shiller real estate index help us better illustrate different aspects of the global crisis.

Chapter 2: Risk and Return: Part I
We added a new box on the risk that remains even for long-term investors, "What Does Risk Really Mean?" We added two additional boxes on risk, "How Risky Is a Large Portfolio of Stocks?" and "Another Kind of Risk: The Bernie Madoff Story."

Chapter 3: Risk and Return: Part II
We added a box on *The Wall Street Journal* contest between dart throwers and investors, "Skill or Luck?" We expanded our discussion of the Fama-French three-factor model and included a table showing returns of portfolios formed by sorting on size and the book-to-market ratio.

Chapter 4: Bond Valuation
We added five new boxes related to the global economic crisis: (1) "Betting With or Against the U.S. Government: The Case of Treasury Bond Credit Default Swaps," (2) "Insuring with Credit Default Swaps: Let the Buyer Beware!" (3) "U.S. Treasury Bonds Downgraded!" (4) "The Few, the Proud, the … AAA-Rated Companies!" and (5) "Are Investors Rational?" We also added a new table summarizing corporate bond default rates and annual changes in ratings.

Chapter 5: Basic Stock Valuation
We added a new box on behavioral issues, "Rational Behavior versus Animal Spirits, Herding, and Anchoring Bias." We also added a new section, "The Market Stock Price versus Intrinsic Value."

Chapter 6: Financial Options
We completely rewrote the description of the binomial option pricing model. In addition to the hedge portfolio, we also discuss replicating portfolios. We now provide the binomial formula, and we show the complete solution to the two-period model. To provide greater continuity, the company used to illustrate the binomial example is now the same company used to illustrate the Black-Scholes model. Our discussion of put options now includes the Black-Scholes put formula.

Chapter 7: Accounting for Financial Management
We added a new box on the global economic crisis that explains the problems associated with off-balance-sheet assets, "Let's Play Hide-and-Seek!" We added a new figure illustrating the uses of free cash flow. We now have two end-of-chapter spreadsheet problems, one focusing on the articulation between the income statement and statement of cash flows and one focusing on free cash flow.

Chapter 8: Analysis of Financial Statements
We added a new box on marking to market, "The Price Is Right! (Or Wrong!)," and a new box on international accounting standards, "The World Might Be Flat, but Global Accounting Is Bumpy! The Case of IFRS versus FASB." We have included discussion of the price/EBITDA ratio, gross profit margin, and operating profit margin; we also explain how to use the statement of cash flows in financial analysis.

Chapter 9: Financial Planning and Forecasting Financial Statements
It is difficult to do financial planning without using spreadsheet software, so we completely rewrote the chapter and explicitly integrated the text and the *Excel Tool Kit* model. We illustrate the ways that financial policies (i.e., dividend payout and capital structure choices) affect financial projections, including ways to ensure that balance sheets balance. The *Excel Tool Kit* model now shows a very simple way to incorporate financing feedback effects.

Chapter 10: Determining the Cost of Capital

We added a new figure to highlight the similarities and differences among capital structure weights based on book values, market values, and target values. We added a new box, "GE and Warren Buffett: The Cost of Preferred Stock." We completely rewrote our discussion of the market risk premium, which now includes the impact of stock repurchases on estimating the market risk premium. We also present data from surveys identifying the market risk premia used by CFOs and professors.

Chapter 11: Corporate Valuation and Value-Based Management

We added three new boxes. The first describes corporate governance issues at IBM, "Let's Go to Miami! IBM's 2009 Annual Meeting." The second discusses leadership at bailout recipients, "Would the U.S. Government Be an Effective Board Director?" The third discusses the 2009 proxy season, "Shareholder Reactions to the Crisis."

Chapter 12: Capital Budgeting: Decision Criteria

We reworked the numerical examples in this chapter and the next so that they represent a single, consistent company. We also added a new box, "Why NPV Is Better Than IRR."

Chapter 13: Capital Budgeting: Estimating Cash Flow and Analyzing Risk

We reworked the numerical examples in this chapter and in the previous one so they represent a single, consistent company. We also incorporated two additional decimal places in the MACRS depreciation schedules to reflect the actual rates in the federal tax tables. We now show how to use tornado diagrams in sensitivity analysis. We rewrote our discussion of Monte Carlo simulation and show how to conduct a simulation analysis without using add-ins but instead using only *Excel*'s built-in features (Data Tables and random number generators). We have included an example of replacement analysis and an example of a decision tree showing abandonment. We added a new box, "Are Bank Stress Tests Stressful Enough?"

Chapter 15: Capital Structure Decisions: Part I

We improved our discussion of recapitalizations within the context of the FCF valuation model. We added a new box, "Deleveraging," that discusses the changes in leverage many companies and individuals are making in light of the global economic crisis.

Chapter 17: Distributions to Shareholders: Dividends and Repurchases

We consolidated the coverage of stock repurchases that had been spread over two chapters and located it here. We also use the FCF valuation model to illustrate the different impacts of stock repurchases versus dividend payments. We added two new boxes. The first discusses recent dividend cuts, "Will Dividends Ever Be the Same?" and the second discusses Sun Microsystem's stock splits and recent reverse split, "Talk About a Split Personality!"

Chapter 18: Initial Public Offerings, Investment Banking, and Financial Restructuring

We added a new section on investment banking activities. We added a new box on "Investment Banks and the Global Economic Crisis."

Chapter 19: Lease Financing

A new box addresses the FASB/IASB movement to capitalize all leases, "Off-Balance Sheet Financing: Is It Going to Disappear?"

Chapter 20: Hybrid Financing: Preferred Stock, Warrants, and Convertibles

A new box discusses the use of payment-in-kind preferred stock in the merger of Dow Chemical Company and Rohm & Haas, "The Romance Had No Chemistry, but It Had a Lot of Preferred Stock!"

Chapter 21: Working Capital Management

We reorganized the chapter so that we now discuss working capital holdings and financing before discussing the cash conversion cycle. We rewrote our coverage of the cash conversion cycle to explain the general concepts and then apply them to actual financial statement data. We added three new boxes, "Some Firms Operate with Negative Working Capital!" "Your Check Isn't in the Mail," and "A Wag of the Finger or Tip of the Hat? The Colbert Report and Small Business Payment Terms." We added a new section on the cost of bank loans.

Chapter 24: Derivatives and Risk Management

We added a new box on "Value at Risk and Enterprise Risk Management." Throughout the chapter we discuss the failure of risk management during the global economic crisis.

Chapter 25: Bankruptcy, Reorganization, and Liquidation

We added a new box on personal and small business bankruptcies, "A Nation of Defaulters?"

Chapter 26: Mergers, LBOs, Divestitures, and Holding Companies

We added a section explaining how the stock-swap ratio is determined for mergers where the payment is in the form of the acquiring company's stock.

Chapter 27: Multinational Financial Management

We added two new boxes. The first is on regulating international bribery and taxation, "Greasing the Wheels of International Business." The second new box discusses the wave of foreign companies partnering with Chinese banks to provide consumer finance services, "Consumer Finance in China."

Test Bank

The instructor's test bank has been updated and revised with many new questions and problems.

Other Ways the Book Can be Used

The second corporate finance course can be taught in a variety of other ways, depending on a school's curriculum structure and the instructor's personal preferences. We have been focusing on the BOC questions and discussions, but we have used alternative formats, and all can work out very nicely. Therefore, we designed the book so that it can be flexible.

Mini Cases as a framework for lectures. We originally wrote the Mini Cases specifically for use in class. We had students read the chapter and the Mini Case, and then we systematically went through it in class to "explain" the chapter. (See the section titled "The Instructional Package" later in this Preface for a discussion of lecture aids available from Cengage Learning.) Here we use a *PowerPoint* slide show, which is provided on the Instructor's Resource CD and on the Instructors website, and which we make available to students on our own course website. Students bring a printout of the slides to class, which makes it easier to take good notes. Generally, it takes us about two hours to frame the issues with the opening questions and then go through a Mini Case, so we allocate that much time. We want to facilitate questions and class discussion, and the Mini Case format stimulates both.

The Mini Cases themselves provide case content, so it is not as necessary to use regular cases as it would be if we used lectures based entirely on text chapters. Still, we like to use a number of the free-standing cases that are available from TextChoice, Cengage Learning's online case library, at **www .textchoice2.com/casenet**, and we have teams of students present their findings in class. The presenters play the role of consultants teaching newly hired corporate staff members (the rest of the class) how to analyze a particular problem, and we as instructors play the role of "chief consultant"—normally silent but available to answer questions if the student "consultants" don't know the answers (which is rare). We use this format because it is more realistic to have students think about *how to analyze* problems than to focus on the final decision, which is really the job of corporate executives with far more experience than undergraduate students.

To ensure that nonpresenting students actually study the case, we call on them randomly before the presentation begins, we grade them on class participation, and our exams are patterned closely after the material in the cases. Therefore, nonpresenting students have an incentive to study and understand the cases and to participate when the cases are discussed in class. This format has worked well, and we have obtained excellent results with a relatively small amount of preparation time. Indeed, some of our Ph.D. students with no previous teaching experience have taught the course entirely on their own, following our outline and format, and also obtained excellent results.

An emphasis on basic material. If students have not gained a thorough understanding of the basic concepts from their earlier finance courses, instructors may want to place more emphasis on the basics and thus cover Chapters 2 through 5 in detail rather than merely as a review. We even provide a chapter (Web Chapter 28) on time value of money skills on the textbook's website for students who need an even more complete review. Then, Chapters 6 through 17 can be covered in detail, and any remaining time can be used to cover some of the other chapters. This approach gives students a sound background on the core of financial management, but it does not leave sufficient time to cover a number of interesting and important topics. However, because the book is written in a modular format, if students understand the fundamental core topics they should be able to cover the remaining chapters on their own, if and when the need arises.

A case-based course. At the other extreme, where students have an exceptionally good background, hence little need to review topics that were covered in the basic finance course, instructors can spend less time on the early chapters and concentrate on advanced topics. When we take this approach, we assign Web Chapter 29 as a quick review and then assign cases that deal with the topics covered in the early chapters. We tell students to review the other relevant chapters on their own to the extent necessary to work the cases, thus freeing up class time for the more advanced material. This approach works best with relatively mature students, including evening students with some business experience.

Comprehensive Learning Solutions

Intermediate Financial Management includes a broad range of ancillary materials designed both to enhance students' learning and to help instructors prepare for and conduct classes.

Supplemental Student Resources

Students: Access all of the below resources [except the Study Guide] by visiting **www.cengagebrain.com**, searching ISBN 9781111530266, and clicking "Access Now" under "Study Tools" to go to the student textbook companion site.

Beginning of chapter (BOC) spreadsheets. Many of the integrative questions that appear at the start of each chapter have a spreadsheet model that illustrates the topic. There is also an index of the *Excel* techniques covered in the BOC *Excel* models. This index is in the *Excel* file, *Excel Locations.xls,* and it provides a quick way to locate examples of *Excel* programming techniques

End-of-chapter Build-A-Model spreadsheet problems. In addition to the Tool Kits and Beginning of Chapter models, most chapters have a "Build a Model" spreadsheet problem. These spreadsheets contain financial data plus instructions for solving a particular problem. The model is partially completed, with headings but no formulas, so the models must literally be built. The partially completed spreadsheets for these "Build a Model" problems are on the student companion website, with the completed versions available to instructors.

Mini Case spreadsheets. These *Excel* spreadsheets do all the calculations required in the Mini Cases. They are similar to the Tool Kits for the chapter, except (a) the numbers in the examples correspond to the Mini Case rather than to the chapter per se, and (b) there are some features that make it possible to do "what-if" analyses on a real-time basis in class.

Web Chapters and Web Extensions. Web chapters provide a chapter-length discussion of specialized topics that are not of sufficient general interest to warrant inclusion in the printed version of the text. Web extensions provide additional discussion or examples pertaining to material that is in the text.

Study Guide (ISBN 9781111530273). This printed supplement outlines the key sections of each chapter, and it provides sets of questions and problems similar to those in the text, along with worked-out solutions.

Instructor Resources

Instructors: Access the above chapter resources and the following instructor ancillaries [except the ExamView Test Bank and Study Guide] by going to **login.cengage.com**, logging in with your faculty account username and password, and using ISBN 9781111530266 to search for and to add resources to your account "Bookshelf."

Unless otherwise noted, all resources and ancillaries are available on both the instructor companion site and the Instructor Resource CD (IRCD).

Instructor's Resource CD (ISBN 9781111530389). The IRCD contains electronic versions of the Instructor's Manual, Test Bank, and Study Guide in Microsoft Word® format. It also has the PPT slides and all of the student companion site spreadsheet content with applicable solutions.

- ***Instructor's Manual (ISBN 9781111530280).*** This comprehensive manual contains answers to all the Beginning of Chapter Questions, end-of-chapter questions and problems, and Mini Cases. The Instructor's Manual is also available in print format.

- **PowerPoint® slides.** Created by the authors, the PowerPoint® slides cover essential topics for each chapter. Graphs, tables, and lists are developed sequentially for your convenience and can be easily modified for your needs. There are *also* slides that are specifically based on each chapter's Mini Case and in which graphs, tables, lists, and calculations are developed sequentially.
- **Test Bank (ISBN 9781111530297).** The *Test Bank* that contains more than 1,200 class-tested questions and problems. Information regarding the topic and degree of difficulty, along with the complete solution for all numerical problems, is provided with each question. The Test Bank is also available in print format.

ExamView® Test Bank (ISBN 9781111530310). This easy-to-use, computerized test creation software contains all of the questions in the Microsoft Word® Test Bank and is compatible with Microsoft® Windows®. Add or edit questions, instructions, and answers, and select questions by previewing them on the screen, selecting them randomly, or selecting them by number. Instructors can also create and administer quizzes online, whether over the Internet, a local area network (LAN), or a wide area network (WAN). Contact your Cengage Learning representative for more information. The ExamView® Test Bank is only available as a standalone CD.

Additional Course Tools

New! Aplia for *Intermediate Financial Management.*

Engage, prepare and educate your students with this ideal online learning solution. Aplia™ Finance improves comprehension and outcomes by increasing student effort and engagement. Students stay on top of coursework with regularly scheduled homework assignments while automatic grading provides detailed, immediate feedback. Aplia™ assignments match the language, style, and structure of the text which allows your students to apply what they learn directly to homework. Find out more at **www.aplia.com/finance**.

- Grade It Now
- End-of-Chapter Problems
- Auto-Graded Problem Sets
- Preparing for Finance Tutorials
- News Analyses
- Course Management System
- Digital Textbook

CengageNOW™ for *Intermediate Financial Management.* Designed by instructors for instructors, CengageNOW™ mirrors your natural workflow and provides time-saving, performance-enhancing tools for you and your students—all in one program!

CengageNOW™ takes the best of current technology tools including online homework management; fully customizable algorithmic end-of-chapter problems and test bank; and course support materials such as online quizzing, videos, and tutorials to support your course goals and save you significant preparation and grading time!

- **Plan** student assignments with an easy online homework management component
- **Manage** your grade book with ease
- **Teach** today's student using valuable course support materials
- **Reinforce** student comprehension with Personalized Study
- **Test** with customizable algorithmic end-of-chapter problems and test bank
- **Grade** automatically for seamless, immediate results

TextChoice. More than 100 cases written by Eugene F. Brigham, Linda Klein, and Chris Buzzard are now available via TextChoice, Cengage Learning's online case library. Cases are organized in a database that allows instructors to select individual cases or to create customized casebooks. Most cases have optional spreadsheet models that reduce number crunching, which allows more time for students to consider conceptual issues. The models also show students how computers can be used to make better financial decisions. Cases that we have found particularly useful for the different chapters are listed in the end-of-chapter references. The cases, case solutions, and spreadsheet models can be previewed and ordered by professors at **www.textchoice2.com/casenet**.

Cengage Learning Custom Solutions. Whether you need print, digital, or hybrid course materials, Cengage Learning Custom Solutions can help you create your perfect learning solution. Draw from Cengage Learning's extensive library of texts and collections, add or create your own original work, and create customized media and technology to match your learning and course objectives. Our editorial team will work with you through each step, allowing you to concentrate on the most important thing—your students. Learn more about all our services at **www.cengage.com/custom**.

The Cengage Global Economic Watch (GEW) Resource Center. This is your source for turning today's challenges into tomorrow's solutions. This online portal houses the most current and up-to-date content concerning the economic crisis.

Organized by discipline, the GEW Resource Center offers the solutions instructors and students need in an easy-to-use format. Included are an overview and timeline of the historical events leading up to the crisis, links to the latest news and resources, discussion and testing content, an instructor feedback forum, and a Global Issues Database. Visit **www.cengage.com/thewatch** for more information.

Acknowledgments

This book reflects the efforts of a great many people over a number of years. First, we would like to thank Fred Weston, Joel Houston, Mike Ehrhardt, and Scott Besley, who worked with us on other books published by Cengage Learning from which we borrowed liberally to create *IFM*. We also owe Lou Gapenski special thanks for his many past contributions to earlier editions of this text.

The following professors and professionals, who are experts on specific topics, provided extensive feedback on this edition. We are grateful for their insights.

Thomas J. Alexander
Z. Ayca Altintig
Onur Arugaslan
Steve Beach
Kevin K. Boeh
Mary R. Brown
James J. Cordeiro
Tony Crawford
Ross Dickens
David A. Dumpe
Theodore Engel
John Griffith
Axel Grossmann

George Hachey
Thomas Hall
Tim Jares
Young Kim
Merouane Lakehal-Ayat
Richard N. LaRocca
Yingchou Lin
Barbara MacLeod
Ohaness Paskelian
Bruce Payne
Edward Pyatt
Howard Qi
Alicia Rodriguez

Kenneth Roskelley
Atul Saxena
Mark Sipper
Stephen V. Smith
G. Kevin Spellman
Tom Stuckey
Diane Rizzuto Suhler
Qian Sun
Denver Swaby
A. Tessmer
Manish Tewari

In addition, we would like to thank the following people, whose reviews and comments on prior editions and companion books have contributed to this edition: Mike Adler, Syed Ahmad, Sadhana M. Alangar, Edward I. Altman, Mary Schary Amram, Bruce Anderson, Ron Anderson, Bob Angell, Vince Apilado, Henry Arnold, Nasser Arshadi, Bob Aubey, Abdul Aziz, Gil Babcock, Peter Bacon, Kent Baker, Tom Bankston, Les Barenbaum, Charles Barngrover, John R. Becker-Blease, Bill Beedles, Moshe Ben-Horim, William (Bill) Beranek, Tom Berry, Bill Bertin, Roger Bey, Dalton Bigbee, John Bildersee, Lloyd P. Blenman, Russ Boisjoly, Keith Boles, Gordon R. Bonner, Geof Booth, Kenneth Boudreaux, Helen Bowers, Lyle Bowlin, Oswald Bowlin, Don Boyd, G. Michael Boyd, Pat Boyer, Ben S. Branch, Joe Brandt, Elizabeth Brannigan, Greg Brauer, Mary Broske, Dave Brown, David T. Brown, Kate Brown, Bill Brueggeman, Kirt Butler, Robert Button, Julie Cagle, Bill (B. J.) Campsey, Bob Carleson, Severin Carlson, David Cary, Steve Celec, Don Chance, Antony Chang, Susan Chaplinsky, Jay Choi, S. K. Choudhury, Lal Chugh, Maclyn Clouse, Margaret Considine, Phil Cooley, Joe Copeland, David Cordell, John Cotner, Charles Cox, David Crary, John Crockett, Roy Crum, Brent Dalrymple, Bill Damon, William H. Dare, Joel Dauten, Steve Dawson, Sankar De, Miles Delano, Fred Dellva, Anand Desai, Bernard Dill, Greg Dimkoff, Les Dlabay, Mark Dorfman, Gene Drycimski, Dean Dudley, David Durst, Ed Dyl, Dick Edelman, Charles Edwards, John Ellis, Dave Ewert, John Ezzell, Richard Fendler, Michael Ferri, Jim Filkins, John Finnerty, Susan Fischer, Mark Flannery, Steven Flint, Russ Fogler, Jennifer Foo, E. Bruce Frederickson, Dan French, Tina Galloway, Phil Gardial, Michael Garlington, Jim Garvin, Adam Gehr, Jim Gentry, Philip Glasgo, Rudyard Goode, Myron Gordon, Walt Goulet, Bernie Grablowsky, Theoharry Grammatikos, Ed Grossnickle, John Groth, Alan Grunewald, Manak Gupta, Sam Hadaway, Don Hakala, Sally Hamilton, Gerald Hamsmith, William Hardin, Joel Harper, John Harris, Paul Hastings, Bob Haugen, Steve Hawkey, Del Hawley, Hal Heaton, Robert Hehre, John Helmuth, K. L. Henebry, George Hettenhouse, Hans Heymann, Kendall Hill, Roger Hill, Tom Hindelang, Linda Hittle, Ralph Hocking, J. Ronald Hoffmeister, Jim Horrigan, John Houston, John Howe, Keith Howe, Jim Hsieh, Hugh Hunter, Steve Isberg, James E. Jackson, Jim Jackson, Vahan Janjigian, Kose John, Craig Johnson, Keith H. Johnson, Ramon Johnson, Ken Johnston, Ray Jones, Manuel Jose, Tejendra Kalia, Gus Kalogeras, Mike Keenan, Bill Kennedy, Joe Kiernan, Robert Kieschnick, Rick Kish, Linda Klein, Don Knight, Dorothy Koehl, Raj K. Kohli, Jaroslaw Komarynsky, Duncan Kretovich, Harold Krogh, Charles Kroncke, Joan Lamm, P. Lange, Howard Lanser, Martin Laurence, Ed Lawrence, Richard LeCompte, Wayne Lee, Jim LePage, Ilene Levin, Jules Levine, John Lewis, Kartono Liano, James T. Lindley, Chuck Linke, Bill Lloyd, Susan Long, Judy Maese, Bob Magee, Ileen Malitz, Phil Malone, Terry Maness, Chris Manning, Terry Martell, D. J. Masson, John Mathys, John McAlhany, Andy McCollough, Bill McDaniel, Robin McLaughlin, Tom McCue, Jamshid Mehran, Ilhan Meric, Larry Merville, Rick Meyer, Stuart Michelson, Jim Millar, Ed Miller, John Mitchell, Carol Moerdyk, Bob Moore, Barry Morris, Gene Morris, Fred Morrissey, Chris Muscarella, David Nachman, Tim Nantell, Don Nast, Bill Nelson, Bob Nelson, Bob Niendorf, Tom O'Brien, Dennis O'Connor, John O'Donnell, Jim Olsen, Robert Olsen, R. Daniel Pace, Coleen Pantalone, Jim Pappas, Stephen Parrish, Glenn Petry, Jim Pettijohn, Rich Pettit, Dick Pettway, Hugo Phillips, John Pinkerton, Gerald Pogue, Ralph A. Pope, R. Potter, Franklin Potts, R. Powell, Chris Prestopino, Jerry Prock, Howard Puckett, Herbert Quigley, George Racette, Bob Radcliffe, Allen Rappaport, Bill Rentz, Ken Riener, Charles Rini, John Ritchie, Jay Ritter, Pietra Rivoli, Fiona Robertson, Antonio Rodriguez, E. M. Roussakis, Dexter Rowell, Michael Ryngaert, Jim Sachlis, Abdul Sadik, Thomas Scampini, Kevin Scanlon, Frederick Schadler,

James Schallheim, Mary Jane Scheuer, Carl Schweser, John Settle, Alan Severn, Sol Shalit, Frederic Shipley, Dilip Shome, Ron Shrieves, Neil Sicherman, J. B. Silvers, Clay Singleton, Joe Sinkey, Stacy Sirmans, Jaye Smith, Steve Smith, Don Sorenson, David Speairs, Andrew Spieler, Ken Stanly, Ed Stendardi, Alan Stephens, Don Stevens, Jerry Stevens, G. Bennett Stewart, Glen Strasburg, Robert Strong, Philip Swensen, Ernie Swift, Paul Swink, Eugene Swinnerton, Robert Taggart, Gary Tallman, Dennis Tanner, Russ Taussig, Richard Teweles, Ted Teweles, Andrew Thompson, Jonathan Tiemann, Sheridan Titman, George Trivoli, George Tsetsekos, Alan L. Tucker, Mel Tysseland, David Upton, Howard Van Auken, Pretorious Van den Dool, Pieter Vanderburg, Paul Vanderheiden, David Vang, Jim Verbrugge, Patrick Vincent, Steve Vinson, Susan Visscher, John Wachowicz, Joe Walker, Mike Walker, Sam Weaver, Kuo Chiang Wei, Bill Welch, Gary R. Wells, Fred Weston, Norm Williams, Tony Wingler, Ed Wolfe, Larry Wolken, Annie Wong, Bob G. Wood, Jr., Don Woods, Thomas Wright, Michael Yonan, Miranda Zhang, Zhong-guo Zhou, David Ziebart, Dennis Zocco, and Kent Zumwalt.

Special thanks are due to Fred Weston, Myron Gordon, Merton Miller, and Franco Modigliani, who have done much to help develop the field of financial management and who provided us with instruction and inspiration; to Roy Crum, who coauthored the multinational finance chapter; to Jay Ritter, who helped us with the materials on financial markets and IPOs; to Larry Wolken, who offered his hard work and advice for the development of the *PowerPoint* slides; to Dana Aberwald Clark, Susan Ball, and Chris Buzzard, who helped us develop the spreadsheet models; and to Susan Whitman, Amelia Bell, Stephanie Hodge, and Kirsten Benson, who provided editorial support.

Both our colleagues and our students at the Universities of Florida and Tennessee gave us many useful suggestions, and the Cengage Learning and Cenveo Publisher Services staffs—especially Scott Dillon, Jaci Featherly, Lori Hazzard, Kendra Brown, Nate Anderson, Michelle Kunkler, Scott Fidler, Adele Scholtz, Suellen Ruttkay, and Mike Reynolds of Cengage Learning—helped greatly with all phases of text development, production, and marketing.

Errors in the Text

At this point, authors generally say something like this: "We appreciate all the help we received from the people listed above, but any remaining errors are, of course, our own responsibility." And in many books, there are plenty of remaining errors. Having experienced difficulties with errors ourselves, both as students and as instructors, we resolved to avoid this problem in *Intermediate Financial Management*. As a result of our error detection procedures, we are convinced that the book is relatively free of mistakes.

Partly because of our confidence that few such errors remain, but primarily because we want to detect those errors that may have slipped by to correct them in subsequent printings, we decided to offer a reward of $10 per error to the first person who reports it to us. For purposes of this reward, errors are defined as misspelled words, nonrounding numerical errors, incorrect statements, and any other error that inhibits comprehension. Typesetting problems such as irregular spacing and differences in opinion regarding grammatical or punctuation conventions do not qualify for this reward. Finally, any qualifying error that has follow-through effects is counted as two errors only. Please report any errors to Phillip Daves at the following email address: pdaves@utk.edu.

Conclusion

Finance is, in a real sense, the cornerstone of the free enterprise system. Good financial management is therefore vitally important to the economic health of business firms, hence to the nation and the world. Because of its importance, financial management should be thoroughly understood. However, this is easier said than done. The field is relatively complex, and it is undergoing constant change in response to shifts in economic conditions. All of this makes financial management stimulating and exciting, but also challenging and sometimes perplexing. We sincerely hope that the Eleventh Edition of *Intermediate Financial Management* will help you understand the financial problems faced by businesses today, as well as the best ways to solve those problems.

Eugene F. Brigham
College of Business Administration
University of Florida
Gainesville, Florida 32611-7167
gene.brigham@cba.ufl.edu

Phillip R. Daves
College of Business Administration
University of Tennessee
Knoxville, Tennessee 37996-0540
pdaves@utk.edu

March 2012

Chapter 5

Basic Stock Valuation

In Chapter 2, we examined stocks' risks and the factors that affect their required returns. In this chapter, we use those findings to estimate the *intrinsic value* of a stock. The concepts and models developed here will also be used when we estimate the cost of capital in Chapter 10, a key concept used in many important decisions, especially decisions to invest or not invest in new assets.

Some companies are so small that their common stocks are not actively traded; they are owned by only a few people, usually the companies' managers. The stock in such firms is said to be closely held. In contrast, the stocks of most large companies are owned by many investors, most of whom are not active in management. These are publicly held stocks. Institutions such as pension plans, mutual funds, hedge funds, foreign investors, and insurance companies hold about half the market value of all stocks and buy and sell relatively actively. As a result, they account for about 75% of all transactions and thus have a heavy influence on the valuation of individual stocks. But before plunging into stock valuation, it is useful to begin with a closer look at what it means to be a stockholder.

WEB

The textbook's Web site contains an *Excel* file that will guide you through the chapter's calculations. The file for this chapter is ***Ch05 Tool Kit.xls***, and we encourage you to open the file and follow along as you read the chapter.

Beginning of Chapter Questions

As you read the chapter, consider how you would answer the following questions. You *should not* necessarily be able to answer the questions before you read the chapter. Rather, you should use them to get a sense of the issues covered in the chapter. After reading the chapter, you should be able to give at least partial answers to the questions, and you should be able to give better answers after the chapter has been discussed in class. Note, too, that it is often useful, when answering conceptual questions, to use hypothetical data to illustrate your answer. We illustrate the answers with an *Excel* model that is available on the textbook's Web site. Accessing the model and working through it is a useful exercise, and it provides insights that are useful when answering the questions.

1. Assuming that the required rate of return is determined by the CAPM, explain how you would use the dividend growth model to estimate the price for Stock i. Indicate what data you would need, and give an example of a "reasonable" value for each data input.

2. How would the stock's calculated price be affected if g, r_{RF}, IP (the premium for inflation), r_M, and b_i each (a) "improved" or (b) "became worse" by some arbitrary but "reasonable" amount? "Improved" means caused the stock price to increase, and "became worse" means lowered the price. "Reasonable" means that the condition has existed in the recent past for the economy and/or some particular company. You can look at our model for examples.

3. How could you use the nonconstant growth model to find the value of the stock? Here you can assume that the expected growth rate starts at a high level, then declines for several years, and finally reaches a steady state where growth is constant.

4. Suppose you were offered a chance to buy a stock at a specified price. The stock paid a dividend last year, and the dividend is expected to grow at a very high rate for several years, at a moderate rate for several more years, and at a constant rate from then on. How could you estimate the expected rate of return on the stock?

5. In general, what are some characteristics of stocks for which a dividend growth model is appropriate? What are some characteristics of stocks for which these models are not appropriate? How could you evaluate this second type of stock?

6. What does each of the three forms of the Efficient Markets Hypothesis say about each of the following?
   a. Technical trading rules—that is, rules based on past movements in the stock
   b. Fundamental analysis—that is, trying to identify undervalued or overvalued stocks based on publicly available financial information
   c. Insider trading
   d. Hot tips from (1) Internet chat rooms, (2) close friends unconnected with the company, or (3) close friends who work for the company

5.1 Legal Rights and Privileges of Common Stockholders

The common stockholders are the *owners* of a corporation, and as such they have certain rights and privileges as discussed in this section.

5.1a Control of the Firm

A firm's common stockholders have the right to elect its directors, who, in turn, elect the officers who manage the business. In a small firm, the largest stockholder typically serves as president and chairperson of the board. In a large, publicly owned firm, the managers typically have some stock, but their personal holdings are generally

CORPORATE VALUATION AND STOCK PRICES

In Chapter 1, we told you that managers should strive to maximize intrinsic value and that the value of a firm is determined by the size, timing, and risk of its free cash flows (FCF). Recall that one use of FCF is to pay dividends. One way to estimate the intrinsic value of stock is to discount the cash flows to stockholders (dividends, D_t) at the rate of return required by stockholders (r_s). The result is the intrinsic value to stockholders.

You may say, "But what about capital gains? Don't investors buy stocks expecting to realize capital gains?" The answer is "yes," but we will see that this model actually incorporates capital gains.

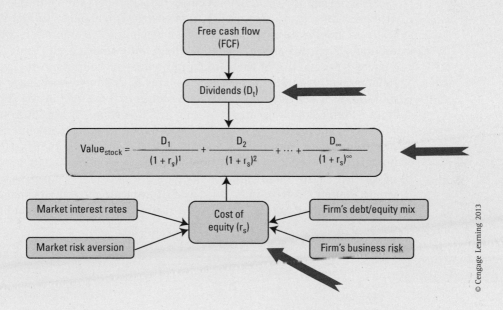

insufficient to give them voting control. Thus, the managers of most publicly owned firms can be removed by the stockholders if the management team is not effective.

Corporations must hold periodic elections to select directors, usually once a year, with the vote taken at the annual meeting. At some companies, all directors are elected each year for a 1-year term. At other companies, the terms are staggered. For example, one-third of the directors are elected each year for a 3-year term.

Each share of stock has one vote, so the owner of 1,000 shares has 1,000 votes for each director.[1] Stockholders can appear at the annual meeting and vote in

---

1. In the situation described, a 1,000-share stockholder could cast 1,000 votes for each of three directors if there were three contested seats on the board. An alternative procedure that may be prescribed in the corporate charter calls for *cumulative voting*. Here the 1,000-share stockholder would get 3,000 votes if there were three vacancies, and he or she could cast all of them for one director. Cumulative voting helps minority stockholders (i.e., those who do not own a majority of the shares) get representation on the board.

person, but typically they transfer their right to vote to another party by means of a **proxy.** Management always solicits stockholders' proxies and usually gets them. However, if earnings are poor and stockholders are dissatisfied, an outside group may solicit the proxies in an effort to overthrow management and take control of the business. This is known as a **proxy fight.** Proxy fights are discussed in detail in Chapter 11.

5.1b The Preemptive Right

Common stockholders often have the right, called the **preemptive right,** to purchase any additional shares sold by the firm. In some states, the preemptive right is automatically included in every corporate charter; in others, it is used only if it is specifically inserted into the charter.

The preemptive right enables current stockholders to maintain control, and it also prevents a transfer of wealth from current stockholders to new stockholders. If it were not for this safeguard, the management of a corporation could issue additional shares at a low price and purchase these shares itself. Management could thereby seize control of the corporation and steal value from the current stockholders. For example, suppose 1,000 shares of common stock, each with a price of $100, were outstanding, making the total market value of the firm $100,000. If an additional 1,000 shares were sold at $50 a share, or for $50,000, this would raise the total market value to $150,000. When total market value is divided by new total shares outstanding, a value of $75 a share is obtained. The old stockholders thus lose $25 per share, and the new stockholders have an instant profit of $25 per share. Thus, selling common stock at a price below the market value would dilute its price and transfer wealth from the present stockholders to those who were allowed to purchase the new shares. The preemptive right prevents such occurrences.

Self Test	What is a proxy fight?
	What are the two primary reasons for using preemptive rights?

www

Note that **finance.yahoo .com** provides an easy way to find stocks meeting specified criteria. Under the Investing tab, select Stocks and then Stock Screener. To find the largest companies in terms of market value, for example, choose More Preset Screens, then select Largest Market Cap. You can also create custom screens to find stocks meeting other criteria.

5.2 Types of Common Stock

Although most firms have only one type of common stock, in some instances **classified stock** is used to meet a company's special needs. Generally, when special classifications are used, one type is designated *Class A*, another *Class B*, and so on. Small, new companies seeking funds from outside sources frequently use different types of common stock. For example, when Genetic Concepts went public, its Class A stock was sold to the public and paid a dividend, but this stock had no voting rights for 5 years. Its Class B stock, which was retained by the firm's organizers, had full voting rights for 5 years, but the legal terms stated that dividends could not be paid on the Class B stock until the company had established its earning power and built up retained earnings to a designated level. The use of classified stock thus enabled the public to take a position in a conservatively financed growth company without sacrificing income, while the founders retained absolute control during the crucial early stages of the firm's development. At the same time, outside investors were protected against excessive withdrawals of funds by the original owners. As is often the case in such situations, the Class B stock was called **founders' shares.**[2]

As these examples illustrate, the right to vote is often a distinguishing characteristic between different classes of stock. Suppose two classes of stock differ in only one respect: One class has voting rights but the other does not. As you would expect, the stock with voting rights would be more valuable. In the United States, which has a legal system with fairly strong protection for minority stockholders (that is, noncontrolling stockholders), voting stock typically sells at a price 4% to 6% above that of otherwise similar nonvoting stock. Thus, if a stock with no voting rights sold for $50, then one with voting rights would probably sell for $52 to $53. In countries with legal systems that provide less protection for minority stockholders, the right to vote is far more valuable. For example voting stock in Israel sells for 45% more on average than nonvoting stock, and voting stock in Italy has an 82% higher value than nonvoting stock.

Some companies have multiple lines of business, with each line having very different growth prospects. Because cash flows for all business lines are mingled on financial statements, some companies worry that investors are not able to value the high-growth business lines correctly. To separate the cash flows and to allow separate valuations, occasionally a company will have classes of stock with dividends tied to a particular part of a company. This is called **tracking stock,** or **target stock.** For example, in 2006 Liberty Media Corporation, a conglomerate that owned such entertainment assets as the Starz movie channel and investments in Time Warner, issued two different tracking stocks to track the two different lines of its business. One of these, Liberty Interactive tracking stock, was designed to track the performance of its QVC home shopping network and other high-growth Internet-based interactive assets. The other, Liberty Capital Group, comprised slower-growth holdings like the Starz Entertainment Group. The idea was that investors would assign a higher value to the high-growth portion of the company if it traded separately.

However, many analysts are skeptical as to whether tracking stock increases a company's total market value. Companies still report consolidated financial statements for the entire company and have considerable leeway in allocating costs, deploying capital, and reporting the financial results for the various divisions, even those with tracking stock. Thus, a tracking stock is far from identical to the stock of an independent, stand-alone company.

What are some reasons why a company might use classified stock?	**Self Test**

5.3 The Market Stock Price versus Intrinsic Value

We saw in Chapter 1 that managers should seek to maximize the value of their firms' stocks. In that chapter, we also emphasized the difference between stock price and intrinsic value. The stock price is simply the current market price, and it is easily observed for publicly traded companies. By contrast, intrinsic value, which

2. Note that "Class A," "Class B," and so on have no standard meanings. Most firms have no classified shares, but a firm that does could designate its Class B shares as founders' shares and its Class A shares as those sold to the public and another firm might reverse these designations.

represents the "true" value of the company's stock, cannot be directly observed and must instead be estimated. Figure 5-1 illustrates the connection between stock price and intrinsic value.

As the figure suggests, market equilibrium occurs when the stock's price equals its intrinsic value. If the stock market is reasonably efficient, then gaps between the stock price and intrinsic value should not be very large, and they should not persist for very long. However, there are cases when an individual stock price may be much higher or lower than its intrinsic value, and such divergence may persist for quite a while. During several years leading up to the crash of 2008–2009, most of the large investment banks were reporting record profits and selling at record prices. However, much of those earnings were illusory in that they did not reflect the huge risks that existed in the sub-prime mortgages they were buying. So, with hindsight, we now know that the market prices of most financial firms' stocks exceeded their intrinsic values just prior to 2008. Then, when the market realized what was happening, those stock prices crashed. Citigroup, Merrill Lynch, and others lost over 80% of their value in a few short months, and others suffered even worse declines. It clearly pays to question market prices at times!

5.3a Why Do Investors and Companies Care about Intrinsic Value?

The remainder of this chapter focuses primarily on different approaches for estimating a stock's intrinsic value. Before describing these approaches, it is worth asking why it is important for investors and companies to understand how to estimate intrinsic values.

When investing in common stocks, the goal is to purchase stocks that are undervalued (i.e., the price is below the stock's intrinsic value) and avoid stocks that are overvalued. Consequently, Wall Street analysts, institutional investors who control mutual funds and pension funds, and even many individual investors are

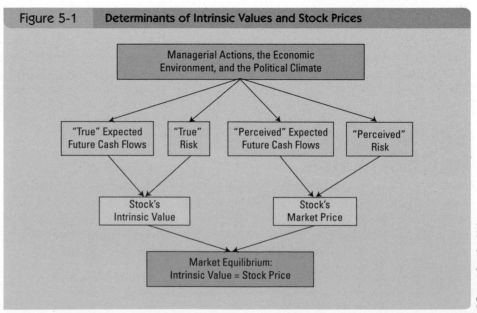

Figure 5-1   Determinants of Intrinsic Values and Stock Prices

© Cengage Learning 2013

quite interested in finding reliable models that help predict intrinsic value. Investors obviously care about intrinsic value, but managers also must understand how intrinsic value is estimated. First, managers need to know how alternative actions are likely to affect stock prices, and the models of intrinsic value that we cover help demonstrate the connection between managerial decisions and firm value. Second, managers should consider whether their stock is significantly undervalued or overvalued before making certain decisions. For example, firms should consider carefully the decision to issue new shares if they believe their stock is undervalued, and an estimate of their stock's intrinsic value is the key to such decisions.

Two basic models are used to estimate intrinsic values: The *discounted dividend model* and the *corporate valuation model*. The dividend model focuses on dividends, while the corporate model drills down below dividends and focuses on sales, costs, and free cash flows. We cover the discounted dividend model in this chapter and the corporate valuation model in Chapter 11.

Self Test

What's the difference between a stock's price and its intrinsic value?

Why do investors and managers need to understand how a firm's intrinsic value is estimated?

5.4 Stock Market Reporting

Fifty years ago, investors who wanted real-time information would sit in brokerage firms' offices watching a "ticker tape" go by that displayed prices of stocks as they were traded. Those who did not need current information could find the previous day's prices from the business section of a daily newspaper like *The Wall Street Journal*. Today, though, one can get quotes throughout the day from many different Internet sources, including Yahoo!.[3] Figure 5-2 shows the quote for General Electric, which is traded on the NYSE under the symbol GE, on February 8, 2011. GE ended the regular trading day (4 p.m. EST) at $21.28, up $0.41, which was a 1.96% increase from the previous day. However, the stock rose by 4 cents in after-hours trading. The data also show that GE opened the day at $20.96 and traded in a range from $20.91 to $21.31. If this quote had been obtained during trading hours, it would also have provided information about the quotes at which the stock could be bought (the Ask quote) or sold (the Bid quote). During the past year, the price hit a high of $21.31 and a low of $13.75. A total of 54.94 million GE shares traded that day, which was a little below the average trading volume of 59.2 million shares.

The screen with the stock quote information also gives the total market value of GE's common stock (the Market Cap); the dividend and dividend yield; the most recent "ttm," or "trailing twelve months," EPS and P/E ratios; and a graph showing the stock's performance during the day. (However, the graph can be changed to show the stock's performance over a number of time periods up to and including 5 years.) In addition to this information, the Web page has links to financial

---

3. Most free sources actually provide quotes that are delayed by 20 minutes, but if you subscribe to a paid site like *The Wall Street Journal*'s online service, or if you have a brokerage account, you can generally get online real-time quotes.

Figure 5-2   **Stock Quote and Other Key Data for GE, February 8, 2011**

General Electric Company Common (NYSE: GE)
After Hours: 21.32 ↑ 0.04 (0.19%) 7:27PM EST

Last Trade:	**21.28**	Day's Range:	**20.91 - 21.31**
Trade Time:	**4:00PM EST**	52wk Range:	**13.75 - 21.31**
Change:	↑ **0.41 (1.96%)**	Volume:	**54,937,383**
Prev Close:	**20.87**	Avg Vol (3m):	**59,199,500**
Open:	**20.96**	Market Cap:	**226.33B**
Bid:	**21.30 x 900**	P/E (ttm):	**20.11**
Ask:	**21.32 x 300**	EPS (ttm):	**1.06**
1y Target Est:	**22.64**	Div & Yield:	**0.56 (2.70%)**

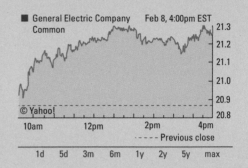

Source: **finance.yahoo.com**.

statements, research reports, historical ratios, analysts' forecasts of EPS and EPS growth rates, and a wealth of other data.

Self Test   What information is provided on the Internet in addition to the stock's latest price?

5.5 Valuing Common Stocks

Common stocks are expected to provide a stream of future cash flows, and a stock's value is found the same way as the values of other financial assets—namely, as the present value of its expected future cash flow stream. The expected cash flows consist of two elements: (1) the dividends expected in each year and (2) the price investors expect to receive when they sell the stock. The expected final stock price includes the return of the original investment plus an expected capital gain.

5.5a Definitions of Terms Used in Stock Valuation Models

We saw in Chapter 1 that a manager should seek to maximize the intrinsic value of the firm's stock. To do this, a manager needs to know how her actions are likely to affect the stock's price. Therefore, we develop some models in this section to show how the value of a share of stock is determined, and we begin by defining some key terms as follows.

D_t = Dividend the stockholder *expects* to receive at the end of Year t. D_0 is the most recent dividend, which has already been paid; D_1 is the first dividend expected, which will be paid at the end of this year; D_2 is the dividend expected at the end of Year 2; and so forth. D_1 represents the first cash flow that a new purchaser of the stock will receive, because D_0 has just been paid. D_0 is known with certainty, but all future dividends are expected values, so the estimate of D_t may differ among investors.[4]

P_0 = Actual **market price** of the stock today.

$\hat{P}_t$ = Expected price of the stock at the end of each Year t (pronounced "P hat t"). $\hat{P}_0$ is the **intrinsic**, or **fundamental, value** of the stock today as seen by the particular investor doing the analysis; $\hat{P}_1$ is the price expected at the end of 1 year; and so on. Note that $\hat{P}_0$ is the intrinsic value of the stock today based on a particular investor's estimate of the stock's expected dividend stream and the risk of that stream. Hence, whereas the market price P_0 is fixed and is identical for all investors, $\hat{P}_0$ could differ among investors depending on how optimistic they are regarding the company. The caret, or "hat," is used to indicate that $\hat{P}_t$ is an estimated future value. $\hat{P}_0$, the individual investor's estimate of the intrinsic value today, could be above or below P_0, the current stock price, but an investor would buy the stock only if his estimate of $\hat{P}_0$ were equal to or greater than P_0.

Since there are many investors in the market, there can be many values for $\hat{P}_0$. However, we can think of a group of "average," or "marginal," investors whose actions actually determine the market price. For these marginal investors, P_0 must equal $\hat{P}_0$; otherwise, a disequilibrium would exist, and buying and selling in the market would cause P_0 to change until $P_0 = \hat{P}_0$ as seen by the marginal investor.

D_1/P_0 = Expected **dividend yield** during the coming year. If the stock is expected to pay a dividend of $D_1 = \$1$ during the next 12 months and if its current price is $P_0 = \$10$, then the expected dividend yield is $\$1/\$10 = 0.10 = 10\%$.

$\dfrac{\hat{P}_1 - P_0}{P_0}$ = Expected **capital gains yield** during the coming year. If the stock sells for $10 today and if it is expected to rise to $10.50 at the end of one year, then the expected capital gain is $\hat{P}_1 - P_0 = \$10.50 - \$10.00 = \$0.50$, and the expected capital gains yield is $\$0.50/\$10 = 0.05 = 5\%$.

g = Expected **growth rate** in dividends as predicted by a marginal investor. If dividends are expected to grow at a constant rate, then g is also the expected rate of growth in earnings and the stock's price. Different investors may use different values of g to evaluate a firm's stock, but the market price, P_0, is set on the basis of g as estimated by the marginal investor.

---

4. Stocks generally pay dividends quarterly, so theoretically we should evaluate them on a quarterly basis. However, in stock valuation, most analysts work on an annual basis because the data generally are not precise enough to warrant refinement to a quarterly model. For additional information on the quarterly model, see Robert Brooks and Billy Helms, "An N-Stage, Fractional Period, Quarterly Dividend Discount Model," *Financial Review*, November 1990, pp. 651–657.

r_s = Minimum acceptable return, or **required rate of return,** on the stock, considering both its risk and the returns available on other investments. Again, this term generally relates to the marginal investor. The primary determinants of r_s include the real rate of return, expected inflation, and risk.

$\hat{r}_s$ = **Expected rate of return** that an investor who buys the stock expects to receive in the future. $\hat{r}_s$ (pronounced "r hat s") could be above or below r_s, but one would buy the stock only if $\hat{r}_s \geq r_s$. Note that the expected return ($\hat{r}_s$) is equal to the expected dividend yield (D_1/P_0) plus the expected capital gains yield ($[\hat{P}_1 - P_0]/P_0$). In our example, $\hat{r}_s = 10\% + 5\% = 15\%$.

$\bar{r}_s$ = **Actual,** or **realized,** *after-the-fact* **rate of return,** pronounced "r bar s." You may *expect* to obtain a return of $\hat{r}_s = 15\%$ if you buy Exxon-Mobil today, but if the market declines then you may end up next year with an actual realized return that is much lower and perhaps even negative.

5.5b Expected Dividends as the Basis for Stock Values

Like all financial assets, the value of a stock is estimated by finding the present value of a stream of expected future cash flows. What are the cash flows that corporations are expected to provide to their stockholders? First, think of yourself as an investor who buys a stock with the intention of holding it (in your family) forever. In this case, all that you (and your heirs) will receive is a stream of dividends, and the value of the stock today is calculated as the present value of an infinite stream of dividends:

(5–1)

$$\text{Value of stock} = \hat{P}_0 = \text{PV of expected future dividends}$$

$$= \frac{D_1}{(1+r_s)^1} + \frac{D_2}{(1+r_s)^2} + \cdots + \frac{D_\infty}{(1+r_s)^\infty}$$

$$= \sum_{t=1}^{\infty} \frac{D_t}{(1+r_s)^t}$$

What about the more typical case, where you expect to hold the stock for a finite period and then sell it—what is the value of $\hat{P}_n$ in this case? Unless the company is likely to be liquidated or sold and thus to disappear, *the value of the stock is again determined by Equation 5-1.* To see this, recognize that for any individual investor, the expected cash flows consist of expected dividends plus the expected sale price of the stock. However, the sale price a current investor receives will depend on the dividends some future investor expects. Therefore, for all present and future investors in total, expected cash flows must be based on expected future dividends. Put another way, unless a firm is liquidated or sold to another concern, the cash flows it provides to its stockholders will consist only of a stream of dividends. Therefore, the value of a share of its stock must be the present value of that expected dividend stream.

The general validity of Equation 5-1 can also be confirmed by solving the following problem. Suppose I buy a stock and expect to hold it for 1 year. I will receive dividends during the year plus the value $\hat{P}_1$ when I sell at the end of the year. But what will determine the value of $\hat{P}_1$? The answer is that it will be determined as the present value of the dividends expected during Year 2 plus the stock price at the end of that year, which, in turn, will be determined as the present value of another set of future dividends and an even more distant stock price. This process can be continued ad infinitum, and the ultimate result is Equation 5-1.[5]

What are the two components of most stocks' expected total return?

How does one calculate the capital gains yield and the dividend yield of a stock?

If D_1 = \$3.00, P_0 = \$50, and $\hat{P}_1$ = \$52, what are the stock's expected dividend yield, expected capital gains yield, and expected total return for the coming year? (**6%, 4%, 10%**)

5.6 Valuing a Constant Growth Stock

Equation 5-1 is a generalized stock valuation model in that the time pattern of D_t can be anything: D_t can be rising, falling, fluctuating randomly, or even zero for several years, yet Equation 5-1 will still hold. With a computer spreadsheet we can easily use this equation to find a stock's intrinsic value for any pattern of dividends.[6] In practice, the hard part is getting an accurate forecast of the future dividends. However, in many cases the stream of dividends is expected to grow at a constant rate, and if so then Equation 5-1 can be rewritten as follows:

$$\hat{P}_0 = \frac{D_0(1+g)^1}{(1+r_s)^1} + \frac{D_0(1+g)^2}{(1+r_s)^2} + \cdots + \frac{D_0(1+g)^\infty}{(1+r_s)^\infty}$$

$$= D_0 \sum_{t=1}^{\infty} \frac{(1+g)^t}{(1+r_s)^t}$$

$$= \frac{D_0(1+g)}{r_s-g} = \frac{D_1}{r_s-g}$$

(5–2)

5. It is ironic that investors periodically lose sight of the long-run nature of stocks as investments and forget that, in order to sell a stock at a profit, one must find a buyer who will pay the higher price. If you analyze a stock's value in accordance with Equation 5-1, conclude that the stock's market price exceeds a reasonable value, and then buy the stock anyway, then you would be following the "bigger fool" theory of investment—you think that you may be a fool to buy the stock at its excessive price, but you think that when you get ready to sell it, you can find someone who is an even bigger fool. The bigger fool theory was widely followed in the spring of 2000, just before the Nasdaq market lost more than one-third of its value, and then again in the housing market before it peaked in mid-2006.
6. Actually, we can only find an approximate price. However, if we project dividends for 100 or so years, the present value of that finite dividend stream is approximately equal to the present value of the infinite dividend stream.

WEB

The last term in Equation 5-2 is derived in **Web Extension 5A** on the textbook's Web site.

The last term of Equation 5-2 is called the **constant growth model,** or the **Gordon model,** after Myron J. Gordon, who did much to develop and popularize it.

A necessary condition for the validity of Equation 5-2 is that r_s be greater than g. Look back at the second form of Equation 5-2. If g is larger than r_s, then $(1 + g)^t/(1 + r_s)^t$ must always be greater than 1. In this case, the second line of Equation 5-2 is the sum of an infinite number of terms, with each term being larger than 1. Therefore, if g were constant and greater than r_s, the resulting stock price would be infinite! Since no company is worth an infinite amount, it is impossible to have a constant growth rate that is greater than r_s forever. Similarly, a student will occasionally plug a value for g that is greater than r_s into the last form of Equation 5-2 and report a negative stock price. This is nonsensical. The last form of Equation 5-2 is valid only when g is less than r_s. *If g is greater than r_s then the constant growth model cannot be used, and the answer you would get from using Equation 5-2 would be wrong and misleading.*

5.6a Illustration of a Constant Growth Stock

Assume that MicroDrive just paid a dividend of $1.15 (that is, $D_0 = \$1.15$). Its stock has a required rate of return, r_s, of 13.4%, and investors expect the dividend to grow at a constant 8% rate in the future. The estimated dividend 1 year hence would be $D_1 = \$1.15(1.08) = \$1.24$; D_2 would be $1.34; and the estimated dividend 5 years hence would be $1.69:

$$D_t = D_0(1 + g)^t = \$1.15(1.08)^5 = \$1.69$$

We could use this procedure to estimate each future dividend and then use Equation 5-1 to determine the current stock value, $\hat{P}_0$. In other words, we could find each expected future dividend, calculate its present value, and then sum all the present values to find the intrinsic value of the stock.

Such a process would be time-consuming, but we can take a shortcut—just insert the illustrative data into Equation 5-2 to find the stock's intrinsic value, $23:

$$\hat{P}_0 = \frac{\$1.15(1.08)}{0.134 - 0.08} = \frac{\$1.242}{0.054} = \$23.00$$

The concept underlying the valuation process for a constant growth stock is graphed in Figure 5-3. Dividends are growing at the rate g = 8%, but because r_s > g, the present value of each future dividend is declining. For example, the dividend in Year 1 is $D_1 = D_0(1 + g)^1 = \$1.15(1.08) = \$1.242$. However, the present value of this dividend, discounted at 13.4%, is $PV(D_1) = \$1.242/(1.134)^1 = \$1.095$. The dividend expected in Year 2 grows to $1.242(1.08) = \$1.341$, but the present value of this dividend falls to $1.043. Continuing, $D_3 = \$1.449$ and $PV(D_3) = \$0.993$, and so on. Thus, the expected dividends are growing, but the present value of each successive dividend is declining, because the dividend growth rate (8%) is less than the rate used for discounting the dividends to the present (13.4%).

If we summed the present values of each future dividend, this summation would be the value of the stock, $\hat{P}_0$. When g is a constant, this summation is equal to $D_1/(r_s - g)$, as shown in Equation 5-2. Therefore, if we extended the lower step-function curve in Figure 5-3 on out to infinity and added up the present values of each future dividend, the summation would be identical to the value given by Equation 5-2, $23.00.

Although Equation 5-2 assumes there are *infinite* time periods, most of the value is based on dividends during a *finite* time period. In our example, 70% of the

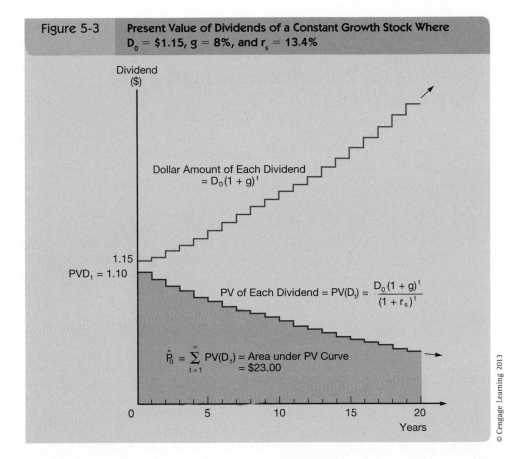

Figure 5-3   **Present Value of Dividends of a Constant Growth Stock Where $D_0 = \$1.15$, $g = 8\%$, and $r_s = 13.4\%$**

Dividend ($)

Dollar Amount of Each Dividend $= D_0(1 + g)^t$

1.15
$PVD_1 = 1.10$

PV of Each Dividend $= PV(D_t) = \dfrac{D_0(1 + g)^t}{(1 + r_s)^t}$

$\hat{P}_0 = \sum\limits_{t=1}^{\infty} PV(D_t) =$ Area under PV Curve $= \$23.00$

0   5   10   15   20

Years

© Cengage Learning 2013

value is attributed to the first 25 years, 91% to the first 50 years, and 99.4% to the first 100 years. This means that companies don't have to survive forever to justify using the Gordon growth model.

5.6b Dividend and Earnings Growth

Because a stock price depends on *all future dividends*, not just next year's dividend, increasing next year's dividend will not have much impact on stock price unless investors expect the dividend increase to be sustainable. Dividends are paid with cash, which means sustainable dividend growth must come from sustainable cash flow growth. The cash flow that is available for distribution to shareholders depends on profitability, investments in operating capital, and the level of debt. Dividends, profitability, capital investments, and capital structure are all interrelated, especially in the long term. A dollar used to pay dividends can't be used for reinvestment in the firm or to pay down debt, so everything else equal, higher dividends must be associated with lower growth or a higher debt level. Growth in dividends can be supported by increasing debt, but to avoid unacceptably high levels of debt, long-term dividend growth must be limited to long-term earnings growth.

Earnings per share (EPS) growth depends on economy-wide factors (such as recessions and inflation), industry-wide factors (such as technological innovations), and firm-specific factors (management skill, brand identity, patent protection, etc.). For a firm to grow faster than the economy, either the industry must become a bigger part of the economy or the firm must take market share from its competitors. In the long run, competition and market saturation will tend to limit EPS growth to the sum of population growth and inflation. And as we just explained, the long-term dividend growth rate cannot exceed the long-term EPS growth rate.

5.6c Do Stock Prices Reflect Long-Term or Short-Term Events?

Managers often complain that the stock market is shortsighted and that investors care only about conditions over the next few years. Let's use the constant growth model to test this assertion. MicroDrive's most recent dividend was $1.15, and it is expected to grow at a rate of 8% per year. Since we know the growth rate, we can forecast the dividends for each of the next 5 years and then find their present values:

$$
\begin{aligned}
PV &= \frac{D_0(1+g)^1}{(1+r_s)^1} + \frac{D_0(1+g)^2}{(1+r_s)^2} + \frac{D_0(1+g)^3}{(1+r_s)^3} + \frac{D_0(1+g)^4}{(1+r_s)^4} + \frac{D_0(1+g)^5}{(1+r_s)^5} \\[2mm]
&= \frac{\$1.15(1.08)^1}{(1.134)^1} + \frac{\$1.15(1.08)^2}{(1.134)^2} + \frac{\$1.15(1.08)^3}{(1.134)^3} + \frac{\$1.15(1.08)^4}{(1.134)^4} + \frac{\$1.15(1.08)^5}{(1.134)^5} \\[2mm]
&= \frac{\$1.242}{(1.134)^1} + \frac{\$1.341}{(1.134)^2} + \frac{\$1.449}{(1.134)^3} + \frac{\$1.565}{(1.134)^4} + \frac{\$1.690}{(1.134)^5} \\[2mm]
&= 1.095 + 1.043 + 0.993 + 0.946 + 0.901 \\[2mm]
&\approx \$5.00
\end{aligned}
$$

Recall that MicroDrive's stock price is $23.00. Therefore, only $5.00, or $5/$23 = 0.22 = 22%, of the $23.00 stock price is attributable to short-term cash flows. This means that MicroDrive's managers will affect the stock price more by working to increase long-term cash flows than by focusing on short-term flows. This situation holds for most companies. Indeed, a number of professors and consulting firms have used actual company data to show that more than 80% of a typical company's stock price is due to cash flows expected farther than 5 years in the future.

This brings up an interesting question. If most of a stock's value is due to long-term cash flows, then why do managers and analysts pay so much attention to quarterly earnings? Part of the answer lies in the information conveyed by short-term earnings. For example, when actual quarterly earnings are lower than expected not because of fundamental problems but only because a company has increased its research and development (R&D) expenditures, studies have shown that the stock price probably won't decline and may actually increase. This makes sense, because R&D should increase future cash flows. On the other hand, if quarterly earnings are lower than expected because customers don't like the company's new products, then this new information will have negative implications for future values of g, the long-term growth rate. As we show later in this chapter, even small changes in g can lead to large changes in stock prices. Therefore, quarterly earnings themselves might not be that important, but the information they convey about future prospects can be extremely important.

Another reason many managers focus on short-term earnings is that some firms pay managerial bonuses on the basis of current earnings rather than stock prices (which reflect future earnings). For these managers, the concern with quarterly earnings is not due to their effect on stock prices—it's due to their effect on bonuses.[7]

---

7. Many apparent puzzles in finance can be explained either by managerial compensation systems or by peculiar features of the Tax Code. So, if you can't explain a firm's behavior in terms of economic logic, look to compensation procedures or taxes as possible explanations.

5.6d When Can the Constant Growth Model Be Used?

The constant growth model is most appropriate for mature companies with a stable history of growth. Expected growth rates vary somewhat among companies, but dividend growth for most mature firms is generally expected to continue in the future at about the same rate as nominal gross domestic product (real GDP plus inflation). On this basis, one might expect the dividends of an average, or "normal," company to grow at a rate of 5% to 8% a year. Note, though, that the 2008–2009 recession caused many analysts to lower their expectations for long-run growth, and those lowered expectations contributed mightily to the stock market crash.

Note too that Equation 5-2 is sufficiently general to handle the case of a **zero growth stock,** where the dividend is expected to remain constant over time. If $g = 0$, then Equation 5-2 reduces to Equation 5-3:

$$\hat{P}_0 = \frac{D}{r_s}$$

(5–3)

This is essentially the equation for a perpetuity, and it is simply the dividend divided by the discount rate.

Self Test

Write out and explain the valuation formula for a constant growth stock.

Are stock prices affected more by long-term or short-term performance? Explain.

A stock is expected to pay a dividend of $2 at the end of the year. The required rate of return is $r_s = 12\%$. What would the stock's price be if the constant growth rate in dividends were 4%? (**$25.00**) What would the price be if $g = 0\%$? (**$16.67**)

5.7 Expected Rate of Return on a Constant Growth Stock

When using Equation 5-2, we first estimated D_0 and r_s, the *required* rate of return on the stock; then we solved for the stock's intrinsic value, which we compared to its actual market price. We can also reverse the process, observing the actual stock price, substituting it into Equation 5-2, and solving for the rate of return. In doing so, we are finding the *expected* rate of return, which will also equal the *required* rate of return, $\hat{r}_s = r_s$, if the market is in equilibrium:[8]

$$
\begin{aligned}
\hat{r}_s &= \begin{matrix}\text{Expected rate} \\ \text{of return}\end{matrix} = \begin{matrix}\text{Expected} \\ \text{dividend yield}\end{matrix} + \begin{matrix}\text{Expected capital} \\ \text{gains yield}\end{matrix} \\
&= \begin{matrix}\text{Expected} \\ \text{dividend yield}\end{matrix} + \begin{matrix}\text{Expected} \\ \text{growth rate}\end{matrix} \\
&= \frac{D_1}{P_0} + g
\end{aligned}
$$

(5–4)

---

8. We say that a stock is in *equilibrium* when $r_s = \hat{r}_s$ and $\hat{P}_0 = P_0$. We discuss this in more detail later in the chapter.

Thus, if you buy a stock for a price $P_0 = \$23$, and if you expect the stock to pay a dividend $D_1 = \$1.242$ 1 year from now and to grow at a constant rate $g = 8\%$ in the future, then your expected rate of return will be 13.4%:

$$\hat{r}_s = \frac{\$1.242}{\$23} + 8\% = 5.4\% + 8\% = 13.4\%$$

In this form, we see that $\hat{r}_s$ is the *expected total return* and that it consists of an *expected dividend yield*, $D_1/P_0 = 5.4\%$, plus an *expected growth rate* (which is also the *expected capital gains yield*) of $g = 8\%$.

Suppose that the current price, P_0, is equal to $23 and that the Year-1 expected dividend, D_1, is equal to $1.242. What is the expected price at the end of the first year, immediately after D_1 has been paid? First, we can estimate the expected Year-2 dividend as $D_2 = D_1(1 + g) = \$1.242(1.08) = \$1.3414$. Then we can apply a version of Equation 5-2 that is shifted ahead by 1 year, using D_2 instead of D_1 and solving for $\hat{P}_1$ instead of $\hat{P}_0$:

$$\hat{P}_1 = \frac{D_2}{r_s - g} = \frac{\$1.3414}{0.134 - 0.08} = \$24.84$$

www

The popular Motley Fool Web site **www.fool.com/school/introduction tovaluation.htm** provides a good description of some benefits and drawbacks of a few of the more commonly used valuation procedures.

Even easier, notice that $\hat{P}_1$ must be 8% larger than $23, the price found 1 year earlier for P_0:

$$\$23(1.08) = \$24.84$$

Either way, we expect a capital gain of $\$24.84 - \$23.00 = \$1.84$ during the year, which is a capital gains yield of 8%:

$$\text{Capital gains yield} = \frac{\text{Capital gains}}{\text{Beginning price}} = \frac{\$1.84}{\$23.00} = 0.08 = 8\%$$

We could extend the analysis, and in each future year the expected capital gains yield would always equal g, the expected dividend growth rate.

The dividend yield during the year could be estimated as follows:

$$\text{Dividend yield} = \frac{D_2}{\hat{P}_1} = \frac{\$1.3414}{\$24.84} = 0.054 = 5.4\%$$

The dividend yield for the following year could also be calculated, and again it would be 5.4%. Thus, *for a constant growth stock,* the following conditions must hold:

1. The dividend is expected to grow forever at a constant rate, g.
2. The stock price will also grow at this same rate.
3. The expected dividend yield is constant.
4. The expected capital gains yield is also constant and is equal to g, the dividend (and stock price) growth rate.
5. The expected total rate of return, $\hat{r}_s$, is equal to the expected dividend yield plus the expected growth rate: $\hat{r}_s$ = dividend yield + g.

The term *expected* should be clarified—it means "expected" in a probabilistic sense, as the "statistically expected" outcome. Thus, if we say the growth rate is expected to remain constant at 8%, we mean that the best prediction for the growth rate in any future year is 8%, not that we literally expect the growth rate to be exactly 8% in each future year. In this sense, the constant growth assumption is a reasonable one for many large, mature companies.

5.8 Valuing Nonconstant Growth Stocks

For many companies, it is not appropriate to assume that dividends will grow at a constant rate. Firms typically go through *life cycles*. During their early years, their growth is much faster than that of the economy as a whole; then they match the economy's growth; and finally their growth is slower than that of the economy.[9] Automobile manufacturers in the 1920s, software companies such as Microsoft in the 1990s, and technology firms such as Cisco in the 2000s are examples of firms in the early part of the cycle; these firms are called **supernormal,** or **nonconstant, growth** firms. Figure 5-4 illustrates nonconstant growth and also compares it with normal growth, zero growth, and negative growth.[10]

In Figure 5-4, the dividends of the nonconstant growth firm are expected to grow at a 30% rate for 3 years, after which the growth rate is expected to fall to 8%, the assumed average for the economy. The value of this firm, like any other, is the present value of its expected future dividends as determined by Equation 5-1. When D_t is growing at a constant rate, we simplify Equation 5-1 to $\hat{P}_0 = D_1/(r_s - g)$. In the nonconstant case, however, the expected growth rate is not a constant—it declines at the end of the nonconstant growth period.

Because Equation 5-2 requires a constant growth rate, we obviously cannot use it to value stocks that have nonconstant growth. However, assuming a company currently experiencing nonconstant growth will eventually slow down and become a constant growth stock, we can use Equation 5-2 to help find the stock's value. First,

---

9. The concept of life cycles could be broadened to *product cycle,* which would include both small start-up companies and large companies like Apple, which periodically introduce new products that give sales and earnings a boost. We should also mention *business cycles,* which alternately depress and boost sales and profits. The growth rate just after a major new product has been introduced, or just after a firm emerges from the depths of a recession, is likely to be much higher than the "expected long-run average growth rate," which is the number that should be used in a DCF analysis.

10. A negative growth rate indicates a declining company. A mining company whose profits are falling because of a declining ore body is an example. Someone buying such a company would expect its earnings, and consequently its dividends and stock price, to decline each year, and this would lead to capital losses rather than capital gains. Obviously, a declining company's stock price will be relatively low, and its dividend yield must be high enough to offset the expected capital loss and still produce a competitive total return. Students sometimes argue that they would never be willing to buy a stock whose price was expected to decline. However, if the annual dividends are large enough to *more than offset* the falling stock price, the stock could still provide a fair return.

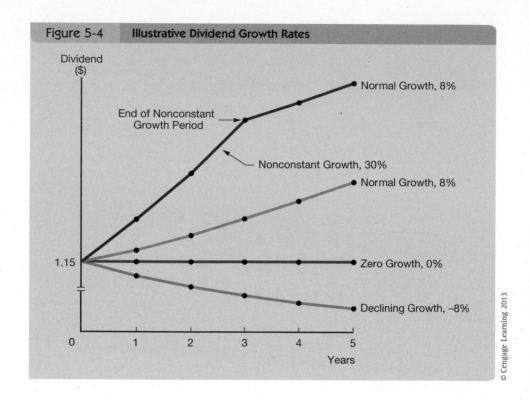

Figure 5-4   Illustrative Dividend Growth Rates

we assume that the dividend will grow at a nonconstant rate (generally a relatively high rate) for N periods, after which it will grow at a constant rate, g. Often N is called the **horizon date** or the **terminal date**.

Recall that a stock's current intrinsic value, $\hat{P}_0$, is the present value of all dividends after Time 0, discounted back to Time 0. Similarly, the intrinsic value of a stock at Time N is the present value of all dividends beyond Time N, discounted back to Time N. When dividends beyond Time N are expected to grow at a constant rate, we can use a variation of the constant growth formula, Equation 5-2, to estimate the stock's intrinsic value at Time N. The intrinsic value at Time N is often called the **horizon value** or the **terminal value**:

(5–5)
$$\text{Horizon value} = \hat{P}_N = \frac{D_{N+1}}{r_s - g} = \frac{D_N(1 + g)}{r_s - g}$$

A stock's intrinsic value today, $\hat{P}_0$, is the present value of the dividends during the nonconstant growth period plus the present value of the dividends after the horizon date:

$$\hat{P}_0 = \underbrace{\frac{D_1}{(1 + r_s)^1} + \frac{D_2}{(1 + r_s)^2} + \cdots + \frac{D_N}{(1 + r_s)^N}}_{\substack{\text{PV of dividends during the} \\ \text{nonconstant growth period} \\ t = 1 \text{ to } N}} + \underbrace{\frac{D_{N+1}}{(1 + r_s)^{N+1}} + \cdots + \frac{D_\infty}{(1 + r_s)^\infty}}_{\substack{\text{PV of dividends during the} \\ \text{constant growth period} \\ t = N + 1 \text{ to } \infty}}$$

The horizon value is the value of all dividends beyond Time N discounted back to Time N. Discounting the horizon value from Time N to Time 0 provides an estimate of the present value of all dividends beyond the nonconstant growth period. Thus, the stock's current intrinsic value is the present value of all dividends during the nonconstant growth period plus the present value of the horizon value:

$$\hat{P}_0 = \left[\frac{D_1}{(1+r_s)^1} + \frac{D_2}{(1+r_s)^2} + \cdots + \frac{D_N}{(1+r_s)^N}\right] + \frac{\hat{P}_N}{(1+r_s)^N}$$

$$= \left[\frac{D_1}{(1+r_s)^1} + \frac{D_2}{(1+r_s)^2} + \cdots + \frac{D_N}{(1+r_s)^N}\right] + \frac{[(D_{N+1})/(r_s-g)]}{(1+r_s)^N}$$

(5–6)

To implement Equation 5-6, we go through the following three steps.

1. Estimate the expected dividends for each year during the period of nonconstant growth.
2. Find the expected price of the stock at the end of the nonconstant growth period, at which point it has become a constant growth stock.
3. Find the present values of the expected dividends during the nonconstant growth period and the present value of the expected stock price at the end of the nonconstant growth period. Their sum is the intrinsic value of the stock, $\hat{P}_0$.

To illustrate the process for valuing nonconstant growth stocks, we make the following assumptions.

r_s = Stockholders' required rate of return = 13.4%. This rate is used to discount all the cash flows.

N = Years of nonconstant growth = 3.

$g_{t,t+1}$ = Rate of growth in both earnings and dividends during the nonconstant growth period from period t to the next period. $g_{0,1}$ = 30%, $g_{1,2}$ = 20%, and $g_{2,3}$ = 10%. These rates are shown directly on the time line.

g_1 = Rate of constant long-term growth after the nonconstant period = 8%. This rate is also shown on the time line, between Years 3 and 4.

D_0 = Last dividend the company paid = $1.15.

The valuation process as diagrammed in Figure 5-5 is explained in the steps set forth below the time line. The estimated value of the nonconstant growth stock is $31.13.

WEB

See *Ch05 Tool Kit.xls* on the textbook's Web site.

Self Test

Explain how one would find the value of a nonconstant growth stock.

Explain what is meant by the terms "horizon (terminal) date" and "horizon (terminal) value."

Suppose D_0 = $5.00 and r_s = 10%. The expected growth rate from Year 0 to Year 1 (g_1) = 20%, the expected growth rate from Year 1 to Year 2 (g_2) = 10%, and the constant growth rate beyond Year 2 is g_L = 5%. What are the expected dividends for Year 1 and Year 2? **($6.00 and $6.60)** What is the expected horizon value price at Year 2 ($\hat{P}_2$)? **($138.60)** What is $\hat{P}_0$? **($125.45)**

Figure 5-5	Process for Finding the Value of a Nonconstant Growth Stock

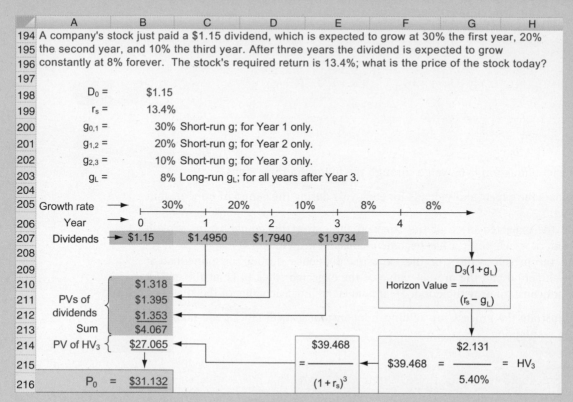

	A	B	C	D	E	F	G	H
194	A company's stock just paid a $1.15 dividend, which is expected to grow at 30% the first year, 20%
195	the second year, and 10% the third year. After three years the dividend is expected to grow
196	constantly at 8% forever. The stock's required return is 13.4%; what is the price of the stock today?
197								
198	D_0 =	$1.15						
199	r_s =	13.4%						
200	$g_{0,1}$ =	30% Short-run g; for Year 1 only.						
201	$g_{1,2}$ =	20% Short-run g; for Year 2 only.						
202	$g_{2,3}$ =	10% Short-run g; for Year 3 only.						
203	g_L =	8% Long-run g_L; for all years after Year 3.						

Notes:

Step 1: Calculate the dividends expected at the end of each year during the nonconstant growth period. Calculate the first dividend, $D_1 = D_0(1 + g_{0,1}) = \$1.15(1.30) = \$1.4950$. Here $g_{0,1}$ is the growth rate (30%) during the first year of the nonconstant growth period. Show the $1.4950 on the time line as the cash flow at Year 1. Then calculate $D_2 = D_1(1 + g_{1,2}) = \$1.4950(1.20) = \$1.7940$ and then $D_3 = D_2(1 + g_{2,3}) = \$1.7940(1.10) = \$1.9734$. (The figure shows the values rounded to four decimal places, but all calculations used nonrounded values.) Show these values on the time line as the cash flows at Year 2 and Year 3. Note that D_0 is used only to calculate D_1.

Step 2: At Year 3, the stock becomes a constant growth stock. Therefore, we can use the constant growth formula to find $\hat{P}_3$, which is the PV of the dividends from Year 4 to infinity as evaluated at Year 3. First we determine $D_4 = \$1.9734(1.08) = \$2.1313$ for use in the formula, and then we calculate $\hat{P}_3$ as follows:

$$\hat{P}_3 = \frac{D_4}{r_s - g_n} = \frac{\$2.1313}{0.134 - 0.08} = \$39.4680$$

We show this $39.468 on the time line as a second cash flow at Year 3. The $39.468 is a Year-3 cash flow in the sense that the owner of the stock could sell it for $39.468 at Year 3 and also in the sense that $39.468 is the value at Year 3 of the dividend cash flows from Year 4 to infinity.

Step 3: Now that the cash flows have been placed on the time line, we can discount each cash flow at the required rate of return, $r_s = 13.4\%$. This produces the PVs shown to the left below the time line, and the sum of the PVs is the value of the nonconstant growth stock, $31.13.

In the figure we show the setup for an *Excel* solution. With a financial calculator, you could use the cash flow (CFLO) register of your calculator. Enter 0 for CF_0 because you get no cash flow at Time 0, $CF_1 = 1.495$, $CF_2 = 1.7940$, and $CF_3 = 1.9734 + 39.468 = 41.4414$. Then enter I/YR = 13.4 and press the NPV key to find the value of the stock, $31.1315.

5.9 Stock Valuation by the Free Cash Flow Approach

The box at the beginning of the chapter showed that the value of a firm is the present value of its future expected free cash flows (FCFs) discounted at the weighted average cost of capital (WACC). The following example illustrates how the firm's total value can be used to find the value of its stock.

Suppose Crum Inc. had a free cash flow of $200 million at the end of the most recent year. Chapter 9 shows how to forecast financial statements and free cash flows, but for now let's assume that Crum's FCFs are expected to grow at a constant rate of 5% per year forever. Chapter 10 explains how to estimate the weighted average cost of capital, but for now let's assume that Crum's WACC is 9%. The present value of the expected future free cash flows is the PV of a growing annuity, so we can use a variation of Equation 5-2, the value of a constantly growing stream of dividends:

$$V = \frac{FCF(1+g)}{WACC-g} = \frac{\$200(1.05)}{0.09-0.05} = \$5{,}250 \text{ million}$$

(5–7)

FCF is the cash flow available for distribution to *all* of the firm's investors, bondholders as well as stockholders. Also, the WACC is the average rate of return required by *all* of the firm's investors, not just shareholders. Therefore, V is the value of the entire firm's operations, not just the value of its equity. If the firm had any nonoperating assets, such as short-term investments in marketable securities, then we would add them to V to find the firm's total value. Crum has no nonoperating assets, so its total value is $5,250 million. To find the value of its equity, subtract the value of claims held by all investors other than common shareholders, such as debtholders and preferred stockholders. If the value of debt plus preferred stock is $2,000 million, then Crum's common equity has a value of $5,250 − $2,000 = $3,250 million. If 325 million shares of stock are outstanding, then the intrinsic value of the stock is $3,250/325 = $10 per share. This example should give you the general idea behind the free cash flow approach to stock price valuation, but see Chapter 11 for a more comprehensive example, including a situation in which free cash flows are growing at a nonconstant rate.

Explain how to find a firm's stock price using the free cash flow approach.

Self Test

5.10 Market Multiple Analysis

If a company is publicly traded, then we can simply look up its most recent stock price to get an estimate of the stock's value. However, we must take another approach if the firm is privately owned. We could estimate the firm's cost of equity based on data for a sample of companies, forecast its earnings and dividends, and apply the DCF method to find the value of its stock. However, another method, **market multiple analysis**, can and generally would be used. Here we would take a metric for the firm—say, its EPS—and then multiply by a market-determined multiple such as the average P/E ratio for a sample of similar companies. This would give us an estimate of the stock's intrinsic value. Market multiples can also be applied to total net income, to sales, to book value, or to number of subscribers for businesses such as cable TV or cellular telephone systems. Whereas the discounted dividend method applies valuation concepts in a precise manner by focusing on expected cash flows, market multiple analysis is more judgmental.

To illustrate the concept, suppose Tapley Products is a privately held firm whose forecasted earnings per share are $7.70, and suppose the average price/earnings (P/E) ratio for a set of similar publicly traded companies is 12. To estimate the intrinsic value of Tapley's stock we would simply multiply its $7.70 EPS by the multiple 12, obtaining the value $7.70(12) = $92.40.

Another commonly used metric is *earnings before interest, taxes, depreciation, and amortization (EBITDA)*. The EBITDA *multiple* is the total value of a company (the market value of its equity plus that of its debt) divided by EBITDA. This multiple is based on total value, since EBITDA is used to compensate the firm's stockholders and bondholders. Therefore, it is called an **entity multiple.** The EBITDA market multiple is the average EBITDA multiple for a group of similar publicly traded companies. This procedure gives an estimate of the company's total value, and to find the estimated intrinsic value of the stock we would subtract the value of the debt from total value and then divide by the shares of stock outstanding.

As suggested previously, in some businesses, such as cable TV and cellular telephone, a critical factor is the number of customers the company has. For example, when a telephone company acquires a cellular operator, it might pay a price that is based on the number of customers. Managed care companies such as HMOs have applied similar logic in acquisitions, basing valuations primarily on the number of people insured. Some Internet companies have been valued by the number of "eyeballs," which is the number of hits on the site.

If you examine the prospectus for a firm that is having an IPO, or information regarding the acquisition of one firm by another, you will almost certainly see references to market multiple analysis. Security analysts also use this approach, sometimes as a primary measure and sometimes as a supplement to a DCF analysis, when estimating firms' intrinsic values.

Self Test	What is market multiple analysis?
	What is an entity multiple?

5.11 Preferred Stock

Preferred stock is a *hybrid*—it's similar to bonds in some respects and to common stock in others. Like bonds, preferred stock has a par value, and a fixed amount of dividends must be paid before dividends can be paid on the common stock. However, if the preferred dividend is not earned, the directors can omit (or "pass") it without throwing the company into bankruptcy. So, although preferred stock has a fixed payment like bonds, a failure to make this payment will not lead to bankruptcy.

The dividends on preferred stocks are fixed, and if they are scheduled to go on forever, the issue is a perpetuity whose value is found as follows:

(5–8)

$$V_{ps} = \frac{D_{ps}}{r_{ps}}$$

V_{ps} is the value of the preferred stock, D_{ps} is the preferred dividend, and r_{ps} is the required rate of return. MicroDrive has preferred stock outstanding that pays a dividend of $10 per year. If the required rate of return on this preferred stock is 10%, then its value is $100:

$$V_{ps} = \frac{\$10.00}{0.10} = \$100.00$$

If we know the current price of a preferred stock and its dividend, we can transpose terms and solve for the expected rate of return as follows:

$$\hat{r}_{ps} = \frac{D_{ps}}{V_{ps}} \qquad\qquad (5\text{--}9)$$

Some preferred stocks have a stated maturity, say, 50 years. If a firm's preferred stock matures in 50 years, pays a $10 annual dividend, has a par value of $100, and has a required return of 8%, then we can find its price using a financial calculator: Enter N = 50, I/YR = 8, PMT = 10, and FV = 100. Then press PV to find the price, V_{ps} = $124.47. If you know the price of a share of preferred stock, you can solve for I/YR to find the expected rate of return, $\hat{r}_{ps}$.

Most preferred stocks pay dividends quarterly. This is true for MicroDrive, so we could find the effective rate of return on its preferred stock as follows:

$$\text{EFF\%} = \text{EAR} = \left(1 + \frac{r_{NOM}}{M}\right)^{M} - 1 = \left(1 + \frac{0.10}{4}\right)^{4} - 1 = 10.38\%$$

If an investor wanted to compare the returns on MicroDrive's bonds and its preferred stock, it would be best to convert the nominal rates on each security to effective rates and then compare these "equivalent annual rates."

Self Test

Explain the following statement: "Preferred stock is a hybrid security."

Is the equation used to value preferred stock more like the one used to evaluate perpetual bonds or the one used for common stock? Explain.

A preferred stock has an annual dividend of $5. The required return is 8%. What is the V_{ps}? (**$62.50**)

5.12 Stock Market Equilibrium

Recall that r_i, the required return on Stock i, can be found using the Capital Asset Pricing Model (CAPM) as discussed in Chapter 2:

$$r_i = r_{RF} + (RP_M)b_i$$

If the risk-free rate of return is 8%, the market risk premium, RP_M, is 4%, and Stock i has a beta of 2, then its required rate of return is 16%:

$$r_i = 8\% + (4\%)2.0$$

$$= 16\%$$

The **marginal investor** will want to buy Stock i if its expected rate of return is more than 16%, will want to sell it if the expected rate of return is less than 16%, and will be indifferent—and hence will hold but not buy or sell it—if the expected rate of return is exactly 16%.

Now suppose a typical investor's portfolio contains Stock i, and suppose she analyzes the stock's prospects and concludes that its earnings, dividends, and price can be expected to grow at a constant rate of 5% per year. The last dividend was $D_0 = \$2.8571$, so the next expected dividend is

$$D_1 = \$2.8571(1.05) = \$3$$

Our investor observes that the present price of the stock, P_0, is $30. Should she purchase more of Stock i, sell the stock, or maintain the present position?

The investor can calculate Stock i's *expected rate of return* as follows:

$$\hat{r}_i = \frac{D_1}{P_0} + g = \frac{\$3}{\$30} + 5\% = 15\%$$

Because the expected rate of return, 15%, is less than the required return, 16%, the investor would want to sell the stock, as would most other holders if this one is typical. However, few people would want to buy at the $30 price, so the present owners would be unable to find buyers unless they cut the price of the stock. Thus, the price would decline, and this decline would continue until the price reached $27.27, at which point the stock would be in **equilibrium**, defined as the price at which the expected rate of return, 16%, is equal to the required rate of return as seen by the marginal investor:

$$\hat{r}_i = \frac{\$3}{\$27.27} + 5\% = 11\% + 5\% = 16\% = r_i$$

Had the stock initially sold for less than $27.27, say, for $25, then events would have been reversed. Investors would have wanted to buy the stock because its expected rate of return would have exceeded its required rate of return, and buy orders would have driven the stock's price up to $27.27.

To summarize, in equilibrium two related conditions must hold:

1. A stock's expected rate of return as seen by the marginal investor must equal its required rate of return: $\hat{r}_i = r_i$.
2. The actual market price of the stock must equal its intrinsic value as estimated by the marginal investor: $P_0 = \hat{P}_0$.

Of course, some individual investors probably believe that $\hat{r}_i > r_i$ and $\hat{P}_0 > P_0$, hence they would invest in the stock, while other investors have the opposite view and would sell all of their shares. However, it is the marginal investor who establishes the actual market price, and for the marginal investor we must have $\hat{r}_i = r_i$ and $P_0 = \hat{P}_0$. If these conditions do not hold, trading will occur until they do.

5.12a Changes in Equilibrium Stock Prices and Market Volatility

Stock prices are not constant—as we demonstrated earlier in this chapter and elsewhere, they undergo violent changes at times. Indeed, many stocks declined by 80% or more during 2008, and a few enjoyed gains of up to 200% or even more. At the risk of understatement, the stock market is volatile!

To see how such changes can occur, assume that Stock i is in equilibrium, selling at a price of $27.27. If all expectations are met exactly, during the next year the price would gradually rise by 5%, to $28.63. However, many different events could occur to cause a change in the equilibrium price. To illustrate, consider again the set of inputs used to develop Stock i's price of $27.27, along with a new set of expected inputs:

	Variable Value	
	Original	New
Risk-free rate, r_{RF}	8%	7%
Market risk premium, $r_M - r_{RF}$	4%	3%
Stock i's beta coefficient, b_i	2.0	1.0
Stock i's expected growth rate, g_i	5%	6%
D_0	$2.8571	$2.8571
Price of Stock i	$27.27	?

Now give yourself a test: Would each of the indicated changes, by itself, lead to an increase, a decrease, or no change in the price, and what is your guess as to the new stock price?

Every change, taken alone, would lead to a higher price. Taken together, the first three would lower r_i from 16% to 10%:

$$\text{Original } r_i = 8\% + 4\%(2.0) = 16\%$$
$$\text{New } r_i = 7\% + 3\%(1.0) = 10\%$$

Using these values together with the new g = 6%, we find that $\hat{P}_0$ rises from $27.27 to $75.71:[11]

$$\text{Original } \hat{P}_0 = \frac{\$2.8571(1.05)}{0.16 - 0.05} = \frac{\$3}{0.11} = \$27.27$$

$$\text{New } \hat{P}_0 = \frac{\$2.8571(1.06)}{0.10 - 0.06} = \frac{\$3.0285}{0.04} = \$75.71$$

---

11 A price change of this magnitude is by no means rare. The prices of *many* stocks double or halve during any given year. For example, IDT Corporation, a provider of domestic and international long distance calling cards, increased 571% in 2010, while DJSP Enterprises, a company that specialized in providing non-legal support to the home foreclosure industry, lost 93.3% of its value.

At the new price, the expected and required rates of return are equal:[12]

$$\hat{r}_i = \frac{\$3.0285}{\$75.71} + 6\% = 10\% = r_i$$

This indicates that the stock is in equilibrium at the new and higher price. As this example illustrates, even small changes in the size of expected future dividends or in their risk, as reflected in the required return, can cause large changes in stock prices as the price moves from one equilibrium condition to another. What might cause investors to change their expectations about future dividends? It could be new information about the company, such as preliminary results for an R&D program, initial sales of a new product, or the discovery of harmful side effects from the use of an existing product. Or new information that will affect many companies could arrive, such as the collapse of the debt markets in 2008. Given the existence of computers and telecommunications networks, new information hits the market on an almost continuous basis, and it causes frequent and sometimes large changes in stock prices. In other words, *ready availability of information causes stock prices to be volatile.*

If a stock's price is stable, this probably means that little new information is arriving. But if you think it's risky to invest in a volatile stock, imagine how risky it would be to invest in a company that rarely releases new information about its sales or operations. It may be bad to see your stock's price jump around, but it would be a lot worse to see a stable quoted price most of the time and then to see huge moves on the rare days when new information is released.[13] Fortunately, in our economy timely information is readily available, and evidence suggests that stocks—especially those of large companies—adjust rapidly to new information. Consequently, equilibrium ordinarily exists for any given stock, and required and expected returns are generally equal. Stock prices certainly change, sometimes violently and rapidly, but this simply reflects changing conditions and expectations.

There are times, of course, when a stock appears to react for several months to favorable or unfavorable developments. However, this does not necessarily signify a long adjustment period; rather, it could simply indicate that, as more new pieces of information about the situation come out, the market adjusts to them. The ability of the market to adjust to new information is discussed in the next section.

Self Test

What two conditions must hold for a stock to be in equilibrium?

Why doesn't a volatile stock price imply irrational pricing?

---

12   It should be obvious by now that *actual realized* rates of return are not necessarily equal to expected and required returns. Thus, an investor might have *expected* to receive a return of 15% if he had bought IDT stock, but after the fact, the realized return was far above 15% in 2010. On the other hand, the 2010 actual realized return on DJSP stock was far below 15%.

13   Note, however, that if information came out infrequently, stock prices would probably be stable for a time and then experience large price swings when news did come out. This would be a bit like not having a lot of little earthquakes (frequent new information) that relieve stress along the fault and instead building up stress for a number of years before a massive earthquake.

5.13 The Efficient Markets Hypothesis

A body of theory called the **Efficient Markets Hypothesis (EMH)** asserts that (1) stocks are always in equilibrium and (2) it is impossible for an investor to "beat the market" and consistently earn a higher rate of return than is justified by the stock's risk. Those who believe in the EMH note that there are 100,000 or so full-time, highly trained, professional analysts and traders operating in the market, while there are fewer than 3,000 major stocks. Therefore, if each analyst followed 30 stocks (which is about right, as analysts tend to specialize in a specific industry), there would on average be 1,000 analysts following each stock. Furthermore, these analysts work for organizations such as Morgan Stanley, Goldman Sachs, CALPERS, Prudential Financial, and the like, which have billions of dollars available with which to take advantage of bargains. In addition, as a result of SEC disclosure requirements and electronic information networks, as new information about a stock becomes available, these analysts generally receive and evaluate it at the same time. Therefore, the price of a stock will adjust almost immediately to any new development. That, in a nutshell, is the logic behind the efficient markets hypothesis. However, there are variations on the theory, as we discuss next.

5.13a Weak-Form Efficiency

Technical analysts believe that past trends or patterns in stock prices can be used to predict future stock prices. In contrast, those who believe in the **weak form** of the EMH argue that all information contained in past price movements is fully reflected in current market prices. If the weak form were true, then information about recent trends in stock prices would be of no use in selecting stocks—the fact that a stock has risen for the past three days, for example, would give us no useful clues as to what it will do today or tomorrow. Those who believe that weak-form efficiency exists also believe that technical analysts, also known as "chartists," are wasting their time.

To illustrate the arguments, after studying the past history of the stock market, a technical analyst might "discover" the following pattern: If a stock falls for three consecutive days, its price typically rises by 10% the following day. The technician would then conclude that investors could make money by purchasing a stock whose price has fallen three consecutive days.

Weak-form advocates argue that if this pattern truly existed then other investors would soon discover it, and if so, why would anyone be willing to sell a stock after it had fallen for three consecutive days? In other words, why sell if you know that the price is going to increase by 10% the next day? Those who believe in weak-form efficiency argue that if the stock were really likely to rise to $44 tomorrow, then its price *today, right now,* would actually rise to somewhere close to $44, thereby eliminating the trading opportunity. Consequently, weak-form efficiency implies that any information that comes from past stock prices is rapidly incorporated into the current stock price.

5.13b Semistrong-Form Efficiency

The **semistrong form** of the EMH states that current market prices reflect all *publicly available* information. Therefore, if semistrong-form efficiency exists, it would do no good to pore over annual reports or other published data because market prices would have adjusted to any good or bad news contained in such reports back when the news came out. With semistrong-form efficiency, investors should expect to earn returns commensurate with risk, but they should not expect to do any better or worse other than by chance.

Another implication of semistrong-form efficiency is that whenever information is released to the public, stock prices will respond only if the information is different from what had been expected. For example, if a company announces a 30% increase in earnings and if that increase is about what analysts had been expecting, then the announcement should have little or no effect on the company's stock price. On the other hand, the stock price would probably fall if analysts had expected earnings to increase by more than 30%, but it probably would rise if they had expected a smaller increase.

5.13c Strong-Form Efficiency

The **strong form** of the EMH states that current market prices reflect all pertinent information, whether publicly available or privately held. If this form holds, even insiders would find it impossible to earn consistently abnormal returns in the stock market.

5.13d Is the Stock Market Efficient?

Many empirical studies have been conducted to test the validity of the three forms of market efficiency. Most empirical studies are joint tests of the EMH and an asset pricing model (usually the CAPM, discussed in Chapter 2 or the Fama-French three-factor model, discussed in Chapter 3). They are joint tests in the sense that they examine whether a particular strategy can beat the market, where "beating the market" means earning a return higher than that predicted by the particular asset pricing model. Most studies suggest that the stock market is highly efficient in the weak form and reasonably efficient in the semistrong form, at least for the larger and more widely followed stocks.[14] The evidence suggests that the strong form EMH does not hold, because those who possessed inside information could and did (illegally) make abnormal profits.

However, skeptics of the EMH point to the stock market bubbles that burst in 2000 and 2008 and suggest that, at the height of these booms, the stocks of many companies—especially in the technology sector—vastly exceeded their intrinsic values. These skeptics suggest that investors are not simply machines that rationally process all available information; rather, a variety of psychological and perhaps irrational factors also come into play. Indeed, researchers have begun to incorporate elements of cognitive psychology in an effort to better understand how individuals and entire

---

14. The vast majority of academic studies have shown that no excess returns (defined as returns above those predicted by the CAPM or other asset pricing models) can be earned with technical analysis—that is, using past stock prices to predict future stock prices—especially after considering transactions costs. A possible exception is in the area of long-term reversals, where several studies show that portfolios of stocks with poor past long-term performance tend to do slightly better than average in the future long term, and vice versa. Another possible exception is in the area of momentum, where studies show that stocks with strong performance in the short-term past tend to do slightly better than average in the short-term future, and likewise for weak performance. For example, see N. Jegadeesh and S. Titman, "Returns to Buying Winners and Selling Losers: Implications for Stock Market Efficiency," *Journal of Finance*, March 1993, pp. 69–91, and W. F. M. DeBondt and R. H. Thaler, "Does the Stock Market Overreact?" *Journal of Finance*, July 1985, pp. 793–808. However, when a way to "beat" the market becomes known, the actions of investors tend to eliminate it.

markets respond to different circumstances. In other words, if people aren't rational in their daily decisions, why should we expect them to be rational in their financial decisions? For example, studies show that investors tend to hold on too long to stocks that have performed poorly in the past (i.e., losers) but that they sell winners too quickly. This field of study is called *behavioral finance.*[15]

Keep in mind that the EMH does not assume that all investors are rational. Instead, it assumes that stock market prices track intrinsic values fairly closely. As we described earlier, new information should cause a stock's intrinsic value to move rapidly to a new level that reflects the new information. The EMH also assumes that if stock prices deviate from their intrinsic values, investors will *quickly* take advantage of this mispricing by buying undervalued stocks and selling overvalued stocks. Thus, investors' actions work to drive prices to their new equilibrium level based on new information. Even if some investors behave irrationally, as by holding losers too long and/or selling winners too quickly, this does not imply that the markets are not efficient. Thus, it is possible to have irrational investors in a rational market.

On the other hand, if the market itself is inherently irrational (i.e., if mispricings persist for long periods), then rational investors can lose a lot of money even if they are ultimately proven to be correct. For example, a "rational" investor in mid-1999 might have concluded that the Nasdaq was overvalued when it was trading at 3,000. If such an investor had acted on that assumption and sold stock short, he would have lost a lot of money the following year, when the Nasdaq soared to over 5,000 as "irrational exuberance" pushed the prices of already overvalued stocks to even higher levels. Ultimately, if our "rational investor" had the courage, patience, and financial resources to hold on, he would have been vindicated in the long run, because the Nasdaq subsequently fell from over 5,000 to about 1,300. But as the economist John Maynard Keynes said, "In the long run we are all dead."

What is the bottom line on market efficiency? Based on our reading of the evidence, we believe that for most stocks, for most of the time, it is generally safe to assume that the market is reasonably efficient in the sense that the intrinsic price is approximately equal to the actual market price ($\hat{P}_0 \approx P_0$). However, major shifts can and do occur periodically, causing most stocks to move strongly up or down. In the early 1980s, inflation was running over 10% per year and interest rates on AAA corporate bonds hit 15%. That knocked most stocks way below their intrinsic values, so when inflation fears receded, stock prices roared ahead. A similar situation, but in reverse, may have occurred in 2008 and 2009. Stock prices fell sharply, probably to a level below their intrinsic values, since they recovered substantially by 2011. In other words, we may have experienced a "reverse bubble."

5.13e Implications of Market Efficiency for Financial Decisions

What bearing does the EMH have on financial decisions? First, many investors have given up trying to beat the market because the professionals who manage

15. Three noteworthy sources for students interested in behavioral finance are: Richard H. Thaler, Editor, *Advances in Behavioral Finance* (New York: Russell Sage Foundation, 1993); Andrei Shleifer, *Inefficient Markets: An Introduction to Behavioral Finance* (New York: Oxford University Press, 2000); and Nicholas Barberis and Richard Thaler, "A Survey of Behavioral Finance," Chapter 18 in *Handbook of the Economics of Finance*, edited by George Constantinides, Milt Harris, and René Stulz (Amsterdam: Elsevier/North-Holland, 2003). Students interested in learning more about the Efficient Markets Hypothesis should consult Burton G. Malkiel, *A Random Walk Down Wall Street* (New York: W.W. Norton & Company, 2007).

mutual fund portfolios, on average, do not outperform the overall stock market as measured by an index like the S&P 500.[16] Indeed, the relatively poor performance of actively managed mutual funds helps explain the growing popularity of index funds, where administrative costs are lower than for actively managed funds. Rather than spending time and money trying to find undervalued stocks, index funds try instead to match overall market returns by buying the basket of stocks that makes up a particular index, such as the S&P 500.

Second, market efficiency also has important implications for managerial decisions, especially stock issues, stock repurchases, and tender offers. If the market prices stocks fairly, then managerial decisions based on the premise that a stock is undervalued or overvalued might not make sense. Managers may have better information about their

RATIONAL BEHAVIOR VERSUS ANIMAL SPIRITS, HERDING, AND ANCHORING BIAS

If investors were completely rational, they would carefully analyze all the available information about stocks and then make well-informed decisions to buy, sell, or hold them. Most academics have argued that investors with enough clout to move the market behave in this manner. However, the stock market bubbles of 2000 and 2008 suggest that something other than pure rationality is alive and well.

The great economist John Maynard Keynes, writing during the 1920s and 1930s, suggested that **animal spirits** influence markets. After a period of rising prosperity and stock prices, Keynes believed that investors begin to think that the good times will last forever, a feeling that is driven by happy talk and high spirits rather than cool reasoning. Indeed, psychologists have demonstrated that many people do in fact anchor too closely on recent events when predicting future events, a phenomenon called **anchoring bias.** Therefore, when the market is performing better than average, they tend to think it will continue to perform better than average. Even worse, when one group of investors does well, other investors begin to emulate them, acting like a herd of sheep following one another merrily down the road. Such **herding behavior** makes it easy for hedge funds to raise enormous sums and for con men like Bernie Madoff to find new marks.

Overinflated markets and bubbles eventually burst, and when they do, the same psychological factors act in reverse, often causing bigger declines than can be explained by rational models. Eventually, though, markets bottom out, and before long the next bubble starts to inflate. Historically, such cycles have existed for as far back as our data go, and these cycles are inconsistent with the idea of rational, data-driven investors. This is the realm of behavioral finance as discussed earlier in the chapter.

How can we reconcile theories that assume investors and decision makers are rational and data-driven with the fact that businesses and the stock market are influenced by people subject to animal spirits and herding instincts? Our conclusion is that there is some truth in both theories—markets are rational to a large extent, but they are also subject to irrational behavior at times. Our advice is to do careful, rational analyses, using the tools and techniques described in this book, but also to recognize that actual prices can differ from intrinsic values—sometimes by large amounts and for long periods. That's the bad news. The good news is that differences between actual prices and intrinsic values provide wonderful opportunities for those able to capitalize on them.

---

16. For a discussion of the performance of actively managed funds, see Jonathan Clements, "Resisting the Lure of Managed Funds," *The Wall Street Journal,* February 27, 2001, p. C1.

own companies than outsiders, but it would be illegal to use this information for their own advantage, and they cannot deliberately defraud investors by knowingly putting out false information.

What is the Efficient Markets Hypothesis (EMH)?
What are the differences among the three forms of the EMH?
What are the implications of the EMH for financial decisions?

Self Test

Summary

Corporate decisions should be analyzed in terms of how alternative courses of action are likely to affect a firm's value. However, it is necessary to know how stock prices are established before attempting to measure how a given decision will affect a firm's value. This chapter showed how stock values are determined and also how investors go about estimating the rates of return they expect to earn. The key concepts covered are listed below.

- A **proxy** is a document that gives one person the power to act for another, typically the power to vote shares of common stock. A **proxy fight** occurs when an outside group solicits stockholders' proxies in an effort to overthrow the current management.
- A **takeover** occurs when a person or group succeeds in ousting a firm's management and takes control of the company.
- Stockholders often have the right to purchase any additional shares sold by the firm. This right, called the **preemptive right,** protects the present stockholders' control and prevents dilution of their value.
- Although most firms have only one type of common stock, in some instances **classified stock** is used to meet the special needs of the company. One type is **founders' shares.** This is stock owned by the firm's founders that carries sole voting rights but restricted dividends for a specified number of years.
- A **closely held company** is one whose stock is owned by a few individuals who are typically associated with the firm's management.
- A **publicly held company** is one whose stock is owned by a relatively large number of individuals who are not actively involved in the firm's management. Publicly held companies are generally regulated by the SEC or other governmental bodies.
- The **intrinsic value of a share of stock** is calculated as the **present value of the stream of dividends** the stock is expected to provide in the future.

- The equation used to find the **intrinsic,** or **expected, value of a constant growth stock** is

$$\hat{P}_0 = \frac{D_1}{r_s - g}$$

  Web Extension 5A provides a derivation of this formula.
- The **expected total rate of return** from a stock consists of an **expected dividend yield** plus an **expected capital gains yield.** For a constant growth firm, both the dividend yield and the capital gains yield are expected to remain constant in the future.
- The equation for $\hat{r}_s$, the **expected rate of return on a constant growth stock,** is

$$\hat{r}_s = \frac{D_1}{P_0} + g$$

- A **zero growth stock** is one whose future dividends are not expected to grow at all. A **nonconstant growth stock** is one whose earnings and dividends are expected to grow much faster than the economy as a whole over some specified time period and then to grow at the "normal" rate.
- To find the **present value of a nonconstant growth stock,** (1) find the dividends expected during the nonconstant growth period, (2) find the price of the stock at the end of the nonconstant growth period, (3) discount the dividends and the projected price back to the present, and (4) sum these PVs to find the current intrinsic, or expected, value of the stock, $\hat{P}_0$.
- The **horizon (terminal) date** is the date when individual dividend forecasts are no longer made because the dividend growth rate is assumed to be constant thereafter.
- The **horizon (terminal) value** is the value at the horizon date of all future dividends after that date:

$$\hat{P}_N = \frac{D_{N+1}}{r_s - g}$$

- **Preferred stock** is a hybrid security having some characteristics of debt and some of equity.
- The **value of a share of perpetual preferred stock** is found as the dividend divided by the required rate of return:

$$V_{ps} = \frac{D_{ps}}{r_{ps}}$$

- **Preferred stock** that has a finite maturity is evaluated with a formula that is identical in form to the bond value formula.
- The **marginal investor** is a representative investor whose actions reflect the beliefs of those people who are currently trading a stock. It is the marginal investor who determines a stock's price.
- **Equilibrium** is the condition under which the expected return on a security as seen by the marginal investor is just equal to its required return, $\hat{r}_s = r_s$. Also, the stock's intrinsic value must be equal to its market price, $\hat{P}_0 = P_0$.

- The **Efficient Markets Hypothesis (EMH)** holds that (1) stocks are always in equilibrium and (2) it is impossible for an investor who does not have inside information to consistently "beat the market." Therefore, according to the EMH, stocks are always fairly valued ($\hat{P}_0 = P_0$) and have a required return equal to their expected return ($r_s = \hat{r}_s$).
- **Animal spirits** refers to the tendency of investors to become excited and let their emotions affect their behavior; **herding instincts** refers to the tendency of investors to follow the crowd, relying on others rather than their own analysis; and **anchoring bias** is the human tendency to "anchor" too closely on recent events when predicting future events. These three factors can interfere with basing decisions on pure rational analysis.

Questions

5-1 Define each of the following terms:
  a. Proxy; proxy fight; takeover; preemptive right; classified stock; founders' shares
  b. Closely held stock; publicly owned stock
  c. Intrinsic value ($\hat{P}_0$); market price (P_0)
  d. Required rate of return, r_s; expected rate of return, $\hat{r}_s$; actual, or realized, rate of return, $\bar{r}_s$
  e. Capital gains yield; dividend yield; expected total return
  f. Normal, or constant, growth; nonconstant growth; zero growth stock
  g. Preferred stock
  h. Equilibrium; Efficient Markets Hypothesis (EMH); three forms of EMH
  i. Purely rational behavior; animal spirits; herding instincts; anchoring; behavioral finance

5-2 Two investors are evaluating General Electric's stock for possible purchase. They agree on the expected value of D_1 and also on the expected future dividend growth rate. Further, they agree on the risk of the stock. However, one investor normally holds stocks for 2 years and the other normally holds stocks for 10 years. On the basis of the type of analysis done in this chapter, they should both be willing to pay the same price for General Electric's stock. True or false? Explain.

5-3 A bond that pays interest forever and has no maturity date is a perpetual bond, also called a perpetuity or a consol. In what respect is a perpetual bond similar to (1) a no-growth common stock and (2) a share of preferred stock?

5-4 In this chapter and elsewhere we have argued that a stock's market price can deviate from its intrinsic value. Discuss the following question: If all investors attempt to behave in an entirely rational manner, could these differences still exist? In answering this question, think about information that's available to insiders versus outsiders, the difficulty of estimating the probabilities of financial events versus physical events, and the validity of the concepts of animal spirits, herding, and anchoring.

Problems   Answers Appear in Appendix B

Easy Problems 1–5

5-1   **DPS Calculation**   Thress Industries just paid a dividend of $1.50 a share (i.e., $D_0 = \$1.50$). The dividend is expected to grow 5% a year for the next 3 years and then 10% a year thereafter. What is the expected dividend per share for each of the next 5 years?

5-2   **Constant Growth Valuation**   Boehm Incorporated is expected to pay a $1.50 per share dividend at the end of this year (i.e., $D_1 = \$1.50$). The dividend is expected to grow at a constant rate of 6% a year. The required rate of return on the stock, r_s, is 13%. What is the value per share of Boehm's stock?

5-3   **Constant Growth Valuation**   Woidtke Manufacturing's stock currently sells for $22 a share. The stock just paid a dividend of $1.20 a share (i.e., $D_0 = \$1.20$), and the dividend is expected to grow forever at a constant rate of 10% a year. What stock price is expected 1 year from now? What is the required rate of return on Woidtke's stock?

5-4   **Preferred Stock Valuation**   Nick's Enchiladas Incorporated has preferred stock outstanding that pays a dividend of $5 at the end of each year. The preferred sells for $50 a share. What is the stock's required rate of return?

5-5   **Nonconstant Growth Valuation**   A company currently pays a dividend of $2 per share ($D_0 = \$2$). It is estimated that the company's dividend will grow at a rate of 20% per year for the next 2 years, then at a constant rate of 7% thereafter. The company's stock has a beta of 1.2, the risk-free rate is 7.5%, and the market risk premium is 4%. What is your estimate of the stock's current price?

Intermediate Problems 6–16

5-6   **Constant Growth Rate, g**   A stock is trading at $80 per share. The stock is expected to have a year-end dividend of $4 per share ($D_1 = \$4$), and it is expected to grow at some constant rate g throughout time. The stock's required rate of return is 14%. If markets are efficient, what is your forecast of g?

5-7   **Constant Growth Valuation**   Crisp Cookware's common stock is expected to pay a dividend of $3 a share at the end of this year ($D_1 = \$3.00$); its beta is 0.8; the risk-free rate is 5.2%; and the market risk premium is 6%. The dividend is expected to grow at some constant rate g, and the stock currently sells for $40 a share. Assuming the market is in equilibrium, what does the market believe will be the stock's price at the end of 3 years (i.e., what is $\hat{P}_3$)?

5-8   **Preferred Stock Rate of Return**   What is the nominal rate of return on a preferred stock with a $50 par value, a stated dividend of 7% of par, and a current market price of (a) $30, (b) $40, (c) $50, and (d) $70?

5-9   **Declining Growth Stock Valuation**   Brushy Mountain Mining Company's coal reserves are being depleted, so its sales are falling. Also, environmental costs increase each year, so its costs are rising. As a result, the company's earnings and dividends are declining at the constant rate of 4% per year. If $D_0 = \$6$ and $r_s = 14\%$, what is the value of Brushy Mountain's stock?

5-10 **Rates of Return and Equilibrium** The beta coefficient for Stock C is $b_C = 0.4$ and that for Stock D is $b_D = -0.5$. (Stock D's beta is negative, indicating that its rate of return rises whenever returns on most other stocks fall. There are very few negative-beta stocks, although collection agency and gold mining stocks are sometimes cited as examples.)

   a. If the risk-free rate is 9% and the expected rate of return on an average stock is 13%, what are the required rates of return on Stocks C and D?

   b. For Stock C, suppose the current price, P_0, is $25; the next expected dividend, D_1, is $1.50; and the stock's expected constant growth rate is 4%. Is the stock in equilibrium? Explain, and describe what would happen if the stock were not in equilibrium.

5-11 **Nonconstant Growth Stock Valuation** Assume that the average firm in your company's industry is expected to grow at a constant rate of 6% and that its dividend yield is 7%. Your company is about as risky as the average firm in the industry, but it has just successfully completed some R&D work that leads you to expect that its earnings and dividends will grow at a rate of 50% $[D_1 = D_0(1 + g) = D_0(1.50)]$ this year and 25% the following year, after which growth should return to the 6% industry average. If the last dividend paid (D_0) was $1, what is the value per share of your firm's stock?

5-12 **Nonconstant Growth Stock Valuation** Simpkins Corporation does not pay any dividends because it is expanding rapidly and needs to retain all of its earnings. However, investors expect Simpkins to begin paying dividends, with the first dividend of $0.50 coming 3 years from today. The dividend should grow rapidly—at a rate of 80% per year—during Years 4 and 5. After Year 5, the company should grow at a constant rate of 7% per year. If the required return on the stock is 16%, what is the value of the stock today?

5-13 **Preferred Stock Valuation** Several years ago, Rolen Riders issued preferred stock with a stated annual dividend of 10% of its $100 par value. Preferred stock of this type currently yields 8%. Assume dividends are paid annually.

   a. What is the value of Rolen's preferred stock?

   b. Suppose interest rate levels have risen to the point where the preferred stock now yields 12%. What would be the new value of Rolen's preferred stock?

5-14 **Return on Common Stock** You buy a share of The Ludwig Corporation stock for $21.40. You expect it to pay dividends of $1.07, $1.1449, and $1.2250 in Years 1, 2, and 3, respectively, and you expect to sell it at a price of $26.22 at the end of 3 years.

   a. Calculate the growth rate in dividends.

   b. Calculate the expected dividend yield.

   c. Assuming that the calculated growth rate is expected to continue, you can add the dividend yield to the expected growth rate to obtain the expected total rate of return. What is this stock's expected total rate of return?

5-15 **Constant Growth Stock Valuation** Investors require a 13% rate of return on Brooks Sisters's stock ($r_s = 13\%$).

   a. What would the value of Brooks's stock be if the previous dividend were $D_0 = \$3.00$ and if investors expect dividends to grow at a constant annual rate of (1) −5%, (2) 0%, (3) 5%, and (4) 10%?

   b. Using data from part a, what is the constant growth model's value for Brooks Sisters's stock if the required rate of return is 13% and the expected growth rate is (1) 13% or (2) 15%? Are these reasonable results? Explain.

   c. Is it reasonable to expect that a constant growth stock would have $g > r_s$?

5-16 **Equilibrium Stock Price** The risk-free rate of return, r_{RF}, is 11%; the required rate of return on the market, r_M, is 14%; and Schuler Company's stock has a beta coefficient of 1.5.

a. If the dividend expected during the coming year, D_1, is $2.25, and if g is a constant 5%, then at what price should Schuler's stock sell?

b. Now suppose that the Federal Reserve Board increases the money supply, causing a fall in the risk-free rate to 9% and in r_M to 12%. How would this affect the price of the stock?

c. In addition to the change in part b, suppose investors' risk aversion declines; this fact, combined with the decline in r_{RF}, causes r_M to fall to 11%. At what price would Schuler's stock now sell?

d. Suppose Schuler has a change in management. The new group institutes policies that increase the expected constant growth rate to 6%. Also, the new management stabilizes sales and profits and thus causes the beta coefficient to decline from 1.5 to 1.3. Assume that r_{RF} and r_M are equal to the values in part c. After all these changes, what is Schuler's new equilibrium price? (*Note:* D_1 goes to $2.27.)

Challenging Problems 17–19

5-17 **Constant Growth Stock Valuation** You are analyzing Jillian's Jewelry (JJ) stock for a possible purchase. JJ just paid a dividend of $1.50 *yesterday*. You expect the dividend to grow at the rate of 6% per year for the next 3 years; if you buy the stock, you plan to hold it for 3 years and then sell it.

a. What dividends do you expect for JJ stock over the next 3 years? In other words, calculate D_1, D_2, and D_3. Note that D_0 = $1.50.

b. JJ's stock has a required return of 13%, and so this is the rate you'll use to discount dividends. Find the present value of the dividend stream; that is, calculate the PV of D_1, D_2, and D_3, and then sum these PVs.

c. JJ stock should trade for $27.05 3 years from now (i.e., you expect $\hat{P}_3$ = $27.05). Discounted at a 13% rate, what is the present value of this expected future stock price? In other words, calculate the PV of $27.05.

d. If you plan to buy the stock, hold it for 3 years, and then sell it for $27.05, what is the most you should pay for it?

e. Use the constant growth model to calculate the present value of this stock. Assume that g = 6% and is constant.

f. Is the value of this stock dependent on how long you plan to hold it? In other words, if your planned holding period were 2 years or 5 years rather than 3 years, would this affect the value of the stock today, $\hat{P}_0$? Explain your answer.

5-18 **Nonconstant Growth Stock Valuation** Reizenstein Technologies (RT) has just developed a solar panel capable of generating 200% more electricity than any solar panel currently on the market. As a result, RT is expected to experience a 15% annual growth rate for the next 5 years. By the end of 5 years, other firms will have developed comparable technology, and RT's growth rate will slow to 5% per year indefinitely. Stockholders require a return of 12% on RT's stock. The most recent annual dividend (D_0), which was paid yesterday, was $1.75 per share.

a. Calculate RT's expected dividends for t = 1, t = 2, t = 3, t = 4, and t = 5.

b. Calculate the intrinsic value of the stock today, $\hat{P}_0$. Proceed by finding the present value of the dividends expected at t = 1, t = 2, t = 3, t = 4, and t = 5 plus the present value of the stock price that should exist at t = 5, $\hat{P}_5$. The $\hat{P}_5$ stock price can be found by using the constant growth equation. Note that to find $\hat{P}_5$ you use the dividend expected at t = 6, which is 5% greater than the t = 5 dividend.

c. Calculate the expected dividend yield ($D_1/\hat{P}_0$), the capital gains yield expected during the first year, and the expected total return (dividend yield plus capital gains yield) during the first year. (Assume that $\hat{P}_0 = P_0$, and recognize that the capital gains yield is equal to the total return minus the dividend yield.) Also calculate these same three yields for t = 5 (e.g., $D_6/\hat{P}_5$).

d. If your calculated intrinsic value differed substantially from the current market price, and if your views are consistent with those of most investors (the marginal investor), what would happen in the marketplace? What would happen if your views were *not* consistent with those of the marginal investor and you turned out to be correct?

5-19 Nonconstant Growth Stock Valuation Conroy Consulting Corporation (CCC) has been growing at a rate of 30% per year in recent years. This same nonconstant growth rate is expected to last for another 2 years ($g_{0,1} = g_{1,2} = 30\%$).

a. If $D_0 = \$2.50$, $r_s = 12\%$, and $g_L = 7\%$, then what is CCC's stock worth today? What is its expected dividend yield and its capital gains yield at this time?

b. Now assume that CCC's period of nonconstant growth is to last another 5 years rather than 2 years ($g_{0,1} = g_{1,2} = g_{2,3} = g_{3,4} = g_{4,5} = 30\%$). How would this affect its price, dividend yield, and capital gains yield? Answer in words only.

c. What will CCC's dividend yield and capital gains yield be once its period of nonconstant growth ends? (*Hint:* These values will be the same regardless of whether you examine the case of 2 or 5 years of nonconstant growth, and the calculations are very easy.)

d. Of what interest to investors is the relationship over time between dividend yield and capital gains yield?

Spreadsheet Problem

5-20 Build a Model: Nonconstant Growth and Corporate Valuation Start with the partial model in the file *Ch05 P20 Build a Model.xls* on the textbook's Web site. Rework parts a, b, and c of Problem 5-19 using a spreadsheet model. For part b, calculate the price, dividend yield, and capital gains yield as called for in the problem.

 THOMSON REUTERS

Use the Thomson ONE—Business School Edition online database to work this chapter's questions.

Estimating ExxonMobil's Intrinsic Stock Value

In this chapter we described the various factors that influence stock prices and the approaches analysts use to estimate a stock's intrinsic value. By comparing these intrinsic value estimates to the current price, an investor can assess whether it makes sense to buy or sell a particular stock. Stocks trading at a price far below their estimated intrinsic values may be good candidates for purchase, whereas stocks trading at prices far in excess of their intrinsic value may be good stocks to avoid or sell.

Although estimating a stock's intrinsic value is a complex exercise that requires reliable data and good judgment, we can use the data available in Thomson ONE to arrive at a quick "back of the envelope" calculation of intrinsic value.

Discussion Questions

1. For the purposes of this exercise, let's take a closer look at the stock of Exxon-Mobil Corporation (XOM). Looking at the COMPANY OVERVIEW, we can immediately see the company's current stock price and its performance relative to the overall market in recent months. What is ExxonMobil's current stock price? How has the stock performed relative to the market over the past few months?

2. Click on the "NEWS" tab to see the recent news stories for the company. Have there been any recent events affecting the company's stock price, or have things been relatively quiet?

3. To provide a starting point for gauging a company's relative valuation, analysts often look at a company's price-to-earnings (P/E) ratio. Returning to the COMPANY OVERVIEW page, you can see XOM's current P/E ratio. To put this number in perspective, it is useful to compare this ratio with other companies in the same industry and to take a look at how this ratio has changed over time. If you want to see how XOM's P/E ratio stacks up to its peers, click on the tab labeled PEERS. Click on FINANCIALS on the next row of tabs and then select KEY FINANCIAL RATIOS. Toward the bottom of the table you should see information on the P/E ratio in the section titled Market Value Ratios. Toward the top, you should see an item that says CLICK HERE TO SELECT NEW PEER SET—do this if you want to compare XOM to a different set of firms.

   For the most part, is XOM's P/E ratio above or below that of its peers? Off the top of your head, can these factors explain why XOM's P/E ratio differs from its peers?

4. To see how XOM's P/E ratio has varied over time, return to the COMPANY OVERVIEW page. Next click FINANCIALS—GROWTH RATIOS and then select WORLDSCOPE—INCOME STATEMENT RATIOS. Is XOM's current P/E ratio well above or well below its historical average? If so, do you have any explanation for why the current P/E deviates from its historical trend? On the basis of this information, does XOM's current P/E suggest that the stock is undervalued or overvalued? Explain.

5. In the text, we discussed using the dividend growth model to estimate a stock's intrinsic value. To keep things as simple as possible, let's assume at first that XOM's dividend is expected to grow at some constant rate over time. Then its intrinsic value would equal $D_1/(r_s - g)$, where D_1 is the expected annual dividend 1 year from now, r_s is the stock's required rate of return, and g is the dividend's constant growth rate. To estimate the dividend growth rate, it's helpful first to look at XOM's dividend history. Staying on the current Web page (WORLDSCOPE—INCOME STATEMENT RATIOS), you should immediately find the company's annual dividend for the past several years. On the basis of this information, what has been the average annual dividend growth rate? Another

way to obtain estimates of dividend growth rates is to look at analysts' fore-casts for future dividends, which can be found on the ESTIMATES tab. Scrolling down the page, you should see an area marked Consensus Estimates and a tab under Available Measures. Here you click on the down arrow key and select Dividends Per Share (DPS). What is the median year-end dividend forecast? You can use this as an estimate of D_1 in your measure of intrinsic value. You can also use this forecast along with the historical data to arrive at a measure of the forecasted dividend growth rate, g.

6. The required return on equity, r_s, is the final input needed to estimate intrinsic value. For our purposes you can either assume a number (say, 8% or 9%) or use the CAPM to calculate an estimated cost of equity using the data available in Thomson ONE. (For more details, take a look at the Thomson ONE exercise for Chapter 2). Having decided on your best estimates for D_1, r_s, and g, you can then calculate XOM's intrinsic value. How does this estimate compare with the current stock price? Does your preliminary analysis suggest that XOM is under-valued or overvalued? Explain.

7. Often it is useful to perform a sensitivity analysis, in which you show how your estimate of intrinsic value varies according to different estimates of D_1, r_s, and g. To do so, recalculate your intrinsic value estimate for a range of different estimates for each of these key inputs. One convenient way to do this is to set up a simple data table in *Excel*. Refer to the *Excel* tutorial accessed through the textbook's Web site for instructions on data tables. On the basis of this analysis, what inputs justify the current stock price?

8. On the basis of the dividend history you uncovered in question 5 and your assessment of XOM's future dividend payout policies, do you think it is reason-able to assume that the constant growth model is a good proxy for intrinsic value? If not, how would you use the available data in Thomson ONE to estimate intrinsic value using the nonconstant growth model?

9. Finally, you can also use the information in Thomson ONE to value the entire corporation. This approach requires that you estimate XOM's annual free cash flows. Once you estimate the value of the entire corporation, you subtract the value of debt and preferred stock to arrive at an estimate of the company's equity value. Divide this number by the number of shares of common stock outstanding, which yields an alternative estimate of the stock's intrinsic value. This approach may take some more time and involve more judgment concerning forecasts of future free cash flows, but you can use the financial statements and growth forecasts in Thomson ONE as useful starting points. Go to Worldscope's Cash Flow Ratios Report (which you find by clicking on FINANCIALS, FUNDA-MENTAL RATIOS, and WORLDSCOPE RATIOS) to find an estimate of "free cash flow per share." Although this number is useful, Worldscope's definition of free cash flow subtracts out dividends per share; therefore, to make it comparable to the measure used in this text, you must add back dividends. To see Worldscope's definition of free cash flow (or any term), click on SEARCH FOR COMPANIES from the left toolbar and then select the ADVANCED SEARCH tab. In the middle of your screen, on the right-hand side, you will see a dialog box with terms. Use the down arrow to scroll through the terms, highlighting the term for which you would like to see a definition. Then, click on the DEFINITION button immedi-ately below the dialog box.

MINI CASE

Sam Strother and Shawna Tibbs are senior vice presidents of Mutual of Seattle. They are co-directors of the company's pension fund management division, with Strother having responsibility for fixed income securities (primarily bonds) and Tibbs responsible for equity investments. A major new client, the Northwestern Municipal Alliance, has requested that Mutual of Seattle present an investment seminar to the mayors of the cities in the association, and Strother and Tibbs, who will make the actual presentation, have asked you to help them.

To illustrate the common stock valuation process, Strother and Tibbs have asked you to analyze the Temp Force Company, an employment agency that supplies word processor operators and computer programmers to businesses with temporarily heavy workloads. You are to answer the following questions.

a. Describe briefly the legal rights and privileges of common stockholders.

b. (1) Write out a formula that can be used to value any stock, regardless of its dividend pattern.

(2) What is a constant growth stock? How are constant growth stocks valued?

(3) What happens if a company has a constant g that exceeds its r_s? Will many stocks have expected $g > r_s$ in the short run (i.e., for the next few years)? In the long run (i.e., forever)?

c. Assume that Temp Force has a beta coefficient of 1.2, that the risk-free rate (the yield on T-bonds) is 7.0%, and that the market risk premium is 5%. What is the required rate of return on the firm's stock?

d. Assume that Temp Force is a constant growth company whose last dividend (D_0, which was paid yesterday) was $2.00 and whose dividend is expected to grow indefinitely at a 6% rate.

(1) What is the firm's expected dividend stream over the next 3 years?

(2) What is the firm's current intrinsic stock price?

(3) What is the stock's expected value 1 year from now?

(4) What are the expected dividend yield, the expected capital gains yield, and the expected total return during the first year?

e. Now assume that the stock is currently selling at $30.29. What is its expected rate of return?

f. What would the stock price be if the dividends were expected to have zero growth?

g. Now assume that Temp Force's dividend is expected to experience nonconstant growth of 30% from Year 0 to Year 1, 25% from Year 1 to Year 2, and 15% from Year 2 to Year 3. After Year 3, dividends will grow at a constant rate of 6%. What is the stock's intrinsic value under these conditions? What are the expected dividend yield and capital gains yield during the first year? What are the expected dividend yield and capital gains yield during the fourth year (from Year 3 to Year 4)?

h. Is the stock price based more on long-term or short-term expectations? Answer this by finding the percentage of Temp Force's current stock price that is based on dividends expected more than 3 years in the future.

i. Suppose Temp Force is expected to experience zero growth during the first 3 years and then to resume its steady-state growth of 6% in the fourth year. What is the stock's intrinsic value now? What are its expected dividend yield and its capital gains yield in Year 1? In Year 4?

j. Now suppose that Temp Force's earnings and dividends are expected to decline by a constant 6% per year forever—that is, g = −6%. Why would anyone be willing to buy such a stock, and at what price should it sell? What would be the dividend yield and capital gains yield in each year?

k. What is market multiple analysis?

l. Temp Force recently issued preferred stock that pays an annual dividend of $5 at a price of $50 per share. What is the expected return to an investor who buys this preferred stock?

m. Why do stock prices change? Suppose the expected D_1 is $2, the growth rate is 5%, and r_s is 10%. Using the constant growth model, what is the stock's price? What is the impact on the stock price if g falls to 4% or rises to 6%? If r_s increases to 9% or to 11%?

n. What does market equilibrium mean?

o. If equilibrium does not exist, how will it be established?

p. What is the Efficient Markets Hypothesis, what are its three forms, and what are its implications?

q. Assume that all the growth rates used in the preceding answers were averages of the growth rates published by well-known and respected security analysts. Would you then say that your results are based on a purely rational analysis? If not, what factors might have led to "irrational results"?

Selected Additional Cases

The following cases from TextChoice, *Cengage Learning's online case library, cover many of the concepts discussed in this chapter and are available at* **www.textchoice2.com/casenet.**

Klein-Brigham Series:
Case 3, "Peachtree Securities, Inc. (B)"; Case 71, "Swan Davis"; Case 78, "Beatrice Peabody"; and Case 101, "TECO Energy."

Brigham-Buzzard Series:
Case 4, "Powerline Network Corporation (Stocks)."

Chapter 7

Accounting for Financial Management

A manager's primary goal is to maximize the fundamental, or intrinsic, value of the firm's stock. This value is based on the stream of cash flows the firm is expected to generate in the future. But how does an investor go about estimating future cash flows, and how does a manager decide which actions are most likely to increase cash flows? The first step is to understand the financial statements that publicly traded firms must provide to the public. Thus, we begin with a discussion of financial statements, including how to interpret them and how to use them. Because value depends on usable, after-tax cash flows, we highlight the difference between accounting income and cash flow. In fact, it is *after-tax* cash flow that is important, so we also provide an overview of the federal income tax system.

Beginning of Chapter Questions

As you read the chapter, consider how you would answer the following questions. You *should not* necessarily be able to answer the questions before you read the chapter. Rather, you should use them to get a sense of the issues covered in the chapter. After reading the chapter, you should be able to give at least partial answers to the questions, and you should be able to give better answers after the chapter has been discussed in class. Note, too, that it is often useful, when answering conceptual questions, to use hypothetical data to illustrate your answer. We illustrate the answers with an *Excel* model that is available on the textbook's Web site. Accessing the model and working through it is a useful exercise, and it provides insights that are useful when answering the questions.

1. How are the balance sheet and the income statement *related* to one another? How would you explain to a layperson the *primary purpose* of each of the statements? Which of the numbers in the income statement is considered to be most important?
2. WorldCom capitalized some costs that should, under standard accounting practices, have been expensed. Enron and some other companies took similar actions to inflate their reported income and to hide debts. (a) Explain how such improper and illegal actions would affect the firms' financial statements and stock prices. (b) What effect did the revelations about these actions have on the specific companies' stock prices and the prices of other stocks? (c) Could such actions affect the entire economy?
3. How could (accurate) balance sheet and income statement information be used, along with other information, to make a **statement of cash flows?** What is the primary purpose of this statement?
4. Differentiate between **net income, EPS, EBITDA, net cash flow, NOPAT, free cash flow, MVA,** and **EVA.** What is the primary purpose of each item; that is, when and how is it used?
5. How and why are regular accounting data *modified* for use in financial management? (*Hint:* Think about cash and operations.)
6. The **income statement** shows "flows" over a period of time, while the **balance sheet** shows accounts at a given point in time. Explain how these two concepts are combined when we calculate **free cash flow.**
7. **Taxes** affect many financial decisions. Explain how (a) **interest and dividend payments** are treated for tax purposes, from both a company's and an investor's perspective, and (b) how **dividends and capital gains** are treated for tax purposes by individuals. In your answers, explain how these tax treatments influence corporations' and investors' behavior.
8. If Congress wants to *stimulate* the economy, explain how it might alter each of the following: (a) **personal and corporate tax rates,** (b) **depreciation schedules,** and (c) the **differential between the tax rate on personal income and long-term capital gains.** How would these changes affect corporate profitability and free cash flow? How would they affect investors' choices regarding which securities to hold in their portfolios? Might any of these actions affect the general level of interest rates?

7.1 Financial Statements and Reports

A company's **annual report** usually begins with the chairman's description of the firm's operating results during the past year and a discussion of new developments that will affect future operations. The annual report also presents four basic financial statements—the *balance sheet,* the *income statement,* the *statement of stockholders' equity,* and the *statement of cash flows.*[1]

---

1. Firms also provide less comprehensive quarterly reports. Larger firms file even more detailed statements, giving breakdowns for each major division or subsidiary, with the Securities and Exchange Commission (SEC). These reports, called *10-Q* and *10-K reports,* are available on the SEC's Web site at www.sec.gov under the heading "EDGAR."

INTRINSIC VALUE, FREE CASH FLOW, AND FINANCIAL STATEMENTS

In Chapter 1, we told you that managers should strive to make their firms more valuable and that the intrinsic value of a firm is determined by the present value of its free cash flows (FCF) discounted at the weighted average cost of capital (WACC). This chapter focuses on FCF, including its calculation from financial statements and its interpretation when evaluating a company and manager.

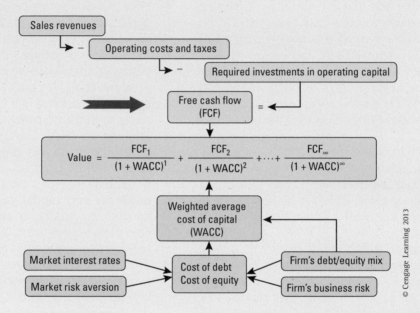

© Cengage Learning 2013

The quantitative and written materials are equally important. The financial statements report *what has actually happened* to assets, earnings, dividends, and cash flows during the past few years, whereas the written materials attempt to explain why things turned out the way they did.

For illustrative purposes, we use a hypothetical company, MicroDrive Inc., which produces hard drives for microcomputers. Formed in 1982, MicroDrive has grown steadily and has a reputation as one of the best firms in the microcomputer components industry.

Self Test	
	What is the annual report, and what two types of information are given in it?
	What four types of financial statements are typically included in the annual report?

7.2 The Balance Sheet

Table 7-1 shows MicroDrive's most recent **balance sheets**, which represent "snapshots" of its financial position on the last day of each year. Although most companies report their balance sheets only on the last day of a given period, the

TABLE 7-1	MicroDrive Inc.: December 31 Balance Sheets (Millions of Dollars)					
Assets	**2012**	**2011**	**Liabilities and Equity**	**2012**	**2011**
Cash and equivalents	$ 10	$ 15	Accounts payable	$ 60	$ 30
Short-term investments	0	65	Notes payable	110	60
Accounts receivable	375	315	Accruals	140	130
Inventories	615	415	Total current liabilities	$ 310	$ 220
Total current assets	$1,000	$ 810	Long-term bonds	754	580
Net plant and equipment	1,000	870	Total liabilities	$1,064	$ 800
			Preferred stock (400,000 shares)	40	40
			Common stock (50,000,000 shares)	130	130
			Retained earnings	766	710
			Total common equity	$ 896	$ 840
Total assets	$2,000	$1,680	Total liabilities and equity	$2,000	$1,680

© Cengage Learning 2013

"snapshot" actually changes daily as inventories are bought and sold, as fixed assets are added or retired, or as loan balances are increased or paid down. Moreover, a retailer will have much larger inventories before Christmas than later in the spring, so balance sheets for the same company can look quite different at different times during the year.

WEB

See *Ch07 Tool Kit.xls* for details.

The left side of a balance sheet lists assets, which are the "things" the company owns. They are listed in order of "liquidity," or length of time it typically takes to convert them to cash at fair market values. The right side lists the claims that various groups have against the company's value, listed in the order in which they must be paid. For example, suppliers may have a claim called "accounts payable" that is due within 30 days, banks may have claims called "notes payable" that are due within 90 days, and bondholders may have claims that are not due for 20 years or more.

Stockholders come last, for two reasons. First, their claim represents ownership (or equity) and need never be "paid off." Second, they have a residual claim in the sense that they may receive payments only if the other claimants have already been paid. The nonstockholder claims are liabilities from the stockholders' perspective. The amounts shown on the balance sheets are called **book values** because they are based on the amounts recorded by bookkeepers when assets are purchased or liabilities are issued. As you will see throughout this textbook, book values may be very different from **market values**, which are the current values as determined in the marketplace.

Self Test

What is the balance sheet, and what information does it provide?

What determines the order of the information shown on the balance sheet?

Why might a company's December 31 balance sheet differ from its June 30 balance sheet?

A firm has $8 million in total assets. It has $3 million in current liabilities, $2 million in long-term debt, and $1 million in preferred stock. What is the total value of common equity? (**$2 million**)

THE GLOBAL ECONOMIC CRISIS

Let's Play Hide-and-Seek!
In a shameful lapse of regulatory accountability, banks and other financial institutions were allowed to use "structured investment vehicles" (SIVs) to hide assets and liabilities off their balance sheets and simply not report them. Here's how SIVs worked and why they subsequently failed. The SIV was set up as a separate legal entity that the bank owned and managed. The SIV would borrow money in the short-term market (backed by the credit of the bank) and then invest in long-term securities. As you might guess, many SIVs invested in mortgage-backed securities. When the SIV paid only 3% on its borrowings but earned 10% on its investments, the managing bank was able to report fabulous earnings, especially if it also earned fees for creating the mortgage securities that went into the SIV.

But this game of hide-and-seek doesn't have a happy ending. Mortgage-backed securities began defaulting in 2007 and 2008, causing the SIVs to pass losses through to the banks. SunTrust, Citigroup, Bank of America, and Northern Rock are just a few of the many banks that reported enormous losses in the SIV game. Investors, depositors, and the government eventually found the hidden assets and liabilities, but by then the assets were worth a lot less than the liabilities.

In a case of too little and too late, regulators are closing these loopholes, and it doesn't look like there will be any more SIVs in the near future. But the damage has been done, and the entire financial system is at risk in large part because of this high-stakes game of hide-and-seek.

7.3 The Income Statement

See **Ch07 Tool Kit.xls** for details.

WEB

Table 7-2 shows the **income statements** for MicroDrive. Income statements can cover any period of time, but they are usually prepared monthly, quarterly, and annually. Unlike the balance sheet, which is a snapshot of a firm at a point in time, the income statement reflects performance during the period.

Subtracting operating costs from net sales but excluding depreciation and amortization results in **EBITDA**, which stands for earnings before interest, taxes, depreciation, and amortization. Depreciation and amortization are annual charges that reflect the estimated costs of the assets used up each year. Depreciation applies to tangible assets, such as plant and equipment, whereas amortization applies to intangible assets such as patents, copyrights, trademarks, and goodwill.[2] Because neither depreciation nor amortization is paid in cash, some analysts claim that EBITDA is a better measure of financial strength than is net income. However, as we show later in the chapter, EBITDA is not as important as free cash flow. In fact, some financial wags have stated that EBITDA really stands for "earnings before anything bad happens."

The net income available to common shareholders, which is revenues less expenses, taxes, and preferred dividends (but before paying common dividends), is generally referred to as **net income**, although it is also called **profit** or **earnings**,

---

2. The accounting treatment of goodwill resulting from mergers has changed in recent years. Rather than an annual charge, companies are required to periodically evaluate the value of goodwill and reduce net income only if the goodwill's value has decreased materially ("become impaired," in the language of accountants). For example, in 2002 AOL Time Warner wrote off almost $100 billion associated with the AOL merger. It doesn't take too many $100 billion expenses to really hurt net income!

TABLE 7-2	MicroDrive Inc.: Income Statements for Years Ending December 31 (Millions of Dollars, Except for Per Share Data)		
		2012	**2011**
Net sales		$3,000	$2,850
Operating costs excluding depreciation and amortization		2,617	2,500
Earnings before interest, taxes, depreciation, and amortization (EBITDA)		$ 383	$ 350
Depreciation and amortization		100	90
Earnings before interest and taxes (EBIT, or operating income)		$ 283	$ 260
Less interest		88	60
Earnings before taxes (EBT)		$ 195	$ 200
Taxes (40%)		78	80
Net income before preferred dividends		$ 117	$ 120
Preferred dividends		4	4
Net income		$ 113	$ 116
Additional Information			
Common dividends		$ 57	$ 53
Addition to retained earnings		$ 56	$ 63
Per Share Data			
Common stock price		$23.00	$26.00
Earnings per share (EPS)		$ 2.26	$ 2.32
Dividends per share (DPS)		$ 1.14	$ 1.06
Book value per share (BVPS)		$17.92	$16.80
Cash flow per share (CFPS)		$ 4.26	$ 4.12

Notes:
There are 50,000,000 shares of common stock outstanding. Note that EPS is based on earnings after preferred dividends—that is, on net income available to common stockholders. Calculations of the most recent EPS, DPS, BVPS, and CFPS values are as follows:

$$\text{Earnings per share} = \text{EPS} = \frac{\text{Net income}}{\text{Common shares outstanding}} = \frac{\$113,000,000}{50,000,000} = \$2.26$$

$$\text{Dividends per share} = \text{DPS} = \frac{\text{Dividends paid to common stockholders}}{\text{Common shares outstanding}} = \frac{\$57,000,000}{50,000,000} = \$1.14$$

$$\text{Book value per share} = \text{BVPS} = \frac{\text{Total common equity}}{\text{Common shares outstanding}} = \frac{\$896,000,000}{50,000,000} = \$17.92$$

$$\text{Cash flow per share} = \text{CFPS} = \frac{\text{Net income} + \text{Depreciation} + \text{Amortization}}{\text{Common shares outstanding}} = \frac{\$213,000,000}{50,000,000} = \$4.26$$

particularly in the news or financial press. Dividing net income by the number of shares outstanding gives earnings per share (EPS), which is often called "the bottom line." Throughout this book, unless otherwise indicated, net income means net income available to common stockholders.[3]

Self Test

What is an income statement, and what information does it provide?

What is often called "the bottom line?"

What is EBITDA?

Regarding the time period reported, how does the income statement differ from the balance sheet?

A firm has $2 million in earnings before taxes. The firm has an interest expense of $300,000 and depreciation of $200,000; it has no amortization. What is its EBITDA? **($2.5 million)**

7.4 Statement of Stockholders' Equity

Changes in stockholders' equity during the accounting period are reported in the **statement of stockholders' equity.** Table 7-3 shows that MicroDrive earned $113 million during 2012, paid out $57 million in common dividends, and plowed $56 million back into the business. Thus, the balance sheet item "Retained earnings" increased from $710 million at year-end 2011 to $766 million at year-end 2012.[4] The last column shows the beginning stockholders' equity, any changes, and the end-of-year stockholders' equity.

Note that "retained earnings" does not represent assets but is instead a *claim against assets.* In 2012, MicroDrive's stockholders allowed it to reinvest $56 million instead of distributing the money as dividends, and management spent this money on new assets. Thus, retained earnings, as reported on the balance sheet, does not represent cash and is not "available" for the payment of dividends or anything else.[5]

---

3. Companies also report "comprehensive income," which is the sum of net income and any "comprehensive" income item, such as unrealized gain or loss when an asset is marked-to-market. For our examples, we assume that there are no comprehensive income items.

   Some companies also choose to report "pro forma income." For example, if a company incurs an expense that it doesn't expect to recur, such as the closing of a plant, it might calculate pro forma income as though it had not incurred the one-time expense. There are no hard-and-fast rules for calculating pro forma income, so many companies find ingenious ways to make pro forma income higher than traditional income. The SEC and the Public Company Accounting Oversight Board (PCAOB) are taking steps to reduce deceptive uses of pro forma reporting.

4. If they had been applicable, then columns would have been used to show "Additional Paid-in Capital" and "Treasury Stock." Also, additional rows would have contained information on such things as new issues of stock, treasury stock acquired or reissued, stock options exercised, and unrealized foreign exchange gains or losses.

5. The amount reported in the retained earnings account is *not* an indication of the amount of cash the firm has. Cash (as of the balance sheet date) is found in the cash account, an asset account. A positive number in the retained earnings account indicates only that in the past the firm earned some income, but its dividends paid were less than its earnings. Even though a company reports record earnings and shows an increase in its retained earnings account, it still may be short of cash.

   The same situation holds for individuals. You might own a new BMW (no loan), lots of clothes, and an expensive stereo—and hence have a high net worth—but if you have only 23 cents in your pocket plus $5 in your checking account, you will still be short of cash.

TABLE 7-3	MicroDrive Inc.: Statement of Stockholders' Equity, December 31, 2012 (Millions of Dollars)			
	Common Stock (Millions)			
	Shares	Amount	Retained Earnings	Total Equity
Balances, Dec. 31, 2011	50	$130	$710	$840
Net income			$113	$113
Cash dividends			(57)	(57)
Issuance of common stock	0	0		
Balances, Dec. 31, 2012	50	$130	$766	$896

Note: Here and throughout the book, parentheses are used to denote negative numbers.

What is the statement of stockholders' equity, and what information does it provide?

Why do changes in retained earnings occur?

Explain why the following statement is true: "The retained earnings reported on the balance sheet does not represent cash and is not available for the payment of dividends or anything else."

A firm had a retained earnings balance of $3 million in the previous year. In the current year, its net income is $2.5 million. If it pays $1 million in common dividends in the current year, what is its resulting retained earnings balance? **($4.5 million)**

7.5 Net Cash Flow

A business's **net cash flow** generally differs from its *accounting profit* because some of the revenues and expenses listed on the income statement were not received or paid in cash during the year. The relationship between net cash flow and net income is:

$$\text{Net cash flow} = \text{Net income} - \text{Noncash revenues} + \text{Noncash charges} \qquad (7\text{--}1)$$

The primary examples of noncash charges are depreciation and amortization. These items reduce net income but are not paid out in cash, so we add them back to net income when calculating net cash flow. Another example of a noncash charge is deferred taxes. In some instances, companies are allowed to defer tax payments to a later date even though the tax payment is reported as an expense on the income statement. Therefore, deferred tax payments are added to net income when calculating net cash flow.[6] Sometimes a customer will purchase services or products that

---

6. Deferred taxes may arise, for example, if a company uses accelerated depreciation for tax purposes but straight-line depreciation for reporting its financial statements to investors. If deferred taxes are increasing, then the company is paying less in taxes than it reports to the public.

FINANCIAL ANALYSIS ON THE WEB

A wide range of valuable financial information is available on the Web. With just a couple of clicks, an investor can easily find the key financial statements for most publicly traded companies. Here's a partial (by no means a complete) list of places you can go to get started.

- One of the very best sources of financial information is Thomson Financial. Go to the textbook's Web site and follow the directions to access Thomson ONE—Business School Edition. An especially useful feature is the ability to download up to 10 years of financial statements in spreadsheet form. First, enter the ticker for a company and click Go. From the menu at left (in dark blue), select Financials. A new menu (in light blue) will expand and selecting Thomson Financials under the Financial Statements heading will reveal Balance Sheets, Income Statements, and Cash Flow Statements items. Select any of these and a menu item for 5YR and 10YR statements will pop up. Select the 10YR item and 10 years of the selected financial statements will be displayed. To download the financial statements into a spreadsheet, click on the *Excel* icon toward the right of the light blue row at the top of the Thomson ONE panel. This will bring up a dialog box that lets you download the *Excel* file to your computer.

- Try Yahoo! Finance's Web site, **finance.yahoo.com**. Here you will find updated market information along with links to a variety of interesting research sites. Enter a stock's ticker symbol, click GET QUOTES, and you will see the stock's current price along with recent news about the company. The panel on the left has links to key statistics and to the company's income statement, balance sheet, statement of cash flows, and more.

The Web site also has a list of insider transactions, so you can tell if a company's CEO and other key insiders are buying or selling their company's stock. In addition, there is a message board where investors share opinions about the company, and there is a link to the company's filings with the SEC. Note that, in most cases, a more complete list of the SEC filings can be found at **www.sec.gov**.

- Other sources for up-to-date market information are **http://money.cnn.com** and **www.zacks.com**. These sites also provide financial statements in standardized formats.

- Both **www.bloomberg.com** and **www.marketwatch.com** have areas where you can obtain stock quotes along with company financials, links to Wall Street research, and links to SEC filings.

- If you are looking for charts of key accounting variables (for example, sales, inventory, depreciation and amortization, and reported earnings) as well as financial statements, take a look at **www.smartmoney.com**.

- Another good place to look is **www.investor.reuters.com**. Here you can find links to analysts' research reports along with the key financial statements.

- Zacks (already mentioned) and **www.hoovers.com** have free research available along with more detailed information provided to subscribers.

In addition to this information, you may be looking for sites that provide opinions regarding the direction of the overall market and views regarding individual stocks. Two popular sites in this category are The Motley Fool's Web site, **www.fool.com**, and the Web site for The Street.com, **www.thestreet.com**.

extend beyond the reporting date, such as iPhone subscriptions at Apple. Even if the company collects the cash at the time of the purchase, the company will spread the reported revenues over the life of the purchase. This causes income to be lower than cash flow in the first year and higher in any subsequent years, so adjustments are made when calculating net cash flow.

Depreciation and amortization usually are the largest noncash items, and in many cases the other noncash items roughly net out to zero. For this reason, many analysts assume that net cash flow equals net income plus depreciation and amortization:

$$\text{Net cash flow} = \text{Net income} + \text{Depreciation and amortization} \qquad (7\text{--}2)$$

We will generally assume that Equation 7-2 holds. However, you should remember that Equation 7-2 will not accurately reflect net cash flow when there are significant noncash items other than depreciation and amortization.

We can illustrate Equation 7-2 with 2012 data for MicroDrive taken from Table 7-2:

$$\text{Net cash flow} = \$113 + \$100 = \$213 \text{ million}$$

To illustrate depreciation's effect, suppose a machine with a life of 5 years and zero expected salvage value was purchased in late 2011 for $100,000 and placed into service in early 2012. This $100,000 cost is not expensed in the purchase year; rather, it is charged against production over the machine's 5-year depreciable life. If the depreciation expense were not taken, then profits would be overstated and taxes would be too high. Therefore, the annual depreciation charge is deducted from sales revenues, along with such other costs as labor and raw materials, to determine income. However, because the $100,000 was actually expended back in 2011, the depreciation charged against income in 2012 and subsequent years is not a cash outflow. *Depreciation is a noncash charge, so it must be added back to net income to obtain the net cash flow.* If we assume that all other noncash items (including amortization) sum to zero, then net cash flow is simply equal to net income plus depreciation.

Self Test

Differentiate between net cash flow and accounting profit.

A firm has net income of $5 million. Assuming that depreciation of $1 million is its only noncash expense, what is the firm's net cash flow? **($6 million)**

7.6 Statement of Cash Flows

Even if a company reports a large net income during a year, the *amount of cash* reported on its year-end balance sheet may be the same or even lower than its beginning cash. The reason is that its net income can be used in a variety of ways, not just kept as cash in the bank. For example, the firm may use its net income to pay dividends, to increase inventories, to finance accounts receivable, to invest in fixed assets, to reduce debt, or to buy back common stock. Indeed, the company's *cash position* as reported on its balance sheet is affected by a great many factors, which include the following.

1. **Net income before preferred dividends.** Other things held constant, a positive net income will lead to more cash in the bank. However, as we shall discuss, other things generally are not held constant.

2. **Noncash adjustments to net income.** To calculate cash flow, it is necessary to adjust net income to reflect noncash revenues and expenses, such as depreciation and deferred taxes, as shown previously in the calculation of net cash flow.

3. **Changes in working capital.** Increases in current assets other than cash (such as inventories and accounts receivable) decrease cash, whereas decreases in these accounts increase cash. For example, if inventories are to increase, then the firm must use some of its cash to acquire the additional inventory. Conversely, if inventories decrease, this generally means the firm is selling inventories and not replacing all of them, hence generating cash. On the other hand, if payables increase then the firm has received additional credit from its suppliers, which saves cash, but if payables decrease, this means it has used cash to pay off its suppliers. Therefore, increases in current liabilities such as accounts payable increase cash, whereas decreases in current liabilities decrease cash.

4. **Investments.** If a company invests in fixed assets or short-term financial investments, this will reduce its cash position. On the other hand, if it sells some fixed assets or short-term investments, this will increase cash.

5. **Security transactions and dividend payments.** If a company issues stock or bonds during the year, the funds raised will increase its cash position. On the other hand, if the company uses cash to buy back outstanding stock or to pay off debt, or if it pays dividends to its shareholders, this will reduce cash.

Each of these five factors is reflected in the **statement of cash flows,** which summarizes the changes in a company's cash position. The statement separates activities into three categories, plus a summary section, as follows.

1. **Operating activities,** which includes net income, depreciation, changes in current assets and liabilities other than cash, short-term investments, and short-term debt.

2. **Investing activities,** which includes investments in or sales of fixed assets and short-term financial investments.

3. **Financing activities,** which includes raising cash by issuing short-term debt, long-term debt, or stock. Also, because dividend payments, stock repurchases, and principal payments on debt reduce a company's cash, such transactions are included here.

Accounting texts explain how to prepare the statement of cash flows, but the statement is used to help answer questions such as these: Is the firm generating enough cash to purchase the additional assets required for growth? Is the firm generating any extra cash that can be used to repay debt or to invest in new products? Such information is useful both for managers and investors, so the statement of cash flows is an important part of the annual report.

Table 7-4 shows MicroDrive's statement of cash flows as it would appear in the company's annual report. The top section shows cash generated by and used in operations—for MicroDrive, operations provided net cash flows of *minus* $3 million. This subtotal, the minus $3 million net cash flow provided by operating activities, is in many respects the most important figure in any of the financial statements. Profits as reported on the income statement can be "doctored" by such tactics as depreciating assets too slowly, not recognizing bad debts promptly, and the like. However, it is far more difficult to simultaneously doctor profits and the working capital accounts. Therefore, it is not uncommon for a company to report positive net income right up to the day it declares bankruptcy. In such cases, however, the net cash flow from operations almost always began to deteriorate much earlier, and analysts who kept an eye on cash flow could have predicted trouble. Therefore, if you are ever analyzing a

TABLE 7-4	MicroDrive Inc.: Statement of Cash Flows for 2012 (Millions of Dollars)	
		Cash Provided or Used
Operating Activities		
Net income before preferred dividends		$117
Adjustments:		
Noncash adjustments:		
Depreciation and amortization[a]		100
Due to changes in working capital:[b]		
Increase in accounts receivable		(60)
Increase in inventories		(200)
Increase in accounts payable		30
Increase in accruals		10
Net cash provided (used) by operating activities		($ 3)
Investing Activities		
Cash used to acquire fixed assets[c]		($230)
Sale of short-term investments		$ 65
Net cash provided (used) by investing activities		($165)
Financing Activities		
Increase in notes payable		$ 50
Increase in bonds outstanding		174
Payment of preferred and common dividends		(61)
Net cash provided (used) by financing activities		$163
Summary		
Net change in cash		($ 5)
Cash at beginning of year		15
Cash at end of year		$ 10

See *Ch07 Tool Kit.xls* for details.

© Cengage Learning 2013

[a]Depreciation and amortization is a noncash expense that was deducted when calculating net income. It must be added back to show the correct cash flow from operations.
[b]An increase in a current asset *decreases* cash. An increase in a current liability *increases* cash. For example, inventories increased by $200 million and therefore reduced cash by a like amount.
[c]The net increase in fixed assets is $130 million; however, this net amount is after a deduction for the year's depreciation expense. Depreciation expense would have to be added back to find the increase in gross fixed assets. From the company's income statement, we see that the 2012 depreciation expense is $100 million; thus, expenditures on fixed assets were actually $230 million.

company and are pressed for time, look first at the trend in net cash flow provided by operating activities, because it will tell you more than any other number.

The second section shows investing activities. MicroDrive purchased fixed assets totaling $230 million and sold $65 million of short-term investments, for a net cash flow from investing activities of *minus* $165 million.

FILLING IN THE GAAP

While U.S. companies adhere to "Generally Accepted Accounting Principles," or GAAP, when preparing financial statements, most other developed countries use "International Financial Reporting Standards," or IFRS. The U.S. GAAP system is "rules-based," with thousands of instructions, or "guidances," for how individual transactions should be reported in financial statements. IFRS, on the other hand, is a "principles-based" system in which myriad detailed instructions are replaced by fewer overall guiding principles. For example, whereas GAAP provides extensive and detailed rules about when to recognize revenue from any conceivable activity, IFRS provides just four categories of revenue and two overall principles for timing recognition. This means that even the most basic accounting measure, revenue, is different under the two standards—Total Revenue, or Sales, under GAAP won't typically equal Total Revenue under IFRS. Thus, financial statements prepared under GAAP cannot be compared directly to IFRS financial statements, making comparative financial analysis of U.S. and international companies difficult. Perhaps more problematic is that the IFRS principles allow for more company discretion in recording transactions. This means that two different companies may treat an identical transaction differently when using IFRS, which makes company-to-company comparisons more difficult.

The U.S. Financial Accounting Standards Board (FASB) and the International Accounting Standards Board (IASB) have been working on a project to merge the two standards since 2002. If the current timetable holds, the joint standards will be completed by the end of 2011, with adoption by U.S. firms by 2015.

What does this mean for you? There will still be an income statement, a balance sheet, and an equivalent to the statement of cash flows. Line item summary measures may change a bit, and the technical details about how individual transactions are recorded will certainly change. Accounting systems will be re-programmed, accounting texts will be re-written, and CPAs will have to re-train. The end result, though, will be a better ability to compare U.S. and international companies' financial statements.

To keep abreast of developments in IFRS/GAAP convergence, visit the IASB Web site at **www.iasb.org** and the FASB Web site at **www.fasb.org**. For discussions of the issues companies face with convergence, see **www.pwc.com/us/en/issues/ifrs-reporting/publications/ifrs-and-us-gaap-similarities-and-differences-september-2010.jhtml** and **www.ey.com/Publication/vwLUAssets/IFRS_v_GAAP_basics_Jan09/$file/IFRS_v_GA AP_basics_Jan09.pdf**.

The third section, financing activities, includes borrowing from banks (notes payable), selling new bonds, and paying dividends on common and preferred stock. Micro-Drive raised $224 million by borrowing, but it paid $61 million in preferred and common dividends. Therefore, its net inflow of funds from financing activities was $163 million.

In the summary, when all of these sources and uses of cash are totaled, we see that MicroDrive's cash outflows exceeded its cash inflows by $5 million during 2012; that is, its net change in cash was a *negative* $5 million.

MicroDrive's statement of cash flows should be worrisome to its managers and to outside analysts. The company had a $3 million cash shortfall from operations, it spent an additional $230 million on new fixed assets, and it paid out another $61 million in dividends. It covered these cash outlays by borrowing heavily and by liquidating $65 million of short-term investments. Obviously, this situation cannot continue year after year, so something will have to be done. In Chapter 9, when we discuss financial planning, we consider some of the actions that MicroDrive's financial staff might recommend.[7]

---

7. For a more detailed discussion of financial statement analysis, see Lyn M. Fraser and Aileen Ormiston, *Understanding Financial Statements*, 9th ed. (Upper Saddle River, NJ: Prentice-Hall, 2010).

What types of questions does the statement of cash flows answer?

Identify and briefly explain the three different categories of activities shown in the statement of cash flows.

A firm has inventories of $2 million for the previous year and $1.5 million for the current year. What impact does this have on net cash provided by operations? **(Increase of $500,000)**

7.7 Modifying Accounting Data for Managerial Decisions

Thus far in the chapter we have focused on financial statements as they are presented in the annual report. When you studied income statements in accounting, the emphasis was probably on the firm's net income, which is its **accounting profit.** However, the intrinsic value of a company's operations is determined by the stream of cash flows that the operations will generate now and in the future. To be more specific, the value of operations depends on all the future expected **free cash flows (FCF),** defined as after-tax operating profit minus the amount of new investment in working capital and fixed assets necessary to sustain the business. *Therefore, the way for managers to make their companies more valuable is to increase free cash flow now and in the future.*

Notice that FCF is the cash flow *available for distribution to all the company's investors after the company has made all investments necessary to sustain ongoing operations.* How well have MicroDrive's managers done in generating FCF? In this section, we will calculate MicroDrive's FCF and evaluate the performance of MicroDrive's managers.

Figure 7-1 shows the five steps in calculating free cash flow. As we explain each individual step in the following sections, refer back to Figure 7-1 to keep the big picture in mind.

7.7a Net Operating Profit after Taxes (NOPAT)

If two companies have different amounts of debt and hence different amounts of interest charges, they could have identical operating performances but different net incomes—the one with more debt would have a lower net income. Net income is certainly important, but it does not always reflect the true performance of a company's operations or the effectiveness of its operating managers. A better measurement for comparing managers' performance is **net operating profit after taxes,** or **NOPAT,** which is the amount of profit a company would generate if it had no debt and held no financial assets. NOPAT is defined as follows:[8]

---

8. For firms with a more complicated tax situation, it is better to define NOPAT as follows: NOPAT = (Net income before preferred dividends) + (Net interest expense)(1 − Tax rate). Also, if firms are able to defer paying some of their taxes, perhaps by the use of accelerated depreciation, then NOPAT should be adjusted to reflect the taxes that the company actually paid on its operating income. See P. Daves, M. Ehrhardt, and R. Shrieves, *Corporate Valuation: A Guide for Managers and Investors* (Mason, OH: Thomson South-Western, 2004) for a detailed explanation of these and other adjustments. Also see Tim Koller, Marc Goedhart, and David Wessels, *Valuation: Measuring and Managing the Value of Companies* (Hoboken, NJ: Wiley, 2005), and G. Bennett Stewart, *The Quest for Value* (New York: Harper Collins, 1991).

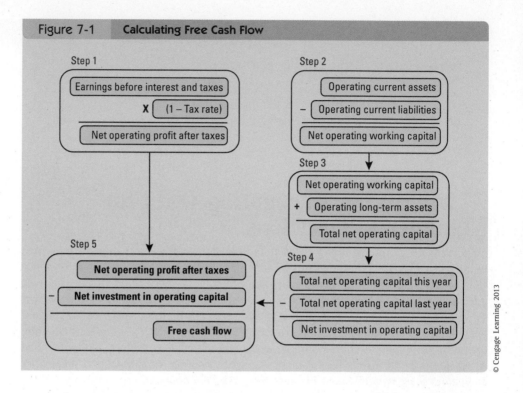

Figure 7-1   Calculating Free Cash Flow

© Cengage Learning 2013

$$(7\text{--}3) \qquad \text{NOPAT} = \text{EBIT}(1 - \text{Tax rate})$$

Using data from the income statements of Table 7-2, MicroDrive's 2012 NOPAT is

$$\text{NOPAT} = \$283(1 - 0.4) = \$283(0.6) = \$169.8 \text{ million}$$

This means MicroDrive generated an after-tax operating profit of $169.8 million, a little better than its previous NOPAT of $260(0.6) = $156.0 million. However, the income statements in Table 7-2 show that MicroDrive's earnings per share actually declined. This decrease in EPS was caused by an increase in interest expense, and not by a decrease in operating profit.

7.7b Net Operating Working Capital

Most companies need some current assets to support their operating activities. For example, all companies must carry some cash to "grease the wheels" of their operations. Companies continuously receive checks from customers and write checks to suppliers, employees, and so on. Because inflows and outflows do not coincide perfectly, a company must keep some cash in its bank account. In other words, some cash is required to conduct operations. The same is true for most other current assets, such as inventory and accounts receivable, which are required for normal operations. The short-term assets normally used in a company's operating activities are called **operating current assets.**

Not all current assets are operating current assets. For example, holdings of short-term securities generally result from investment decisions made by the treasurer and not as a natural consequence of operating activities. Therefore, short-term investments are **nonoperating assets** and normally are excluded when calculating operating current assets.[9] A useful rule of thumb is that if an asset pays interest, it should not be classified as an operating asset.

Some current liabilities—especially accounts payable and accruals—arise in the normal course of operations. Such short-term liabilities are called **operating current liabilities.** Not all current liabilities are operating current liabilities. For example, consider the current liability shown as notes payable to banks. The company could have raised an equivalent amount as long-term debt or could have issued stock, so the choice to borrow from the bank was a financing decision and not a consequence of operations. Again, the rule of thumb is that if a liability charges interest, it is not an operating liability.

If you are ever uncertain about whether an item is an operating asset or operating liability, ask yourself whether the item is a natural consequence of operations or if it is a discretionary choice, such as a particular method of financing or an investment in a particular financial asset. If it is discretionary, then the item is not an operating asset or liability.

Notice that each dollar of operating current liabilities is a dollar that the company does not have to raise from investors in order to conduct its short-term operating activities. Therefore, we define **net operating working capital (NOWC)** as operating current assets minus operating current liabilities. In other words, net operating working capital is the working capital acquired with investor-supplied funds. Here is the definition in equation form:

$$\text{Net operating working capital} = \text{Operating current assets} - \text{Operating current liabilities} \tag{7–4}$$

We can apply these definitions to MicroDrive, using the balance sheet data given in Table 7-1. Here is its net operating working capital at year-end 2012:

$$
\begin{aligned}
\text{NOWC} &= \text{Operating current assets} - \text{Operating current liabilities} \\
&= (\text{Cash} + \text{Accounts receivable} + \text{Inventories}) \\
&\quad - (\text{Accounts payable} + \text{Accruals}) \\
&= (\$10 + \$375 + \$615) - (\$60 + \$140) \\
&= \$800 \text{ million}
\end{aligned}
$$

For the previous year, net operating working capital was

$$
\begin{aligned}
\text{NOWC} &= (\$15 + \$315 + \$415) - (\$30 + \$130) \\
&= \$585 \text{ million}
\end{aligned}
$$

---

9. If the marketable securities are held as a substitute for cash and therefore reduce the cash requirements, then they may be classified as part of operating working capital. Generally, though, large holdings of marketable securities are held as a reserve for some contingency or else as a temporary "parking place" for funds prior to an acquisition, a major capital investment program, or the like.

7.7c Total Net Operating Capital

In addition to working capital, most companies also use long-term assets to support their operations. These include land, buildings, factories, equipment, and the like. **Total net operating capital** is the sum of NOWC and operating long-term assets:

$$(7\text{--}5) \qquad \text{Total net operating capital} = \text{NOWC} + \text{Operating long-term assets}$$

Because MicroDrive's operating long-term assets consist only of net plant and equipment, its total net operating capital at year-end 2012 was

$$\text{Total net operating capital} = \$800 + \$1,000$$
$$= \$1,800 \text{ million}$$

FINANCIAL BAMBOOZLING: HOW TO SPOT IT

Recent accounting frauds by Enron, WorldCom, Xerox, Merck, Arthur Andersen, Tyco, and many others have shown that analysts can no longer blindly assume that a firm's published financial statements are the best representation of its financial position. Clearly, many companies were "pushing the envelope," if not outright lying, in an effort to make their companies look better.

A recent *Fortune* article points out that there are only three basic ways to manipulate financial statements: moving earnings from the future to the present, avoiding taxes, or hiding debt. For example, suppose one telecom firm (think WorldCom or Global Crossing) sold the right to use parts of its fiber-optic network for 10 years to another telecom firm for $100 million. The seller would immediately record revenues of $100 million. The buyer, however, could spread the expense over 10 years and report an expense of only $10 million this year. The buyer would simultaneously sell similar rights to the original seller for $100 million. This way, no cash changes hands, both companies report an extra $100 million in revenue, but each reports a cost of only $10 million. Thus, both companies "created" an extra $90 million in pre-tax profits without actually doing anything. Of course, both companies will have to report an extra $10 million expense each year for the remaining 9 years, but they have each boosted short-term profits and thus this year's executive bonuses. To boost earnings next year, all they have to do is play the same game, but on a bigger scale.

For hiding debt, it's hard to beat Enron's special purpose entities (SPEs). These SPEs owed hundreds of millions of dollars, and it turned out that Enron was responsible for this debt, even though it never showed up on Enron's financial statements.

How can you spot bamboozling? Here are some tips. When companies have lots of write-offs or charges for restructuring, it could be that they are planning on managing earnings in the future. In other words, they sandbag this year to pad next year's earnings. Beware of serial acquirers, especially if they use their own stock to buy other companies. This can increase reported earnings, but it often erodes value since the acquirer usually pays a large premium for the target. Watch out for companies that depreciate their assets much more slowly than others in the industry (this is shown in the financial statements' footnotes). This causes their current earnings to look larger than their competitors', even though they aren't actually performing any better. Perhaps the best evidence of bamboozling is if earnings are consistently growing faster than cash flows, which almost always indicates a financial scam.

Sources: Geoffrey Colvin, "Bamboozling: A Field Guide," *Fortune,* July 8, 2002, 51; and Shawn Tully, "Don't Get Burned," *Fortune,* February 18, 2002, 87–90.

For the previous year, its total net operating capital was

$$\text{Total net operating capital} = \$585 + \$870$$
$$= \$1,455 \text{ million}$$

Notice that we have defined total net operating capital as the sum of net operating working capital and operating long-term assets. In other words, our definition is in terms of operating assets and liabilities. However, we can also calculate total net operating capital by adding up the funds provided by investors, such as notes payable, long-term bonds, preferred stock, and common equity. For MicroDrive, the total capital provided by investors at year-end 2011 was $60 + $580 + $40 + $840 = $1,520 million. Of this amount, $65 million was tied up in short-term investments, which are not directly related to MicroDrive's operations. Therefore, only $1,520 − $65 = $1,455 million of investor-supplied capital was used in operations. Notice that this is exactly the same value as calculated before. This shows that we can calculate total net operating capital either from net operating working capital and operating long-term assets or from the investor-supplied funds. We usually base our calculations on operating data because this approach allows us to analyze a division, factory, or work center, whereas the approach based on investor-supplied capital is applicable only for the entire company.

The expression "total net operating capital" is a mouthful, so we often call it *operating capital* or even just *capital*. Also, unless we specifically say "investor-supplied capital," we are referring to total net operating capital.

7.7d Net Investment in Operating Capital

As calculated previously, MicroDrive had $1,455 million of total net operating capital at the end of 2011 and $1,800 million at the end of 2012. Therefore, during 2012, it made a **net investment in operating capital** of

$$\text{Net investment in operating capital} = \$1,800 - \$1,455 = \$345 \text{ million}$$

Most of this investment was made in net operating working capital, which rose from $585 million to $800 million, or by $215 million. This 37% increase in net operating working capital, in view of a sales increase of only 5% (from $2,850 to $3,000 million), should set off warning bells in your head: Why did MicroDrive tie up so much additional cash in working capital? Is the company gearing up for a big increase in sales, or are inventories not moving and receivables not being collected? We will address these questions in detail in Chapter 8, when we cover ratio analysis.

7.7e Calculating Free Cash Flow

Free cash flow is defined as

$$\text{FCF} = \text{NOPAT} - \text{Net investment in operating capital} \qquad (7\text{--}6)$$

MicroDrive's free cash flow in 2012 was

$$\text{FCF} = \$169.8 - (\$1,800 - \$1,455)$$
$$= \$169.8 - \$345$$
$$= -\$175.2 \text{ million}$$

Although we prefer this approach to calculating FCF, sometimes the financial press calculates FCF with a different approach. The results are the same either way, but you should be aware of this alternative approach. The difference lies in how depreciation is treated. To see this, notice that net fixed assets rose from $870 to $1,000 million, or by $130 million. However, MicroDrive reported $100 million of depreciation, so its gross investment in fixed assets was $130 + $100 = $230 million for the year. With this background, the **gross investment in operating capital** is

(7–7)
$$\text{Gross investment in operating capital} = \text{Net investment in operating capital} + \text{Depreciation}$$

For MicroDrive, the gross investment in operating capital was:

$$\text{Gross investment in operating capital} = \$345 + \$100 = \$445 \text{ million}$$

Because depreciation is a noncash expense, some analysts calculate **operating cash flow** as

(7–8)
$$\text{Operating cash flow} = \text{NOPAT} + \text{Depreciation}$$

MicroDrive's most recent operating cash flow is

$$\text{Operating cash flow} = \text{NOPAT} + \text{Depreciation} = \$169.8 + \$100 = \$269.8$$

An algebraically equivalent expression for free cash flow in terms of operating cash flow and gross investment in operating capital is

(7–9)
$$\text{FCF} = (\text{NOPAT} + \text{Depreciation}) - \left(\text{Net investment in operating capital} + \text{Depreciation}\right)$$

$$= \text{Operating cash flow} - \text{Gross investment in operating capital}$$

$$= \text{Operating cash flow} - \text{Gross investment in long-term operating assets} - \text{Investment in NOWC}$$

For MicroDrive, this definition produces FCF of −$175.2, the same value as found earlier:

$$\text{FCF} = (\$169.8 + \$100) - \$445$$
$$= -\$175.2 \text{ million}$$

Equations 7-6 and 7-9 are equivalent because depreciation is added to both NOPAT and net investment in Equation 7-6 to arrive at Equation 7-9. We usually use Equation 7-6, because it saves us this step, but you should be aware of this alternative approach.

7.7f The Uses of FCF

Recall that free cash flow (FCF) is the amount of cash that is available for distribution to all investors, including shareholders and debtholders. There are five good uses for FCF:

1. Pay interest to debtholders, keeping in mind that the net cost to the company is the after-tax interest expense.
2. Repay debtholders; that is, pay off some of the debt.
3. Pay dividends to shareholders.
4. Repurchase stock from shareholders.
5. Buy short-term investments or other nonoperating assets.

Consider MicroDrive, with its FCF of –$175.2 million in 2012. How did MicroDrive use the FCF?

MicroDrive's income statement shows an interest expense of $88 million. With a tax rate of 40%, the after-tax interest payment for the year is

$$\text{After-tax interest payment} = \$88(1 - 40\%) = \$52.8 \text{ million}$$

The net amount of debt that is repaid is equal to the amount at the beginning of the year minus the amount at the end of the year. This includes notes payable and long-term debt. If the amount of ending debt is less than the beginning debt, the company paid down some of its debt. But if the ending debt is greater than the beginning debt, the company actually borrowed additional funds from creditors. In that case, it would be a negative use of FCF. For MicroDrive, the net debt repayment for 2012 is

$$\text{Net reduction in debt} = (\$60 + \$580) - (\$754 + \$110) = -\$224 \text{ million}$$

This is a "negative use" of FCF because it increased the debt balance. This is typical of most companies because growing companies usually add debt each year.

MicroDrive paid $4 million in preferred dividends and $57 in common dividends for a total of

$$\text{Dividend payments} = \$4 + \$57 = \$61 \text{ million}$$

The net amount of stock that is repurchased is equal to the amount at the beginning of the year minus the amount at the end of the year. This includes preferred stock and common stock. If the amount of ending stock is less than the beginning stock, then the company made net repurchases. But if the ending stock is greater than the beginning stock, the company actually made net issuances. In that case, it would be a negative use of FCF. Even though MicroDrive neither issued nor repurchased stock during the year, many companies use FCF to repurchase stocks as a replacement for or supplement to dividends, as we discuss in Chapter 17.

The amount of net purchases of short-term investments is equal to the amount at the end of the year minus the amount at the beginning of the year. If the amount of ending investments is greater than the beginning investments, then the company made net purchases. But if the ending investments are less than the beginning investments, the company actually sold investments. In that case, it would be a negative use of FCF. MicroDrive's net purchases of short-term investments in 2012 are:

$$\text{Net purchases of short-term investments} = \$0 - \$65 = -\$65 \text{ million}$$

Notice that this is a "negative use" because MicroDrive sold short-term investments instead of purchasing them.

We combine these individual uses of FCF to find the total uses.

1. After-tax interest:	$ 52.8
2. Net debt repayments:	−224.0
3. Dividends:	61.0
4. Net stock repurchases:	0.0
5. Net purchases of ST investments:	−65.0
Total uses of FCF:	−$175.2

The −$175.2 total for uses of FCF is identical to the value of FCF from operations that we calculated previously. If it were not equal, then we would have made an error somewhere in our calculations.

Observe that a company does not use FCF to acquire operating assets, because the calculation of FCF already takes into account the purchase of operating assets needed to support growth. Unfortunately, there is evidence to suggest that some companies with high FCF tend to make unnecessary investments that don't add value, such as paying too much to acquire another company. Thus, high FCF can cause waste if managers fail to act in the best interests of shareholders. As discussed in Chapter 1, this is called an agency cost, since managers are hired as agents to act on behalf of stockholders. We discuss agency costs and ways to control them in Chapter 11, where we discuss value-based management and corporate governance, and in Chapter 15, where we discuss the choice of capital structure.

7.7g FCF and Corporate Value

Free cash flow is the amount of cash available for distribution to investors; so the fundamental value of a company to its investors depends on the present value of its expected future FCFs, discounted at the company's weighted average cost of capital (WACC). Subsequent chapters will develop the tools needed to forecast FCFs and evaluate their risk. Chapter 11 ties all this together with a model that is used to calculate the value of a company. Even though you do not yet have all the tools to apply the model, it's important that you understand this basic concept: *FCF is the cash flow available for distribution to investors. Therefore, the fundamental value of a firm primarily depends on its expected future FCF.*

7.7h Evaluating FCF, NOPAT, and Operating Capital

Even though MicroDrive had a positive NOPAT, its very high investment in operating assets resulted in a negative FCF. Because free cash flow is the cash flow available for distribution to investors, MicroDrive's negative FCF meant that MicroDrive had to sell short-term investments and so investors actually had to provide *additional* money to keep the business going.

Is a negative free cash flow always bad? The answer is, "Not necessarily; it depends on why the free cash flow was negative." It's a bad sign if FCF was negative because NOPAT was negative, since then the company is probably experiencing operating problems. However, many high-growth companies have positive NOPAT but negative FCF because they are making large investments in operating assets to support growth. There is nothing wrong with profitable growth, even if it causes negative cash flows.

One way to determine whether growth is profitable is by examining the **return on invested capital (ROIC)**, which is the ratio of NOPAT to total operating capital. If the ROIC exceeds the rate of return required by investors, then a negative free cash flow caused by high growth is nothing to worry about. Chapter 11 discusses this in detail.

To calculate the ROIC, we first calculate NOPAT and operating capital. The return on invested capital is a performance measure that indicates how much NOPAT is generated by each dollar of operating capital:

$$\text{ROIC} = \frac{\text{NOPAT}}{\text{Operating capital}} \qquad (7\text{--}10)$$

If ROIC is greater than the rate of return that investors require, which is the weighted average cost of capital (WACC), then the firm is adding value.

As noted previously, a negative FCF is not necessarily bad, provided it is due to high, profitable growth.[10] For example, Qualcomm's sales grew by 26% in 2008, which led to large capital investments and an FCF of *negative* $4.6 billion. However, its ROIC was about 29%, so the growth was profitable. Qualcomm experienced negative growth in 2009 and only slow growth in 2010 as a result of the global recession, and with slower growth came smaller capital requirements and higher FCF; FCF soared to about $2.5 billion in 2010 with an ROIC of 14%. Certainly Qualcomm would have preferred to maintain its 26% growth rate and high ROIC, but the silver lining behind the decline in growth was the substantial increase in FCF.

MicroDrive had an ROIC in 2012 of 9.43%: $169.8/$1,800 = 0.0943. Is this enough to cover its cost of capital? We'll answer that question in the next section.

Self Test

What is net operating working capital? Why does it exclude most short-term investments and also notes payable?

What is total net operating capital? Why is it important for managers to calculate a company's capital requirements?

Why is NOPAT a better performance measure than net income?

What is free cash flow? Why is it important?

A firm's total net operating capital for the previous year was $2 million. For the current year, its total net operating capital is $2.5 million and its NOPAT is $1.2 million. What is its free cash flow for the current year? (**$700,000**)

---

10. If g is the growth rate in capital, then with a little (or a lot of!) algebra, free cash flow is

$$\text{FCF} = \text{Capital}\left(\text{ROIC} - \frac{g}{1+g}\right)$$

This shows that when the growth rate gets almost as high as ROIC, then FCF will be negative.

7.8 MVA and EVA

Neither traditional accounting data nor the modified data discussed in the preceding section incorporates stock prices, even though the primary goal of management is to maximize the firm's stock price. Financial analysts have therefore developed two additional performance measures, Market Value Added (MVA) and Economic Value Added (EVA). These concepts are discussed in this section.[11]

7.8a Market Value Added (MVA)

The primary goal of most firms is to maximize shareholders' wealth. This goal obviously benefits shareholders, but it also helps to ensure that scarce resources are allocated efficiently, which benefits the economy. Shareholder wealth is maximized by maximizing the *difference* between the market value of the firm's stock and the amount of equity capital that was supplied by shareholders. This difference is called the **Market Value Added (MVA):**

(7–11)
$$\text{MVA} = \text{Market value of stock} - \text{Equity capital supplied by shareholders}$$
$$= (\text{Shares outstanding})(\text{Stock price}) - \text{Total common equity}$$

www

For an updated estimate of Coca-Cola's MVA, go to **finance.yahoo.com**, enter KO, and click GO. This shows the market value of equity, called Mkt Cap. To get the book value of equity, select Balance Sheet from the left panel.

To illustrate, consider Coca-Cola. In December 2010, its total market equity value was $152.0 billion while its balance sheet showed that stockholders had put up only $24.8 billion. Thus, Coca-Cola's MVA was $152.0 − $24.8 = $127.2 billion. This $127.2 billion represents the difference between the money that Coca-Cola's stockholders have invested in the corporation since its founding—including indirect investment by retaining earnings—and the cash they could get if they sold the business. The higher its MVA, the better the job management is doing for the firm's shareholders.

Sometimes MVA is defined as the total market value of the company minus the total amount of investor-supplied capital:

(7–11a)
$$\text{MVA} = \text{Total market value} - \text{Total investor-supplied capital}$$
$$= (\text{Market value of stock} + \text{Market value of debt})$$
$$- \text{Total investor-supplied capital}$$

For most companies, the total amount of investor-supplied capital is the sum of equity, debt, and preferred stock. We can calculate the total amount of investor-supplied capital directly from their reported values in the financial statements. The total market value of a company is the sum of the market values of common equity, debt, and preferred stock. It is easy to find the market value of equity, since stock prices are readily available, but it is not always easy to find the market value of debt. Hence, many analysts use the value of debt that is reported in the financial statements, which is the debt's book value, as an estimate of its market value.

For Coca-Cola, the total amount of reported debt was about $23.9 billion, and Coca-Cola had no preferred stock. Using this as an estimate of the market value

---

11. The concepts of EVA and MVA were developed by Joel Stern and Bennett Stewart, co-founders of the consulting firm Stern Stewart & Company. Stern Stewart copyrighted the terms "EVA" and "MVA," so other consulting firms have given other names to these values. Still, EVA and MVA are the terms most commonly used in practice.

of debt, Coke's total market value was $152.0 + $23.9 = $175.9 billion. The total amount of investor-supplied funds was $24.8 + $23.9 = $48.7 billion. Using these total values, the MVA was $175.9 - $48.7 = $127.2 billion. Note that this is the same answer as when we used the previous definition of MVA. Both methods will give the same result if the market value of debt is approximately equal to its book value.

7.8b Economic Value Added (EVA)

Whereas MVA measures the effects of managerial actions since the very inception of a company, **Economic Value Added (EVA)** focuses on managerial effectiveness in a given year. The basic EVA formula is:

$$
\begin{aligned}
\text{EVA} &= \text{Net operating profit after taxes (NOPAT)} \\
&\quad - \text{After-tax dollar cost of capital used to support operations} \\
&= \text{EBIT}(1 - \text{Tax rate}) - (\text{Total net operating capital})(\text{WACC})
\end{aligned}
\tag{7–12}
$$

We can also calculate EVA in terms of ROIC:

$$
\text{EVA} = (\text{Operating capital})(\text{ROIC} - \text{WACC})
\tag{7–13}
$$

As this equation shows, a firm adds value—that is, has a positive EVA—if its ROIC is greater than its WACC. If WACC exceeds ROIC, then new investments in operating capital will reduce the firm's value.

Economic Value Added is an estimate of a business's true economic profit for the year, and it differs sharply from accounting profit.[12] EVA represents the residual income that remains after the cost of *all* capital, including equity capital, has been deducted, whereas accounting profit is determined without imposing a charge for equity capital. As we discuss in Chapter 10, equity capital has a cost because shareholders give up the opportunity to invest and earn returns elsewhere when they provide capital to the firm. This cost is an *opportunity cost* rather than an *accounting cost,* but it is quite real nevertheless.

Note that when calculating EVA we do not add back depreciation. Although it is not a cash expense, depreciation is a cost because worn-out assets must be replaced, and it is therefore deducted when determining both net income and EVA. Our calculation of EVA assumes that the true economic depreciation of the company's fixed assets exactly equals the depreciation used for accounting and tax purposes. If this were not the case, adjustments would have to be made to obtain a more accurate measure of EVA.

Economic Value Added measures the extent to which the firm has increased shareholder value. Therefore, if managers focus on EVA, this will help to ensure that they operate in a manner that is consistent with maximizing shareholder wealth. Note too that EVA can be determined for divisions as well as for the company as a

---

12. The most important reason EVA differs from accounting profit is that the cost of equity capital is deducted when EVA is calculated. Other factors that could lead to differences include adjustments that might be made to depreciation, to research and development costs, to inventory valuations, and so on. These other adjustments also can affect the calculation of investor-supplied capital, which affects both EVA and MVA. See Stewart, *The Quest for Value,* cited in footnote 8.

TABLE 7-5   MVA and EVA for MicroDrive Inc. (Millions of Dollars)

	2012	2011
MVA Calculation		
Price per share	$ 23.0	$ 26.0
Number of shares (millions)	50.0	50.0
Market value of equity = Share price × Number of shares	$1,150.0	$1,300.0
Book value of equity	$ 896.0	$ 840.0
MVA = Market value − Book value	$ 254.0	$ 460.0
EVA Calculation		
EBIT	$ 283.0	$ 260.0
Tax rate	40.0%	40.0%
NOPAT = EBIT(1 − T)	$ 169.8	$ 156.0
Total investor-supplied operating capital[a]	$1,800.0	$1,455.0
Weighted average cost of capital, WACC (%)	11.0%	10.8%
Dollar cost of capital = Operating capital × WACC	$ 198.0	$ 157.1
EVA = NOPAT − Dollar cost of capital	($ 28.2)	($ 1.1)
ROIC = NOPAT ÷ Operating capital	9.43%	10.72%
ROIC − Cost of capital = ROIC − WACC	(1.57%)	(0.08%)
EVA = Operating capital × (ROIC − WACC)	($ 28.2)	($ 1.1)

[a]Investor-supplied operating capital equals the sum of notes payable, long-term debt, preferred stock, and common equity, less short-term investments. It could also be calculated as total liabilities and equity minus accounts payable, accruals, and short-term investments. It is also equal to total net operating capital.

© Cengage Learning 2013

WEB

See *Ch07 Tool Kit.xls* for details.

whole, so it provides a useful basis for determining managerial performance at all levels. Consequently, EVA is being used by an increasing number of firms as the primary basis for determining managerial compensation.

Table 7-5 shows how MicroDrive's MVA and EVA are calculated. The stock price was $23 per share at year-end 2012, down from $26 per share the previous year. Its WACC, which is the percentage after-tax cost of capital, was 10.8% in 2011 and 11.0% in 2012, and its tax rate was 40%. Other data in Table 7-5 were given in the basic financial statements provided earlier in the chapter.

Note first that the lower stock price and the higher book value of equity (due to retaining earnings during 2012) combined to reduce the MVA. The 2012 MVA is still positive, but $460 − $254 = $206 million of stockholders' value was lost during the year.

Economic Value Added for 2011 was virtually zero, and in 2012 it was negative. Operating income (NOPAT) rose, but EVA still declined, primarily because the amount of capital rose more sharply than NOPAT—by about 24% versus 9%—and the cost of this additional capital pulled EVA down.

Recall also that net income fell, but not nearly so dramatically as the decline in EVA. Net income does not reflect the amount of equity capital employed, but EVA does. Because of this omission, net income is not as useful as EVA for setting corporate goals and measuring managerial performance.

SARBANES-OXLEY AND FINANCIAL FRAUD

Investors need to be cautious when they review financial statements. Although companies are required to follow generally accepted accounting principles (GAAP), managers still have quite a lot of discretion in deciding how and when to report certain transactions. Consequently, two firms in exactly the same operating situation may report financial statements that convey different impressions about their financial strength. Some variations may stem from legitimate differences of opinion about the correct way to record transactions. In other cases, managers may choose to report numbers in a way that helps them present either higher earnings or more stable earnings over time. As long as they follow GAAP, such actions are not illegal, but these differences make it harder for investors to compare companies and gauge their true performances.

Unfortunately, there have also been cases where managers overstepped the bounds and reported fraudulent statements. Indeed, a number of high-profile executives have faced criminal charges because of their misleading accounting practices. For example, in June 2002 it was discovered that WorldCom (now called MCI) had committed the most massive accounting fraud of all time by recording over $7 billion of ordinary operating costs as capital expenditures, thus overstating net income by the same amount.

WorldCom's published financial statements fooled most investors—investors bid the stock price up to $64.50, and banks and other lenders provided the company with more than $30 billion of loans. Arthur Andersen, the firm's auditor, was faulted for not detecting the fraud. WorldCom's CFO and CEO were convicted, and Arthur Andersen went bankrupt. But that didn't help the investors who relied on the published financial statements.

In response to these and other abuses, Congress passed the Sarbanes-Oxley Act of 2002. One of its provisions requires both the CEO and the CFO to sign a statement certifying that the "financial statements and disclosures fairly represent, in all material respects, the operations and financial condition" of the company. This will make it easier to haul off in handcuffs a CEO or CFO who has been misleading investors. Whether this will prevent future financial fraud remains to be seen.

We will have more to say about both MVA and EVA later in the book, but we can close this section with two observations. First, there is a relationship between MVA and EVA, but it is not a direct one. If a company has a history of negative EVAs, then its MVA will probably be negative; conversely, its MVA probably will be positive if the company has a history of positive EVAs. However, the stock price, which is the key ingredient in the MVA calculation, depends more on expected future performance than on historical performance. Therefore, a company with a history of negative EVAs could have a positive MVA, provided investors expect a turnaround in the future.

The second observation is that when EVAs or MVAs are used to evaluate managerial performance as part of an incentive compensation program, EVA is the measure that is typically used. The reasons are: (1) EVA shows the value added during a given year, whereas MVA reflects performance over the company's entire life, perhaps even including times before the current managers were born; and (2) EVA can be applied to individual divisions or other units of a large corporation, whereas MVA must be applied to the entire corporation.

Self Test

Define "Market Value Added (MVA)" and "Economic Value Added (EVA)."

How does EVA differ from accounting profit?

A firm has $100 million in total net operating capital. Its return on invested capital is 14%, and its weighted average cost of capital is 10%. What is its EVA? **($4 million)**

7.9 The Federal Income Tax System

The value of any financial asset (including stocks, bonds, and mortgages), as well as most real assets such as plants or even entire firms, depends on the after-tax stream of cash flows produced by the asset. The following sections describe the key features of corporate and individual taxation.

7.9a Corporate Income Taxes

The corporate tax structure, shown in Table 7-6, is relatively simple. The **marginal tax rate** is the rate paid on the last dollar of income, while the **average tax rate** is the average rate paid on all income. To illustrate, if a firm had $65,000 of taxable income, its tax bill would be

$$\text{Taxes} = \$7,500 + 0.25(\$65,000 - \$50,000)$$
$$= \$7,500 + \$3,750 = \$11,250$$

Its marginal rate would be 25%, and its average tax rate would be $11,250/$65,000 = 17.3%. Note that corporate income above $18,333,333 has an average and marginal tax rate of 35%.[13]

---

13. Prior to 1987, many large, profitable corporations such as General Electric and Boeing paid no income taxes. The reasons for this were as follows: (1) expenses, especially depreciation, were defined differently for calculating taxable income than for reporting earnings to stockholders, so some companies reported positive profits to stockholders but losses—hence no taxes—to the Internal Revenue Service; and (2) some companies that did have tax liabilities used various tax credits to offset taxes that would otherwise have been payable. This situation was effectively eliminated in 1987.

   The principal method used to eliminate this situation is the Alternative Minimum Tax (AMT). Under the AMT, both corporate and individual taxpayers must figure their taxes in two ways, the "regular" way and the AMT way, and then pay the higher of the two. The AMT is calculated as follows: (1) Figure your regular taxes. (2) Take your taxable income under the regular method and then add back certain items, especially income on certain municipal bonds, depreciation in excess of straight-line depreciation, certain research and drilling costs, itemized or standard deductions (for individuals), and a number of other items. (3) The income determined in (2) is defined as AMT income, and it must then be multiplied by the AMT tax rate to determine the tax due under the AMT system. An individual or corporation must then pay the higher of the regular tax or the AMT tax. In 2011, there were two AMT tax rates for individuals (26% and 28%, depending on the level of AMT income and filing status). Most corporations have an AMT of 20%. However, there is no AMT for very small companies, defined as those that have had average sales of less than $7.5 million for the past 3 years. Even with the AMT, however, GE, for example, still pays taxes at a rate well under 20% due to other loopholes in the tax code.

TABLE 7-6	Corporate Tax Rates as of January 2011		
If a Corporation's Taxable Income Is	It Pays This Amount on the Base of the Bracket	Plus This Percentage on the Excess Over the Base	Average Tax Rate at Top of Bracket
Up to $50,000	$ 0	15%	15.0%
$50,000–$75,000	$ 7,500	25	18.3
$75,000–$100,000	$ 13,750	34	22.3
$100,000–$335,000	$ 22,250	39	34.0
$335,000–$10,000,000	$ 113,900	34	34.0
$10,000,000–$15,000,000	$3,400,000	35	34.3
$15,000,000–$18,333,333	$5,150,000	38	35.0
Over $18,333,333	$6,416,667	35	35.0

© Cengage Learning 2013

Interest and Dividend Income Received by a Corporation

Interest income received by a corporation is taxed as ordinary income at regular corporate tax rates. However, *70% of the dividends received by one corporation from another is excluded from taxable income, while the remaining 30% is taxed at the ordinary tax rate.*[14] Thus, a corporation earning more than $18,333,333 and paying a 35% marginal tax rate would pay only $(0.30)(0.35) = 0.105 = 10.5\%$ of its dividend income as taxes, so its effective tax rate on dividends received would be 10.5%. If this firm had $10,000 in pre-tax dividend income, then its after-tax dividend income would be $8,950:

$$\frac{\text{After-tax}}{\text{income}} = \frac{\text{Before-tax}}{\text{income}} - \text{Taxes}$$

$$= \frac{\text{Before-tax}}{\text{income}} - \left(\frac{\text{Before-tax}}{\text{income}}\right)(\text{Effective tax rate})$$

$$= \left(\frac{\text{Before-tax}}{\text{income}}\right)(1 - \text{Effective tax rate})$$

$$= \$10,000[1 - (0.30)(0.35)]$$

$$= \$10,000(1 - 0.105) = \$10,000(0.895) = \$8,950$$

WEB

See *Ch07 Tool Kit.xls* for details.

If the corporation pays its own after-tax income out to its stockholders as dividends, then the income is ultimately subjected to *triple taxation:* (1) the original corporation is first taxed, (2) the second corporation is then taxed on the dividends it received, and (3) the individuals who receive the final dividends are taxed again. This is the reason for the 70% exclusion on intercorporate dividends.

If a corporation has surplus funds that can be invested in marketable securities, the tax treatment favors investment in stocks, which pay dividends, rather than

---

14. The size of the dividend exclusion actually depends on the degree of ownership. Corporations that own less than 20% of the stock of the dividend-paying company can exclude 70% of the dividends received; firms that own more than 20% but less than 80% can exclude 80% of the dividends; and firms that own more than 80% can exclude the entire dividend payment. We will, in general, assume a 70% dividend exclusion.

in bonds, which pay interest. For example, suppose Home Depot had $100,000 to invest, and suppose it could buy either bonds that paid interest of $8,000 per year or preferred stock that paid dividends of $7,000. Home Depot is in the 35% tax bracket; therefore, its tax on the interest, if it bought bonds, would be 0.35($8,000) = $2,800, and its after-tax income would be $5,200. If it bought preferred (or common) stock, its tax would be 0.35[(0.30)($7,000)] = $735, and its after-tax income would be $6,265. Other factors might lead Home Depot to invest in bonds, but the tax treatment certainly favors stock investments when the investor is a corporation.[15]

Interest and Dividends Paid by a Corporation

A firm's operations can be financed with either debt or equity capital. If the firm uses debt then it must pay interest on this debt, but if the firm uses equity then it is expected to pay dividends to the equity investors (stockholders). The interest *paid* by a corporation is deducted from its operating income to obtain its taxable income, but dividends paid are not deductible. Therefore, a firm needs $1 of pre-tax income to pay $1 of interest, but if it is in the 40% federal-plus-state tax bracket, it must earn $1.67 of pre-tax income to pay $1 of dividends:

$$\text{Pre-tax income needed to pay \$1 of dividends} = \frac{\$1}{1 - \text{Tax rate}} = \frac{\$1}{0.60} = \$1.67$$

Working backward, if a company has $1.67 in pre-tax income, it must pay $0.67 in taxes: (0.4)($1.67) = $0.67. This leaves the firm with after-tax income of $1.00.

Of course, it is generally not possible to finance exclusively with debt capital, and the risk of doing so would offset the benefits of the higher expected income. Still, *the fact that interest is a deductible expense has a profound effect on the way businesses are financed: Our corporate tax system favors debt financing over equity financing.* This point is discussed in more detail in Chapters 10 and 15.

Corporate Capital Gains

Before 1987, corporate long-term capital gains were taxed at lower rates than corporate ordinary income, so the situation was similar for corporations and individuals. Under current law, however, corporations' capital gains are taxed at the same rates as their operating income.

Corporate Loss Carryback and Carryforward

Ordinary corporate operating losses can be carried back (**carryback**) to each of the preceding 2 years and forward (**carryforward**) for the next 20 years and thus be used to offset taxable income in those years. For example, an operating loss in 2012 could be carried back and used to reduce taxable income in 2010 and 2011 as well as forward, if necessary, to reduce taxes in 2013, 2014, and so on, to the year 2032.

---

15. This illustration demonstrates why corporations favor investing in lower-yielding preferred stocks over higher-yielding bonds. When tax consequences are considered, the yield on the preferred stock, [1 − 0.35(0.30)](7.0%) = 6.265%, is higher than the yield on the bond, (1 − 0.35)(8.0%) = 5.2%. Also, note that corporations are restricted in their use of borrowed funds to purchase other firms' preferred or common stocks. Without such restrictions, firms could engage in *tax arbitrage,* whereby the interest on borrowed funds reduces taxable income on a dollar-for-dollar basis while taxable income is increased by only $0.30 per dollar of dividend income. Thus, current tax laws reduce the 70% dividend exclusion in proportion to the amount of borrowed funds used to purchase the stock.

After carrying back 2 years, any remaining loss is typically carried forward first to the next year, then to the one after that, and so on, until losses have been used up or the 20-year carryforward limit has been reached.

To illustrate, suppose Apex Corporation had $2 million of *pre-tax* profits (taxable income) in 2010 and 2011, and then, in 2012, Apex lost $12 million. Also, assume that Apex's federal-plus-state tax rate is 40%. As shown in Table 7-7, the company would use the carryback feature to recompute its taxes for 2010, using $2 million of the 2012 operating losses to reduce the 2010 pre-tax profit to zero. This would permit it to recover the taxes paid in 2010. Therefore, in 2012 Apex would receive a refund of its 2010 taxes because of the loss experienced in 2012. Because $10 million of the unrecovered losses would still be available, Apex would repeat this procedure for 2011. Thus, in 2012 the company would pay zero taxes for 2012 and also would receive a refund for taxes paid in 2010 and 2011. Apex would still have $8 million of unrecovered losses to carry forward, subject to the 20-year limit. This $8 million could be used to offset future taxable income. The purpose of this loss treatment is to avoid penalizing corporations whose incomes fluctuate substantially from year to year.

Improper Accumulation to Avoid Payment of Dividends

Corporations could refrain from paying dividends and thus permit their stockholders to avoid personal income taxes on dividends. To prevent this, the Tax Code contains an **improper accumulation** provision that states that earnings accumulated by a corporation are subject to penalty rates *if the purpose of the accumulation is to enable stockholders to avoid personal income taxes*. A cumulative total of $250,000 (the balance sheet item "retained earnings") is by law exempted from the improper accumulation tax for most corporations. This is a benefit primarily to small corporations.

WEB

See **Ch07 Tool Kit.xls** for details.

TABLE 7-7	Apex Corporation: Calculation of $12 Million Loss Carryback and Amount Available for Carryforward		
	Past Year 2010	Past Year 2011	Current Year 2012
Original taxable income	$2,000,000	$2,000,000	−$12,000,000
Carryback credit	2,000,000	2,000,000	
Adjusted profit	$ 0	$ 0	
Taxes previously paid (40%)	800,000	800,000	
Difference = Tax refund due	$ 800,000	$ 800,000	
Total tax refund received			$ 1,600,000
Amount of loss carryforward available			
Current loss			−$12,000,000
Carryback losses used			4,000,000
Carryforward losses still available			−$ 8,000,000

The improper accumulation penalty applies only if the retained earnings in excess of $250,000 are *shown by the IRS to be unnecessary to meet the reasonable needs of the business.* A great many companies do indeed have legitimate reasons for retaining more than $250,000 of earnings. For example, earnings may be retained and used to pay off debt, to finance growth, or to provide the corporation with a cushion against possible cash drains caused by losses. How much a firm should be allowed to accumulate for uncertain contingencies is a matter of judgment. We shall consider this matter again in Chapter 17, which deals with corporate dividend policy.

Consolidated Corporate Tax Returns

If a corporation owns 80% or more of another corporation's stock, then it can aggregate income and file one consolidated tax return; thus, the losses of one company can be used to offset the profits of another. (Similarly, one division's losses can be used to offset another division's profits.) No business ever wants to incur losses (you can go broke losing $1 to save 35¢ in taxes), but tax offsets do help make it more feasible for large, multidivisional corporations to undertake risky new ventures or ventures that will suffer losses during a developmental period.

Taxes on Overseas Income

Many U.S. corporations have overseas subsidiaries, and those subsidiaries must pay taxes in the countries where they operate. Often, foreign tax rates are lower than U.S. rates. As long as foreign earnings are reinvested overseas, no U.S. tax is due on those earnings. However, when foreign earnings are repatriated to the U.S. parent, they are taxed at the applicable U.S. rate, less a credit for taxes paid to the foreign country. As a result, U.S. corporations such as IBM, Coca-Cola, and Microsoft have been able to defer billions of dollars of taxes. This procedure has stimulated overseas investments by U.S. multinational firms—they can continue the deferral indefinitely, but only if they reinvest the earnings in their overseas operations.[16]

7.9b Taxation of Small Businesses: S Corporations

The Tax Code provides that small businesses that meet certain restrictions may be set up as corporations and thus receive the benefits of the corporate form of organization—especially limited liability—yet still be taxed as proprietorships or partnerships rather than as corporations. These corporations are called **S corporations.** ("Regular" corporations are called C corporations.) If a corporation elects S corporation status for tax purposes, then all of the business's income is reported as personal income by its stockholders, on a pro rata basis, and thus is taxed at the rates that apply to individuals. This is an important benefit to the owners of small corporations in which

---

16. This is a contentious political issue. U.S. corporations argue that our tax system is similar to systems in the rest of the world, and if they were taxed immediately on all overseas earnings then they would be at a competitive disadvantage vis-à-vis their global competitors. Others argue that taxation encourages overseas investments at the expense of domestic investments, contributing to the jobs outsourcing problem and also to the federal budget deficit.

all or most of the income earned each year will be distributed as dividends, because then the income is taxed only once, at the individual level.

7.9c Personal Taxes

Web Extension 7A provides a more detailed treatment of individual taxation, but the key elements are presented here. **Ordinary income** consists primarily of wages or profits from a proprietorship or partnership, plus investment income. For the 2010 tax year, individuals with less than $8,375 of taxable income are subject to a federal income tax rate of 10%. For those with higher income, tax rates increase and go up to 35%, depending on the level of income. This is called a **progressive tax,** because the higher one's income, the larger the percentage paid in taxes.

As noted before, individuals are taxed on investment income as well as earned income, but with a few exceptions and modifications. For example, interest received from most state and local government bonds, called **municipals** or **"munis,"** is not subject to federal taxation. However, interest earned on most other bonds or lending is taxed as ordinary income. This means that a lower-yielding muni can provide the same after-tax return as a higher-yielding corporate bond. For a taxpayer in the 35% marginal tax bracket, a muni yielding 5.5% provides the same after-tax return as a corporate bond with a pre-tax yield of 8.46%: $8.46\%(1 - 0.35) = 5.5\%$.

Assets such as stocks, bonds, and real estate are defined as capital assets. If you own a capital asset and its price goes up, then your wealth increases, but you are not liable for any taxes on your increased wealth until you sell the asset. If you sell the asset for more than you originally paid, the profit is called a **capital gain;** if you sell it for less, then you suffer a **capital loss.** The length of time you owned the asset determines the tax treatment. If held for less than 1 year, then your gain or loss is simply added to your other ordinary income. If held for more than a year, then gains are called *long-term capital gains* and are taxed at a lower rate. See *Web Extension 7A* for details, but the long-term capital gains rate is 15% for most situations.

Under the 2003 tax law changes, dividends are now taxed as though they were capital gains. As stated earlier, corporations may deduct interest payments but not dividends when computing their corporate tax liability, which means that dividends are taxed twice, once at the corporate level and again at the personal level. This differential treatment motivates corporations to use debt relatively heavily and to pay small (or even no) dividends. The 2003 tax law did not eliminate the differential treatment of dividends and interest payments from the corporate perspective, but it did make the tax treatment of dividends more similar to that of capital gains from investors' perspectives. To see this, consider a company that doesn't pay a dividend but instead reinvests the cash it could have paid. The company's stock price should increase, leading to a capital gain, which would be taxed at the same rate as the dividend. Of course, the stock price appreciation isn't actually taxed until the stock is sold, whereas the dividend is taxed in the year it is paid, so dividends will still be more costly than capital gains for many investors.

Finally, note that the income of S corporations *and* noncorporate businesses is reported as income by the firms' owners. Since there are far more S corporations, partnerships, and proprietorships than C corporations (which are subject to the corporate tax), individual tax considerations play an important role in business finance.

WEB

See *Web Extension 7A* on the textbook's Web site for details concerning personal taxation.

Self Test

Explain what is meant by this statement: "Our tax rates are progressive."

If a corporation has $85,000 in taxable income, what is its tax liability? **($17,150)**

Explain the difference between marginal tax rates and average tax rates.

What are municipal bonds, and how are these bonds taxed?

What are capital gains and losses, and how are they taxed?

How does the federal income tax system treat dividends received by a corporation versus those received by an individual?

What is the difference in the tax treatment of interest and dividends paid by a corporation? Does this factor favor debt or equity financing?

Briefly explain how tax loss carryback and carryforward procedures work.

Summary

The primary purposes of this chapter were (1) to describe the basic financial statements, (2) to present some background information on cash flows, and (3) to provide an overview of the federal income tax system. The key concepts covered are listed below.

- The four basic statements contained in the **annual report** are the balance sheet, the income statement, the statement of stockholders' equity, and the statement of cash flows.
- The **balance sheet** shows assets on the left-hand side and liabilities and equity, or claims against assets, on the right-hand side. (Sometimes assets are shown at the top and claims at the bottom of the balance sheet.) The balance sheet may be thought of as a snapshot of the firm's financial position at a particular point in time.
- The **income statement** reports the results of operations over a period of time, and it shows earnings per share as its "bottom line."
- The **statement of stockholders' equity** shows the change in retained earnings between balance sheet dates. Retained earnings represent a claim against assets, not assets per se.
- The **statement of cash flows** reports the effect of operating, investing, and financing activities on cash flows over an accounting period.
- **Net cash flow** differs from **accounting profit** because some of the revenues and expenses reflected in accounting profits may not have been received or paid out in cash during the year. Depreciation is typically the largest noncash item, so net cash flow is often expressed as net income plus depreciation.
- **Operating current assets** are the current assets that are used to support operations, such as cash, inventory, and accounts receivable. They do not include short-term investments.

- **Operating current liabilities** are the current liabilities that occur as a natural consequence of operations, such as accounts payable and accruals. They do not include notes payable or any other short-term debts that charge interest.
- **Net operating working capital** is the difference between operating current assets and operating current liabilities. Thus, it is the working capital acquired with investor-supplied funds.
- **Operating long-term assets** are the long-term assets used to support operations, such as net plant and equipment. They do not include any long-term investments that pay interest or dividends.
- **Total net operating capital** (which means the same as **operating capital** and **net operating assets**) is the sum of net operating working capital and operating long-term assets. It is the total amount of capital needed to run the business.
- **NOPAT** is net operating profit after taxes. It is the after-tax profit a company would have if it had no debt and no investments in nonoperating assets. Because it excludes the effects of financial decisions, it is a better measure of operating performance than is net income.
- **Free cash flow (FCF)** is the amount of cash flow remaining after a company makes the asset investments necessary to support operations. In other words, FCF is the amount of cash flow available for distribution to investors, so *the value of a company is directly related to its ability to generate free cash flow.* FCF is defined as NOPAT minus the net investment in operating capital.
- **Market Value Added (MVA)** represents the difference between the total market value of a firm and the total amount of investor-supplied capital. If the market values of debt and preferred stock equal their values as reported on the financial statements, then MVA is the difference between the market value of a firm's stock and the amount of equity its shareholders have supplied.
- **Economic Value Added (EVA)** is the difference between after-tax operating profit and the total dollar cost of capital, including the cost of equity capital. EVA is an estimate of the value created by management during the year, and it differs substantially from accounting profit because no charge for the use of equity capital is reflected in accounting profit.
- Interest income received by a corporation is taxed as **ordinary income**; however, 70% of the dividends received by one corporation from another are excluded from **taxable income.**
- Because interest paid by a corporation is a **deductible expense** whereas dividends are not, our tax system favors debt over equity financing.
- Ordinary corporate operating losses can be **carried back** to each of the preceding 2 years and **carried forward** for the next 20 years in order to offset taxable income in those years.
- **S corporations** are small businesses that have the limited-liability benefits of the corporate form of organization yet are taxed as partnerships or proprietorships.
- In the United States, tax rates are **progressive**—the higher one's income, the larger the percentage paid in taxes.
- Assets such as stocks, bonds, and real estate are defined as **capital assets.** If a capital asset is sold for more than its cost, the profit is called a **capital gain;** if the asset is sold for a loss, it is called a **capital loss.** Assets held for more than a year provide **long-term gains** or **losses.**
- Dividends are taxed as though they were capital gains.
- **Personal taxes** are discussed in more detail in *Web Extension 7A.*

Questions

7-1 Define each of the following terms:
  a. Annual report; balance sheet; income statement
  b. Common stockholders' equity, or net worth; retained earnings
  c. Statement of stockholders' equity; statement of cash flows
  d. Depreciation; amortization; EBITDA
  e. Operating current assets; operating current liabilities; net operating working capital; total net operating capital
  f. Accounting profit; net cash flow; NOPAT; free cash flow
  g. Market Value Added; Economic Value Added
  h. Progressive tax; taxable income; marginal and average tax rates
  i. Capital gain or loss; tax loss carryback and carryforward
  j. Improper accumulation; S corporation

7-2 What four statements are contained in most annual reports?

7-3 If a "typical" firm reports $20 million of retained earnings on its balance sheet, can the firm definitely pay a $20 million cash dividend?

7-4 Explain the following statement: "Whereas the balance sheet can be thought of as a snapshot of the firm's financial position *at a point in time*, the income statement reports on operations *over a period of time*."

7-5 What is operating capital, and why is it important?

7-6 Explain the difference between NOPAT and net income. Which is a better measure of the performance of a company's operations?

7-7 What is free cash flow? Why is it the most important measure of cash flow?

7-8 If you were starting a business, what tax considerations might cause you to prefer to set it up as a proprietorship or a partnership rather than as a corporation?

Problems   Answers Appear in Appendix B

Note: By the time this book is published, Congress may have changed rates and/or other provisions of current tax law—as noted in the chapter, such changes occur fairly often. Work all problems on the assumption that the information in the chapter is applicable.

Easy Problems 1–6

7-1 **Personal After-Tax Yield** An investor recently purchased a corporate bond that yields 9%. The investor is in the 36% combined federal and state tax bracket. What is the bond's after-tax yield?

7-2 **Personal After-Tax Yield** Corporate bonds issued by Johnson Corporation currently yield 8%. Municipal bonds of equal risk currently yield 6%. At what tax rate would an investor be indifferent between these two bonds?

7-3 **Income Statement** Molteni Motors Inc. recently reported $6 million of net income. Its EBIT was $13 million, and its tax rate was 40%. What was its interest expense? (*Hint:* Write out the headings for an income statement and then fill in the known values. Then divide $6 million net income by $1 - T = 0.6$ to find the pre-tax income. The difference between EBIT and taxable income must be the interest expense. Use this same procedure to work some of the other problems.)

7-4 Income Statement Talbot Enterprises recently reported an EBITDA of $8 million and net income of $2.4 million. It had $2.0 million of interest expense, and its corporate tax rate was 40%. What was its charge for depreciation and amortization?

7-5 Net Cash Flow Kendall Corners Inc. recently reported net income of $3.1 million and depreciation of $500,000. What was its net cash flow? Assume it had no amortization expense.

7-6 Statement of Retained Earnings In its most recent financial statements, Del-Castillo Inc. reported $70 million of net income and $900 million of retained earnings. The previous retained earnings were $855 million. How much in dividends was paid to shareholders during the year?

Intermediate Problems 7–11

7-7 Corporate Tax Liability The Talley Corporation had a taxable income of $365,000 from operations after all operating costs but before (1) interest charges of $50,000, (2) dividends received of $15,000, (3) dividends paid of $25,000, and (4) income taxes. What are the firm's income tax liability and its after-tax income? What are the company's marginal and average tax rates on taxable income?

7-8 Corporate Tax Liability The Wendt Corporation had $10.5 million of taxable income.
a. What is the company's federal income tax bill for the year?
b. Assume the firm receives an additional $1 million of interest income from some bonds it owns. What is the tax on this interest income?
c. Now assume that Wendt does not receive the interest income but does receive an additional $1 million as dividends on some stock it owns. What is the tax on this dividend income?

7-9 Corporate After-Tax Yield The Shrieves Corporation has $10,000 that it plans to invest in marketable securities. It is choosing among AT&T bonds, which yield 7.5%, state of Florida muni bonds, which yield 5% (but are not taxable), and AT&T preferred stock, with a dividend yield of 6%. Shrieves's corporate tax rate is 35%, and 70% of the dividends received are tax exempt. Find the after-tax rates of return on all three securities.

7-10 Cash Flows The Moore Corporation has operating income (EBIT) of $750,000. The company's depreciation expense is $200,000. Moore is 100% equity financed, and it faces a 40% tax rate. What is the company's net income? What is its net cash flow?

7-11 Income and Cash Flow Analysis The Berndt Corporation expects to have sales of $12 million. Costs other than depreciation are expected to be 75% of sales, and depreciation is expected to be $1.5 million. All sales revenues will be collected in cash, and costs other than depreciation must be paid for during the year. Berndt's federal-plus-state tax rate is 40%. Berndt has no debt.
a. Set up an income statement. What is Berndt's expected net cash flow?
b. Suppose Congress changed the tax laws so that Berndt's depreciation expenses doubled. No changes in operations occurred. What would happen to reported profit and to net cash flow?
c. Now suppose that Congress, instead of doubling Berndt's depreciation, reduced it by 50%. How would profit and net cash flow be affected?
d. If this were your company, would you prefer Congress to cause your depreciation expense to be doubled or halved? Why?

Challenging Problems 12–13

7-12 **Free Cash Flows** Using Rhodes Corporation's financial statements (shown below), answer the following questions.
   a. What is the net operating profit after taxes (NOPAT) for 2012?
   b. What are the amounts of net operating working capital for both years?
   c. What are the amounts of total net operating capital for both years?
   d. What is the free cash flow for 2012?
   e. What is the ROIC for 2012?
   f. How much of the FCF did Rhodes use for each of the following purposes: after-tax interest, net debt repayments, dividends, net stock repurchases, and net purchases of short-term investments? (*Hint:* Remember that a net use can be negative.)

Rhodes Corporation: Income Statements for Year Ending December 31 (Millions of Dollars)

	2012	2011
Sales	$11,000	$10,000
Operating costs excluding depreciation	9,360	8,500
Depreciation and amortization	380	360
Earnings before interest and taxes	$ 1,260	$ 1,140
Less interest	120	100
Earnings before taxes	$ 1,140	$ 1,040
Taxes (40%)	456	416
Net income available to common stockholders	$ 684	$ 624
Common dividends	$ 220	$ 200

Rhodes Corporation: Balance Sheets as of December 31 (Millions of Dollars)

	2012	2011
Assets		
Cash	$ 550	$ 500
Short-term investments	110	100
Accounts receivable	2,750	2,500
Inventories	1,650	1,500
Total current assets	$5,060	$4,600
Net plant and equipment	3,850	3,500
Total assets	$8,910	$8,100

	2012	2011
Liabilities and Equity		
Accounts payable	$1,100	$1,000
Accruals	550	500
Notes payable	384	200
Total current liabilities	$2,034	$1,700
Long-term debt	1,100	1,000
Total liabilities	$3,134	$2,700
Common stock	4,312	4,400
Retained earnings	1,464	1,000
Total common equity	$5,776	$5,400
Total liabilities and equity	$8,910	$8,100

7-13 **Loss Carryback and Carryforward** The Bookbinder Company has made $150,000 before taxes during each of the last 15 years, and it expects to make $150,000 a year before taxes in the future. However, in 2012 the firm incurred a loss of $650,000. The firm will claim a tax credit at the time it files its 2012 income tax return, and it will receive a check from the U.S. Treasury. Show how it calculates this credit, and then indicate the firm's tax liability for each of the next 5 years. Assume a 40% tax rate on *all* income to ease the calculations.

Spreadsheet Problems

7-14 **Build a Model: Financial Statements, EVA, and MVA** Begin with the partial model in the file *Ch07 P14 Build a Model.xls* on the textbook's Web site.
  a. Cumberland Industries's 2012 sales were $455,000,000; operating costs (excluding depreciation) were equal to 85% of sales; net fixed assets were $67,000,000; depreciation amounted to 10% of net fixed assets; interest expenses were $8,550,000; the state-plus-federal corporate tax rate was 40%; and Cumberland paid 25% of its net income out in dividends. Given this information, construct Cumberland's 2012 income statement. Also calculate total dividends and the addition to retained earnings. (*Hint:* Start with the partial model in the file and report all dollar figures in thousands to reduce clutter.)
  b. Cumberland Industries's partial balance sheets are shown below. Cumberland issued $10,000,000 of new common stock in 2012. Using this information and the results from part a, fill in the missing values for common stock, retained earnings, total common equity, and total liabilities and equity.

Cumberland Industries: Balance Sheets as of December 31
(Thousands of Dollars)

	2012	2011
Assets		
Cash	$ 91,450	$ 74,625
Short-term investments	11,400	15,100
Accounts receivable	108,470	85,527
Inventories	38,450	34,982
Total current assets	$249,770	$210,234
Net fixed assets	67,000	42,436
Total assets	$316,770	$252,670

	2012	2011
Liabilities and Equity		
Accounts payable	$ 30,761	$ 23,109
Accruals	30,405	22,656
Notes payable	12,717	14,217
Total current liabilities	$ 73,883	$ 59,982
Long-term debt	80,263	63,914
Total liabilities	$154,146	$123,896
Common stock	?	$ 90,000
Retained earnings	?	38,774
Total common equity	?	$128,774
Total liabilities and equity	?	$252,670

    c. Construct the statement of cash flows for 2012.

7-15 **Build a Model: Free Cash Flows, EVA, and MVA** Begin with the partial model in the file *Ch07 P15 Build a Model.xls* on the textbook's Web site.

    a. Using the financial statements shown below for Lan & Chen Technologies, calculate net operating working capital, total net operating capital, net operating profit after taxes, free cash flow, and return on invested capital for 2012. (*Hint:* Start with the partial model in the file and report all dollar figures in thousands to reduce clutter.)

    b. Assume there were 15 million shares outstanding at the end of 2012, the year-end closing stock price was $65 per share, and the after-tax cost of capital was 8%. Calculate EVA and MVA for 2012.

Lan & Chen Technologies: Income Statements for Year Ending December 31 (Thousands of Dollars)

	2012	2011
Sales	$945,000	$900,000
Expenses excluding depreciation and amortization	812,700	774,000
EBITDA	$132,300	$126,000
Depreciation and amortization	33,100	31,500
EBIT	$ 99,200	$ 94,500
Interest expense	10,470	8,600
EBT	$ 88,730	$ 85,900
Taxes (40%)	35,492	34,360
Net income	$ 53,238	$ 51,540
Common dividends	$ 43,300	$ 41,230
Addition to retained earnings	$ 9,938	$ 10,310

Lan & Chen Technologies: December 31 Balance Sheets (Thousands of Dollars)

	2012	2011
Assets		
Cash and cash equivalents	$ 47,250	$ 45,000
Short-term investments	3,800	3,600
Accounts receivable	283,500	270,000
Inventories	141,750	135,000
Total current assets	$476,300	$453,600
Net fixed assets	330,750	315,000
Total assets	$807,050	$768,600
Liabilities and Equity		
Accounts payable	$ 94,500	$ 90,000
Accruals	47,250	45,000
Notes payable	26,262	9,000
Total current liabilities	$168,012	$144,000
Long-term debt	94,500	90,000
Total liabilities	$262,519	$234,000
Common stock	444,600	444,600
Retained earnings	99,938	90,000
Total common equity	$544,538	$534,600
Total liabilities and equity	$807,050	$768,600

 # THOMSON REUTERS

Use the Thomson ONE–Business School Edition online database to work this chapter's questions.

Exploring Starbucks's Financial Statements

Over the past decade, Starbucks coffee shops have become an increasingly familiar part of the urban landscape. The Thomson ONE–Business School Edition online database can provide a wealth of financial information for companies such as Starbucks. Begin by entering the company's ticker symbol, SBUX, and then selecting GO. The opening screen includes a summary of what Starbucks does, a chart of its recent stock price, EPS estimates, some recent news stories, and a list of key financial data and ratios.

For recent stock price performance, look at the top of the Stock Price Chart and click on the section labeled Interactive Chart. From this point, we are able to obtain a chart of the company's stock price performance relative to the overall market, as measured by the S&P 500. To obtain a 10-year chart, go to Time Frame, click on the down arrow, and select 10 years. Then click on Draw, and a 10-year price chart should appear.

You can also find Starbucks's recent financial statements. On the left side of your screen, click on the Financials tab to find the company's balance sheet, income statement, and statement of cash flows for the past 5 years. Clicking on the Microsoft *Excel* icon downloads these statements directly to a spreadsheet.

Discussion Questions

1. Looking at the most recent year available, what is the amount of total assets on Starbucks's balance sheet? What percentage is fixed assets, such as plant and equipment, and what percentage is current assets? How much has the company grown over the years shown?
2. Does Starbucks have a lot of long-term debt? What are Starbucks's primary sources of financing?
3. Looking at the statement of cash flows, what factors can explain the change in the company's cash position over the last couple of years?
4. Looking at the income statement, what are the company's most recent sales and net income? Over the past several years, what has been the sales growth rate? What has been the growth rate in net income?

MINI CASE

Jenny Cochran, a graduate of the University of Tennessee with 4 years of experience as an equities analyst, was recently brought in as assistant to the chairman of the board of Computron Industries, a manufacturer of computer components.

The company doubled its plant capacity, opened new sales offices outside its home territory, and launched an expensive advertising campaign. Computron's results were not satisfactory, to put it mildly. Its board of directors, which consisted of its president and vice-president plus its major stockholders (who were all local business-people), was most upset when directors learned how the expansion was going. Suppliers were being paid late and were unhappy, and the bank was complaining about the deteriorating situation and threatening to cut off credit. As a result, Robert Edwards, Computron's president, was informed that changes would have to be made—and quickly—or he would be fired. At the board's insistence, Jenny Cochran was given the job of assistant to Gary Meissner, a retired banker who was Computron's chairman and largest stockholder. Meissner agreed to give up a few of his golfing days and to help nurse the company back to health, with Cochran's assistance.

Cochran began by gathering financial statements and other data.

	2011	2012
Balance Sheets		
Assets		
Cash	$ 9,000	$ 7,282
Short-term investments	48,600	20,000
Accounts receivable	351,200	632,160
Inventories	715,200	1,287,360
Total current assets	$1,124,000	$1,946,802
Gross fixed assets	491,000	1,202,950
Less: Accumulated depreciation	146,200	263,160
Net fixed assets	$ 344,800	$ 939,790
Total assets	$1,468,800	$2,886,592
Liabilities and Equity		
Accounts payable	$ 145,600	$ 324,000
Notes payable	200,000	720,000
Accruals	136,000	284,960
Total current liabilities	$ 481,600	$1,328,960
Long-term debt	323,432	1,000,000
Common stock (100,000 shares)	460,000	460,000
Retained earnings	203,768	97,632
Total equity	$ 663,768	$ 557,632
Total liabilities and equity	$1,468,800	$2,886,592

	2011	2012
Income Statements		
Sales	$3,432,000	$5,834,400
Cost of goods sold	2,864,000	4,980,000
Other expenses	340,000	720,000
Depreciation and amortization	18,900	116,960
Total operating costs	$3,222,900	$5,816,960
EBIT	$ 209,100	$ 17,440
Interest expense	62,500	176,000
EBT	$ 146,600	($ 158,560)
Taxes (40%)	58,640	(63,424)
Net income	$ 87,960	($ 95,136)

(Continued)

	2011	2012
Other Data		
Stock price	$ 8.50	$ 6.00
Shares outstanding	100,000	100,000
EPS	$ 0.880	($ 0.951)
DPS	$ 0.220	$ 0.110
Tax rate	40%	40%

	2012
Statement of Cash Flows	
Operating Activities	
Net income	($ 95,136)
Adjustments:	
Noncash adjustments:	
Depreciation and amortization	116,960
Changes in working capital:	
Change in accounts receivable	(280,960)
Change in inventories	(572,160)
Change in accounts payable	178,400
Change in accruals	148,960
Net cash provided (used) by operating activities	($ 503,936)
Investing Activities	
Cash used to acquire fixed assets	($ 711,950)
Change in short-term investments	28,600
Net cash provided (used) by investing activities	($ 683,350)
Financing Activities	
Change in notes payable	$ 520,000
Change in long-term debt	676,568
Change in common stock	—
Payment of cash dividends	(11,000)
Net cash provided (used) by financing activities	$1,185,568
Summary	
Net change in cash	($ 1,718)
Cash at beginning of year	9,000
Cash at end of year	$ 7,282

Assume that you are Cochran's assistant and that you must help her answer the following questions for Meissner.

a. What effect did the expansion have on sales and net income? What effect did the expansion have on the asset side of the balance sheet? What effect did it have on liabilities and equity?

b. What do you conclude from the statement of cash flows?

c. What is free cash flow? Why is it important? What are the five uses of FCF?

d. What is Computron's net operating profit after taxes (NOPAT)? What are operating current assets? What are operating current liabilities? How much net operating working capital and total net operating capital does Computron have?

e. What is Computron's free cash flow (FCF)? What are Computron's "net uses" of its FCF?

f. Calculate Computron's return on invested capital. Computron has a 10% cost of capital (WACC). Do you think Computron's growth added value?

g. Cochran also has asked you to estimate Computron's EVA. She estimates that the after-tax cost of capital was 10% in both years.

h. What happened to Computron's Market Value Added (MVA)?

i. Assume that a corporation has $100,000 of taxable income from operations plus $5,000 of interest income and $10,000 of dividend income. What is the company's federal tax liability?

j. Assume that you are in the 25% marginal tax bracket and that you have $5,000 to invest. You have narrowed your investment choices down to California bonds with a yield of 7% or equally risky ExxonMobil bonds with a yield of 10%. Which one should you choose and why? At what marginal tax rate would you be indifferent to the choice between California and ExxonMobil bonds?

Chapter **8**

Analysis of Financial Statements

WEB

The textbook's Web site contains an *Excel* file that will guide you through the chapter's calculations. The file for this chapter is ***Ch08 Tool Kit.xls***, and we encourage you to open the file and follow along as you read the chapter.

Financial statement analysis involves (1) comparing a firm's performance with that of other firms in the same industry and (2) evaluating trends in the firm's financial position over time. Managers use financial analysis to identify situations needing attention; potential lenders use financial analysis to determine whether a company is creditworthy; and stockholders use financial analysis to help predict future earnings, dividends, and free cash flow. As we explain in this chapter, there are similarities and differences among these uses.[1]

---

1. Widespread accounting fraud has cast doubt on whether all firms' published financial statements can be trusted. New regulations by the SEC and the exchanges, as well as new laws enacted by Congress, have improved oversight of the accounting industry and increased the criminal penalties on management for fraudulent reporting.

Beginning of Chapter Questions

As you read the chapter, consider how you would answer the following questions. You *should not* necessarily be able to answer the questions before you read the chapter. Rather, you should use them to get a sense of the issues covered in the chapter. After reading the chapter, you should be able to give at least partial answers to the questions, and you should be able to give better answers after the chapter has been discussed in class. Note, too, that it is often useful, when answering conceptual questions, to use hypothetical data to illustrate your answer. We illustrate the answers with an *Excel* model that is available on the textbook's Web site. Accessing the model and working through it is a useful exercise, and it provides insights that are useful when answering the questions.

1. Why are **financial ratios** used? Name five categories of ratios, and then list several ratios in each category. Would a bank loan officer, a bond analyst, a stock analyst, and a manager be likely to put the same emphasis and interpretation on each ratio?

2. Suppose a company has a DSO that is considerably higher than its industry average. If the company could reduce its accounts receivable to the point where its DSO was equal to the industry average *without affecting its sales or its operating costs*, how would this affect (a) Its **free cash flow**, (b) **its return on common equity**, (c) its

debt ratio, (d) its **times-interest-earned ratio**, (e) its **loan/EBITDA ratio**, (f) **its price/earnings ratio**, and (g) its **market/book ratio?**

3. How do managers, bankers, and security analysts use (a) **trend analysis**, (b) **benchmarking**, (c) **percent change analysis**, and (d) **common size analysis?**

4. Explain how **ratio analysis** in general, and the **Du Pont model** in particular, can be used by managers to help maximize their firms' stock prices.

5. How would each of the following factors affect ratio analysis? (a) The firm's sales are highly seasonal. (b) The firm uses some type of window dressing. (c) The firm issues more debt and uses the proceeds to repurchase stock. (d) The firm leases more of its fixed assets than most firms in its industry. (e) In an effort to stimulate sales, the firm eases its credit policy by offering 60-day credit terms rather than the current 30-day terms. How might one use sensitivity analysis to help quantify the answers?

6. How might one establish norms (or target values) for the financial ratios of a company that is just getting started? Where might data for this purpose be obtained? Could information of this type be used to help determine how much debt and equity capital a new firm would require?

8.1 Financial Analysis

When we perform a financial analysis, we conduct the following steps.

8.1a Gather Data

The first step in financial analysis is to gather data. As we discussed in Chapter 7, financial statements can be downloaded from many different Web sites. One of our favorites is Zacks Investment Research, which provides financial statements in a standardized format. If you cut and paste financial statements from Zacks into a spreadsheet and then perform a financial analysis, you can quickly repeat the analysis on a different company by simply pasting that company's financial statements into the same cells as the original company's statements. In other words, there is no need to reinvent the wheel each time you analyze a company.

8.1b Examine the Statement of Cash Flows

Some financial analysis can be done with virtually no calculations. For example, we always look to the statement of cash flows first, particularly the net cash provided

WWW

See **www.zacks.com** for a source of standardized financial statements.

INTRINSIC VALUE AND ANALYSIS OF FINANCIAL STATEMENTS

The intrinsic value of a firm is determined by the present value of the expected future free cash flows (FCF) when discounted at the weighted average cost of capital (WACC). This chapter explains how to use financial statements to evaluate a company's profitability, required capital investments, business risk, and mix of debt and equity.

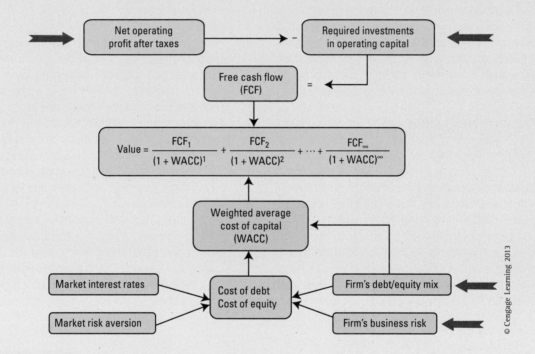

© Cengage Learning 2013

by operating activities. Downward trends or negative net cash flow from operations almost always indicate problems. The statement of cash flows section on investing activities shows whether the company has made a big acquisition, especially when compared with the prior years' net cash flows from investing activities. A quick look at the section on financing activities also reveals whether or not a company is issuing debt or buying back stock; in other words, is the company raising capital from investors or returning it to them?

8.1c Calculate and Examine the Return on Invested Capital

After examining the statement of cash flows, we calculate the return on invested capital (ROIC) as described in Chapter 7. The ROIC provides a vital measure of a firm's overall performance. If ROIC is greater than the company's weighted average cost of capital (WACC), then the company usually is adding value. If ROIC is less than WACC, then the company usually has serious problems. No matter what ROIC tells us about the firm's overall performance, it is important to examine specific areas within the firm, and for that we use ratios.

8.1d Begin Ratio Analysis

Financial ratios are designed to extract important information that might not be obvious simply from examining a firm's financial statements. For example, suppose Firm A owes $5 million of debt while Firm B owes $50 million of debt. Which company is in a stronger financial position? It is impossible to answer this question without first standardizing each firm's debt relative to total assets, earnings, and interest. Such standardized comparisons are provided through *ratio analysis*.

We will calculate the 2012 financial ratios for MicroDrive Inc., using data from the balance sheets and income statements given in Table 8-1. We will also evaluate the ratios in relation to the industry averages. Note that dollar amounts are in millions.

8.2 Liquidity Ratios

As shown in Table 8-1, MicroDrive has current liabilities of $310 million that must be paid off within the coming year. Will it have trouble satisfying those obligations? **Liquidity ratios** attempt to answer this type of question: We discuss two commonly used liquidity ratios in this section.

WEB

See *Ch08 Tool Kit.xls* for all calculations.

8.2a The Current Ratio

The **current ratio** is calculated by dividing current assets by current liabilities:

$$\text{Current ratio} = \frac{\text{Current assets}}{\text{Current liabilities}}$$

$$= \frac{\$1,000}{\$310} = 3.2$$

Industry average = 4.2

Current assets normally include cash, marketable securities, accounts receivable, and inventories. Current liabilities consist of accounts payable, short-term notes payable, current maturities of long-term debt, accrued taxes, and other accrued expenses.

MicroDrive has a lower current ratio than the average for its industry. Is this good or bad? Sometimes the answer depends on who is asking the question. For example, suppose a supplier is trying to decide whether to extend credit to MicroDrive. In general, creditors like to see a high current ratio. If a company is getting into financial difficulty, it will begin paying its bills (accounts payable) more slowly, borrowing from its bank, and so on, so its current liabilities will be increasing. If current liabilities are rising faster than current assets then the current ratio will fall, and this could spell trouble. Because the current ratio provides the best single indicator of the extent to which the claims of short-term creditors are covered by assets that are expected to be converted to cash fairly quickly, it is the most commonly used measure of short-term solvency.

TABLE 8-1	MicroDrive Inc.: Balance Sheets and Income Statements for Years Ending December 31 (Millions of Dollars, Except for Per Share Data)					
Assets	**2012**	**2011**	**Liabilities and Equity**	**2012**	**2011**	
Cash and equivalents	$ 10	$ 15	Accounts payable	$ 60	$ 30	
Short-term investments	0	65	Notes payable	110	60	
Accounts receivable	375	315	Accruals	140	130	
Inventories	615	415	Total current liabilities	$ 310	$ 220	
Total current assets	$1,000	$ 810	Long-term bonds[a]	754	580	
Net plant and equipment	1,000	870	Total liabilities	$1,064	$ 800	
			Preferred stock (400,000 shares)	40	40	
			Common stock (50,000,000 shares)	130	130	
			Retained earnings	766	710	
			Total common equity	$ 896	$ 840	
Total assets	$2,000	$1,680	Total liabilities and equity	$2,000	$1,680	

	2012	**2011**
Net sales	$3,000	$2,850
Operating costs excluding depreciation and amortization[b]	2,617	2,500
Earnings before interest, taxes, depreciation, and amortization (EBITDA)	$ 383	$ 350
Depreciation and amortization	100	90
Earnings before interest and taxes (EBIT, or operating income)	$ 283	$ 260
Less interest	88	60
Earnings before taxes (EBT)	$ 195	$ 200
Taxes (40%)	78	80
Net income before preferred dividends	$ 117	$ 120
Preferred dividends	4	4
Net income	$ 113	$ 116
Common dividends	$ 57	$ 53
Addition to retained earnings	$ 56	$ 63
Per-Share Data		
Common stock price	$ 23.00	$ 26.00
Earnings per share (EPS)	$ 2.26	$ 2.32
Book value per share (BVPS)	$ 17.92	$ 16.80
Cash flow per share (CFPS)	$ 4.26	$ 4.12

[a]The bonds have a sinking fund requirement of $20 million a year.
[b]The costs include lease payments of $28 million a year.

Now consider the current ratio from the perspective of a shareholder. A high current ratio could mean that the company has a lot of money tied up in nonproductive assets, such as excess cash or marketable securities. Or perhaps the high current ratio is due to large inventory holdings, which might well become obsolete before they can be sold. Thus, shareholders might not want a high current ratio.

An industry average is not a magic number that all firms should strive to maintain—in fact, some very well-managed firms will be above the average, while other good firms will be below it. However, if a firm's ratios are far removed from the averages for its industry, this is a red flag, and analysts should be concerned about why the variance occurs. For example, suppose a low current ratio is traced to low inventories. Is this a competitive advantage resulting from the firm's mastery of just-in-time inventory management, or is it an Achilles' heel that is causing the firm to miss shipments and lose sales? Ratio analysis doesn't answer such questions, but it does point to areas of potential concern.

8.2b The Quick, or Acid Test, Ratio

The **quick**, or **acid test, ratio** is calculated by deducting inventories from current assets and then dividing the remainder by current liabilities:

$$\text{Quick, or acid test, ratio} = \frac{\text{Current assets} - \text{Inventories}}{\text{Current liabilities}}$$

$$= \frac{\$385}{\$310} = 1.2$$

$$\text{Industry average} = 2.1$$

A **liquid asset** is one that trades in an active market and hence can be converted quickly to cash at the going market price. Inventories are typically the least liquid of a firm's current assets; hence they are the current assets on which losses are most likely to occur in a bankruptcy. Therefore, a measure of the firm's ability to pay off short-term obligations without relying on the sale of inventories is important.

The industry average quick ratio is 2.1, so MicroDrive's 1.2 ratio is low in comparison with other firms in its industry. Still, if the accounts receivable can be collected, the company can pay off its current liabilities without having to liquidate its inventory.

Self Test

Identify two ratios that are used to analyze a firm's liquidity position, and write out their equations.

What are the characteristics of a liquid asset? Give some examples.

Which current asset is typically the least liquid?

A company has current liabilities of $800 million, and its current ratio is 2.5. What is its level of current assets? **($2,000 million)** If this firm's quick ratio is 2, how much inventory does it have? **($400 million)**

8.3 Asset Management Ratios

Asset management ratios measure how effectively a firm is managing its assets. If a company has excessive investments in assets, then its operating capital will be unduly high, which will reduce its free cash flow and ultimately its stock price. On the other hand, if a company does not have enough assets then it will lose sales, which will hurt profitability, free cash flow, and the stock price. Therefore, it is important to have the *right* amount invested in assets. Ratios that analyze the different types of assets are described in this section.

8.3a Evaluating Inventories: The Inventory Turnover Ratio

The **inventory turnover ratio** is defined as sales divided by inventories:

$$\text{Inventory turnover ratio} = \frac{\text{Sales}}{\text{Inventories}}$$

$$= \frac{\$3,000}{\$615} = 4.9$$

Industry average $= 9.0$

As a rough approximation, each item of MicroDrive's inventory is sold out and restocked, or "turned over," 4.9 times per year.[2]

MicroDrive's turnover of 4.9 is much lower than the industry average of 9.0. This suggests that MicroDrive is holding too much inventory. High levels of inventory add to net operating working capital (NOWC), which reduces FCF, which leads to lower stock prices. In addition, MicroDrive's low inventory turnover ratio makes us wonder whether the firm is actually holding obsolete goods not worth their stated value.[3]

Note that sales occur over the entire year, whereas the inventory figure is measured at a single point in time. For this reason, it is better to use an average inventory measure.[4]

---

2. "Turnover" is a term that originated many years ago with the old Yankee peddler who would load up his wagon with goods and then go off to peddle his wares. If he made 10 trips per year, stocked 100 pans, and made a gross profit of $5 per pan, his annual gross profit would be $(100)(\$5)(10) = \$5,000$. If he "turned over" (i.e., sold) his inventory faster and made 20 trips per year, then his gross profit would double, other things held constant. So, his turnover directly affected his profits.

3. A problem arises when calculating and analyzing the inventory turnover ratio. Sales are stated at market prices, so if inventories are carried at cost, as they generally are, then the calculated turnover overstates the true turnover ratio. Therefore, it would be more appropriate to use cost of goods sold in place of sales in the formula's numerator. However, established compilers of financial ratio statistics such as Dun & Bradstreet use the ratio of sales to inventories carried at cost. To develop a figure that can be compared with those published by Dun & Bradstreet and similar organizations, it is necessary to measure inventory turnover with sales in the numerator, as we do here.

4. Preferably, the average inventory value should be calculated by summing the monthly figures during the year and dividing by 12. If monthly data are not available, one can add the beginning and ending annual figures and divide by 2. However, most industry ratios are calculated as shown here, using end-of-year values.

THE GLOBAL ECONOMIC CRISIS

The Price Is Right! (Or Wrong!)

How much is an asset worth if no one is buying or selling? The answer to that question matters because an accounting practice called "mark to market" requires that some assets be adjusted on the balance sheet to reflect their "fair market value." The accounting rules are complicated, but the general idea is that if an asset is available for sale, then the balance sheet would be most accurate if it showed the asset's market value. For example, suppose a company purchased $100 million of Treasury bonds and the value of those bonds later fell to $90 million. With mark to market, the company would report the bonds' value on the balance sheet as $90 million, not the original purchase price of $100 million. Notice that marking to market can have a significant impact on financial ratios and thus on investors' perception of a firm's financial health.

But what if the assets are mortgage-backed securities that were originally purchased for $100 million? As defaults increased during 2008, the value of such securities fell rapidly, and then investors virtually stopped trading them. How should the company

report them? At the $100 million original price, at a $60 million price that was observed before the market largely dried up, at $25 million when a hedge fund in desperate need for cash to avoid a costly default sold a few of these securities, or at $0, since there are no current quotes? Or should they be reported at a price generated by a computer model or in some other manner?

The answer to this question is especially important during times of economic stress. Congress, the SEC, FASB, and the U.S. Treasury all are working to find the right answers. If they come up with a price that is too low, it could cause investors mistakenly to believe that some companies are worth much less than their intrinsic values, and this could trigger runs on banks and bankruptcies for companies that might otherwise survive. But if the price is too high, some "walking dead" or "zombie" companies could linger on and later cause even larger losses for investors, including the U.S. government, which is now the largest investor in many financial institutions. Either way, an error in pricing could perhaps trigger a domino effect that might topple the entire financial system. So let's hope the price is right!

If the firm's business is highly seasonal, or if there has been a strong upward or downward sales trend during the year, then it is especially useful to make some such adjustment. To maintain comparability with industry averages, however, we did not use the average inventory figure.

8.3b Evaluating Receivables: The Days Sales Outstanding

Days sales outstanding (DSO), also called the "average collection period" (ACP), is used to appraise accounts receivable, and it is calculated by dividing accounts receivable by average daily sales to find the number of days' sales that are tied up in receivables.[5] Thus, the DSO represents the average length of time that the firm

---

5. It would be better to use *average* receivables, but we have used year-end values for comparability with the industry average.

must wait after making a sale before receiving cash, which is the average collection period. MicroDrive's DSO is 46, well above the 36-day industry average:

$$DSO = \frac{Days\ sales}{outstanding} = \frac{Receivables}{Average\ sales\ per\ day} = \frac{Receivables}{Annual\ sales/365}$$

$$= \frac{\$375}{\$3,000/365} = \frac{\$375}{\$8.2192} = 45.6\ days \approx 46\ days$$

Industry average = 36 days

MicroDrive's sales terms call for payment within 30 days. The fact that 46 days of sales are outstanding indicates that customers, on average, are not paying their bills on time. As with inventory, high levels of accounts receivable cause high levels of NOWC, which hurts FCF and stock price.

A customer who is paying late may well be in financial trouble, in which case MicroDrive may have a hard time ever collecting the receivable. Therefore, if the trend in DSO has been rising but the credit policy has not been changed, steps should be taken to review credit standards and to expedite the collection of accounts receivable.

8.3c Evaluating Fixed Assets: The Fixed Assets Turnover Ratio

The **fixed assets turnover ratio** measures how effectively the firm uses its plant and equipment. It is the ratio of sales to net fixed assets:

$$Fixed\ assets\ turnover\ ratio = \frac{Sales}{Net\ fixed\ assets}$$

$$= \frac{\$3,000}{\$1,000} = 3.0$$

Industry average = 3.0

MicroDrive's ratio of 3.0 is equal to the industry average, indicating that the firm is using its fixed assets about as intensively as are other firms in its industry. Therefore, MicroDrive seems to have about the right amount of fixed assets in relation to other firms.

A potential problem can exist when interpreting the fixed assets turnover ratio. Recall from accounting that fixed assets reflect the historical costs of the assets. Inflation has caused the current value of many assets that were purchased in the past to be seriously understated. Therefore, if we were comparing an old firm that had acquired many of its fixed assets years ago at low prices with a new company that had acquired its fixed assets only recently, we would probably find that the old firm had the higher fixed assets turnover ratio. However, this would be more reflective of the difficulty accountants have in dealing with inflation than of any inefficiency on the part of the new firm. You should be alert to this potential problem when evaluating the fixed assets turnover ratio.

8.3d Evaluating Total Assets: The Total Assets Turnover Ratio

The **total assets turnover ratio** is calculated by dividing sales by total assets:

$$\text{Total assets turnover ratio} = \frac{\text{Sales}}{\text{Total assets}}$$

$$= \frac{\$3,000}{\$2,000} = 1.5$$

$$\text{Industry average} = 1.8$$

MicroDrive's ratio is somewhat below the industry average, indicating that the company is not generating a sufficient volume of business given its total asset investment. Sales should be increased, some assets should be sold, or a combination of these steps should be taken.

> **Self Test**
>
> Identify four ratios that are used to measure how effectively a firm is managing its assets, and write out their equations.
>
> What problem might arise when comparing different firms' fixed assets turnover ratios?
>
> A firm has annual sales of $200 million, $40 million of inventory, and $60 million of accounts receivable. What is its inventory turnover ratio? **(5)** What is its DSO based on a 365-day year? **(109.5 days)**

8.4 Debt Management Ratios

The extent to which a firm uses debt financing, or **financial leverage**, has three important implications: (1) By raising funds through debt, stockholders can maintain control of a firm without increasing their investment. (2) If the firm earns more on investments financed with borrowed funds than it pays in interest, then its shareholders' returns are magnified, or "leveraged," but their risks are also magnified. (3) Creditors look to the equity, or owner-supplied funds, to provide a margin of safety, so the higher the proportion of funding supplied by stockholders, the less risk creditors face. Chapter 15 explains the first two points in detail, while the following ratios examine leverage from a creditor's point of view.

8.4a How the Firm Is Financed: Total Liabilities to Total Assets

The ratio of total liabilities to total assets is called the **debt ratio**, or sometimes the **total debt ratio**. It measures the percentage of funds provided by current liabilities and long-term debt:

$$\text{Debt ratio} = \frac{\text{Total liabilities}}{\text{Total assets}}$$

$$= \frac{\$310 + \$754}{\$2,000} = \frac{\$1,064}{\$2,000} = 53.2\%$$

$$\text{Industry average} = 40.0\%$$

Creditors prefer low debt ratios because the lower the ratio, the greater the cushion against creditors' losses in the event of liquidation. Stockholders, on the other hand, may want more leverage because it magnifies their return, as we explain in Section 8.8 when we discuss the Du Pont model.

MicroDrive's debt ratio is 53.2% but its debt ratio in the previous year was 47.6%, which means that creditors are now supplying more than half the total financing. In addition to an upward trend, the level of the debt ratio is well above the industry average. Creditors may be reluctant to lend the firm more money because a high debt ratio is associated with a greater risk of bankruptcy.

Some sources report the debt-to-equity ratio, defined as:

$$\text{Debt-to-equity ratio} = \frac{\text{Total liabilities}}{\text{Total assets} - \text{Total liabilities}}$$

$$= \frac{\$310 + \$754}{\$2,000 - (\$310 + \$754)} = \frac{\$1,064}{\$936} = 1.14$$

$$\text{Industry average} = 0.67$$

The debt-to-equity ratio and the debt ratio contain the same information but present that information slightly differently.[6] The debt-to-equity ratio shows that MicroDrive has $1.14 of debt for every dollar of equity, whereas the debt ratio shows that 53.2% of MicroDrive's financing is in the form of liabilities. We find it more intuitive to think about the percentage of the firm that is financed with debt, so we usually use the debt ratio. However, the debt-to-equity ratio is also widely used, so you should know how to interpret it.

Sometimes it is useful to express debt ratios in terms of market values. It is easy to calculate the market value of equity, which is equal to the stock price multiplied by the number of shares. MicroDrive's market value of equity is $23(50) = \$1,150$. Often it is difficult to estimate the market value of liabilities, so many analysts define the market debt ratio as

$$\text{Market debt ratio} = \frac{\text{Total liabilities}}{\text{Total liabilities} + \text{Market value of equity}}$$

$$= \frac{\$1,064}{\$1,064 + (\$23 \times 50)} = \frac{\$1,064}{\$2,214} = 48.1\%$$

MicroDrive's market debt ratio in the previous year was 38.1%. The big increase was due to two major factors: Liabilities increased and the stock price fell. The stock price reflects a company's prospects for generating future cash flows, so a decline in stock price indicates a likely decline in future cash flows. Thus, the market debt ratio reflects a source of risk that is not captured by the conventional book debt ratio.

---

6. The debt ratio and debt-to-equity ratios are simply transformations of each other:

$$\text{Debt-to-equity} = \frac{\text{Debt ratio}}{1 - \text{Debt ratio}} \quad \text{and Debt ratio} = \frac{\text{Debt-to-equity}}{1 + \text{Debt-to-equity}}$$

If you use a debt ratio that you did not calculate yourself, be sure to find out how the ratio was defined. Some sources define the numerator to be only long-term debt, others define it to be all interest-bearing debt, while others do as we do, which is to define it to be total liabilities, so be sure to check your source's definition.

8.4b Ability to Pay Interest: Times-Interest-Earned Ratio

The **times-interest-earned (TIE) ratio**, also called the **interest coverage ratio**, is determined by dividing earnings before interest and taxes (EBIT in Table 8-1) by the interest expense:

$$\text{Times-interest-earned (TIE) ratio} = \frac{\text{EBIT}}{\text{Interest expense}}$$

$$= \frac{\$283}{\$88} = 3.2$$

Industry average $= 6.0$

The TIE ratio measures the extent to which operating income can decline before the firm is unable to meet its annual interest costs. Failure to meet this obligation can bring legal action by the firm's creditors, possibly resulting in bankruptcy. Note that earnings before interest and taxes, rather than net income, is used in the numerator. Because interest is paid with pre-tax dollars, the firm's ability to pay current interest is not affected by taxes.

MicroDrive's interest is covered 3.2 times. The industry average is 6, so Micro-Drive is covering its interest charges by a relatively low margin of safety. Thus, the TIE ratio reinforces the conclusion from our analysis of the debt ratio that MicroDrive would face difficulties if it attempted to borrow additional funds.

8.4c Ability to Service Debt: EBITDA Coverage Ratio

The TIE ratio is useful for assessing a company's ability to meet interest charges on its debt, but this ratio has two shortcomings: (1) Interest is not the only fixed financial charge—companies must also reduce debt on schedule, and many firms lease assets and thus must make lease payments. If they fail to repay debt or meet lease payments, they can be forced into bankruptcy. (2) EBIT does not represent all the cash flow available to service debt, especially if a firm has high depreciation and/or amortization charges. The **EBITDA coverage ratio** accounts for these deficiencies:[7]

---

7. Different analysts define the EBITDA coverage ratio in different ways. For example, some omit the lease payment information; others "gross up" principal payments by dividing them by 1 − T since these payments are not tax deductions and hence must be made with after-tax cash flows. We included lease payments because for many firms they are quite important, and failing to make them can lead to bankruptcy just as surely as can failure to make payments on "regular" debt. We did not gross up principal payments because, if a company is in financial difficulty, then its tax rate will probably be zero; hence the gross up is not necessary whenever the ratio is really important.

$$\text{EBITDA coverage ratio} = \frac{\text{EBITDA} + \text{Lease payments}}{\text{Interest} + \text{Principle payments} + \text{Lease payments}}$$

$$= \frac{\$383 + \$28}{\$88 + \$20 + \$28} = \frac{\$411}{\$136} = 3.0$$

Industry average $= 4.3$

MicroDrive had $383 million of earnings before interest, taxes, depreciation, and amortization (EBITDA). Also, lease payments of $28 million were deducted while calculating EBITDA. That $28 million was available to meet financial charges; hence it must be added back, bringing the total available to cover fixed financial charges to $411 million. Fixed financial charges consisted of $88 million of interest, $20 million of sinking fund payments, and $28 million for lease payments, for a total of $136 million.[8] Therefore, MicroDrive covered its fixed financial charges by 3.0 times. However, if EBITDA declines then the coverage will fall, and EBITDA certainly can decline. Moreover, MicroDrive's ratio is well below the industry average, so again the company seems to have a relatively high level of debt.

The EBITDA coverage ratio is most useful for relatively short-term lenders such as banks, which rarely make loans (except real estate-backed loans) for longer than about 5 years. Over a relatively short period, depreciation-generated funds can be used to service debt. Over a longer time, those funds must be reinvested to maintain the plant and equipment or else the company cannot remain in business. Therefore, banks and other relatively short-term lenders focus on the EBITDA coverage ratio, whereas long-term bondholders focus on the TIE ratio.

Self Test

How does the use of financial leverage affect current stockholders' control position?

Explain the following statement: "Analysts look at both balance sheet and income statement ratios when appraising a firm's financial condition."

Name three ratios that are used to measure the extent to which a firm uses financial leverage, and write out their equations.

A company has EBITDA of $600 million, interest payments of $60 million, lease payments of $40 million, and required principal payments (due this year) of $30 million. What is its EBITDA coverage ratio? **(4.9)**

8.5 Profitability Ratios

Profitability is the net result of a number of policies and decisions. The ratios examined thus far provide useful clues as to the effectiveness of a firm's operations, but the **profitability ratios** go on to show the combined effects of liquidity, asset management, and debt on operating results.

---

8. A sinking fund is a required annual payment designed to reduce the balance of a bond or preferred stock issue.

8.5a Net Profit Margin

The **net profit margin**, which is also called the **profit margin on sales**, is calculated by dividing net income by sales. It gives the profit per dollar of sales:

$$\text{Net profit margin} = \frac{\text{Net income available to common stockholders}}{\text{Sales}}$$

$$= \frac{\$113}{\$3,000} = 3.8\%$$

$$\text{Industry average} = 5.0\%$$

MicroDrive's net profit margin is below the industry average of 5%, but why is this so? Is it due to inefficient operations, high interest expenses, or both?

Instead of just comparing net income to sales, many analysts also break the income statement into smaller parts to identify the sources of a low net profit margin. For example, the **operating profit margin** is defined as

$$\text{Operating profit margin} = \frac{\text{EBIT}}{\text{Sales}}$$

The operating profit margin identifies how a company is performing with respect to its operations before the impact of interest expenses is considered. Some analysts drill even deeper by breaking operating costs into their components. For example, the **gross profit margin** is defined as

$$\text{Gross profit margin} = \frac{\text{Sales} - \text{Cost of goods sold}}{\text{Sales}}$$

The gross profit margin identifies the gross profit per dollar of sales before any other expenses are deducted.

Rather than calculate each type of profit margin here, later in the chapter we will use common size analysis and percent change analysis to focus on different parts of the income statement. In addition, we will use the Du Pont equation to show how the ratios interact with one another.

Sometimes it is confusing to have so many different types of profit margins. To help simplify the situation, we will focus primarily on the net profit margin throughout the book and simply call it the "profit margin."

8.5b Basic Earning Power (BEP) Ratio

The **basic earning power (BEP) ratio** is calculated by dividing earnings before interest and taxes (EBIT) by total assets:

$$\text{Basic earning power (BEP) ratio} = \frac{\text{EBIT}}{\text{Total assets}}$$

THE WORLD MIGHT BE FLAT, BUT GLOBAL ACCOUNTING ISN'T: IFRS VERSUS FASB

In a flat world, distance is no barrier. Work flows to where it can be accomplished most efficiently, and capital flows to where it can be invested most profitably. If a radiologist in India is more efficient than one in the United States, then images will be e-mailed to India for diagnosis; if rates of return are higher in Brazil, then investors throughout the world will provide funding for Brazilian projects. One key to "flattening" the world is agreement on common standards. For example, there are common Internet standards so that users throughout the world are able to communicate.

A glaring exception to standardization is in accounting. The Securities and Exchange Commission (SEC) in the United States requires firms to comply with standards set by the Financial Accounting Standards Board (FASB). But the European Union requires all EU-listed companies to comply with the International Financial Reporting Standards (IFRS) as defined by the International Accounting Standards Board (IASB).

IFRS tends to rely on general principles, whereas FASB standards are rules-based. As the recent accounting scandals demonstrate, many U.S. companies have been able to comply with U.S. rules while violating the principle, or intent, underlying the rules. The United States is likely to adopt IFRS, or a slightly modified IFRS, but the question is "When?" The SEC estimated that a large company is likely to incur costs of up to $32 million when switching to IFRS. So even though a survey by the accounting firm KPMG indicates that most investors and analysts favor adoption of IFRS, the path to adoption is likely to be bumpy.

Sources: See the Web sites of the IASB and the FASB, **www.iasb.org.uk** and **www.fasb.org**. Also see David M. Katz and Sarah Johnson, "Top Obama Advisers Clash on Global Accounting Standards," January 15, 2009, at **www.cfo.com**; and "Survey Favors IFRS Adoption," February 3, 2009, at **www.webcpa.com**.

$$= \frac{\$283}{\$2,000} = 14.2\%$$

Industry average $= 17.2\%$

This ratio shows the raw earning power of the firm's assets before the influence of taxes and leverage, and it is useful for comparing firms with different tax situations and different degrees of financial leverage. Because of its low turnover ratios and low profit margin on sales, MicroDrive is not getting as high a return on its assets as is the average company in its industry.[9]

---

9. Notice that EBIT is earned throughout the year, whereas the total assets figure is an end-of-the-year number. Therefore, it would be better, conceptually, to calculate this ratio as EBIT/(Average assets) = EBIT/[(Beginning assets + Ending assets)/2]. We have not made this adjustment because the published ratios used for comparative purposes do not include it. However, when we construct our own comparative ratios, we do make this adjustment. The same adjustment would also be appropriate for the next two ratios, ROA and ROE.

8.5c Return on Total Assets

The ratio of net income to total assets measures the **return on total assets (ROA)** after interest and taxes. This ratio is also called the **return on assets** and is defined as follows:

$$\frac{\text{Return on}}{\text{total assets}} = \text{ROA} = \frac{\text{Net income available to common stockholders}}{\text{Total assets}}$$

$$= \frac{\$113}{\$2,000} = 5.7\%$$

Industry average = 9.0%

MicroDrive's 5.7% return is well below the 9% average for the industry. This low return is due to (1) the company's low basic earning power and (2) high interest costs resulting from its above-average use of debt; both of these factors cause Micro Drive's net income to be relatively low.

8.5d Return on Common Equity

The ratio of net income to common equity measures the **return on common equity (ROE)**:

$$\frac{\text{Return on}}{\text{common equity}} = \text{ROE} = \frac{\text{Net income available to common stockholders}}{\text{Common equity}}$$

$$= \frac{\$113}{\$896} = 12.6\%$$

Industry average = 15.0%

Stockholders invest to earn a return on their money, and this ratio tells how well they are doing in an accounting sense. MicroDrive's 12.6% return is below the 15% industry average, but not as far below as its return on total assets. This somewhat better result is due to the company's greater use of debt, a point that we explain in detail later in the chapter.

8.6 Market Value Ratios

Market value ratios relate a firm's stock price to its earnings, cash flow, and book value per share. Market value ratios are a way to measure the value of a company's stock relative to that of another company.

8.6a Price/Earnings Ratio

The **price/earnings (P/E) ratio** shows how much investors are willing to pay per dollar of reported profits. MicroDrive's stock sells for $23, so with an earnings per share (EPS) of $2.27 its P/E ratio is 10.2:

$$\text{Price/earnings (P/E) ratio} = \frac{\text{Price per share}}{\text{Earnings per share}}$$

$$= \frac{\$23.00}{\$2.26} = 10.2$$

Industry average $= 12.5$

Price/earnings ratios are higher for firms with strong growth prospects, other things held constant, but they are lower for riskier firms. Because MicroDrive's P/E ratio is below the average, this suggests that the company is regarded as being somewhat riskier than most, as having poorer growth prospects, or both. In early 2011, the average P/E ratio for firms in the S&P 500 was 18.12, indicating that investors were willing to pay $18.12 for every dollar of earnings.

8.6b Price/Cash Flow Ratio

Stock prices depend on a company's ability to generate cash flows. Consequently, investors often look at the **price/cash flow ratio**, where cash flow is defined as net income plus depreciation and amortization:

$$\text{Price/cash flow ratio} = \frac{\text{Price per share}}{\text{Cash flow per share}}$$

$$= \frac{\$23.00}{\$4.26} = 5.4$$

Industry average $= 6.8$

MicroDrive's price/cash flow ratio is also below the industry average, once again suggesting that its growth prospects are below average, its risk is above average, or both.

The **price/EBITDA ratio** is similar to the price/cash flow ratio, except the price/EBITDA ratio measures performance before the impact of interest expenses and taxes, making it a better measure of operating performance. MicroDrive's EBITDA per share is $383/50 = $7.66, so its price/EBITDA is $23/$7.66 = 3.0. The industry average price/EBITDA ratio is 4.6, so we see again that MicroDrive is below the industry average.

Note that some analysts look at other multiples as well. For example, depending on the industry, some may look at measures such as price/sales or price/customers. Ultimately, though, value depends on free cash flows, so if these "exotic" ratios do not forecast future free cash flow, they may turn out to be misleading. This was true in the case of the dot-com retailers before they crashed and burned in 2000, costing investors many billions.

8.6c Market/Book Ratio

The ratio of a stock's market price to its book value gives another indication of how investors regard the company. Companies with relatively high rates of return on equity generally sell at higher multiples of book value than those with low returns. First, we find MicroDrive's book value per share:

$$\text{Book value per share} = \frac{\text{Common equity}}{\text{Shares outstanding}}$$

$$= \frac{\$896}{50} = \$17.92$$

Now we divide the market price by the book value to get a **market/book (M/B) ratio** of 1.3 times:

$$\text{Market/book ratio} = \text{M/B} = \frac{\text{Market price per share}}{\text{Book value per share}}$$

$$= \frac{\$23.00}{\$17.92} = 1.3$$

Industry average $= 1.7$

Investors are willing to pay relatively little for a dollar of MicroDrive's book value.

The average company in the S&P 500 had a market/book ratio of about 2.90 in early 2011. Since M/B ratios typically exceed 1.0, this means that investors are willing to pay more for stocks than their accounting book values. The book value is a record of the past, showing the cumulative amount that stockholders have invested, either directly by purchasing newly issued shares or indirectly through retaining earnings. In contrast, the market price is forward-looking, incorporating investors' expectations of future cash flows. For example, in early 2011 Bank of America had a market/book ratio of only 0.68, reflecting the financial services industry's problems, whereas Apple's market/book ratio was 6.22, indicating that investors expected Apple's past successes to continue.

Table 8-2 summarizes MicroDrive's financial ratios. As the table indicates, the company has many problems.

Self Test

Describe three ratios that relate a firm's stock price to its earnings, cash flow, and book value per share, and write out their equations.

What does the price/earnings (P/E) ratio show? If one firm's P/E ratio is lower than that of another, what are some factors that might explain the difference?

How is book value per share calculated? Explain why book values often deviate from market values.

A company has $6 billion of net income, $2 billion of depreciation and amortization, $80 billion of common equity, and 1 billion shares of stock. If its stock price is $96 per share, what is its price/earnings ratio? **(16)** Its price/cash flow ratio? **(12)** Its market/book ratio? **(1.2)**

TABLE 8-2	MicroDrive Inc.: Summary of Financial Ratios (Millions of Dollars)					
Ratio	**Formula**	**Calculation**		**Ratio**	**Industry Average**	**Comment**
Liquidity						
Current	$\dfrac{\text{Current assets}}{\text{Current liabilities}}$	$\dfrac{\$1,000}{\$310}$	=	3.2	4.2	Poor
Quick	$\dfrac{\text{Current assets} - \text{Inventories}}{\text{Current liabilities}}$	$\dfrac{\$385}{\$310}$	=	1.2	2.1	Poor
Asset Management						
Inventory turnover	$\dfrac{\text{Sales}}{\text{Inventories}}$	$\dfrac{\$3,000}{\$615}$	=	4.9	9.0	Poor
Days sales outstanding (DSO)	$\dfrac{\text{Receivables}}{\text{Annual sales}/365}$	$\dfrac{\$375}{\$8.219}$	=	45.6	36.0	Poor
Fixed assets turnover	$\dfrac{\text{Sales}}{\text{Net fixed assets}}$	$\dfrac{\$3,000}{\$1,000}$	=	3.0	3.0	OK
Total assets turnover	$\dfrac{\text{Sales}}{\text{Total assets}}$	$\dfrac{\$3,000}{\$2,000}$	=	1.5	1.8	Poor
Debt Management						
Debt ratio	$\dfrac{\text{Total liabilities}}{\text{Total assets}}$	$\dfrac{\$1,064}{\$2,000}$	=	53.2%	40.0%	High (risky)
Times-interest-earned (TIE)	$\dfrac{\text{Earnings before interest and taxes (EBIT)}}{\text{Interest charges}}$	$\dfrac{\$283}{\$88}$	=	3.2	6.0	Low (risky)
EBITDA coverage	$\dfrac{\text{EBITDA} + \text{Lease pmts.}}{\text{Interest} + \text{Principle payments} + \text{Lease pmts.}}$	$\dfrac{\$411}{\$136}$	=	3.0	4.3	Low (risky)
Profitability						
Profit margin on sales	$\dfrac{\text{Net income available to common stockholders}}{\text{Sales}}$	$\dfrac{\$113}{\$3,000}$	=	3.8%	5.0%	Poor
Basic earning power (BEP)	$\dfrac{\text{Earnings before interest and taxes (EBIT)}}{\text{Total assets}}$	$\dfrac{\$283}{\$2,000}$	=	14.2%	17.2%	Poor
Return on total assets (ROA)	$\dfrac{\text{Net income available to common stockholders}}{\text{Total assets}}$	$\dfrac{\$113}{\$2,000}$	=	5.7%	9.0%	Poor
Return on common equity (ROE)	$\dfrac{\text{Net income available to common stockholders}}{\text{Common equity}}$	$\dfrac{\$113}{\$896}$	=	12.6%	15.0%	Poor
Market Value						
Price/earnings (P/E)	$\dfrac{\text{Price per share}}{\text{Earnings per share}}$	$\dfrac{\$23.00}{\$2.26}$	=	10.2	12.5	Low
Price/cash flow	$\dfrac{\text{Price per share}}{\text{Cash flow per shares}}$	$\dfrac{\$23.00}{\$4.26}$	=	5.4	6.8	Low
Market/book (M/B)	$\dfrac{\text{Market price per share}}{\text{Book value per share}}$	$\dfrac{\$23.00}{\$17.92}$	=	1.3	1.7	Low

8.7 Trend Analysis, Common Size Analysis, and Percentage Change Analysis

Trends give clues as to whether a firm's financial condition is likely to improve or deteriorate. To do a **trend analysis**, you examine a ratio over time, as shown in Figure 8-1. This graph shows that MicroDrive's rate of return on common equity has been declining since 2009, even though the industry average has been relatively stable. All the other ratios could be analyzed similarly.

In a **common size analysis,** all income statement items are divided by sales and all balance sheet items are divided by total assets. Thus, a common size income statement shows each item as a percentage of sales, and a common size balance sheet shows each item as a percentage of total assets.[10] The advantage of common size analysis is that it facilitates comparisons of balance sheets and income statements over time and across companies.

Common size statements are easy to generate if the financial statements are in a spreadsheet. In fact, if you obtain your data from a source that uses standardized financial statements, then it is easy to cut and paste the data for a new company over your original company's data, and all of your spreadsheet formulas will be valid for the new company. We generated Figure 8-2 in the *Excel* file *Ch08 Tool Kit.xls.* Figure 8-2 shows MicroDrive's 2011 and 2012 common size income statements, along with the composite statement for the industry. (*Note:* Rounding may cause

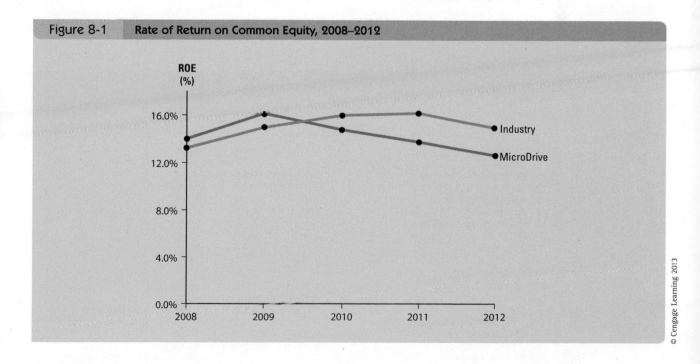

Figure 8-1	Rate of Return on Common Equity, 2008–2012

---

10. Some sources of industry data, such as Risk Management Associates (formerly known as Robert Morris Associates), are presented exclusively in common size form.

addition/subtraction differences in Figures 8-2, 8-3, and 8-4.) MicroDrive's EBIT is slightly below average, and its interest expenses are slightly above average. The net effect is a relatively low profit margin.

Figure 8-3 shows MicroDrive's common size balance sheets along with the industry composite. Its accounts receivable are significantly higher than the industry average, its inventories are significantly higher, and it uses much more debt than the average firm.

Figure 8-2   MicroDrive Inc.: Common Size Income Statement

	A	B	C	D Industry Composite 2012	E MicroDrive 2012	F 2011
169	Net sales			100.0%	100.0%	100.0%
170	Operating costs			87.6%	87.2%	87.7%
171	Earnings before interest, taxes, depr. & amort. (EBITDA)			12.4%	12.8%	12.3%
172	Depreciation and amortization			2.8%	3.3%	3.2%
173	Earnings before interest and taxes (EBIT)			9.6%	9.4%	9.1%
174	Less interest			1.3%	2.9%	2.1%
175	Earnings before taxes (EBT)			8.3%	6.5%	7.0%
176	Taxes (40%)			3.3%	2.6%	2.8%
177	Net income before preferred dividends			5.0%	3.9%	4.2%
178	Preferred dividends				0.1%	0.1%
179	Net income available to common stockholders (profit margin)			5.0%	3.8%	4.1%

Figure 8-3   MicroDrive Inc.: Common Size Balance Sheet

	A	B	C Industry Composite 2012	D MicroDrive 2012	E 2011
187	*Assets*				
188	Cash and equivalents		1.0%	0.5%	0.9%
189	Short-term investments		2.2%	0.0%	3.9%
190	Accounts receivable		17.8%	18.8%	18.8%
191	Inventories		19.8%	30.8%	24.7%
192	Total current assets		40.8%	50.0%	48.2%
193	Net plant and equipment		59.2%	50.0%	51.8%
194	Total assets		100.0%	100.0%	100.0%
195					
196	*Liabilities and equity*				
197	Accounts payable		1.8%	3.0%	1.8%
198	Notes payable		4.4%	5.5%	3.6%
199	Accruals		3.6%	7.0%	7.7%
200	Total current liabilities		9.8%	15.5%	13.1%
201	Long-term bonds		30.2%	37.7%	34.5%
202	Total liabilities		40.0%	53.2%	47.6%
203	Preferred stock		0.0%	2.0%	2.4%
204	Total common equity		60.0%	44.8%	50.0%
205	Total liabilities and equity		100.0%	100.0%	100.0%

© Cengage Learning 2013

Figure 8-4	MicroDrive Inc.: Income Statement Percentage Change Analysis

	A	B	C	D
213	Base year = 2011			Percent Change in
214				2012
215	Net sales			5.3%
216	Operating costs			4.7%
217	Earnings before interest, taxes, depr. & amort. (EBITDA)			9.4%
218	Depreciation and amortization			11.1%
219	Earnings before interest and taxes (EBIT)			8.8%
220	Less interest			46.7%
221	Earnings before taxes (EBT)			(2.5%)
222	Taxes (40%)			(2.5%)
223	Net income before preferred dividends			(2.5%)
224	Preferred dividends			0.0%
225	Net income available to common stockholders			(2.6%)
226				

© Cengage Learning 2013

In **percentage change analysis**, growth rates are calculated for all income statement items and balance sheet accounts relative to a base year. To illustrate, Figure 8-4 contains MicroDrive's income statement percentage change analysis for 2012 relative to 2011. Sales increased at a 5.3% rate during 2012, but EBITDA increased by 9.4%. This "good news" was offset by a 46.7% increase in interest expense. The significant growth in interest expense caused growth in net income to be negative. Thus, the percentage change analysis points out that the decrease in net income in 2012 resulted almost exclusively from an increase in interest expense. This conclusion could be reached by analyzing dollar amounts, but percentage change analysis simplifies the task. We apply the same type of analysis to the balance sheets (see the file *Ch08 Tool Kit.xls*), which shows that inventories grew at a whopping 48.2% rate. With only a 5.3% growth in sales, the extreme growth in inventories should be of great concern to MicroDrive's managers.

WEB
See *Ch08 Tool Kit.xls* for details.

Self Test

What is a trend analysis, and what important information does it provide?

What is common size analysis?

What is percentage change analysis?

8.8 Tying the Ratios Together: The Du Pont Equation

In ratio analysis, it is sometimes easy to miss the forest for all the trees. The **Du Pont equation** provides a framework that ties together a firm's profitability, asset efficiency, and use of debt. The return on assets (ROA) can be expressed as the profit margin multiplied by the total assets turnover ratio:

(8–1)
$$\text{ROA} = \text{Profit margin} \times \text{Total assets turnover}$$
$$= \frac{\text{Net income}}{\text{Sales}} \times \frac{\text{Sales}}{\text{Total assets}}$$

For MicroDrive, the ROA is

$$\text{ROA} = 3.77\% \times 1.5 = 5.65\%$$

MicroDrive made 3.8%, or 3.8 cents, on each dollar of sales, and its assets were turned over 1.5 times during the year. Therefore, the company earned a return of 5.65% on its assets.

To find the return on equity (ROE), multiply the ROA by the *equity multiplier,* which is the ratio of assets to common equity:

(8–2)
$$\text{Equity multiplier} = \frac{\text{Total assets}}{\text{Common equity}}$$

Firms that have a lot of leverage (i.e., a lot of liabilities or preferred stock) have a high equity multiplier because the assets are financed with a relatively smaller amount of equity. Therefore, the return on equity (ROE) depends on the ROA and the use of leverage:

(8–3)
$$\text{ROE} = \text{ROA} \times \text{Equity multiplier}$$
$$= \frac{\text{Net income}}{\text{Total assets}} \times \frac{\text{Total assets}}{\text{Common equity}}$$

MicroDrive's ROE is

$$\text{ROE} = 5.65\% \times \$2,000/\$896$$
$$= 5.65\% \times 2.23$$
$$= 12.6\%$$

Combining Equations 8-1 and 8-3 gives the *extended, or modified, Du Pont equation,* which shows how the profit margin, the total assets turnover ratio, and the equity multiplier combine to determine the ROE:

(8–4)
$$\text{ROE} = (\text{Profit margin})(\text{Total assets turnover})(\text{Equity multiplier})$$
$$= \frac{\text{Net income}}{\text{Sales}} \times \frac{\text{Sales}}{\text{Total assets}} \times \frac{\text{Total assets}}{\text{Common equity}}$$

For MicroDrive, we have

$$ROE = (3.77\%)(1.5)(2.23)$$
$$= 12.6\%$$

The insights provided by the Du Pont model are valuable, and the model can be used for "quick and dirty" estimates of the impact that operating changes have on returns. For example, holding all else equal, if MicroDrive can implement lean production techniques and increase to 1.8 its ratio of sales to total assets, then its ROE will improve to $(3.77\%)(1.8)(2.23) = 15.13\%$. For a more complete "what if" analysis, most companies use a forecasting model such as the one described in Chapter 9.

8.9 Comparative Ratios and Benchmarking

Ratio analysis involves comparisons. A company's ratios are compared with those of other firms in the same industry—that is, with industry average figures. However, like most firms, MicroDrive's managers go one step further: They also compare their ratios with those of a smaller set of the leading computer companies. This technique is called **benchmarking**, and the companies used for the comparison are called **benchmark companies**. For example, MicroDrive benchmarks against five other firms that its management considers to be the best-managed companies with operations similar to its own.

Many companies also benchmark various parts of their overall operation against top companies, whether they are in the same industry or not. For example, Micro-Drive has a division that sells hard drives directly to consumers through catalogs and the Internet. This division's shipping department benchmarks against L.L.Bean, even though they are in different industries, because L.L.Bean's shipping department is one of the best. MicroDrive wants its own shippers to strive to match L.L.Bean's record for on-time shipments.

Comparative ratios are available from a number of sources, including *Value Line*, Dun and Bradstreet (D&B), and the *Annual Statement Studies* published by Risk Management Associates, which is the national association of bank loan officers. Table 8-3 reports selected ratios from Reuters for Apple and its industry, revealing that Apple has a much higher profit margin and lower debt ratio than its peers.

Each data-supplying organization uses a somewhat different set of ratios designed for its own purposes. For example, D&B deals mainly with small firms, many of which are proprietorships, and it sells its services primarily to banks and other lenders. Therefore, D&B is concerned largely with the creditor's viewpoint, and its ratios emphasize current assets and liabilities, not market value ratios. So, when you select a comparative

TABLE 8-3	Comparative Ratios for Apple Inc., the Computer Hardware Industry, the Technology Sector, and the S&P 500			
Ratio	Apple	Computer Hardware Industry[a]	Technology Sector[b]	S&P 500
P/E ratio	21.43	16.00	24.84	18.12
Market to book	6.22	2.27	3.87	2.90
Price to tangible book	6.38	4.55	4.68	7.54
Price to cash flow	19.80	9.16	9.88	10.99
Net profit margin	21.48	4.35	10.52	10.84
Quick ratio	1.96	1.10	1.16	0.66
Current ratio	2.01	1.49	2.23	0.98
Long-term debt to equity	0.00	22.71	14.85	119.81
Total debt to equity	0.00	58.07	23.33	175.73
Interest coverage (TIE)[c]	–	0.28	1.44	16.50
Return on assets	22.84	7.27	10.10	5.88
Return on equity	35.28	17.90	15.57	17.36
Inventory turnover	52.51	12.14	239.32	6.61
Asset turnover	1.06	1.98	0.82	0.54

[a]The computer hardware industry is composed of fifty firms, including IBM, Dell, Apple, Sun Microsystems, Gateway, and Silicon Graphics.
[b]The technology sector contains eleven industries, including communications equipment, computer hardware, computer networks, semiconductors, and software and programming.
[c]Apple had more interest income than interest expense.

Source: Adapted from **www.reuters.com**, December 28, 2010.

data source, you should be sure that your own emphasis is similar to that of the agency whose ratios you plan to use. Additionally, there are often definitional differences in the ratios presented by different sources, so before using a source, be sure to verify the exact definitions of the ratios to ensure consistency with your own work.

Self Test

Differentiate between trend analysis and comparative ratio analysis.

What is benchmarking?

8.10 Uses and Limitations of Ratio Analysis

Ratio analysis provides useful information concerning a company's operations and financial condition, but it has limitations that necessitate care and judgment. Some potential problems include the following.

1. Many large firms operate different divisions in different industries, and for such companies it is difficult to develop a meaningful set of industry averages. Therefore, industry averages are more applicable to small, narrowly focused firms than to large, multidivisional ones.

2. To set goals for high-level performance, it is best to benchmark on the industry *leaders'* ratios rather than the industry *average* ratios.

3. Inflation may have badly distorted firms' balance sheets—reported values are often substantially different from "true" values. Further, because inflation affects depreciation charges and inventory costs, reported profits are also affected. Thus, inflation can distort a ratio analysis for one firm over time or a comparative analysis of firms of different ages.

4. Seasonal factors can also distort a ratio analysis. For example, the inventory turnover ratio for a food processor will be radically different if the balance sheet figure used for inventory is the one just before versus the one just after the close of the canning season. This problem can be minimized by using monthly averages for inventory (and receivables) when calculating turnover ratios.

5. Firms can employ **"window dressing" techniques** to make their financial statements look stronger. To illustrate, suppose a company takes out a 2-year loan in late December. Because the loan is for more than 1 year, it is not included in current liabilities even though the cash received through the loan is reported as a current asset. This improves the current and quick ratios and makes the year-end balance sheet look stronger. If the company pays the loan back in January, then the transaction was strictly window dressing.

6. Companies' choices of different accounting practices can distort comparisons. For example, choices of different inventory valuation and depreciation methods affect financial statements differently, making comparisons among companies less meaningful. As another example, if one firm leases a substantial amount of its productive equipment, then its assets may appear low relative to sales (because leased assets often do not appear on the balance sheet) and its debt may appear low (because the liability associated with the lease obligation may not be shown as debt).[11]

In summary, conducting ratio analysis in a mechanical, unthinking manner is dangerous, but when ratio analysis is used intelligently and with good judgment, it can provide useful insights into a firm's operations and identify the right questions to ask.

RATIO ANALYSIS ON THE WEB

A great source for comparative ratios is **www.reuters.com**. Enter a company's ticker at the top of the page. This brings up a table with the stock quote, company information, and additional links. Select Financials, which brings up a page with a detailed ratio analysis for the company and includes comparative ratios for other companies in the same sector, the same industry, and the S&P 500. (*Note:* You may have to register to get extra features, but registration is free.)

---

11. This may change when FASB and IASB complete their joint project on leasing. As of the middle of 2011, the FASB and IASB plan to provide a draft of the revised standards by the end of 2011. See **72.3.243.42/project/leases.shtml** for updates.

8.11 Looking beyond the Numbers

Sound financial analysis involves more than just calculating and comparing ratios—qualitative factors must be considered. Here are some questions suggested by the American Association of Individual Investors (AAII).

1. To what extent are the company's revenues tied to one key customer or to one key product? To what extent does the company rely on a single supplier? Reliance on single customers, products, or suppliers increases risk.
2. What percentage of the company's business is generated overseas? Companies with a large percentage of overseas business are exposed to risk of currency exchange volatility and political instability.
3. What are the probable actions of current competitors and the likelihood of additional new competitors?
4. Do the company's future prospects depend critically on the success of products currently in the pipeline or on existing products?
5. How does the legal and regulatory environment affect the company?

Summary

This chapter explained techniques used by investors and managers to analyze financial statements. The key concepts covered are listed below.

- **Liquidity ratios** show the relationship of a firm's current assets to its current liabilities and thus its ability to meet maturing debts. Two commonly used liquidity ratios are the **current ratio** and the **quick,** or **acid test, ratio.**
- **Asset management ratios** measure how effectively a firm is managing its assets. These ratios include **inventory turnover, days sales outstanding, fixed assets turnover,** and **total assets turnover.**
- **Debt management ratios** reveal (1) the extent to which the firm is financed with debt and (2) its likelihood of defaulting on its debt obligations. They include the **debt ratio,** the **times-interest-earned ratio,** and the **EBITDA coverage ratio.**
- **Profitability ratios** show the combined effects of liquidity, asset management, and debt management policies on operating results. They include the **net profit margin** (also called the **profit margin on sales**), the **basic earning power ratio,** the **return on total assets,** and the **return on common equity.**

- **Market value ratios** relate the firm's stock price to its earnings, cash flow, and book value per share, thus giving management an indication of what investors think of the company's past performance and future prospects. These include the **price/earnings ratio**, the **price/cash flow ratio**, and the **market/book ratio**.
- **Trend analysis**, in which one plots a ratio over time, is important because it reveals whether the firm's condition has been improving or deteriorating over time.
- The **Du Pont model** is designed to show how the profit margin on sales, the assets turnover ratio, and the use of debt all interact to determine the rate of return on equity. The firm's management can use the Du Pont model to analyze ways of improving performance.
- **Benchmarking** is the process of comparing a particular company with a group of similar successful companies.

Ratio analysis has limitations, but when used with care and judgment it can be very helpful.

Questions

8–1 Define each of the following terms:
    a. *Liquidity ratios:* current ratio; quick, or acid test, ratio
    b. *Asset management ratios:* inventory turnover ratio; days sales outstanding (DSO); fixed assets turnover ratio; total assets turnover ratio
    c. *Financial leverage ratios:* debt ratio; times-interest-earned (TIE) ratio; coverage ratio
    d. *Profitability ratios:* profit margin on sales; basic earning power (BEP) ratio; return on total assets (ROA); return on common equity (ROE)
    e. *Market value ratios:* price/earnings (P/E) ratio; price/cash flow ratio; market/book (M/B) ratio; book value per share
    f. Trend analysis; comparative ratio analysis; benchmarking
    g. Du Pont equation; window dressing; seasonal effects on ratios

8–2 Financial ratio analysis is conducted by managers, equity investors, long-term creditors, and short-term creditors. What is the primary emphasis of each of these groups in evaluating ratios?

8–3 Over the past year, M. D. Ryngaert & Co. has realized an increase in its current ratio and a drop in its total assets turnover ratio. However, the company's sales, quick ratio, and fixed assets turnover ratio have remained constant. What explains these changes?

8–4 Profit margins and turnover ratios vary from one industry to another. What differences would you expect to find between a grocery chain such as Safeway and a steel company? Think particularly about the turnover ratios, the profit margin, and the Du Pont equation.

8–5 How might (a) seasonal factors and (b) different growth rates distort a comparative ratio analysis? Give some examples. How might these problems be alleviated?

8–6 Why is it sometimes misleading to compare a company's financial ratios with those of other firms that operate in the same industry?

Problems   Answers Appear in Appendix B

Easy Problems 1–5

8-1 **Days Sales Outstanding** Greene Sisters has a DSO of 20 days. The company's average daily sales are $20,000. What is the level of its accounts receivable? Assume there are 365 days in a year.

8-2 **Debt Ratio** Vigo Vacations has an equity multiplier of 2.5. The company's assets are financed with some combination of long-term debt and common equity. What is the company's debt ratio?

8-3 **Market/Book Ratio** Winston Washers's stock price is $75 per share. Winston has $10 billion in total assets. Its balance sheet shows $1 billion in current liabilities, $3 billion in long-term debt, and $6 billion in common equity. It has 800 million shares of common stock outstanding. What is Winston's market/book ratio?

8-4 **Price/Earnings Ratio** Reno Revolvers has an EPS of $1.50, a cash flow per share of $3.00, and a price/cash flow ratio of 8.0. What is its P/E ratio?

8-5 **ROE** Needham Pharmaceuticals has a profit margin of 3% and an equity multiplier of 2.0. Its sales are $100 million and it has total assets of $50 million. What is its ROE?

Intermediate Problems 6–10

8-6 **Du Pont Analysis** Gardial & Son has an ROA of 12%, a 5% profit margin, and a return on equity equal to 20%. What is the company's total assets turnover? What is the firm's equity multiplier?

8-7 **Current and Quick Ratios** Ace Industries has current assets equal to $3 million. The company's current ratio is 1.5, and its quick ratio is 1.0. What is the firm's level of current liabilities? What is the firm's level of inventories?

8-8 **Profit Margin and Debt Ratio** Assume you are given the following relationships for the Haslam Corporation:

Sales/total assets	1.2
Return on assets (ROA)	4%
Return on equity (ROE)	7%

Calculate Haslam's profit margin and debt ratio.

8-9 **Current and Quick Ratios** The Nelson Company has $1,312,500 in current assets and $525,000 in current liabilities. Its initial inventory level is $375,000, and it will raise funds as additional notes payable and use them to increase inventory. How much can Nelson's short-term debt (notes payable) increase without pushing its current ratio below 2.0? What will be the firm's quick ratio after Nelson has raised the maximum amount of short-term funds?

8-10 **Times-Interest-Earned Ratio** The Morris Corporation has $600,000 of debt outstanding, and it pays an interest rate of 8% annually. Morris's annual sales are $3 million, its average tax rate is 40%, and its net profit margin on sales is 3%. If the company does not maintain a TIE ratio of at least 5 to 1, then its bank will refuse to renew the loan and bankruptcy will result. What is Morris's TIE ratio?

Challenging Problems 11–14

8-11 **Balance Sheet Analysis** Complete the balance sheet and sales information in the table that follows for J. White Industries using the following financial data:

Debt ratio: 40%
Quick ratio: 0.80
Total assets turnover: 1.5
Days sales outstanding: 36.5 days[a]
Gross profit margin on sales: (Sales – Cost of goods sold)/Sales = 25%
Inventory turnover ratio: 5.0

[a]Calculation is based on a 365-day year.

Balance Sheet

Cash	_____	Accounts payable	_____
Accounts receivable	_____	Long-term debt	50,000
Inventories	_____	Common stock	_____
Fixed assets	_____	Retained earnings	100,000
Total assets	$400,000	Total liabilities and equity	_____
Sales	=========	Cost of goods sold	=========

8-12 **Comprehensive Ratio Calculations** The Kretovich Company had a quick ratio of 1.4, a current ratio of 3.0, an inventory turnover of 6 times, total current assets of $810,000, and cash and marketable securities of $120,000. What were Kretovich's annual sales and its DSO? Assume a 365-day year.

8-13 **Comprehensive Ratio Analysis** Data for Lozano Chip Company and its industry averages follow.
   a. Calculate the indicated ratios for Lozano.
   b. Construct the extended Du Pont equation for both Lozano and the industry.
   c. Outline Lozano's strengths and weaknesses as revealed by your analysis.
   d. Suppose Lozano had doubled its sales as well as its inventories, accounts receivable, and common equity during 2012. How would that information affect the validity of your ratio analysis? (*Hint:* Think about averages and the effects of rapid growth on ratios if averages are not used. No calculations are needed.)

Lozano Chip Company: Balance Sheet as of December 31, 2012 (Thousands of Dollars)

Cash	$ 225,000	Accounts payable	$ 601,866
Receivables	1,575,000	Notes payable	326,634
Inventories	1,125,000	Other current liabilities	525,000
Total current assets	$2,950,000	Total current liabilities	$1,453,500
Net fixed assets	1,350,000	Long-term debt	1,068,750
		Common equity	1,752,750
Total assets	$4,275,000	Total liabilities and equity	$4,275,000

Lozano Chip Company: Income Statement for Year Ended December 31, 2012 (Thousands of Dollars)

Sales	$ 7,500,000
Cost of goods sold	6,375,000
Selling, general, and administrative expenses	825,000
Earnings before interest and taxes (EBIT)	$ 300,000
Interest expense	111,631
Earnings before taxes (EBT)	$ 188,369
Federal and state income taxes (40%)	75,348
Net income	$ 113,022

Ratio	Lozano	Industry Average
Current assets/Current liabilities	_____	2.0
Days sales outstanding[a]	_____	35.0 days
Sales/Inventory	_____	6.7
Sales/Fixed assets	_____	12.1
Sales/Total assets	_____	3.0
Net income/Sales	_____	1.2%
Net income/Total assets	_____	3.6%
Net income/Common equity	_____	9.0%
Total liabilities/Total assets	_____	60.0%

[a]Calculation is based on a 365-day year.

8-14 **Comprehensive Ratio Analysis** The Jimenez Corporation's forecasted 2013 financial statements follow, along with some industry average ratios.

a. Calculate Jimenez's 2013 forecasted ratios, compare them with the industry average data, and comment briefly on Jimenez's projected strengths and weaknesses.

b. What do you think would happen to Jimenez's ratios if the company initiated cost-cutting measures that allowed it to hold lower levels of inventory and substantially decreased the cost of goods sold? No calculations are necessary; think about which ratios would be affected by changes in these two accounts.

Jimenez Corporation: Forecasted Balance Sheet as of December 31, 2013

Assets	
Cash	$ 72,000
Accounts receivable	439,000
Inventories	894,000
Total current assets	$ 1,405,000
Fixed assets	431,000
Total assets	$ 1,836,000
Liabilities and Equity	
Accounts and notes payable	$ 432,000
Accruals	170,000
Total current liabilities	$ 602,000
Long-term debt	404,290
Common stock	575,000
Retained earnings	254,710
Total liabilities and equity	$ 1,836,000

Jimenez Corporation: Forecasted Income Statement for 2013

Sales	$4,290,000
Cost of goods sold	3,580,000
Selling, general, and administrative expenses	370,320
Depreciation and amortization	159,000
Earnings before taxes (EBT)	$ 180,680
Taxes (40%)	72,272
Net income	$ 108,408

Per Share Data

EPS	$ 4.71
Cash dividends per share	$ 0.95
P/E ratio	5.0
Market price (average)	$ 23.57
Number of shares outstanding	23,000

Industry Financial Ratios (2012)[a]

Quick ratio	1.0
Current ratio	2.7
Inventory turnover[b]	7.0
Days sales outstanding[c]	32.0 days
Fixed assets turnover[b]	13.0
Total assets turnover[b]	2.6
Return on assets	9.1%
Return on equity	18.2%
Debt ratio	50.0%
Profit margin on sales	3.5%
P/E ratio	6.0
Price/Cash flow ratio	3.5

[a]Industry average ratios have been constant for the past 4 years.
[b]Based on year-end balance sheet figures.
[c]Calculation is based on a 365-day year

Spreadsheet Problem

8-15 **Build a Model: Ratio Analysis** Start with the partial model in the file *Ch08 P15 Build a Model.xls* from the textbook's Web site. Joshua & White (J&W) Technologies's financial statements are also shown below. Answer the following questions. (*Note:* Industry average ratios are provided in *Ch08 P15 Build a Model.xls.*)

a. Has J&W's liquidity position improved or worsened? Explain.

b. Has J&W's ability to manage its assets improved or worsened? Explain.

c. How has J&W's profitability changed during the last year?

d. Perform an extended Du Pont analysis for J&W for 2011 and 2012. What do these results tell you?

e. Perform a common size analysis. What has happened to the composition (that is, percentage in each category) of assets and liabilities?

f. Perform a percentage change analysis. What does this tell you about the change in profitability and asset utilization?

Joshua & White Technologies: December 31 Balance Sheets
(Thousands of Dollars)

Assets	2012	2011	Liabilities & Equity	2012	2011
Cash and cash equivalents	$ 21,000	$ 20,000	Accounts payable	$ 33,600	$ 32,000
Short-term investments	3,759	3,240	Accruals	12,600	12,000
Accounts receivable	52,500	48,000	Notes payable	19,929	6,480
Inventories	84,000	56,000	Total current liabilities	$ 66,129	$ 50,480
Total current assets	$161,259	$127,240	Long-term debt	67,662	58,320
Net fixed assets	218,400	200,000	Total liabilities	$133,791	$108,800
Total assets	$379,659	$327,240	Common stock	183,793	178,440
			Retained earnings	62,075	40,000
			Total common equity	$245,868	$218,440
			Total liabilities & equity	$379,659	$327,240

Joshua & White Technologies December 31 Income Statements
(Thousands of Dollars)

	2012	2011
Sales	$420,000	$400,000
Expenses excluding depreciation and amortization	327,600	320,000
EBITDA	$ 92,400	$ 80,000
Depreciation and amortization	19,660	18,000
EBIT	$ 72,740	$ 62,000
Interest expense	5,740	4,460
EBT	$ 67,000	$ 57,540
Taxes (40%)	26,800	23,016
Net income	$ 40,200	$ 34,524
Common dividends	$ 18,125	$ 17,262

Other Data	2012	2011
Year-end stock price	$ 90.00	$ 96.00
Number of shares (Thousands)	4,052	4,000
Lease payment (Thousands of Dollars)	$20,000	$20,000
Sinking fund payment (Thousands of Dollars)	$ 0	$ 0

THOMSON REUTERS

Use the Thomson ONE—Business School Edition online database to work this chapter's questions.

Analysis of Ford's Financial Statements

Use Thomson ONE to analyze Ford Motor Company. Enter Ford's ticker symbol (F) and select GO. By selecting the menu at left labeled Financials, you can find Ford's key financial statements for the past several years. Under the Financial Ratios heading select Thomson Ratios and then Annual Ratios to see an in-depth summary of Ford's various ratios over the past 5 years.

Click on the Comparables menu at left and scroll down to find the submenu items for Key Financials and Key Financial Ratios for Ford and a few of its peers. If you scroll up, still in the Comparables menu, you can select a different the list of peer firms to be included in the analysis. The default group is "Peers by SIC code."

Discussion Questions

1. What has happened to Ford's liquidity position over the past 3 years? How does Ford's liquidity compare with its peers? (*Hint:* You may use both the peer key financial ratios and liquidity comparison to answer this question.)
2. Take a look at Ford's inventory turnover ratio. How does this ratio compare with its peers? Have there been any interesting changes over time in this measure? Do you consider Ford's inventory management to be a strength or a weakness?
3. Construct a simple Du Pont analysis for Ford and its peers. What are Ford's strengths and weaknesses relative to its competitors?

MINI CASE

The first part of the case, presented in Chapter 7, discussed the situation of Computron Industries after an expansion program. A large loss occurred in 2012, rather than the expected profit. As a result, its managers, directors, and investors are concerned about the firm's survival.

Jenny Cochran was brought in as assistant to Gary Meissner, Computron's chairman, who had the task of getting the company back into a sound financial position. Computron's 2011 and 2012 balance sheets and income statements, together with projections for 2013, are shown in the following tables. The tables also show the 2011 and 2012 financial ratios, along with industry average data. The 2013 projected financial statement data represent Cochran's and Meissner's best guess for 2013 results, assuming that some new financing is arranged to get the company "over the hump."

Balance Sheets

	2011	2012	2013E
Assets			
Cash	$ 9,000	$ 7,282	$ 14,000
Short-term investments	48,600	20,000	71,632
Accounts receivable	351,200	632,160	878,000
Inventories	715,200	1,287,360	1,716,480
Total current assets	$1,124,000	$1,946,802	$2,680,112
Gross fixed assets	491,000	1,202,950	1,220,000
Less: Accumulated depreciation	146,200	263,160	383,160
Net fixed assets	$ 344,800	$ 939,790	$ 836,840
Total assets	$1,468,800	$2,886,592	$3,516,952
Liabilities and Equity			
Accounts payable	$ 145,600	$ 324,000	$ 359,800
Notes payable	200,000	720,000	300,000
Accruals	136,000	284,960	380,000
Total current liabilities	$ 481,600	$1,328,960	$1,039,800
Long-term debt	323,432	1,000,000	500,000
Common stock (100,000 shares)	460,000	460,000	1,680,936
Retained earnings	203,768	97,632	296,216
Total equity	$ 663,768	$ 557,632	$1,977,152
Total liabilities and equity	$1,468,800	$2,886,592	$3,516,952

Note: "E" denotes "estimated"; the 2013 data are forecasts.

Income Statements

	2011	2012	2013E
Sales	$3,432,000	$5,834,400	$7,035,600
Cost of goods sold	2,864,000	4,980,000	5,800,000
Other expenses	340,000	720,000	612,960
Depreciation and amortization	18,900	116,960	120,000
Total operating costs	$3,222,900	$5,816,960	$6,532,960
EBIT	$ 209,100	$ 17,440	$ 502,640
Interest expense	62,500	176,000	80,000
EBT	$ 146,600	($ 158,560)	$ 422,640
Taxes (40%)	58,640	(63,424)	169,056
Net income	$ 87,960	($ 95,136)	$ 253,584
Other Data			
Stock price	$ 8.50	$ 6.00	$ 12.17
Shares outstanding	100,000	100,000	250,000

	2011	2012	2013E
EPS	$ 0.880	($ 0.951)	$ 1.014
DPS	$ 0.220	0.110	0.220
Tax rate	40%	40%	40%
Book value per share	$ 6.638	$ 5.576	$ 7.909
Lease payments	$40,000	$40,000	$40,000

Note: "E" denotes "estimated"; the 2013 data are forecasts.

Ratio Analysis

	2011	2012	2013E	Industry Average
Current	2.3	1.5	_____	2.7
Quick	0.8	0.5	_____	1.0
Inventory turnover	4.8	4.5	_____	6.1
Days sales outstanding	37.3	39.6	_____	32.0
Fixed assets turnover	10.0	6.2	_____	7.0
Total assets turnover	2.3	2.0	_____	2.5
Debt ratio	54.8%	80.7%	_____	50.0%
TIE	3.3	0.1	_____	6.2
EBITDA coverage	2.6	0.8	_____	8.0
Profit margin	2.6%	−1.6%	_____	3.6%
Basic earning power	14.2%	0.6%	_____	17.8%
ROA	6.0%	−3.3%	_____	9.0%
ROE	13.3%	−17.1%	_____	17.9%
Price/Earnings (P/E)	9.7	−6.3	_____	16.2
Price/Cash flow	8.0	27.5	_____	7.6
Market/Book	1.3	1.1	_____	2.9

Note: "E" denotes "estimated."

Cochran must prepare an analysis of where the company is now, what it must do to regain its financial health, and what actions should be taken. Your assignment is to help her answer the following questions. Provide clear explanations, not yes or no answers.

a. Why are ratios useful? What three groups use ratio analysis and for what reasons?

b. Calculate the 2013 current and quick ratios based on the projected balance sheet and income statement data. What can you say about the company's liquidity position in 2011, 2012, and as projected for 2013? We often think of ratios as being useful (1) to managers to help run business, (2) to bankers for credit analysis, and (3) to stockholders for stock valuation. Would these different types of analysts have an equal interest in the liquidity ratios?

c. Calculate the 2013 inventory turnover, days sales outstanding (DSO), fixed assets turnover, and total assets turnover. How does Computron's utilization of assets stack up against that of other firms in its industry?

d. Calculate the 2013 debt, times-interest-earned, and EBITDA coverage ratios. How does Computron compare with the industry with respect to financial leverage? What can you conclude from these ratios?

e. Calculate the 2013 profit margin, basic earning power (BEP), return on assets (ROA), and return on equity (ROE). What can you say about these ratios?

f. Calculate the 2013 price/earnings ratio, price/cash flow ratio, and market/book ratio. Do these ratios indicate that investors are expected to have a high or low opinion of the company?

g. Perform a common size analysis and percentage change analysis. What do these analyses tell you about Computron?

h. Use the extended Du Pont equation to provide a summary and overview of Computron's financial condition as projected for 2013. What are the firm's major strengths and weaknesses?

i. What are some potential problems and limitations of financial ratio analysis?

j. What are some qualitative factors that analysts should consider when evaluating a company's likely future financial performance?

Selected Additional Cases

The following cases from TextChoice, Cengage Learning's online case library, cover many of the concepts discussed in this chapter and are available at www.textchoice2.com/casenet.

Klein-Brigham Series:
Case 35, "Mark X Company (A)," which illustrates the use of ratio analysis in the evaluation of a firm's existing and potential financial positions; Case 36, "Garden State Container Corporation," which is similar in content to Case 35; Case 51, "Safe Packaging Corporation," which updates Case 36; Case 68, "Sweet Dreams Inc.," which also updates Case 36; and Case 71, "Swan-Davis, Inc.," which illustrates how financial analysis—based on both historical statements and forecasted statements—is used for internal management and lending decisions.

PART II

Corporate Valuation

Chapter 9

Financial Planning and Forecasting Financial Statements

WEB

The textbook's Web site contains an *Excel* file that will guide you through the chapter's calculations. The file for this chapter is ***Ch09 Tool Kit.xls***, and we encourage you to open the file and follow along as you read the chapter.

Our primary objective in this book is to explain how financial managers can make their companies more valuable. However, value creation is impossible unless the company has well-designed strategic and tactical operating plans. As Yogi Berra once said, "You've got to be careful if you don't know where you're going, because you might not get there." An important component of these operating plans is financial projections.

Managers use **pro forma,** or **projected, financial statements** in four ways: (1) By looking at projected statements, they can assess whether the firm's anticipated performance is in line with the firm's own general targets and with investors' expectations. (2) Pro forma statements can be used to estimate the effect of proposed operating changes, enabling managers to conduct "what if" analyses. (3) Managers use pro forma statements to anticipate the firm's future financing needs. (4) Managers forecast free cash flows under different operating plans, forecast their capital requirements, and then choose the plan that maximizes shareholder value. Security analysts make the same types of projections, forecasting future earnings, cash flows, and stock prices.

Beginning of Chapter Questions

As you read the chapter, consider how you would answer the following questions. You *should not* necessarily be able to answer the questions before you read the chapter. Rather, you should use them to get a sense of the issues covered in the chapter. After reading the chapter, you should be able to give at least partial answers to the questions, and you should be able to give better answers after the chapter has been discussed in class. Note, too, that it is often useful, when answering conceptual questions, to use hypothetical data to illustrate your answer. We illustrate the answers with an *Excel* model that is available on the textbook's Web site. Accessing the model and working through it is a useful exercise, and it provides insights that are useful when answering the questions.

1. List and discuss briefly the major components of a firm's **strategic plan.** What role do projections of financial statements play in the development of the strategic plan?

2. One forecasting technique is called the **forecasted financial statement approach,** and it is used to forecast future financial statements. If you had a company's balance sheets and income statements for the past 5 years but no other information, how could you use the forecasted financial statement approach to forecast the following items for the coming year? (a) Its sales revenues. (b) Its financial statements. (c) Its

funds requirements (AFN). (d) Its financial condition and profitability as shown by its ROE and other key ratios.

3. If you had a set of industry average ratios for the firm you were analyzing, how might you use these data?

4. All forecasts are subject to error. Do you think top managers would be concerned about the effects on the firm if sales revenues or unit costs, for example, turned out to be different from the forecasted level? How could you provide information on the effects of such errors?

5. Define the following terms and then explain the role they might play in your forecast. (a) **Economies of scale.** (b) **Lumpy assets.** (c) **Excess capacity.**

6. The funds requirement can be forecasted by the forecasted financial statement approach, but you could also use the **AFN equation.** What is this equation, and how does it operate? What are its advantages and disadvantages relative to the financial statement method?

7. For most firms, there is some sales growth rate at which they could grow without needing any external financing, that is, where AFN = $0. How could you determine that growth rate? What variables under management's control would affect this **sustainable growth rate?**

9.1 Overview of Financial Planning

Most companies have strategic plans, operating plans, and financial plans.

9.1a Strategic Plans

Strategic plans usually have statements for mission, corporate scope, corporate objectives, and strategies.

Mission Statement

Strategic plans usually begin with a *mission statement*, which is a statement of the firm's overall purpose. Many companies are very clear about their corporate mission, and for most this is typical: "Our mission is to maximize shareowner value over time." Before the economic crisis of 2008 and 2009, many companies forgot

WEB

The textbook's Web site contains an *Excel* file that will guide you through the chapter's calculations. The file for this chapter is **Ch09 Tool Kit.xls**, and we encourage you to open the file and follow along as you read the chapter.

CORPORATE VALUATION AND FINANCIAL PLANNING

The value of a firm is determined by the size, timing, and risk of its expected future free cash flows (FCF). This chapter explains how to project financial statements and use them to calculate expected future free cash flows under different operating plans. The next chapter takes the analysis further, showing how to identify optimal plans and then design incentive compensation systems that will lead to optimal results.

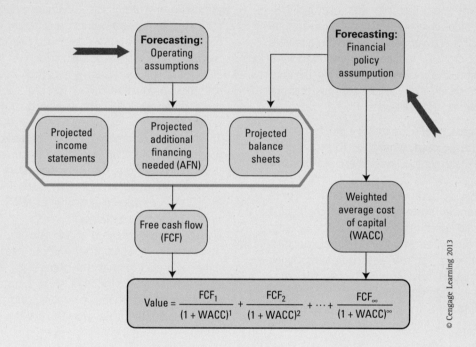

© Cengage Learning 2013

about the "over time" part, focusing instead on "maximizing the stock price on the date the CEO's options vest." Stockholders and directors have, fortunately, brought "over time" back into focus.

The goal of creating wealth for the company's owners is not as common abroad as it is in the United States. For example, Veba AG (now part of the German energy company E.ON), one of Germany's largest companies, created a stir when it made the following statement in its annual report: "Our commitment is to create value for you, our shareholders." This was quite different from the usual German model, because German companies generally have representatives from labor on their boards of directors and explicitly state their commitments to labor and a variety of other stakeholders. As one might expect, Veba's stock consistently outperformed the average German stock. As the trend in international investing continues, more and more non-U.S. companies are adopting a corporate purpose similar to that of Veba.

Corporate Scope

A firm's corporate scope defines its line or lines of business and its geographic area of operations. For example, Coca-Cola limits its products to soft drinks, but it operates on a global scale. PepsiCo followed Coke's lead by spinning off its food service businesses, as several studies have found that the market tends to value focused firms more highly than diversified ones.[1] During the bull market that led up to the 2008–2009 crash, many companies expanded into areas management knew little about, seeking sales growth as much or more than profits. For example, electric utilities bought insurance companies, and conservative banks bought shady mortgage originators. Those misguided ventures led to many disasters, so today companies are paying more attention to having a well-defined and reasonable corporate scope.

Statement of Corporate Objectives

This statement sets forth specific goals or targets to help operating managers focus on the firm's primary objectives. Most organizations have both quantitative and qualitative objectives. A typical quantitative objective might be attaining a 50% market share, a 20% ROE, and a 10% earnings growth rate. Qualitatively, their stated objective might be: "To provide better information systems to lower the cost and improve the efficiency of the U.S. medical system."

Corporate Strategies

Once a firm has defined its purpose, scope, and objectives, it must develop a strategy for achieving its goals. Corporate strategies are broad approaches rather than detailed plans. For example, one airline may have a strategy of offering no-frills service to a limited number of cities, while another's strategy may be to offer "a stateroom in the sky." Any such strategy should, of course, be compatible with the firm's purpose, scope, and objectives.

Overall, the strategic plan provides a "vision" of what the firm's top management expects, and without such a vision, the firm is not likely to be successful.

9.1b Operating Plans

Operating plans provide detailed implementation guidance to help the firm realize its strategic vision. These plans can be developed for any time horizon, but most companies use a 5-year horizon, with the plan being quite detailed for the first year but less and less specific for each succeeding year. The plan explains who is responsible for each particular function, when specific tasks are to be accomplished, targets for sales and profits, and the like. Large, multidivisional companies such as General Electric break their operating plans down by divisions, so each division has its own goals, mission, and plan for meeting its objectives. These plans are then consolidated to form the overall corporate plan.

---

1. See, for example, Philip G. Berger and Eli Ofek, "Diversification's Effect on Firm Value," *Journal of Financial Economics,* January 1995, pp. 39–66; and Larry Lang and René Stulz, "Tobin's Q, Corporate Diversification, and Firm Performance," *Journal of Political Economy,* Vol. 102, 1994, pp. 1248–1280.

9.1c The Financial Plan

The financial planning process generally involves five steps.

1. The firm forecasts financial statements under alternative versions of the operating plan in order to analyze the effects of different operating procedures on projected profits and financial ratios.

2. Next, it determines the amount of capital that will be needed to support the plan; that is, it finds out how much the new assets needed to achieve the target sales will cost, since without adequate capital, the plan obviously cannot be realized.

3. Then the firm forecasts the funds that will be generated internally. If internal funds are insufficient to cover the required new investment, then it must identify sources from which the required external capital can be raised, taking account of any constraints due to bond covenants that limit its debt ratio and other financial ratios. Market conditions must also be recognized. For example, in 2009 banks reduced many firms' lines of credit and also increased the fees and interest rates on such lines. This surprised firms that were not keeping up with conditions in financial markets.

4. The firm establishes a performance-based management compensation system that rewards employees for creating shareholder wealth. The emphasis here should be on the long run, not on profits over the next few quarters or even years. A failure in this area was an important factor leading to the worldwide financial and economic crisis that hit in 2008 and 2009.

5. Finally, management must monitor operations after implementing the plan to spot any deviations and then take corrective actions. Computer software is helping greatly here, and it's changing the way companies do business. In particular, corporate information systems are reducing the need for "middle managers" and flattening firms' management structures.

In the remainder of this chapter, we explain how to create a financial plan, including its three key components: (1) the sales forecast, (2) forecasted financial statements, and (3) methods for raising any needed external financing. Later, in Chapter 11, we discuss in more detail the relationships among incentives, compensation, and performance.

Self Test	Briefly explain the following terms: (1) mission statement, (2) corporate scope, (3) corporate objectives, and (4) corporate strategies.
	Briefly describe the key elements of an operating plan.
	Identify the five steps involved in the financial planning process as discussed in this section.

9.2 Sales Forecast

The **sales forecast** generally starts with a review of sales during the past 5 to 10 years, expressed in a graph such as that in Figure 9-1. The first part of the graph shows 5 years of historical sales for MicroDrive, the fictional firm we discussed in Chapters 7 and 8. The graph could have contained 10 years of sales data, but MicroDrive typically focuses on sales for the latest 5 years because its studies have shown that its future growth is more closely related to recent events than to the distant past.

Entire courses are devoted to forecasting sales, so we only touch on the basic elements here. However, forecasting the future sales growth rate always begins with

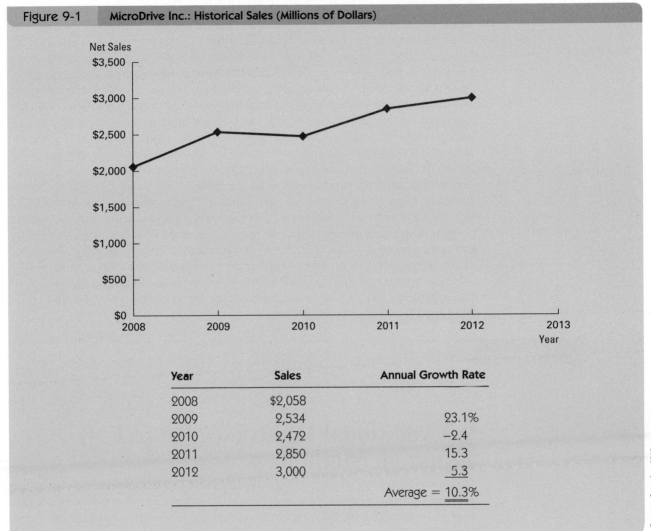

Figure 9-1   **MicroDrive Inc.: Historical Sales (Millions of Dollars)**

Year	Sales	Annual Growth Rate
2008	$2,058	
2009	2,534	23.1%
2010	2,472	−2.4
2011	2,850	15.3
2012	3,000	5.3
		Average = 10.3%

a look at past growth. MicroDrive's recent annual growth rates have averaged 10.3%, and the compound growth rate from 2008 to 2012 is the value for g in this equation:[2]

$$\$2,058(1 + g)^4 = \$3,000$$

The value of g can be found by solving the equation with a financial calculator. Enter N = 4, PV = −2058, PMT = 0, and FV = 3000; then, press I/YR to get g = 9.9%.[3]

No sensible manager would ever just forecast a continuation of past sales growth without taking account of current conditions in both the national and global economies, the firm's and its competitors' new products, planned advertising programs, and so on. But in the end, a sales forecast will emerge. In MicroDrive's case,

2. Unless we indicate otherwise, we report values from MicroDrive's financial statements in millions of dollars, as shown in Figure 9-1.
3. See this chapter's *Excel Tool Kit* for an explanation of projecting sales using a trend line or the average exponential growth rate.

the conclusion is that sales are most likely to grow at a 10% rate. Note, though, that actual sales could turn out to be materially higher or lower, depending on a number of factors that cannot be forecasted at this time.

If the sales forecast is off and the company does not have sufficient flexibility built into its plans, the consequences could be serious. First, if the market expands by *more* than MicroDrive has anticipated, the company will not be able to meet demand. Its customers will end up buying competitors' products, and MicroDrive will lose market share that might be hard to regain. On the other hand, if its projections are overly optimistic then it could wind up with too much plant, equipment, and inventory, which would hurt its profits, free cash flow, and intrinsic stock value. Moreover, if the firm had financed an expansion with debt, high interest charges and mandatory debt repayments would compound its problem. Thus, an accurate sales forecast is critical to the firm's well-being. After much discussion and analysis, MicroDrive's managers decided that a 10% increase in sales was the most appropriate forecast.

The firm's next questions include these: How much new capital will be needed to fund the increased sales? Can this capital be raised internally, or will new external funds be needed? And in view of current economic conditions, will it be feasible to raise the needed capital? We answer these questions in the following sections using two approaches: (1) the additional funds needed (AFN) equation method, and (2) the forecasted financial statements method.

Self Test	List some factors that should be considered when developing a sales forecast.
	Why is an accurate sales forecast critical to profitability?

9.3 Additional Funds Needed (AFN) Equation Method

MicroDrive is typical of most companies in that it expects growth in sales, which means its assets also must grow. Asset growth requires additional funds, so the firm may have to raise additional external capital if it has insufficient internal funds. If we assume that none of the firm's ratios will change (an assumption that we later modify), we can use a simple approach, the **additional funds needed (AFN)** equation method, to forecast financial requirements. The logic of the AFN equation approach is discussed in the next few sections.

9.3a Required Increase in Assets

In a steady-state situation in which no excess capacity exists, the firm must have additional plant and equipment, more delivery trucks, higher inventories, and so forth if sales are to increase. In addition, more sales will lead to more accounts receivable, and those receivables must be financed from the time of the sale until they are collected. Therefore, both fixed and current assets must increase if sales are to increase. Of course, if assets are to increase, liabilities and equity must also increase by a like amount to make the balance sheet balance.

9.3b Spontaneous Liabilities

The first sources of expansion funding are the "spontaneous" increases that will occur in MicroDrive's accounts payable and accrued wages and taxes. The company's suppliers give it 10 days to pay for inventory purchases, and since purchases will increase with sales, accounts payable will automatically rise. For example, if sales rise by 10% then inventory purchases will also rise by 10%, and this will cause accounts payable to rise spontaneously by the same 10%. Similarly, because the company pays workers every 2 weeks, more workers and a larger payroll will mean more accrued wages payable. Finally, higher expected income will mean more accrued income taxes, and its higher wage bill will mean more accrued withholding taxes. No interest normally is paid on these spontaneous funds, but their amount is limited by credit terms, contracts with workers, and tax laws. Therefore, *spontaneous funds will thus be used to the extent possible, but there is little flexibility in their usage.*

9.3c Addition to Retained Earnings

The second source of funds for expansion comes from net income. Part of MicroDrive's profit will be paid out in dividends, but the remainder will be reinvested in operating assets, as shown in the Assets section of the balance sheet; a corresponding amount will be reported as an addition to retained earnings in the Liabilities and equity section of the balance sheet. There is some flexibility in the amount of funds that will be generated from new reinvested earnings because dividends can be increased or decreased, but if the firm plans to hold its dividend steady or to increase it at a target rate, as most do, then flexibility is limited.

9.3d Calculating Additional Funds Needed (AFN)

If we start with the required new assets and then subtract both spontaneous funds and additions to retained earnings, we are left with the additional funds needed, or AFN. The AFN must come from *external sources*; hence it is sometimes called EFN. The typical sources of external funds are bank loans, new long-term bonds, new preferred stock, and newly issued common stock. The mix of the external funds used should be consistent with the firm's financial policies, especially its target debt ratio.

9.3e Using MicroDrive's Data to Implement the AFN Equation Method

Figure 9-2 reports MicroDrive's 2011 and 2012 financial statements.

Equation 9-1 summarizes the logic underlying the AFN equation method. Figure 9-3 defines the notation in Equation 9-1 and applies it to identify MicroDrive's AFN. The **additional funds needed (AFN) equation** is:

$$
\begin{array}{ccccc}
\text{Required} & & \text{Increase in} & \text{Increase in} & & \text{Additional} \\
\text{increase} & - & \text{spontaneous} & \text{retained} & = & \text{funds} \\
\text{in assets} & & \text{liabilities} & \text{earnings} & & \text{needed}
\end{array}
$$

$$
(A_0^*/S_0)\Delta S \; - \; (L_0^*/S_0)\Delta S \; - \; S_1 \times M \times (1 - \text{Payout Ratio}) \; = \; \text{AFN}
$$

(9–1)

We see from Part II of Figure 9-3 that, for sales to increase by $300 million, MicroDrive must increase assets by $200 million. Therefore, liabilities and capital must also increase by $200 million. Of this total, $20 million will come from spontaneous liabilities, and another $61.6 million will come from new retained earnings. The remaining $118.4 million must be raised from external sources—probably some

Figure 9-2   **MicroDrive's Most Recent Financial Statements (Millions of Dollars, Except for Per Share Data)**

	A	B	C	D	E	F	G	H
103	INCOME STATEMENTS		2011	2012	BALANCE SHEETS		2011	2012
104					*Assets*			
105	Sales		$2,850.0	$3,000.0	Cash		$15.0	$10.0
106	Costs except depreciation		2,500.0	2,617.0	ST Investments		65.0	0.0
107	Depreciation		90.0	100.0	Accounts receivable		315.0	375.0
108	Total operating costs		$2,590.0	$2,717.0	Inventories		415.0	615.0
109	EBIT		260.0	283.0	Total current assets		$810.0	$1,000.0
110	Less interest (INT)		60.0	88.0	Net plant and equip.		870.0	1,000.0
111	Earnings before taxes (EBT)		$200.0	$195.0	Total assets		$1,680.0	$2,000.0
112	Taxes (40%)		80.0	78.0				
113	Income before pref. dividends		$120.0	$117.0	*Liabilities and equity*			
114	Preferred dividends		4.0	4.0	Accounts payable		$30.0	$60.0
115	Net income for common (NI)		$116.0	$113.0	Accruals		130.0	140.0
116					Notes payable		60.0	110.0
117	Dividends to common (DIVs)		$53.0	$57.0	Total current liab.		$220.0	$310.0
118	Add. to retained earnings:				Long-term bonds		580.0	754.0
119	(NI – DIVs)		$63.0	$56.0	Total liabilities		$800.0	$1,064.0
120	Shares of common stock		50	50	Preferred stock		40.0	40.0
121	Earnings per share (EPS)		$2.32	$2.26	Common stock		130.0	130.0
122	Dividends per share (DPS)		$1.06	$1.14	Retained earnings		710.0	766.0
123	Price per share (P)		$26.00	$23.00	Total common equity		$840.0	$896.0
124					Total liab. & equity		$1,680.0	$2,000.0
125								

© Cengage Learning 2013

combination of short-term bank loans, long-term bonds, preferred stock, and common stock.

9.3f Key Factors in the AFN Equation

The AFN equation shows that external financing requirements depend on five key factors.

1. **Sales growth (g).** Rapidly growing companies require large increases in assets and a corresponding large amount of external financing, other things held constant. When capital is in short supply, as was the case during the financial crisis of 2009, companies may be forced to limit their growth.

2. **Capital intensity (A_0^*/S_0).** The amount of assets required per dollar of sales, A_0^*/S_0, is the **capital intensity ratio**, which has a major effect on capital requirements. Companies with relatively high assets-to-sales ratios require a relatively large amount of new assets for any given increase in sales; hence they have a greater need for external financing. If a firm can find a way to lower this ratio—for instance, by adopting a just-in-time inventory system, by going to two shifts in its manufacturing plants, or by outsourcing rather than manufacturing parts—then it can achieve a given level of growth with fewer assets and thus less new external capital.

3. **Spontaneous liabilities-to-sales ratio (L_0^*/S_0).** If a company can increase its spontaneously generated liabilities, this will reduce its need for external financing. One way of raising this ratio is by paying suppliers in, say, 20 days rather than 10 days. Such a change may be possible but, as we shall see in Chapter 21, it would probably have serious adverse consequences.

Figure 9-3   Additional Funds Needed (AFN) (Millions of Dollars)

	A	B	C	D	E	F	G	H	I
131	Part I. Inputs and Definitions								
132	S_0:		Last year's sales, i.e., 2012 sales:						$3,000
133	g:		Forecasted growth rate in sales:						10.00%
134	S_1:		Coming year's sales, i.e., 2013 sales = $S_0 \times (1 + g)$:						$3,300
135	gS_0:		Change in sales = $S_1 - S_0 = \Delta S$:						$300
136	$A_0{}^*$:		Assets that must increase to support the increase in sales:						$2,000
137	$A_0{}^* / S_0$:		Required assets per dollar of sales:						66.67%
138	$L_0{}^*$:		Last year's spontaneous liabilities i.e., payables + accruals:						$200
139	$L_0{}^* / S_0$:		Spontaneous liabilities per dollar of sales:						6.67%
140	Profit margin (M):		2012 profit margin = net income/sales:						3.77%
141	Payout ratio (POR):		Last year's dividends / net income = % of income paid out:						50.44%
142									
143	Part II. Additional Funds Needed (AFN) to Support Growth								
144									
145	AFN =	Required Increase in Assets			–	Spontaneous Increase		–	Addition to Retained
146	=	$(A_0{}^*/S_0)\Delta S$			–	$(L_0{}^*/S_0)\Delta S$		–	$S_1 \times M \times (1 - POR)$
147					–			–	
148	=	$(A_0{}^*/S_0)(gS_0)$			–	$(L_0{}^*/S_0)(gS_0)$		–	$(1+g)S_0 \times M \times (1 - POR)$
149					–			–	
150	=	(0.667)($300)			–	(0.067)($300)		–	$3,300(0.0377)(1 - 0.504)
151	=	$200			–	$20.00		–	$61.60
152	AFN =	$118.40 million							

Notes:

1. Under the assumed conditions, the firm must raise $118.42 million externally to support its planned growth. However, the model assumes (1) that no excess capacity existed in 2012, so all assets were needed to produce the indicated sales; and (2) that the key ratios will remain constant at their 2012 levels. We explain later how to relax these assumptions, but it is better to use forecasted financial statements to deal with these issues, as we do on **Tab 2** of the *Excel Tool Kit* model.
2. Under the conditions set forth in Figure 9-3, a growth rate of 3.21% could be achieved without any AFN. This 3.21% is called the "sustainable growth rate," and we explain how it is calculated in a later section and also in the chapter's *Excel **Tool Kit*** model.

4. **Profit margin (M = Net Income/Sales).** The higher the profit margin, the more net income is available to support increases in assets—and hence the less the need for external financing. A firms' profit margin is normally as high as management can get it, but sometimes a change in operations can boost the sales price or reduce costs, thus raising the margin further. If so, this will permit a faster growth rate with less external capital.

5. **Payout ratio (POR = DPS/EPS).** The less of its income a company distributes as dividends, the larger its addition to retained earnings—and hence the less its need for external capital. Companies typically like to keep their dividends stable or to increase them at a steady rate—stockholders like stable, dependable dividends, so such a dividend policy will generally lower the cost of equity and thus maximize the stock price. So even though reducing the dividend is one way a company can reduce its need for external capital, companies generally resort to this method only if they are under financial duress.

9.3g The Self-Supporting Growth Rate

One interesting question is: "What is the maximum growth rate the firm could achieve if it had no access to external capital?" This rate is called the "self-supporting growth rate," and it can be found as the value of g that, when used in the AFN equation, results in an AFN of zero. We first replace ΔS in the AFN equation with gS_0 and S_1 with $(1+g)S_0$ so that the only unknown is g; we then solve for g to obtain the following equation for the self-supporting growth rate:

$$(9\text{-}2) \qquad \text{Self-supporting } g = \frac{M(1 - POR)(S_0)}{A_0^* - L_0^* - M(1 - POR)(S_0)}$$

The definitions of the terms used in this equation are shown in Figure 9-3.

If the firm has any positive earnings and pays out less than 100% in dividends, then it will have some additions to retained earnings, and those additions could be combined with spontaneous funds to enable the company to grow at some rate without having to raise external capital. As explained in the chapter's *Excel **Tool Kit***, this value can be found either algebraically or with *Excel's* Goal Seek function. For MicroDrive, the self-supporting growth rate is 3.21%; this means it could grow at that rate even if capital markets dried up completely, with everything else held constant.

WEB

See *Ch09 Tool Kit.xls* on the textbook's Web site for details.

9.3h A Potential Problem with the AFN Equation: Excess Capacity

As noted previously, when we use the AFN equation we are implicitly assuming that the key ratios remain constant at their base-year levels. However, this assumption may not always be true. For example, in 2010 many firms were operating at significantly less than their full capacity because of the recession. Let's suppose MicroDrive had been operating its fixed assets at only 50% of capacity. It could then double its sales, which is a 100% increase, without adding any fixed assets at all. Similarly, if it had 25% more inventories at the start of the year than it required, it could increase sales by 25% without increasing its inventories. We could adjust the AFN equation to account for excess capacity, and we explain how to do so in the *Tool Kit*. However, a far better procedure is simply to recognize that while the AFN is useful for quickly obtaining a "back of the envelope" estimate of external financing requirements, the forecasted financial statements method, which is explained in the next section, is vastly superior for realistic financial planning.

Self Test

If all ratios are expected to remain constant, an equation can be used to forecast AFN. Write out the equation and briefly explain it.

Describe how the following factors affect external capital requirements: (1) payout ratio, (2) capital intensity, (3) profit margin.

In what sense do accounts payable and accruals provide "spontaneous funds" to a growing firm?

Is it possible for the calculated AFN to be negative? If so, what would this imply?

Refer to data in the MicroDrive example presented, but now assume that MicroDrive's growth rate in sales is forecasted to be 15% rather than 10%. If all ratios remain constant, what would the AFN be? **($205.6 million)**

9.4 Forecasted Financial Statements Method

As its name implies, the objective of the **forecasted financial statements (FFS) method** is to project a complete set of financial statements. Because financial statements contain numerous accounts, forecasting is almost always done using computer software such as *Excel*. There are many different ways to do this, and entire books have been written on the topic.[4] In the following analysis, we explain one particular approach that we have found to be effective, particularly for a company considering changes to its capital structure or dividend policy.[5] In addition, it is easy to modify this forecasting approach to incorporate changes in assumptions.

Forecasting financial statements is conceptually similar to the AFN equation, but it is easy to get lost in the details. *Excel*'s calculations don't necessarily follow this sequence, but keep these conceptual steps in mind as we describe MicroDrive's forecasted financial statements.

1. Forecast the operating items on the income statement and balance sheet; these include sales, costs, operating assets, and spontaneous operating liabilities. Notice that these are the items required to calculate free cash flow.
2. Forecast items that depend on the firm's choice of financial policies, such as the dividend payout policy and the planned financing from debt and equity.
3. Forecast interest expense and preferred dividends, given the levels of debt and preferred stock that were forecast according to the financing plan.
4. Use the forecasted interest expense and preferred dividends to complete the income statement.
5. Determine the total common dividend payments.
6. Issue or repurchase additional common stock to make the balance sheets balance.
7. Calculate AFN as the amount of funding needed in excess of the amount of funding planned.

Forecasting is an iterative process. It begins with a set of initial operating assumptions and financial policies. The resulting forecasted statements are used to estimate free cash flow, EPS, and financial ratios. Managers then go through a set of "what if" questions and examine their operating assumptions and financial policies, as we describe next.

9.4a Background on the Company and the Forecast

MicroDrive's board recently installed a new management team: A new CEO, CFO, marketing manager, sales manager, inventory manager, and credit manager—only

---

4. For a much more detailed treatment of financial forecasting, see P. Daves, M. Ehrhardt, and R. Shrieves, *Corporate Valuation: A Guide for Managers and Investors* (Mason, OH: Thomson/South-Western, 2004).

5. One point about *Excel* models is worth noting. It is generally fairly easy to set up a model to study a given issue, but the complexity of the model rises exponentially as you attempt to deal with more and more different issues within the model. Therefore, in our experience it's generally better to develop limited-scope, single-issue models and then modify them to create new models—rather than trying to develop one model that can "do everything." Also, and crucially, it's much easier to debug single-purpose models than all-inclusive ones. Furthermore, if others are planning to use and perhaps modify the model, it's far easier for them to work with a simple model. There have been numerous occasions when we were given a complex model, had a hard time understanding it, and then abandoned it to make our own model that could do what we needed. These statements about "keeping it simple" are, of course, more appropriate for time-constrained students than for business people.

the production manager was retained. The new team was charged with improving the company's performance. As we noted in Chapter 8, many of MicroDrive's ratios are below industry averages.

The management team met in late 2012, when the industry was in a recession, for a 3-day retreat. The new CFO developed an *Excel* model to forecast financial statements under several different sets of assumptions, or scenarios. The first scenario assumes that operations maintain the status quo, the second that operations improve, and the third that conditions deteriorate. During the 3-day meeting, the CFO developed a fourth scenario based on discussions among the managers regarding changes that could be made to improve the firm's performance. (We report the details of these discussions in a later section.) They concluded that many changes could be implemented almost immediately and that the effects of those changes would be reflected in the 2013 results.

WEB

See *Ch09 Tool Kit.xls* on the textbook's Web site for details.

9.4b Input Data for the Forecast: Alternative Scenarios

The forecast begins with Figure 9-4, which shows the data used in the three preliminary forecasts as well as the final forecast. Industry averages and MicroDrive's actual operating and financial data for the most recent year are given in Columns C and D. Ignore Column E for the moment and look at Columns F, G, H, and I, which show the inputs used in four alternative scenarios.

Inputs for the Status Quo Scenario

The Status Quo scenario in Column F assumes that the firm in 2013 has essentially the same operating and financial ratios as it had in 2012, except that its rate of sales growth increases from 5.26% to 10%. Operating costs, operating assets, and operating spontaneous liabilities are assumed to be the same percentage of sales in 2013 as in 2012. Depreciation is assumed to be a fixed percentage of the net plant and equipment.

The components of MicroDrive's investor-supplied capital are notes payable, long-term bonds, preferred stock, and common equity. For this initial forecast, the target proportions of these components as percentages of total investor-supplied capital are held constant. The interest rates on its debt and the dividend rate on its preferred stock are assumed to remain at 2012 levels. The payout ratio for total common dividends is also assumed to stay at approximately the 2012 level in the Status Quo scenario.

If additional financing is needed, it is assumed that new shares of common stock can be issued at $23 per share, the 2012 year-end price. If a surplus of funds arises, then MicroDrive will pay down some of its debt and repurchase shares of preferred and common stock.

Inputs for the Best-Case Scenario

The data in Column G are for the Best case. Here the CEO assumes that MicroDrive is able to achieve industry average operating results immediately. However, the CEO also assumes that the company continues to use its current capital structure, which calls for more debt than the industry average. The improved operating performance would lower the costs of debt and preferred stock. However, the higher than average debt level would offset this factor to some extent, so the end result would be somewhat higher than industry average cost rates for notes payable, long-term debt, and preferred stock.

Figure 9-4	Input Data for the Forecast (Millions, Except for Percentages and Per Share Data)

	A	B	C	D	E	F	G	H	I
84									
85			2012			2013			
86	Inputs		Actual Values			Forecasted Input Values for Scenarios			
87					Active				
88			Industry	MicroDrive	Scenario:	Status Quo	Best	Worst	Final
89	Operating Ratios:				Final				
90	Growth rate in sales		10.00%	5.26%	10.00%	10.00%	10.00%	−10.00%	10.00%
91	Op costs except depr'n / Sales		83.00%	87.23%	86.00%	87.23%	83.00%	92.21%	86.00%
92	Depr'n / Net plant & equip.		10.20%	10.00%	10.20%	10.00%	10.00%	10.00%	10.20%
93	Cash / Sales		0.25%	0.33%	0.25%	0.33%	0.33%	0.33%	0.25%
94	Accounts Rec. / Sales		9.80%	12.50%	11.00%	12.50%	9.80%	15.00%	11.00%
95	Inventory / Sales		11.11%	20.50%	16.00%	20.50%	11.11%	25.50%	16.00%
96	Net plant & equip. / Sales		33.33%	33.33%	33.33%	33.33%	33.33%	40.00%	33.33%
97	Accounts Pay. / Sales		2.00%	2.00%	2.00%	2.00%	2.00%	2.00%	2.00%
98	Accruals / Sales		4.00%	4.67%	4.00%	4.67%	2.00%	4.67%	4.00%
99	Tax rate:		40.00%	40.00%	40.00%	40.00%	40.00%	40.00%	40.00%
100	Financing Data:								
101	Notes payable/Investor-sup cap		5.00%	6.11%	5.00%	6.11%	6.11%	6.11%	5.00%
102	LT bonds/Investor-sup capital		32.00%	41.89%	37.00%	41.89%	41.89%	41.89%	37.00%
103	Pref. stock/Investor-sup cap.		3.00%	2.22%	3.00%	2.22%	2.22%	2.22%	3.00%
104	Comm equity/Investor-sup cap		60.00%	49.78%	55.00%	49.78%	49.78%	49.78%	55.00%
105	Interest rate on notes payable		8.00%	9.00%	8.50%	9.00%	8.50%	11.00%	8.50%
106	Interest rate on L-T bonds		10.00%	11.00%	10.50%	11.00%	10.50%	11.50%	10.50%
107	Dividend rate on pfd stock		9.00%	10.00%	9.50%	10.00%	9.50%	10.00%	9.50%
108	Target dividend payout ratio		40.00%	50.44%	40.00%	50.67%	50.67%	50.67%	40.00%
109			2012	2013	2013	2013	2013	2013	2013
110	Key Results		MicroDrive	Final	Status Quo	Best	Worst	Final	
111	Free cash flow (FCF)		−$175.20	$208.63	$6.98	$401.59	−$141.01	$208.63	
112	Return on inv. capital (ROIC)		9.43%	11.65%	9.44%	16.21%	3.07%	11.65%	
113	Earnings per share (EPS)		$2.26	$3.11	$2.42	$5.07	−$0.10	$3.11	
114	Return on equity (ROE)		12.61%	15.70%	12.60%	25.97%	−0.55%	15.70%	
115	# Shares, end-of-year		50.00	50.06	51.23	42.54	54.62	50.06	
116	Dividends per share (DPS)		$1.14	$1.24	$1.23	$2.57	$0.00	$1.24	

Inputs for the Worst-Case Scenario

The data in Column H, the Worst case, assume a continued long, bad recession, in which case the growth rate would be negative and the operating and financial ratios would be poor. It is likely that the stock price would decline during the year, but the CFO assumes that new shares could still have been issued at the beginning of the year for $23 per share, before investors and managers learned how bad things were going to get.

Inputs for the Final Scenario

The fourth set of input data, given in Column I and called "Final," was developed during the 3-day management conference held in late 2012. All of the operating executives were there, and all aspects of the business (including the ratios shown in Figure 9-4) were discussed. Some of the executives were relatively optimistic while others were relatively pessimistic, but all tried their best to be realistic. We will discuss these Final inputs in the next section.

Inputs for the Active Scenario

Now look at Column E in Figure 9-4, the one labeled "Active Scenario: Final." With *Excel*'s Scenario Manager, you choose a scenario and *Excel* replaces the input data in Column E with the data for the chosen scenario (we had chosen the Final scenario when we created Figure 9-4, so that is the scenario showing in Column E). These inputs are then linked to the section of the spreadsheet where the financial statements are forecast. (The forecasted statements are shown in Figure 9-5.)

After forecasting the financial statements, the model calculates performance measures, including the forecasted free cash flow (FCF), return on invested capital (ROIC), EPS, ROE, number of shares at the end of the year, and DPS. These six key results also are shown at the bottom of Figure 9-4; we will discuss them later.

9.4c Discussion of the Forecasted Operating Input Data

The CFO had taken a two-part computer course in college. The first module was taught by a computer science expert who focused on the mechanics of programming and computer usage in general. The second module was taught by an economist who discussed how to apply computers to specific tasks, including various types of forecasting. The economist's favorite term was GIGO, which stands for "garbage in, garbage out," and she repeated it constantly. No matter how well a model is set up, if the inputs used aren't accurate then the output won't be accurate, either. The CFO began the discussion by reminding the management team of this critical fact.

The sales growth rate is the first input item shown in Figure 9-4 and is followed by the most important driver of profitability, the ratio of operating costs (excluding depreciation) to sales. MicroDrive's 2012 operating cost ratio was 87.23%, well above the 83% industry average. This ratio is affected by operating costs, sales prices, and unit sales, and it was discussed at length during the planning conference. The CFO showed the forecasted results for the status quo, best-case, and worst-case scenarios, after which the CEO led a discussion of what the firm could actually achieve in 2013. After much discussion, the management team concluded that, because of licensing fees and other costs, it was not feasible for the firm to achieve the industry average operating cost ratio of 83% in the foreseeable future. However, the team believed that a figure of 86%, down from 2012's 87.23%, was "attainable." They agreed that over time it might be possible to reduce this ratio a bit further, but that 86% was the most realistic choice to use in the forecast.

Intrinsic value is affected by many factors, including the level of inventory. If MicroDrive carries too much inventory then storage costs, deterioration, and obsolescence will drive up operating costs. The CFO had studied the inventory/sales ratio earlier and had pointed out that MicroDrive had almost twice as much inventory for its sales as an average firm in the industry. The CEO stated that the production, sales, and purchasing managers were jointly responsible for inventory in MicroDrive's supply chain. The managers said that they had already been working on a plan to fix this problem. Because MicroDrive's production facilities are farther from their suppliers and customers than are those of most other firms in the industry, MicroDrive must hold a higher than average level of inventory to avoid running out of stock if sales surge. In the end, it was agreed that the inventory/sales ratio could be lowered from 20.5% to 16%, a significant improvement but still above the 11.11% industry average.

The CFO also pointed out that accounts receivable were much higher than the industry average level. This meant that too much capital was tied up in receivables. If a firm continues to sell to a customer who does not pay on time, the account balance will rise significantly, and if the customer then defaults, the selling firm will suffer a larger bad debt loss than if it had stopped selling to the customer sooner. In addition, collection costs rise with the amount of old receivables, which is another reason to keep a tight rein on credit operations. During the discussion, the sales manager noted that tightening its credit policy would lose the firm some sales. However, the lost sales would not be excessive, because most of the late-paying customers were financially sound but were just taking advantage of the "float" MicroDrive was giving them. After the discussion, the credit manager, sales manager, and treasurer jointly agreed that it would be feasible to reduce the receivables/sales ratio to 11% in 2013. That was still above the 9.8% industry average but below MicroDrive's 2012 level of 12.5%. Therefore, 11% was built into the final forecast.

The CFO also brought up the net plant/sales ratio but noted that this ratio was in line with the industry average—the production manager, who was not replaced during the management change, had been forecasting sales accurately and holding equipment purchases to the level actually required. This was facilitated by the outsourcing of production to make up for shortfalls if more orders came during a given period than had been expected. This smart use of outsourcing enabled the firm to operate without carrying excess capacity in "normal" times in order to meet demand when orders surged. Thus, the 2012 ratio of 33.3% for net plant and equipment to sales was used in the forecast.

9.4d Financial Policy Issues

The discussion next turned to two key financial policies: capital structure and dividends. The CFO noted that MicroDrive's debt ratio was significantly above the industry average. This high leverage boosted ROE and EPS during good times, but it also raised the interest rates for debt as well as the required return on common stock. Further, an excessive amount of debt increased the risk of bankruptcy and reduced the firm's ability to maintain stable operations in times of stress. The treasurer noted that the company's banks were concerned about its high debt usage and that banks nationwide were reducing the credit lines of companies deemed to have too much debt. MicroDrive's credit lines had not been reduced to date, but if the firm were to have even one bad quarter then a reduction might well occur, and that would be devastating. Credit is the lifeblood of a business, and if its credit were curtailed then MicroDrive might not be able to purchase supplies, pay workers, and so on, which would be fatal. After this discussion, the decision was made to increase the common equity ratio from its current 49.8% level of investor-supplied capital to 55.0%.[6]

The discussion then turned to dividend policy. In recent years, MicroDrive has been increasing the dividend by about 8% per year, and the board of directors has stated that it would like to continue this policy. However, the CFO recently disclosed to the board that many companies that formerly increased their dividends at a steady rate had re-examined that policy and had lowered the targeted rate of increase. An 8% annual increase during the long boom from the 1980s until 2008 had been feasible, but in the current and likely future economic climate a different policy might be necessary. The CFO also pointed out that the average mature firm in the industry was distributing about 40% of its earnings as dividends, compared with MicroDrive's 50.4%. At the conclusion of this discussion, it was decided to use the 40% industry average payout for the forecast, determine the resulting dividend per share, review the resulting

---

6. Capital structure decisions are discussed in detail in Chapter 15.

performance measures, and then discuss the dividend policy recommendation with the board. The CEO agreed with this plan but clearly hoped that the forecast would support a dividend growth rate of 8% or more.

The next item discussed was the timing of new financing. The treasurer argued that it would be best to issue any required new stock early in the year to ensure that these funds would be available—stock prices are volatile, and the market for new stock could slam shut later in the year. Also, if the firm raised equity early, that would make it easier to issue new debt later. The CFO and CEO agreed, so the decision was made to sell any required new stock early and to borrow throughout the year as needed.

A question was asked about the price at which new stock would be sold. The CFO noted that the most recent price was $23 per share, and that was the most likely price at which new shares could be sold early in the year. Interest rates on the existing debt floated, moving up and down with rates in the general economy and the company's financial condition.[7] The CFO thought interest rates probably would fluctuate to some extent, but there was no more reason to believe that rates would go up than go down. However, by mid-year the company's own financial condition would be known sufficiently well to influence its cost of debt. Therefore, as indicated in Figure 9-4, the rates vary depending on the scenarios—low rates under good conditions and high rates under bad conditions. The preferred dividend also floated, so its rate also varied with the scenarios.

Based on an earlier back-of-the-envelope calculation using the AFN model, the CFO had concluded that if operations improved significantly, the firm might not need any new external funds and might even have a surplus. For example, if the profit margin could be increased, this would lower external capital requirements. Even more importantly, if the ratios of inventories and accounts receivable to sales could be lowered, as the management team had discussed earlier, then this would greatly reduce the need for new capital, especially during 2013. Those considerations prompted the CEO to raise the following question: "If excess funds become available, what should we do with them?" The CFO had actually considered several possibilities: (1) increase the dividend, (2) repurchase stock and repay debt in amounts that would keep the capital structure constant, (3) invest excess funds in marketable securities, or (4) embark on a merger program to acquire other firms. They decided that the best alternative for modeling purposes was to simply use surplus funds to repay debt and buy back stock. If the surplus was projected to extend on into the long run, then a strategic decision would have to be made regarding what to do with it, but that would require input from the board.

Debt could be repaid at book value and preferred stock repurchased at close to book value. If the common stock repurchase occurred early in the year, then it could probably be bought at close to the current price. This brought up the question of when any surplus funds would actually be available—would they be available early or late, or would they come in regularly throughout the year? It might make sense to *raise* new funds early, but excess funds could not be *used* until they were actually in hand, and that would probably occur throughout the year. The decision was made to repurchase stock early in the year and repay debt later in the year. The CFO also planned to revisit this issue when developing the projected 2013 cash budget. (Cash budgets are discussed in Chapter 21; they are typically done on a monthly basis.)

---

7. All of the debt—both short-term bank loans and long-term bonds—had floating rates. The spread between the bank loan rate and the London Interbank Offered Rate (LIBOR) was based on the firm's interest coverage ratio (EBIT to interest charges). The long-term bond rate was determined similarly. The bank loan rate was reset quarterly, and the long-term rate was reset every 6 months.

9.4e The Forecasted Financial Statements

Using input from the Final scenario as shown in column E of Figure 9-4, MicroDrive's forecasted financial statements (balance sheet and income statement) are reported in Figure 9-5.[8] The following points explain how to forecast the statements shown in Figure 9-5.

WEB

See *Ch09 Tool Kit.xls* on the textbook's Web site for details.

1. Forecast next year's sales based on the assumed growth rate: $S_{2013} = S_{2012} \times (1 + g)$.
2. Forecast each of the operating assets (cash, accounts receivable, inventories, and net plant and equipment) and the spontaneous current liabilities (accounts payable and accruals) as a percentage of forecasted sales. This completes the assets section of the balance sheet and partially completes the liabilities section.
3. Use the forecasted operating data from Step 2 to calculate the required investor-supplied capital, which is found as Total assets – (Accounts payable + Accruals). Note that this amount of investor-supplied capital is precisely the amount of funding that, when combined with Accounts payable and Accruals, will make the balance sheet balance.
4. Multiply the investor-supplied capital found in Step 3 by the inputs for the target capital structure percentages shown in Figure 9-4 to forecast the amounts of notes payable, long-term bonds, preferred stock, and total common equity. This completes the balance sheet except for dividing the forecasted total common equity into its two components, common stock and retained earnings.
5. Calculate operating costs as a percentage of forecasted sales and calculate depreciation as a percentage of forecasted net plant and equipment. Subtract these costs from sales to find EBIT.
6. It is assumed that new debt will be borrowed throughout the year, so interest expenses will be based on the average amount of debt outstanding during the year. This amount is equal to the average of the beginning-of-year debt and the end-of-year debt forecast in Step 4. Multiply this average by the interest rate to determine the forecasted interest expense. Note that we have separate lines for notes payable interest expense and long-term bond interest expense since their interest rates differ.
7. Subtract interest expense from EBIT to find taxable income (EBT). Calculate taxes and subtract them from EBT to get net income before preferred dividends.
8. Forecast preferred dividends in a similar manner as the forecasted interest expense in Step 6: (1) find the average amount of preferred stock outstanding during the year and then (2) multiply it by the preferred stock's dividend rate.
9. Subtract the forecasted preferred dividends from the net income before preferred dividends to find the net income available to common stockholders.
10. Multiply the net income by the target payout ratio to forecast the total amount of common dividends paid. If net income is negative, set common dividends to zero.
11. Subtract common dividends from net income to find the addition to retained earnings.
12. The forecasted total retained earnings shown on the balance sheet is equal to the prior year's retained earnings plus the addition to retained earnings calculated in Step 11.
13. The forecasted total common stock must be equal to the difference between forecasted total common equity from Step 4 and the forecasted retained earnings balance from Step 12: Common stock = Total common equity – Retained earnings.

---

8. Columns E and I are identical in Figure 9-4. *Excel*'s Scenario Manager replaces the values in Column E with the values shown in Column I when the Final scenario is selected. Similarly, the Scenario Manager replaces data in Column E with the values shown in Columns F, G, or H when those scenarios are selected.

Figure 9-5   **Forecasted Financial Statements (Millions of Dollars, Except for Per Share Data)**

	A	B	C	D	E	F	G
129	Scenario Shown: Final						Final
130			Most Recent				Forecast
131	Part 1. Balance Sheet		2012	Factors	Basis for 2013 Forecast		2013
132	*Assets*						
133	Cash		$10.0	0.25%	Factor × 2013 Sales		$8.25
134	Accounts receivable		375.0	11.00%	Factor × 2013 Sales		$363.00
135	Inventories		615.0	16.00%	Factor × 2013 Sales		$528.00
136	Total current assets		$1,000.0				$899.25
137	Net plant and equipment		1,000.0	33.33%	Factor × 2013 Sales		$1,100.00
138	Total assets (TA)		$2,000.0				$1,999.25
139	*Liabilities and equity*						
140	Accounts payable		$60.0	2.00%	Factor × 2013 Sales		$66.00
141	Accruals		140.0	4.00%	Factor × 2013 Sales		$132.00
142	Notes payable[a]		110.0	5.00%	% of investor-sup. cap.		$90.06
143	Total current liabilities		$310.0				$288.06
144	Long-term bonds[a]		754.0	37.00%	% of investor-sup. cap.		$666.46
145	Total liabilities		$1,064.0				$954.52
146	Preferred stock[a]		$40.0	3.00%	% of investor-sup. cap.		$54.04
147	Common stock		130.0		Tot. Com. Eq − Ret. Earn		$131.35
148	Retained earnings		766.0		Old RE + Add. to RE		$859.34
149	Total common equity[a]		$896.0	55.00%	% of investor-sup. cap.		$990.69
150	Total liabilities and equity		$2,000.0				$1,999.25
151	[a] Investor-supplied capital		$1,800.0		TA − accts. pay. − accruals		$1,801.25
152	Scenario Shown: Final						Final
153			Most Recent				Forecast
154	Part 2. Income Statement		2012	Factor	Basis for 2013 Forecast		2013
155	Sales		$3,000.0	110%	Factor × 2012 Sales		$3,300.00
156	Costs except depreciation		2,617.0	86.00%	Factor × 2013 Sales		$2,838.00
157	Depreciation		100.0	10.20%	Factor × 2013 Net plant		$112.20
158	Total operating costs		$2,717.0				$2,950.20
159	EBIT		$283.0				$349.80
160	Less: Interest on notes		9.9	8.50%	Interest rate × Avg notes		$8.50
161	Interest on bonds		78.1	10.50%	Interest rate × Avg bonds		$74.57
162	Earnings before taxes (EBT)		$195.0				$266.72
163	Taxes (40%)		78.0	40.00%	Tax rate × 2013 EBT		$106.69
164	NI before preferred dividends		$117.0				$160.03
165	Preferred dividends		4.0	9.50%	Pfd div rate × Avg preferred		$4.47
166	NI available to common		$113.0				$155.57
167	Dividends paid out		$57.0	40.00%	Net income × Payout rate		$62.23
168	Addition to retained earnings		$56.0		Net income − Dividends		$93.34
169	Change in shares outstanding				(Change in Com. stk.)/P_{2012}		0.06
170	Ending shares outstanding		50.00		$Shares_{2012} + \Delta$ shares		50.06
171	Earnings per share, EPS		$2.26		Net income/Total shares		$3.11
172	Dividends per share, DPS		$1.14		Total dividends/Total shares		$1.24

Note: Calculations in the model have been shown to one decimal, so rounding differences may occur.

© Cengage Learning 2013

14. The required additional dollars of common stock issued or repurchased are equal to the change in common stock: Additional dollars of stock issued or repurchased = Common stock in 2013 − Common stock in 2012. If the amount is negative, it means that stock will be repurchased rather than issued.

15. The number of new shares either issued or repurchased is equal to the additional dollars of common stock found in Step 14 divided by the price per share. Because the stock is assumed to be sold at the beginning of 2013, the assumed stock price is $23, the price at the end of 2012. We calculate this as: Change in shares = (Additional dollars of common stock) ÷ (Stock price at the beginning of the year).
16. The number of shares outstanding at the end of the year is equal to the number of outstanding shares at the beginning of the year plus the change in the number of shares calculated in Step 15.

9.4f Analyzing the Forecasted Results

After the Final set of inputs had been chosen, the CFO created a summary sheet showing key results for the different scenarios, as shown in Figure 9-6. After projecting the key results on a big screen, the team discussed each of the scenarios. Everyone dismissed the worst-case results, because if things started getting that bad there would be an emergency meeting in which actions would be taken to modify the plan. Similarly, the status quo and best-case results were given short shrift, and then the team focused on the Final scenario results.

The jump in EPS looked good, and even with the assumed 40% payout ratio, DPS rose by about 9%, which pleased the CEO.

The ROE improved nicely, rising from 12.6% to 15.7%, which exceeded the industry average. However, the CFO pointed out that the firm's debt ratio, even after the capital structure change, still exceeded the industry average, and that its greater leverage was largely responsible for the above-average ROE.

Free cash flow was projected to make a tremendous improvement, from −$175 million in 2012 to +$209 million in 2013. The CFO noted, though, that a similar improvement would not occur in the future, because most of the gain in free cash flow

Figure 9-6   Summary of Key Results for Forecasted Scenarios (Millions, Except for Per Share Data)

	A	B	C	D	E	F	G	H
240			2012 Actual			2013 Forecasts		
241			Industry	MicroDrive				
242	Key Results				Final	Status Quo	Best	Worst
243	Net operating profit after taxes		NA	$170	$210	$187	$271	$61
244	Net operating working capital		NA	$800	$701	$880	$569	$922
245	Total operating capital		NA	$1,800	$1,801	$1,980	$1,669	$2,002
246	FCF = NOPAT − Δ op. capital		NA	−$175	$209	$7	$402	−$141
247	Return on invested capital		11.0%	9.4%	11.7%	9.5%	16.2%	3.1%
248	EPS		NA	$2.26	$3.11	$2.43	$5.07	−$0.10
249	DPS		NA	$1.14	$1.24	$1.23	$2.57	$0.00
250	Return on equity (ROE)		15.0%	12.6%	15.7%	12.6%	26.0%	−0.5%
251	Return on assets (ROA)		9.0%	5.7%	7.8%	5.7%	12.0%	−0.2%
252	Inventory turnover		9.0	4.9	6.3	4.9	9.0	3.9
253	Days sales outstanding		36.0	45.6	40.2	45.6	35.8	54.8
254	Total liabilities / TA		46.0%	53.2%	47.7%	53.2%	51.8%	52.3%
255	Times interest earned		6.0	3.2	4.2	3.2	5.3	1.0
256	Shares outstanding		NA	50.00	50.06	51.22	42.54	54.62
257	Payout ratio		40.0%	50.4%	40.0%	50.7%	50.7%	0.0%
258	AFN[a]		NA	$224	−$92	$118	−$237	$208

260 [a]The AFN equation calculates the additional financing required compared to the most recent year. With
261 forecasted financial statements, AFN is the additional financing over the planned amount of financing and
262 is calculated as AFN = required assets − planned liabilites and equity = TA − Accts. pay. − Accruals −
263 Planned NP − Planned LT bonds − Planned pf. stk − Planned common stk − RE. Here, planned NP,
264 bonds, pf. stk, and common stock are equal to their current levels.

was attributable to the one-time reduction in inventories and accounts receivable. AFN, the last item in Figure 9-6, is the additional funding that would be required if no additional notes payable, bonds, preferred stock, or common stock were issued. AFN is negative, indicating a surplus of funds in 2013, and is negative for the same reason free cash flow is positive—the reduction in inventories and accounts receivable. The lower payout and higher profit margin also helped reduce the AFN, but the one-time reduction in inventories and receivables was the key driver here.

The forecasted statement of cash flows in Figure 9-7 tells a similar story: (1) cash flow from operations is positive and large (with large cash flows resulting from improved asset utilization); (2) cash flow from investments is negative because of the expansion in fixed assets needed to support growth; and (3) the cash flow from financing activities shows that MicroDrive would be able to pay large dividends and reduce its debt.

At the conclusion of the CFO's summary, the CEO said that the firm would be in great shape and that nice bonuses and stock options would result if the targets were met and maintained over the long run.

9.4f Alternative Financial Policies and Multi-Year Forecasts

When the CEO and CFO presented the plan to the board of directors, the board was pleased overall but had a few questions. Several board members, including the

Figure 9-7   Forecasted Statement of Cash Flows (Millions of Dollars, Except for Per Share Data)

	A	B	C	D	E	F
268	Scenario Shown: Final				Actual	Forecast
269					2012	2013
270	Operating Activities					
271	Net Income before preferred dividends				$117.0	$160.0
272	Noncash adjustments					
273	Depreciation and amortization				100.0	112.2
274	Due to changes in working capital					
275	Increase(−)/Decrease(+) in accounts receivable				−60.0	12.0
276	Increase(−)/Decrease(+) in inventories				−200.0	87.0
277	Increase(−)/Decrease(+) in payables				30.0	6.0
278	Increase(−)/Decrease(+) in accruals				10.0	−8.0
279	Net cash provided by operating activities				−$3.0	$369.2
280						
281	Long-term investing activities					
282	Cash used to acquire fixed assets				−$230.0	−$212.2
283	Sale of short-term investments				65.0	0.0
284	Net cash provided by investing activities				−$165.0	−$212.2
285						
286	Financing Activities					
287	Increase(+)/Decrease(−) in notes payable				$50.0	−$19.9
288	Increase(+)/Decrease(−) in bonds				174.0	−87.5
289	Preferred stock issue(+)/repurchase(−)				0.0	14.0
290	Payment of common and preferred dividends				−61.0	−66.7
291	Common stock issue(+)/repurchase(−)				0.0	1.3
292	Net cash provided by financing activities				$163.0	−$158.8
293						
294	Net cash flow				−$5.0	−$1.7
295	Cash at beginning of the year				15.0	10.0
296	Cash at end of the year				$10.0	$8.3

chairman and founder of the company, were concerned that the plan included issuing new shares of common stock. They were also uneasy about the assumed price at which shares of stock could be repurchased later in the year if there were surplus funds. In addition, the board thought that determining dividends as a fixed percentage payout of net income might introduce quite a bit of volatility in DPS. Because of these concerns, the board asked the CFO to provide forecasted statements using the following different assumptions regarding the financial policies.

For the purposes of this additional forecast, the board specified the following financial policies: (1) let the regular DPS grow at a specified rate; (2) do not change the level of existing notes payable; and (3) do not issue or repurchase bonds, preferred stock, or common stock. If additional financing is needed, the board suggested forecasting the AFN as a draw against an existing line of credit on a temporary basis (even though the interest rate would be high) until the board could meet and decide on a final financing plan. If instead a surplus of funds is available at the end of the year, the board suggested that the surplus be paid to shareholders in the form of a special dividend.[9]

Figure 9-8 **One-Year Forecasted Financial Statements under an Alternative Financial Policy: Scenario = Maintain (Millions, Except for Per Share Data)**

	A	B	C	D	E	F	G	H
94	Scenario Shown:	Maintain				Planned		With
95		Actual	Factor	Basis for		(w/o AFN)	AFN	AFN
96	Balance Sheet	2012	or Rate	2013 Forecast		2013	Adjust.	2013
97	Assets							
98	Cash	$10.0	0.33% ×	2013 Sales		$11.0		$11.0
99	Acc. rec.	375.0	12.50% ×	2013 Sales		412.5		412.5
100	Inventories	615.0	20.50% ×	2013 Sales		676.5		676.5
101	Total CA	$1,000.0				$1,100.0		$1,100.0
102	Net plant & equip.	1,000.0	33.33% ×	2013 Sales		1,100.0		1,100.0
103	Total assets (TA)	$2,000.0				$2,200.0		$2,200.0
104	Liab. & equity							
105	Accounts payable	$60.0	2.00% ×	2013 Sales		$66.0		$66.0
106	Accruals	140.0	4.67% ×	2013 Sales		154.1		154.1
107	Notes pay. (NP)	110.0		Carry over		110.0		110.0
108	Line of credit (LOC)[a]			Blank			$109.3	109.3
109	Total CL	$310.0				$330.1		$439.4
110	LT bonds	754.0		Carry over		754.0		754.0
111	Tot. liab.	$1,064.0				$1,084.1		$1,193.4
112	Pref. stock	40.0		Carry over		40.0		40.0
113	Com. stock	130.0		Carry over		130.0		130.0
114	Ret. earnings	766.0		2012 RE + ΔRE		836.5		836.5
115	Total CE	$896.0				$966.5		$966.5
116	Total L&E	$2,000.0				$2,090.6		$2,200.0
117								
118	AFN[b]	=	TA − Planned total liabilities & equity				$109.3	
119	Line of credit[c]	=	AFN if AFN > 0 (additional financing needed)				$109.3	
120	Special dividend[d]	=	−AFN if AFN ≤ 0 (surplus funds available)				$0.0	
121								

(Continued)

9. In actuality, the board would decide at that time whether to repurchase shares of stock instead, if that seemed preferable given the prevailing stock price.

Figure 9-8   One-Year Forecasted Financial Statements under an Alternative Financial Policy: Scenario = Maintain (Millions, Except for Per Share Data) (Continued)

	A	B	C	D	E	F	G	H
122	Scenario Shown:	Maintain				Planned		With
123		Actual	Factor	Basis for		(w/o AFN)	AFN	AFN
124	Income Statement	2012	or Rate	2013 Forecast		2013	Adjust.	2013
125	Sales	$3,000.0	1.10 ×	2012 Sales		$3,300.0		$3,300.0
126	Costs (excl. depr.)	2,617.0	87.21% ×	2013 Sales		2,877.9		2,877.9
127	Depreciation	100.0	10.00% ×	2013 Net plant		110.0		110.0
128	Total op. costs	$2,717.0				$2,987.9		$2,987.9
129	EBIT	$283.0				$312.1		$312.1
130	Int. on planned NP	9.9	9.00% ×	Avg notes		9.9		9.9
131	Int. on planned bonds	78.1	11.00% ×	Avg bonds		82.9		82.9
132	Int. on LOC[e]		9.00%	Blank			$0.0	0.0
133	EBT	$195.0				$219.2		$219.2
134	Taxes (T = 40%)	78.0	40.00% ×	2013 EBT		87.7		87.7
135	NI before pref. div.	$117.0				$131.5		$131.5
136	Pref. div.	4.0	10.00% ×	Avg preferred		4.0		4.0
137	NI to common	$113.0				$127.5		$127.5
138								
139	# of shares (n)	50.0		Carry over		50.0		50.0
140	Regular DPS	$1.14	1.00 ×	2012 DPS		$1.14		$1.14
141	Regular dividends	$57.0		n × 2013 DPS		$57.0		$57.0
142	Special dividend[f]	0.0				0.0	$0.0	0.0
143	Add. To RE (ΔRE)	$56.0		NI − Dividends		$70.5		$70.5

[a]If additional financing is needed, the line of credit will be used on a temporary basis.
[b]The AFN in forecasted financial statements is equal to the required assets minus the planned liabilities and equity (i.e., the liabilities and equity assuming AFN is zero).
[c]If AFN > 0, then additional financing will be raised by borrowing via the line of credit.
[d]If AFN ≤ 0, then surplus funds will be used to pay a special dividend.
[e]This forecast assumes that any temporary borrowing will be undertaken at the end of the year; thus, there will be no additional interest expense.
[f]Any surplus funds will be paid out as a special dividend.

The board asked to see two scenarios. The first is similar to the Status Quo scenario previously discussed, except that the board's three financial policies just described are employed (the board suggested a zero growth rate for regular DPS). Because there is no change in operating performance, this is called the Maintain scenario. The second scenario is similar to the Final scenario discussed earlier, except that the board's financial policy is applied (the board suggested an 8% growth in regular DPS for this scenario). Because there are significant improvements in operating performance, this is called the Improve scenario. The board asked to see the Maintain scenario first, which is shown in Figure 9-8 (see *Tab 3* in *Ch09 Tool Kit.xls* for details).

The operating items are forecasted in the same way as shown before. All liabilities and equity accounts (except the line of credit) are planned in the sense that they are specified by the financial policies. For the policies used here, there are no changes in notes payable, bonds, or common stock; in addition, regular dividends are specified, so the addition to retained earnings is specified. Column F in Figure 9-8 shows these planned forecasts, but notice that the balance sheets don't balance: The total assets line equals $2,200, but total liabilities and equity sum only to $2,090.6. Thus, there is a $2,200 − $2,090.6 = $109.3 million shortfall. In other words, the AFN is $109.3, as shown in Row 118. Because additional financing is needed, there will be an adjustment to the statements by borrowing $109.3 through the line of credit, as shown in Column G. Because we assume that the borrowing occurs at the end of the year, there will be no additional interest in this forecast. Column H shows the forecasted statements after including the AFN.

Figure 9-9 reports the forecasted statements for the Improve scenario. The balance sheets in Column F again do not balance, but this is because there is more financing (total liabilities and equity = $2,089.4) than assets (total assets = $1,999.2). Thus, Row 118 shows a negative AFN, −$90.2 million. This will be paid out as a special dividend, as shown in Column G. Column H reports the forecasted statements after including the AFN.

The board expressed two additional concerns. First, they thought it unrealistic to assume that the line of credit was only used on the last day of the year and thus caused no additional interest expense. The board felt it would be more appropriate to assume that the line of credit was accessed at regular intervals

Figure 9-9   **One-Year Forecasted Financial Statements under an Alternative Financial Policy: Scenario = Improve (Millions, Except for Per Share Data)**

	A	B	C	D	E	F	G	H
94	Scenario Shown:	Improve				Planned		With
95		Actual	Factor	Basis for		(w/o AFN)	AFN	AFN
96	Balance Sheet	2012	or Rate	2013 Forecast		2013	Adjust.	2013
97	Assets							
98	Cash	$10.0	0.25% ×	2013 Sales		$8.3		$8.3
99	Acc. rec.	375.0	11.00% ×	2013 Sales		363.0		363.0
100	Inventories	615.0	16.00% ×	2013 Sales		528.0		528.0
101	Total CA	$1,000.0				$899.3		$899.3
102	Net plant & equip.	1,000.0	33.33% ×	2013 Sales		1,100.0		1,100.0
103	Total assets (TA)	$2,000.0				$1,999.2		$1,999.2
104	Liab. & equity							
105	Accounts payable	$60.0	2.00% ×	2013 Sales		$66.0		$66.0
106	Accruals	140.0	4.00% ×	2013 Sales		132.0		132.0
107	Notes pay. (NP)	110.0		Carry over		110.0		110.0
108	Line of credit (LOC)[a]			Blank			$0.0	0.0
109	Total CL	$310.0				$308.0		$308.0
110	LT bonds	754.0		Carry over		754.0		754.0
111	Tot. liab.	$1,064.0				$1,062.0		$1,062.0
112	Pref. stock	40.0		Carry over		40.0		40.0
113	Com. stock	130.0		Carry over		130.0		130.0
114	Ret. earnings	766.0		2012 RE + ΔRE		857.4		767.2
115	Total CE	$896.0				$987.4		$897.2
116	Total L&E	$2,000.0				$2,089.4		$1,999.2
117								
118	AFN[b]		= TA − Planned total liabilities & equity			−$90.2		
119	Line of credit[c]		= AFN if AFN > 0 (additional financing needed)			$0.0		
120	Special dividend[d]		= −AFN if AFN ≤ 0 (surplus funds available)			$90.0		
121								

(Continued)

Figure 9-9   **One-Year Forecasted Financial Statements under an Alternative Financial Policy: Scenario = Improve (Millions, Except for Per Share Data)** *(Continued)*

	A	B	C	D	E	F	G	H
122	Scenario Shown:	Improve				Planned		With
123		Actual	Factor	Basis for		(w/o AFN)	AFN	AFN
124	Income Statement	2012	or Rate	2013 Forecast		2013	Adjust.	2013
125	Sales	$3,000.0	1.10 ×	2012 Sales		$3,300.0		$3,300.0
126	Costs (excl. depr.)	2,617.0	86.00% ×	2013 Sales		2,838.0		2,838.0
127	Depreciation	100.0	10.20% ×	2013 Net plant		112.2		112.2
128	Total op. costs	$2,717.0				$2,950.2		$2,950.2
129	EBIT	$283.0				$349.8		$349.8
130	Int. on planned NP	9.9	8.50% ×	Avg notes		9.4		9.4
131	Int. on planned bonds	78.1	10.50% ×	Avg bonds		79.2		79.2
132	Int. on LOC[e]		8.50%	Blank			$0.0	0.0
133	EBT	$195.0				$261.3		$261.3
134	Taxes (T = 40%)	78.0	40.00% ×	2013 EBT		104.5		104.5
135	NI before pref. div.	$117.0				$156.8		$156.8
136	Pref. div.	4.0	9.50% ×	Avg preferred		3.8		3.8
137	NI to common	$113.0				$153.0		$153.0
138								
139	# of shares (n)	50.0		Carry over		50.0		50.0
140	Regular DPS	$1.14	1.08 ×	2012 DPS		$1.23		$1.23
141	Regular dividends	$57.0		n × 2013 DPS		$61.6		$61.6
142	Special dividend[f]	0.0				0.0	$90.2	90.2
143	Add. To RE (ΔRE)	$56.0		NI − Dividends		$91.4		$1.2

[a]If additional financing is needed, the line of credit will be used on a temporary basis.
[b]The AFN in forecasted financial statements is equal to the required assets minus the planned liabilities and equity (i.e., the liabilities and equity assuming AFN is zero).
[c]If AFN > 0, then additional financing will be raised by borrowing via the line of credit.
[d]If AFN ≤ 0, then surplus funds will be used to pay a special dividend.
[e]This forecast assumes that any temporary borrowing will be undertaken at the end of the year; thus, there will be no additional interest expense.
[f]Any surplus funds will be paid out as a special dividend.

throughout the year, which would lead to additional interest expense. The CFO explained that when the AFN leads to additional interest expense it reduces net income, which reduces the addition to retained earnings and then increases the AFN, with the cycle being repeated in a circular manner. This is called **financing feedback**, and there are a variety of ways to incorporate feedback effects into the forecast. The CFO agreed that adding debt throughout the year was a more realistic assumption but said that the end-of-year assumption usually produced results fairly close to those that incorporated feedback effects. However, the CFO agreed to incorporate financing feedback in the next set of forecasts, but rather than use valuable board time explaining feedback adjustments in detail, the CFO suggested that interested board members take a look at *Tab 4* in *Ch09 Tool Kit.xls*.

The board also wanted to see multi-year projections. After updating the forecasting model to incorporate feedback effects and multi-year forecasts, the CFO returned to the board meeting and presented the results shown in Figure 9-10. (See *Tab 5* in *Ch09 Tool Kit.xls* for calculations.)

Figure 9-10   **Summary of Forecasted Key Results for the "Improve" Scenario (Millions, Except for Percentages and Per Share Data)**

	A	B	C	D	E	F	G	H	I
			Actual		Forecast	Forecast	Forecast	Forecast	Forecast
211			2012		2013	2014	2015	2016	2017
212									
213			Industry	MicroDrive	Improve	Improve	Improve	Improve	Improve
214	Key Results								
215	Net operating profit after taxes		NA	$170	$210	$231	$254	$279	$307
216	Net operating working capital		NA	$800	$701	$771	$849	$933	$1,027
217	Total operating capital		NA	$1,800	$1,801	$1,981	$2,180	$2,397	$2,637
218	FCF = NOPAT − Δ op capital		NA	−$175	$209	$51	$56	$61	$68
219	Return on invested capital		11.0%	9.4%	11.7%	11.7%	11.7%	11.7%	11.7%
220	EPS		NA	$2.26	$3.06	$3.43	$3.79	$4.19	$4.63
221	DPS		NA	$1.14	$1.23	$1.33	$1.44	$1.55	$1.68
222	Return on equity (ROE)		15.0%	12.6%	17.0%	17.1%	16.9%	16.7%	16.5%
223	Return on assets (ROA)		9.0%	5.7%	7.7%	7.8%	7.8%	7.9%	7.9%
224	Inventory turnover		9.0	4.9	6.3	6.3	6.3	6.3	6.3
225	Days sales outstanding		36.0	45.6	40.2	40.2	40.2	40.2	40.2
226	Total liabilities / TA		46.0%	53.2%	53.1%	52.6%	52.1%	51.5%	50.8%
227	Times interest earned		6.0	3.2	4.0	4.3	4.8	5.3	5.8
228	Shares outstanding		NA	50.00	50.00	50.00	50.00	50.00	50.00
229	Payout ratio		40.0%	50.4%	40.2%	38.8%	37.9%	37.0%	36.2%
230	AFN		NA	$224	−$90	$75	$156	$242	$334
231	Line of credit balance		NA	$0	$0	$75	$156	$242	$334
232	Special dividend		NA	$0	$90	$0	$0	$0	$0

The dramatic increase in FCF during 2013 would be a result of the improved operations, including less inventory and fewer receivables. After this one-time improvement, FCF drops in 2014 but then increases each year. The improved operations are reflected in the increased return on invested capital, which in turn leads to strong growth in EPS and thus enables growth in DPS. With the projected increase in the times interest earned ratio and the decrease in the ratio of total liabilities to total assets, the board discussed whether MicroDrive could support more debt. They decided to discuss a possible recapitalization at their next meeting, in which MicroDrive might issue bonds and use the proceeds to pay off the line of credit and possibly repurchase shares of stock, topics we discuss in Chapters 15 and 17.

Self Test

Is the AFN as calculated using the forecasted financial statements method, with all the ratios held constant, the same (except for rounding errors) as the AFN found using the AFN equation? Explain.

Why does the text argue that the forecasted financial statements method is preferable to the AFN equation method?

What does the acronym GIGO stand for? Is this important for forecasting?

9.5 Forecasting When the Ratios Change

The AFN equation assumes that the ratios of assets and liabilities to sales $(A_0^*/S_0$ and $L_0^*/S_0)$ remain constant over time. This assumption can be relaxed when we use the forecasted financial statement method, but in our forecast we made a one-time change in these ratios and then held them constant thereafter. This implies that each "spontaneous" asset and liability item increases at the same rate as sales. In graph form, this implies the type of relationship shown in Panel a of Figure 9-11, a relationship whose graph (1) is linear and (2) passes through the origin. Under those conditions, if the company's sales increase from $200 million to $400 million, or by 100%, then inventory will also increase by 100%, from $100 million to $200 million.

The assumption of constant ratios and identical growth rates is appropriate at times, but there are times when it is incorrect. Three such conditions are described in the following sections.

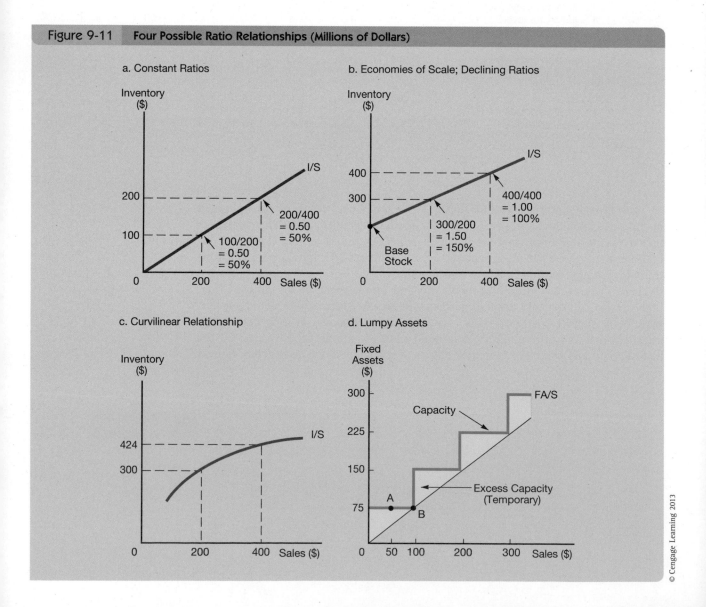

Figure 9-11   Four Possible Ratio Relationships (Millions of Dollars)

a. Constant Ratios

b. Economies of Scale; Declining Ratios

c. Curvilinear Relationship

d. Lumpy Assets

9.5a Economies of Scale

There are economies of scale in the use of many kinds of assets, and when economies of scale occur, the ratios are likely to change over time as the size of the firm increases. For example, retailers often need to maintain base stocks of different inventory items even if current sales are quite low. As sales expand, inventories may then grow less rapidly than sales, so the ratio of inventory to sales (I/S) declines. This situation is depicted in Panel b of Figure 9-11. Here we see that the inventory/sales ratio is 1.5 (or 150%) when sales are $200 million but declines to 1.0 when sales climb to $400 million.

The relationship in Panel b is linear, but nonlinear relationships often exist. Indeed, if the firm uses one popular model for establishing inventory levels (the Economic Ordering Quantity, or EOQ, model), its inventories will rise with the *square root* of sales. This situation is shown in Panel c of Figure 9-11, which shows a curved line whose slope decreases at higher sales levels. In this situation, very large increases in sales would require very little additional inventory.[10]

9.5b Lumpy Assets

In many industries, technological considerations dictate that if a firm is to be competitive, it must add fixed assets in large, discrete units; such assets are often referred to as **lumpy assets**. In the paper industry, for example, there are strong economies of scale in basic paper mill equipment, so when a paper company expands capacity, it must do so in large, lumpy increments. This type of situation is depicted in Panel d of Figure 9-11. Here we assume that the minimum economically efficient plant has a cost of $75 million, and that such a plant can produce enough output to reach a sales level of $100 million. If the firm is to be competitive, it simply must have at least $75 million of fixed assets.

Lumpy assets have a major effect on the ratio of fixed assets to sales (FA/S) at different sales levels and, consequently, on financial requirements. At Point A in Panel d, which represents a sales level of $50 million, the fixed assets are $75 million and so the ratio FA/S = $75/$50 = 1.5. Sales can expand by $50 million, out to $100 million, with no additions to fixed assets. At that point, represented by Point B, the ratio FA/S = $75/$100 = 0.75. However, since the firm is operating at capacity (sales of $100 million), even a small increase in sales would require a doubling of plant capacity, so a small projected sales increase would bring with it a large financial requirement.[11]

---

10. See **Web Extension 09A** for more on forecasting when things like inventories are not constant in relation to sales.
11. Several other points should be noted about Panel d of Figure 9-11. First, if the firm is operating at a sales level of $100 million or less, then any expansion that calls for a sales increase of more than $100 million would require a *doubling* of the firm's fixed assets. A much smaller percentage increase would be involved if the firm were large enough to be operating a number of plants. Second, firms generally go to multiple shifts and take other actions to minimize the need for new fixed asset capacity as they approach Point B. However, these efforts can only go so far, and eventually a fixed asset expansion will be required. Third, firms often make arrangements to share excess capacity with other firms in their industry. For example, the situation in the electric utility industry is very much like that depicted in Panel d. However, electric companies often build jointly owned plants, or else they "take turns" building plants, and then they buy power from or sell power to other utilities to avoid building new plants that would be underutilized.

9.5c Excess Capacity Adjustments

If a firm has excess capacity, then sales can grow before the firm must add capacity. The level of full capacity sales is

(9-3)

$$\text{Full capacity sales} = \frac{\text{Actual sales}}{\text{Percentage of capacity at which fixed assets were operated}}$$

For example, consider MicroDrive and use the data from its financial statements in Figure 9-2, but now assume that excess capacity exists in fixed assets. Specifically, assume that fixed assets in 2012 were being utilized to only 96% of capacity. If fixed assets had been used to full capacity, then 2012 sales could have been as high as $3,125 million versus the $3,000 million in actual sales:

$$\text{Full capacity sales} = \frac{\text{Actual sales}}{\text{Percentage of capacity at which fixed assets were operated}}$$

$$= \frac{\$3,000 \text{ million}}{0.96} = \$3,125 \text{ million}$$

The target fixed assets/sales ratio can be defined in terms of the full capacity sales:

(9-4)

$$\text{Target fixed assets/Sales} = \frac{\text{Actual fixed sales}}{\text{Full capacity sales}}$$

MicroDrive's target fixed assets/sales ratio should be 32% rather than 33.3%:

$$\text{Target fixed assets/Sales} = \frac{\text{Actual fixed assets}}{\text{Full capacity sales}}$$

$$= \frac{\$1,000}{\$3,125} = 0.32 = 32\%$$

The required level of fixed assets depends upon this target fixed assets/sales ratio:

(9-5)

$$\text{Required level of fixed assets} = \left(\frac{\text{Target fixed assets}}{\text{Sales}} \right) \left(\begin{array}{c} \text{Projected} \\ \text{sales} \end{array} \right)$$

Therefore, if MicroDrive's sales increase to $3,300 million, its fixed assets would have to increase to $1,056 million:

$$\text{Required level of fixed assets} = \left(\frac{\text{Target fixed assets}}{\text{Sales}} \right) \left(\begin{array}{c} \text{Projected} \\ \text{sales} \end{array} \right)$$

$$= 0.32(\$3,300) = \$1,056 \text{ million}$$

We previously forecasted that MicroDrive would need to increase fixed assets at the same rate as sales, or by 10%. That meant an increase of $100 million, from $1,000 million to $1,100 million. Under the new assumptions, the actual required increase in fixed assets is only from $1,000 million to $1,056 million, or $56 million. Thus, the capacity-adjusted forecast is $100 − $56 = $44 million less than the earlier forecast. With a smaller fixed asset requirement, the projected AFN would decline from an estimated $118 million to $118 − $44 = $74 million.

Note also that when excess capacity exists, sales can grow to the capacity sales as calculated above with no increase in fixed assets, but sales beyond that level would require additions of fixed assets as in our example. The same situation could occur with respect to inventories, and the required additions would be determined in exactly the same manner as for fixed assets. Theoretically, the same situation could occur with other types of assets, but as a practical matter excess capacity normally exists only with respect to fixed assets and inventories.

How do economies of scale and lumpy assets affect financial forecasting?   **Self Test**

Summary

- **Financial forecasting** generally begins with a forecast of the firm's sales in terms of both units and dollars.
- Either the **forecasted financial statements (FFS) method** or the **additional funds needed (AFN) equation** can be used to forecast financial requirements. If conditions are likely to change, the financial statements method is more reliable, and it also provides ratios and other data that can be used to evaluate alternative business plans. The AFN equation is typically used to arrive at an approximation for AFN.
- A firm can determine its **AFN** by estimating the amount of new assets necessary to support the forecasted level of sales and then subtracting from this amount the spontaneous funds that will be generated from operations. The firm can then plan how to raise the AFN most efficiently.
- The higher a firm's **sales growth rate** and the higher its **payout ratio**, the greater will be its need for additional financing.
- The greatest benefit of the forecasted financial statements method is its use in planning to optimize operations and thereby increase the firm's intrinsic value and thus its stock price.
- Adjustments must be made if **economies of scale** exist in the use of assets, if **excess capacity** exists, or if growth must occur in large increments (**lumpy assets**).
- **Linear regression** and **excess capacity adjustments** can be used to forecast asset requirements in situations in which assets are not expected to grow at the same rate as sales. See **Web Extension 9A** for more discussion of these issues.

Questions

9-1 Define each of the following terms:
a. Mission statement; corporate scope; statement of corporate objectives; corporate strategies
b. Operating plan; financial plan; sales forecast
c. Spontaneous liabilities; profit margin; payout ratio
d. Additional funds needed (AFN); AFN equation; capital intensity ratio; self-supporting growth rate
e. Forecasted financial statement approach
f. Excess capacity; lumpy assets; economies of scale
g. Full capacity sales; target fixed assets/sales ratio; required level of fixed assets
h. Financing feedback effects

9-2 Some liability and net worth items increase spontaneously with increases in sales. Put a check (✓) by those items listed below that typically increase spontaneously:

Accounts payable	_____	Mortgage bonds	_____
Notes payable to banks	_____	Common stock	_____
Accrued wages	_____	Retained earnings	_____
Accrued taxes	_____		

9-3 The following equation is sometimes used to forecast financial requirements:

$$AFN = (A_0^*/S_0)(\Delta S) - (L_0^*/S_0)(\Delta S) - MS_1(1 - POR)$$

What key assumption do we make when using this equation? Under what conditions might this assumption not hold true?

9-4 Name five key factors that affect a firm's external financing requirements.

9-5 What is meant by the term "self-supporting growth rate"? How is this rate related to the AFN equation, and how can that equation be used to calculate the self-supporting growth rate?

9-6 Suppose a firm makes the policy changes listed below. If a change means that external, nonspontaneous financial requirements (AFN) will increase, indicate this by a (+); indicate a decrease by a (−); and indicate no effect or an indeterminate effect by a (0). Think in terms of the *immediate, short-run* effect on funds requirements.
a. The dividend payout ratio is increased.   _____
b. The firm decides to pay all suppliers on delivery, rather than after a 30-day delay, to take advantage of discounts for rapid payment.   _____
c. The firm begins to offer credit to its customers, whereas previously all sales had been on a cash basis.   _____
d. The firm's profit margin is eroded by increased competition, although sales hold steady.   _____
e. The firm sells its manufacturing plants for cash to a contractor and simultaneously signs an outsourcing contract to purchase from that contractor goods that the firm formerly produced.   _____
f. The firm negotiates a new contract with its union that lowers its labor costs without affecting its output.   _____

9–7 Assume that you recently received your MBA and now work as assistant to the CFO of a relatively large corporation. Your boss has asked you to prepare a financial forecast for the coming year, using an *Excel* model, and then to present your forecast to the firm's executive committee. Describe how you would deal with the following issues.

a. Would you want to set up the model with a number of scenarios whose results could be presented to the executives?

b. What are "financing feedbacks," and what are the pros and cons of incorporating such feedbacks into your model?

c. What are the pros and cons of assuming that all necessary outside funds are obtained from a single source (such as a bank loan) versus assuming that a mix of funds is raised so as to keep the capital structure at its target level?

d. What are the pros and cons of providing the capability to examine the results of changing dividend policy and capital structure policy as well as various operating policies such as credit policy, outsourcing policy, and so forth?

e. What does the acronym GIGO stand for, and how important is this for someone who is developing a financial model? For someone using a forecasting model? How might post-audits and incentive compensation plans help reduce GIGO?

Answers Appear in Appendix B

Problems

Easy Problems 1–3

9–1 **AFN Equation** Broussard Skateboard's sales are expected to increase by 15% from $8 million in 2012 to $9.2 million in 2013. Its assets totaled $5 million at the end of 2012. Broussard is already at full capacity, so its assets must grow at the same rate as projected sales. At the end of 2012, current liabilities were $1.4 million, consisting of $450,000 of accounts payable, $500,000 of notes payable, and $450,000 of accruals. The after-tax profit margin is forecasted to be 6%, and the forecasted payout ratio is 40%. Use the AFN equation to forecast Broussard's additional funds needed for the coming year.

9–2 **AFN Equation** Refer to Problem 9-1. What would be the additional funds needed if the company's year-end 2012 assets had been $7 million? Assume that all other numbers, including sales, are the same as in Problem 9-1 and that the company is operating at full capacity. Why is this AFN different from the one you found in Problem 9-1? Is the company's "capital intensity" ratio the same or different?

9–3 **AFN Equation** Refer to Problem 9-1. Return to the assumption that the company had $5 million in assets at the end of 2012, but now assume that the company pays no dividends. Under these assumptions, what would be the additional funds needed for the coming year? Why is this AFN different from the one you found in Problem 9-1?

Intermediate Problems 4–6

9–4 Sales Increase Maggie's Muffins, Inc., generated $5,000,000 in sales during 2012, and its year-end total assets were $2,500,000. Also, at year-end 2012, current liabilities were $1,000,000, consisting of $300,000 of notes payable, $500,000 of accounts payable, and $200,000 of accruals. Looking ahead to 2013, the company estimates that its assets must increase at the same rate as sales, its spontaneous liabilities will increase at the same rate as sales, its profit margin will be 7%, and its payout ratio will be 80%. How large a sales increase can the company achieve without having to raise funds externally; that is, what is its self-supporting growth rate?

9–5 Long-Term Financing Needed At year-end 2012, Wallace Landscaping's total assets were $2.17 million and its accounts payable were $560,000. Sales, which in 2012 were $3.5 million, are expected to increase by 35% in 2013. Total assets and accounts payable are proportional to sales, and that relationship will be maintained. Wallace typically uses no current liabilities other than accounts payable. Common stock amounted to $625,000 in 2012, and retained earnings were $395,000. Wallace has arranged to sell $195,000 of new common stock in 2013 to meet some of its financing needs. The remainder of its financing needs will be met by issuing new long-term debt at the end of 2013. (Because the debt is added at the end of the year, there will be no additional interest expense due to the new debt.) Its net profit margin on sales is 5%, and 45% of earnings will be paid out as dividends.
a. What were Wallace's total long-term debt and total liabilities in 2012?
b. How much new long-term debt financing will be needed in 2013? (*Hint:* AFN – New stock = New long-term debt.)

9–6 Additional Funds Needed The Booth Company's sales are forecasted to double from $1,000 in 2012 to $2,000 in 2013. Here is the December 31, 2012, balance sheet:

Cash	$ 100	Accounts payable	$ 50
Accounts receivable	200	Notes payable	150
Inventories	200	Accruals	50
Net fixed assets	500	Long-term debt	400
		Common stock	100
		Retained earnings	250
Total assets	$1,000	Total liabilities and equity	$1,000

Booth's fixed assets were used to only 50% of capacity during 2012, but its current assets were at their proper levels in relation to sales. All assets except fixed assets must increase at the same rate as sales, and fixed assets would also have to increase at the same rate if the current excess capacity did not exist. Booth's after-tax profit margin is forecasted to be 5% and its payout ratio to be 60%. What is Booth's additional funds needed (AFN) for the coming year?

Challenging Problems 7–9

9–7 Forecasted Statements and Ratios Upton Computers makes bulk purchases of small computers, stocks them in conveniently located warehouses, ships them to its chain of retail stores, and has a staff to advise customers and help them set up their new computers. Upton's balance sheet as of December 31, 2012, is shown here (millions of dollars):

Cash	$ 3.5	Accounts payable	$ 9.0
Receivables	26.0	Notes payable	18.0
Inventories	58.0	Accruals	8.5
Total current assets	$ 87.5	Total current liabilities	$ 35.5
Net fixed assets	35.0	Mortgage loan	6.0
		Common stock	15.0
		Retained earnings	66.0
Total assets	$122.5	Total liabilities and equity	$122.5

Sales for 2012 were $350 million and net income for the year was $10.5 million, so the firm's profit margin was 3.0%. Upton paid dividends of $4.2 million to common stockholders, so its payout ratio was 40%. Its tax rate is 40%, and it operated at full capacity. Assume that all assets/sales ratios, spontaneous liabilities/sales ratios, the profit margin, and the payout ratio remain constant in 2013.

a. If sales are projected to increase by $70 million, or 20%, during 2013, use the AFN equation to determine Upton's projected external capital requirements.
b. Using the AFN equation, determine Upton's self-supporting growth rate. That is, what is the maximum growth rate the firm can achieve without having to employ nonspontaneous external funds?
c. Use the forecasted financial statement method to forecast Upton's balance sheet for December 31, 2013. Assume that all additional external capital is raised as a bank loan at the end of the year and is reflected in notes payable (because the debt is added at the end of the year, there will be no additional interest expense due to the new debt). Assume Upton's profit margin and dividend payout ratio will be the same in 2013 as they were in 2012. What is the amount of notes payable reported on the 2013 forecasted balance sheets? (*Hint:* You don't need to forecast the income statements because you are given the projected sales, profit margin, and dividend payout ratio; these figures allow you to calculate the 2013 addition to retained earnings for the balance sheet.)

9–8 **Additional Funds Needed** Stevens Textiles's 2012 financial statements are shown below:

Balance Sheet as of December 31, 2012 (Thousands of Dollars)

Cash	$ 1,080	Accounts payable	$ 4,320
Receivables	6,480	Accruals	2,880
Inventories	9,000	Notes payable	2,100
Total current assets	$16,560	Total current liabilities	$ 9,300
Net fixed assets	12,600	Mortgage bonds	3,500
		Common stock	3,500
		Retained earnings	12,860
Total assets	$29,160	Total liabilities and equity	$29,160

Income Statement for December 31, 2012 (Thousands of Dollars)

Sales	$36,000
Operating costs	32,440
Earnings before interest and taxes	$ 3,560
Interest	460
Earnings before taxes	$ 3,100
Taxes (40%)	1,240
Net income	$ 1,860
Dividends (45%)	$ 837
Addition to retained earnings	$ 1,023

a. Suppose 2013 sales are projected to increase by 15% over 2012 sales. Use the forecasted financial statement method to forecast a balance sheet and income statement for December 31, 2013. The interest rate on all debt is 10%, and cash earns no interest income. Assume that all additional debt is added at the end of the year, which means that you should base the forecasted interest expense on the balance of debt at the beginning of the year. Use the forecasted income statement to determine the addition to retained earnings. Assume that the company was operating at full capacity in 2012, that it cannot sell off any of its fixed assets, and that any required financing will be borrowed as notes payable. Also, assume that assets, spontaneous liabilities, and operating costs are expected to increase by the same percentage as sales. Determine the additional funds needed.

b. What is the resulting total forecasted amount of notes payable?

c. In your answers to Parts a and b, you should not have charged any interest on the additional debt added during 2013 because it was assumed that the new debt was added at the end of the year. But now suppose that the new debt is added throughout the year. Don't do any calculations, but how would this change the answers to parts a and b?

9-9 **Additional Funds Needed** Garlington Technologies Inc.'s 2012 financial statements are shown below:

Balance Sheet as of December 31, 2012

Cash	$ 180,000	Accounts payable	$ 360,000
Receivables	360,000	Notes payable	156,000
Inventories	720,000	Accruals	180,000
Total current assets	$1,260,000	Total current liabilities	$ 696,000
Fixed assets	1,440,000	Common stock	1,800,000
		Retained earnings	204,000
Total assets	$2,700,000	Total liabilities and equity	$2,700,000

Income Statement for December 31, 2012

Sales	$3,600,000
Operating costs	3,279,720
EBIT	$ 320,280
Interest	18,280
EBT	$ 302,000
Taxes (40%)	120,800
Net income	$ 181,200
Dividends	$ 108,000

Suppose that in 2013 sales increase by 10% over 2012 sales and that 2013 dividends will increase to $112,000. Forecast the financial statements using the forecasted financial statement method. Assume the firm operated at full capacity in 2012. Use an interest rate of 13%, and assume that any new debt will be added at the end of the year (so forecast the interest expense based on the debt balance at the beginning of the year). Cash does not earn any interest income. Assume that the AFN will be in the form of notes payable.

Spreadsheet Problems

9–10 **Build a Model: Forecasting Financial Statements** Start with the partial model in the file *Ch09 P10 Build a Model.xls* on the textbook's Web site, which contains the 2012 financial statements of Zieber Corporation. Forecast Zeiber's 2013 income statement and balance sheets. Use the following assumptions: (1) Sales grow by 6%. (2) The ratios of expenses to sales, depreciation to fixed assets, cash to sales, accounts receivable to sales, and inventories to sales will be the same in 2013 as in 2012. (3) Zeiber will not issue any new stock or new long-term bonds. (4) The interest rate is 9% for short-term debt and 11% for long-term debt. (5) No interest is earned on cash. (6) Dividends grow at an 8% rate. (6) Calculate the additional funds needed (AFN). If new financing is required, assume it will be raised as notes payable. Assume that any new notes payable will be borrowed on the last day of the year, so there will be no additional interest expense for the new notes payable. If surplus funds are available, pay a special dividend.
   a. What are the forecasted levels of notes payable and special dividends?
   b. Now assume that the growth in sales is only 3%. What are the forecasted levels of notes payable and special dividends?

9–11 **Build a Model: Forecasting Financial Statements** Start with the partial model in the file *Ch09 P11 Build a Model.xls* on the textbook's Web site, which shows Matthews Industries's most recent balance sheet, income statement, and other data. Matthews Industries's financial planners must forecast the company's financial results for the coming year. The forecast will be based on the forecasted financial statement method, and any additional funds needed will be obtained by using notes payable. Complete the partial model and answer the following questions.
   a. Assume that the firm's 2012 profit margin, payout ratio, capital intensity ratio, and spontaneous liabilities-to-sales ratio remain constant. If sales grow by 10% in 2013, what is the required external capital the firm will need in 2013 as calculated by the AFN equation?
   b. If 2012 ratios remain constant, what is Matthews's self-supporting growth rate? Describe how the self-supporting growth rate will change in response to each of the following: (1) the profit margin declines, (2) the payout ratio increases, (3) the capital intensity ratio declines.
   c. Matthews's management has reviewed its financial statements and arrived at two possible scenarios for 2013. The first scenario assumes a steady state while the second scenario, the target scenario, shows some improvement in ratios toward industry average values. Forecasted values for the scenarios are shown in the partially completed file *Ch09 P11 Build a Model.xls*. If Matthews assumes that external financing is achieved through notes payable and that financing feedbacks are not considered because the new notes

payable are added at the end of the year, then what are the firm's forecasted AFN, EPS, DPS, and year-end stock price under each scenario?

d. Matthews's management realizes that interest for additional notes payable should be included in the analysis. Assume that notes will be issued midway through the year, so that interest on these notes is incurred for only half the year. If Matthews assumes now that external financing is achieved through notes payable and if financing feedbacks are considered, then what are the firm's forecasted AFN, EPS, DPS, and year-end stock price under each scenario?

 THOMSON REUTERS

Use the Thomson ONE–Business School Edition online database to work this chapter's questions.

Forecasting the Future Performance of Abercrombie & Fitch

Clothing retailer Abercrombie & Fitch enjoyed phenomenal success in the late 1990s. Between 1996 and 2000, its sales grew almost fourfold, from $335 million to more than $1.2 billion, and its stock price soared by more than 500%. More recently, however, its growth rate has begun to slow down, and Abercrombie has had a hard time meeting its quarterly earnings targets. These problems were compounded by the global recession in 2009 with the stock price in November 2009 falling by 90% from its high 1 year before. Abercrombie's struggles resulted from increased competition, a sluggish economy, and the challenges of staying ahead of the fashion curve.

Since 2009, the company's stock has rebounded strongly but questions remain about the firm's long-term growth prospects. Given the questions about Abercrombie's future growth rate, analysts have focused on the company's earnings reports. Thomson ONE provides a convenient and detailed summary of the company's recent earnings history along with a summary of analysts' earnings forecasts.

To access this information, we begin by entering the company's ticker symbol, ANF, on Thomson ONE's main screen and then selecting GO. This takes us to an overview of the company's recent performance. After checking out the overview, you should click on the tab labeled Estimates, near the top of your screen. Here you will find a wide range of information about the company's past and projected earnings.

Discussion Questions

1. What are the mean and median forecasts for Abercrombie's earnings per share over the next fiscal year?
2. Based on analysts' forecasts, what is the firm's expected long-term growth rate in earnings?
3. Have analysts made any significant changes to their forecasted earnings for Abercrombie & Fitch in the past few months?
4. Historically, have Abercrombie's reported earnings generally met, exceeded, or fallen short of analysts' forecasted earnings?
5. How has Abercrombie's stock performed this year relative to the S&P 500?

MINI CASE

Hatfield Medical Supplies's stock price had been lagging its industry averages, so its board of directors brought in a new CEO, Adam Lee. Lee asked for the company's long-run strategic plan; when he learned that no formal plan existed, he decided to develop one himself. Lee had brought in Rick Novak, a finance MBA who had been working for a consulting company, to replace the old CFO, and he asked Rick to develop the financial planning section of the strategic plan. In his previous job, Novak's primary task had been to help clients develop financial forecasts, and that was one reason Lee hired him.

Novak began as he always did, by comparing Hatfield's financial ratios to the industry averages. If any ratio was substandard, he discussed it with the responsible manager to see what could be done to improve the situation. Figure 9-MC-1 provides Hatfield's latest financial statements plus some ratios and other data that Novak plans to use in his analysis. Notice that the figure is extracted from an *Excel* spreadsheet. Novak learned back in his university days that, because of interactions among variables, any realistic financial forecast must be based on a computer model. (The model is available to your instructor on the textbook's Web site.) Of course, he is also aware of the well-known computer axiom—garbage in, garbage out (GIGO). Novak therefore plans to discuss the model's inputs carefully with Hatfield's operating managers, individually and also collectively in the company's financial planning conference.

a. Do you think Adam Lee should develop a strategic plan for the company? Why? What are the central elements of such a plan? What is the role of finance in a strategic plan?

b. Given the data in Figure 9-MC-1, how well run would you say Hatfield appears to be in comparison with other firms in its industry? What are its primary strengths and weaknesses? Be specific in your answer, and point to various ratios that support your position. Also, use the Du Pont equation (see Chapter 8) as one part of your analysis.

c. Use the AFN equation to estimate Hatfield's required new external capital for 2013 if the 15% expected growth takes place. Assume that the firm's 2012 ratios will remain the same in 2013.

d. Define the term *capital intensity*. Explain how a decline in capital intensity would affect the AFN, other things held constant. Would economies of scale combined with rapid growth affect capital intensity, other things held constant? Also, explain how changes in each of the following would affect AFN, holding other things constant: the growth rate, the amount of accounts payable, the profit margin, and the payout ratio.

e. Define the term *self-supporting growth rate*. Based on the Figure 9-MC-1 data, what is Hatfield's self-supporting growth rate? Would the self-supporting growth rate be affected by a change in the capital intensity ratio or the other factors mentioned in question d? Other things held constant, would the calculated capital intensity ratio change over time if the company were growing and were also subject to economies of scale and/or lumpy assets?

f. Forecast the financial statements for 2013 using the following assumptions. (1) Operating ratios remain unchanged. (2) No additional notes payable, LT bonds, or common stock will be issued. (3) The interest rate on all debt is 10%. (4) If additional financing is needed, then it will be raised through a line of credit. The line of credit would be tapped on the last day of the year, so it would create no additional interest expenses for that year. (5) Interest expenses for notes payable and LT bonds are based on the average balances during the year. (6) If surplus funds are available, the surplus will be paid out as a special dividend payment. (7) Regular dividends will grow by 15%. (8) Sales will grow by 15%. We call this the Steady scenario because operations remain unchanged.

(1) How much new capital will the firm need (i.e., what is the forecasted AFN); how does

Figure 9-MC-1   **Financial Statements and Other Data (Millions, Except for Per Share Data)**

	A	B	C	D	E	F	G
4	Balance Sheet, Hatfield, 12/31/12				Income Statement, Hatfield, 2012		
5	Cash and securities		$20		Sales		$2,000
6	Accounts receivable		290		Total operating costs		1,900
7	Inventories		390		EBIT		$100
8	Total current assets		$700		Interest		60
9	Net fixed assets		500		EBT		$40
10	Total assets		$1,200		Taxes (40%)		16
11					Net income		$24
12	Accounts pay. + accruals		$100		Dividends		$9
13	Notes payable		80		Add. to retain. earnings		$15
14	Total current liabilities		$180		Shares outstanding		10
15	Long-term debt		520		EPS		$2.40
16	Total liabilities		$700		DPS		$0.90
17	Common stock		300		Year-end stock price		$24.00
18	Retained earnings		200				
19	Total common equity		$500				
20	Total liab. & equity		$1,200				
21							
22	Selected Ratios and Other Data, 2012			Hatfield	Industry		
23	Sales, 2012 (S_0):			$2,000	$2,000		Sales set equal to
24	Expected growth in sales:			15.0%	15.0%		Hatfield to make the
25	Profit margin (M):			1.2%	2.74%		data comparable.
26	Assets/Sales (A_0^*/S_0):			60.0%	50.0%		
27	Payout ratio (POR):			37.5%	35.0%		
28	Equity multiplier (Assets/Equity):			2.40	2.13		
29	Total liability/Total assets			58.3%	53.0%		
30	Times interest earned (EBIT/Interest):			1.67	5.20		
31	Increase in sales ($\Delta S = gS_0$):			$300	$300		
32	(Payables + Accruals)/Sales (L_0^*/S_0):			5.0%	4.0%		
33	Operating costs/Sales:			95.0%	93.0%		
34	Cash/Sales:			1.0%	1.0%		
35	Receivables/Sales:			14.5%	11.0%		
36	Inventories/Sales:			19.5%	15.0%		
37	Fixed assets/Sales:			25.0%	23.0%		
38	Tax rate:			40.0%	40.0%		
39	Interest rate on all debt:			10.00%	9.5%		
40	Price/Earning (P/E):			10.0	12.0		
41	ROE (Net income/Common equity):			4.80%	11.64%		

Note: Hatfield was operating at full capacity in 2012.

it compare with the amount you calculated using the AFN equation; and why does any difference exist?

(2) Calculate the firm's free cash flow, return on invested capital, EPS, DPS, ROE, and any other ratios you think would be useful in considering the situation.

(3) Assuming all of the inputs turn out to be exactly correct, would these answers also be exactly correct? If not, why not?

g. Repeat the analysis performed for Question f but now assume that Hatfield is able to achieve industry averages for the following input variables: operating costs/sales, receivables/sales, inventories/sales, and fixed assets/sales. Answer parts (1) and (2) of Question f under the new assumptions.

h. Could a strategic plan that included an incentive compensation program affect the firm's ability to move toward industry average operating performance?

i. What is financing feedback?

Selected Additional Cases

The following cases from TextChoice, *Cengage Learning's online case library, cover many of the concepts discussed in this chapter and are available at* **www.textchoice2.com/casenet.**

Klein-Brigham Series:

Case 37, "Space-Age Materials, Inc."; Case 38, "Automated Banking Management, Inc."; Case 52, "Expert Systems"; and Case 69, "Medical Management Systems, Inc."

Chapter 11

Corporate Valuation and Value-Based Management

As we have emphasized throughout the book, maximizing intrinsic value should be management's primary objective. However, to maximize value, managers need a tool for estimating the effects of alternative strategies. In this chapter, we develop and illustrate such a tool—the **corporate valuation model**, which is the present value of expected future free cash flows discounted at the weighted average cost of capital. In a sense, the corporate valuation model is the culmination of all the material covered thus far, because it pulls together financial statements, cash flows, financial projections, time value of money, risk, and the cost of capital. Some companies practice **value-based management** by systematically using the corporate valuation model to guide their decisions. The degree to which a company employs principles of value-based management often depends on its **corporate governance**, which is the set of laws, rules, and procedures that influence its operations and the decisions made by its managers. This chapter addresses all these topics, beginning with corporate valuation.

Beginning of Chapter Questions

As you read the chapter, consider how you would answer the following questions. You *should not* necessarily be able to answer the questions before you read the chapter. Rather, you should use them to get a sense of the issues covered in the chapter. After reading the chapter, you should be able to give at least partial answers to the questions, and you should be able to give better answers after the chapter has been discussed in class. Note, too, that it is often useful, when answering conceptual questions, to use hypothetical data to illustrate your answer. We illustrate the answers with an *Excel* model that is available on the textbook's Web site. Accessing the model and working through it is a useful exercise, and it provides insights that are useful when answering the questions.

1. What's the difference between **operating** and **nonoperating assets,** and between **net operating working capital** and **net working capital?** Why are these distinctions important to someone who is estimating the value of a business?
2. What is the definition of **free cash flow (FCF),** and how is it related to the **value of a firm's operations** as determined using the **corporate valuation model?**
3. What is **value-based management,** and how is it related to the corporate valuation model? Is

value-based management a good way to run a business, or can you think of alternative systems that are likely to produce better results?
4. Define **EVA** and **MVA,** and indicate how those concepts are related to value-based management.
5. Why is **corporate governance** important to investors? Explain how each of the following is related to corporate governance: (a) management entrenchment, (b) hostile takeovers, (c) incentive compensation plans, (d) greenmail, (e) poison pills, (f) strong boards of directors, (g) vesting periods for options, and (h) ESOPs.
6. How does the **free cash flow model** differ from the **dividend growth model,** and what are the advantages and disadvantages of each model? Do these models produce the same answers to the total value of a firm and the value of its stock?
7. How have events such as the accounting frauds at AIG, Enron, WorldCom, and several other companies affected people's ideas about corporate governance, the government's role in corporate governance, and the use of options for management compensation?

11.1 Overview of Corporate Valuation

As stated earlier, managers should evaluate the effects of alternative strategies on their firms' values. This really means forecasting financial statements under alternative strategies, finding the present value of each strategy's cash flow stream, and then choosing the strategy that provides the maximum value. The financial statements should be projected using the techniques and procedures discussed in Chapter 9, and the discount rate should be the risk-adjusted cost of capital as discussed in Chapter 10. But what model should managers use to discount the cash flows? One possibility is the dividend growth model from Chapter 5. However, that model is often unsuitable for managerial purposes. For example, suppose a start-up company is formed to develop and market a new product. Its managers will focus on product development, marketing, and raising capital. They will probably be thinking about an eventual IPO, or perhaps the sale of the company to a larger firm—Cisco, Microsoft, Intel, IBM, or another of the industry leaders that buy hundreds of successful new companies each year. For the managers of such a start-up, the decision to initiate dividend payments in the foreseeable future will be totally off the radar screen. Thus, the dividend growth model is not useful for valuing most start-up companies.

Also, many established firms pay no dividends. Investors may expect them to pay dividends sometime in the future—but when, and how much? As long as internal

CORPORATE VALUATION: PUTTING THE PIECES TOGETHER

The intrinsic value of a firm is determined by the size, timing, and risk of its expected future free cash flows (FCF). Chapter 9 showed how to project financial statements, and Chapter 7 showed how to calculate free cash flows. Chapter 10 explained how to estimate the weighted average cost of capital. This chapter puts the pieces together and shows how to calculate the value of a firm. It also shows how to use the valuation model as a guide for choosing among different corporate strategies and operating tactics.

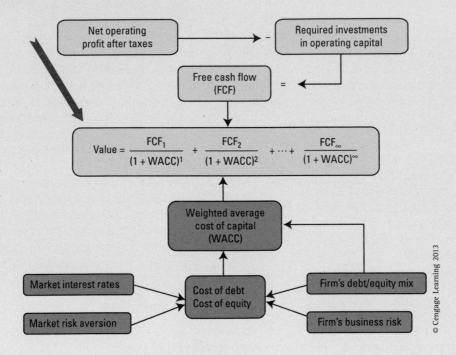

$$\text{Value} = \frac{FCF_1}{(1 + WACC)^1} + \frac{FCF_2}{(1 + WACC)^2} + \cdots + \frac{FCF_\infty}{(1 + WACC)^\infty}$$

© Cengage Learning 2013

opportunities and acquisitions are so attractive, the initiation of dividends will be postponed, and this makes the dividend growth model of little use. Even Microsoft, one of the world's most successful companies, paid no dividends until 2003.

Finally, the dividend growth model is generally of limited use for internal management purposes, even for a dividend-paying company. If the firm consisted of just one big asset and if that asset produced all of the cash flows used to pay dividends, then alternative strategies could be judged through the use of the dividend growth model. However, most firms have several different divisions with many assets, so the corporation's value depends on the cash flows from many different assets and on the actions of many managers. These managers need a way to measure the effects of their decisions on corporate value, but the discounted dividend model isn't very useful because individual divisions don't pay dividends.

Fortunately, the corporate valuation model does not depend on dividends, and it can be applied to divisions and subunits as well as to the entire firm.

Another important aspect of value-based management is the concept of corporate governance. The corporate valuation model shows how corporate decisions affect *stockholders*. However, corporate decisions are made by managers, not stockholders, and maximizing shareholder wealth is not the same as individual managers maximizing their own "satisfaction." Thus, a key aspect of value-based management is making sure that managers focus on the goal of maximizing stockholder wealth. The set of laws, rules, and procedures that influence a company's operations and motivate its managers falls under the general heading of *corporate governance.*

This chapter discusses the corporate valuation model, value-based management, and corporate governance, beginning with the corporate valuation model.

Self Test

Why is the corporate valuation model applicable in more circumstances than the dividend growth model?

What is value-based management?

What is corporate governance?

11.2 The Corporate Valuation Model

There are two types of corporate assets: **operating** and **nonoperating**. Operating assets, in turn, take two forms: **assets-in-place** and **growth options**. Assets-in-place include such tangible assets as land, buildings, machines, and inventory as well as intangible assets such as patents, customer lists, reputation, and general know-how. Growth options are opportunities to expand that arise from the firm's current operating knowledge, experience, and other resources. The assets-in-place provide an expected stream of cash flows, and so do the growth options. For instance, Wal-Mart has stores, inventory, widespread name recognition, a reputation for low prices, and considerable expertise in business processes. These tangible and intangible assets produce current sales and cash flows, and they also provide opportunities for new investments that will produce additional cash flows in the future. Similarly, Merck owns manufacturing plants, patents, and other real assets; it also has a knowledge base that facilitates the development of new drugs and thus new cash flow streams.

Most companies also own some nonoperating assets, which come in two forms. The first is a marketable securities portfolio over and above the cash needed to operate the business. For example, Ford Motor Company's automotive operation held about $14.2 billion in marketable securities at the end of December 2010, and this was in addition to $6.3 billion in cash. Second, Ford also had $2.4 billion of investments in other businesses, which were reported on the asset side of the balance sheet as "Equity in Net Assets of Affiliated Companies." In total, Ford had $14.2 + $2.4 = $16.6 billion of nonoperating assets, amounting to 26% of its $64.6 billion of total automotive assets. For most companies, the percentage is much lower. For example, as of the end of October 2010, Wal-Mart's percentage of nonoperating assets was less than 1%, which is more typical.

We see, then, that for most companies operating assets are far more important than nonoperating assets. Moreover, companies can influence the values of their operating assets, whereas the values of nonoperating assets are largely beyond their direct control. Therefore, value-based management—and hence this chapter—focuses on operating assets.

11.2a Estimating the Value of Operations

Figures 11-1 and 11-2 contain the actual 2012 and projected 2013 to 2016 financial statements for MagnaVision Inc., which produces optical systems for use in medical photography. (See Chapter 9 for more details on how to project financial statements.) Growth has been rapid in the past, but the market is becoming saturated, so the sales growth rate is expected to decline from 21% in 2013 to a sustainable rate of 5% in 2016 and beyond. Profit margins are expected to improve as the production process becomes more efficient and because MagnaVision will no longer be incurring marketing costs associated with the introduction of a major product. All items on the financial statements are projected to grow at a 5% rate after 2016. Note that the company does not pay a dividend, but it is expected to start paying out about 75% of its earnings beginning in 2015. (Chapter 17 explains in more detail how companies decide how much to pay out in dividends.)

Recall that free cash flow (FCF) is the cash from operations that is actually available for distribution to investors, including stockholders, bondholders, and preferred stockholders. The value of operations is the present value of the free cash flows the firm is expected to generate out into the future. Therefore, MagnaVision's value can be calculated as the present value of its expected future free cash flows from operations, discounted at its weighted average cost of capital (WACC), plus the value of its nonoperating assets. Here is the equation for the value of operations, which is the firm's value as a going concern:

Figure 11-1   MagnaVision Inc.: Income Statements (Millions of Dollars, Except for Per Share Data)

	A	B	C	D	E	F	G
			Actual		Projected		
26			2012	2013	2014[a]	2015	2016
28	Net Sales		$700.0	$850.0	$1,000.0	$1,100.0	$1,155.0
29	Costs (except depreciation)		599.0	734.0	911.0	935.0	982.0
30	Depreciation		28.0	31.0	34.0	36.0	38.0
31	Total operating costs		$627.0	$765.0	$945.0	$971.0	$1,020.0
32	Earning before int. & tax (EBIT)		$73.0	$85.0	$55.0	$129.0	$135.0
33	Less: Net interest[b]		13.0	15.0	16.0	17.0	19.0
34	Earning before taxes		$60.0	$70.0	$39.0	$112.0	$116.0
35	Taxes (40%)		24.0	28.0	15.6	44.8	46.4
36	Net income before pref. div.		$36.0	$42.0	$23.4	$67.2	$69.6
37	Preferred div.		6.0	7.0	7.4	8.0	8.3
38	Net income avail. for com. div.		$30.0	$35.0	$16.0	$59.2	$61.3
39	Common dividends		$0.0	$0.0	$0.0	$44.2	$45.3
40	Addition to retained earnings		$30.0	$35.0	$16.0	$15.0	$16.0
41							
42	Number of shares		100	100	100	100	100
43	Dividends per share		$0.000	$0.000	$0.000	$0.442	$0.453

[a]Net income is projected to decline in 2014. This is due to the projected cost for a one-time marketing program in that year.
[b]"Net interest" is interest paid on debt minus interest earned on marketable securities. Both items could be shown separately on the income statements, but for this example we combine them and show net interest. MagnaVision pays more interest than it earns; hence its net interest is subtracted.

| Figure 11-2 | MagnaVision Inc.: Balance Sheets (Millions of Dollars) | | | | | |

	A	B	C	D	E	F	G
52			Actual	Projected			
53	Assets		2012	2013	2014	2015	2016
54	Cash		$17.0	$20.0	$22.0	$23.0	$24.0
55	Marketable Securities[a]		63.0	70.0	80.0	84.0	88.0
56	Accounts receivable		85.0	100.0	110.0	116.0	121.0
57	Inventories		170.0	200.0	220.0	231.0	243.0
58	Total current assets		$335.0	$390.0	$432.0	$454.0	$476.0
59	Net plant and equipment		279.0	310.0	341.0	358.0	376.0
60	Total Assets		$614.0	$700.0	$773.0	$812.0	$852.0
61							
62	Liabilities and Equity						
63	Accounts Payable		$16.0	$20.0	$22.0	$23.0	$24.0
64	Notes payable		123.0	140.0	160.0	168.0	176.0
65	Accruals		44.0	50.0	55.0	58.0	61.0
66	Total current liabilities		$183.0	$210.0	$237.0	$249.0	$261.0
67	Long-term bonds		124.0	140.0	160.0	168.0	176.0
68	Preferred stock		62.0	70.0	80.0	84.0	88.0
69	Common Stock[b]		$200.0	$200.0	$200.0	$200.0	$200.0
70	Retained earnings		45.0	80.0	96.0	111.0	127.0
71	Common equity		$245.0	$280.0	$296.0	$311.0	$327.0
72	Total liabilities and equity		$614.0	$700.0	$773.0	$812.0	$852.0

[a]All assets except marketable securities are operating assets required to support sales. The marketable securities are financial assets not required in operations.
[b]Par plus paid-in capital.

Value of operations = V_{op} = PV of expected future free cash flows

$$= \frac{FCF_1}{(1 + WACC)^1} + \frac{FCF_2}{(1 + WACC)^2} + \cdots + \frac{FCF_\infty}{(1 + WACC)^\infty}$$

(11–1)

$$= \sum_{t=1}^{\infty} \frac{FCF_t}{(1 + WACC)^t}$$

MagnaVision's cost of capital is 10.84%. To find its value of operations as a going concern, we use an approach similar to the nonconstant dividend growth model for stocks in Chapter 5 and proceed as follows.

1. Assume that the firm will experience nonconstant growth for N years, after which it will grow at some constant rate.
2. Calculate the expected free cash flow for each of the N nonconstant growth years.
3. Recognize that growth after Year N will be constant, so we can use the constant growth formula to find the firm's value at Year N. This is the sum of the PVs for year N + 1 and all subsequent years, discounted back to Year N.
4. Find the PV of the free cash flows for each of the N nonconstant growth years. Also, find the PV of the firm's value at Year N.
5. Now sum all the PVs, those of the annual free cash flows during the nonconstant period plus the PV of the Year-N value, to find the firm's value of operations.

Figure 11-3   Calculating MagnaVision's Expected Free Cash Flow (Millions of Dollars)

	A	B	C	D	E	F	G
			Actual		Projected		
81							
82	Step 1: Calculate FCF		2012	2013	2014[b]	2015	2016
83	1. Net operating working capital[a]		$212.0	$250.0	$275.0	$289.0	$303.0
84	2. Net plant and equipment		279.0	310.0	341.0	358.0	376.0
85	3. Net operating capital		$491.0	$560.0	$616.0	$647.0	$679.0
86	4. Investment in operating capital			69.0	56.0	31.0	32.0
87	5. NOPAT		$43.8	$51.0	$33.0	$77.4	$81.0
88	6. Less: Investment in op. capital			69.0	56.0	31.0	32.0
89	7. Free cash flow			-$18.0	-$23.0	$46.4	$49.0

[a]We use the terms "total net operating capital," "operating capital," and "net operating assets" interchangeably.
[b]NOPAT declines in 2014 because of a marketing expenditure projected for that year. See Note a in Figure 11-1.

© Cengage Learning 2013

WEB

See *Ch11 Tool Kit.xls* on the textbook's Web site.

Figure 11-3 calculates free cash flow for each year, using procedures discussed in Chapter 7. Line 1, with data for 2013 from the balance sheets in Figure 11-2, shows the required net operating working capital, or operating current assets minus operating current liabilities, for 2012:

$$\begin{array}{c}\text{Required net}\\\text{operating}\\\text{working capital}\end{array} = \left(\begin{array}{c}\text{Cash}\\+ \text{Accounts receivable}\\+ \text{Inventories}\end{array}\right) - \left(\begin{array}{c}\text{Accounts payable}\\+ \text{Accruals}\end{array}\right)$$

$$= (\$17.00 + \$85.00 + \$170.00) - (\$16.00 + \$44.00)$$
$$= \$212.00$$

Line 2 shows required net plant and equipment; Line 3, which is the sum of Lines 1 and 2, shows the required net operating assets, also called total net operating capital or just operating capital. For 2012, operating capital is $212 + $279 = $491 million.

Line 4 shows the required annual addition to operating capital, found as the change in operating capital from the previous year. For 2013, the required investment in operating capital is $560 − $491 = $69 million.

Line 5 shows NOPAT, or net operating profit after taxes. Note that EBIT is operating earnings *before* taxes, while NOPAT is operating earnings *after* taxes. Therefore, NOPAT = EBIT(1 – T). With a 2013 EBIT of $85 million (as shown in Figure 11-1) and a tax rate of 40%, the NOPAT projected for 2013 is $51 million:

$$\text{NOPAT} = \text{EBIT}(1 - \text{T}) = \$85(1.0 - 0.4) = \$51 \text{ million}$$

Although MagnaVision's operating capital is projected to produce $51 million of after-tax profits in 2013, the company must invest $69 million in new operating capital in 2013 to support its growth plan. Therefore, the free cash flow for 2013, shown on Line 7, is a negative $18 million:

$$\text{Free cash flow (FCF)} = \$51 - \$69 = -\$18 \text{ million}$$

This negative free cash flow in the early years is typical for young, high-growth companies. Even though net operating profit after taxes (NOPAT) is positive in all years, free cash flow is negative because of the need to invest in operating assets. The negative free cash flow means the company will have to obtain new funds from investors, and the balance sheets in Figure 11-2 show that notes payable, long-term bonds, and preferred stock all increase from 2012 to 2013. Stockholders will also help fund MagnaVision's growth—they will receive no dividends until 2015, so all of the net income from 2013 and 2014 will be reinvested. However, as growth slows, free cash flow will become positive, and MagnaVision plans to use some of its FCF to pay dividends beginning in 2015.[1]

A variant of the constant growth dividend model is shown as Equation 11-2. This equation can be used to find the value of MagnaVision's operations at time N, when its free cash flows stabilize and begin to grow at a constant rate. This is the value of all FCFs beyond time N, discounted back to time N (which is 2016 for MagnaVision):

$$V_{op(at\ time\ N)} = \sum_{t=N+1}^{\infty} \frac{FCF_t}{(1+WACC)^{t-N}}$$

$$= \frac{FCF_{N+1}}{WACC-g} = \frac{FCF_N(1+g)}{WACC-g}$$

(11–2)

Based on a 10.84% cost of capital, $49 million of free cash flow in 2016, and a 5% growth rate, the value of MagnaVision's operations as of December 31, 2016, is forecasted to be $880.99 million:

$$V_{op(12/31/16)} = \frac{FCF_{12/31/16}(1+g)}{WACC-g}$$

$$= \frac{\$49(1+0.05)}{0.1084-0.05} = \frac{\$51.45}{0.1084-0.05} = \$880.99$$

(11–2a)

This $880.99 million figure is called the company's **horizon value** because it is the value at the end of the forecast period. It is also sometimes called a **continuing value** or **terminal value**. It is the amount that MagnaVision could expect to receive if it sold its operating assets on December 31, 2016.

Figure 11-4 shows the free cash flow for each year during the nonconstant growth period along with the horizon value of operations in 2016. To find the value of operations as of "today," December 31, 2012, we find the PV of the horizon value and each annual free cash flow in Figure 11-4, discounting at the 10.84% cost of capital:

$$V_{op(12/31/12)} = \frac{-\$18.00}{(1+0.1084)^1} + \frac{-\$23.00}{(1+0.1084)^2} + \frac{\$46.40}{(1+0.1084)^3} + \frac{\$49.00}{(1+0.1084)^4} + \frac{\$880.99}{(1+0.1084)^4}$$

$$= \$615.27$$

See **Ch11 Tool Kit.xls** on the textbook's Web site.

---

1. MagnaVision plans to increase its debt and preferred stock each year so as to maintain a constant capital structure. We discuss capital structure in detail in Chapter 15.

Figure 11-4   MagnaVision's Value of Operations (Millions of Dollars)

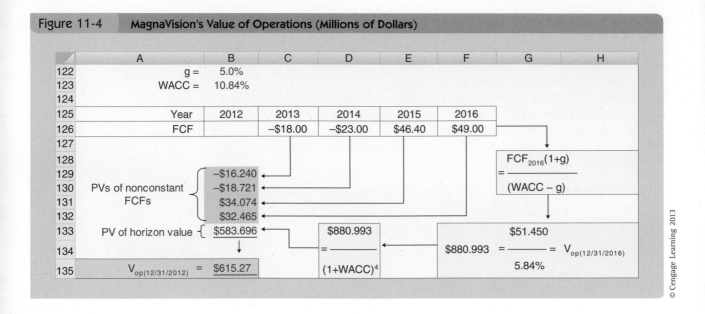

WEB

See **Ch11 Tool Kit.xls** on the textbook's Web site.

The sum of the PVs is approximately $615 million, and it represents an estimate of the price MagnaVision could expect to receive if it sold its operating assets "today," December 31, 2012.

11.2b Estimating the Price Per Share

The total value of any company is the value of its operations plus the value of its nonoperating assets.[2] As shown in the Figure 11-2 balance sheet for December 31, 2012, MagnaVision had $63 million of marketable securities on that date. Unlike for operating assets, we don't need to calculate a present value for marketable securities because short-term financial assets as reported on the balance sheet are at (or close to) their market value. Therefore, MagnaVision's total value on December 31, 2012, is $615.27 + $63 = $678.27 million.

If the company's total value on December 31, 2012, is $678.27 million, then what is the value of its common equity? First, the sum of notes payable and long-term debt is $123 + $124 = $247 million, and these securities have the first claim on assets and income.[3] The preferred stock has a claim of $62 million, and it also ranks above the common. Therefore, the value left for common stockholders is $678.27 − $247 − $62 = $369.27 million.

Figure 11-5 is a bar chart that provides a breakdown of MagnaVision's value. The left bar shows the company's total value as the sum of its nonoperating assets and its value of operations. Next, the middle bar shows the claim of each class of investors on that total value. Debtholders have the highest priority claim, and Magna Vision owes $123 million on notes payable and $124 million on long-term bonds for a total of $247 million. The preferred stockholders have the next claim, $62 million. The remaining value belongs to the common equity, and it amounts to

---

2. The total value also includes the value of growth options not associated with assets-in-place, but MagnaVision has no such options.
3. Accounts payable and accruals were part of the calculation of FCF, so their impact on value is already incorporated into the valuation of the company's operations. It would be double-counting to subtract them now from the value of operations.

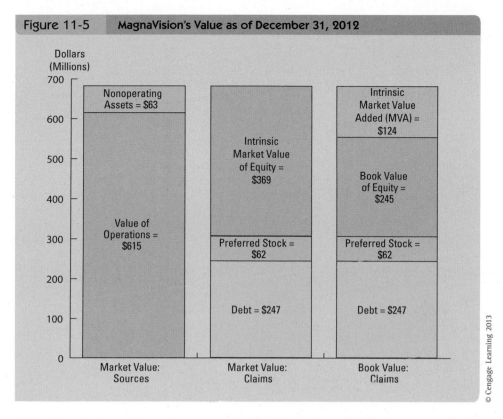

Figure 11-5   MagnaVision's Value as of December 31, 2012

$678.27 − $247 − $62 = $369.27 million.[4] This is MagnaVision's intrinsic value of equity.

In Chapter 7, we defined the Market Value Added (MVA) as the difference between the market value of equity and the book value of equity capital supplied by shareholders. Here we focus on the *intrinsic* MVA, which is the difference between the intrinsic market value of stock and the book value of equity. The bar on the right side of Figure 11-5 divides the estimated market value of equity into these two components.

Figure 11-6 summarizes the calculations used to find MagnaVision's stock value. There are 100 million shares outstanding, and their total intrinsic value is $369.27 million. Therefore, the intrinsic value of a single share is $369.27/100 = $3.69.

11.2c The Dividend Growth Model Applied to MagnaVision

MagnaVision has not yet begun to pay dividends. However, as we saw in Figure 11-1, a cash dividend of $0.442 per share is forecasted for 2015. The dividend is expected to grow by about 2.5% in 2016 and at a constant 5% rate thereafter. MagnaVision's cost of equity is 14%. In this situation, we can apply the nonconstant dividend growth model as developed earlier in Chapter 5. Figure 11-7 shows that the value of MagnaVision's stock, based on this model, is $3.70 per share,

---

4. When estimating the intrinsic market value of equity, it would be better to subtract the market values of debt and preferred stock rather than their book values. However, in most cases (including this one), the book values of fixed-income securities are close to their market values. When this is true, one can simply use book values.

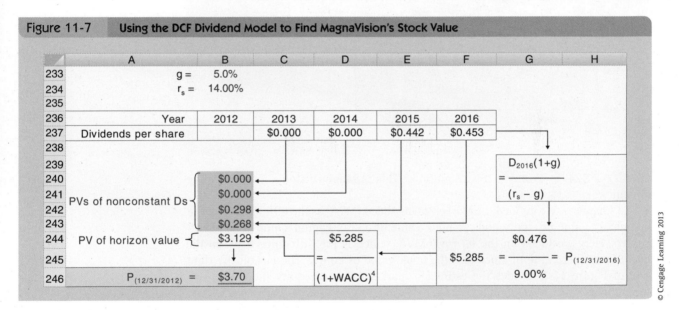

Figure 11-6 Finding the Value of MagnaVision's Intrinsic Stock Price (Millions, Except for Per Share Data)

	A	B	C	D
196		Process	MagnaVision	
197				
198		Value of operations	$615.27	
199		+ Value of nonoperating assets	63.00	
200		Total intrinsic value of firm	$678.27	
201		− Debt	247.00	
202		− Preferred stock	62.00	
203		Intrinsic value of equity	$369.27	
204		÷ Number of shares	100.00	
205				
206		Intrinsic stock price per share =	$3.69	

© Cengage Learning 2013

Figure 11-7 Using the DCF Dividend Model to Find MagnaVision's Stock Value

	A	B	C	D	E	F	G	H
233	g =	5.0%						
234	r_s =	14.00%						
235								
236	Year	2012	2013	2014	2015	2016		
237	Dividends per share		$0.000	$0.000	$0.442	$0.453		
238								
239							$\dfrac{D_{2016}(1+g)}{(r_s - g)}$	
240		$0.000						
241	PVs of nonconstant Ds	$0.000						
242		$0.298						
243		$0.268						
244	PV of horizon value	$3.129		$5.285		$0.476		
245			$= \dfrac{}{(1+WACC)^4}$		$5.285	$= \dfrac{0.476}{9.00\%} = P_{(12/31/2016)}$		
246	$P_{(12/31/2012)}$ =	$3.70						

© Cengage Learning 2013

WEB

See *Ch11 Tool Kit.xls* on the textbook's Web site.

which is the same (except for a rounding difference) as the value found using the corporate valuation model.[5]

11.2d Comparing the Corporate Valuation and Dividend Growth Models

Because the corporate valuation and dividend growth models give the same answer, does it matter which model you choose? In general, it does. For example, if you were a financial analyst estimating the value of a mature company whose dividends are expected to grow steadily in the future, it would probably be more efficient to use the dividend growth model. In this case you would need to estimate only the growth rate in dividends, not the entire set of forecasted financial statements.

However, if a company is paying a dividend but is still in the high-growth stage of its life cycle, you would need to project the future financial statements

---

5. The small difference is due to rounding the cost of capital to four significant digits.

before you could make a reasonable estimate of future dividends. Then, because you would have already estimated future financial statements, it would be a toss-up as to whether the corporate valuation model or the dividend growth model would be easier to apply. Intel, which pays a dividend of about 78 cents per share on earnings of about $2.31 per share, is an example of a company to which you could apply either model.

Now suppose you were trying to estimate the value of a company that has never paid a dividend, or a new firm that is about to go public, or a division that GE or some other large company is planning to sell. In each of these situations there would be no choice: You would have to estimate future financial statements and use the corporate valuation model.

Actually, much can be learned from the corporate valuation model even if a company is paying steady dividends; hence, many analysts today use it for all valuation analyses. The process of projecting future financial statements can reveal quite a bit about a company's operations and financing needs. Also, such an analysis can provide insights into actions that might be taken to increase the company's value. This is the essence of value-based management, which we discuss in the next section.[6]

Self Test

Give some examples of assets-in-place, growth options, and nonoperating assets.

Write out the equation for the value of operations.

What is the *horizon value?* Why is it also called the *terminal value* or *continuing value?*

Explain how to estimate the price per share using the corporate valuation model.

A company expects FCF of −$10 million at Year 1 and FCF of $20 million at Year 2; after Year 2, FCF is expected to grow at a 5% rate. If the WACC is 10%, then what is the horizon value of operations, $V_{op(Year 2)}$? (**$420 million**) What is the current value of operations, $V_{op(Year 0)}$? (**$354.55 million**)

A company has a current value of operations of $800 million, and it holds $100 million in short-term investments. If the company has $400 million in debt and has 10 million shares outstanding, what is the price per share? (**$50.00**)

11.3 Value-Based Management

WEB

See *Ch11 Tool Kit.xls* on the textbook's Web site.

Bell Electronics Inc. has two divisions, Memory and Instruments, with total sales of $1.5 billion and operating capital of $1.07 billion. Based on its current stock and bond prices, the company's total market value is about $1.215 billion, giving it an MVA of $145 million: $1.215 − $1.070 = $0.145 billion = $145 million. Because it has a positive MVA, Bell has created value for its investors. Even so, management

---

6. For a more detailed explanation of corporate valuation, see P. Daves, M. Ehrhardt, and R. Shrieves, *Corporate Valuation: A Guide for Managers and Investors* (Mason, OH: Thomson/South-Western, 2004).

is considering several new strategic plans in its efforts to increase the firm's value. All of Bell's assets are used in operations.

The Memory division produces memory chips for such handheld electronic devices as smart phones, while the Instruments division produces devices for measuring and controlling sewage and water treatment facilities. Table 11-1 shows the latest financial results for the two divisions and for the company as a whole.

As the table shows, Bell Memory is the larger of the two divisions, with higher sales and more operating capital. Bell Memory is also more profitable, with a NOPAT/Sales ratio of 7.9% versus 7.2% for Bell Instruments. This year, as in other recent years, the focus of the initial strategic planning sessions was on the Memory division. Bell Memory has grown rapidly because of the phenomenal growth in consumer electronics, and this division rocketed past Instruments several years ago. Although Memory's growth has tapered off, senior management generally agreed that this division should receive the lion's share of corporate attention and resources because it is larger, more profitable, and, frankly, more exciting. After all, Bell Memory is associated with the glamorous market for telecommunications and personal electronic devices, whereas Bell Instruments is associated with sewage and sludge.

The financial assumptions and projections associated with the preliminary strategic plans for the two divisions are shown in Figures 11-8 and 11-9. The initial strategic plans project that each division will have 5% annual growth for the next 5 years and thereafter. These plans also assume that the cost structures of the two divisions will remain unchanged from the current year, 2012. Only partial financial projections are shown in Figures 11-8 and 11-9. However, when Bell's management decides on a final strategic plan, it will develop complete financial statements for the company as a whole and use them to determine financing requirements, as described in Chapter 9.

To evaluate the plans, Bell's management applied the corporate valuation model to each division, thus valuing them using the free cash flow valuation technique. Each division has a WACC of 10.5%, and Figure 11-10 shows the results. The three key items are NOPAT, the required investment in operating capital, and the resulting free cash flows for each year. In addition, the table shows each division's horizon value of operations at 2017, which is the end of the 5 years of explicit forecasts, as calculated via Equation 11-2. The value of operations at 2012 is the present value of the free cash flows and the horizon value, discounted at the weighted average cost of capital. As expected, Bell Memory has the greater value of operations, $709.6 million versus $505.5 million for Bell Instruments. However, the managers were surprised to see that Bell Memory's Market Value Added (MVA) is *negative*:

TABLE 11-1	2012 Financial Results for Bell Electronics Inc. (Millions of Dollars, Except for Percentages)		
	Division 1: Bell Memory	Division 2: Bell Instruments	Total Company
Sales	$1,000.0	$500.0	$1,500.0
Operating capital	870.0	200.0	1,070.0
Earnings before interest and taxes (EBIT)	131.0	60.0	191.0
Net operating profit after taxes (NOPAT)	78.6	36.0	114.6
Operating profitability (NOPAT/Sales)	7.9%	7.2%	7.6%

Figure 11-8	Initial Projections for the Bell Memory Division (Millions of Dollars, Except for Percentages)

	A	B	C	D	E	F	G
13		Actual	Projected	Projected	Projected	Projected	Projected
14	Panel A: Inputs	2012	2013	2014	2015	2016	2017
15	Sales Growth Rate		5%	5%	5%	5%	5%
16	Costs / Sales	81%	81%	81%	81%	81%	81%
17	Depreciation / Net plant & equip.	10%	10%	10%	10%	10%	10%
18	Cash / Sales	1%	1%	1%	1%	1%	1%
19	Acct. Rec. / Sales	8%	8%	8%	8%	8%	8%
20	Inventories / Sales	30%	30%	30%	30%	30%	30%
21	Net plant & equip. / Sales	59%	59%	59%	59%	59%	59%
22	Acct. Pay. / Sales	5%	5%	5%	5%	5%	5%
23	Accruals / Sales	6%	6%	6%	6%	6%	6%
24	Tax rate	40%	40%	40%	40%	40%	40%
25							
26	Panel 2: Partial Income Statement	2012	2013	2014	2015	2016	2017
27	Net Sales	$1,000.0	$1,050.0	$1,102.5	$1,157.6	$1,215.5	$1,276.3
28	Costs (except depreciation)	$810.0	$850.5	$893.0	$937.7	$984.6	$1,033.8
29	Depreciation	59.0	62.0	65.0	68.3	71.7	75.3
30	Total operating costs	$869.0	$912.5	$958.1	$1,006.0	$1,056.3	$1,109.1
31	Op. profit before int. & tax	$131.0	$137.6	$144.4	$151.6	$159.2	$167.2
32							
33	Panel C: Partial Balance Sheets						
34	Operating Assets	2012	2013	2014	2015	2016	2017
35	Cash	$10.0	$10.5	$11.0	$11.6	$12.2	$12.8
36	Accounts receivable	80.0	84.0	88.2	92.6	97.2	102.1
37	Inventories	300.0	315.0	330.8	347.3	364.7	382.9
38	Operating current assets	$390.0	$409.5	$430.0	$451.5	$474.0	$497.7
39	Net plant and equipment	$590.0	$619.5	$650.5	$683.0	$717.1	$753.0
40							
41	Operating Liabilities						
42	Accounts Payable	$50.0	$52.5	$55.1	$57.9	$60.0	$63.8
43	Accruals	60.0	63.0	66.2	69.5	72.9	76.6
44	Operating current liabilities	$110.0	$115.5	$121.3	$127.3	$133.7	$140.4

$709.6 value of operations − $870.0 operating capital = −$160.4 million.[7] In contrast, Bell Instruments's MVA is positive: $505.5 value of operations − $200 operating capital = $305.5 million.

A second strategic planning meeting was called to address this unexpected result. In it, Bell Memory's managers proposed a $20 million marketing campaign to boost

WEB

See *Ch11 Tool Kit.xls* on the textbook's Web site.

---

7. Earlier in this chapter, we estimated MVA as the estimated value of equity minus the book value of equity. We can also define MVA as

$$MVA = \text{Total market value} - \text{Total investor-supplied capital}$$

(see Chapter 7). By subtracting the value of any short-term investments from total market value, we get the value of operations. If we subtract short-term investments from total capital, we get investor-supplied operating capital. Therefore, MVA can be estimated as

$$MVA = \text{Value of operations} - \text{Investor-supplied operating capital}$$

Recall from Chapter 7 that investor-supplied operating capital is equal to total net operating capital, which we also call total capital. Therefore, we can estimate MVA for a division or for a privately held company as

$$MVA = \text{Value of operations} - \text{Total operating capital}$$

Figure 11-9   Initial Projections for the Bell Instruments Division (Millions of Dollars, Except for Percentages)

	A	B	C	D	E	F	G
49		Actual	Projected	Projected	Projected	Projected	Projected
50	Panel A: Inputs	2012	2013	2014	2015	2016	2017
51	Sales Growth Rate		5%	5%	5%	5%	5%
52	Costs / Sales	85%	85%	85%	85%	85%	85%
53	Depreciation / Net plant & equip.	10%	10%	10%	10%	10%	10%
54	Cash / Sales	1%	1%	1%	1%	1%	1%
55	Acct. Rec. / Sales	5%	5%	5%	5%	5%	5%
56	Inventories / Sales	15%	15%	15%	15%	15%	15%
57	Net plant & equipment / Sales	30%	30%	30%	30%	30%	30%
58	Acct. Pay. / Sales	5%	5%	5%	5%	5%	5%
59	Accruals / Sales	6%	6%	6%	6%	6%	6%
60	Tax rate	40%	40%	40%	40%	40%	40%
61							
62	Panel B: Partial Income Statement	2012	2013	2014	2015	2016	2017
63	Net Sales	$500.0	$525.0	$551.3	$578.8	$607.8	$638.1
64	Costs (except depreciation)	425.0	446.3	468.6	492.0	516.6	542.4
65	Depreciation	15.0	15.8	16.5	17.4	18.2	19.1
66	Total operating costs	$440.0	$462.0	$485.1	$509.4	$534.8	$561.6
67	Earning before int. & tax	$60.0	$63.0	$66.2	$69.5	$72.9	$76.6
68							
69	Panel C: Partial Balance Sheets						
70	Operating Assets	2012	2013	2014	2015	2016	2017
71	Cash	$5.0	$5.3	$5.5	$5.8	$6.1	$6.4
72	Accounts receivable	25.0	26.3	27.6	28.9	30.4	31.9
73	Inventories	75.0	78.8	82.7	86.8	91.2	95.7
74	Operating current assets	$105.0	$110.3	$115.8	$121.6	$127.6	$134.0
75	Net plant and equipment	$150.0	$157.5	$165.4	$173.6	$182.3	$191.4
76							
77	Operating Liabilities						
78	Accounts Payable	$25.0	$26.3	$27.6	$28.9	$30.4	$31.9
79	Accruals	30.0	31.5	33.1	34.7	36.5	38.3
80	Operating current liabilities	$55.0	$57.8	$60.6	$63.7	$66.9	$70.2

their sales growth rate from 5% to 6%. They argued that because Bell Memory is so profitable, its value would be much higher if they could push up sales. Before accepting this proposal, though, the proposed changes were run through the valuation model. The managers changed the Bell Memory division's growth rate from 5% to 6%; see the file *Ch11 Tool Kit.xls* on the textbook's Web site for details. To their surprise, the division's value of operations fell to $691.5 million, and its MVA also declined, from −$160.4 million to −$178.5 million. Although Bell Memory was profitable, increasing its sales growth actually reduced its value!

To better understand these results, we can express the firm's value in terms of four fundamental wealth drivers:

$$g = \text{Growth in sales}$$

$$OP = \text{Operating profitability (OP)} = \text{NOPAT/Sales}$$

$$CR = \text{Capital requirements (CR)} = \text{Operating capital/Sales}$$

$$WACC = \text{Weighted average cost of capital}$$

Figure 11-10 **Initial FCF Valuation of Each Division (Millions of Dollars, Except for Percentages)**

	A	B	C	D	E	F	G
87	Panel A: FCF Valuation of the						
88	Bell Memory Division	Actual	Projected	Projected	Projected	Projected	Projected
89	Calculation of FCF:	2012	2013	2014	2015	2016	2017
90	Net operating working capital	$280.0	$294.0	$308.7	$324.1	$340.3	$357.4
91	Net plant & equipment	590.0	619.5	650.5	683.0	717.1	753.0
92	Net operating capital	$870.0	$913.5	$959.2	$1,007.1	$1,057.5	$1,110.4
93	Investment in operating capital		$43.5	$45.7	$48.0	$50.4	$52.9
94	NOPAT (Tax rate = 40%)	$78.6	$82.5	$86.7	$91.0	$95.5	$100.3
95	Free cash flow (FCF)		$39.0	$41.0	$43.0	$45.2	$47.4
96	Growth in FCF			5%	5%	5%	5%
97	Value of Operations:						
98	WACC	10.5%					
99	Horizon value						$905.7
100	Total cash flow		$ 39.0	$ 41.0	$ 43.0	$ 45.2	$953.1
101	Value of operations =	$709.6					
102	Divisional MVA						
103	(Val. of ops - total op. capital) =	($160.4)					
104							
105	Panel B: FCF Valuation of the						
106	Bell Instruments Division	Actual	Projected	Projected	Projected	Projected	Projected
107	Calculation of FCF	2012	2013	2014	2015	2016	2017
108	Net operating working capital	$50.0	$52.5	$55.1	$57.9	$60.8	$63.8
109	Net plant & equipment	150.0	157.5	165.4	173.6	182.3	191.4
110	Net operating capital	$200.0	$210.0	$220.5	$231.5	$243.1	$255.3
111	Investment in operating capital		$10.0	$10.5	$11.0	$11.6	$12.2
112	NOPAT (Tax rate – 40%)	$36.0	$37.8	$39.7	$41.7	$43.8	$45.9
113	Free cash flow (FCF)		$27.8	$29.2	$30.6	$32.2	$33.8
114	Growth in FCF			5%	5%	5%	5%
115	Value of Operations						
116	WACC	10.5%					
117	Horizon value						$645.1
118	Total cash flow		$ 27.8	$ 29.2	$ 30.6	$ 32.2	$678.9
119	Value of operations =	$305.5					
120	Divisional MVA						
121	(Val. of ops - total op. capital) =	$305.5					
122							

Notes: The WACC is 10.5% for each division. The horizon value (HV) at 2017 is calculated using Equation 11-2, the constant growth formula for free cash flows:

$$HV_{2017} = [FCF_{2017}(1 + g)] \div (WACC - g)$$

The value of operations is the present value of the horizon value and the free cash flows discounted at the WACC; it is calculated in a manner similar to Figure 11-3. Projected figures may not total exactly because of rounding. See **Ch11 Tool Kit.xls** on the textbook's Web site for all calculations.

How do these drivers affect the value of a firm? First, the sales growth rate usually (but not always) has a positive effect on value, provided the company is profitable enough. However, the effect can be negative if growth requires a great deal of capital and if the cost of capital is high. Second, operating profitability, which measures the after-tax profit per dollar of sales, always has a positive effect—the higher the better. Third, the capital requirements ratio, which measures how much operating capital is needed to generate a dollar of sales, also has a consistent effect: The lower the CR the better, since a low CR means that the company can generate new sales with smaller amounts of new capital. Finally, the fourth factor, the WACC, also has a consistent effect: The lower it is, the higher the firm's value.

Another important metric in the corporate valuation model is the **expected return on invested capital (EROIC)**, defined as the expected NOPAT for the coming year divided by the amount of operating capital at the beginning of the year (which is the end of the preceding year). It can also be defined in terms of the fundamental value drivers for profitability (OP) and capital requirements (CR). Thus, EROIC represents the expected return on the capital that has already been invested:

(11–3)

$$EROIC_N = \frac{NOPAT_{N+1}}{Capital_N}$$

$$= \frac{OP_{N+1}}{CR_N}$$

To illustrate, the EROIC of the Bell Memory division for 2017, the last year in the forecast period, is

WEB

See *Ch11 Tool Kit.xls* on the textbook's Web site for details.

$$EROIC_{2017} = \frac{NOPAT_{2018}}{Capital_{2017}} = \frac{NOPAT_{2017}(1+g)}{Capital_{2017}} = \frac{\$100.3(1.05)}{\$1,110.4} = 9.5\%$$

To see exactly how the four value drivers and EROIC determine value for a constant growth firm, we can start with Equation 11-2 (which we repeat here),

$$V_{op(at\ time\ N)} = \frac{FCF_{N+1}}{WACC - g}$$

and rewrite it in terms of the value drivers:

(11–4)

$$V_{op(at\ time\ N)} = Capital_N + \left\{ \left[\frac{Sales_N(1+g)}{WACC - g} \right] \left[OP - WACC\left(\frac{CR}{1+g}\right) \right] \right\}$$

Equation 11-4 shows that the value of operations can be divided into two components: (1) the dollars of operating capital that investors have provided; and (2) the additional value that management has added or subtracted, which is equivalent to MVA.

Note that the first [bracketed] fraction in Equation 11-4 represents the present value of growing sales, discounted at the WACC. This would be the MVA of a firm that has no costs and that never needs to invest additional capital. But firms do have costs and capital requirements, and their effect is captured by the term in the second set of brackets. Here we see that, holding g constant, MVA will improve if operating profitability (OP) increases, if WACC decreases, and/or if capital requirements (CR) decrease.

Observe that an increase in growth will not necessarily increase value. OP could be positive, but if CR is quite high—meaning that a lot of new capital is needed to support a given increase in sales—then the second bracketed term can be negative. In this situation, growth causes the first bracketed term to increase; however, since it's being multiplied by a negative term (the second bracket), the net result will be a decrease in MVA.

We can also rewrite Equation 11-2 in terms of EROIC (or profitability and capital requirements) as follows:

$$V_{op(at\ time\ N)} = Capital_N + \frac{Capital_N\,(EROIC_N - WACC)}{WACC - g}$$

$$= Capital_N + \frac{Capital_N\left(\dfrac{OP_{N+1}}{CR_N} - WACC\right)}{WACC - g}$$

(11–5)

Equation 11-5 also breaks value into two components, the value of capital and the MVA, shown in the second term. This term for MVA shows that value depends on the EROIC, the WACC, and the spread between the expected return on invested capital. Notice that the EROIC in turn depends on profitability and required capital. If the combination of profitability and required capital produces an EROIC greater than WACC, then the return on capital is greater than the return investors expect and management is adding value. In this case, an increase in the growth rate causes value to go up. If EROIC is exactly equal to WACC then the firm is, in an economic sense, "breaking even." It has positive accounting profits and cash flow, but these cash flows are just sufficient to satisfy investors, causing value to exactly equal the amount of capital that has been provided. If EROIC is less than WACC then the term in parentheses is negative, management is destroying value, and growth is harmful. This is one case where the faster the growth rate, the lower the firm's value.

We should also note that the insights from Equations 11-4 and 11-5 apply to all firms, but the equations themselves can be applied only to relatively stable firms whose growth has leveled out at a constant rate. For example, in 2010 World Fuel Services's sales grew at 69% per year, so we cannot apply Equations 11-4 and 11-5 directly (although we could always apply Equation 11-1). World Fuel Services is an extremely low-margin business and its NOPAT/Sales ratio was only 0.8%, but it was nonetheless quite profitable. Despite its profits, it had a negative free cash flow of about $276 million! If World Fuel Services can maintain profitability as its growth slows to sustainable levels, it will generate huge amounts of FCF. This explains why its MVA was over $1.3 billion in 2010 even though its FCF was negative.

Table 11-2 shows the value drivers for Bell's two divisions as measured at 2017, the end of the forecast period. We report these for the *end* of the forecast period because ratios can change during the forecast period in response to input changes. By the end of the forecast period, however, all inputs and ratios should be stable.

Both divisions have the same growth rate and the same WACC, as shown in Table 11-2. Bell Memory is more profitable, but it also has much higher capital requirements. The result is that Bell Memory's EROIC is only 9.5%, well below its 10.5% WACC. Thus, growth doesn't help Bell Memory—indeed, it reduces the division's value.

TABLE 11-2 Bell Electronics's Forecasted Value Drivers for 2017

	Division 1: Bell Memory	Division 2: Bell Instruments
Growth: g	5.0%	5.0%
Profitability: $(NOPAT_{2017}/Sales_{2017})$	7.9	7.2
Capital requirement: $(Capital_{2017}/Sales_{2017})$	87.0	40.0
WACC	10.5	10.5
Expected return on invested capital, EROIC: $NOPAT_{2017}(1 + g)/Capital_{2017}$	9.5	18.9

© Cengage Learning 2013

Based on this analysis, Bell Memory's managers decided not to request funds for a marketing campaign. Instead, they developed a plan to reduce capital requirements. The new plan called for spending $50 million on an integrated supply chain information system that would allow them to cut their inventory/sales ratio from 30% to 20% and also reduce the ratio of net plant to sales from 59% to 50%. Table 11-3 shows projected operating results based on this new plan. The value of operations would increase from $709.6 million to $1.1574 billion, or by $447.8 million. Because this amount is well over the $50 million required to implement the plan, top management decided to approve it. Note also that the plan shows MVA becoming positive at $287.4 million (a substantial improvement on the preliminary plan's negative $160.4 million) and the divisional EROIC rising to 13.0%, well over the 10.5% WACC.

Bell Instruments's managers also used the valuation model to assess changes in plans for their division. Given their high EROIC, the Instruments division proposed

TABLE 11-3 Comparison of the Preliminary and Final Plans (Millions of Dollars, Except for Percentages)

	Bell Memory		Bell Instruments	
	Preliminary	Final	Preliminary	Final
Inputs				
Sales growth rate, g	5%	5%	5%	6%
Inventories/Sales	30	20	15	16
Net plant/Sales	59	50	30	30
Results				
EROIC (2017)[a]	9.5%	13.0%	18.9%	18.6%
Invested (operating) capital (2017)[a]	$1,110.4	$ 867.9	$255.3	$274.3
Current value of operations (2012)[b]	709.6	1,157.4	505.5	570.1
Current MVA (2012)[b]	(160.4)	287.4	305.5	370.1

© Cengage Learning 2013

[a]We report EROIC and capital for the end of the forecast period because ratios can change during the forecast period if inputs change during that period. By the end of the forecast period, however, all inputs and ratios should be stable.
[b]We report the value of operations and the MVA as of the current date, 2012, because we want to see what effect the proposed plans would have on the current value of the two divisions.

(1) an aggressive marketing campaign and (2) an increase in inventories that would allow faster delivery and fewer stockouts. Together, these changes would boost the growth rate from 5% to 6%. The direct cost to implement the plan was $20 million, but there was also an indirect cost in that more inventories would have to be carried: The ratio of inventories to sales was forecasted to increase from 15% to 16%.

Should Instruments's new plan be implemented? Table 11-3 shows the forecasted results. The capital requirements associated with the increased inventory caused the EROIC to fall from 18.9% to 18.6%, but (1) the 18.6% return greatly exceeds the 10.5% WACC, and (2) the spread between 18.6% and 10.5% would be earned on additional capital. This caused the forecasted value of operations to increase from $505.5 to $570.1 million, or by $64.6 million. An 18.6% return on $274.3 million of capital is more valuable than an 18.9% return on $255.3 million of capital.[8] (To see this, note that you, or one of Bell's stockholders, would surely rather have an asset that provides a 50% return on an investment of $1,000 than one that provides a 100% return on an investment of $1.) Therefore, the new plan should be accepted, even though it lowers the Instruments division's EROIC.

Sometimes companies focus on their profitability and growth without giving adequate consideration to their capital requirements. This is a big mistake—*all* the wealth creation drivers, not just growth, must be taken into account. Fortunately for Bell's investors, the revised plan was accepted. However, as this example illustrates, it is easy for a company to mistakenly focus only on profitability and growth. They are important, but so are the other value drivers: capital requirements and the weighted average cost of capital. Value-based management explicitly includes the effects of all the value drivers because it uses the corporate valuation model, and the drivers are all embodied in that model.[9]

Self Test

What are the four drivers of value?

How is it possible for sales growth to *decrease* the value of a profitable firm?

You are given the following forecasted information for a constant growth company: sales = $10 million, operating profitability (OP) = 5%, capital requirements (CR) = 40%, growth (g) = 6%, and the weighted average cost of capital (WACC) = 10%. What is the current level of capital? (**$4 million**) What is the current level of NOPAT? (**$0.5 million**) What is the EROIC? (**13.25%**) What is the value of operations? (**$7.25 million**)

---

8. A potential fly in the ointment is that Bell's compensation plan might be based on rates of return and not on changes in wealth. In such a plan, which is fairly typical, the managers might reject the new proposed strategic plan if it lowers ROIC and hence their bonuses, even though the plan is good for the company's stockholders. We discuss the effect of compensation plans in more detail later in the chapter.

9. For more on corporate valuation and value-based management, see Sheridan Titman and John D. Martin, *Valuation: The Art and Science of Corporate Investment Decisions*, 2nd ed. (Boston: Prentice Hall, 2011); Tim Koller, Marc Goedhart, and David Wessels, *Valuation: Measuring and Managing the Value of Companies*, 4th ed. (Hoboken, NJ: John Wiley & Sons, 2005); John D. Martin and J. William Petty, *Value Based Management: The Corporate Response to the Shareholder Revolution* (Boston: Harvard Business School Press, 2000); John D. Martin, J. William Petty, and James S. Wallace, *Value Based Management with Corporate Social Responsibility* (New York: Oxford University Press, 2009); James M. McTaggart, Peter W. Kontes, and Michael C. Mankins, *The Value Imperative* (New York: The Free Press, 1994); and G. Bennett Stewart, *The Quest for Value* (New York: Harper Collins, 1991). For an application to small-firm valuation, see Michael S. Long and Thomas A. Bryant, *Valuing the Closely Held Firm* (New York: Oxford University Press, 2008).

11.4 Managerial Behavior and Shareholder Wealth

Shareholders want companies to hire managers who are able and willing to take legal and ethical actions to maximize intrinsic stock prices.[10] This obviously requires managers with technical competence, but it also requires managers who are willing to put forth the extra effort necessary to identify and implement value-adding activities. However, managers are people, and people have both personal and corporate goals. Logically, therefore, managers can be expected to act in their own self-interests, and if their self-interests are not aligned with those of stockholders, then corporate value will not be maximized. There are six ways in which a manager's behavior might harm a firm's intrinsic value.

1. Managers might not expend the time and effort required to maximize firm value. Rather than focusing on corporate tasks, they might spend too much time on external activities, such as serving on boards of other companies, or on nonproductive activities, such as golfing, lunching, and traveling.

2. Managers might use corporate resources on activities that benefit themselves rather than shareholders. For example, they might spend company money on such perquisites as lavish offices, memberships at country clubs, museum-quality art for corporate apartments, large personal staffs, and corporate jets. Because these perks are not actually cash payments to the managers, they are called **nonpecuniary benefits**.

3. Managers might avoid making difficult but value-enhancing decisions that harm friends in the company. For example, a manager might not close a plant or terminate a project if the manager has personal relationships with those who are adversely affected by such decisions, even if termination is the economically sound action.

4. Managers might take on too much risk or they might not take on enough risk. For example, a company might have the opportunity to undertake a risky project with a positive NPV. If the project turns out badly, then the manager's reputation will be harmed and the manager might even be fired. Thus, a manager might choose to avoid risky projects even if they are desirable from a shareholder's point of view. On the other hand, a manager might take on projects with too much risk. Consider a project that is not living up to expectations. A manager might be tempted to invest even more money in the project rather than admit that the project is a failure. Or a manager might be willing to take on a second project with a negative NPV if it has even a slight chance of a very positive outcome, since hitting a home run with this second project might cover up the first project's poor performance. In other words, the manager might throw good money after bad.

---

10. Notice that we said both legal and ethical actions. The accounting frauds perpetrated by Enron, WorldCom, and others that were uncovered in 2002 raised stock prices in the short run, but only because investors were misled about the companies' financial positions. Then, when the correct financial information was finally revealed, the stocks tanked. Investors who bought shares based on the fraudulent financial statements lost tens of billions of dollars. Releasing false financial statements is illegal. Aggressive earnings management and the use of misleading accounting tricks to pump up reported earnings is unethical, and executives can go to jail as a result of their shenanigans. When we speak of taking actions to maximize stock prices, we mean making operational or financial changes designed to maximize intrinsic stock value, not fooling investors with false or misleading financial reports.

5. If a company is generating positive free cash flow, a manager might "stockpile" it in the form of marketable securities instead of returning FCF to investors. This potentially harms investors because it prevents them from allocating these funds to other companies with good growth opportunities. Even worse, positive FCF often tempts a manager into paying too much for the acquisition of another company. In fact, most mergers and acquisitions end up as break-even deals, at best, for the acquiring company because the premiums paid for the targets are often very large.

   Why would a manager be reluctant to return cash to investors? First, extra cash on hand reduces the company's risk, which appeals to many managers. Second, a large distribution of cash to investors is an admission that the company doesn't have enough good investment opportunities. Slow growth is normal for a maturing company, but it isn't very exciting for a manager to admit this. Third, there is a lot of glamour associated with making a large acquisition, and this can provide a large boost to a manager's ego. Fourth, compensation usually is higher for executives at larger companies; cash distributions to investors make a company smaller, not larger.

6. Managers might not release all the information that is desired by investors. Sometimes, they might withhold information to prevent competitors from gaining an advantage. At other times, they might try to avoid releasing bad news. For example, they might "massage" the data or "manage the earnings" so that the news doesn't look so bad. If investors are unsure about the quality of information provided by managers, they tend to discount the company's expected free cash flows at a higher cost of capital, which reduces the company's intrinsic value.

   If senior managers believe there is little chance that they will be removed, we say that they are *entrenched*. Such a company faces a high risk of being poorly run, because entrenched managers are able to act in their own interests rather than in the interests of shareholders.

Name six types of managerial behaviors that can reduce a firm's intrinsic value.   **Self Test**

11.5 Corporate Governance

A key requirement for successful implementation of value-based management is to influence executives and other managers so that they do not behave in the ways described in the previous section but instead behave in a way that maximizes a firm's intrinsic value. Corporate governance can provide just such an influence. Corporate governance can be defined as the set of laws, rules, and procedures that influence a company's operations and the decisions made by its managers. At the risk of oversimplification, most corporate governance provisions come in two forms, sticks and carrots. The primary stick is the *threat of removal*, either as a decision by the board of directors or as the result of a hostile takeover. If a firm's managers are maximizing the value of the resources entrusted to them, they need not fear the loss of their jobs. On the other hand, if managers are not maximizing value, they should be removed by their own boards of directors, by dissident stockholders, or by other companies seeking to profit by installing a better management team. The main carrot is *compensation*. Managers have greater incentives to maximize intrinsic stock value if their compensation is linked to their firm's performance rather than being strictly in the form of salary.

Almost all corporate governance provisions affect either the threat of removal or compensation. Some provisions are internal to a firm and are under its control.[11] These internal provisions and features can be divided into five areas: (1) monitoring and discipline by the board of directors, (2) charter provisions and bylaws that affect the likelihood of hostile takeovers, (3) compensation plans, (4) capital structure choices, and (5) accounting control systems. In addition to the corporate governance provisions that are under a firm's control, there are also environmental factors outside of a firm's control, such as the regulatory environment, block ownership patterns, competition in the product markets, the media, and litigation. Our discussion begins with the internal provisions.

11.5a Monitoring and Discipline by the Board of Directors

Shareholders are a corporation's owners, and they elect the board of directors to act as agents on their behalf. In the United States, it is the board's duty to monitor senior managers and discipline them if they do not act in the interests of shareholders, either by removal or by a reduction in compensation.[12] This is not necessarily the case outside the United States. For example, many companies in Europe are required to have employee representatives on the board. Also, many European and Asian companies have bank representatives on the board. But even in the United States, many boards fail to act in the shareholders' best interests. How can this be?

Consider the election process. The board of directors has a nominating committee. These directors choose the candidates for the open director positions, and the ballot for a board position usually lists only one candidate. Although outside candidates can run a "write-in" campaign, only those candidates named by the board's nominating committee are on the ballot.[13] At many companies, the CEO is also the chairman of the board and has considerable influence on this nominating committee. This means that in practice it often is the CEO who, in effect, nominates candidates for the board. High compensation and prestige go with a position on the board of a major company, so board seats are prized possessions. Board members typically want to retain their positions, and they are grateful to whomever helped get them on the board. Thus, the nominating process often results in a board that is favorably disposed to the CEO.

At most companies, a candidate is elected simply by having a majority of votes cast. The proxy ballot usually lists all candidates, with a box for each candidate to check if the shareholder votes "For" the candidate and a box to check if the shareholder "Withholds" a vote on the candidate—you can't actually vote "No"; you can only withhold your vote. In theory, a candidate could be elected with a single "For" vote if all other votes were withheld. In practice, though, most shareholders either vote "For" or assign to management their right to vote (proxy is defined as the authority to act for another, which is why it is called a proxy statement). In practice,

---

11. We have adapted this framework from the one provided by Stuart L. Gillan, "Recent Developments in Corporate Governance: An Overview," *Journal of Corporate Finance*, June 2006, pp. 381–402. Gillan provides an excellent discussion of the issues associated with corporate governance, and we highly recommend this article to the reader who is interested in an expanded discussion of the issues in this section.

12. There are a few exceptions to this rule. For example, some states have laws allowing the board to take into consideration the interests of other stakeholders, such as employees and members of the community.

13. There is currently (early 2011) a movement under way to allow shareholders to nominate candidates for the board, but only time will tell whether this movement is successful.

then, the nominated candidates virtually always receive a majority of votes and are thus elected.

Occasionally there is a "Just vote no" campaign in which a large investor (usually an institution such as a pension fund) urges stockholders to withhold their votes for one or more directors. Although such campaigns do not directly affect the director's election, they do provide a visible way for investors to express their dissatisfaction. Recent evidence shows that "Just vote no" campaigns at poorly performing firms lead to better subsequent firm performance and a greater probability that the CEO will be dismissed.[14]

Voting procedures also affect the ability of outsiders to gain positions on the board. If the charter specifies cumulative voting, then each shareholder is given a number of votes equal to his or her shares multiplied by the number of board seats up for election. For example, the holder of 100 shares of stock will receive 1,000 votes if 10 seats are to be filled. Then, the shareholder can distribute those votes however he or she sees fit. One hundred votes could be cast for each of 10 candidates, or all 1,000 votes could be cast for one candidate. If noncumulative voting is used, our hypothetical stockholder cannot concentrate votes in this way—no more than 100 votes can be cast for any one candidate.

With noncumulative voting, if management controls 51% of the shares then they can fill every seat on the board, leaving dissident stockholders without any representation on the board. With cumulative voting, however, if 10 seats are to be filled then dissidents could elect a representative, provided they have 10% plus 1 additional share of the stock.

Note also that bylaws specify whether the entire board is to be elected annually or if directors are to have staggered terms with, say, one-third of the seats to be

LET'S GO TO MIAMI! IBM'S 2009 ANNUAL MEETING

IBM invited its stockholders to its annual meeting held on April 28, 2009, in Miami. The agenda included election of each board member for a 1-year term, ratification of PricewaterhouseCoopers as its independent auditing firm, approval of long-term incentive plans for executives, and three stockholder proposals: (1) adopt cumulative voting; (2) remove consideration of pension income that does not reflect operating performance from the measure of income used for bonuses; (3) adopt an advisory shareholder vote each year ratifying (or not) executive compensation. IBM's board recommended that shareholders vote against all three proposals.

About 8 pages of the proxy statement described nominees for the board and their compensation, about 53 pages explained executive compensation, and about 4½ pages covered the stockholders' proposals, with much of that being management's explanation for why it opposed them.

Stockholders were permitted to vote over the Web, by telephone, by mail, or in person at the meeting. When the result were tallied, IBM revealed that all board nominees had been elected by a majority and that all three stockholder proposals had been defeated, although the last two proposals garnered over 43% of the votes in their favor.

IBM's annual meeting might not have been as exciting as the TV show *CSI: Miami*, but we think the evidence shows that there will be more stockholder proposals in the future and that many will win approval.

14. See Diane Del Guercio, Laura Seery, and Tracie Woidtke, "Do Boards Pay Attention When Institutional Investor Activists 'Just Vote No'?" *Journal of Financial Economics,* October 2008, pp. 84–103.

filled each year and directors to serve 3-year terms. With staggered terms, fewer seats come up each year, making it harder for dissidents to gain representation on the board. Staggered boards are also called **classified boards**.

Many board members are "insiders"—that is, people who hold managerial positions within the company, such as the CFO. Because insiders report to the CEO, it may be difficult for them to oppose the CEO at a board meeting. To help mitigate this problem, several exchanges, such as the NYSE and Nasdaq, now require that listed companies have a majority of outside directors.

Some "outside" board members often have strong connections with the CEO through professional relationships, personal friendships, and consulting or other fee-generating activities. In fact, outsiders sometimes have very little expert business knowledge but have "celebrity" status from nonbusiness activities. Some companies also have **interlocking boards of directors**, where Company A's CEO sits on Company B's board and B's CEO sits on A's board. In these situations, even the outside directors are not truly independent and impartial.

Large boards (those with more than about ten members) often are less effective than smaller boards. As anyone who has been on a committee can attest, individual participation tends to fall as committee size increases. Thus, there is a greater likelihood that members of a large board will be less active than those on smaller boards.

The compensation of board members has an impact on the board's effectiveness. When board members have exceptionally high compensation, the CEO also tends to have exceptionally high compensation. This suggests that such boards tend to be too lenient with the CEO.[15] The form of board compensation also affects board performance. Rather than compensating board members with only salary, many companies now include restricted stock grants or stock options in an effort to better align board members with stockholders.

Studies show that corporate governance usually improves if (1) the CEO is not also the chairman of the board, (2) the board has a majority of true outsiders who bring some type of business expertise to the board and are not too busy with other activities, (3) the board is not too large, and (4) board members are compensated appropriately (not too high and not all cash, but including exposure to equity risk through options or stock). The good news for the shareholder is that the boards at many companies have made significant improvements in these directions during the past decade. Fewer CEOs are also board chairmen and, as power has shifted from CEOs to boards as a whole, there has been a tendency to replace insiders with strong, independent outsiders. Today, the typical board has about one-third insiders and two-thirds outsiders, and most outsiders are truly independent. Moreover, board members are compensated primarily with stock or options rather than a straight salary. These changes clearly have decreased the patience of boards with poorly performing CEOs. Within the past several years the CEOs of Wachovia, Sprint Nextel, Gap, Hewlett-Packard, Home Depot, Citigroup, Pfizer, Ford, and Dynegy, to name just a few, have been removed by their boards. This would have been unheard of 30 years ago.

11.5b Charter Provisions and Bylaws That Affect the Likelihood of Hostile Takeovers

Hostile takeovers usually occur when managers have not been willing or able to maximize the profit potential of the resources under their control. In such a

---

15. See I. E. Brick, O. Palmon, and J. Wald, "CEO Compensation, Director Compensation, and Firm Performance: Evidence of Cronyism?" *Journal of Corporate Finance*, June 2006, pp. 403–423.

situation, another company can acquire the poorly performing firm, replace its managers, increase free cash flow, and improve MVA. The following paragraphs describe some provisions that can be included in a corporate charter to make it harder for poorly performing managers to remain in control.[16]

A shareholder-friendly charter should ban **targeted share repurchases**, also known as **greenmail**. For example, suppose a company's stock is selling for $20 per share. Now a hostile bidder, or raider, who plans to replace management if the takeover is successful, buys 5% of the company's stock at the $20 price.[17] The raider then makes an offer to purchase the remainder of the stock for $30 per share. The company might offer to buy back the raider's stock at a price of, say, $35 per share. This is called a targeted share repurchase since the stock will be purchased only from the raider and not from any other shareholders. A raider who paid only $20 per share for the stock would be making a quick profit of $15 per share, which could easily total several hundred million dollars. As a part of the deal, the raider would sign a document promising not to attempt to take over the company for a specified number of years; hence the buyback also is called greenmail. Greenmail hurts shareholders in two ways. First, they are left with $20 stock when they could have received $30 per share. Second, the company purchased stock from the bidder at $35 per share, which represents a direct loss by the remaining shareholders of $15 for each repurchased share.

Managers who buy back stock in targeted repurchases typically argue that their firms are worth more than the raiders offered and that, in time, the "true value" will be revealed in the form of a much higher stock price. This situation might be true if a company were in the process of restructuring itself, or if new products with high potential were in the pipeline. But if the old management had been in power for a long time and had a history of making empty promises, then one should question whether the true purpose of the buyback was to protect stockholders or management.

Another characteristic of a stockholder-friendly charter is that it does not contain a **shareholder rights provision**, better described as a **poison pill**. These provisions give the shareholders of target firms the right to buy a specified number of shares in the company at a very low price if an outside group or firm acquires a specified percentage of the firm's stock. Therefore, if a potential acquirer tries to take over a company, its other shareholders will be entitled to purchase additional shares of stock at a bargain price, thus seriously diluting the holdings of the raider. For this reason, these clauses are called poison pills, because if they are in the charter, the acquirer will end up swallowing a poison pill if the acquisition is successful. Obviously, the existence of a poison pill makes a takeover more difficult, and this helps to entrench management.

A third management entrenchment tool is a **restricted voting rights** provision, which automatically cancels the voting rights of any shareholder who owns more

---

16. Some states have laws that go further than others to protect management. This is one reason that many companies are incorporated in manager-friendly Delaware. Some companies have even shifted their state of incorporation to Delaware because their managers felt that a hostile takeover attempt was likely. Note that a "shareholder-friendly charter" could and would waive the company's right to strong anti-takeover protection, even if the state allowed it.

17. Someone can, under the law, acquire up to 5% of a firm's stock without announcing the acquisition. Once the 5% limit has been hit, the acquirer has 10 days to "announce" the acquisition by filing Schedule 13D with the SEC. Schedule 13D reports not only the acquirer's number of shares but also his or her intentions, such as a passive investment or a takeover. These reports are monitored closely, so as soon as one is filed, management is alerted to the possibility of an imminent takeover.

THE GLOBAL ECONOMIC CRISIS

Would the U.S. Government Be an Effective Board Director?

In response to the global economic crisis that began with the recession of 2007, many governments are becoming major stakeholders in heretofore publicly traded companies. For example, the U.S. government has invested billions in Fannie Mae and Freddie Mac, taking them into conservatorship and having a direct say in the companies' leadership and operations, including the dismissal of former Fannie Mae CEO Daniel Mudd in 2008.

The U.S. government has made multibillon-dollar investments in banks (among them, Citigroup, Bank of America, JPMorgan Chase, and Wells Fargo), insurance companies, AIG (spectacularly), and auto companies (GM and Chrysler). Much of this has been in the form of preferred stock, which does not give the government any direct voting or decision-making authority. However, the government has certainly applied moral suasion, as evidenced by the removal of GM's former CEO Rick Wagoner. The government also imposed limits on executive compensation at firms receiving additional government funds.

For the most part, however, the government does not have voting rights at bailout recipients, nor does it have representation on their boards of directors. It will be interesting to see if this changes and if the government takes a more direct role in corporate governance.

Source: See **http://projects.nytimes.com/creditcrisis/recipients/table** for updates on TARP recipients.

---

than a specified amount of the company's stock. The board can grant voting rights to such a shareholder, but this is unlikely if that shareholder plans to take over the company.

11.5c Using Compensation to Align Managerial and Shareholder Interests

The typical CEO today receives a fixed salary, a cash bonus based on the firm's performance, and stock-based compensation, either in the form of stock grants or option grants. Cash bonuses often are based upon short-run operating factors, such as this year's growth in earnings per share, or medium-term operating performance, such as earnings growth over the past 3 years.

Stock-based compensation is often in the form of options. Chapter 6 explains option valuation in detail, but here we discuss how a standard **stock option compensation plan** works. Suppose IBM decides to grant an option to an employee, allowing her to purchase a specified number of IBM shares at a fixed price, called the **strike price** (or **exercise price**), regardless of the actual price of the stock. The strike price is usually set equal to the current stock price at the time the option is granted. Thus, if IBM's current price were $100, then the option would have an exercise price of $100. Options usually cannot be exercised until after some specified period (the **vesting period**), which is usually 1 to 5 years. Some grants have **cliff vesting**, which means that all the granted options vest at the same date, such as 3 years after the grant. Other grants have **annual vesting**, which means that a certain percentage vest each year. For example, one-third of the options in the grant might vest each year. The options have an **expiration date**, usually 10 years after issue. For our IBM example, assume that the options have cliff vesting in 3 years and have an expiration date in 10 years. Thus, the employee can exercise the option 3 years after issue or wait as long as 10 years. Of course, the employee would not exercise unless IBM's stock is above the $100 exercise price, and if the price never rose above $100, the option would expire unexercised. However, if the stock price were above $100 on the expiration date, the option would surely be exercised.

Suppose the stock price had grown to $134 after 5 years, at which point the employee decided to exercise the option. She would buy stock from IBM for $100, so IBM would get only $100 for stock worth $134. The employee would (probably) sell the stock the same day she exercised the option and hence would receive in cash the $34 difference between the $134 stock price and the $100 exercise price. There are two important points to note in this example. First, most employees sell stock soon after exercising the option. Thus, the incentive effects of an option grant typically end when the option is exercised. Second, option pricing theory shows that it is not optimal to exercise a conventional call option on stock that does not pay dividends before the option expires: An investor is always better off selling the option in the marketplace rather than exercising it. But because employee stock options are not tradable, grantees often exercise the options well before they expire. For example, people often time the exercise of options to the purchase of a new home or some other large expenditure. But early exercise occurs not just for liquidity reasons, such as needing cash to purchase a house, but also because of behavioral reasons. For example, exercises occur more frequently after stock run-ups, which suggests that grantees view the stock as overpriced.

In theory, stock options should align a manager's interests with those of shareholders, influencing the manager to behave in a way that maximizes the company's value. But in practice there are two reasons why this does not always occur.

First, suppose a CEO granted options on 1 million shares. If we use the same stock prices as in our previous example then the grantee would receive $34 for each option, or a total of $34 million. Keep in mind that this is in addition to an annual salary and cash bonuses. The logic behind employee options is that they motivate people to work harder and smarter, thus making the company more valuable and benefiting shareholders. But take a closer look at this example. If the risk-free rate is 5.5%, the market risk premium is 6%, and IBM's beta is 1.19, then the expected return, based on the CAPM, is 5.5% + 1.19(6%) = 12.64%. IBM's dividend yield is only 0.8%, so the expected annual price appreciation must be about 11.84% (12.64% − 0.8% = 11.84%). Now note that if IBM's stock price grew from $100 to $134 over 5 years, that would translate to an annual growth rate of only 6%, not the 11.84% shareholders expected. Thus, the executive would receive $34 million for helping run a company that performed below shareholders' expectations. As this example illustrates, standard stock options do not necessarily link executives' wealth with that of shareholders.

Second, and even worse, the events of the early 2000s showed that some executives were willing to illegally falsify financial statements in order to drive up stock prices just prior to exercising their stock options.[18] In some notable cases, the subsequent stock

---

18. Several academic studies show that option-based compensation leads to a greater likelihood of earnings restatements (which means having to refile financial statements with the SEC because there was a material error) and outright fraud. See A. Agrawal and S. Chadha, "Corporate Governance and Accounting Scandals," *Journal of Law and Economics*, 2006, pp. 371–406; N. Burns and S. Kedia, "The Impact of Performance-Based Compensation on Misreporting," *Journal of Financial Economics*, January 2006, pp. 35–67; and D. J. Denis, P. Hanouna, and A. Sarin, "Is There a Dark Side to Incentive Compensation?" *Journal of Corporate Finance*, June 2006, pp. 467–488.

price drop and loss of investor confidence have forced firms into bankruptcy. Such behavior is certainly not in shareholders' best interests!

As a result, companies today are experimenting with different types of compensation plans that involve different vesting periods and different measures of performance. For example, from a legal standpoint it is more difficult to manipulate EVA (Economic Value Added) than earnings per share.[19] Therefore, many companies incorporate EVA-type measures in their compensation systems. Also, many companies have quit granting options and instead are granting restricted stock that cannot be sold until it has vested.

Just as "all ships rise in a rising tide," so too do most stocks rise in a bull market such as that of 2003–2007. In a strong market, even the stocks of companies whose performance ranks in the bottom 10% of their peer group can rise and thus trigger handsome executive bonuses. This situation is leading to compensation plans that are based on *relative* as opposed to *absolute* stock price performance. For example, some compensation plans have indexed options whose exercise prices depend on the performance of the market or a subset of competitors.

Finally, the empirical results from academic studies show that the correlation between executive compensation and corporate performance is mixed. Some studies suggest that the type of compensation plan used affects company performance, while others find little effect, if any. But we can say with certainty that managerial compensation plans will continue to receive lots of attention from researchers, the popular press, and boards of directors.

11.5d Capital Structure and Internal Control Systems

Capital structure decisions can affect managerial behavior. As the debt level increases, so does the probability of bankruptcy. This increased threat of bankruptcy brings with it two effects on behavior. First, as discussed earlier in this chapter, managers may waste money on unnecessary expenditures and perquisites. This behavior is more likely when times are good and firms are flush with cash; it is less likely in the face of high debt levels and possible bankruptcy. Thus high levels of debt tend to reduce managerial waste. Second, however, high levels of debt may also reduce a manager's willingness to undertake positive-NPV but risky projects. Most managers have their personal reputation and wealth tied to a single company. If that company has a lot of debt then a particularly risky project, even if it has a positive NPV, may be just too risky for the manager to tolerate because a bad outcome could lead to bankruptcy and loss of the manager's job. Stockholders, on the other hand, are diversified and would want the manager to invest in positive-NPV projects even if they are risky. When managers forgo risky but value-adding projects, the resulting **underinvestment problem** reduces firm value. So increasing debt might increase firm value by reducing wasteful expenditures, but it also might reduce value by inducing underinvestment by managers. Empirical tests have not been able to establish exactly which effect dominates.

Internal control systems have become an increasingly important issue since the passage of the Sarbanes-Oxley Act of 2002. Section 404 of the act requires companies to establish effective internal control systems. The Securities and Exchange Commission,

---

19. For a discussion of EVA, see Al Ehrbar, *EVA: The Real Key to Creating Wealth* (New York: John Wiley & Sons, 1998); and Pamela P. Peterson and David R. Peterson, *Company Performance and Measures of Value Added* (The Research Foundation of the Institute of Chartered Financial Analysts, 1996).

THE GLOBAL ECONOMIC CRISIS

Shareholder Reactions to the Crisis

It is safe to say that shareholders were dismayed by the market's decline in 2008, and it looks like they are seeking more control. RiskMetrics Group provides data on the shareholder proposals that are included in proxy statements, with votes tallied at the annual meetings. The 2009 proxy season saw an enormous number of proposals related to corporate governance, especially compensation, as shown below.

	Number of proposals
Executive Pay Issues	
Advisory vote on compensation	85
Vote on golden parachutes	9
Anti–gross-ups policy	2
Vote on executive death benefits	12
Retention period for stock awards	14
Establish bonus banks	3
Board Issues	
Independent board chairman	33
Allow for cumulative voting	34
Require majority vote to elect directors	51
Takeover Defenses/Other	
Right to call special meeting	61
End supermajority vote requirement	15
Repeal classified board	71

It will be interesting to see how companies respond to these votes and whether more shareholder power translates into better performance.

Source: RiskMetrics Group, **www.riskmetrics.com/knowledge/proxy_season_scorecard_2009**.

which is charged with the implementation of Sarbanes-Oxley, defines an effective internal control system as one that provides "reasonable assurance regarding the reliability of financial reporting and the preparation of financial statements for external purposes in accordance with generally accepted accounting principles." In other words, investors should be able to trust a company's reported financial statements.

11.5e Environmental Factors Outside of a Firm's Control

As noted earlier, corporate governance is also affected by environmental factors that are outside of a firm's control, including the regulatory/legal environment, block ownership patterns, competition in the product markets, the media, and litigation.

THE SARBANES-OXLEY ACT OF 2002 AND CORPORATE GOVERNANCE

In 2002, Congress passed the Sarbanes-Oxley Act, known in the industry as SOX, as a measure to improve transparency in financial accounting and to prevent fraud. SOX consists of eleven chapters, or *titles*, which establish wide-ranging new regulations for auditors, CEOs and CFOs, boards of directors, investment analysts, and investment banks. These regulations are designed to ensure that (a) companies that perform audits are sufficiently independent of the companies that they audit, (b) a key executive in each company *personally* certifies that the financial statements are complete and accurate, (c) the board of directors's audit committee is relatively independent of management, (d) financial analysts are relatively independent of the companies they analyze, and (e) companies publicly and promptly release all important information about their financial condition. The individual titles are briefly summarized below.

Title I establishes the Public Company Accounting Oversight Board, whose charge is to oversee auditors and establish quality control and ethical standards for audits.

Title II requires that auditors be independent of the companies that they audit. Basically this means they can't provide consulting services to the companies they audit. The purpose is to remove financial incentives for auditors to help management cook the books.

Title III requires that the board of directors's audit committee must be composed of "independent" members. Section 302 requires that the CEO and CFO must review the annual and quarterly financial statements and reports and personally certify that they are complete and accurate. Penalties for certifying reports that executives know are false range up to a $5 million fine, 20 years in prison, or both. Under Section 304, if the financial statements turn out to be false and must be *restated,* then certain bonuses and equity-based compensation that executives earn must be reimbursed to the company.

Title IV's Section 401(a) requires prompt disclosure and more extensive reporting on off–balance sheet transactions. Section 404 requires that management evaluate its internal financial controls and report whether they are "effective." The external auditing firm must also indicate whether it agrees with management's evaluation of its internal controls. Section 409 requires that a company disclose to the public promptly and *in plain English* any material changes to its financial condition. Title IV also places restrictions on the loans that a company can make to its executives.

Title V addresses the relationship between financial analysts, the investment banks they work for, and the companies they cover. It requires that analysts and brokers who make stock recommendations disclose any conflicts of interest they might have concerning the stocks they recommend.

Titles VI and VII are technical in nature, dealing with the SEC's budget and powers and requiring that several studies be undertaken by the SEC.

Title VIII establishes penalties for destroying or falsifying audit records. It also provides "whistle-blower protection" for employees who report fraud.

Title IX increases the penalties for a variety of white-collar crimes associated with securities fraud, such as mail and wire fraud. Section 902 also makes it a crime to alter, destroy, or hide documents that might be used in an investigation. It also makes it a crime to conspire to do so.

Title X requires that the CEO sign the company's federal income tax return.

Title XI provides penalties for obstructing an investigation and grants the SEC authority to remove officers or directors from a company if they have committed fraud.

Regulations and Laws

The regulatory/legal environment includes the agencies that regulate financial markets, such as the SEC. Even though the fines and penalties levied on firms for financial misrepresentation by the SEC are relatively small, the damage to a firm's reputation can have significant costs, leading to extremely large reductions in the firm's value.[20] Thus, the regulatory system has an enormous impact on corporate governance and firm value.

The regulatory/legal environment also includes the laws and legal system under which a company operates. These vary greatly from country to country. Studies show that firms located in countries with strong legal protection for investors have stronger corporate governance and that this is reflected in better access to financial markets, a lower cost of equity, increases in market liquidity, and less noise in stock prices.[21]

Block Ownership Patterns

Prior to the 1960s, most U.S. stock was owned by a large number of individual investors, each of whom owned a diversified portfolio of stocks. Because each individual owned a small amount of any given company's stock, there was little that he or she could do to influence its operations. Also, with such a small investment, it was not cost effective for the investor to monitor companies closely. Indeed dissatisfied stockholders would typically just "vote with their feet" by selling the stock. This situation began to change as institutional investors such as pension funds and mutual funds gained control of larger and larger shares of investment capital—and as they then acquired larger and larger percentages of all outstanding stock. Given their large block holdings, it now makes sense for institutional investors to monitor management, and they have the clout to influence the board. In some cases, they have actually elected their own representatives to the board. For example, when TIAA-CREF, a huge private pension fund, became frustrated with the performance and leadership of Furr's/Bishop, a cafeteria chain, the fund led a fight that ousted the entire board and then elected a new board consisting only of outsiders.

In general, activist investors with large blocks in companies have been good for all shareholders. They have searched for firms with poor profitability and then replaced management with new teams that are well versed in value-based management techniques, thereby improving profitability. Not surprisingly, stock prices usually rise on the news that a well-known activist investor has taken a major position in an underperforming company.

Note that activist investors can improve performance even if they don't go so far as to take over a firm. More often, they either elect their own representatives to the board or simply point out the firm's problems to other board members. In such cases, boards often change their attitudes and become less tolerant when they realize that the management team is not following the dictates of value-based management. Moreover, the firm's top managers recognize what will happen if they don't whip the company into shape, and they go about doing just that.

---

20. For example, see Jonathan M. Karpoff, D. Scott Lee, and Gerald S. Martin, "The Cost to Firms of Cooking the Books," *Journal of Financial and Quantitative Analysis,* September 2008, pp. 581–612.
21. For example, see R. La Porta, F. Lopez-de-Silanes, A. Shleifer, and R. Vishny, "Legal Determinants of External Finance," *Journal of Finance,* January 1997, pp. 1131–1150; Hazem Daouk, Charles M. C. Lee, and David Ng, "Capital Market Governance: How Do Security Laws Affect Market Performance?" *Journal of Corporate Finance,* June 2006, pp. 560–593; and Li Jin and Stewart C. Myers, "R² Around the World: New Theory and New Tests," *Journal of Financial Economics,* February 2006, pp. 257–292.

Competition in Product Markets

The degree of competition in a firm's product market has an impact on its corporate governance. For example, companies in industries with lots of competition don't have the luxury of tolerating poorly performing CEOs. As might be expected, CEO turnover is higher in competitive industries than in those with less competition.[22] When most firms in an industry are fairly similar, you might expect it to be easier to find a qualified replacement from another firm for a poorly performing CEO. This is exactly what the evidence shows: As industry homogeneity increases, so does the incidence of CEO turnover.[23]

The Media and Litigation

Corporate governance, especially compensation, is a hot topic in the media. The media can have a positive impact by discovering or reporting corporate problems, such as the Enron scandal. Another example is the extensive coverage that was given to option backdating, in which the exercise prices of executive stock options were set *after* the options officially were granted. Because the exercise prices were set at the lowest stock price during the quarter in which the options were granted, the options were in-the-money and more valuable when their "official" lives began. Several CEOs have already lost their jobs over this practice, and more firings are likely.

However, the media can also hurt corporate governance by focusing too much attention on a CEO. Such "superstar" CEOs often command excessive compensation packages and spend too much time on activities outside the company, resulting in too much pay for too little performance.[24]

In addition to penalties and fines from regulatory bodies such as the SEC, civil litigation also occurs when companies are suspected of fraud. Recent research indicates that such suits lead to improvements in corporate governance.[25]

Self Test

What are the two primary forms of corporate governance provisions that correspond to the stick and the carrot?

What factors improve the effectiveness of a board of directors?

What are three provisions in many corporate charters that deter takeovers?

Describe how a typical stock option plan works. What are some problems with a typical stock option plan?

---

22. See M. De Fond and C. Park, "The Effect of Competition on CEO Turnover," *Journal of Accounting and Economics*, Vol. 27, 1999, pp. 35–56; and T. Fee and C. Hadlock, "Management Turnover and Product Market Competition: Empirical Evidence from the U.S. Newspaper Industry," *Journal of Business*, April 2000, pp. 205–243.
23. See R. Parrino, "CEO Turnover and Outside Succession: A Cross-Sectional Analysis," *Journal of Financial Economics*, Vol. 46, 1997, pp. 165–197.
24. See U. Malmendier and G. A. Tate, "Superstar CEOs," *Quarterly Journal of Economics*, November 2009, pp. 1593–1638.
25. For example, see D. B. Farber, "Restoring Trust after Fraud: Does Corporate Governance Matter?" *Accounting Review*, April 2005, pp. 539–561; and Stephen P. Ferris, Tomas Jandik, Robert M. Lawless, and Anil Makhija, "Derivative Lawsuits as a Corporate Governance Mechanism: Empirical Evidence on Board Changes Surrounding Filings," *Journal of Financial and Quantitative Analysis*, March 2007, pp. 143–166.

INTERNATIONAL CORPORATE GOVERNANCE

Corporate governance includes the following factors: (1) the likelihood that a poorly performing firm can be taken over; (2) whether the board of directors is dominated by insiders or outsiders; (3) the extent to which most of the stock is held by a few large "blockholders" versus many small shareholders; and (4) the size and form of executive compensation. An interesting study compared corporate governance in Germany, Japan, and the United States.

First, note from the accompanying table that the threat of a takeover serves as a stick in the United States but not in Japan or Germany. This threat, which reduces management entrenchment, should benefit shareholders in the United States relative to the other two countries. Second, German and Japanese boards are larger than those in the United States. Japanese boards consist primarily of insiders, unlike German and American boards, which have similar inside/outside mixes. It should be noted, though, that the boards of most large German corporations include representatives of labor, whereas U.S. boards represent only shareholders. Thus, it would appear that U.S. boards, with a higher percentage of outsiders, would have interests most closely aligned with those of shareholders.

German and Japanese firms are also more likely to be controlled by large blocks of stock than those in the United States. Although pension and mutual funds, as well as other institutional investors, are increasingly important in the United States, block ownership is still less prevalent than in Germany and Japan. In both Germany and Japan, banks often own large blocks of stock, something that is not permitted by law in the United States, and corporations also own large blocks of stock in other corporations. In Japan, combinations of companies, called *keiretsus*, have cross-ownership of stock among the member companies, and these interlocking blocks distort the definition of an outside board member. For example, when the performance of a company in a keiretsu deteriorates, new directors are often appointed from the staffs of other members of the keiretsu. Such appointees might be classified officially as insiders, but they represent interests other than those of the troubled company's CEO.

In general, large blockholders are better able to monitor management than are small investors, so one might expect the blockholder factor to favor German and Japanese shareholders. However, these blockholders have other relationships with the company that might be detrimental to outside shareholders. For example, if one company buys from another, transfer pricing might be used to shift wealth to a favored company, or a company might be forced to buy from a sister company in spite of the availability of lower-cost resources from outside the group.

Executive compensation packages differ dramatically across the three countries, with U.S. executives receiving by far the highest compensation. However, compensation plans are remarkably similar in terms of how sensitive total compensation is to corporate performance.

Which country's system of corporate governance is best from the standpoint of a shareholder whose goal is stock price maximization? There is no definitive answer. U.S. stocks have had the best performance in recent years. Moreover, German and Japanese companies are slowly moving toward the U.S. system with respect to size of compensation, and compensation plans in all three countries are being linked ever more closely to performance. At the same time, however, U.S. companies are moving toward the others in the sense of having larger ownership blocks; because those blocks are primarily held by pension and mutual funds (rather than banks and related corporations), they better represent the interests of shareholders.

Source: Steven N. Kaplan, "Top Executive Incentives in Germany, Japan, and the USA: A Comparison," in *Executive Compensation and Shareholder Value*, Jennifer Carpenter and David Yermack, eds. (Boston: Kluwer Academic Publishers, 1999), pp. 3–12.

International Characteristics of Corporate Governance

	Germany	Japan	United States
Threat of a takeover	Moderate	Low	High
Board of directors			
Size of board	26	21	14
Percent insiders	27%	91%	33%
Percent outsiders	73%	9%	67%
Are large blocks of stock typically owned by			
A controlling family?	Yes	No	No
Another corporation?	Yes	Yes	No
A bank?	Yes	Yes	No
Executive compensation			
Amount of compensation	Moderate	Low	High
Sensitivity to performance	Low to moderate	Low to moderate	Low to moderate

www

See **www.esopasso-ciation.org** for more on ESOPs.

11.6 Employee Stock Ownership Plans (ESOPs)

Studies show that 90% of the employees who receive stock under option plans sell the stock as soon as they exercise their options, so the plans motivate employees only for a limited period.[26] Moreover, many companies limit their stock option plans to key managers and executives. To help provide long-term productivity gains and improve retirement incomes for all employees, Congress authorized the use of **Employee Stock Ownership Plans (ESOPs)**. Today about 9,000 privately held companies and 1,000 publicly held firms have ESOPs, and more are being created every day. Typically, the ESOP's major asset is shares of the common stock of the company that created it, and of the 10,000 total ESOPs, about 2,500 of them actually own a majority of their company's stock.[27]

To illustrate how an ESOP works, consider Gallagher & Abbott Inc. (G&A), a construction company located in Knoxville, Tennessee. G&A's simplified balance sheet is shown below:

G&A's Balance Sheet prior to ESOP (Millions of Dollars)

Assets		Liabilities and Equity	
Cash	$ 10	Debt	$100
Other	190	Equity (1 million shares)	100
Total	$200	Total	$200

Now G&A creates an ESOP, which is a new legal entity. The company issues 500,000 shares of new stock at $100 per share, or $50 million in total, which it

---

26. See Gary Laufman, "To Have and Have Not," *CFO,* March 1998, pp. 58–66.
27. See Eugene Pilotte, "Employee Stock Ownership Plans, Management Motives, and Shareholder Wealth: A Review of the Evidence," *Journal of Financial Education,* Spring 1997, pp. 41–46; and Daniel Eisenberg, "No ESOP Fable," *Time,* May 10, 1999, p. 95.

sells to the ESOP. The company's employees are the ESOP's stockholders, and each employee receives an ownership interest based on the size of his or her salary and years of service. The ESOP borrows the $50 million to buy the newly issued stock.[28] Financial institutions are willing to lend the ESOP the money because G&A signs a guarantee for the loan. Here is the company's new balance sheet:

G&A's Balance Sheet after the ESOP (Millions of Dollars)

Assets		Liabilities and Equity	
Cash	$ 60	Debt[a]	$100
Other	190	Equity (1.5 million shares)	150
Total	$250	Total	$250

[a]The company has guaranteed the ESOP's loan, and it has promised to make payments to the ESOP sufficient to retire the loan, but this does not show up on the balance sheet.

The company now has an additional $50 million of cash and $50 million more of book equity, but it has a de facto liability owing to its guarantee of the ESOP's debt. It could use the cash to finance an expansion, but many companies use the cash to repurchase their own common stock, so we assume that G&A will do likewise. The company's new balance sheets, and that of the ESOP, are shown below:

G&A's Balance Sheet after the ESOP and Share Repurchase (Millions of Dollars)

Assets		Liabilities and Equity	
Cash	$ 10	Debt	$100
Other	190	Equity (1 million shares)	150
		Treasury stock	(50)
Total	$200	Total	$200

ESOP's Initial Balance Sheet (Millions of Dollars)

Assets		Liabilities and Equity	
G&A stock	$50	Debt	$50
		Equity	0
Total	$50	Total	$50

Note that although the company's balance sheet looks exactly as it did initially, there is actually a huge difference—the company has guaranteed the ESOP's debt and hence it has an off–balance sheet liability of $50 million. Moreover, because the ESOP has no equity, the guarantee is very real indeed. Finally, observe that operating assets have not been increased at all, but the total debt outstanding supported by those assets has increased by $50 million.[29]

---

28. Our description is somewhat simplified. Technically, the stock would be placed in a suspense account and then be allocated to employees as the debt is repaid.

29. We assumed that the company used the $50 million paid to it by the ESOP to repurchase common stock and thus to increase its de facto debt. It could have used the $50 million to retire debt, in which case its true debt ratio would remain unchanged, or it could have used the money to support an expansion.

If this were the whole story, then there would be no reason to have an ESOP. However, G&A has promised to make payments to the ESOP in sufficient amounts to enable the ESOP to pay interest and principal charges on the debt, amortizing it over 15 years. Thus, after 15 years, the debt will be paid off and the ESOP's equity holders (the employees) will have equity with a book value of $50 million and a market value that could be much higher if G&A's stock increases, as it should over time. Then, as employees retire, the ESOP will distribute a pro rata amount of the G&A stock to each employee, who can then use it as a part of his or her retirement plan.

An ESOP is clearly beneficial for employees, but why would a company want to establish one? There are five primary reasons.

1. Congress passed the enabling legislation in hopes of enhancing employees' productivity and thus making the economy more efficient. In theory, employees who have equity in the enterprise will work harder and smarter. Note too that if employees are more productive and creative then this will benefit outside shareholders, because productivity enhancements that benefit ESOP shareholders also benefit outside shareholders.

2. The ESOP represents additional compensation to employees: In our example, there is a $50 million (or more) transfer of wealth from existing shareholders to employees over the 15-year period. Presumably, if the ESOP were not created then some other form of compensation would have been required, and that alternative compensation might not have the secondary benefit of enhancing productivity. Also note that the ESOP's payments to employees (as opposed to the payment by the company) come primarily at retirement, and Congress wanted to boost retirement incomes.

3. Depending on when an employee's rights to the ESOP are vested, the ESOP may help the firm retain employees.

4. There are strong tax incentives that encourage a company to form an ESOP. First, Congress decreed that when the ESOP owns 50% or more of the company's common stock, financial institutions that lend money to ESOPs can exclude from taxable income 50% of the interest they receive on the loan. This improves the financial institutions' after-tax returns, which allows them to lend to ESOPs at below-market rates. Therefore, a company that establishes an ESOP can borrow through the ESOP at a lower rate than would otherwise be available—in our example, the $50 million of debt would be at a reduced rate.

   There is also a second tax advantage. If the company were to borrow directly, it could deduct interest but not principal payments from its taxable income. However, companies typically make the required payments to their ESOPs in the form of cash dividends. Dividends are not normally deductible from taxable income, but *cash dividends paid on ESOP stock are deductible if the dividends are paid to plan participants or are used to repay the loan.* Thus, companies whose ESOPs own 50% of their stock can in effect borrow on ESOP loans at subsidized rates and then deduct both the interest and principal payments made on the loans. American Airlines and Publix Supermarkets are two of the many firms that have used ESOPs to obtain this benefit, along with motivating employees by giving them an equity interest in the enterprise.

5. A less desirable use of ESOPs is to help companies avoid being acquired by another company. The company's CEO, or someone appointed by the CEO, typically acts as trustee for its ESOP, and the trustee is supposed to vote the ESOP's shares according to the will of the plan participants. Moreover, the

participants, who are the company's employees, usually oppose takeovers because they frequently involve labor cutbacks. Therefore, if an ESOP owns a significant percentage of the company's shares, then management has a powerful tool for warding off takeovers. This is not good for outside stockholders.

Are ESOPs good for a company's shareholders? In theory, ESOPs motivate employees by providing them with an ownership interest. That should increase productivity and thereby enhance stock values. Moreover, tax incentives mitigate the costs associated with some ESOPs. However, an ESOP can be used to help entrench management, and that could hurt stockholders. How do the pros and cons balance out? The empirical evidence is not entirely clear, but certain findings are worth noting. First, if an ESOP is established to help defend against a takeover, then the firm's stock price typically falls when plans for the ESOP are announced. The market does not like the prospect of entrenching management and having to give up the premium normally associated with a takeover. However, if the ESOP is established for tax purposes and/or to motivate employees, the stock price generally goes up at the time of the announcement. In these cases, the company typically has a subsequent improvement in sales per employee and other long-term performance measures, which stimulates the stock price. Indeed, a study showed that companies with ESOPs enjoyed a 26% average annual stock return compared to a return of only 19% for peer companies without ESOPs.[30] It thus appears that ESOPs, if used appropriately, can be a powerful tool for creating shareholder value.

What are ESOPs? What are some of their advantages and disadvantages?	**Self Test**

Summary

- **Corporate assets** consist of operating assets and financial, or nonoperating, assets.
- **Operating assets** take two forms: assets-in-place and growth options.
- **Assets-in-place** include the land, buildings, machines, and inventory that the firm uses in its operations to produce products and services.
- **Growth options** refer to opportunities the firm has to increase sales. They include opportunities arising from R&D expenditures, customer relationships, and the like.
- **Nonoperating assets** are distinguished from operating assets and include **financial assets** such as investments in marketable securities and noncontrolling interests in the stock of other companies.
- The **value of nonoperating assets** is usually close to the figure reported on the balance sheet.

30. See Daniel Eisenberg, "No ESOP Fable," *Time*, May 10, 1999, p. 95.

- The **value of operations** is the present value of all the future free cash flows expected from operations when discounted at the weighted average cost of capital:

$$V_{op(\text{at time }0)} = \sum_{t=1}^{\infty} \frac{\text{FCF}_t}{(1 + \text{WACC})^t}$$

- The **horizon value** is the value of operations at the end of the explicit forecast period. It is also called the **terminal value** or **continuing value,** and it is equal to the present value of all free cash flows beyond the forecast period, discounted back to the end of the forecast period at the weighted average cost of capital:

$$\text{Continuing value} = V_{op(\text{at time }N)} = \frac{\text{FCF}_{N+1}}{\text{WACC} - g} = \frac{\text{FCF}_N(1 + g)}{\text{WACC} - g}$$

- The **corporate valuation model** can be used to calculate the total value of a company by finding the value of operations plus the value of nonoperating assets.
- The intrinsic **value of equity** is the total value of the company minus the value of the debt and preferred stock. The intrinsic **price per share** is the total value of the equity divided by the number of shares.
- **Value-based management** involves the systematic use of the corporate valuation model to evaluate a company's potential decisions.
- The four **value drivers** are (1) the growth rate (g) of sales; (2) operating profitability (OP), which is measured by the ratio of NOPAT to sales; (3) capital requirements (CR), as measured by the ratio of operating capital to sales; and (4) the weighted average cost of capital (WACC).
- **Expected return on invested capital (EROIC)** is equal to expected NOPAT divided by the amount of capital that is available at the beginning of the year.
- A company creates value when the spread between EROIC and WACC is positive—that is, when EROIC − WACC > 0.
- **Corporate governance** involves the manner in which shareholders' objectives are implemented, and it is reflected in a company's policies and actions.
- The two primary mechanisms used in corporate governance are (1) the threat of removal of a poorly performing CEO and (2) the type of plan used to compensate executives and managers.
- Poorly performing managers can be removed either by a takeover or by the company's own board of directors. Provisions in the corporate charter affect the difficulty of a successful takeover, and the composition of the board of directors affects the likelihood of a manager being removed by the board.
- **Managerial entrenchment** is most likely when a company has a weak board of directors coupled with strong anti-takeover provisions in its corporate charter. In this situation, the likelihood that badly performing senior managers will be fired is low.
- **Nonpecuniary benefits** are noncash perks such as lavish offices, memberships at country clubs, corporate jets, foreign junkets, and the like. Some of these expenditures may be cost effective, but others are wasteful and simply reduce profits. Such fat is almost always cut after a hostile takeover.

- **Targeted share repurchases,** also known as **greenmail,** occur when a company buys back stock from a potential acquirer at a price higher than the market price. In return, the potential acquirer agrees not to attempt to take over the company.
- **Shareholder rights provisions,** also known as **poison pills,** allow existing shareholders to purchase additional shares of stock at a price lower than the market value if a potential acquirer purchases a controlling stake in the company.
- A **restricted voting rights** provision automatically deprives a shareholder of voting rights if he or she owns more than a specified amount of stock.
- **Interlocking boards of directors** occur when the CEO of Company A sits on the board of Company B and also B's CEO sits on A's board.
- A **stock option** provides for the purchase of a share of stock at a fixed price, called the **exercise price,** no matter what the actual price of the stock is. Stock options have an **expiration date,** after which they cannot be exercised.
- An **Employee Stock Ownership Plan (ESOP)** is a plan that facilitates employees' ownership of stock in the company for which they work.

Questions

11–1 Define each of the following terms:
    a. Assets-in-place; growth options; nonoperating assets
    b. Net operating working capital; operating capital; NOPAT; free cash flow
    c. Value of operations; horizon value; corporate valuation model
    d. Value-based management; value drivers; EROIC
    e. Managerial entrenchment; nonpecuniary benefits
    f. Greenmail; poison pills; restricted voting rights
    g. Stock option; ESOP

11–2 Explain how to use the corporate valuation model to find the price per share of common equity.

11–3 Explain how it is possible for sales growth to decrease the value of a profitable company.

11–4 What are some actions an entrenched management might take that would harm shareholders?

11–5 How is it possible for an employee stock option to be valuable even if the firm's stock price fails to meet shareholders' expectations?

Problems   Answers Appear in Appendix B

Easy Problems 1–5

11–1 **Free Cash Flow** Use the following income statements and balance sheets to calculate Garnet Inc.'s free cash flow for 2012.

Garnet Inc.

	2013	2012
Income Statement (Millions of Dollars)		
Net sales	$530.0	$500.0
Costs (except depreciation)	400.0	380.0
Depreciation	30.0	25.0
Total operating costs	$430.0	$405.0
Earnings before interest and taxes (EBIT)	100.0	95.0
Less interest	23.0	21.0
Earnings before taxes	$ 77.0	$ 74.0
Taxes (40%)	30.8	29.6
Net income	$ 46.2	$ 44.4

Balance Sheet	2013	2012
Assets		
Cash	$ 28.0	$ 27.0
Marketable securities	69.0	66.0
Accounts receivable	84.0	80.0
Inventories	112.0	106.0
Total current assets	$293.0	$279.0
Net plant and equipment	281.0	265.0
Total assets	$574.0	$544.0
Liabilities and Equity		
Accounts payable	$ 56.0	$ 52.0
Notes payable	138.0	130.0
Accruals	28.0	28.0
Total current liabilities	$222.0	$210.0
Long-term bonds	173.0	164.0
Common stock	100.0	100.0
Retained earnings	79.0	70.0
Common equity	$179.0	$170.0
Total liabilities and equity	$574.0	$544.0

11-2 **Value of Operations of Constant Growth Firm** EMC Corporation has never paid a dividend. Its current free cash flow of $400,000 is expected to grow at a constant rate of 5%. The weighted average cost of capital is WACC = 12%. Calculate EMC's value of operations.

11-3 **Horizon Value** Current and projected free cash flows for Radell Global Operations are shown below. Growth is expected to be constant after 2014, and the weighted average cost of capital is 11%. What is the horizon (continuing) value at 2014?

	Actual	Projected		
	2012	2013	2014	2015
Free cash flow (millions of dollars)	$606.82	$667.50	$707.55	$750.00

11-4 **EROIC and MVA of Constant Growth Firm** A company has capital of $200 million. It has an EROIC of 9%, forecasted constant growth of 5%, and a WACC of 10%. What is its value of operations? What is its intrinsic MVA? (*Hint:* Use Equation 11-5.)

11-5 **Value Drivers and Horizon Value of Constant Growth Firm** You are given the following forecasted information for the year 2016: sales = $300,000,000, operating profitability (OP) = 6%, capital requirements (CR) = 43%, growth (g) = 5%, and the weighted average cost of capital (WACC) = 9.8%. If these values remain constant, what is the horizon value (i.e., the 2016 value of operations)? (*Hint:* Use Equation 11-4.)

Intermediate Problems 6–7

11-6 **Value of Operations** Brooks Enterprises has never paid a dividend. Free cash flow is projected to be $80,000 and $100,000 for the next 2 years, respectively; after the second year, FCF is expected to grow at a constant rate of 8%. The company's weighted average cost of capital is 12%.
   a. What is the terminal, or horizon, value of operations? (*Hint:* Find the value of all free cash flows beyond Year 2 discounted back to Year 2.)
   b. Calculate the value of Brooks's operations.

11-7 **Corporate Valuation** Dozier Corporation is a fast-growing supplier of office products. Analysts project the following free cash flows (FCFs) during the next 3 years, after which FCF is expected to grow at a constant 7% rate. Dozier's weighted average cost of capital is WACC = 13%.

	Year		
	1	**2**	**3**
Free cash flow ($ millions)	−$20	$30	$40

   a. What is Dozier's terminal, or horizon, value? (*Hint:* Find the value of all free cash flows beyond Year 3 discounted back to Year 3.)
   b. What is the current value of operations for Dozier?
   c. Suppose Dozier has $10 million in marketable securities, $100 million in debt, and 10 million shares of stock. What is the intrinsic price per share?

Challenging Problems 8–10

11-8 **Value of Equity** The balance sheet of Hutter Amalgamated is shown below. If the 12/31/2012 value of operations is $756 million, what is the 12/31/2012 intrinsic market value of equity?

Balance Sheet, December 31, 2012 (Millions of Dollars)

Assets		Liabilities and Equity	
Cash	$ 20.0	Accounts payable	$ 19.0
Marketable securities	77.0	Notes payable	151.0
Accounts receivable	100.0	Accruals	51.0
Inventories	200.0	Total current liabilities	$221.0
Total current assets	$397.0	Long-term bonds	190.0
Net plant and equipment	279.0	Preferred stock	76.0
		Common stock	100.0
		(par plus PIC)	
		Retained earnings	89.0
		Common equity	$189.0
Total assets	$676.0	Total liabilities and equity	$676.0

11-9 **Price per Share** The balance sheet of Roop Industries is shown below. The 12/31/2012 value of operations is $651 million, and there are 10 million shares of common equity. What is the intrinsic price per share?

Balance Sheet, December 31, 2012 (Millions of Dollars)

Assets		Liabilities and Equity	
Cash	$ 20.0	Accounts payable	$ 19.0
Marketable securities	47.0	Notes payable	65.0
Accounts receivable	100.0	Accruals	51.0
Inventories	200.0	Total current liabilities	$135.0
Total current assets	$367.0	Long-term bonds	131.0
Net plant and equipment	279.0	Preferred stock	33.0
		Common stock	160.0
		(par plus PIC)	
		Retained earnings	187.0
		Common equity	$347.0
Total assets	$646.0	Total liabilities and equity	$646.0

11-10 **Corporate Valuation** The financial statements of Lioi Steel Fabricators are shown below—both the actual results for 2012 and the projections for 2013. Free cash flow is expected to grow at a 6% rate after 2013. The weighted average cost of capital is 11%.
   a. If operating capital as of 12/31/2012 is $502.2 million, what is the free cash flow for 12/31/2013?
   b. What is the horizon value as of 12/31/2013?
   c. What is the value of operations as of 12/31/2012?
   d. What is the total value of the company as of 12/31/2012?
   e. What is the intrinsic price per share for 12/31/2012?

Income Statements for the Year Ending December 31
(Millions of Dollars Except for Per Share Data)

	Actual 2012	Projected 2013
Net sales	$500.0	$530.0
Costs (except depreciation)	360.0	381.6
Depreciation	37.5	39.8
Total operating costs	$397.5	$421.4
Earnings before interest and taxes	$102.5	$108.6
Less interest	13.9	16.0
Earnings before taxes	$ 88.6	$ 92.6
Taxes (40%)	35.4	37.0
Net income before preferred dividends	$ 53.2	$ 55.6
Preferred dividends	6.0	7.4
Net income available for common dividends	$ 47.2	$ 48.2
Common dividends	$ 40.8	$ 29.7
Addition to retained earnings	$ 6.4	$ 18.5
Number of shares	10.0	10.0
Dividends per share	$ 4.08	$ 2.97

Balance Sheets for December 31
(Millions of Dollars)

	Actual 2012	Projected 2013
Assets		
Cash	$ 5.3	$ 5.6
Marketable securities	49.9	51.9
Accounts receivable	53.0	56.2
Inventories	106.0	112.4
Total current assets	$214.2	$226.1
Net plant and equipment	375.0	397.5
Total assets	$589.2	$623.6
Liabilities and Equity		
Accounts payable	$ 9.6	$ 11.2
Notes payable	69.9	74.1
Accruals	27.5	28.1
Total current liabilities	$107.0	$113.4
Long-term bonds	140.8	148.2
Preferred stock	35.0	37.1
Common stock (par plus PIC)	160.0	160.0
Retained earnings	146.4	164.9
Common equity	$306.4	$324.9
Total liabilities and equity	$589.2	$623.6

Spreadsheet Problem

11-11 **Build a Model: Corporate Valuation** Start with the partial model in the file *Ch11 P11 Build a Model.xls* on the textbook's Web site. The Henley Corporation is a privately held company specializing in lawn care products and services. The most recent financial statements are shown below.

Income Statement for the Year Ending December 31
(Millions of Dollars Except for Per Share Data)

	2012
Net sales	$800.0
Costs (except depreciation)	576.0
Depreciation	60.0
Total operating costs	$636.0
Earnings before interest and taxes	$164.0
Less interest	32.0
Earnings before taxes	$132.0
Taxes (40%)	52.8
Net income before preferred dividends	$ 79.2
Preferred dividends	1.4
Net income available for common dividends	$ 77.9
Common dividends	$ 31.1
Addition to retained earnings	$ 46.7
Number of shares (in millions)	10.0
Dividends per share	$ 3.11

Balance Sheet for December 31 (Millions of Dollars)

Assets	2012	Liabilities and Equity	2012
Cash	$ 8.0	Accounts payable	$ 16.0
Marketable securities	20.0	Notes payable	40.0
Accounts receivable	80.0	Accruals	40.0
Inventories	160.0	Total current liabilities	$ 96.0
Total current assets	$268.0	Long-term bonds	300.0
Net plant and equipment	600.0	Preferred stock	15.0
		Common stock (par plus PIC)	257.0
		Retained earnings	200.0
		Common equity	$457.0
Total assets	$868.0	Total liabilities and equity	$868.0

Projected ratios and selected information for the current and projected years are shown below.

	Actual	Projected			
	2012	2013	2014	2015	2016
Sales growth rate		15%	10%	6%	6%
Costs/Sales	72%	72	72	72	72
Depreciation/Net PPE	10	10	10	10	10
Cash/Sales	1	1	1	1	1
Accounts receivable/Sales	10	10	10	10	10

(Continued)

	Actual	Projected			
	2012	**2013**	**2014**	**2015**	**2016**
Inventories/Sales	20	20	20	20	20
Net PPE/Sales	75	75	75	75	75
Accounts payable/Sales	2	2	2	2	2
Accruals/Sales	5	5	5	5	5
Tax rate	40	40	40	40	40
Weighted average cost of capital (WACC)	10.5	10.5	10.5	10.5	10.5

a. Forecast the parts of the income statement and balance sheet that are necessary for calculating free cash flow.

b. Calculate free cash flow for each projected year. Also calculate the growth rates of free cash flow each year to verify that there is constant growth (that is, the same as the constant growth rate in sales) by the end of the forecast period.

c. Calculate operating profitability (OP = NOPAT/Sales), capital requirements (CR = Operating capital/Sales), and expected return on invested capital (EROIC = Expected NOPAT/Operating capital at beginning of year). Based on the spread between EROIC and WACC, do you think that the company will have a positive Market Value Added (MVA = Market value of company – Book value of company = Value of operations – Operating capital)?

d. Calculate the value of operations and MVA. (*Hint:* First calculate the horizon value at the end of the forecast period, which is equal to the value of operations at the end of the forecast period.) Assume that the annual growth rate beyond the horizon is 6%.

e. Calculate the price per share of common equity as of 12/31/2012.

MINI CASE

You have been hired as a consultant to Kulpa Fishing Supplies (KFS), a company that is seeking to increase its value. The company's CEO and founder, Mia Kulpa, has asked you to estimate the value of two privately held companies that KFS is considering acquiring. But first, the senior management of KFS would like for you to explain how to value companies that don't pay any dividends. You have structured your presentation around the following items.

a. List the two types of assets that companies own.

b. What are assets-in-place? How can their value be estimated?

c. What are nonoperating assets? How can their value be estimated?

d. What is the total value of a corporation? Who has claims on this value?

e. The first acquisition target is a privately held company in a mature industry owned by two brothers, each with 5 million shares of stock. The company currently has free cash flow of $24 million. Its WACC is 11%, and the FCF is expected to grow at a constant rate of 5%. The company owns marketable securities of $100 million. It is financed with $200 million of debt, $50 million of preferred stock, and $210 million of book equity.

(1) What is its value of operations?

(2) What is its total corporate value?

(3) What is its intrinsic value of equity?

(4) What is its intrinsic stock price per share?

(5) What is its intrinsic MVA (MVA = Total corporate value − Total book value of capital supplied by investors)?

f. The second acquisition target is a privately held company in a growing industry. The target has recently borrowed $40 million to finance its expansion; it has no other debt or preferred stock. It pays no dividends and currently has no marketable securities. KFS expects the company to produce free cash flows of −$5 million in 1 year, $10 million in 2 years, and $20 million in 3 years. After 3 years, free cash flow will grow at a rate of 6%. The target's WACC is 10% and it currently has 10 million shares of stock outstanding.

(1) What is the company's horizon value (i.e., its value of operations at Year 3)? What is its current value of operations (i.e., at Time 0)?

(2) What is its intrinsic value of equity on a price-per-share basis?

g. KFS is also interested in applying value-based management to its own divisions. Explain what value-based management is.

h. What are the four value drivers? How does each of them affect value?

i. What is the expected return on invested capital (EROIC)? Why is the spread between EROIC and WACC so important?

j. KFS has two divisions. Both have current sales of $1,000 million, current expected growth of 5%, and a WACC of 10%. Division A has high profitability (OP = 6%) but high capital requirements (CR = 78%). Division B has low profitability (OP = 4%) but low capital requirements (CR = 27%). Given the current growth rate of 5%, determine the intrinsic MVA of each division. What is the intrinsic MVA of each division if growth is instead 6%?

k. What is the EROIC of each division for 5% growth and for 6% growth? How is this related to intrinsic MVA?

l. List six potential managerial behaviors that can harm a firm's value.

m. The managers at KFS have heard that corporate governance can affect shareholder value. What is corporate governance? List five corporate governance provisions that are internal to a firm and are under its control.

n. What characteristics of the board of directors usually lead to effective corporate governance?

o. List three provisions in the corporate charter that affect takeovers.

p. Briefly describe the use of stock options in a compensation plan. What are some potential problems with stock options as a form of compensation?

q. What is block ownership? How does it affect corporate governance?

r. Briefly explain how regulatory agencies and legal systems affect corporate governance.

Selected Additional Cases

The following cases from TextChoice, Cengage Learning's online case library, cover many of the concepts discussed in this chapter and are available at **www.textchoice2.com/casenet.**

Klein-Brigham Series:
Case 41, "Advanced Fuels Corporation," and Case 93, "Electro Technology Corporation," discuss financing and valuing a new venture.

Brigham-Buzzard Series:
Case 14, "Maris Distributing Company," discusses valuation techniques used in a court case.

Chapter 12

Capital Budgeting:
Decision Criteria

WEB

The textbook's Web site contains an *Excel* file that will guide you through the chapter's calculations. The file for this chapter is ***Ch12 Tool Kit.xls***, and we encourage you to open the file and follow along as you read the chapter.

In Chapters 12 and 13, we discuss *capital budgeting*. Here *capital* refers to long-term assets used in production, and a *budget* is a plan that outlines projected expenditures during a future period. Thus, *the capital budget* is a summary of planned investments of assets that will last for more than a year, and **capital budgeting** is the whole process of analyzing projects and deciding which ones to accept and thus include in the capital budget. Chapter 12 focuses on the basics of capital budgeting, especially the primary criteria used to evaluate projects, and it explains why one method—the net present value (NPV)—is the best single criterion. We use simplified examples in this chapter to explain the basic theory and then, in Chapter 13, we go on to discuss how cash flows are estimated, how risk is measured, and how capital budgeting decisions are actually made.

Beginning of Chapter Questions

A s you read the chapter, consider how you would answer the following questions. You *should not* necessarily be able to answer the questions before you read the chapter. Rather, you should use them to get a sense of the issues covered in the chapter. After reading the chapter, you should be able to give at least partial answers to the questions, and you should be able to give better answers after the chapter has been discussed in class. Note, too, that it is often useful, when answering conceptual questions, to use hypothetical data to illustrate your answer. We illustrate the answers with an *Excel* model that is available on the textbook's Web site. Accessing the model and working through it is a useful exercise, and it provides insights that are useful when answering the questions.

1. Describe the **six primary capital budgeting decision criteria.** What are their pros and cons, and how are they related to maximizing shareholder wealth? Should managers use just one criterion, or are there good reasons for using two or more criteria in the decision process?
2. Why do conflicts sometimes arise between the **net present value (NPV)** and **internal rate of**

return **(IRR)** methods; that is, what conditions can lead to conflicts? Can similar conflicts arise between **modified internal rate of return (MIRR)** and NPV rankings, or between rankings by the MIRR and IRR methods?
3. If management's goal is to maximize shareholder wealth, should it focus on the regular IRR or the MIRR? Explain your answer.
4. Under what conditions might you find more than one IRR for a project? How would you decide whether or not to accept the project? If you were comparing two mutually exclusive projects, one with a single IRR of 12% and the other with two different IRRs of 10% and 15%, how should you choose between the projects?
5. What is the **unequal life problem,** under what conditions is it relevant, and how should it be dealt with?
6. What is a **post-audit,** and what is the purpose of this audit?
7. What is **capital rationing,** what conditions lead to it, and how should it be dealt with?

12.1 An Overview of Capital Budgeting

Capital budgeting is based on the same procedures used in the corporate valuation model, but with one major difference. Whereas we used the corporate valuation model to evaluate existing companies or divisions, capital budgeting involves both analyzing and creating investment projects. If companies execute their plans well, then capital budgeting projects will be successful, but poor execution will lead to project failures. Still, in both corporate valuation and capital budgeting, we forecast a set of cash flows, find the present value of those flows, and then make the investment if and only if the PV of the expected future cash flows exceeds the investment's cost.

A firm's growth, and even its ability to remain competitive and to survive, depends on a constant flow of ideas for new products, improvements in existing products, and ways to operate more efficiently. Accordingly, well-managed firms go to great lengths to develop good capital budgeting proposals. For example, the executive vice president of one successful corporation told us that his company takes the following steps to generate projects.

Our R&D department constantly searches for new products and ways to improve existing products. In addition, our Executive Committee, which consists of senior executives in marketing, production, and finance, identifies the products and markets in which our company should compete, and the Committee sets long-run targets for each division. These targets, which are spelled out in the corporation's strategic business plan, provide a general guide to the operating executives who must meet them. The operating

CORPORATE VALUATION AND CAPITAL BUDGETING

You can calculate the cash flows (CF) for a project in much the same way as for a firm. When the project's cash flows are discounted at the appropriate risk-adjusted weighted average cost of capital ("r" for simplicity), the result is the project's value. Note that when valuing an entire firm we discount its free cash flows at the overall weighted average cost of capital, but when valuing a project we discount its cash flows at the project's own risk-adjusted cost of capital. Note also that the firm's free cash flows are the total of all the net cash flows from its past projects. Thus, if a project is accepted and put into operation, it will provide cash flows that add to the firm's free cash flows and thus to the firm's value.

Subtracting the initial cost of the project from the discounted future expected cash flows gives the project's net present value (NPV). A project that has a positive NPV adds value to the firm. In fact, the firm's Market Value Added (MVA) is the sum of all its projects' NPVs. The key point, though, is that the process of evaluating projects, or capital budgeting, is absolutely critical for a firm's success.

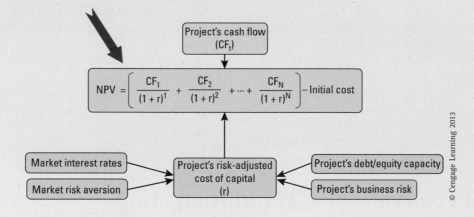

$$NPV = \left[\frac{CF_1}{(1+r)^1} + \frac{CF_2}{(1+r)^2} + \cdots + \frac{CF_N}{(1+r)^N} \right] - \text{Initial cost}$$

© Cengage Learning 2013

executives then seek new products, set expansion plans for existing products, and look for ways to reduce production and distribution costs. Since bonuses and promotions are based on each unit's ability to meet or exceed its targets, these economic incentives encourage our operating managers to seek out profitable investment opportunities.

While our senior executives are judged and rewarded on the basis of how well their units perform, people further down the line are given bonuses and stock options for suggestions that lead to profitable investments. Additionally, a percentage of our corporate profit is set aside for distribution to nonexecutive employees, and we have an Employees' Stock Ownership Plan (ESOP) to provide further incentives. Our objective is to encourage employees at all levels to keep an eye out for good ideas, especially those that lead to capital investments.

Analyzing capital expenditure proposals is not costless—benefits can be gained, but analysis does have a cost. For certain types of projects, an extremely detailed analysis may be warranted, whereas simpler procedures are adequate for other projects. Accordingly, firms generally categorize projects and analyze those in each category somewhat differently:

1. *Replacement needed to continue profitable operations.* An example would be an essential pump on a profitable offshore oil platform. The platform manager could make this investment without an elaborate review process.
2. *Replacement to reduce costs.* An example would be the replacement of serviceable but obsolete equipment in order to lower costs. A fairly detailed analysis would be needed, with more detail required for larger expenditures.
3. *Expansion of existing products or markets.* These decisions require a forecast of growth in demand, so a more detailed analysis is required. Go/no-go decisions are generally made at a higher level than are replacement decisions.
4. *Expansion into new products or markets.* These investments involve strategic decisions that could change the fundamental nature of the business. A detailed analysis is required, and the final decision is made by top officers, possibly with board approval.
5. *Contraction decisions.* Especially during bad recessions, companies often find themselves with more capacity than they are likely to need in the foreseeable future. Then, rather than continue to operate plants at, say, 50% of capacity and incur losses as a result of excessive fixed costs, they decide to downsize. That generally requires payments to laid off workers and additional costs for shutting down selected operations. These decisions are made at the board level.
6. *Safety and/or environmental projects.* Expenditures necessary to comply with environmental orders, labor agreements, or insurance policy terms fall into this category. How these projects are handled depends on their size, with small ones being treated much like the Category 1 projects and large ones requiring expenditures that might even cause the firm to abandon the line of business.
7. *Other.* This catch-all includes items such as office buildings, parking lots, and executive aircraft. How they are handled varies among companies.
8. *Mergers.* Buying a whole firm (or division) is different from buying a machine or building a new plant. Still, basic capital budgeting procedures are used when making merger decisions.

Relatively simple calculations, and only a few supporting documents, are required for most replacement decisions, especially maintenance investments in profitable plants. More detailed analyses are required as we move on to more complex expansion decisions, especially for investments in new products or areas. Also, within each category projects are grouped by their dollar costs: Larger investments require increasingly detailed analysis and approval at higher levels. Thus, a plant manager might be authorized to approve maintenance expenditures up to $10,000 using a simple payback analysis, but the full board of directors might have to approve decisions that involve either amounts greater than $1 million or expansions into new products or markets.

If a firm has capable and imaginative executives and employees, and if its incentive system is working properly, then many ideas for capital investment will be forthcoming. Some ideas will be good and should be funded, but others should be killed. Therefore, the following procedures have been established for screening projects and deciding which to accept or reject:[1]

1. Net Present Value (NPV)
2. Internal Rate of Return (IRR)
3. Modified Internal Rate of Return (MIRR)

---

1. One other rarely used criterion, the Accounting Rate of Return, is covered in the chapter's *Excel Tool Kit* model and *Web Extension 12A.*

4. Profitability Index (PI)
5. Regular Payback
6. Discounted Payback

As we shall see, the NPV is the best single criterion, primarily because it is directly related to the firm's central goal of maximizing the stock's intrinsic value. However, all of the methods provide some useful information, and all are used in practice.

In the sections that follow, we will use these six procedures to analyze the decisions that Guyton Products Company (GPC) faces. GPC is a high-tech "lab-bench-to-market" development company that takes cutting-edge research advances and translates them into consumer products. GPC has recently licensed a nano-fabrication coating technology from a university that promises to significantly increase the efficiency with which solar energy can be harvested and stored as heat. GPC is considering using this technology in two different product lines. In the first, code-named "Project S" for "solid," the technology would be used to coat rock and concrete structures to be used as passive heat sinks and sources for energy-efficient residential and commercial buildings. In the second, code-named "Project L" for "liquid," it would be used to coat the collectors in a high-efficiency solar water heater. GPC must decide whether to undertake either of these two projects.

In Chapter 13, we will discuss in detail how to estimate the cash flows for Project L and how to deal with uncertainty and risk in making capital budgeting decisions, but for now we will take the two projects' cash flows as given so that we can focus on how to use the six procedures.[2]

Self Test

How is capital budgeting similar to security valuation? How is it different?

What are some ways that firms generate ideas for capital projects?

Identify the major project classification categories, and explain how and why they are used.

List six procedures used for screening projects and deciding which to accept or reject.

12.2 Net Present Value (NPV)

The **net present value (NPV)**, defined as the present value of a project's cash inflows minus the present value of its costs, tells us how much the project contributes to shareholder wealth—the larger the NPV, the more value the project adds and thus the higher the stock's price. NPV is generally regarded as the best single screening criterion. We use the data for GPC's Projects S and L shown in Figure 12-1 to illustrate the calculations for the NPV and the other criteria. Although Projects S and L are GPC's "solid" and "liquid" projects, you may also find it helpful to think of S and L as standing for *Short* and *Long*: Project S is a short-term project in the sense that most of its cash inflows come in relatively soon; Project L has more total cash inflows, but most are realized in the later years.

The projects are equally risky, and they both have a 10% cost of capital. Furthermore, the cash flows have been adjusted to incorporate the impact of depreciation,

---

2. We will see in Chapter 13 that the cash flows we analyze are, in fact, free cash flows as calculated in Chapters 8 and 9 and analyzed in Chapter 11.

Figure 12-1   **Cash Flows (CF$_t$) and Selected Evaluation Criteria for Projects S and L**

	A	B	C	D	E	F
22	Panel A: Project Cash Flows and Cost of Capital					
23	Project cost of capital, r, for each project:		10%			
24						
25		Initial Cost	After-Tax, End of Year, Project Cash Flows, CF$_t$			
26	Year	0	1	2	3	4
27	Project S	−$10,000	$5,300	$4,300	$1,874	$1,500
28	Project L	−$10,000	$1,900	$2,700	$2,345	$7,800
29						
30	Panel B: Summary of Selected Evaluation Criteria					
31			Project S	Project L		
32		NPV	$804.38	$1,048.02		
33		IRR	14.69%	13.79%		
34		MIRR	12.15%	12.78%		
35		PI	1.08	1.10		
36		Payback	2.21	3.39		
37		Discounted Payback	3.21	3.80		

© Cengage Learning 2013

WEB

See *Ch12 Tool Kit.xls* on the textbook's Web site.

taxes, and salvage values.[3] The investment outlays are shown under Year 0, and they include investments in fixed assets and any necessary working capital. All subsequent cash flows occur at the end of the year. All of the calculations can be done easily with a financial calculator, but since capital budgeting in the real world is generally done using a spreadsheet, we show how problems would be set up in *Excel*.

We can find the NPVs as follows.

1. Calculate the present value of each cash flow discounted at the project's risk-adjusted cost of capital, which is r − 10% in our example.
2. The sum of the discounted cash flows is defined as the project's NPV.

The equation for the NPV, set up with input data for Project S, is

$$NPV = CF_0 + \frac{CF_1}{(1+r)^1} + \frac{CF_2}{(1+r)^2} + \cdots + \frac{CF_N}{(1+r)^N}$$

$$= \sum_{t=0}^{N} \frac{CF_t}{(1+r)^t}$$

(12–1)

Applying Equation 12-1 to Project S, we have

$$NPV_S = -\$10,000 + \frac{\$5,300}{(1.10)^1} + \frac{\$4,300}{(1.10)^2} + \frac{\$1,874}{(1.10)^3} + \frac{\$1,500}{(1.10)^4}$$

$$= -\$10,000 + \$4,818.18 + \$3,553.72 + \$1,407.96 + \$1,024.52$$

$$= \$804.38$$

---

3. The most difficult aspect of capital budgeting is estimating the "relevant" cash flows, which are defined as the cash flows generated by the project that are available for distribution to investors. We illustrate this for Project L in Chapter 13.

Here CF_t is the expected net cash flow at Time t, r is the project's risk-adjusted cost of capital (or WACC), and N is its life. Projects generally require an initial investment— for example, developing the product, buying the equipment needed to make it, building a factory, and stocking inventory. The initial investment is a negative cash flow. For Projects S and L, only CF_0 is negative, but for a large project such as an FPL power plant, outflows would occur for several years before cash inflows begin.

Figure 12-2 shows, on Row 51, the cash flow time line for project S as taken from Figure 12-1. The cost is −$10,000, which is not discounted because it occurs at t = 0. The PV of each cash inflow, and the sum of the PVs, is shown in Column B. You could find the PVs of the cash flows with a calculator or with *Excel*, and the end result would be the numbers in Column B of the figure. When we sum the PVs of the inflows and subtract the cost, the result is $804.38, which is NPV_S. The NPV for Project L, $1,048.02, can be found similarly.

The step-by-step procedure shown for Project S is useful for illustrating how the NPV is calculated, but in practice (and on exams) it is far more efficient to use a financial calculator or *Excel*. Different calculators are set up somewhat differently, but (as we discuss in Chapter 28) they all have a "cash flow register" that can be used to evaluate uneven cash flows such as those for Projects S and L. Equation 12-1 is actually programmed into these calculators, and all we need to do is enter the cash flows (with the correct signs) along with r = I/YR = 10. Once the data have been entered, you can press the NPV key to get the answer, 804.38, on the screen.[4] If you are familiar with *Excel*, you can use it to find the NPVs for S and L:

$$NPV_S = \$804.38$$
$$NPV_L = \$1,048.02$$

We provide the model used to obtain these values in the chapter's *Excel Tool Kit*. If you are familiar with *Excel* then you should look at the model, as this is how most people in the real world deal with capital budgeting problems.

Before using these NPVs in the decision process, we need to know whether Projects S and L are **independent** or **mutually exclusive**. Independent projects are those whose cash flows are not affected by other projects. If Wal-Mart were considering a new store in Boise and another in Atlanta, those projects would

WEB

See *Ch12 Tool Kit.xls* on the textbook's Web site.

Figure 12-2　Finding the NPV for Projects S and L

	A	B	C	D	E	F
49		r = 10%				
50	Year	0	1	2	3	4
51	Project S	−10,000.00	5,300	4,300	1,874	1,500
52		4,818.18				
53		3,553.72				
54		1,407.96				
55		1,024.52				
56	NPV_S =	$804.38	Long way: Sum the PVs of the CFs to find NPV			
57						
58	Year	0	1	2	3	4
59	Project L	−10,000.00	1,900	2,700	2,345	7,800
60	NPV_L =	$1,048.02	Short way: Use *Excel's* NPV function =NPV(C49,C59:F59)+B59			

© Cengage Learning 2013

---

4. The keystrokes for finding the NPV are shown for several calculators in the calculator tutorials we provide on the textbook's Web site.

be independent, and if both had positive NPVs, Wal-Mart should accept both. In the case of Projects S and L, GPC is targeting two different heating markets—one for passive solar heating and one for hot water, and so the projects are independent. Mutually exclusive projects, on the other hand, are two different ways of accomplishing the same result, so if one project is accepted then the other must be rejected. A conveyor-belt system to move goods in a warehouse and a fleet of forklifts for the same purpose would be mutually exclusive—accepting one implies rejecting the other. If, instead of two different uses of the nano-coatings, Projects S and L had been two different ways to manufacture the solar water heaters, then they would have been mutually exclusive.

What should the decision be if Projects S and L are independent? In this case, both should be accepted because both have positive NPVs and thus add value to the firm. However, if they are mutually exclusive, then Project L should be chosen because it has the higher NPV and thus adds more value than S. We can summarize these criteria with the following rules.

12.2a NPV Decision Rules

Independent projects: If NPV exceeds zero, accept the project. Since S and L both have positive NPVs, accept them both if they are independent.

Mutually exclusive projects: Accept the project with the highest positive NPV. If no project has a positive NPV, then reject them all. If S and L are mutually exclusive, the NPV criterion would select L.

Projects must be either independent or mutually exclusive, so one or the other of these rules applies to every project.[5]

Why is NPV the primary capital budgeting decision criterion?

What is the difference between "independent" and "mutually exclusive" projects?

Projects SS and LL have the following cash flows:

End-of-Year Cash Flows

	0	1	2	3
SS	−700	500	300	100
LL	−700	100	300	600

If the cost of capital is 10%, then what are the projects' NPVs?
(NPV$_{SS}$ = 77.61; NPV$_{LL}$ = 89.63)

What project or set of projects would be in your capital budget if SS and LL were (a) independent or (b) mutually exclusive? **(Both; LL)**

12.3 Internal Rate of Return (IRR)

In Chapter 4 we discussed the yield to maturity on a bond, and we explained that if you hold a bond to maturity then you will earn the yield to maturity on your

---

5. This is a simplification. For example, some projects can benefit others—these are "complementary" projects. Other projects harm others—these are called "cannibalizing" projects. These concepts are addressed in Chapter 13.

investment. The YTM is found as the discount rate that forces the present value of the cash inflows to equal the price of the bond. This same concept is used in capital budgeting when we calculate a project's **internal rate of return,** or **IRR:**

A project's IRR is the discount rate that forces the PV of the inflows to equal the initial cost (or to equal the PVs of all the costs if costs are incurred over several years). This is equivalent to forcing the NPV to equal zero. The IRR is an estimate of the project's rate of return, and it is comparable to the YTM on a bond.

To calculate the IRR, we begin with Equation 12-1 for the NPV, replace r in the denominator with the term "IRR," and set the NPV equal to zero. This transforms Equation 12-1 into Equation 12-2, the one used to find the IRR. The rate that forces NPV to equal zero is the IRR.[6]

(12–2)

$$NPV = CF_0 + \frac{CF_1}{(1 + IRR)^1} + \frac{CF_2}{(1 + IRR)^2} + \ldots + \frac{CF_N}{(1 + IRR)^N} = 0$$

$$= \sum_{t=0}^{N} \frac{CF_t}{(1 + IRR)^t} = 0$$

For Project S, we have

$$NPV_s = 0 = -\$10,000 + \frac{\$5,300}{(1 + IRR)^1} + \frac{\$4,300}{(1 + IRR)^2} + \frac{\$1,874}{(1 + IRR)^3} + \frac{\$1,500}{(1 + IRR)^4}$$

WEB

See *Ch12 Tool Kit.xls* on the textbook's Web site.

Figure 12-3 illustrates the process for finding the IRR of Project S.

Three procedures can be used to find the **IRR:**

1. *Trial-and-error.* We could use a trial-and-error procedure: Try a discount rate, see if the equation solves to zero, and if it doesn't, try a different rate. Continue until we find the rate that forces the NPV to zero, and that rate will be the IRR. No

Figure 12-3   **Finding the IRR**

	A	B	C	D	E	F
84		r = 14.686%				
85	Year	0	1	2	3	4
86	Project S	−10,000.00	5,300	4,300	1,874	1,500
87		4,621.33				
88		3,269.26				
89		1,242.34				
90		867.07				
91	Sum of PVs =	$0.00	= NPV at r = 14.686%. NPV = 0, so IRR = 14.686%			
92	IRR_S =	14.69%	=IRR(B86:F86) using IRR function			
93						
94	Year	0	1	2	3	4
95	Project L	−10,000.00	1,900	2,700	2,345	7,800
96	IRR_L =	13.79%	=IRR(B95:F95) using IRR function			

© Cengage Learning 2013

---

6. For a large, complex project like an FPL power plant, costs are incurred for several years before cash inflows begin. That simply means that we have a number of negative cash flows before the positive cash flows begin.

one does this, however. Instead, IRR is always calculated using either a financial calculator or *Excel* (or some other computer program) as described below.

2. *Calculator solution.* Enter the cash flows into the calculator's cash flow register just as we did to find the NPV, and then press the calculator key labeled "IRR." Instantly, you get the internal rate of return. Here are the values for Projects S and L:[7]

$$IRR_S = 14.686\%$$
$$IRR_L = 13.786\%$$

3. *Excel solution.* It is even easier to find IRRs using *Excel,* as we demonstrate in this chapter's *Tool Kit.*[8]

Why is the discount rate that causes a project's NPV to equal zero so special? The reason is that the IRR is an estimate of the project's rate of return. If this return exceeds the cost of the funds used to finance the project, then the difference is a bonus that goes to the firm's stockholders and causes the stock's price to rise. Project S has an estimated return of 14.686% versus a 10% cost of capital, so its bonus is 4.686%. On the other hand, if the IRR is less than the cost of capital then stockholders must make up the shortfall, which would hurt the stock price.

Note again that the IRR formula, Equation 12-2, is simply the NPV formula, Equation 12-1, solved for the particular discount rate that forces the NPV to zero. Thus, the same basic equation is used for both methods. The only difference is that with the NPV method, the discount rate is given and we find the NPV, whereas with the IRR method, the NPV is set equal to zero and we find the interest rate that provides this equality.

If the IRR criterion is used to rank projects, then the decision rules are as follows.

Independent projects: If IRR exceeds the project's WACC, then the project should be accepted. If IRR is less than the project's WACC, reject it. Projects S and L both have positive IRRs, so they would both be accepted by the IRR method. Note that both projects were also accepted by the NPV criterion, so the NPV and IRR criteria provide the same result if the projects are independent.

Mutually exclusive projects: Accept the mutually exclusive project with the highest IRR, provided that the project's IRR is greater than its WACC. Reject any project whose IRR does not exceed the firm's WACC. Since Project S has the higher IRR, it should be accepted (and L rejected) if the projects are mutually exclusive. However, recall that Project L had the larger NPV, so the NPV method ranked L over S and thus would choose L. Therefore, a conflict will exist between the NPV and the IRR criteria if the projects are mutually exclusive.

---

7. See our calculator tutorials on the textbook's Web site. Note that once the cash flows have been entered into the cash flow register, you can find both the NPV and the IRR. To find the NPV, enter the interest rate (I/YR) and then press the NPV key. Then, with no further entries, press the IRR key to find the IRR. Thus, once you set up the calculator to find the NPV, it is easy to find the IRR. This is one reason most firms calculate both the NPV and the IRR. If you calculate one, it is easy to also calculate the other, and both provide information that decision makers find useful. The same is true with *Excel:* After estimating cash flows, it is easy to calculate both NPV and IRR.

8. Note that to calculate the IRR with *Excel* the full data range is specified, because *Excel's* IRR function assumes that the first cash flow (the negative $10,000) occurs at t = 0. You can use the function wizard if you don't have the formula memorized.

The IRR is logically appealing—it is useful to know the rates of return on proposed investments. However, as we see from Projects L and S, NPV and IRR can produce conflicting conclusions when one is choosing between mutually exclusive projects, and when conflicts occur the NPV criterion is generally better. A simple, but extreme, example should make this very clear. Consider Projects A and B, which are mutually exclusive and each has a 10% cost of capital. Project A costs $1 and will generate cash flows of $0.60 a year for 10 years. Project B costs $100,000 and will generate cash flows of $20,000 a year for 10 years. Project A's IRR is 59.4% and its NPV is $2.60. Project B's IRR is much smaller, only 15.1%, but its NPV is $22,891. Provided the company can obtain the capital it needs to invest in profitable projects, then clearly Project B is better—the company is worth $22,891 more if Project B is selected, but only $2.60 more if Project A is selected, so Project B should be selected despite its lower IRR.

Self Test

In what sense is a project's IRR similar to the YTM on a bond?

The cash flows for Projects SS and LL are as follows:

	End-of-Year Cash Flows			
	0	1	2	3
SS	−700	500	300	100
LL	−700	100	300	600

Assume that the firm's WACC = r = 10%. What are the two projects' IRRs? **(IRR$_{SS}$ = 18.0%; IRR$_{LL}$ = 15.6%)**

Which project would the IRR method select if the firm has a 10% cost of capital and the projects are (a) independent or (b) mutually exclusive? **(Both; SS)**

12.4 Multiple Internal Rates of Return[9]

One problem with the IRR is that, under certain conditions, a project may have more than one IRR. First, note that a project is said to have *normal* cash flows if it has one or more cash outflows (costs) followed by a series of cash inflows. If, however, a cash *outflow* occurs sometime after the inflows have started, meaning that the signs of the cash flows change *more than once*, then the project is said to have *nonnormal* cash flows. Here's an illustration of these concepts:

Normal: − + + + +   or   − − − + + + +
Nonnormal: − + + + + −   or   − + + + − + + +

An example of a project with nonnormal flows would be a strip coal mine where the company first spends money to buy the property and prepare the site for mining, has positive inflows for several years, and then spends more money to return the land to its original condition. In this case, the project might have two IRRs—that is, **multiple IRRs**.[10]

---

9. This section is relatively technical, and some instructors may choose to omit it without loss of continuity.
10. Equation 12-2 is a polynomial of degree n, so it has n different roots, or solutions. All except one of the roots are imaginary numbers when investments have normal cash flows (one or more cash outflows followed by cash inflows), so in the normal case only one value of IRR appears. However, the possibility of multiple real roots, and hence of multiple IRRs, arises when negative net cash flows occur after the project has been placed in operation.

To illustrate multiple IRRs, suppose a firm is considering a potential strip mine (Project M) that has a cost of $1.6 million and will produce a cash flow of $10 million at the end of Year 1; then, at the end of Year 2, the firm must spend $10 million to restore the land to its original condition. Therefore, the project's expected net cash flows are as follows (in millions):

	Year 0	End of Year 1	End of Year 2
Cash flows	−$1.6	+$10	−$10

We can substitute these values into Equation 12-2 and then solve for the IRR:

$$NPV = \frac{-\$1.6 \text{ million}}{(1 + IRR)^0} + \frac{\$10 \text{ million}}{(1 + IRR)^1} + \frac{-\$10 \text{ million}}{(1 + IRR)^2} = 0$$

For these cash flows, the NPV equals 0 when IRR = 25%, but it also equals 0 when IRR = 400%.[11] Therefore, Project M has one IRR of 25% and another of 400%, and we don't know which one to use. This relationship is depicted graphically in Figure 12-4.[12] The graph is constructed by plotting the project's NPV at different discount rates.

Observe that no dilemma regarding Project M would arise if the NPV method were used; we would simply find the NPV at the appropriate cost of capital and use it to evaluate the project. We would see that if Project M's cost of capital were 10% then its NPV would be −$0.774 million and the project should be rejected. If r were between 25% and 400% then the NPV would be positive, but any such number would probably not be realistic or useful for anything. (At such a high cost of capital, the firm's typical projects would have negative NPVs.)

WEB

See **Ch12 Tool Kit.xls** on the textbook's Web site for all calculations.

Self Test

What condition regarding cash flows would cause more than one IRR to exist?

Project MM has the following cash flows:

End-of-Year Cash Flows			
0	1	2	3
−$1,000	$2,000	$2,000	−$3,350

Calculate MM's NPV at discount rates of 0%, 10%, 12.2258%, 25%, 122.147%, and 150%. (**−$350; −$46; $0; $165; $0; −$94**)

What are MM's IRRs? (**12.23% and 122.15%**)

If the cost of capital were 10%, should the project be accepted or rejected? (**Reject because NPV < 0**)

---

11. If you attempt to find Project M's IRR with an HP calculator, you will get an error message, whereas TI calculators give only the IRR that's closest to zero. When you encounter either situation, you can find the approximate IRRs by first calculating NPVs using several different values for r = I/YR, constructing a graph with NPV on the vertical axis and cost of capital on the horizontal axis, and then visually determining approximately where NPV = 0. The intersection with the x-axis gives a rough idea of the IRRs' values. With some calculators and also with *Excel*, you can find both IRRs by entering guesses, as we explain in our calculator and *Excel* tutorials.

12. Figure 12-4 is called an *NPV profile*. Profiles are discussed in more detail in Section 12.7.

Figure 12-4   **Graph for Multiple IRRs: Project M (Millions of Dollars)**

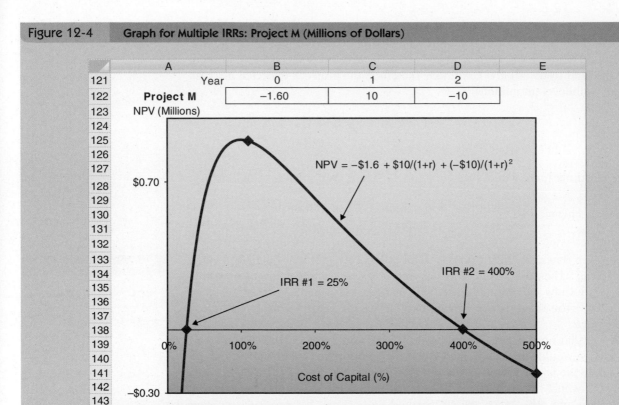

Note:
The data table shown below calculates Project M's NPV at the rates shown in the left column. These data are plotted to form the graph shown above. Notice that NPV = 0 at both 25% and 400%. Since the definition of the IRR is the rate at which the NPV = 0, we see that there are two IRRs.

r	NPV
0%	−$1.600
10%	−$0.774
25%	$0.000 = IRR #1 = 25%
110%	$0.894
400%	$0.000 = IRR #2 = 400%
500%	−$0.211

WEB

See **Ch12 Tool Kit.xls** on the textbook's Web site.

12.5 Reinvestment Rate Assumptions

The NPV calculation is based on the assumption that cash inflows can be reinvested at the project's risk-adjusted WACC, whereas the IRR calculation is based on the assumption that cash flows can be reinvested at the IRR itself. To see why this is so, think about the following diagram, which illustrates the future value of $100 when the interest rate is 5%:

$$0 \quad\; 5\% \quad\; 1 \quad\; 5\% \quad\; 2 \quad\; 5\% \quad\; 3$$

Going from PV to FV: PV = $100.00 ---▶ $105.00 ---▶ $110.25 ---▶ $115.76 = FV

Observe that the FV calculation assumes that the interest earned during each year can itself be reinvested to earn the same 5% in each succeeding year.

Now recall that to find the PV we reversed the process, discounting rather than compounding at the 5% rate. The following diagram can be used to demonstrate this point:

$$
\begin{array}{ccccccc}
0 & 5\% & 1 & 5\% & 2 & 5\% & 3
\end{array}
$$

Going from FV to PV: PV $=\$100.00\blacktriangleleft$---$\$105.00\blacktriangleleft$---$\$110.25\blacktriangleleft$---$\$115.76 =$ FV

We are thus led to the following conclusion: *When we calculate a present value, we are implicitly assuming that cash flows can be reinvested at a specified interest rate* (5% in our example). This applies to Projects S and L: When we calculated their NPVs, we discounted at their WACC of 10%, which means that we assumed that their cash flows could be reinvested at 10%.

Now consider the IRR. In Section 12.3 we presented a cash flow diagram set up to show the PVs of the cash flows when discounted at the IRR. We saw that the sum of the PVs is equal to the cost at a discount rate of 14.686%, so by definition 14.686% is the IRR. Now we can ask this question: What reinvestment rate is built into the IRR?

Because discounting at a given rate assumes that cash flows can be reinvested at that same rate, the IRR assumes that cash flows are reinvested at the IRR itself.

So the NPV assumes reinvestment at the WACC, whereas the IRR assumes reinvestment at the IRR itself. Which assumption is more reasonable? For most firms, assuming reinvestment at the WACC is better, for the following reasons.

- If a firm has reasonably good access to the capital markets then it can raise all the capital it needs at the going rate, which in our example is 10%.
- Since the firm can obtain capital at 10%, if it has investment opportunities with positive NPVs then it should take them on, and it can finance them at a 10% cost.
- If we assume that the firm operates in a reasonably competitive industry, then its return on investment opportunities should be relatively close to its cost of capital; if it were much higher, then new firms would enter the market and drive prices (and thus returns) down to near the cost of capital.
- If the firm uses internally generated cash flows from past projects rather than external capital, this will simply save it the 10% cost of capital. Thus, 10% is the *opportunity cost* of the cash flows, and that is the effective return on reinvested funds.

As an illustration, suppose a project's IRR is 50%, the firm's WACC is 10%, and it has good access to the capital markets and operates in a competitive industry. Thus, the firm can raise all the capital it needs at the 10% rate. Given the existence of competition, the 50% return would attract new entry, which would make it hard to find new projects with a similar high return, which is what the IRR assumes. Moreover, even if the firm does find such projects, it would take them on with external capital that costs 10%. The logical conclusion is that the original project's cash flows will simply save the 10% cost of the external capital and that 10%, not 50%, is the effective return on those flows.

If a firm does not have good access to external capital, and if it also has a lot of potential projects with high IRRs, then it might be reasonable to assume that a project's cash flows could be reinvested at rates close to their IRRs. However, that situation rarely occurs, since firms with good investment opportunities generally *do* have good access to debt and equity markets.

Our conclusion is that the assumption built into the IRR—that cash flows can be reinvested at the IRR, no matter how high it is—is flawed, whereas the assumption built into the NPV—that cash flows can be reinvested at the WACC—is generally correct. Moreover, if the true reinvestment rate is less than the IRR, then the true rate of return on the investment must be less than the calculated IRR; thus the IRR is misleading as a measure of a project's profitability. This point is discussed further in the next section.

Self Test

Why is a reinvestment rate implicitly assumed whenever we find the present value of a future cash flow? Would it be possible to find the PV of a FV without specifying an implicit reinvestment rate?

What reinvestment rate is built into the NPV calculation? The IRR calculation?

For a firm that has adequate access to capital markets, is it more reasonable to assume reinvestment at the WACC or the IRR? Why?

12.6 Modified Internal Rate of Return (MIRR)

It is logical for managers to want to know the expected rate of return on investments, and this is what the IRR is supposed to tell us. However, the IRR is based on the assumption that projects' cash flows can be reinvested at the IRR itself, and this assumption is usually wrong: *The IRR overstates the expected return for accepted projects because cash flows cannot generally be reinvested at the IRR itself.* Therefore, the IRR for accepted projects is generally greater than the true expected rate of return. This imparts an upward bias on corporate projections based on IRRs. Given this fundamental flaw, is there a percentage evaluator that is better than the regular IRR? The answer is "yes": *We can modify the IRR to make it a better measure of profitability.*

This new measure, the **Modified IRR (MIRR)**, is illustrated for Project S in Figure 12-5. It is similar to the regular IRR, except it is based on the assumption that cash flows are reinvested at the WACC (or some other explicit rate if that is a more reasonable assumption). Refer to Figure 12-5 as you read about the construction of this measure.

1. Project S has just one outflow, a negative $10,000 at t = 0. Since it occurs at Time 0, it is not discounted, and its PV is −$10,000. If the project had additional outflows, we would find the PV at t = 0 for each one and then sum them for use in the MIRR calculation.
2. Next, we find the future value of each *inflow,* compounded at the WACC out to the "terminal year," which is the year the last inflow is received. We assume that cash flows are reinvested at the WACC. For Project S, the first cash flow, $5,300, is compounded at WACC = 10% for 3 years, and it grows to $7,054. The second inflow, $4,300, grows to $5,203, and the third inflow, $1,874, grows to $2,061. The last inflow, $1,500, is received at the end, so it is not compounded at all. The sum of the future values, $15,819, is called the "terminal value," or TV.
3. We now have the cost at t = 0, −$10,000, and the TV at Year 4, $15,819. There is some discount rate that will cause the PV of the terminal value to equal the cost. *That interest rate is defined as the Modified Internal Rate of Return (MIRR).* In a calculator, enter N = 4, PV = −10000, PMT = 0, and FV = 15819. Then pressing the I/YR key yields the MIRR, 12.15%.

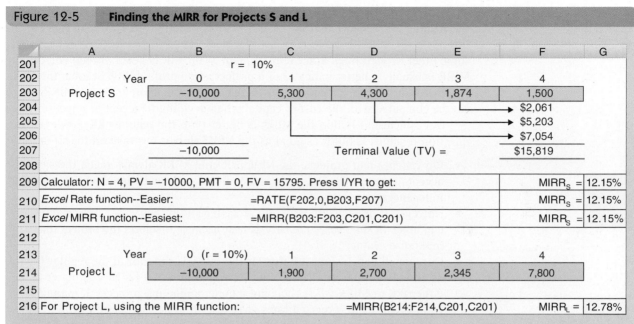

Figure 12-5   **Finding the MIRR for Projects S and L**

	A	B	C	D	E	F	G
201			r = 10%					
202		Year	0	1	2	3	4	
203	Project S		−10,000	5,300	4,300	1,874	1,500	
204							$2,061	
205							$5,203	
206							$7,054	
207			−10,000			Terminal Value (TV) =	$15,819	
208								
209	Calculator: N = 4, PV = −10000, PMT = 0, FV = 15795. Press I/YR to get:						MIRR$_S$ =	12.15%
210	*Excel* Rate function--Easier:		=RATE(F202,0,B203,F207)				MIRR$_S$ =	12.15%
211	*Excel* MIRR function--Easiest:		=MIRR(B203:F203,C201,C201)				MIRR$_S$ =	12.15%
212								
213		Year	0 (r = 10%)	1	2	3	4	
214	Project L		−10,000	1,900	2,700	2,345	7,800	
215								
216	For Project L, using the MIRR function:				=MIRR(B214:F214,C201,C201)		MIRR$_L$ =	12.78%

Notes:

1. In this figure we find the rate that forces the present value of the terminal value to equal the project's cost. That rate is defined as the MIRR. We have $10,000 = TV/(1 + MIRR)^N = $15,819/(1 + MIRR)^4$. We can find the MIRR with a calculator or *Excel*.

2. If S and L are independent, then both should be accepted because both MIRRs exceed the cost of capital. If the projects are mutually exclusive, then L should be chosen because it has the higher MIRR.

4. The MIRR can be found in a number of ways. Figure 12-5 illustrates exactly how the MIRR is calculated: We compound each cash inflow, sum them to determine the TV, and then find the rate that causes the PV of the TV to equal the cost. That rate in this example is 12.15%. However, *Excel* and some of the better calculators have a built-in MIRR function that streamlines the process. We explain how to use the MIRR function in our calculator tutorials, and we explain how to find MIRR with *Excel* in this chapter's *Excel Tool Kit*.[13]

---

13. If we let COF_t and CIF_t denote cash outflows and inflows, respectively, then Equations 12-2a and 12-2b summarize the steps just described:

$$\sum_{t=0}^{N} \frac{COF_t}{(1 + r)^t} = \frac{\sum_{t=0}^{N} CIF_t(1 + r)^{N-t}}{(1 + MIRR)^N} \qquad (12\text{–}2a)$$

$$PV\ Costs = \frac{TV}{(1 + MIRR)^N} \qquad (12\text{–}2b)$$

Also, note that there are alternative definitions for the MIRR. One difference relates to whether negative cash flows after the positive cash flows begin should be compounded and treated as part of the TV or discounted and treated as a cost. A related issue is whether negative and positive flows in a given year should be netted or treated separately. For more discussion, see David M. Shull, "Interpreting Rates of Return: A Modified Rate of Return Approach," *Financial Practice and Education*, Fall 1993, pp. 67–71.

The MIRR has two significant advantages over the regular IRR. First, whereas the regular IRR assumes that the cash flows from each project are reinvested at the IRR itself, the MIRR assumes that cash flows are reinvested at the cost of capital (or some other explicit rate). Since reinvestment at the IRR is generally not correct, the MIRR is usually a better indicator of a project's true profitability. Second, the MIRR eliminates the multiple IRR problem—there can never be more than one MIRR, and it can be compared with the cost of capital when deciding to accept or reject projects.

Our conclusion is that the MIRR is better than the regular IRR; however, this question remains: Is MIRR as good as the NPV? Here is our take on the situation.

- For *independent* projects, the NPV, IRR, and MIRR always reach the same accept–reject conclusion, so the three criteria are equally good when evaluating independent projects.
- However, if projects are *mutually exclusive* and if they differ in size, conflicts can arise. In such cases the NPV is best because it selects the project that maximizes value.[14]
- Our overall conclusions are that (1) the MIRR is superior to the regular IRR as an indicator of a project's "true" rate of return, but (2) NPV is better than either IRR or MIRR when choosing among competing projects. If managers want to know the expected rates of return on projects, it would be better to give them MIRRs rather than IRRs because MIRRs are more likely to be the rates that are actually earned.

Self Test

What's the primary difference between the MIRR and the regular IRR?

Which provides a better estimate of a project's "true" rate of return, the MIRR or the regular IRR? Explain your answer.

Projects A and B have the following cash flows:

	0	1	2
A	−$1,000	$1,150	$100
B	−$1,000	$100	$1,300

The cost of capital is 10%. What are the projects' IRRs, MIRRs, and NPVs? (IRR$_A$ = 23.1%, IRR$_B$ = 19.1%; MIRR$_A$ = 16.8%, MIRR$_B$ = 18.7%; NPV$_A$ = $128.10, NPV$_B$ = $165.29)

Which project would each method select? (IRR: A; MIRR: B; NPV: B)

12.7 NPV Profiles

Figure 12-4 from our discussion of multiple internal rates of return was a **net present value profile** for Project M; to make it, we plotted M's NPV at many different discount rates and connected the values to create a graph. M's (in this case, two different) IRRs were found at the discount rates where the NPV profile crossed the horizontal axis. Figure 12-6 shows the NPV profiles for Projects S and L plotted on the same axes. From this picture, we can observe the following points:

---

14. For projects of equal size but different lives, the MIRR will always lead to the same decision as the NPV if the MIRRs are both calculated using as the terminal year the life of the longer project. (Just fill in zeros for the shorter project's missing cash flows.)

Figure 12-6	NPV Profiles for Projects S and L

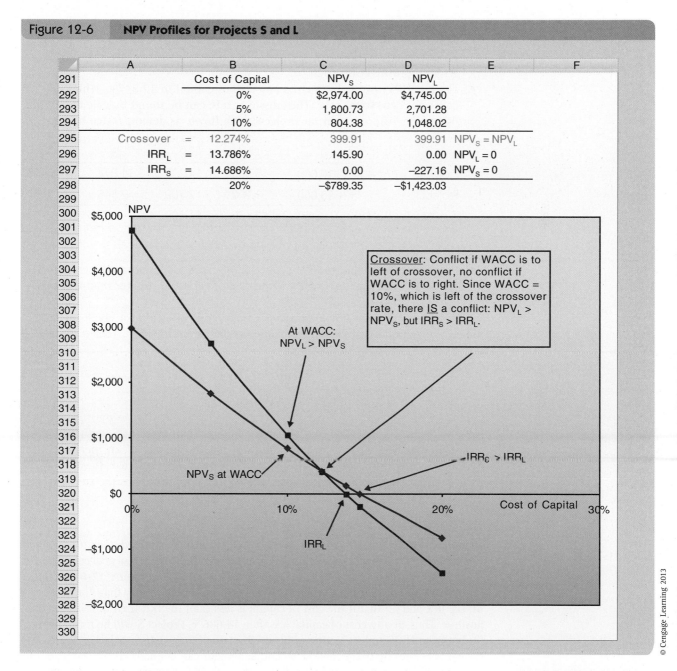

	A	B	C	D	E	F
291		Cost of Capital	NPV$_S$	NPV$_L$		
292		0%	$2,974.00	$4,745.00		
293		5%	1,800.73	2,701.28		
294		10%	804.38	1,048.02		
295	Crossover =	12.274%	399.91	399.91	NPV$_S$ = NPV$_L$	
296	IRR$_L$ =	13.786%	145.90	0.00	NPV$_L$ = 0	
297	IRR$_S$ =	14.686%	0.00	−227.16	NPV$_S$ = 0	
298		20%	−$789.35	−$1,423.03		

Crossover: Conflict if WACC is to left of crossover, no conflict if WACC is to right. Since WACC = 10%, which is left of the crossover rate, there <u>IS</u> a conflict: NPV$_L$ > NPV$_S$, but IRR$_S$ > IRR$_L$.

At WACC: NPV$_L$ > NPV$_S$

NPV$_S$ at WACC

IRR$_C$ > IRR$_L$

IRR$_L$

- The NPVs vary depending on the cost of capital. At a zero cost of capital, the NPV is just the sum of all of the cash flows while for a normal project, with a cash outflow at the start and positive cash flows thereafter, the higher the cost of capital, the lower the NPV. Observe also that L's NPV declines faster than does S's with increases in the cost of capital.[15]

WEB

See **Ch12 Tool Kit.xls** on the textbook's Web site.

---

15. Project M's NPV profile in Figure 12-4 looks different from the NPV profiles for S and L in that it initially increases, reaches a maximum, and then decreases. This is because M has nonnormal cash flows—an outflow followed by an inflow and then an outflow again. Projects S and L have normal cash flows—they only have outflows at the beginning followed by inflows, and so their NPV profiles both slope downward.

- The IRR is the rate at which the NPV profile crosses the horizontal axis and so doesn't depend on the cost of capital at all. Project L's IRR is less than Project S's IRR since L's NPV profile crosses the horizontal axis to the left of where S's NPV profile crosses it.
- The two NPV profile lines cross at a cost of capital of 12.247%, which is called the **crossover rate**. The crossover rate can be found by calculating the IRR of the differences in the projects' cash flows, as demonstrated below:

	0	1	2	3	4
Project S	−$10,000	$5,300	$4,300	$1,874	$1,500
Project L	−10,000	1,900	2,700	2,345	7,800
$\Delta = CF_S - CF_L$	$0	$3,400	$1,600	−$471	−$6,300

IRR Δ = 12.274%

- Project L has the higher NPV if the cost of capital is less than the crossover rate, but S has the higher NPV if the cost of capital is greater than that rate.

Notice that Project L has the steeper slope, indicating that a given increase in the cost of capital causes a larger decline in NPV_L than in NPV_S. To see why this is so, recall the equation for the NPV:

$$NPV = CF_0 + \frac{CF_1}{(1+r)^1} + \frac{CF_2}{(1+r)^2} + \cdots + \frac{CF_N}{(1+r)^N}$$

Now recognize (1) that L's cash flows come in later than those of S, with L's highest cash flows coming when N is large, and (2) that the impact of an increase in the discount rate is much greater on distant than on near-term cash flows. Thus L's NPV is more sensitive to interest rates and so its NPV profile has the steeper slope.

Independent Projects

If an independent project with normal cash flows is being evaluated, then the NPV and IRR criteria always lead to the same accept/reject decision: If NPV says accept then IRR also says accept, and vice versa. To see why this is so, look at Figure 12-6 and notice (1) that the IRR says accept Project S if the cost of capital is less than (or to the left of) the IRR and (2) that if the cost of capital is less than the IRR then the NPV must be positive. Thus, at any cost of capital less than 14.686%, Project S will be recommended by both the NPV and IRR criteria, but both methods reject the project if the cost of capital is greater than 14.686%. A similar statement can be made for Project L, or any other normal project, and we would always reach the same conclusion: *For normal, independent projects, if the IRR says to accept it, then so will the NPV.*

Mutually Exclusive Projects

Now assume that Projects S and L are mutually exclusive rather than independent. Therefore, we can choose either S or L, or we can reject both, but we can't accept both. Now look at Figure 12-6 and note these points.

- $IRR_S > IRR_L$, so the IRR decision rule would say to accept Project S over Project L.

- As long as the cost of capital is *greater than* the crossover rate of 12.274%, both methods agree that Project S is better: $NPV_S > NPV_L$ and $IRR_S > IRR_L$. Therefore, if r is *greater* than the crossover rate, no conflict occurs.
- However, if the cost of capital is *less than* the crossover rate, a conflict arises: NPV ranks L higher, but IRR ranks S higher.

There are two basic conditions that cause NPV profiles to cross and thus lead to conflicts.[16]

1. *Timing differences.* If most of the cash flows from one project come in early while most of those from the other project come in later, then the NPV profiles may cross and result in a conflict. This is the reason for the conflict between our Projects S and L.
2. *Project size (or scale) differences.* If the amount invested in one project is larger than the other, this can also lead to profiles crossing and a resulting conflict. Section 12.3 has an extreme example of this size difference conflict.

When either size or timing differences occur, the firm will have different amounts of funds to invest in other projects in the various years, depending on which of the two mutually exclusive projects it chooses. If it chooses S, then it will have more funds to invest in Year 1 because S has a larger inflow that year. Similarly, if one project costs more than the other, then the firm will have more money to invest at t = 0 if it selects the smaller project.

Given this situation, the rate of return at which differential cash flows can be reinvested is a critical issue. We saw earlier that the NPV assumes reinvestment at the cost of capital, and that this is generally a more reasonable assumption. Therefore, *whenever conflicts exist between mutually exclusive projects, use the NPV method.*

Describe in words how an NPV profile is constructed. How does one determine the intercepts for the x-axis and the y-axis?

What is the "crossover rate," and how does it interact with the cost of capital to determine whether or not a conflict exists between NPV and IRR?

What two characteristics can lead to conflicts between the NPV and the IRR when evaluating mutually exclusive projects?

12.8 Profitability Index (PI)

A fourth method used to evaluate projects is the **profitability index (PI)**:

$$PI = \frac{\text{PV of future cash flows}}{\text{Initial cost}} = \frac{\sum\limits_{t=1}^{N} \dfrac{CF_t}{(1+r)^t}}{CF_0} \qquad (12\text{--}3)$$

---

16. Also, if mutually exclusive projects have different lives (as opposed to different cash flow patterns over a common life), this introduces further complications; thus, for meaningful comparisons, some mutually exclusive projects must be evaluated over a common life. This point is discussed later in the chapter.

Here CF_t represents the expected future cash flows and CF_0 represents the initial cost. The PI shows the *relative* profitability of any project, or the present value per dollar of initial cost. As we can see from Figure 12-7, the PI for Project S, based on a 10% cost of capital, is $10,804.38/$10,000 = 1.0804; the PI for Project L is 1.1048. Thus, Project S is expected to produce $1.0804 of present value for each $1 of investment, whereas L should produce $1.1048 for each dollar invested.

A project is acceptable if its PI is greater than 1.0; and the higher the PI, the higher the project's ranking. Therefore, both S and L would be accepted by the PI criterion if they were independent, and L would be ranked ahead of S if they were mutually exclusive.

Mathematically, the NPV, IRR, MIRR, and PI methods will always lead to the same accept/reject decisions for *normal, independent* projects: If a project's NPV is positive, its IRR and MIRR will always exceed r and its PI will always be greater than 1.0. However, these methods can give conflicting rankings for *mutually exclusive* projects if the projects differ in size or in the timing of cash flows. If the PI ranking conflicts with the NPV, then the NPV ranking should be used.

Self Test

Explain how the PI is calculated. What does it measure?

A project has the following expected cash flows: $CF_0 = -\$500$, $CF_1 = \$200$, $CF_2 = \$200$, and $CF_3 = \$400$. If the project's cost of capital is 9%, what is the PI? **(1.32)**

12.9 Payback Period

WEB

See **Ch12 Tool Kit.xls** on the textbook's Web site.

NPV and IRR are the most commonly used methods today, but historically the first selection criterion was the **payback period**, defined as the number of years required to recover the funds invested in a project from its operating cash flows. Equation 12-4 is used for the calculation, and the process is diagrammed in Figure 12-8. We start with the project's cost, a negative number, and then add the cash inflow for each year until the cumulative cash flow turns positive. The payback year is the

---

Figure 12-7   Profitability Index (PI)

	A	B	C	D	E
342	Project S:		PI_S = PV of future cash flows	÷	Initial cost
343			PI_S = $10,804.38	÷	$10,000
344			PI_S = 1.0804		
345					
346	Project L:		PI_L = PV of future cash flows	÷	Initial cost
347			PI_L = $11,048.02	÷	$10,000
348			PI_L = 1.1048		

Notes:
1. If Projects L and S are independent, then both should be accepted because both have PI greater than 1.0. However, if they are mutually exclusive then Project L should be chosen because it has the higher PI.
2. PI and NPV rankings will be consistent if the projects have the same cost, as is true for S and L. However, if they differ in size then conflicts can occur. In the event of a conflict, the NPV ranking should be used.

Figure 12-8   Payback Period

	A	B	C	D	E	F	G
377		Year	0	1	2	3	4
378	Project S	Cash flow	−10,000	5,300	4,300	1,874	1,500
379		Cumulative cash flow	−10,000	−4,700	−400	1,474	2,974
380	Intermediate calculation for payback		-	-	-	2.21	3.98
381							
382						Intermediate calculation:	
383	Manual calculation of Payback S = 2 + $400/$1,874 =			2.21		=IF(F379>0,E377+ABS(E379/F378),"–")	
384	Excel calculation of Payback S =			2.21		2.21	
385							
386		Year	0	1	2	3	4
387	Project L	Cash flow	−10,000	1,900	2,700	2,345	7,800
388		Cumulative cash flow	−10,000	−8,100	−5,400	−3,055	4,745
389							
390	Manual calculation of Payback L = 3 + $3,055/$7,800 =			3.39		Payback is between	
391	Alternative Excel calculation of Payback L =					negative and positive	
392	=PERCENTRANK(C388:G388,0,6)*G386			3.39		cumulative cash flow.	
393							

© Cengage Learning 2013

year *prior to* full recovery, plus a fraction equal to the shortfall at the end of the prior year divided by the cash flow during the year when full recovery occurs:[17]

WEB

See **Ch12 Tool Kit.xls** on the textbook's Web site.

$$\text{Payback} = \begin{array}{c}\text{Number of}\\\text{years prior to}\\\text{full recovery}\end{array} + \frac{\begin{array}{c}\text{Unrecovered cost}\\\text{at start of year}\end{array}}{\begin{array}{c}\text{Cash flow during}\\\text{full recovery year}\end{array}}$$

(12–4)

The cash flows for Projects S and L, together with their paybacks, are shown in Figure 12-8.[18] The shorter the payback, the better the project. Therefore, if the firm requires a payback of 3 years or less, then S would be accepted but L would be rejected. If the projects were mutually exclusive, S would be ranked over L because of its shorter payback.

The regular payback has three flaws: (1) Dollars received in different years are all given the same weight—that is, the time value of money is ignored. (2) Cash flows beyond the payback year are given no consideration whatsoever, regardless of how large they might be. (3) Unlike the NPV or the IRR, which tell us how much wealth a project adds or how much a project's rate of return exceeds the cost of capital, the payback merely tells us how long it takes to recover our investment. There is no necessary relationship between a given payback period and investor wealth, so we don't know how to specify an acceptable payback. The firm might use 2 years, 3 years, or any other number as the minimum acceptable payback, but the choice is purely arbitrary.

To counter the first criticism, financial analysts developed the **discounted payback**, where cash flows are discounted at the WACC and then those discounted cash flows are used to find the payback. In Figure 12-9, we calculate the discounted paybacks for S and L, assuming both have a 10% cost of capital. Each inflow is

17. Equation 12-4 assumes that cash flows come in uniformly during the full recovery year.
18. There is not an *Excel* function for payback. But if the cash flows are normal then the PERCENTRANK function can be used to find payback, as illustrated in Figures 12-8 and 12-9.

Figure 12-9   Discounted Payback

	A	B	C	D	E	F	G
406		Year	0	1	2	3	4
407	Project S	Cash flow	−10,000.00	5,300.00	4,300.00	1,874.00	1,500.00
408		Discounted cash flow	−10,000.00	4,818.18	3,553.72	1,407.96	1,024.52
409		Cumulative discounted CF	−10,000.00	−5,181.82	−1,628.10	−220.14	804.38
410							
411	Discounted Payback S = 3 + $220.14/$1,024.52 =			3.21		Payback is between negative and positive cumulative discounted cash flow.	
412	*Excel* calculation of Discounted Payback S =						
413	=PERCENTRANK(C409:G409,0,6)*G406			3.21			
414							
415		Year	0	1	2	3	4
416	Project L	Cash flow	−10,000.00	1,900.00	2,700.00	2,345.00	7,800.00
417		Discounted cash flow	−10,000.00	1,727.27	2,231.40	1,761.83	5,327.50
418		Cumulative discounted CF	−10,000.00	−8,272.73	−6,041.32	−4,279.49	1,048.02
419							
420	Discounted Payback L = 3 + $4,279.49/$5,327.50 =			3.80		Payback is between negative and positive cumulative discounted cash flow.	
421	*Excel* calculation of Discounted Payback L =						
422	=PERCENTRANK(C418:G418,0,6)*G415			3.80			
423							

WEB

See *Ch12 Tool Kit.xls* on the textbook's Web site.

divided by $(1 + r)^t = (1.10)^t$, where t is the year in which the cash flow occurs and r is the project's cost of capital, and then those PVs are used to find the payback. Project S's discounted payback is 3.21 years and L's is 3.80 years.

Note that the payback is a "break-even" calculation in the sense that if cash flows come in at the expected rate, then the project will at least break even. However, since the regular payback doesn't consider the cost of capital, it doesn't specify the true break-even year. The discounted payback does consider capital costs, but it still disregards cash flows beyond the payback year, which is a serious flaw. Further, if mutually exclusive projects vary in size, both payback methods can conflict with the NPV, and that might lead to poor decisions. Finally, there is no way to determine how short the payback periods must be to justify accepting a project.

Although the payback methods have faults as ranking criteria, they do provide information about *liquidity* and *risk*. The shorter the payback, other things held constant, the greater the project's liquidity. This factor is often important for smaller firms that don't have ready access to the capital markets. Also, cash flows expected in the distant future are generally riskier than near-term cash flows, so the payback period is also a risk indicator.

Self Test

What two pieces of information does the payback method provide that are absent from the other capital budgeting decision methods?

What three flaws does the regular payback method have? Does the discounted payback method correct all of those flaws? Explain.

Project P has a cost of $1,000 and cash flows of $300 per year for 3 years plus another $1,000 in Year 4. The project's cost of capital is 15%. What are P's regular and discounted paybacks? **(3.10, 3.55)** If the company requires a payback of 3 years or less, would the project be accepted? Would this be a good accept/reject decision, considering the NPV and/or the IRR? **(NPV = $256.72, IRR = 24.78%)**

12.10 Conclusions on Capital Budgeting Methods

We have discussed six capital budgeting decision criteria: NPV, IRR, MIRR, PI, payback, and discounted payback. We compared these methods with one another and highlighted their strengths and weaknesses. In the process, we may have created the impression that "sophisticated" firms should use only one method, the NPV. However, virtually all capital budgeting decisions are analyzed by computer, so it is easy to calculate using all six methods. In making the accept–reject decision, large sophisticated firms such as FPL, GE, and Boeing generally calculate and consider all six measures, because each provides a somewhat different piece of information about the decision.

NPV is the single best criterion because it provides a direct measure of the value a project adds to shareholder wealth. IRR and MIRR measure profitability expressed as a percentage rate of return, which decision makers like to consider. The PI also measures profitability but in relation to the amount of the investment. Further, IRR, MIRR, and PI all contain information concerning a project's "safety margin." To illustrate, consider a firm, whose WACC is 10%, that must choose between these two mutually exclusive projects: SS (for small) has a cost of $10,000 and is expected to return $16,500 at the end of 1 year LL (for large) has a cost of $100,000 and is expected to return $115,550 at the end of 1 year. SS has a huge IRR, 65%, while LL's IRR is a more modest 15.6%. The NPV paints a somewhat different picture: At the 10% cost of capital, SS's NPV is $5,000 while LL's is $5,045. By the NPV rule we would choose LL. However, SS's IRR indicates that it has a much larger margin for error: Even if its cash flow were 39% below the $16,500 forecast, the firm would still recover its $10,000 investment. On the other hand, if LL's inflows fell by only 13.5% from its forecasted $115,550, the firm would not recover its investment. Further, if neither project generated any cash flows at all, the firm would lose only $10,000 on SS but would lose $100,000 by accepting LL.

The modified IRR has all the virtues of the IRR, but it incorporates a better reinvestment rate assumption and also avoids the problem of multiple rates of return. So if decision makers want to know projects' rates of return, the MIRR is a better indicator than the regular IRR.

The PI tells a similar story to the IRR. Here PI_{LL} is only 1.05 while PI_{SS} is 1.50. As with the IRR, this indicates that Project SS's cash inflows could decline by 50% before it loses money, whereas a decline of only 5% in LL's cash flows would result in a loss.

Payback and discounted payback provide indications of a project's *liquidity* and *risk*. A long payback means that investment dollars will be locked up for a long time; hence the project is relatively illiquid. In addition, a long payback means that cash flows must be forecast far into the future, and that probably makes the project riskier than one with a shorter payback. A good analogy for this is bond valuation. An investor should never compare the yields to maturity on two bonds without also considering their terms to maturity, because a bond's risk is significantly influenced by its maturity. The same holds true for capital projects.

In summary, the different measures provide different types of useful information. It is easy to calculate all of them: Simply put the cost of capital and the cash flows into an *Excel* model like the one provided in this chapter's **Tool Kit** and the model will instantly calculate all six criteria. Therefore, most sophisticated companies consider all six measures when making capital budgeting decisions. For most decisions, the greatest weight should be given to the NPV, but it would be foolish to ignore the information provided by the other criteria.

Just as it would be foolish to ignore these capital budgeting methods, it would also be foolish to make decisions based *solely* on them. One cannot know at Time 0 the exact cost of future capital or the exact future cash flows. These inputs are simply estimates, and if they turn out to be incorrect then so will be the calculated NPVs and IRRs. Thus, *quantitative methods provide valuable information, but they should not be used as the sole criteria for accept–reject decisions* in the capital budgeting process. Rather, managers should use quantitative methods in the decision-making process but should also consider the likelihood that actual results will differ from the forecasts. Qualitative factors, such as the chances of a tax increase, or a war, or a major product liability suit, should also be considered. In summary, *quantitative methods such as NPV and IRR should be considered as an aid to informed decisions but not as a substitute for sound managerial judgment.*

In this same vein, managers should ask sharp questions about any project that has a large NPV, a high IRR, or a high PI. In a perfectly competitive economy, there would be no positive-NPV projects—all companies would have the same opportunities, and competition would quickly eliminate any positive NPV. The existence of positive-NPV projects must be predicated on some imperfection in the marketplace, and the longer the life of the project, the longer that imperfection must last. Therefore, managers should be able to identify the imperfection and explain why it will persist before accepting that a project will really have a positive NPV. Valid explanations might include patents or proprietary technology, which is how pharmaceutical and software firms create positive-NPV projects. Pfizer's Lipitor (a cholesterol-reducing medicine) and Microsoft's Windows 7 operating system are examples. Companies can also create positive NPV by being the first entrant into a new market or by creating new products that meet some previously unidentified consumer needs. The Post-it notes invented by 3M are an example. Similarly, Dell developed procedures for direct sales of microcomputers and, in the process, created projects with enormous NPV. Also, companies such as Southwest Airlines have managed to train and motivate their workers better than their competitors, and this has led to positive-NPV projects. In all of these cases, the companies developed some source of competitive advantage, and that advantage resulted in positive-NPV projects.

This discussion suggests three things: (1) If you can't identify the reason a project has a positive projected NPV, then its actual NPV will probably not be positive. (2) Positive-NPV projects don't just happen—they result from hard work to develop some competitive advantage. At the risk of oversimplification, the primary job of a manager is to find and develop areas of competitive advantage. (3) Some competitive advantages last longer than others, with their durability depending on competitors' ability to replicate them. Patents, the control of scarce resources, or large size in an industry where strong economies of scale exist can keep competitors at bay. However, it is relatively easy to replicate product features that cannot be patented. The bottom line is that managers should strive to develop nonreplicable sources of competitive advantage. If such an advantage cannot be demonstrated, then you should question projects with high NPV—especially if they have long lives.

Self Test	Describe the advantages and disadvantages of the six capital budgeting methods.
	Should capital budgeting decisions be made solely on the basis of a project's NPV, with no regard to the other criteria? Explain your answer.
	What are some possible reasons that a project might have a high NPV?

12.11 Decision Criteria Used in Practice

Over the years, surveys have been designed and administered to find out which of the criteria managers actually use. Surveys prior to 1999 asked companies to indicate which method they gave the most weight, whereas the most recent one (taken in 1999) asked what method or methods managers actually calculated and used. A summary of all these surveys is shown in Table 12-1, and it reveals some interesting trends.

First, the NPV criterion was not used significantly before the 1980s, but by 1999 it was close to the top in usage. Moreover, informal discussions with companies suggest that if a survey were taken in 2012, NPV would be at the top of this list. Second, the IRR method was used slightly more than the NPV at the time of the last survey (1999), but its recent growth is much less dramatic than that of NPV; if a survey were taken today, we believe that the NPV would predominate. Third, payback was the most important criterion years ago, but its use as the primary criterion had fallen drastically by 1980. Companies still use payback because it is easy to calculate and provides some useful information, but it is rarely used as the primary criterion. Fourth, "other methods," primarily the profitability index and the accounting rate of return (the latter of which is explained in this chapter's *Tool Kit*), have been fading due to the increased use of IRR and especially NPV.

These trends are consistent with our evaluation of the various methods. NPV is the best single criterion, but all of the methods provide useful information and are easy to calculate. Hence all are used, along with judgment and common sense. We will have more to say about all this in the next chapter.

What trends in capital budgeting methodology can be seen from Table 12-1?	Self Test

12.12 Other Issues in Capital Budgeting

Three other issues in capital budgeting are discussed in this section: (1) how to deal with mutually exclusive projects whose lives differ; (2) the potential advantage of

TABLE 12-1	**Capital Budgeting Methods Used in Practice**			
	Firms' Primary Criterion			Firms Use
	1960	**1970**	**1980**	**1999**
NPV	0%	0%	15%	75%
IRR	20	60	65	76
Payback	35	15	5	57
Discounted Payback	NA	NA	NA	29
Other	45	25	15	NA
Totals	100%	100%	100%	

© Cengage Learning 2013

Sources: The 1999 data are from John R. Graham and Campbell R. Harvey, "The Theory and Practice of Corporate Finance: Evidence from the Field," *Journal of Financial Economics,* 2001, pp. 187–244. Data from prior years are our estimates based on averaging data from these studies: J. S. Moore and A. K. Reichert, "An Analysis of the Financial Management Techniques Currently Employed by Large U.S. Corporations," *Journal of Business Finance and Accounting,* Winter 1983, pp. 623–645; and M. T. Stanley and S. R. Block, "A Survey of Multinational Capital Budgeting," *The Financial Review,* March 1984, pp. 36–51.

terminating a project before the end of its physical life; and (3) the optimal capital budget when the cost of capital rises as the size of the capital budget increases.

12.12a Mutually Exclusive Projects with Unequal Lives

When choosing between two mutually exclusive alternatives with significantly different lives, an adjustment is necessary. For example, suppose a company is planning to modernize its production facilities and is considering either a conveyor system (Project C) or a fleet of forklift trucks (Project F) for moving materials. The first two sections of Figure 12-10 show the expected net cash flows, NPVs, and IRRs for these two mutually exclusive alternatives. We see that Project C, when discounted at the firm's 12% cost of capital, has the higher NPV and thus appears to be the better project.

Although the NPVs shown in Figure 12-10 suggest that Project C should be selected, this analysis is incomplete, and the decision to choose Project C is actually incorrect. If we choose Project F, we will have an opportunity to make a similar investment in 3 years, and if cost and revenue conditions continue at the levels shown in Figure 12-10, then this second investment will also be profitable. However, if we choose Project C, we cannot make this second investment. Two different approaches can be used to correctly compare Projects C and F, as shown in Figure 12-10 and discussed next.

Replacement Chains

The key to the *replacement chain,* or *common life, approach* is to analyze both projects over an equal life. In our example, Project C has a 6-year life, so we assume that Project F will be repeated after 3 years and then analyze it over the same 6-year period. We can then calculate the NPV of C and compare it to the extended-life NPV of Project F. The NPV for Project C, as shown in Figure 12-10, is already based on the 6-year common life. For Project F, however, we must add in a second project to extend the overall life to 6 years. The time line for this extended project, denoted as "All CFs for FF," is shown in Figure 12-10. Here we assume (1) that Project F's cost

WEB

See ***Ch12 Tool Kit.xls*** on the textbook's Web site.

Figure 12-10   Analysis of Projects C and F (r = 12%)

	A	B	C	D	E	F	G	H
457	WACC = r = 12.0%							
458	Data on Project C, Conveyor System:							
459	Year	0	1	2	3	4	5	6
460	Cash flows for C	($40,000)	$8,000	$14,000	$13,000	$12,000	$11,000	$10,000
461		NPV$_C$ =	$6,491		IRR$_C$ =	17.5%		
462								
463	Data on Project F, Forklifts							
464	Year	0	1	2	3			
465	Cash flows for F	($20,000)	$7,000	$13,000	$12,000			
466		NPV$_F$ =	$5,155		IRR$_F$ =	25.2%		
467								
468	Common Life Approach with F Repeated (Project FF):							
469	Year	0	1	2	3	4	5	6
470	CF$_t$ for 1st F	($20,000)	$7,000	$13,000	$12,000			
471	CF$_t$ for 2nd F				($20,000)	$7,000	$13,000	$12,000
472	All CFs for FF	($20,000)	$7,000	$13,000	($8,000)	$7,000	$13,000	$12,000
473		NPV$_{FF}$ =	$8,824		IRR$_{FF}$ =	25.2%		

and annual cash inflows will not change if the project is repeated in 3 years and (2) that the cost of capital will remain at 12%.

The NPV of this extended Project F is $8,824, and its IRR is 25.2%. (The IRR of two Project Fs is the same as the IRR for one Project F.) However, the $8,824 extended NPV of Project F is greater than Project C's $6,491 NPV, so Project F should be selected.

Alternatively, we could recognize that Project F has an NPV of $5,155 at Time 0 and a second NPV of that same amount at Time 3, then find the PV of the second NPV at Time 0, and sum the two to find Project F's extended-life NPV of $8,824.

Equivalent Annual Annuities (EAA)

Electrical engineers designing power plants and distribution lines were the first to encounter the unequal life problem. They could install transformers and other equipment that had relatively low initial costs but short lives, or they could use equipment that had higher initial costs but longer lives. The services would be required into the indefinite future, so this was the issue: Which choice would result in a higher NPV in the long run? The engineers converted the annual cash flows under the alternative investments into a constant cash flow stream whose NPV was equal to, or equivalent to, the NPV of the initial stream. This was called the **equivalent annual annuity (EAA) method**. To apply the EAA method to Projects C and F, for each project we simply find the constant payment streams that the projects' NPVs ($6,491 for C and $5,155 for F) would provide over their respective lives. Using a financial calculator for Project C, we enter N = 6, I/YR = 12, PV = −6491, and FV = 0. Then, when we press the PMT key, we find EAA_C = $1,579. For Project F, we enter N = 3, I/YR = 12, PV = −5155, and FV = 0; solving for PMT, we find EAA_F = $2,146. Project F would thus produce a higher cash flow stream over the 6 years, so it is the better project.

Conclusions about Unequal Lives

When should we worry about analysis of unequal lives? The unequal life issue (1) does not arise for independent projects but (2) can arise if mutually exclusive projects with significantly different lives are being compared. However, even for mutually exclusive projects, it is not always appropriate to extend the analysis to a common life. This should be done if and only if there is a high probability that the projects will actually be repeated at the end of their initial lives.

We should note several potentially serious weaknesses inherent in this type of analysis. (1) If inflation occurs, then replacement equipment will have a higher price. Moreover, both sales prices and operating costs would probably change. Thus, the static conditions built into the analysis would be invalid. (2) Replacements that occur down the road would probably employ new technology, which in turn might change the cash flows. (3) It is difficult enough to estimate the lives of most projects, and even more so to estimate the lives of a series of projects. In view of these problems, no experienced financial analyst would be too concerned about comparing mutually exclusive projects with lives of, say, 8 years and 10 years. Given all the uncertainties in the estimation process, such projects would, for all practical purposes, be assumed to have the same life. Still, it is important to recognize that a problem exists if mutually exclusive projects have substantially different lives.

When we encounter situations in practice where significant differences in project lives are encountered, we first use a computer spreadsheet to build expected inflation and/or possible efficiency gains directly into the cash flow estimates and then use the replacement chain approach. We prefer the replacement chain approach for two reasons. First, it is easier to explain to those who are responsible for approving capital budgets. Second, it is easier to build inflation and other modifications into a spreadsheet and then go on to make the replacement chain calculations.

12.12b Economic Life versus Physical Life

Projects are normally evaluated under the assumption that the firm will operate them over their full physical lives. However, this may not be the best plan—it may be better to terminate a project before the end of its potential life. For example, the cost of maintenance for trucks and machinery can become quite high if they are used for too many years, so it might be better to replace them before the end of their potential lives.

Figure 12-11 provides data for an asset with a physical life of 3 years. However, the project can be terminated at the end of any year and the asset sold at the indicated salvage values. All of the cash flows are after taxes, and the firm's cost of capital is 10%. The undiscounted cash flows are shown in Columns C and D in the upper part of the figure, and the present values of these flows are shown in Columns E and F. We find the project's NPV under different assumptions about how long it will be operated. If the project is operated for its full 3-year life, it will have a negative NPV. The NPV will be positive if it is operated for 2 years and then the asset is sold for a relatively high salvage value; the NPV will be negative if the asset is disposed after only 1 year of operation. Therefore, the project's optimal life is 2 years.

This type of analysis is used to determine a project's **economic life**, which is the life that maximizes the NPV and thus shareholder wealth. For our project, the economic life is 2 years versus the 3-year **physical**, or **engineering, life**. Note that this analysis was based on the expected cash flows and the expected salvage values, and it should always be conducted as a part of the capital budgeting evaluation if salvage values are relatively high.

12.12c The Optimal Capital Budget

WEB

See *Ch12 Tool Kit.xls* on the textbook's Web site.

The **optimal capital budget** is defined as the set of projects that maximizes the value of the firm. Finance theory states that all independent projects with positive NPVs

Figure 12-11   Economic Life versus Physical Life

	A	B	C	D	E	F	G
					PVs of the Cash Flows		
511							
512			Operating Cash		Operating Cash		
513		Year	Flow	Salvage Value	Flow	Salvage Value	
514		0	−$4,800				
515		1	2,000	$3,000	$1,818.18	$2,727.27	
516		2	2,000	1,650	1,652.89	1,363.64	
517		3	1,750	0	1,314.80	0.00	
518	WACC = 10%				PV of		PV of
519	NPV at Different Operating Lives:		Intial Cost	+	Operating Cash	+	Salvage
520					Flows		Value
521	Operate for 3 Years:		−$4,800.00	+	$4,785.88	+	$0.00
522	NPV$_3$:	−$14.12					
523	Operate for 2 Years:		−$4,800.00	+	$3,471.07	+	$1,363.64
524	NPV$_2$:	$34.71					
525	Operate for 1 Year:		−$4,800.00	+	$1,818.18	+	$2,727.27
526	NPV$_1$:	−$254.55					

Note: The project is profitable if and only if it is operated for just 2 years.

should be accepted, as should the mutually exclusive projects with the highest NPVs. Therefore, the optimal capital budget consists of that set of projects. However, two complications arise in practice: (1) The cost of capital might increase as the size of the capital budget increases, making it hard to know the proper discount rate to use when evaluating projects; and (2) sometimes firms set an upper limit on the size of their capital budgets, which is also known as *capital rationing.*

An Increasing Cost of Capital

The cost of capital may increase as the capital budget increases—this is called an *increasing marginal cost of capital.* As we discussed in Chapter 10, flotation costs associated with issuing new equity can be quite high. This means that the cost of capital will increase once a company has invested all of its internally generated cash and must sell new common stock. In addition, once a firm has used up its normal credit lines and must seek additional debt capital, it may encounter an increase in its cost of debt. This means that a project might have a positive NPV if it is part of a $10 million capital budget but the same project might have a negative NPV if it is part of a $20 million capital budget because the cost of capital might increase.

Fortunately, these problems rarely occur for most firms, especially those that are stable and well established. When a rising cost of capital is encountered, we would proceed as indicated below. You can look at Figure 12-12 as you read through our points.

- Find the IRR (or MIRR) on all potential projects, arrange them in rank order (along with their initial costs), and then plot them on a graph with the IRR on the vertical axis and the cumulative costs on the horizontal axis. The firm's data are shown in Figure 12-12, and the IRRs are plotted in the graph. The line is called the Investment Opportunity Schedule (IOS), and it shows the marginal return on capital.
- Next, determine how much capital can be raised before it is necessary to issue new common stock or go to higher-cost sources of debt, and identify the amounts of higher-cost capital. Use this information to calculate the WACC that corresponds to the different amounts of capital raised. In this example, the firm can raise $300 before the WACC rises, but the WACC increases as additional capital is raised. The increasing WACC represents the marginal cost of capital, and its graph is called the Marginal Cost of Capital (MCC) schedule.
- The intersection of the IOS and MCC schedules indicates the amount of capital the firm should raise and invest, and it is analogous to the familiar marginal cost versus marginal revenue schedule discussed in introductory economics courses. In our example, the firm should have a capital budget of $400; if it uses a WACC of 10% then it will accept projects A, B, C, and D, which have a cumulative cost of $400. The 10% WACC should be used for average-risk projects, but it should be scaled up or down for more or less risky projects as discussed in Chapter 10.

Our example illustrates the case of a firm that cannot raise all the money it needs at a constant WACC. Firms should not try to be too precise with this process—the data are not good enough for precision—but they should be aware of the concept and get at least a rough idea of how raising additional capital will affect the WACC.

Capital Rationing

Armbrister Pyrotechnics, a manufacturer of fireworks and lasers for light shows, has identified 40 potential independent projects, of which 15 have a positive NPV based on the firm's 12% cost of capital. The total investment required to implement these

Figure 12-12   **IOS and MCC Schedules**

	A	B	C	D	E	F
534	Investment Opportunity Schedule (IOS)			Marginal Cost of Capital (MCC)		
535			Highest to	Cumulative	Lowest to	
536	Projects	Cost	Lowest IRR	Cost	Highest WACC	
537	A	$100	14.0%	$100	9.0%	
538	B	$100	13.0%	$200	9.0%	
539	C	$100	11.5%	$300	9.0%	
540	D	$100	10.0%	$400	10.0%	
541	E	$50	9.5%	$450	11.0%	
542	F	$50	9.0%	$500	12.0%	
543	G	$100	8.5%	$600	15.0%	

MCC and IOS Schedules

Note: Use WACC = 10% as the base rate for finding base risk-adjusted project WACCs.

WEB

See *Ch12 Tool Kit.xls* on the textbook's Web site.

15 projects would be $75 million and so, according to finance theory, the optimal capital budget is $75 million. Thus, Armbrister should accept the 15 projects with positive NPVs and invest $75 million. However, Armbrister's management has imposed a limit of $50 million for capital expenditures during the upcoming year. Because of this restriction, the company must forgo a number of value-adding projects. This is an example of **capital rationing**, defined as a situation in which a firm limits its capital expenditures to an amount less than would be required to fund the optimal capital budget. Despite being at odds with finance theory, this practice is quite common.

Why would any company forgo value-adding projects? Here are some potential explanations, along with some suggestions for better ways to handle these situations.

1. *Reluctance to issue new stock.* Many firms are extremely reluctant to issue new stock, so all of their capital expenditures must be funded out of debt and internally generated cash. Also, most firms try to stay near their target capital

structure, and, when combined with the limit on equity, this limits the amount of debt that can be added during any one year without raising the cost of that debt as well as the cost of equity. The result can be a serious constraint on the amount of funds available for investment in new projects.

The reluctance to issue new stock could be based on some sound reasons: (a) flotation costs can be very expensive; (b) investors might perceive new stock offerings as a signal that the company's equity is overvalued; and (c) the company might have to reveal sensitive strategic information to investors, thereby reducing some of its competitive advantages. To avoid these costs, many companies simply limit their capital expenditures.

However, rather than placing a somewhat artificial limit on capital expenditures, companies might be better off explicitly incorporating the costs of raising external capital into their costs of capital along the lines shown in Figure 12-12. If there still are positive-NPV projects even with the higher cost of capital, then the company should go ahead and raise external equity and accept the projects.

2. *Constraints on nonmonetary resources.* Sometimes a firm simply doesn't have the necessary managerial, marketing, or engineering talent to immediately accept all positive-NPV projects. In other words, the potential projects may be independent from a demand standpoint but not from an internal standpoint, because accepting them all would raise the firm's costs. To avoid potential problems due to spreading existing talent too thinly, many firms simply limit the capital budget to a size that can be accommodated by their current personnel.

A better solution might be to employ a technique called **linear programming**. Each potential project has an expected NPV, and each potential project requires a certain level of support by different types of employees. A linear program can identify the set of projects that maximizes NPV *subject to the constraint* that the total amount of support required for these projects does not exceed the available resources.

3. *Controlling estimation bias.* Many managers become overly optimistic when estimating the cash flows for a project. Some firms try to control this estimation bias by requiring managers to use an unrealistically high cost of capital. Others try to control the bias by limiting the size of the capital budget. Neither solution is generally effective, because managers quickly learn the rules of the game and then increase their own estimates of project cash flows, which might have been biased upward to begin with.

A better solution is to implement a post-audit program and to link the accuracy of forecasts to the compensation of the managers who initiated the projects.

Self Test

Briefly describe the replacement chain (common life) approach and differentiate it from the Equivalent Annual Annuity (EAA) approach.

Differentiate between a project's *physical* life and its *economic* life.

What factors can lead to an increasing marginal cost of capital? How might this affect capital budgeting?

What is capital rationing?

What are three explanations for capital rationing? How might firms otherwise handle these situations?

Summary

This chapter has described six techniques that are used in capital budgeting analysis: NPV, IRR, MIRR, PI, payback, and discounted payback. Each approach provides a different piece of information, so in this age of computers, managers often look at all of them when evaluating projects. However, NPV is the best single measure, and almost all firms now use NPV. The key concepts covered in this chapter are listed below.

- **Capital budgeting** is the process of analyzing potential projects. Capital budgeting decisions are probably the most important ones that managers must make.
- The **net present value (NPV) method** discounts all cash flows at the project's cost of capital and then sums those cash flows. The project should be accepted if the NPV is positive because such a project increases shareholders' value.
- The **internal rate of return (IRR)** is defined as the discount rate that forces a project's NPV to equal zero. The project should be accepted if the IRR is greater than the cost of capital.
- The NPV and IRR methods make the same accept–reject decisions for **independent projects**, but if projects are **mutually exclusive** then ranking conflicts can arise. In such cases, the NPV method should generally be relied upon.
- The NPV method assumes that cash flows will be reinvested at the firm's cost of capital, whereas the IRR method assumes reinvestment at the project's IRR. *Reinvestment at the cost of capital is generally a better assumption* because it is closer to reality.
- The **modified IRR (MIRR) method** corrects some of the problems with the regular IRR. MIRR involves finding the **terminal value (TV)** of the cash inflows, compounding them at the firm's cost of capital, and then determining the discount rate that forces the present value of the TV to equal the present value of the outflows. Thus, the MIRR assumes reinvestment at the cost of capital, not at the IRR. If management wants to know the rate of return on projects, the MIRR is a better estimate than the regular IRR.
- The **profitability index (PI)** is calculated by dividing the present value of cash inflows by the initial cost, so it measures relative profitability—that is, the amount of the present value per dollar of investment.
- The regular **payback period** is defined as the number of years required to recover a project's cost. The regular payback method has three flaws: It ignores cash flows beyond the payback period, it does not consider the time value of money, and it doesn't give a precise acceptance rule. The payback does, however, provide an indication of a project's risk and liquidity, because it shows how long the invested capital will be tied up.
- The **discounted payback** is similar to the regular payback except that it discounts cash flows at the project's cost of capital. It considers the time value of money, but it still ignores cash flows beyond the payback period.
- The chapter's *Tool Kit Excel* model and *Web Extension 12A* describe another but seldom-used evaluation method, the **accounting rate of return**.
- If mutually exclusive projects have **unequal lives**, it may be necessary to adjust the analysis to put the projects on an equal-life basis. This can be done using the **replacement chain (common life) approach** or the **equivalent annual annuity (EAA) approach**.

- A project's true value may be greater than the NPV based on its **physical life** if it can be **terminated** at the end of its **economic life**.
- Flotation costs and increased risk associated with unusually large expansion programs can cause the **marginal cost of capital** to increase as the size of the capital budget increases.
- **Capital rationing** occurs when management places a constraint on the size of the firm's capital budget during a particular period.

Questions

12-1 Define each of the following terms:
   a. Capital budgeting; regular payback period; discounted payback period
   b. Independent projects; mutually exclusive projects
   c. DCF techniques; net present value (NPV) method; internal rate of return (IRR) method; profitability index (PI)
   d. Modified internal rate of return (MIRR) method
   e. NPV profile; crossover rate
   f. Nonnormal cash flow projects; normal cash flow projects; multiple IRRs
   g. Reinvestment rate assumption
   h. Replacement chain; economic life; capital rationing; equivalent annual annuity (EAA)

12-2 What types of projects require the least detailed and the most detailed analysis in the capital budgeting process?

12-3 Explain why the NPV of a relatively long-term project, defined as one for which a high percentage of its cash flows are expected in the distant future, is more sensitive to changes in the cost of capital than is the NPV of a short-term project.

12-4 When two mutually exclusive projects are being compared, explain why the short-term project might be higher ranked under the NPV criterion if the cost of capital is high, whereas the long-term project might be deemed better if the cost of capital is low. Would changes in the cost of capital ever cause a change in the IRR ranking of two such projects?

12-5 In what sense is a reinvestment rate assumption embodied in the NPV, IRR, and MIRR methods? What is the assumed reinvestment rate of each method?

12-6 Suppose a firm is considering two mutually exclusive projects. One has a life of 6 years and the other a life of 10 years. Would the failure to employ some type of replacement chain analysis bias an NPV analysis against one of the projects? Explain.

Problems   Answers Appear in Appendix B

Easy Problems 1–7

12-1 **NPV** A project has an initial cost of $40,000, expected net cash inflows of $9,000 per year for 7 years, and a cost of capital of 11%. What is the project's NPV? (*Hint:* Begin by constructing a time line.)

12-2 **IRR** Refer to Problem 12-1. What is the project's IRR?

12-3 **MIRR** Refer to Problem 12-1. What is the project's MIRR?

12-4 **Profitability Index** Refer to Problem 12-1. What is the project's PI?

12-5 **Payback** Refer to Problem 12-1. What is the project's payback period?

12-6 **Discounted Payback** Refer to Problem 12-1. What is the project's discounted payback period?

12-7 **NPV** Your division is considering two investment projects, each of which requires an up-front expenditure of $15 million. You estimate that the investments will produce the following net cash flows:

Year	Project A	Project B
1	$ 5,000,000	$20,000,000
2	10,000,000	10,000,000
3	20,000,000	6,000,000

a. What are the two projects' net present values, assuming the cost of capital is 5%? 10%? 15%?

b. What are the two projects' IRRs at these same costs of capital?

Intermediate Problems 8–18

12-8 **NPVs, IRRs, and MIRRs for Independent Projects** Edelman Engineering is considering including two pieces of equipment, a truck and an overhead pulley system, in this year's capital budget. The projects are independent. The cash outlay for the truck is $17,100 and that for the pulley system is $22,430. The firm's cost of capital is 14%. After-tax cash flows, including depreciation, are as follows:

Year	Truck	Pulley
1	$5,100	$7,500
2	5,100	7,500
3	5,100	7,500
4	5,100	7,500
5	5,100	7,500

Calculate the IRR, the NPV, and the MIRR for each project, and indicate the correct accept–reject decision for each.

12-9 **NPVs and IRRs for Mutually Exclusive Projects** Davis Industries must choose between a gas-powered and an electric-powered forklift truck for moving materials in its factory. Since both forklifts perform the same function, the firm will choose only one. (They are mutually exclusive investments.) The electric-powered truck will cost more, but it will be less expensive to operate; it will cost $22,000, whereas the gas-powered truck will cost $17,500. The cost of capital that applies to both investments is 12%. The life for both types of truck is estimated to be 6 years, during which time the net cash flows for the electric-powered truck will be $6,290 per year and those for the gas-powered truck will be $5,000 per year. Annual net cash flows include depreciation expenses. Calculate the NPV and IRR for each type of truck, and decide which to recommend.

12-10 **Capital Budgeting Methods** Project S has a cost of $10,000 and is expected to produce benefits (cash flows) of $3,000 per year for 5 years. Project L costs $25,000 and is expected to produce cash flows of $7,400 per year for 5 years. Calculate the two projects' NPVs, IRRs, MIRRs, and PIs, assuming a cost of capital of 12%. Which project would be selected, assuming they are mutually exclusive, using each ranking method? Which should actually be selected?

12-11 **MIRR and NPV** Your company is considering two mutually exclusive projects, X and Y, whose costs and cash flows are shown below:

Year	X	Y
0	−$5,000	−$5,000
1	1,000	4,500
2	1,500	1,500
3	2,000	1,000
4	4,000	500

The projects are equally risky, and their cost of capital is 12%. You must make a recommendation, and you must base it on the modified IRR (MIRR). Which project has the higher MIRR?

12-12 **NPV and IRR Analysis** After discovering a new gold vein in the Colorado mountains, CTC Mining Corporation must decide whether to go ahead and develop the deposit. The most cost-effective method of mining gold is sulfuric acid extraction, a process that could result in environmental damage. Before proceeding with the extraction, CTC must spend $900,000 for new mining equipment and pay $165,000 for its installation. The gold mined will net the firm an estimated $350,000 each year for the 5-year life of the vein. CTC's cost of capital is 14%. For the purposes of this problem, assume that the cash inflows occur at the end of the year.
a. What are the project's NPV and IRR?
b. Should this project be undertaken if environmental impacts were not a consideration?
c. How should environmental effects be considered when evaluating this, or any other, project? How might these concepts affect the decision in part b?

12-13 **NPV and IRR Analysis** Cummings Products is considering two mutually exclusive investments whose expected net cash flows are as follows:

	Expected Net Cash Flows	
Year	Project A	Project B
0	−$400	−$650
1	−528	235
2	−219	235
3	−150	235
4	1,100	235
5	820	235
6	990	235
7	−325	0

a. Construct NPV profiles for Projects A and B.

b. What is each project's IRR?

c. If you were told that each project's cost of capital was 10%, which project, if either, should be selected? If the cost of capital were 17%, what would be the proper choice?

d. What is each project's MIRR at the cost of capital of 10%? At 17%? (*Hint:* Note that B is a 6-year project.)

e. What is the crossover rate, and what is its significance?

12-14 Timing Differences The Ewert Exploration Company is considering two mutually exclusive plans for extracting oil on property for which it has mineral rights. Both plans call for the expenditure of $10 million to drill development wells. Under Plan A, all the oil will be extracted in 1 year, producing a cash flow at t = 1 of $12 million; under Plan B, cash flows will be $1.75 million per year for 20 years.

a. What are the annual incremental cash flows that will be available to Ewert Exploration if it undertakes Plan B rather than Plan A? (*Hint:* Subtract Plan A's flows from B's.)

b. If the company accepts Plan A and then invests the extra cash generated at the end of Year 1, what rate of return (reinvestment rate) would cause the cash flows from reinvestment to equal the cash flows from Plan B?

c. Suppose a firm's cost of capital is 10%. Is it logical to assume that the firm would take on all available independent projects (of average risk) with returns greater than 10%? Further, if all available projects with returns greater than 10% have been taken, would this mean that cash flows from past investments would have an opportunity cost of only 10%, because all the firm could do with these cash flows would be to replace money that has a cost of 10%? Finally, does this imply that the cost of capital is the correct rate to assume for the reinvestment of a project's cash flows?

d. Construct NPV profiles for Plans A and B, identify each project's IRR, and indicate the crossover rate.

12-15 Scale Differences The Pinkerton Publishing Company is considering two mutually exclusive expansion plans. Plan A calls for the expenditure of $50 million on a large-scale, integrated plant that will provide an expected cash flow stream of $8 million per year for 20 years. Plan B calls for the expenditure of $15 million to build a somewhat less efficient, more labor-intensive plant that has an expected cash flow stream of $3.4 million per year for 20 years. The firm's cost of capital is 10%.

a. Calculate each project's NPV and IRR.

b. Set up a Project Δ by showing the cash flows that will exist if the firm goes with the large plant rather than the smaller plant. What are the NPV and the IRR for this Project Δ?

c. Graph the NPV profiles for Plan A, Plan B, and Project Δ.

d. Give a logical explanation, based on reinvestment rates and opportunity costs, as to why the NPV method is better than the IRR method when the firm's cost of capital is constant at some value such as 10%.

12-16 Unequal Lives Shao Airlines is considering two alternative planes. Plane A has an expected life of 5 years, will cost $100 million, and will produce net cash flows of $30 million per year. Plane B has a life of 10 years, will cost $132 million, and will produce net cash flows of $25 million per year. Shao plans to serve the route for only 10 years. Inflation in operating costs, airplane costs, and fares is expected to be zero, and the company's cost of capital is 12%. By how much would the value of the company increase if it accepted the better project (plane)? What is the equivalent annual annuity for each plane?

12-17 **Unequal Lives** The Perez Company has the opportunity to invest in one of two mutually exclusive machines that will produce a product it will need for the foreseeable future. Machine A costs $10 million but realizes after-tax inflows of $4 million per year for 4 years. After 4 years, the machine must be replaced. Machine B costs $15 million and realizes after-tax inflows of $3.5 million per year for 8 years, after which it must be replaced. Assume that machine prices are not expected to rise because inflation will be offset by cheaper components used in the machines. The cost of capital is 10%. By how much would the value of the company increase if it accepted the better machine? What is the equivalent annual annuity for each machine?

12-18 **Unequal Lives** Filkins Fabric Company is considering the replacement of its old, fully depreciated knitting machine. Two new models are available: Machine 190-3, which has a cost of $190,000, a 3-year expected life, and after-tax cash flows (labor savings and depreciation) of $87,000 per year; and Machine 360-6, which has a cost of $360,000, a 6-year life, and after-tax cash flows of $98,300 per year. Knitting machine prices are not expected to rise, because inflation will be offset by cheaper components (microprocessors) used in the machines. Assume that Filkins's cost of capital is 14%. Should the firm replace its old knitting machine? If so, which new machine should it use? By how much would the value of the company increase if it accepted the better machine? What is the equivalent annual annuity for each machine?

Challenging Problems 19–22

12-19 **Multiple Rates of Return** The Ulmer Uranium Company is deciding whether or not it should open a strip mine whose net cost is $4.4 million. Net cash inflows are expected to be $27.7 million, all coming at the end of Year 1. The land must be returned to its natural state at a cost of $25 million, payable at the end of Year 2.
a. Plot the project's NPV profile.
b. Should the project be accepted if $r = 8\%$? If $r = 14\%$? Explain your reasoning.
c. Can you think of some other capital budgeting situations in which negative cash flows during or at the end of the project's life might lead to multiple IRRs?
d. What is the project's MIRR at $r = 8\%$? At $r = 14\%$? Does the MIRR method lead to the same accept–reject decision as the NPV method?

12-20 **Present Value of Costs** The Aubey Coffee Company is evaluating the within-plant distribution system for its new roasting, grinding, and packing plant. The two alternatives are (1) a conveyor system with a high initial cost but low annual operating costs, and (2) several forklift trucks, which cost less but have considerably higher operating costs. The decision to construct the plant has already been made, and the choice here will have no effect on the overall revenues of the project. The cost of capital for the plant is 8%, and the projects' expected net costs are listed in the following table:

	Expected Net Cost	
Year	Conveyor	Forklift
0	−$500,000	−$200,000
1	−120,000	−160,000
2	−120,000	−160,000
3	−120,000	−160,000
4	−120,000	−160,000
5	−20,000	−160,000

a. What is the IRR of each alternative?
b. What is the present value of the costs of each alternative? Which method should be chosen?

12-21 **Payback, NPV, and MIRR** Your division is considering two investment projects, each of which requires an up-front expenditure of $25 million. You estimate that the cost of capital is 10% and that the investments will produce the following after-tax cash flows (in millions of dollars):

Year	Project A	Project B
1	5	20
2	10	10
3	15	8
4	20	6

a. What is the regular payback period for each of the projects?
b. What is the discounted payback period for each of the projects?
c. If the two projects are independent and the cost of capital is 10%, which project or projects should the firm undertake?
d. If the two projects are mutually exclusive and the cost of capital is 5%, which project should the firm undertake?
e. If the two projects are mutually exclusive and the cost of capital is 15%, which project should the firm undertake?
f. What is the crossover rate?
g. If the cost of capital is 10%, what is the modified IRR (MIRR) of each project?

12-22 **Economic Life** The Scampini Supplies Company recently purchased a new delivery truck. The new truck cost $22,500, and it is expected to generate net after-tax operating cash flows, including depreciation, of $6,250 per year. The truck has a 5-year expected life. The expected salvage values after tax adjustments for the truck are given below. The company's cost of capital is 10%.

Year	Annual Operating Cash Flow	Salvage Value
0	−$22,500	$22,500
1	6,250	17,500
2	6,250	14,000
3	6,250	11,000
4	6,250	5,000
5	6,250	0

a. Should the firm operate the truck until the end of its 5-year physical life? If not, then what is its optimal economic life?
b. Would the introduction of salvage values, in addition to operating cash flows, ever *reduce* the expected NPV and/or IRR of a project?

Spreadsheet Problem

12-23 **Build a Model: Capital Budgeting Tools** Start with the partial model in the file *Ch12 P23 Build a Model.xls* on the textbook's Web site. Gardial Fisheries is considering two mutually exclusive investments. The projects' expected net cash flows are as follows:

Expected Net Cash Flows

Year	Project A	Project B
0	−$375	−$575
1	−300	190
2	−200	190
3	−100	190
4	600	190
5	600	190
6	926	190
7	−200	0

a. If each project's cost of capital is 12%, which project should be selected? If the cost of capital is 18%, what project is the proper choice?
b. Construct NPV profiles for Projects A and B.
c. What is each project's IRR?
d. What is the crossover rate, and what is its significance?
e. What is each project's MIRR at a cost of capital of 12%? At r = 18%? (*Hint:* Note that B is a 6-year project.)
f. What is the regular payback period for these two projects?
g. At a cost of capital of 12%, what is the discounted payback period for these two projects?
h. What is the profitability index for each project if the cost of capital is 12%?

MINI CASE

You have just graduated from the MBA program of a large university, and one of your favorite courses was "Today's Entrepreneurs." In fact, you enjoyed it so much you have decided you want to "be your own boss." While you were in the master's program, your grandfather died and left you $1 million to do with as you please. You are not an inventor, and you do not have a trade skill that you can market; however, you have decided that you would like to purchase at least one established franchise in the fast-foods area, maybe two (if profitable). The problem is that you have never been one to stay with any project for too long, so you figure that your time frame is 3 years. After 3 years you will go on to something else.

You have narrowed your selection down to two choices: (1) Franchise L, Lisa's Soups, Salads, & Stuff, and (2) Franchise S, Sam's Fabulous Fried Chicken. The net cash flows shown below include the price you would receive for selling the franchise in Year 3 and the forecast of how each franchise will do over the 3-year period. Franchise L's cash flows will start off slowly but will increase rather quickly as people become more health-conscious, while Franchise S's cash flows will start off high but will trail off as other chicken competitors enter the marketplace and as people become more health-conscious and avoid fried foods. Franchise L serves breakfast and lunch whereas Franchise S serves only dinner, so it is possible for you to invest in both franchises. You see these franchises as perfect complements to one another: You could attract both the lunch and dinner crowds and the health-conscious and not-so-health-conscious crowds without the franchises directly competing against one another.

Here are the net cash flows (in thousands of dollars):

Expected Net Cash Flows

Year	Franchise L	Franchise S
0	−$100	−$100
1	10	70
2	60	50
3	80	20

Depreciation, salvage values, net working capital requirements, and tax effects are all included in these cash flows.

You also have made subjective risk assessments of each franchise and concluded that both franchises have risk characteristics that require a return of 10%. You must now determine whether one or both of the franchises should be accepted.

a. What is capital budgeting?

b. What is the difference between independent and mutually exclusive projects?

c. (1) Define the term *net present value (NPV)*. What is each franchise's NPV?

   (2) What is the rationale behind the NPV method? According to NPV, which franchise or franchises should be accepted if they are independent? Mutually exclusive?

   (3) Would the NPVs change if the cost of capital changed?

d. (1) Define the term *internal rate of return (IRR)*. What is each franchise's IRR?

   (2) How is the IRR on a project related to the YTM on a bond?

   (3) What is the logic behind the IRR method? According to IRR, which franchises should be accepted if they are independent? Mutually exclusive?

   (4) Would the franchises' IRRs change if the cost of capital changed?

e. (1) Draw NPV profiles for Franchises L and S. At what discount rate do the profiles cross?

   (2) Look at your NPV profile graph without referring to the actual NPVs and IRRs. Which franchise or franchises should be accepted if they are independent? Mutually exclusive? Explain. Are your answers correct at any cost of capital less than 23.6%?

f. (1) What is the underlying cause of ranking conflicts between NPV and IRR?

(2) What is the *reinvestment rate assumption,* and how does it affect the NPV-versus-IRR conflict?

(3) Which method is the best? Why?

g. (1) Define the term *modified IRR (MIRR).* Find the MIRRs for Franchises L and S.

(2) What are the MIRR's advantages and disadvantages vis-à-vis the regular IRR? What are the MIRR's advantages and disadvantages vis-à-vis the NPV?

h. What does the profitability index (PI) measure? What are the PIs of Franchises S and L?

i. (1) What is the payback period? Find the paybacks for Franchises L and S.

(2) What is the rationale for the payback method? According to the payback criterion, which franchise or franchises should be accepted if the firm's maximum acceptable payback is 2 years and if Franchises L and S are independent? If they are mutually exclusive?

(3) What is the difference between the regular and discounted payback periods?

(4) What is the main disadvantage of discounted payback? Is the payback method of any real usefulness in capital budgeting decisions?

j. As a separate project (Project P), you are considering sponsorship of a pavilion at the upcoming World's Fair. The pavilion would cost $800,000, and it is expected to result in $5 million of incremental cash inflows during its single year of operation. However, it would then take another year, and $5 million of costs, to demolish the site and return it to its original condition. Thus, Project P's expected net cash flows look like this (in millions of dollars):

Year	Net Cash Flows
0	−$0.8
1	5.0
2	−5.0

The project is estimated to be of average risk, so its cost of capital is 10%.

(1) What are normal and nonnormal cash flows?

(2) What is Project P's NPV? What is its IRR? Its MIRR?

(3) Draw Project P's NPV profile. Does Project P have normal or nonnormal cash flows? Should this project be accepted?

k. In an unrelated analysis, you have the opportunity to choose between the following two mutually exclusive projects:

Expected Net Cash Flows

Year	Project S	Project L
0	−$100,000	−$100,000
1	60,000	33,500
2	60,000	33,500
3	—	33,500
4	—	33,500

The projects provide a necessary service, so whichever one is selected is expected to be repeated into the foreseeable future. Both projects have a 10% cost of capital.

(1) What is each project's initial NPV without replication?

(2) What is each project's equivalent annual annuity?

(3) Now apply the replacement chain approach to determine the projects' extended NPVs. Which project should be chosen?

(4) Now assume that the cost to replicate Project S in 2 years will increase to $105,000 because of inflationary pressures. How should the analysis be handled now, and which project should be chosen?

l. You are also considering another project that has a physical life of 3 years; that is, the machinery will be totally worn out after 3 years. However, if the project were terminated prior to the end of 3 years, the machinery would have a positive salvage value. Here are the project's estimated cash flows:

Year	Initial Investment and Operating Cash Flows	End-of-Year Net Salvage Value
0	−$5,000	$5,000
1	2,100	3,100
2	2,000	2,000
3	1,750	0

Using the 10% cost of capital, what is the project's NPV if it is operated for the full 3 years? Would the NPV change if the company planned to terminate the project at the end of Year 2? At the end of Year 1? What is the project's optimal (economic) life?

m. After examining all the potential projects, you discover that there are many more projects this year with positive NPVs than in a normal year. What two problems might this extra-large capital budget cause?

Selected Additional Cases

The following cases from TextChoice, *Cengage Learning's online case library, cover many of the concepts discussed in this chapter and are available at* **www.textchoice2.com/casenet.**

Klein-Brigham Series:
Case 11, "Chicago Valve Company."

Brigham-Buzzard Series:
Case 6, "Powerline Network Corporation (Basics of Capital Budgeting)."

Chapter 15

Capital Structure Decisions: Part I

As we saw in Chapters 9 and 11, growth in sales requires growth in operating capital, often requiring that external funds must be raised through a combination of equity and debt. The firm's mixture of debt and equity is called its **capital structure**. Although actual levels of debt and equity may vary somewhat over time, most firms try to keep their financing mix close to a **target capital structure**. A firm's **capital structure decision** includes its choice of a target capital structure, the average maturity of its debt, and the specific types of financing it decides to use at any particular time. As with operating decisions, managers should make capital structure decisions that are designed to maximize the firm's intrinsic value.

Beginning of Chapter Questions

As you read this chapter, consider how you would answer the following questions. You *should not* necessarily be able to answer the questions before you read the chapter. Rather, you should use them to get a sense of the issues covered in the chapter. After reading the chapter, you should be able to give at least partial answers to the questions, and you should be able to give better answers after the chapter has been discussed in class. Note, too, that it is often useful, when answering conceptual questions, to use hypothetical data to illustrate your answer. We illustrate the answers with an *Excel* model that is available on the textbook's Web site. Accessing the model and working through it is a useful exercise, and it provides insights that are useful when answering the questions.

1. What is **business risk?** List and then discuss some factors that affect business risk.
2. What is **financial risk?** How is it related to business risk?
3. Who are **Modigliani and Miller (MM),** and what were their conclusions regarding the effect of capital structure on a firm's value and cost of capital under the assumption of no corporate taxes? How do their conclusions change when they introduce corporate taxes? If a firm's managers thought that MM were exactly right, and they

wanted to maximize the firm's value, what capital structure would they choose?
4. Does the MM theory appear to be correct according to either empirical research or observations of firms' actual behavior? How do assumptions affect your conclusion about whether the MM theory appears to be correct?
5. What is the **trade-off theory** of capital structure? How does it differ from MM's theory?
6. In general, does the market view the **announcement of a new stock issue** to be a good **signal?** Does the signaling theory lead to the same conclusions regarding the optimal capital structure as the trade-off theory and/or the MM theory?
7. What does it mean to be at the **optimal capital structure?** What is optimized? What is maximized and what is minimized?
8. Should firms focus on **book value** or **market value** capital structures? How would the calculated WACC be affected by the use of book weights rather than market weights?
9. What would you expect to happen to an all-equity firm's stock price if its management announced a **recapitalization** under which debt would be issued and used to repurchase common stock?

15.1 A Preview of Capital Structure Issues

Recall from Chapter 11 that the value of a firm's operations is the present value of its expected future free cash flows (FCF) discounted at its weighted average cost of capital (WACC):

$$V_{op} = \sum_{t=1}^{\infty} \frac{FCF_t}{(1 + WACC)^t} \qquad (15\text{--}1)$$

The WACC of a firm financed only by debt and common stock depends on the percentages of debt and common stock (w_d and w_s), the cost of debt (r_d), the cost of stock (r_s), and the corporate tax rate (T):

$$WACC = w_d(1 - T)r_d + w_s r_s \qquad (15\text{--}2)$$

CORPORATE VALUATION AND CAPITAL STRUCTURE

A firm's financing choices obviously have a direct effect on the weighted average cost of capital (WACC). Financing choices also have an indirect effect on the costs of debt and equity because they change the risk and required returns of debt and equity. Financing choices can also affect free cash flows if the probability of bankruptcy becomes high. This chapter focuses on the debt–equity choice and its effect on value.

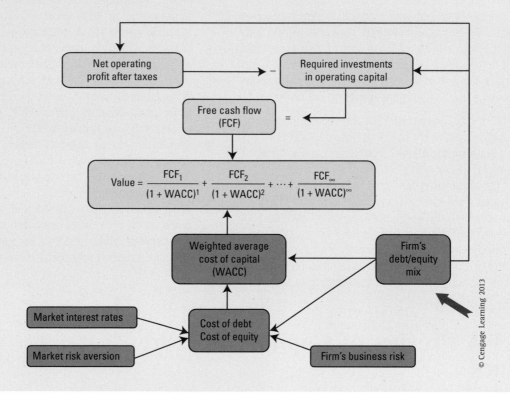

As these equations show, the only way any decision can change a firm's value is by affecting either expected free cash flows or the cost of capital. We discuss below some of the ways that a higher proportion of debt can affect WACC and/or FCF.

15.1a Debt Increases the Cost of Stock, r$_s$

Debtholders have a claim on the company's cash flows that is prior to shareholders, who are entitled only to any residual cash flow after debtholders have been paid. As we show later in a numerical example, the "fixed" claim of the debtholders causes the "residual" claim of the stockholders to become riskier, and this increases the cost of stock, r$_s$.

15.1b Debt Reduces the Taxes a Company Pays

Imagine that a company's cash flows are a pie and that three different groups get pieces of the pie. The first piece goes to the government in the form of taxes, the second goes to debtholders, and the third to shareholders. Companies can deduct interest expenses when calculating taxable income, which reduces the government's piece of the pie and leaves more pie available to debtholders and investors. This reduction in taxes reduces the after-tax cost of debt, as shown in Equation 15-2.

15.1c The Risk of Bankruptcy Increases the Cost of Debt, r_d

As debt increases, the probability of financial distress, or even bankruptcy, goes up. With higher bankruptcy risk, debtholders will insist on a higher interest rate, which increases the pre-tax cost of debt, r_d.

15.1d The Net Effect on the Weighted Average Cost of Capital

As Equation 15-2 shows, the WACC is a weighted average of relatively low-cost debt and high-cost equity. If we increase the proportion of debt, then the weight of low-cost debt (w_d) increases and the weight of high-cost equity (w_s) decreases. If all else remained the same, then the WACC would fall and the value of the firm in Equation 15-1 would increase. But the previous paragraphs show that all else doesn't remain the same: Both r_d and r_s increase. It should be clear that changing the capital structure affects all the variables in the WACC equation, but it's not easy to say whether those changes increase the WACC, decrease it, or balance out exactly and thus leave the WACC unchanged. We'll return to this issue later when discussing capital structure theory.

15.1e Bankruptcy Risk Reduces Free Cash Flow

As the risk of bankruptcy increases, some customers may choose to buy from another company, which hurts sales. This, in turn, decreases net operating profit after taxes (NOPAT), thus reducing FCF. Financial distress also hurts the productivity of workers and managers, who spend more time worrying about their next job than attending to their current job. Again, this reduces NOPAT and FCF. Finally, suppliers tighten their credit standards, which reduces accounts payable and causes net operating working capital to increase, thus reducing FCF. Therefore, the risk of bankruptcy can decrease FCF and reduce the value of the firm.

15.1f Bankruptcy Risk Affects Agency Costs

Higher levels of debt may affect the behavior of managers in two opposing ways. First, when times are good, managers may waste cash flow on perquisites and unnecessary expenditures. This is an agency cost, as described in Chapter 11. The good news is that the threat of bankruptcy reduces such wasteful spending, which increases FCF.

But the bad news is that a manager may become gun-shy and reject positive-NPV projects if they are risky. From the stockholder's point of view, it would be unfortunate if a risky project caused the company to go into bankruptcy, but note that other companies in the stockholder's portfolio may be taking on risky projects that turn out to be successful. Since most stockholders are well diversified, they can afford for a manager to take on risky but positive-NPV projects. But a manager's reputation and wealth are generally tied to a single company, so the project may be unacceptably risky from the manager's point of view. Thus, high debt can cause managers to forgo positive-NPV projects unless they are extremely safe. This is called the **underinvestment problem**, and it is another type of agency cost. Notice that debt can reduce one aspect of agency costs (wasteful spending) but may increase another (underinvestment), so the net effect on value isn't clear.

15.1g Issuing Equity Conveys a Signal to the Marketplace

Managers are in a better position to forecast a company's free cash flow than are investors, and academics call this **informational asymmetry**. Suppose a company's stock price is $50 per share. If managers are willing to issue new stock at $50 per share, investors reason that no one would sell anything for less than its true value. Therefore, the true value of the shares as seen by the managers with their superior information must be less than or equal to $50. Thus, investors perceive an equity issue as a negative signal, and this usually causes the stock price to fall.[1]

In addition to affecting investors' perceptions, capital structure choices also affect FCF and risk, as discussed earlier. The following section focuses on the way that capital structure affects risk.

15.1h A Quick Overview of Actual Debt Ratios

For the average company in the S&P 500, the ratio of long-term debt to equity was about 108% in the winter of 2011. This means that the typical company had about $1.08 in debt for every dollar of equity. However, Table 15-1 shows that there are wide divergences in the average ratios for different business sectors and for different companies within a sector. For example, the technology sector has a very low average ratio (13%) while the utilities sector has a much higher ratio (82%). Even so, within each sector there are some companies with low levels of debt and others with high levels. For example, the average debt ratio for the consumer/noncyclical sector is 24%, but in this sector Starbucks has a ratio of 15% while Kellogg has a ratio of 177%. Why do we see such variation across companies and business sectors? Can a company make itself more valuable through its choice of debt ratio? We address those questions in the rest of this chapter, beginning with a description of business risk and financial risk.

Self Test	Briefly describe some ways in which the capital structure decision can affect the WACC and FCF.

15.2 Business Risk and Financial Risk

Business risk and financial risk combine to determine the total risk of a firm's future return on equity, as we explain in the next sections.

---

1. An exception to this rule is any situation with little informational asymmetry, such as a regulated utility. Also, some companies, such as start-ups or high-tech ventures, are unable to find willing lenders and therefore must issue equity; we discuss this later in the chapter.

TABLE 15-1	Long-Term Debt-to-Equity Ratios for Selected Firms and Industries			
Sector and Company	**Long-Term Debt-to-Equity Ratio**	**Sector and Company**	**Long-Term Debt-to-Equity Ratio**
Technology	13%	**Capital Goods**	24%
Microsoft (MSFT)	21	Winnebago Industries (WGO)	0
Ricoh (RICTEUR.Lp)	64	Caterpillar Inc. (CAT)	207
Energy	17	**Consumer/Noncyclical**	24
ExxonMobil (XOM)	11	Starbucks (SBUX)	15
Chesapeake Energy (CHK)	75	Kellogg Company (K)	177
Transportation	54	**Services**	54
United Parcel Service (UPS)	102	Administaff Inc. (ASF)	0
Delta Airlines (DAL)	1,469	Republic Services (RSG)	75
Basic Materials	19	**Utilities**	82
Anglo American PLC (AAUKYN.MX)	37	Genon Energy Inc. (RRI)	51
Century Aluminum (CENX)	23	CMS Energy (CMS)	220

Source: For updates on a company's ratio, go to **www.reuters.com** and enter the ticker symbol for a stock quote. Click on Financials tab for updates on the sector ratio.

15.2a Business Risk

Business risk is the risk a firm's common stockholders would face if the firm had no debt. In other words, it is the risk inherent in the firm's operations, which arises from uncertainty about future operating profits and capital requirements.

Business risk depends on a number of factors, beginning with variability in product demand. For example, General Motors has more demand variability than does Kroger: When times are tough, consumers quit buying cars but they still buy food. Second, most firms are exposed to variability in sales prices and input costs. Some firms with strong brand identity like Apple may be able to pass unexpected costs through to their customers, and firms with strong market power like Wal-Mart may be able to keep their input costs low, but variability in prices and costs adds significant risk to most firms' operations. Third, firms that are slower to bring new products to market have greater business risk: Think of GM's relatively sluggish time to bring a new model to the market versus that of Toyota. Being faster to the market allows Toyota to more quickly respond to changes in consumer desires. Fourth, international operations add the risk of currency fluctuations and political risk. Fifth, if a high percentage of a firm's costs are fixed and hence do not decline when demand falls, then the firm has high *operating leverage,* which increases its business risk. We focus on operating leverage in the next section.

15.2b Operating Leverage

A high degree of **operating leverage** implies that a relatively small change in sales results in a relatively large change in EBIT, net operating profits after taxes (NOPAT), and return on invested capital (ROIC). Other things held constant, the higher a firm's fixed costs, the greater its operating leverage. Higher fixed costs are generally

Figure 15-1   **Illustration of Operating and Financial Leverage (Millions of Dollars and Millions of Units, Except Per Unit Data)**

	A	B	C	D	E
23	*Input Data*		Plan A	Plan U	Plan L
24	Required capital		$200	$200	$200
25	Book equity		$200	$200	$150
26	Debt				$50
27	Interest rate		8%	8%	8%
28	Sales price (P)		$2.00	$2.00	$2.00
29	Tax rate (T)		40%	40%	40%
30	Expected units sold (Q)		110	110	110
31	Fixed costs (F)		$20	$60	$60
32	Variable costs (V)		$1.50	$1.00	$1.00
33					
34	*Income Statements*		Plan A	Plan U	Plan L
35	Sales revenue (P×Q)		$220.0	$220.0	$220.0
36	Fixed costs		$20.0	$60.0	$60.0
37	Variable costs (V×Q)		$165.0	$110.0	$110.0
38	EBIT		$35.0	$50.0	$50.0
39	Interest		$0.0	$0.0	$4.0
40	EBT		$35.0	$50.0	$46.0
41	Tax		$14.0	$20.0	$18.4
42	Net income		$21.0	$30.0	$27.6
43					
44	*Key Performance Measures*		Plan A	Plan U	Plan L
45	NOPAT = EBIT(1 − T)		$21.0	$30.0	$30.0
46	ROIC = NOPAT/Capital		10.5%	15.0%	15.0%
47	ROE = NI/Equity		10.5%	15.0%	18.4%

associated with (1) highly automated, capital intensive firms; (2) businesses that employ highly skilled workers who must be retained and paid even when sales are low; and (3) firms with high product development costs that must be maintained to complete ongoing R&D projects.

To illustrate the relative impact of fixed versus variable costs, consider Strasburg Electronics Company, a manufacturer of components used in cell phones. Strasburg is considering several different operating technologies and several different financing alternatives. We will analyze its financing choices in the next section, but for now we focus on its operating plans.

Each of Strasburg's plans requires a capital investment of $200 million; assume for now that Strasburg will finance its choice entirely with equity.[2] Each plan is expected to produce 100 million units (Q) per year at a sales price (P) of $2 per unit. As shown in Figure 15-1, Plan A's technology requires a smaller annual fixed cost (F) than Plan U's, but Plan A has higher variable costs (V). (We denote the second plan with U because it has no financial leverage, and we denote the third plan with L because it does have financial leverage; Plan L is discussed in the next section.) Figure 15-1 also shows the projected income statements and selected performance

---

2. Strasburg has improved its supply chain operations to such an extent that its operating current assets are not larger than its operating current liabilities. In fact, its Op CA = Op CL = $10 million. Recall that net operating working capital (NOWC) is the difference between Op CA and Op CL, so Strasburg has NOWC = 0. Even though Strasburg's plans require $210 million in assets, they also generate $10 million in spontaneous operating liabilities, so Strasburg's investors must put up only $200 million in some combination of debt and equity.

measures for the first year. Notice that Plan U has higher net income, higher net operating profit after taxes (NOPAT), higher return on equity (ROE), and higher return on invested capital than does Plan A. So at first blush it seems that Strasburg should accept Plan U instead of Plan A.

Notice that the projections in Figure 15-1 are based on the 110 million units that are expected to be sold. But what if demand is lower than expected? It often is useful to know how far sales can fall before operating profits become negative. The **operating break-even point** occurs when earnings before interest and taxes (EBIT) equal zero:[3]

$$EBIT = PQ - VQ - F = 0 \qquad (15\text{--}3)$$

If we solve for the break-even quantity, Q_{BE}, we get this expression:

$$Q_{BE} = \frac{F}{P - V} \qquad (15\text{--}4)$$

The break-even quantities for Plans A and U are

$$\text{Plan A: } Q_{BE} = \frac{\$20 \text{ million}}{\$2.00 - \$1.50} = 40 \text{ million units}$$

$$\text{Plan U: } Q_{BE} = \frac{\$60 \text{ million}}{\$2.00 - \$1.00} = 60 \text{ million units}$$

Plan A will be profitable if unit sales are above 40 million, whereas Plan U requires sales of 60 million units before it is profitable. This difference is because Plan U has higher fixed costs, so more units must be sold to cover these fixed costs. Panel a of Figure 15-2 illustrates the operating profitability of these two plans for different levels of unit sales. (We discuss Panel b in the next section.) Suppose sales are at 80 million units. In this case, the NOPAT is identical for each plan. As unit sales begin to climb above 80 million, both plans increase in profitability, but NOPAT increases more for Plan U than for Plan A. If sales fall below 80 million then both plans become less profitable, but NOPAT decreases more for Plan U than for Plan A. This illustrates that the combination of higher fixed costs and lower variable costs of Plan U magnifies its gain or loss relative to Plan A. In other words, because Plan U has higher operating leverage, it also has greater business risk.

Notice that business risk is being driven by variability in the number of units that can be sold. It would be straightforward to estimate a probability for each possible level of sales and then calculate the standard deviation of the resulting NOPATs in exactly the same way that we calculated project risk using scenario analysis in Chapter 13. This would produce a quantitative estimate of business

---

3. This definition of the break-even point does not include any fixed financial costs because it focuses on operating profits. We could also examine net income, in which case a levered firm would have negative net income even at the operating break-even point. We introduce financial costs shortly.

Figure 15-2   **Operating Leverage and Financial Leverage**

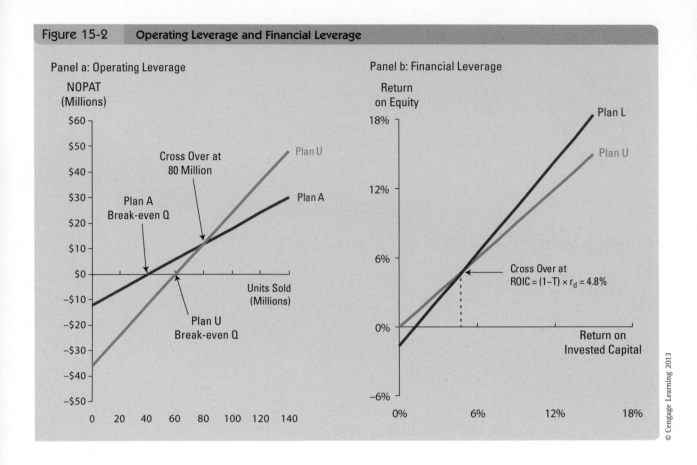

© Cengage Learning 2013

risk.[4] However, for most purposes it is sufficient to recognize that business risk increases if operating leverage increases and then use that insight qualitatively rather than quantitatively when evaluating plans with different degrees of operating leverage.

15.2c Financial Risk

Financial risk is the additional risk placed on the common stockholders as a result of the decision to finance with debt.[5] Conceptually, stockholders face a certain amount of risk that is inherent in a firm's operations—this is its business risk, which is defined as the uncertainty in projections of future EBIT, NOPAT, and ROIC. If a firm uses debt (financial leverage), then the business risk is concentrated on the common stockholders. To illustrate, suppose ten people decide to form a corporation to manufacture flash memory drives. There is a certain amount of business risk in the operation. If the firm is capitalized only with common equity and if each person buys 10% of the stock,

---

4. For this example, we could also directly express the standard deviation of NOPAT, σ_{NOPAT}, in terms of the standard deviation of unit sales, σ_Q: $\sigma_{NOPAT} = (P - V)(1 - T) \times \sigma_Q$. We could also express the standard deviation of ROIC as $\sigma_{ROIC} = [(P - V)(1 - T)/Capital] \times \sigma_Q$. As this shows, volatility in NOPAT (and ROIC) is driven by volatility in unit sales, with a bigger spread between price and variable costs leading to higher volatility. Also, there are several other ways to calculate measures of operating leverage, as we explain in *Web Extension 15A*.

5. Preferred stock also adds to financial risk. To simplify matters, we examine only debt and common equity in this chapter.

then each investor shares equally in the business risk. However, suppose the firm is capitalized with 50% debt and 50% equity, with five of the investors putting up their money by purchasing debt and the other five putting up their money by purchasing equity. In this case, the five debtholders are paid before the five stockholders, so *virtually all* of the business risk is borne by the stockholders. Thus, the use of debt, or **financial leverage**, concentrates business risk on stockholders.[6]

To illustrate the impact of financial risk, we can extend the Strasburg Electronics example. Strasburg initially decided to use the technology of Plan U, which is unlevered (financed with all equity), but now it's considering financing the technology with $150 million of equity and $50 million of debt at an 8% interest rate, as shown for Plan L in Figure 15-1 (recall that L denotes leverage). Compare Plans U and L. Notice that the ROIC of 15% is the same for the two plans because the financing choice doesn't affect operations. Plan L has lower net income ($27.6 million versus $30 million) because it must pay interest, but it has a higher ROE (18.4%) because the net income is shared over a smaller equity base.[7]

Suppose Strasburg is a zero-growth company and pays out all net income as dividends. This means that Plan U has net income of $30 million available for distribution to its investors. Plan L has $27.6 million net income available to pay as dividends and it already pays $4 million in interest to its debtholders, so its total distribution is $27.6 + $4 = $31.6 million. How is it that Plan L is able to distribute a larger total amount to investors? Look closely at the taxes paid under the two plans. Plan L pays only $18.4 million in tax while Plan U pays $20 million. The $1.6 million difference is because interest payments are deductible for tax purposes. Because Plan L pays less in taxes, an extra $1.6 million is available to distribute to investors. If our analysis ended here, we would choose Plan L over Plan U because Plan L distributes more cash to investors and provides a higher ROE for its equity holders.

But there is more to the story. Just as operating leverage adds risk, so does financial leverage. We used the Data Table feature in the file *Ch15 Tool Kit.xls* to generate performance measures for plans U and L at different levels of unit sales, which lead to different levels of ROIC. Panel b of Figure 15-2 shows the ROE of Plan L versus its ROIC. (Keep in mind that the ROIC for Plan U is the same as for Plan L because leverage doesn't affect operating performance; also, Plan U's ROE is the same as its ROIC because it has no leverage.)

Notice that for an ROIC of 4.8%, which is the after-tax cost of debt, Plan U (with no leverage) and Plan L (with leverage) have the same ROE. As ROIC increases above 6%, the ROE increases for each plan, but more for Plan L than for Plan U. However, if ROIC falls below 6%, then the ROE falls further for Plan L than for Plan U. Thus, financial leverage magnifies the ROE for good or ill, depending on the ROIC, and so increases the risk of a levered firm relative to an unlevered firm.[8]

We see, then, that using leverage has both good and bad effects: If expected ROIC is greater than the after-tax cost of debt, then higher leverage increases expected ROE but also increases risk.

---

6. Holders of corporate debt generally do bear some business risk, because they may lose some of their investment if the firm goes bankrupt. We discuss this in more depth later in the chapter.

7. Recall that Strasburg's operating CA are equal to its operating CL. Strasburg has no short-term investments, so its book values of debt and equity must sum up to the amount of operating capital it uses.

8. We could also express the standard deviation of ROE, σ_{ROE}, in terms of the standard deviation of ROIC: $\sigma_{ROE} = (\text{Capital/Equity}) \times \sigma_{ROIC} = (\text{Capital/Equity}) \times [(P - V)(1 - T)/\text{Capital}] \times \sigma_Q$. Thus, volatility in ROE is due to the amount of financial leverage, the amount of operating leverage, and the underlying risk in units sold. This is similar in spirit to the Du Pont model discussed in Chapter 8.

15.2d Strasburg's Valuation Analysis

Strasburg decided to go with Plan L, the one with high operating leverage and $50 million in debt financing. This resulted in a stock price of $20 per share. With 10 million shares, Strasburg's market value of equity is $20(10) = $200 million. Strasburg has no short-term investments, so Strasburg's total enterprise value is the sum of its debt and equity: V = $50 + $200 = $250 million. Notice that this is greater than the required investment, which means that the plan has a positive NPV; another way to view this is that Strasburg's Market Value Added (MVA) is positive. In terms of market values, Strasburg's capital structure has 20% debt (w_d = $50/$250 = 0.20) and 80% equity (w_s = $200/$250 = 0.80). These calculations are reported in Figure 15-3.

Is this the optimal capital structure? We will address the question in more detail later, but for now let's focus on understanding Strasburg's current valuation, beginning with its cost of capital. Strasburg has a beta of 1.25. We can use the Capital Asset Pricing Model (CAPM) to estimate the cost of equity. The risk-free rate, r_{RF}, is 6.3% and the market risk premium, RP_M, is 6%, so the cost of equity is

$$r_s = r_{RF} + b(RP_M) = 6.3\% + 1.25(6\%) = 13.8\%$$

Figure 15-3   Strasburg's Valuation Analysis (Millions of Dollars Except Per Share Data)

	A	B	C	D
104	Input Data (Millions Except Per Share Data)			
105	Tax rate			40.00%
106	Debt (D)			$50.00
107	Number of shares (n)			10.00
108	Stock price per share (P)			$20.00
109	NOPAT			$30.00
110	Free Cash Flow (FCF)			$30.00
111	Growth rate in FCF			0.00%
112				
113	Capital Structure (Millions Except Per Share Data)			
114	Market value of equity (S = P × n)			$200.00
115	Total value (V = D + S)			$250.00
116	Percent financed with debt (w_d = D/V)			20%
117	Percent financed with stock (w_s = S/V)			80%
118				
119	Cost of Capital			
120	Cost of debt (r_d)			8.00%
121	Beta (b)			1.25
122	Risk-free rate (r_{RF})			6.30%
123	Market risk premium (RP_M)			6.00%
124	Cost of equity ($r_s = r_{RF} + b × RP_M$)			13.80%
125	WACC			12.00%
126				
127	Intrinsic Valuation (Millions Except Per Share Data)			
128	Value of operations:			
129	V_{op} = [FCF(1 + g)]/(WACC − g)			$250.00
130	+ Value of ST investments			$0.00
131	Total intrinsic value of firm			$250.00
132	− Debt			$50.00
133	Intrinsic value of equity			$200.00
134	÷ Number of shares			10.00
135	Intrinsic price per share			$20.00

© Cengage Learning 2013

The weighted average cost of capital is

$$\text{WACC} = w_d(1 - T)r_d + w_s r_s$$
$$= 20\%(1 - 0.40)(8\%) + 80\%(13.8\%)$$
$$= 12\%$$

As shown in Figure 15-1, Plan L has a NOPAT of $30 million. Strasburg expects zero growth, which means there are no required investments in capital. Therefore, FCF is equal to NOPAT. Using the constant growth formula, the value of operations is

$$V_{op} = \frac{\text{FCF}(1 + g)}{\text{WACC} - g} = \frac{\$30(1 + 0)}{0.12 - 0} = \$250$$

Figure 15-3 illustrates the calculation of the intrinsic stock price. For Strasburg, the intrinsic stock price and the market price are each equal to $20. Can Strasburg increase its value by changing its capital structure? The next section discusses how the trade-off between risk and return affects the value of the firm, and Section 15.5 estimates the optimal capital structure for Strasburg.

Self Test

What is business risk, and how can it be measured?

What are some determinants of business risk?

How does operating leverage affect business risk?

What is financial risk, and how does it arise?

Explain this statement: "Using leverage has both good and bad effects."

A firm has fixed operating costs of $100,000 and variable costs of $4 per unit. If it sells the product for $6 per unit, what is the break-even quantity? **(50,000)**

15.3 Capital Structure Theory

In the previous section, we showed how capital structure choices affect a firm's ROE and its risk. For a number of reasons, we would expect capital structures to vary considerably across industries. For example, pharmaceutical companies generally have very different capital structures than airline companies. Moreover, capital structures vary among firms within a given industry. What factors explain these differences? In an attempt to answer this question, academics and practitioners have developed a number of theories, and the theories have been subjected to many empirical tests. The following sections examine several of these theories.[9]

---

9. For additional discussion of capital structure theories, see John C. Easterwood and Palani-Rajan Kadapakkam, "The Role of Private and Public Debt in Corporate Capital Structures," *Financial Management,* Autumn 1991, pp. 49–57; Gerald T. Garvey, "Leveraging the Underinvestment Problem: How High Debt and Management Shareholdings Solve the Agency Costs of Free Cash Flow," *Journal of Financial Research,* Summer 1992, pp. 149–166; Milton Harris and Artur Raviv, "Capital Structure and the Informational Role of Debt," *Journal of Finance,* June 1990, pp. 321–349; and Ronen Israel, "Capital Structure and the Market for Corporate Control: The Defensive Role of Debt Financing," *Journal of Finance,* September 1991, pp. 1391–1409.

15.3a Modigliani and Miller: No Taxes

Modern capital structure theory began in 1958, when Professors Franco Modigliani and Merton Miller (MM) published what has been called the most influential finance article ever written.[10] MM's study was based on some strong assumptions, which included the following:

1. There are no brokerage costs.
2. There are no taxes.
3. There are no bankruptcy costs.
4. Investors can borrow at the same rate as corporations.
5. All investors have the same information as management about the firm's future investment opportunities.
6. EBIT is not affected by the use of debt.

Modigliani and Miller imagined two hypothetical portfolios. The first contains all the equity of an unlevered firm, so the portfolio's value is V_U, the value of an unlevered firm. Because the firm has no growth (which means it does not need to invest in any new net assets) and because it pays no taxes, the firm can pay out all of its EBIT in the form of dividends. Therefore, the cash flow from owning this first portfolio is equal to EBIT.

Now consider a second firm that is identical to the unlevered firm *except* that it is partially financed with debt. The second portfolio contains all of the levered firm's stock (S_L) and debt (D), so the portfolio's value is V_L, the total value of the levered firm. If the interest rate is r_d, then the levered firm pays out interest in the amount r_dD. Because the firm is not growing and pays no taxes, it can pay out dividends in the amount EBIT − r_dD. If you owned all of the firm's debt and equity, your cash flow would be equal to the sum of the interest and dividends: r_dD + (EBIT − r_dD) = EBIT. Therefore, the cash flow from owning this second portfolio is equal to EBIT.

Notice that the cash flow of each portfolio is equal to EBIT. Thus, MM concluded that two portfolios producing the same cash flows must have the same value:[11]

(15–5)
$$V_L = V_U = S_L + D$$

Given their assumptions, MM proved that a firm's value is unaffected by its capital structure.

Recall that the WACC is a combination of the cost of debt and the relatively higher cost of equity, r_s. As leverage increases, more weight is given to low-cost debt but equity becomes riskier, which drives up r_s. Under MM's assumptions,

---

10. Franco Modigliani and Merton H. Miller, "The Cost of Capital, Corporation Finance, and the Theory of Investment," *American Economic Review,* June 1958, pp. 261–297. Modigliani and Miller each won a Nobel Prize for their work.

11. They actually showed that if the values of the two portfolios differed, then an investor could engage in riskless arbitrage: The investor could create a trading strategy (buying one portfolio and selling the other) that had no risk, required none of the investor's own cash, and resulted in a positive cash flow for the investor. This would be such a desirable strategy that everyone would try to implement it. But if everyone tries to buy the same portfolio, its price will be driven up by market demand, and if everyone tries to sell a portfolio, its price will be driven down. The net result of the trading activity would be to change the portfolio's values until they were equal and no more arbitrage was possible.

r_s increases by exactly enough to keep the WACC constant. Put another way: If MM's assumptions are correct, then it doesn't matter how a firm finances its operations and so capital structure decisions are irrelevant.

Even though some of their assumptions are obviously unrealistic, MM's irrelevance result is extremely important. By indicating the conditions under which capital structure is irrelevant, MM also provided us with clues about what is required for capital structure to be relevant and hence to affect a firm's value. The work of MM marked the beginning of modern capital structure research, and subsequent research has focused on relaxing the MM assumptions in order to develop a more realistic theory of capital structure.

Modigliani and Miller's thought process was just as important as their conclusion. It seems simple now, but their idea that two portfolios with identical cash flows must also have identical values changed the entire financial world because it led to the development of options and derivatives. It is no surprise that Modigliani and Miller received Nobel awards for their work.

15.3b Modigliani and Miller II: The Effect of Corporate Taxes

In 1963, MM published a follow-up paper in which they relaxed the assumption that there are no corporate taxes.[12] The Tax Code allows corporations to deduct interest payments as an expense, but dividend payments to stockholders are not deductible. The differential treatment encourages corporations to use debt in their capital structures. This means that interest payments reduce the taxes paid by a corporation, and if a corporation pays less to the government then more of its cash flow is available for its investors. In other words, the tax deductibility of the interest payments shields the firm's pre-tax income.

YOGI BERRA ON THE MM PROPOSITION

When a waitress asked Yogi Berra (Baseball Hall of Fame catcher for the New York Yankees) whether he wanted his pizza cut into four pieces or eight, Yogi replied: "Better make it four. I don't think I can eat eight."[a]

Yogi's quip helps convey the basic insight of Modigliani and Miller. The firm's choice of leverage "slices" the distribution of future cash flows in a way that is like slicing a pizza. MM recognized that holding a company's investment activities fixed is like fixing the size of the pizza; no information costs means that everyone sees the same pizza; no taxes means the IRS gets none of the pie; and no "contracting costs" means nothing sticks to the knife.

So, just as the substance of Yogi's meal is unaffected by whether the pizza is sliced into four pieces or eight, the economic substance of the firm is unaffected by whether the liability side of the balance sheet is sliced to include more or less debt—at least under the MM assumptions.

[a]Lee Green, *Sportswit* (New York: Fawcett Crest, 1984), p. 228.

Source: "Yogi Berra on the MM Proposition," *Journal of Applied Corporate Finance,* Winter 1995, p. 6. Reprinted by permission of Stern Stewart Management.

---

12. Franco Modigliani and Merton H. Miller, "Corporate Income Taxes and the Cost of Capital: A Correction," *American Economic Review,* June 1963, pp. 433–443.

As in their earlier paper, MM introduced a second important way of looking at the effect of capital structure: The value of a levered firm is the value of an otherwise identical unlevered firm plus the value of any "side effects." While others have expanded on this idea by considering other side effects, MM focused on the tax shield:

$$(15\text{-}6) \qquad V_L = V_U + \text{Value of side effects} = V_U + \text{Present value of tax shield}$$

Under their assumptions, they showed that the present value of the tax shield is equal to the corporate tax rate, T, multiplied by the amount of debt, D:

$$(15\text{-}7) \qquad V_L = V_U + TD$$

With a tax rate of about 40%, this implies that every dollar of debt adds about 40 cents of value to the firm, and this leads to the conclusion that the optimal capital structure is virtually 100% debt. MM also showed that the cost of equity, r_s, increases as leverage increases but that it doesn't increase quite as fast as it would if there were no taxes. As a result, under MM with corporate taxes the WACC falls as debt is added.

15.3c Miller: The Effect of Corporate and Personal Taxes

Merton Miller (this time without Modigliani) later brought in the effects of personal taxes.[13] The income from bonds is generally interest, which is taxed as personal income at rates (T_d) going up to 35%, while income from stocks generally comes partly from dividends and partly from capital gains. Long-term capital gains are taxed at a rate of 15%, and this tax is deferred until the stock is sold and the gain realized. If stock is held until the owner dies, no capital gains tax whatsoever must be paid. So, on average, returns on stocks are taxed at lower effective rates (T_s) than returns on debt.[14]

Because of the tax situation, Miller argued that investors are willing to accept relatively low before-tax returns on stock relative to the before-tax returns on bonds. (The situation here is similar to that with tax-exempt municipal bonds as discussed in Chapter 4 and preferred stocks held by corporate investors as discussed in Chapter 5.) For example, an investor might require a return of 10% on Strasburg's bonds, and if stock income were taxed at the same rate as bond income, the required rate of return on Strasburg's stock might be 16% because of the stock's greater risk. However, in view of the favorable treatment of income on the stock, investors might be willing to accept a before-tax return of only 14% on the stock.

Thus, as Miller pointed out, (1) the *deductibility of interest* favors the use of debt financing, but (2) the *more favorable tax treatment of income from stock* lowers the required rate of return on stock and thus favors the use of equity financing.

---

13. See Merton H. Miller, "Debt and Taxes," *Journal of Finance,* May 1977, pp. 261–275.
14. The Tax Code isn't quite as simple as this. An increasing number of investors face the Alternative Minimum Tax (AMT); see *Web Extension 7A* for a discussion. The AMT imposes a 28% tax rate on most income and an effective rate of 22% on long-term capital gains and dividends. Under the AMT there is still a spread between the tax rates on interest income and stock income, but the spread is narrower. See Leonard Burman, William Gale, Greg Leiserson, and Jeffrey Rohaly, "The AMT: What's Wrong and How to Fix It," *National Tax Journal,* September 2007, pp. 385–405.

Miller showed that the net impact of corporate and personal taxes is given by this equation:

$$V_L = V_U + \left[1 - \frac{(1 - T_c)(1 - T_s)}{(1 - T_d)}\right]D \qquad \text{(15–8)}$$

Here T_c is the corporate tax rate, T_s is the personal tax rate on income from stocks, and T_d is the tax rate on income from debt. Miller argued that the marginal tax rates on stock and debt balance out in such a way that the bracketed term in Equation 15-8 is zero and so $V_L = V_U$, but most observers believe there is still a tax advantage to debt if reasonable values of tax rates are assumed. For example, if the marginal corporate tax rate is 40%, the marginal rate on debt is 30%, and the marginal rate on stock is 12%, then the advantage of debt financing is

$$V_L = V_U + \left[1 - \frac{(1 - 0.40)(1 - 0.12)}{(1 - 0.30)}\right]D \qquad \text{(15–8a)}$$

$$= V_U + 0.25\,D$$

Thus it appears that the presence of personal taxes reduces but does not completely eliminate the advantage of debt financing.

15.3d Trade-off Theory

The results of Modigliani and Miller also depend on the assumption that there are no **bankruptcy costs**. However, bankruptcy can be quite costly. Firms in bankruptcy have very high legal and accounting expenses, and they also have a hard time retaining customers, suppliers, and employees. Moreover, bankruptcy often forces a firm to liquidate or sell assets for less than they would be worth if the firm were to continue operating. For example, if a steel manufacturer goes out of business it might be hard to find buyers for the company's blast furnaces. Such assets are often illiquid because they are configured to a company's individual needs and also because they are difficult to disassemble and move.

Note, too, that the *threat of bankruptcy,* not just bankruptcy per se, causes many of these same problems. Key employees jump ship, suppliers refuse to grant credit, customers seek more stable suppliers, and lenders demand higher interest rates and impose more restrictive loan covenants if potential bankruptcy looms.

Bankruptcy-related problems are most likely to arise when a firm includes a great deal of debt in its capital structure. Therefore, bankruptcy costs discourage firms from pushing their use of debt to excessive levels.

Bankruptcy-related costs have two components: (1) the probability of financial distress and (2) the costs that would be incurred if financial distress does occur. Firms whose earnings are more volatile, all else equal, face a greater chance of bankruptcy and should therefore use less debt than more stable firms. This is consistent with our earlier point that firms with high operating leverage, and thus greater business risk, should limit their use of financial leverage. Likewise, firms that would face high costs in the event of financial distress should rely less heavily on debt.

For example, firms whose assets are illiquid and thus would have to be sold at "fire sale" prices should limit their use of debt financing.

The preceding arguments led to the development of what is called the trade-off theory of leverage, in which firms trade off the benefits of debt financing (favorable corporate tax treatment) against higher interest rates and bankruptcy costs. In essence, the **trade-off theory** says that the value of a levered firm is equal to the value of an unlevered firm plus the value of any side effects, which include the tax shield and the expected costs due to financial distress. A summary of the trade-off theory is expressed graphically in Figure 15-4, and a list of observations about the figure follows here.

1. Under the assumptions of the MM model with corporate taxes, a firm's value increases linearly for every dollar of debt. The line labeled "MM Result Incorporating the Effects of Corporate Taxation" in Figure 15-4 expresses the relationship between value and debt under those assumptions.

2. There is some threshold level of debt, labeled D_1 in Figure 15-4, below which the probability of bankruptcy is so low as to be immaterial. Beyond D_1, however, expected bankruptcy-related costs become increasingly important, and they reduce the tax benefits of debt at an increasing rate. In the range from D_1 to D_2, expected bankruptcy-related costs reduce but do not completely offset the tax benefits of debt, so the stock price rises (but at a decreasing rate) as the debt ratio increases. However, beyond D_2, expected bankruptcy-related costs exceed the tax benefits, so from this point on increasing the debt ratio lowers the value of the stock. Therefore, D_2 is the optimal capital structure. Of course, D_1 and D_2 vary from firm to firm, depending on their business risks and bankruptcy costs.

3. Although theoretical and empirical work confirms the general shape of the curve in Figure 15-4, this graph must be taken as an approximation and not as a precisely defined function.

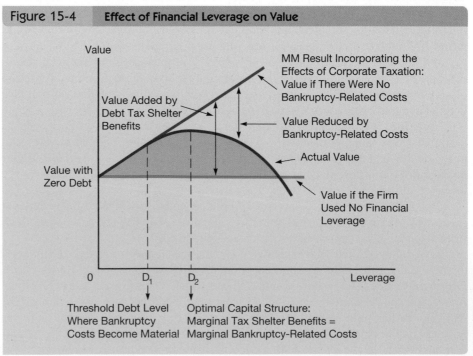

Figure 15-4   Effect of Financial Leverage on Value

15.3e Signaling Theory

It was assumed by MM that investors have the same information about a firm's prospects as its managers—this is called **symmetric information**. However, managers in fact often have better information than outside investors. This is called **asymmetric information**, and it has an important effect on the optimal capital structure. To see why, consider two situations, one in which the company's managers know that its prospects are extremely positive (Firm P) and one in which the managers know that the future looks negative (Firm N).

Suppose, for example, that Firm P's R&D labs have just discovered a nonpatentable cure for the common cold. They want to keep the new product a secret as long as possible to delay competitors' entry into the market. New plants must be built to make the new product, so capital must be raised. How should Firm P's management raise the needed capital? If it sells stock then, when profits from the new product start flowing in, the price of the stock would rise sharply and the purchasers of the new stock would make a bonanza. The current stockholders (including the managers) would also do well, but not as well as they would have done if the company had not sold stock before the price increased, because then they would not have had to share the benefits of the new product with the new stockholders. Therefore, *we should expect a firm with very positive prospects to avoid selling stock and instead to raise required new capital by other means, including debt usage beyond the normal target capital structure.*[15]

Now let's consider Firm N. Suppose its managers have information that new orders are off sharply because a competitor has installed new technology that has improved its products' quality. Firm N must upgrade its own facilities, at a high cost, just to maintain its current sales. As a result, its return on investment will fall (but not by as much as if it took no action, which would lead to a 100% loss through bankruptcy). How should Firm N raise the needed capital? Here the situation is just the reverse of that facing Firm P, which did not want to sell stock so as to avoid having to share the benefits of future developments. *A firm with negative prospects would want to sell stock, which would mean bringing in new investors to share the losses!*[16] The conclusion from all this is that firms with extremely bright prospects prefer not to finance through new stock offerings, whereas firms with poor prospects like to finance with outside equity. How should you, as an investor, react to this conclusion? You ought to say: "If I see that a company plans to issue new stock, this should worry me because I know that management would not want to issue stock if future prospects looked good. However, management *would* want to issue stock if things looked bad. Therefore, I should lower my estimate of the firm's value, other things held constant, if it plans to issue new stock."

If you gave this answer then your views are consistent with those of sophisticated portfolio managers. In a nutshell: *The announcement of a stock offering is generally taken as a signal that the firm's prospects as seen by its own management are not good; conversely, a debt offering is taken as a positive signal.* Notice that Firm N's managers cannot make a false signal to investors by mimicking Firm P and issuing debt. With its unfavorable future prospects, issuing debt could soon force Firm N into bankruptcy. Given the resulting damage to the personal wealth and reputations of N's managers, they cannot afford to mimic Firm P. All of this

15. It would be illegal for Firm P's managers to personally purchase more shares on the basis of their inside knowledge of the new product.
16. Of course, Firm N would have to make certain disclosures when it offered new shares to the public, but it might be able to meet the legal requirements without fully disclosing management's worst fears.

suggests that when a firm announces a new stock offering, more often than not the price of its stock will decline. Empirical studies have shown that this is indeed true.

15.3f Reserve Borrowing Capacity

Because issuing stock sends a negative signal and tends to depress the stock price even if the company's true prospects are bright, a company should try to maintain a **reserve borrowing capacity** so that debt can be used if an especially good investment opportunity comes along. This means that *firms should, in normal times, use more equity and less debt than is suggested by the tax benefit–bankruptcy cost trade-off model depicted in Figure 15-4.*

15.3g The Pecking Order Hypothesis

The presence of flotation costs and asymmetric information may cause a firm to raise capital according to a **pecking order**. In this situation, a firm first raises capital internally by reinvesting its net income and selling its short-term marketable securities. When that supply of funds has been exhausted, the firm will issue debt and perhaps preferred stock. Only as a last resort will the firm issue common stock.[17]

15.3h Using Debt Financing to Constrain Managers

Agency problems may arise if managers and shareholders have different objectives. Such conflicts are particularly likely when the firm's managers have too much cash at their disposal. Managers often use excess cash to finance pet projects or for perquisites such as nicer offices, corporate jets, and sky boxes at sports arenas—none of which have much to do with maximizing stock prices. Even worse, managers might be tempted to pay too much for an acquisition, something that could cost shareholders hundreds of millions of dollars. By contrast, managers with limited "excess cash flow" are less able to make wasteful expenditures.

Firms can reduce excess cash flow in a variety of ways. One way is to funnel some of it back to shareholders through higher dividends or stock repurchases. Another alternative is to shift the capital structure toward more debt in the hope that higher debt service requirements will force managers to be more disciplined. If debt is not serviced as required then the firm will be forced into bankruptcy, in which case its managers would likely lose their jobs. Therefore, a manager is less likely to buy an expensive new corporate jet if the firm has large debt service requirements that could cost the manager his or her job. In short, high levels of debt **bond the cash flow**, since much of it is precommitted to servicing the debt.

A **leveraged buyout (LBO)** is one way to bond cash flow. In an LBO, a large amount of debt and a small amount of cash are used to finance the purchase of a company's shares, after which the firm "goes private." The first wave of LBOs was in the mid-1980s; private equity funds led the buyouts of the late 1990s and early 2000s. Many of these LBOs were specifically designed to reduce corporate waste. As noted, high debt payments force managers to conserve cash by eliminating unnecessary expenditures.

---

17. For more information, see Jonathon Baskin, "An Empirical Investigation of the Pecking Order Hypothesis," *Financial Management*, Spring 1989, pp. 26–35.

Of course, increasing debt and reducing the available cash flow has its downside: It increases the risk of bankruptcy. Ben Bernanke, current (summer 2011) chairman of the Fed, has argued that adding debt to a firm's capital structure is like putting a dagger into the steering wheel of a car.[18] The dagger—which points toward your stomach—motivates you to drive more carefully, but you may get stabbed if someone runs into you—even if you are being careful. The analogy applies to corporations in the following sense: Higher debt forces managers to be more careful with shareholders' money, but even well-run firms could face bankruptcy (get stabbed) if some event beyond their control occurs: a war, an earthquake, a strike, or a recession. To complete the analogy, the capital structure decision comes down to deciding the length of the dagger that stockholders should use to keep managers in line.

Finally, too much debt may overconstrain managers. A large portion of a manager's personal wealth and reputation is tied to a single company, so managers are not well diversified. When faced with a positive-NPV project that is risky, a manager may decide that it's not worth taking on the risk even though well-diversified stockholders would find the risk acceptable. As previously mentioned, this is an underinvestment problem. The more debt the firm has, the greater the likelihood of financial distress and thus the greater the likelihood that managers will forgo risky projects even if they have positive NPVs.

15.3i The Investment Opportunity Set and Reserve Borrowing Capacity

Bankruptcy and financial distress are costly, and, as just reiterated, this can discourage highly levered firms from undertaking risky new investments. If potential new investments, although risky, have positive net present values, then high levels of debt can be doubly costly—the expected financial distress and bankruptcy costs are high, and the firm loses potential value by not making some potentially profitable investments. On the other hand, if a firm has very few profitable investment opportunities then high levels of debt can keep managers from wasting money by investing in poor projects. For such companies, increases in the debt ratio can actually increase the value of the firm.

Thus, in addition to the tax, signaling, bankruptcy, and managerial constraint effects discussed previously, the firm's optimal capital structure is related to its set of investment opportunities. Firms with many profitable opportunities should maintain their ability to invest by using low levels of debt, which is also consistent with maintaining reserve borrowing capacity. Firms with few profitable investment opportunities should use high levels of debt (which have high interest payments) to impose managerial constraint.[19]

15.3j Windows of Opportunity

If markets are efficient, then security prices should reflect all available information; hence they are neither underpriced nor overpriced (except during the time it takes

---

18. See Ben Bernanke, "Is There Too Much Corporate Debt?" *Federal Reserve Bank of Philadelphia Business Review,* September/October 1989, pp. 3–13.

19. See Michael J. Barclay and Clifford W. Smith, Jr., "The Capital Structure Puzzle: Another Look at the Evidence," *Journal of Applied Corporate Finance,* Spring 1999, pp. 8–20.

prices to move to a new equilibrium caused by the release of new information). The *windows of opportunity theory* states that managers don't believe this and supposes instead that stock prices and interest rates are sometimes either too low or too high relative to their true fundamental values. In particular, the theory suggests that managers issue equity when they believe stock market prices are abnormally high and issue debt when they believe interest rates are abnormally low. In other words, they try to time the market.[20] Notice that this differs from signaling theory because no asymmetric information is involved: These managers aren't basing their beliefs on insider information, just on a difference of opinion with the market consensus.

Self Test	Why does the MM theory with corporate taxes lead to 100% debt?
	Explain how *asymmetric information* and *signals* affect capital structure decisions.
	What is meant by *reserve borrowing capacity*, and why is it important to firms?
	How can the use of debt serve to discipline managers?

15.4 Capital Structure Evidence and Implications

There have been hundreds, perhaps even thousands, of papers testing the capital structure theories described in the previous section. We can cover only the highlights here, beginning with the empirical evidence.[21]

15.4a Empirical Evidence

Studies show that firms do benefit from the tax deductibility of interest payments, with a typical firm increasing in value by about $0.10 for every dollar of debt. This is much less than the corporate tax rate, which supports the Miller model (with corporate and personal taxes) more than the MM model (with only corporate taxes). Recent evidence shows that the cost of bankruptcies can be as much as 10% to 20% of the firm's value.[22] Thus, the evidence shows the existence of tax benefits and financial distress costs, which provides support for the trade-off theory.

A particularly interesting study by Professors Mehotra, Mikkelson, and Partch examined the capital structure of firms that were spun off from their parents.[23] The financing choices of existing firms might be influenced by their past financing choices and by the costs of moving from one capital structure to another, but because spin-offs

---

20. See Malcolm Baker and Jeffrey Wurgler, "Market Timing and Capital Structure," *Journal of Finance,* February 2002, pp. 1–32.

21. This section also draws heavily from Barclay and Smith, "The Capital Structure Puzzle," cited in footnote 19; Jay Ritter, ed., *Recent Developments in Corporate Finance* (Northampton, MA: Edward Elgar Publishing Inc., 2005); and a presentation by Jay Ritter at the 2003 FMA meeting, "The Windows of Opportunity Theory of Capital Structure."

22. The *expected cost* of financial distress is the product of bankruptcy costs and the probability of bankruptcy. At moderate levels of debt with low probabilities of bankruptcy, the expected cost of financial distress would be much less than the actual bankruptcy costs if the firm failed.

23. See V. Mehotra, W. Mikkelson, and M. Partch, "The Design of Financial Policies in Corporate Spin-offs," *Review of Financial Studies,* Winter 2003, pp. 1359–1388.

are newly created companies, managers can choose a capital structure without regard to these issues. The study found that more profitable firms (which have a lower expected probability of bankruptcy) and more asset-intensive firms (which have better collateral and thus a lower cost of bankruptcy should one occur) have higher levels of debt. These findings support the trade-off theory.

However, there is also evidence that is inconsistent with the static optimal target capital structure implied by the trade-off theory. For example, stock prices are volatile, which frequently causes a firm's actual market-based debt ratio to deviate from its target. However, such deviations don't cause firms to immediately return to their target by issuing or repurchasing securities. Instead, firms tend to make a partial adjustment each year, moving about one-third of the way toward their target capital structure.[24] This evidence supports the idea of a more dynamic trade-off theory in which firms have target capital structures but don't strive to maintain them too closely.

If a stock price has a big run-up, which reduces the debt ratio, then the trade-off theory suggests that the firm should issue debt to return to its target. However, firms tend to do the opposite, issuing stock after big run-ups. This is much more consistent with the windows of opportunity theory, with managers trying to time the market by issuing stock when they perceive the market to be overvalued. Furthermore, firms tend to issue debt when stock prices and interest rates are low. The maturity of the issued debt seems to reflect an attempt to time interest rates: Firms tend to issue short-term debt if the term structure is upward sloping but long-term debt if the term structure is flat. Again, these facts suggest that managers try to time the market, which is consistent with the windows of opportunity theory.

Firms issue equity much less frequently than debt. On the surface, this seems to support both the pecking order hypothesis and the signaling hypothesis. The pecking order hypothesis predicts that firms with a high level of informational asymmetry, which causes equity issuances to be costly, should issue debt before issuing equity. Yet we often see the opposite, with high-growth firms (which usually have greater informational asymmetry) issuing more equity than debt. Also, many highly profitable firms could afford to issue debt (which comes before equity in the pecking order) but instead choose to issue equity. With respect to the signaling hypothesis, consider the case of firms that have large increases in earnings that were unanticipated by the market. If managers have superior information, then they will anticipate these upcoming performance improvements and issue debt before the increase. Such firms do, in fact, tend to issue debt slightly more frequently than other firms, but the difference isn't economically meaningful.

Many firms have less debt than might be expected, and many have large amounts of short-term investments. This is especially true for firms with high market/book ratios (which indicate many growth options as well as informational asymmetry). This behavior is consistent with the hypothesis that investment opportunities influence attempts to maintain reserve borrowing capacity. It is also consistent with tax considerations, since low-growth firms (which have more debt) are more likely to benefit from the tax shield. This behavior is not consistent with the pecking order hypothesis, where low-growth firms (which often have high free cash flow) would be able to avoid issuing debt by raising funds internally.

To summarize these results, it appears that firms try to capture debt's tax benefits while avoiding financial distress costs. However, they also allow their debt

---

24. See Mark Flannery and Kasturi Rangan, "Partial Adjustment toward Target Capital Structures," *Journal of Financial Economics*, Vol. 79, 2006, pp. 469–506.

TAKING A LOOK AT GLOBAL CAPITAL STRUCTURES

To what extent does capital structure vary across different countries? The accompanying table, which is taken from a study by Raghuram Rajan and Luigi Zingales, gives the median debt ratios of firms in the largest industrial countries.

Rajan and Zingales show that there is considerable variation in capital structure among firms within each of the seven countries. However, they also show that capital structures for the firms in each country are generally determined by a similar set of factors: firm size, profitability, market-to-book ratio, and the ratio of fixed assets to total assets. All in all, the Rajan–Zingales study suggests that the points developed in the chapter apply to firms around the world.

MEDIAN PERCENTAGE OF DEBT TO TOTAL ASSETS IN DIFFERENT COUNTRIES

Country	Book Value Debt Ratio
Canada	32%
France	18
Germany	11
Italy	21
Japan	21
United Kingdom	10
United States	25

Source: Raghuram G. Rajan and Luigi Zingales, "What Do We Know about Capital Structure? Some Evidence from International Data," *Journal of Finance*, December 1995, pp. 1421–1460.

ratios to deviate from the static optimal target ratio implied by the trade-off theory. There is a little evidence indicating that firms follow a pecking order and use security issuances as signals, but there is much more evidence in support of the windows of opportunity theory. Finally, it appears that firms often maintain reserve borrowing capacity, especially firms with many growth opportunities or problems with informational asymmetry.[25]

15.4b Implications for Managers

Managers should explicitly consider tax benefits when making capital structure decisions. Tax benefits obviously are more valuable for firms with high tax rates.

25. For more on empirical tests of capital structure theory, see Gregor Andrade and Steven Kaplan, "How Costly Is Financial (Not Economic) Distress? Evidence from Highly Leveraged Transactions That Became Distressed," *Journal of Finance*, Vol. 53, 1998, pp. 1443–1493; Malcolm Baker, Robin Greenwood, and Jeffrey Wurgler, "The Maturity of Debt Issues and Predictable Variation in Bond Returns," *Journal of Financial Economics*, November 2003, pp. 261–291; Murray Z. Frank and Vidhan K. Goyal, "Testing the Pecking Order Theory of Capital Structure," *Journal of Financial Economics*, February 2003, pp. 217–248; and Michael Long and Ileen Malitz, "The Investment-Financing Nexus: Some Empirical Evidence," *Midland Corporate Finance Journal*, Fall 1985, pp. 53–59.

Firms can utilize tax loss carryforwards and carrybacks, but the time value of money means that tax benefits are more valuable for firms with stable, positive pre-tax income. Therefore, a firm whose sales are relatively stable can safely take on more debt and incur higher fixed charges than a company with volatile sales. Other things being equal, a firm with less operating leverage is better able to employ financial leverage because it will have less business risk and less volatile earnings.

Managers should also consider the expected cost of financial distress, which depends on the probability and cost of distress. Notice that stable sales and lower operating leverage provide tax benefits but also reduce the *probability* of financial distress. One *cost* of financial distress comes from lost investment opportunities. Firms with profitable investment opportunities need to be able to fund them, either by holding higher levels of marketable securities or by maintaining excess borrowing capacity. An astute corporate treasurer made this statement to the authors:

> Our company can earn a lot more money from good capital budgeting and operating decisions than from good financing decisions. Indeed, we are not sure exactly how financing decisions affect our stock price, but we know for sure that having to turn down a promising venture because funds are not available will reduce our long-run profitability.

Another cost of financial distress is the possibility of being forced to sell assets to meet liquidity needs. General-purpose assets that can be used by many businesses are relatively liquid and make good collateral, in contrast to special-purpose assets. Thus, real estate companies are usually highly leveraged, whereas companies involved in technological research are not.

Asymmetric information also has a bearing on capital structure decisions. For example, suppose a firm has just successfully completed an R&D program, and it forecasts higher earnings in the immediate future. However, the new earnings are not yet anticipated by investors and hence are not reflected in the stock price. This company should not issue stock—it should finance with debt until the higher earnings materialize and are reflected in the stock price. Then it could issue common stock, retire the debt, and return to its target capital structure.

Managers should consider conditions in the stock and bond markets. For example, during a recent credit crunch, the junk bond market dried up and there was simply no market at a "reasonable" interest rate for any new long-term bonds rated below BBB. Therefore, low-rated companies in need of capital were forced to go to the stock market or to the short-term debt market, regardless of their target capital structures. When conditions eased, however, these companies sold bonds to get their capital structures back on target.

Finally, managers should always consider lenders' and rating agencies' attitudes. For example, one large utility was recently told by Moody's and Standard & Poor's that its bonds would be downgraded if it issued more debt. This influenced the utility's decision to finance its expansion with common equity. This doesn't mean that managers should never increase debt if it will cause their bond rating to fall, but managers should always factor this into their decision making.[26]

26. For some insights into how practicing financial managers view the capital structure decision, see John Graham and Campbell Harvey, "The Theory and Practice of Corporate Finance: Evidence from the Field," *Journal of Financial Economics,* Vol. 60, 2001, pp. 187–243; Ravindra R. Kamath, "Long-Term Financing Decisions: Views and Practices of Financial Managers of NYSE Firms," *Financial Review,* May 1997, pp. 331–356; and Edgar Norton, "Factors Affecting Capital Structure Decisions," *Financial Review,* August 1991, pp. 431–446.

Which capital structure theories does the empirical evidence seem to support?

What issues should managers consider when making capital structure decisions?

15.5 Estimating the Optimal Capital Structure

Managers should choose the capital structure that maximizes shareholders' wealth. The basic approach is to consider a trial capital structure, based on the market values of the debt and equity, and then estimate the wealth of the shareholders under this capital structure. This approach is repeated until an optimal capital structure is identified. There are several steps in the analysis of each potential capital structure: (1) Estimate the interest rate the firm will pay. (2) Estimate the cost of equity. (3) Estimate the weighted average cost of capital. (4) Estimate the value of operations, which is the present value of free cash flows discounted by the new WACC. The objective is to find the amount of debt financing that maximizes the value of operations. As we will show, this is also the capital structure that maximizes shareholder wealth and the intrinsic stock price. The following sections explain each of these steps, using the company we considered earlier, Strasburg Electronics.

15.5a Estimating the Cost of Debt, r_d

Recall that Strasburg chose Plan L, with high operating leverage and a capital structure consisting of 20% debt. The CFO asked Strasburg's investment bankers to estimate the cost of debt at different capital structures. The investment bankers began by analyzing industry conditions and prospects. They appraised Strasburg's business risk based on its past financial statements and its current technology and customer base. The bankers also forecasted financial statements with different capital structures and analyzed such key ratios as the current ratio and the times-interest-earned ratio. Finally, they factored in current conditions in the financial markets, including interest rates paid by firms in Strasburg's industry. Based on their analysis and judgment, they estimated interest rates at various capital structures as shown in Row 2 of Figure 15-5, starting with a 7.7% cost of debt for the first dollar of debt. This rate increases to 16% if the firm finances 60% of its capital structure with debt. Strasburg's current situation is in Column D and is shown in blue. (We will explain all the rows in Figure 15-5 in the following discussion.)

15.5b Estimating the Cost of Equity, r_s

An increase in the debt ratio also increases the risk faced by shareholders, and this has an effect on the cost of equity, r_s. Recall from Chapter 2 that a stock's beta is the relevant measure of risk for diversified investors. Moreover, it has been demonstrated, both theoretically and empirically, that beta increases with financial leverage. The Hamada equation specifies the effect of financial leverage on beta:[27]

---

27. See Robert S. Hamada, "Portfolio Analysis, Market Equilibrium, and Corporation Finance," *Journal of Finance*, March 1969, pp. 13–31. For a comprehensive framework, see Robert A. Taggart, Jr., "Consistent Valuation and Cost of Capital Expressions with Corporate and Personal Taxes," *Financial Management*, Autumn 1991, pp. 8–20.

Figure 15-5   Estimating Strasburg's Optimal Capital Structure (Millions of Dollars)

	A	B	C	D			
151		Percent of Firm Financed with Debt (w_d)						
152		0%	10%	20%	30%	40%	50%	60%
153 1.	w_s	100.00%	90.00%	80.00%	70.00%	60.00%	50.00%	40.00%
154 2.	r_d	7.70%	7.80%	8.00%	8.50%	9.90%	12.00%	16.00%
155 3.	b	1.09	1.16	1.25	1.37	1.52	1.74	2.07
156 4.	r_s	12.82%	13.26%	13.80%	14.50%	15.43%	16.73%	18.69%
157 5.	r_d (1–T)	4.62%	4.68%	4.80%	5.10%	5.94%	7.20%	9.60%
158 6.	WACC	12.82%	12.40%	12.00%	11.68%	11.63%	11.97%	13.24%
159 7.	V_{op}	$233.98	$241.96	$250.00	$256.87	$257.86	$250.68	$226.65
160 8.	Debt	$0.00	$24.20	$50.00	$77.06	$103.14	$125.34	$135.99
161 9.	Equity	$233.98	$217.76	$200.00	$179.81	$154.72	$125.34	$90.66
162 10.	# shares	12.72	11.34	10.00	8.69	7.44	6.25	5.13
163 11.	Stock price	$18.40	$19.20	$20.00	$20.69	$20.79	$20.07	$17.66
164 12.	Net income	$30.00	$28.87	$27.60	$26.07	$23.87	$20.98	$16.95
165 13.	EPS	$2.36	$2.54	$2.76	$3.00	$3.21	$3.36	$3.30

Notes:
1. The percent financed with equity is: $w_s = 1 - w_d$.
2. The interest rate on debt, r_d, is obtained from investment bankers.
3. Beta is estimated using Hamada's formula, the unlevered beta of 1.09, and a tax rate of 40%:
   $b = b_U [1 + (1 - T) \times (w_d/w_s)]$.
4. The cost of equity is estimated using the CAPM formula with a risk-free rate of 6.3% and a market risk premium of 6%: $r_s = r_{RF} + (RP_M)b$.
5. The after-tax cost of debt is: $r_d(1 - T)$, where T = 40%.
6. The weighted average cost of capital is calculated as WACC = $w_s r_s + w_d r_d(1 - T)$.
7. The value of the firm's operations is calculated as $V_{op} = [FCF(1 + g)] / (WACC - g)$, where FCF = $30 million and g = 0.
8. Debt = $w_d \times V_{op}$.
9. The intrinsic value of equity after the recapitalization and repurchase is $S_{Post} = V_{op} - Debt = w_s \times V_{op}$.
10. The number of shares after the recap has been completed is found using this equation:
    $n_{Post} = n_{Prior} \times [(V_{opNew} - D_{New}) / (V_{opNew} - D_{Old})]$. The subscript "Old" indicates values from the original capital structure, where $w_d = 20\%$; the subscript "New" indicates values at the current capital structure after the recap and repurchase; and the subscript "Post" indicates values after the recap and repurchase.
11. The price after the recap and repurchase is $P_{Post} = S_{Post}/n_{Post}$, but we can also find the price as $P_{Post} = (V_{opNew} - D_{Old})/n_{Prior}$.
12. EBIT is $50 million; see Figure 15-1. Net income is NI = (EBIT - r_dD) (1 - T).
13. Earnings per share is EPS = NI/n_{Post}.

$$b = b_U [1 + (1 - T)(D/S)] \qquad (15\text{–}9)$$

Here D is the market value of the debt and S is the market value of the equity. The Hamada equation shows how increases in the market value debt/equity ratio increase beta. Here b_U is the firm's **unlevered beta** coefficient—that is, the beta it would have if it had no debt. In that case, beta would depend entirely on business risk and thus be a measure of the firm's "basic business risk."

Sometimes it is more convenient to work with the percentages of debt and equity at which the firm is financed (w_d and w_s) rather than the dollar values of D and S. Notice that w_d and w_s are defined as D/(D + S) and S/(D + S), respectively.

This means that the ratio w_d/w_s is equal to the ratio D/S. Substituting these values gives us another form of Hamada's formula:

(15-9a)
$$b = b_U[1 + (1 - T)(w_d/w_s)]$$

Often we know the current capital structure and beta but wish to know the unlevered beta. We find this by rearranging Equation 15-9a as follows:

(15-10)
$$b_U = b/[1 + (1 - T)(w_d/w_s)]$$

For Strasburg, the unlevered beta is

$$b_U = 1.25/[1 + (1 - 0.40)(0.20/0.80)]$$
$$= 1.087$$

Using this unlevered beta, we can then apply Hamada's formula in Equation 15-9a to determine estimates of Strasburg's beta for different capital structures. These results are reported in Line 3 of Figure 15-5.

Recall from Section 15.2 that the risk-free rate is 6.3% and the market risk premium is 6%. We can use the CAPM and the previously estimated betas to estimate Strasburg's cost of equity for different capital structures (which cause Strasburg's beta to change). These results are shown in Line 4 of Figure 15-5. As expected, Strasburg's cost of equity increases as its debt increases. Figure 15-6 graphs Strasburg's required return on equity at different debt ratios. Observe that the cost of

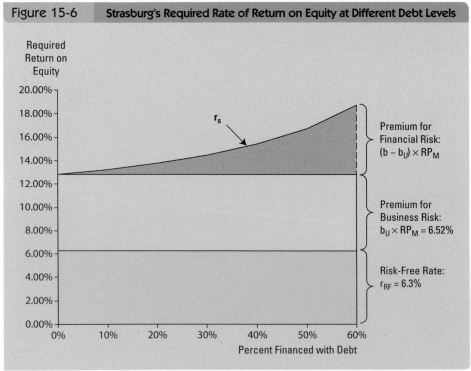

Figure 15-6   Strasburg's Required Rate of Return on Equity at Different Debt Levels

equity consists of the 6.3% risk-free rate, a constant premium for business risk in the amount of $RP_M(b_U) = 6.522\%$, and a premium for financial risk in the amount of $RP_M(b - b_U)$ that starts at zero (because $b = b_U$ for zero debt) but rises at an increasing rate as the debt ratio increases.

15.5c Estimating the Weighted Average Cost of Capital, WACC

Line 6 of Figure 15-5 shows Strasburg's weighted average cost of capital, WACC, at different capital structures. As the debt ratio increases, the costs of both debt and equity rise, at first slowly but then at an accelerating rate. Eventually, the increasing costs of these two components offset the fact that more debt (which is still less costly than equity) is being used. At 40% debt, Strasburg's WACC hits a minimum of 11.63%; Column F is shown in red to indicate that it is the capital structure with the minimum WACC. Notice that the WACC begins to increase for capital structures with more than 40% debt. Figure 15-7 shows how the WACC changes as debt increases.

Note too that, even though the component cost of equity is always higher than that of debt, only using debt would not maximize value. If Strasburg were to issue more than 40% debt, then the costs of both debt and equity would increase in such a way that the overall WACC would increase, because the cost of debt would increase by more than the cost of equity.

15.5d Estimating the Firm's Value

As we showed in Section 15.2, Strasburg currently has a $250 million intrinsic value of operations: $w_d = 20\%$, WACC = 12%, FCF = $30 million, and zero growth in FCF. Using the same approach as in Section 15.2, we can use the data in Figure 15-5 to estimate Strasburg's value of operations at different capital structures; these results are reported in Line 7 of Figure 15-5 and are graphed in Figure 15-8.[28] The maximum

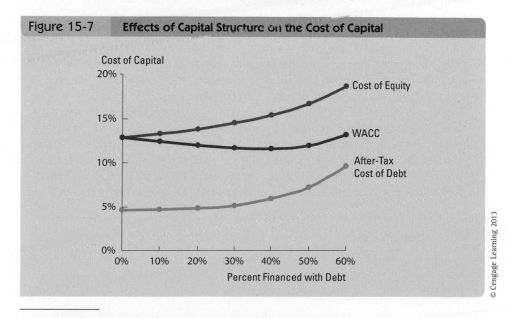

Figure 15-7   Effects of Capital Structure on the Cost of Capital

28. In this analysis we assume that Strasburg's expected EBIT and FCF are constant for the various capital structures. In a more refined analysis we might try to estimate any possible declines in FCF at high levels of debt as the threat of bankruptcy becomes imminent.

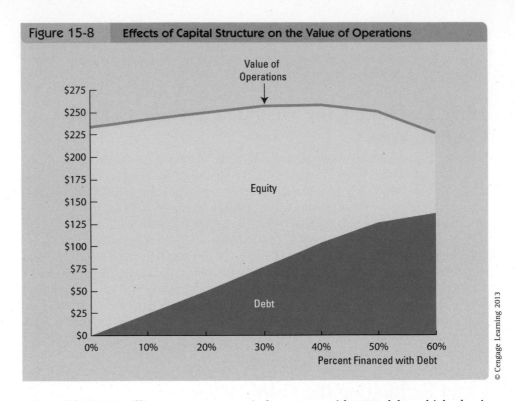

Figure 15-8   Effects of Capital Structure on the Value of Operations

© Cengage Learning 2013

value of $257.86 million occurs at a capital structure with 40% debt, which also is the capital structure that minimizes the WACC.

Notice that the value of the firm initially increases but then begins to fall. As discussed earlier, the value initially rises because the WACC initially falls. But the rising costs of equity and debt eventually cause the WACC to increase, causing the value of the firm to fall. Notice how flat the curve is around the optimal level of debt. Thus, it doesn't make a great deal of difference whether Strasburg's capital structure has 30% debt or 40% debt. Also, notice that the maximum value is about 10% greater than the value with no debt. Although this example is for a single company, the results are typical: The optimal capital structure can add 7% to 15% more value relative to zero debt, and there is a fairly wide range of w_d (from about 20% to 50%) over which value changes very little.

Figures 15-5 and 15-8 also show the values of debt and equity for each capital structure. The value of debt is found by multiplying the value of operations by the percentage of the firm that is financed by debt: $Debt = w_d \times V_{op}$. The intrinsic value of equity is found in a similar manner: $S = V_{op} - Debt = w_s \times V_{op}$. Even though the intrinsic value of equity falls as debt increases, the wealth of shareholders is maximized at the maximum value of operations, as we explain in the next section.

Self Test	What happens to the costs of debt and equity when the leverage increases? Explain.

Use the Hamada equation to calculate the unlevered beta for JAB Industries, assuming the following data: Levered beta = b = 1.4; T = 40%; w_d = 45%. **(0.939)**

Suppose r_{RF} = 6% and RP_M = 5%. What would be the cost of equity for JAB Industries if it had no debt? **(10.7%)** If w_d were 45%? **(13.0%)**

15.6 Anatomy of a Recapitalization

Strasburg should **recapitalize**, meaning that it should issue enough additional debt to optimize its capital structure, and then use the debt proceeds to repurchase stock. As shown in Figure 15-5, a capital structure with 40% debt is optimal. But before tackling the **recap**, as it is commonly called, let's consider the sequence of events, starting with the situation before Strasburg issues any additional debt. Figure 15-3 shows the valuation analysis of Strasburg at a capital structure consisting of 20% debt and 80% equity. These results are repeated in Column 1 of Figure 15-9, along with the shareholder wealth, which consists entirely of $200 million in stock before the repurchase. The next step is to examine the impact of Strasburg's debt issuance.

15.6a Strasburg Issues New Debt but Has Not Yet Repurchased Stock

The next step in the recap is to issue debt and announce the firm's intent to repurchase stock with the newly issued debt. At the optimal capital structure of 40% debt, the value of the firm's operations is $257.86 million, as calculated in Figure 15-5 and repeated in Column 2 of Figure 15-9. This value of operations is greater than the $250 million value of operations for $w_d = 20\%$ because the WACC is lower. Notice that Strasburg raised its debt from $50 million to $103.14 million, an increase of $53.14 million. Because Column 2 reports data prior to the repurchase, Strasburg has short-term investments in the amount of $53.14 million, the amount that was raised in the debt issuance but that has not yet been used to repurchase stock.[29] As Figure 15-9 shows, Strasburg's intrinsic value of equity is $207.86 million.

Because Strasburg has not yet repurchased any stock, it still has 10 million shares outstanding. Therefore, the price per share after the debt issue but prior to the repurchase is

$$P_{Prior} = S_{Prior}/n_{Prior}$$
$$= \$207.86/10 = \$20.79$$

Column 2 of Figure 15-9 summarizes these calculations and also shows the wealth of the shareholders. The shareholders own Strasburg's equity, which is worth $207.86 million. Strasburg has not yet made any cash distributions to shareholders, so the total wealth of shareholders is $207.86 million. The new wealth of $207.86 million is greater than the initial wealth of $200 million, so the recapitalization has added value to Strasburg's shareholders. Notice also that the recapitalization caused the intrinsic stock price to increase from $20.00 to $20.79.

Summarizing these results, we see that the issuance of debt and the resulting change in the optimal capital structure caused (1) the WACC to decrease, (2) the value of operations to increase, (3) shareholder wealth to increase, and (4) the stock price to increase.

15.6b Strasburg Repurchases Stock

What happens to the stock price during the repurchase? In Chapter 17 we discuss repurchases and note that a repurchase does not change the stock price. It is true

---

29. These calculations are shown in the *Excel* file **Ch15 Tool Kit.xls** on the textbook's Web site. The values reported in the text are rounded, but the values used in calculations in the spreadsheet are not rounded.

Figure 15-9	Anatomy of a Recapitalization (Millions, Except Per Share Data)

	A	B	C	D	E	F
335					After Debt	
336				Before Issuing	Issue, but Prior	Post
337				Additional Debt	to Repurchase	Repurchase
338				(1)	(2)	(3)
339						
340		Percent financed with debt: w_d		20%	40%	40%
341						
342		Value of operations		$250.00	$257.86	$257.86
343		+ Value of ST investments		0.00	53.14	0.00
344		Total intrinsic value of firm		$250.00	$311.00	$257.86
345		− Debt		50.00	103.14	103.14
346		Intrinsic value of equity		$200.00	$207.86	$154.72
347		÷ Number of shares		10.00	10.00	7.44
348		Intrinsic price per share		$20.00	$20.79	$20.79
349						
350		Value of stock		$200.00	$207.86	$154.72
351		+ Cash distributed in repurchase		0.00	0.00	53.14
352		Wealth of shareholders		$200.00	$207.86	$207.86

Notes:
1. The value of ST investments in Column 1 is equal to the amount of cash raised by issuing additional debt but that has not been used to repurchase shares: ST investments = $D_{New} - D_{Old}$.
2. The value of ST investments in Column 3 is zero because the funds have been used to repurchase shares of stock.
3. The number of shares in Column 3 reflects the shares repurchased: $n_{Post} = n_{Prior} - (Cash_{Rep}/P_{Prior}) = n_{Prior} - [(D_{New} - D_{Old})/P_{Prior}]$.

that the additional debt will change the WACC and the stock price prior to the repurchase (P_{Prior}), but the subsequent repurchase itself will not affect the post-repurchase stock price (P_{Post}).[30] Therefore, $P_{Post} = P_{Prior}$. (Keep in mind that P_{Prior} is the price immediately prior to the repurchase, not the price prior to the event that led to the cash available for the repurchase, such as the issuance of debt in this example.)

Strasburg uses the entire amount of cash raised by the debt issue to repurchase stock. The total cash raised is equal to $D_{New} - D_{Old}$. The number of shares repurchased is equal to the cash raised by issuing debt divided by the repurchase price:

(15–11)

$$\text{Number of shares repurchased} = \frac{D_{New} - D_{Old}}{P_{Prior}}$$

Strasburg repurchases ($103.14 − $50)/$20.79 = 2.56 million shares of stock.

---

30. As we discuss in Chapter 17, a stock repurchase may be a signal of a company's future prospects or it may be the way a company "announces" a change in capital structure, and either of these situations could have an impact on estimated free cash flows or WACC. However, neither situation applies to Strasburg.

The number of remaining shares after the repurchase, n_{Post}, is equal to the initial number of shares minus the number that is repurchased:

$$n_{Post} = \text{Number of outstanding shares remaining after the repurchase}$$

$$= n_{Prior} - \text{Number of shares repurchased}$$

$$= n_{Prior} - \frac{D_{New} - D_{Old}}{P_{Prior}}$$

(15–12)

For Strasburg, the number of remaining shares after the repurchase is

$$n_{Post} = n_{Prior} - (D_{New} - D_{Old})/P_{Prior}$$
$$= 10 - (\$103.14 - \$50)/\$20.79$$
$$= 7.44 \text{ million}$$

Column 3 of Figure 15-9 summarizes these post-repurchase results. The repurchase doesn't change the value of operations, which remains at $257.86 million. However, the short-term investments are sold and the cash is used to repurchase stock. Strasburg is left with no short-term investments, so the intrinsic value of equity is:

$$S_{Post} = \$257.86 - \$103.14 = \$154.72 \text{ million}$$

After the repurchase, Strasburg has 7.44 million shares of stock. We can verify that the intrinsic stock price has not changed:[31]

$$P_{Post} = S_{Post}/n_{Post} = \$154.72/7.44 = \$20.79$$

Shareholders now own an equity position in the company worth only $154.72 million, but they have received a cash distribution in the amount of $53.14 million, so their total wealth is equal to the value of their equity plus the amount of cash they received: $154.72 + $53.14 = $207.86.

Here are some points worth noting. As shown in Column 3 of Figure 15-9, the change in capital structure clearly added wealth to the shareholders, increased the price per share, and increased the cash (in the form of short-term investments) temporarily held by the company. However, the repurchase itself did not affect shareholder wealth or the price per share. The repurchase did reduce the cash held by the company and the number of shares outstanding, but shareholder wealth stayed constant. After the repurchase, shareholders directly own the funds used in the repurchase; before the repurchase, shareholders indirectly own the funds. In either case, shareholders own the funds. The repurchase simply takes them out of the company's account and puts them into the shareholders' personal accounts.

The approach we've described here is based on the corporate valuation model, and it will always provide the correct value for S_{Post}, and n_{Post}, and P_{Post}. However, there is a quicker way to calculate these values if the firm has no short-term investments

---

31. There may be a small rounding difference due to using rounded numbers in intermediate steps. See the *Excel* file *Ch15 Tool Kit.xls* for the exact calculations.

either before or after the recap (other than the temporary short-term investments held between the time debt was issued and shares repurchased). After the recap is completed, the percentage of equity in the capital structure, based on market values, is equal to $1 - w_d$ if the firm holds no other short-term investments. Therefore, the value of equity after the repurchase is

$$(15\text{--}13) \qquad S_{Post} = V_{opNew}(1 - w_d)$$

where we use the subscript "New" to indicate the value of operations at the new capital structure and the subscript "Post" to indicate the post-repurchase intrinsic value of equity.

The post-repurchase number of shares can be found using this equation:

$$(15\text{--}14) \qquad n_{Post} = n_{Prior}\left[\frac{V_{opNew} - D_{New}}{V_{opNew} - D_{Old}}\right]$$

Given the value of equity and the number of shares, it is straightforward to calculate the intrinsic price per share as $P_{Post} = S_{Post}/n_{Post}$. But we can also calculate the post-repurchase price using

$$(15\text{--}15) \qquad P_{Post} = \frac{V_{opNew} - D_{Old}}{n_{Prior}}$$

Figure 15-5 reports the number of shares and the intrinsic price per share in Lines 9–10. Notice that the number of shares goes down as debt goes up because the debt proceeds are used to buy back stock. Notice also that the capital structure that maximizes stock price, $w_d = 40\%$, is the same capital structure that optimizes the WACC and the value of operations.

Figure 15-5 also reports the earnings per share for the different levels of debt. Figure 15-10 graphs the intrinsic price per share and the earnings per share. Notice that the maximum earnings per share is at 50% debt even though the optimal capital structure is at 40% debt. This means that maximizing EPS will not maximize shareholder wealth.

15.6c Recapitalizations: A Post-Mortem

In Chapter 11, we looked at value-based management and saw how companies can increase their value by improving their operations. Yet there is good news and bad news regarding this connection. The good news is that small improvements in operations can lead to huge increases in value. The bad news is that it's often difficult to improve operations, especially if the company is already well managed and is in a competitive industry.

If instead you seek to increase a firm's value by changing its capital structure, we again have good news and bad news. The good news is that changing capital structure is easy—just call an investment banker and issue debt (or issue equity if

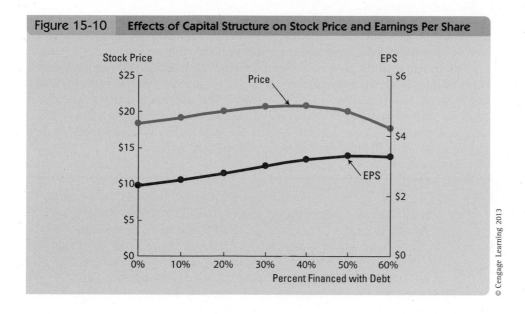

Figure 15-10   **Effects of Capital Structure on Stock Price and Earnings Per Share**

© Cengage Learning 2013

THE GLOBAL ECONOMIC CRISIS

Deleveraging

Many households, nonfinancial businesses, and financial institutions loaded up on easy credit during the run-up to the global economic crisis and found themselves with too much debt during the recession that began in 2007. The process of reducing debt is called *deleveraging*, and it is painful for individuals and the economy.

The debt-to-income ratio for households increased from around 80%–90% during the 1990s to a peak of 133% in 2007. To deleverage, many households are cutting spending on consumer goods and paying off some of their debt. This belt-tightening is difficult for the individual households, but it also is difficult for the economy because decreased spending leads to economic contraction and job losses. Other households are deleveraging by declaring bankruptcy, with over 1.5 million people filing in 2010 and even more expected to file by the end of 2011

Like individuals, businesses can deleverage by paying off debt or by declaring bankruptcy, and many are doing

so during this global economic crisis.
But businesses can also deleverage by issuing equity. For example, Dunkin' Brands Group, owner of the Dunkin' Donuts and Baskin-Robbins brands, issued $427 million in stock in July 2011, part of which will be used to pay down debt. And Wells Fargo and Morgan Stanley issued over $12 billion in stock in May of 2009. A problem with deleveraging via stock issuances is that the stock price usually has been beaten down so much by the time of deleveraging that the new investors get a larger stake in the company, which dilutes the existing stockholders. But the bottom line is that dilution is better than bankruptcy!

Sources: Reuven Glick and Kevin J. Lansing, "U.S. Household Deleveraging and Future Consumption Growth," FRBSF Economic Letter, May 15, 2009, **www.frbsf.org/publications/economics /letter/2009/el2009-16.pdf**; and **BankruptcyAction.com**, **www.bankruptcyaction.com/USbankstats.htm**, August 2011.

the firm has too much debt). The bad news is that this will add only a relatively small amount of value. Of course, any additional value is better than none, so it's hard to understand why there are some mature firms with zero debt.

Finally, some firms have more debt than is optimal and should recapitalize to a lower debt level. This is called *deleveraging*. We can use exactly the same approach and the same formulas as we used for Strasburg. The difference is that the debt will go down and the number of shares will go up. In other words, the company will issue new shares of stock and then use the proceeds to pay off debt, resulting in a capital structure with less debt and lower interest payments.

Self Test

A firm's value of operations is equal to $800 million after a recapitalization (the firm had no debt before the recap). The firm raised $200 million in new debt and used this to buy back stock. The firm had no short-term investments before or after the recap. After the recap, $w_d = 25\%$. The firm had 10 million shares before the recap. What is S (the value of equity after the recap)? **($600 million)** What is P (the stock price after the recap)? **($80/share)** What is n (the number of remaining shares after the recap)? **(7.5 million)**

Summary

This chapter examined the effects of financial leverage on stock prices, earnings per share, and the cost of capital. The key concepts covered are listed below.

- A firm's **optimal capital structure** is the mix of debt and equity that maximizes the stock price. At any point in time, management has a specific **target capital structure** in mind, presumably the optimal one, although this target may change over time.
- Several factors influence a firm's capital structure. These include its (1) **business risk,** (2) **tax position,** (3) need for **financial flexibility,** (4) **managerial conservatism or aggressiveness,** and (5) **growth opportunities.**
- **Business risk** is the risk inherent in the firm's operations if it uses no debt. A firm will have little business risk if the demand for its products is stable, if the prices of its inputs and products remain relatively constant, if it can adjust its prices freely if costs increase, and if a high percentage of its costs are variable and hence will decrease if sales decrease. Other things the same, the lower a firm's business risk, the higher its optimal debt ratio.
- **Financial leverage** is the extent to which fixed-income securities (debt and preferred stock) are used in a firm's capital structure. **Financial risk** is the added risk borne by stockholders as a result of financial leverage.
- **Operating leverage** is the extent to which fixed costs are used in a firm's operations. In business terminology, a high degree of operating leverage, other factors held constant, implies that a relatively small change in sales results in a large change in ROIC. *Web Extension 15A* describes additional measures of operating and financial leverage.

- If there are no corporate or personal taxes, Modigliani and Miller showed that the value of a levered firm is equal to the value of an otherwise identical but unlevered firm:

$$V_L = V_U$$

- If there are only corporate taxes, Modigliani and Miller showed that a firm's value increases as it adds debt due to the interest rate deductibility of debt:

$$V_L = V_U + TD$$

- If there are personal and corporate taxes, Miller showed that

$$V_L = V_U + \left[1 - \frac{(1 - T_C)(1 - T_S)}{(1 - T_d)}\right]D$$

- The **Hamada equation** shows the effect of financial leverage on beta as follows:

$$b = b_U[1 + (1 - T)(D/S)]$$

Firms can use their current beta, tax rate, and debt/equity ratio to derive their **unlevered beta, b_U,** as follows:

$$b_U = b/[1 + (1 - T)(D/S)] = b/[1 + (1 - T)(w_d/w_s)]$$

- **The trade-off theory of capital structure** states that debt initially adds value because interest is **tax deductible** but that debt also brings costs associated with actual or potential bankruptcy. The optimal capital structure strikes a balance between the tax benefits of debt and the costs associated with bankruptcy.
- A firm's decision to use debt versus stock to raise new capital sends a **signal** to investors. A stock issue is viewed as a negative signal, whereas a debt issuance is a positive (or at least a neutral) signal. As a result, companies try to avoid having to issue stock by maintaining a **reserve borrowing capacity,** and this means using less debt in "normal" times than the trade-off theory would suggest.
- A firm's owners may decide to use a relatively large amount of debt to constrain the managers. A **high debt ratio raises the threat of bankruptcy,** which not only carries a cost but also forces managers to be more careful and less wasteful with shareholders' money. Many of the corporate takeovers and leveraged buyouts in recent years were designed to improve efficiency by reducing the cash flow available to managers.

Questions

15-1 Define each of the following terms:
    a. Capital structure; business risk; financial risk
    b. Operating leverage; financial leverage; break-even point
    c. Reserve borrowing capacity
15-2 What term refers to the uncertainty inherent in projections of future ROIC?
15-3 Firms with relatively high nonfinancial fixed costs are said to have a high degree of what?
15-4 "One type of leverage affects both EBIT and EPS. The other type affects only EPS." Explain this statement.

15-5 Why is the following statement true? "Other things being the same, firms with relatively stable sales are able to carry relatively high debt ratios."

15-6 Why do public utility companies usually have capital structures that are different from those of retail firms?

15-7 Why is EBIT generally considered to be independent of financial leverage? Why might EBIT actually be influenced by financial leverage at high debt levels?

15-8 If a firm went from zero debt to successively higher levels of debt, why would you expect its stock price to first rise, then hit a peak, and then begin to decline?

Problems   Answers Appear in Appendix B

Easy Problems 1–6

15-1 **Break-even Quantity** Shapland Inc. has fixed operating costs of $500,000 and variable costs of $50 per unit. If it sells the product for $75 per unit, what is the break-even quantity?

15-2 **Unlevered Beta** Counts Accounting has a beta of 1.15. The tax rate is 40%, and Counts is financed with 20% debt. What is Counts's unlevered beta?

15-3 **Premium for Financial Risk** Ethier Enterprise has an unlevered beta of 1.0. Ethier is financed with 50% debt and has a levered beta of 1.6. If the risk-free rate is 5.5% and the market risk premium is 6%, how much is the additional premium that Ethier's shareholders require to be compensated for financial risk?

15-4 **Value of Equity after Recapitalization** Nichols Corporation's value of operations is equal to $500 million after a recapitalization (the firm had no debt before the recap). It raised $200 million in new debt and used this to buy back stock. Nichols had no short-term investments before or after the recap. After the recap, $w_d = 40\%$. What is S (the value of equity after the recap)?

15-5 **Stock Price after Recapitalization** Lee Manufacturing's value of operations is equal to $900 million after a recapitalization (the firm had no debt before the recap). Lee raised $300 million in new debt and used this to buy back stock. Lee had no short-term investments before or after the recap. After the recap, $w_d = 1/3$. The firm had 30 million shares before the recap. What is P (the stock price after the recap)?

15-6 **Shares Remaining after Recapitalization** Dye Trucking raised $150 million in new debt and used this to buy back stock. After the recap, Dye's stock price is $7.50. If Dye had 60 million shares of stock before the recap, how many shares does it have after the recap?

Intermediate Problems 7–8

15-7 **Break-even Point** Schweser Satellites Inc. produces satellite earth stations that sell for $100,000 each. The firm's fixed costs, F, are $2 million, 50 earth stations are produced and sold each year, profits total $500,000, and the firm's assets (all equity financed) are $5 million. The firm estimates that it can change its production process, adding $4 million to investment and $500,000 to fixed operating costs. This change will (1) reduce variable costs per unit by $10,000 and (2) increase output by 20 units, but (3) the sales price on all units will have to be lowered to $95,000 to permit sales of the additional output. The firm has tax loss carryforwards that render its tax rate zero, its cost of equity is 16%, and it uses no debt.

a. What is the incremental profit? To get a rough idea of the project's profitability, what is the project's expected rate of return for the next year (defined as the incremental profit divided by the investment)? Should the firm make the investment?
b. Would the firm's break-even point increase or decrease if it made the change?
c. Would the new situation expose the firm to more or less business risk than the old one?

15-8 **Capital Structure Analysis** The Rivoli Company has no debt outstanding, and its financial position is given by the following data:

Assets (Market value = book value)	$3,000,000
EBIT	$500,000
Cost of equity, r_s	10%
Stock price, P_0	$15
Shares outstanding, n_0	200,000
Tax rate, T (federal-plus-state)	40%

The firm is considering selling bonds and simultaneously repurchasing some of its stock. If it moves to a capital structure with 30% debt based on market values, its cost of equity, r_s, will increase to 11% to reflect the increased risk. Bonds can be sold at a cost, r_d, of 7%. Rivoli is a no-growth firm. Hence, all its earnings are paid out as dividends. Earnings are expected to be constant over time.

a. What effect would this use of leverage have on the value of the firm?
b. What would be the price of Rivoli's stock?
c. What happens to the firm's earnings per share after the recapitalization?
d. The $500,000 EBIT given previously is actually the expected value from the following probability distribution:

Probability	EBIT
0.10	($ 100,000)
0.20	200,000
0.40	500,000
0.20	800,000
0.10	1,100,000

Determine the times-interest-earned ratio for each probability. What is the probability of not covering the interest payment at the 30% debt level?

Challenging Problems 9–11

15-9 **Capital Structure Analysis** Pettit Printing Company has a total market value of $100 million, consisting of 1 million shares selling for $50 per share and $50 million of 10% perpetual bonds now selling at par. The company's EBIT is $13.24 million, and its tax rate is 15%. Pettit can change its capital structure either by increasing its debt to 70% (based on market values) or decreasing it to 30%. If it decides to *increase* its use of leverage, it must call its old bonds and issue new ones with a 12% coupon. If it decides to *decrease* its leverage, it will call its old bonds and replace them with new 8% coupon bonds. The company will sell or repurchase stock at the new equilibrium price to complete the capital structure change.

The firm pays out all earnings as dividends; hence its stock is a zero-growth stock. Its current cost of equity, r_s, is 14%. If it increases leverage, r_s will be 16%. If it decreases leverage, r_s will be 13%. What is the firm's WACC and total corporate value under each capital structure?

15-10 **Optimal Capital Structure with Hamada** Beckman Engineering and Associates (BEA) is considering a change in its capital structure. BEA currently has $20 million in debt carrying a rate of 8%, and its stock price is $40 per share with 2 million shares outstanding. BEA is a zero-growth firm and pays out all of its earnings as dividends. The firm's EBIT is $14.933 million, and it faces a 40% federal-plus-state tax rate. The market risk premium is 4%, and the risk-free rate is 6%. BEA is considering increasing its debt level to a capital structure with 40% debt, based on market values, and repurchasing shares with the extra money that it borrows. BEA will have to retire the old debt in order to issue new debt, and the rate on the new debt will be 9%. BEA has a beta of 1.0.

a. What is BEA's unlevered beta? Use market value D/S (which is the same as w_d/w_s) when unlevering.

b. What are BEA's new beta and cost of equity if it has 40% debt?

c. What are BEA's WACC and total value of the firm with 40% debt?

15-11 **WACC and Optimal Capital Structure** F. Pierce Products Inc. is considering changing its capital structure. F. Pierce currently has no debt and no preferred stock, but would like to add some debt to take advantage of low interest rates and the tax shield. Its investment banker has indicated that the pre-tax cost of debt under various possible capital structures would be as follows:

Market Debt-to-Value Ratio (w_d)	Market Equity-to-Value Ratio (w_s)	Market Debt-to-Equity Ratio (D/S)	Before-Tax Cost of Debt (r_d)
0.0	1.0	0.00	6.0%
0.2	0.8	0.25	7.0
0.4	0.6	0.67	8.0
0.6	0.4	1.50	9.0
0.8	0.2	4.00	10.0

F. Pierce uses the CAPM to estimate its cost of common equity, r_s and at the time of the analysis the risk-free rate is 5%, the market risk premium is 6%, and the company's tax rate is 40%. F. Pierce estimates that its beta now (which is "unlevered" since it currently has no debt) is 0.8. Based on this information, what is the firm's optimal capital structure, and what would be the weighted average cost of capital at the optimal capital structure?

Spreadsheet Problem

15-12 **Build a Model: WACC and Optimal Capital Structure** Start with the partial model in the file *Ch15 P12 Build a Model.xls* on the textbook's Web site. Reacher Technology has consulted with investment bankers and determined the interest rate it would pay for different capital structures, as shown in the following table. Data for the risk-free rate, the market risk premium, an estimate of Reacher's unlevered beta, and the tax rate are also shown. Based on this information, what is the firm's optimal capital structure, and what is the weighted average cost of capital at the optimal structure?

Percent Financed with Debt (w_d)	Before-Tax Cost Debt (r_d)
0%	6.0%
10	6.1
20	7.0
30	8.0
40	10.0
50	12.5
60	15.5
70	18.0

Input Data	
Risk-free rate	4.5%
Market risk premium	5.5%
Unlevered beta	0.8
Tax rate	40.0%

 THOMSON REUTERS

Use the Thomson ONE—Business School Edition online database to work this chapter's questions.

Exploring the Capital Structures for Three Global Auto Companies

The following discussion questions demonstrate how we can evaluate the capital structures for three global automobile companies: Ford (F), BMW (BMW), and Toyota (J:TYMO). As you gather information on these companies, be mindful of the currencies in which these companies' financial data are reported.

Discussion Questions

1 To get an overall picture of each company's capital structure, it is helpful to see a chart that summarizes the company's capital structure over the past decade. To obtain this chart, choose a company to start with and select FINANCIALS. Next, select MORE>THOMSON REPORTS & CHARTS>CAPITAL STRUCTURE. This should generate a chart that plots the company's long-term debt, common equity, and total current liabilities over the past decade. What, if any, are the major trends that emerge from looking at these charts? Do these companies tend to have relatively high or relatively low levels of debt? Do these companies have significant levels of current liabilities? Have their capital structures changed over time?

2. To obtain more details about the companies' capital structures over the past 5 years, select FINANCIALS>FINANCIAL RATIOS>THOMSON RATIOS. From here you can select ANNUAL RATIOS and/or 5 YEAR AVERAGE RATIOS REPORT. In each case, you can scroll down and look for Leverage Ratios. Here you will find a variety of leverage ratios for the past 5 years. (Notice that these two pages offer different information. The ANNUAL RATIOS page offers year-end leverage ratios, whereas the 5 YEAR AVERAGE RATIOS REPORT offers the average ratio over the previous 5 years for each calendar date. In other words, the 5 YEAR AVERAGE RATIOS REPORT smoothes the changes in capital structure over the

Selected Additional Cases

The following cases from TextChoice, Cengage Learning's online case library, cover many of the concepts discussed in this chapter and are available at **www.textchoice2.com/casenet.**

Klein-Brigham Series:
Case 9, "Kleen Kar, Inc.," Case 43, "Mountain Springs, Inc.," and Case 57, "Greta Cosmetics, Inc.," each present a situation similar to the Strasburg example in the text. Case 74, "The Western Company," and Case 99, "Moore Plumbing Supply," explore capital structure policies.

Brigham-Buzzard Series:
Case 8, "Powerline Network Corporation (Operating Leverage, Financial Leverage, and the Optimal Capital Structure)."

Chapter 16

Capital Structure Decisions: Part II

Chapter 15 presented basic material on capital structure, including an introduction to capital structure theory. We saw that debt concentrates a firm's business risk on its stockholders, thus raising stockholders' risk, but it also increases the expected return on equity. We also saw there is some optimal level of debt that maximizes a company's stock price, and we illustrated this concept with a simple model. Now we go into more detail on capital structure theory. This will give you a deeper understanding of the benefits and costs associated with debt financing.

Beginning of Chapter Questions

As you read the chapter, consider how you would answer the following questions. You *should not* necessarily be able to answer the questions before you read the chapter. Rather, you should use them to get a sense of the issues covered in the chapter. After reading the chapter, you should be able to give at least partial answers to the questions, and you should be able to give better answers after the chapter has been discussed in class. Note, too, that it is often useful, when answering conceptual questions, to use hypothetical data to illustrate your answer. We illustrate the answers with an *Excel* model that is available on the textbook's Web site. Accessing the model and working through it is a useful exercise, and it provides insights that are useful when answering the questions.

1. What is **arbitrage,** and how did Modigliani and Miller use the arbitrage concept in developing their theory that (with no corporate taxes) capital structure has no effect on value or the cost of capital? What real-world impediments exist to creating one's own "homemade" leverage?

2. What is the essence of Miller's contribution to the theory of capital structure, and how does it relate to the earlier MM with-taxes position?

3. MM and Miller assumed that firms do not grow. If they grow, how would this affect the value of the debt tax shield? What does growth do to the required rate of return on equity and the WACC as a firm increases its use of debt?

4. MM and Miller also assumed that debt is riskless. How does the possibility of default on debt cause equity to take on the characteristics of an option? What types of incentives for shareholders does this lead to?

WEB

The textbook's Web site contains an *Excel* file that will guide you through the chapter's calculations. The file for this chapter is ***Ch16 Tool Kit.xls***, and we encourage you to open the file and follow along as you read the chapter.

16.1 Capital Structure Theory: Arbitrage Proofs of the Modigliani-Miller Models

Until 1958, capital structure theory consisted of loose assertions about investor behavior rather than carefully constructed models that could be tested by formal statistical analysis. In what has been called the most influential set of financial papers ever published, Franco Modigliani and Merton Miller (MM) addressed capital structure in a rigorous, scientific fashion, and they set off a chain of research that continues to this day.[1]

16.1a Assumptions

As we explain in this chapter, MM employed the concept of **arbitrage** to develop their theory. Arbitrage occurs if two similar assets—in this case, levered and unlevered stocks—sell at different prices. Arbitrageurs will buy the undervalued stock and simultaneously sell the overvalued stock, earning a profit in the process, and will continue doing so until market forces of supply and demand cause the prices of the two assets to be equal. For arbitrage to work, the assets must be equivalent,

1. See Franco Modigliani and Merton H. Miller, "The Cost of Capital, Corporation Finance and the Theory of Investment," *American Economic Review,* June 1958, pp. 261–297; "The Cost of Capital, Corporation Finance and the Theory of Investment: Reply," *American Economic Review,* September 1958, pp. 655–669; "Taxes and the Cost of Capital: A Correction," *American Economic Review,* June 1963, pp. 433–443; and "Reply," *American Economic Review,* June 1965, pp. 524–527. In a survey of Financial Management Association members, the original MM article was judged to have had the greatest impact on the field of finance of any work ever published. See Philip L. Cooley and J. Louis Heck, "Significant Contributions to Finance Literature," *Financial Management,* Tenth Anniversary Issue, 1981, pp. 23–33. Note that both Modigliani and Miller won Nobel Prizes—Modigliani in 1985 and Miller in 1990.

CORPORATE VALUATION AND CAPITAL STRUCTURE DECISIONS

A firm's financing choices obviously have a direct effect on its weighted average cost of capital (WACC). Financing choices also have an indirect effect because they change the risk and required return of debt and equity. This chapter focuses on the debt–equity choice and its effect on value.

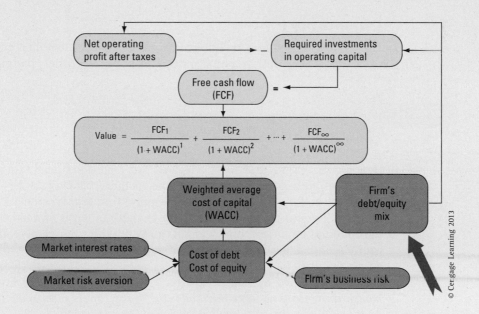

© Cengage Learning 2013

or nearly so. MM show that, under their assumptions, levered and unlevered stocks are sufficiently similar for the arbitrage process to operate.

No one, not even MM, believes their assumptions are sufficiently correct that their models will hold exactly in the real world. However, their models do show how money can be made through arbitrage if one can find ways around problems with the assumptions. Though some of them were later relaxed, here are the initial MM assumptions.

1. There are *no taxes*, either personal or corporate.
2. Business risk can be measured by σ_{EBIT}, and firms with the same degree of business risk are said to be in a *homogeneous risk class.*
3. All present and prospective investors have identical estimates of each firm's future EBIT; that is, investors have *homogeneous expectations* about expected future corporate earnings and the riskiness of those earnings.
4. Stocks and bonds are traded in *perfect capital markets.* This assumption implies, among other things, (a) that there are no brokerage costs and (b) that investors (both individuals and institutions) can borrow at the same rate as corporations.
5. *Debt is riskless.* This applies to both firms and investors, so the interest rate on all debt is the risk-free rate. Further, this situation holds regardless of how much debt a firm (or individual) uses.

6. All cash flows are *perpetuities;* that is, all firms expect zero growth and hence have an "expectationally constant" EBIT, and all bonds are perpetuities. "Expectationally constant" means that the best guess is that EBIT will be constant, although after the fact the realized level could be different from the expected level.

16.1b MM without Taxes

MM first analyzed leverage under the assumption that there are no corporate or personal income taxes. On the basis of their assumptions, they stated and algebraically proved two propositions.[2]

Proposition I

The value of any firm is established by capitalizing its expected net operating income (EBIT) at a constant rate (r_{sU}) that is based on the firm's risk class:

(16–1)
$$V_L = V_U = \frac{EBIT}{WACC} = \frac{EBIT}{r_{sU}}$$

Here the subscript L designates a levered firm and U designates an unlevered firm. Both firms are assumed to be in the same business risk class, and r_{sU} is the required rate of return for an unlevered (i.e., all-equity) firm of this risk class when there are no taxes. For our purposes, it is easiest to think in terms of a single firm that has the option of financing either with all equity or with some combination of debt and equity. Hence, L designates a firm that uses some amount of debt and U designates a firm that uses no debt.

As established by Equation 16-1, V is a constant; therefore, *under the MM model, if there are no taxes then the value of the firm is independent of its leverage.* As we shall see, this also implies the following statements.

1. The weighted average cost of capital, WACC, is completely independent of a firm's capital structure.
2. Regardless of the amount of debt a firm uses, its WACC is equal to the cost of equity that it would have if it used no debt.

Proposition II

When there are no taxes, the cost of equity to a levered firm, r_{sL}, is equal to (1) the cost of equity to an unlevered firm in the same risk class, r_{sU}, plus (2) a risk premium whose size depends on (a) the difference between an unlevered firm's costs of debt and equity and (b) the amount of debt used:

(16–2)
$$r_{sL} = r_{sU} + \text{Risk premium} = r_{sU} + (r_{sU} - r_d)(D/S)$$

Here D is the market value of the firm's debt, S is the market value of its equity, and r_d is the constant cost of debt. Equation 16-2 states that, *as debt increases, the cost*

---

2. Modigliani and Miller actually stated and proved three propositions, but the third one is not material to our discussion here.

of equity rises in a mathematically precise manner (even though the cost of debt does not rise).

Taken together, the two MM propositions imply that using more debt in the capital structure will not increase the value of the firm, because the benefits of cheaper debt will be exactly offset by an increase in the riskiness of the equity and hence in its cost. Thus MM argue that, *in a world without taxes, both the value of a firm and its WACC would be unaffected by its capital structure.*

16.1c MM's Arbitrage Proof

Propositions I and II are important because they showed for the first time that any valuation effects due to the use of debt must arise from taxes or other market frictions. The technique that MM used to prove these propositions is equally important, however, so we discuss it in detail here. They used an *arbitrage proof* to support their propositions, and this proof technique was later used in the development of option pricing models that revolutionized the securities industry.[3] Modigliani and Miller showed that, under their assumptions, if two companies differed only (1) in the way they were financed and (2) in their total market values, then investors would sell shares of the higher-valued firm, buy those of the lower-valued firm, and continue this process until the companies had exactly the same market value. To illustrate, assume that two firms, L and U, are identical in all important respects except that Firm L has $4,000,000 of 7.5% debt while Firm U uses only equity. Both firms have EBIT = $900,000, and σ_{EBIT} is the same for both firms, so they are in the same business risk class.

Modigliani and Miller assumed that all firms are in a zero-growth situation. In other words, EBIT is expected to remain constant; this will occur if ROE is constant, all earnings are paid out as dividends, and there are no taxes. Under the constant EBIT assumption, the total market value of the common stock, S, is the present value of a perpetuity, which is found as follows:

$$S = \frac{\text{Dividends}}{r_{sL}} = \frac{\text{Net income}}{r_{sL}} = \frac{\text{EBIT} - r_d D}{r_{sL}} \qquad \text{(16–3)}$$

Equation 16-3 is merely the value of a perpetuity, where the numerator is the net income available to common stockholders (all of which is paid out as dividends) and the denominator is the cost of common equity. Since there are no taxes, the numerator is not multiplied by $(1 - T)$, as it was when we calculated NOPAT in Chapters 7 and 11.

Assume that initially, *before any arbitrage occurs*, both firms have the same equity capitalization rate (that is, required rate of return on equity): $r_{sU} = r_{sL} = 10\%$. Under this condition, according to Equation 16-3, the following situation would exist.

---

3. By *arbitrage* we mean the simultaneous buying and selling of essentially identical assets that sell at different prices. The buying increases the price of the undervalued asset, and the selling decreases the price of the overvalued asset. Arbitrage operations will continue until prices have adjusted to the point where the arbitrageur can no longer earn a profit, at which point the market is in equilibrium. In the absence of transaction costs, equilibrium requires that the prices of the two assets be equal.

Firm U:

$$\text{Value of Firm U's stock} = S_U = \frac{\text{EBIT} - r_d D}{r_{sU}}$$

$$= \frac{\$900,000 - \$0}{0.10} = \$9,000,000$$

$$\text{Total market value of Firm U} = V_U = D_U + S_U = \$0 + \$9,000,000$$

$$= \$9,000,000$$

Firm L:

$$\text{Value of Firm L's stock} = S_L = \frac{\text{EBIT} - r_d D}{r_{sL}}$$

$$= \frac{\$900,000 - 0.075(\$4,000,000)}{0.10} = \frac{\$600,000}{10}$$

$$= \$6,000,000$$

$$\text{Total market value of Firm L} = V_L = D_L + S_L = \$4,000,000 + \$6,000,000$$

$$= \$10,000,000$$

Thus, before arbitrage (and assuming that $r_{sU} = r_{sL}$, which implies that capital structure has no effect on the cost of equity), the value of the levered Firm L exceeds that of the unlevered Firm U.

Modigliani and Miller argued that this result is a disequilibrium that cannot persist. To see why, suppose you owned 10% of L's stock and so the market value of your investment was 0.10($6,000,000) = $600,000. According to MM, you could increase your income without increasing your exposure to risk. For example, you could (1) sell your stock in L for $600,000, (2) borrow an amount equal to 10% of L's debt ($400,000), and then (3) buy 10% of U's stock for $900,000. Note that you would receive $1,000,000 from the sale of your 10% of L's stock plus your borrowing, and you would be spending only $900,000 on U's stock. Hence you would have an extra $100,000, which you could invest in riskless debt to yield 7.5%, or $7,500 annually. Now consider your income positions:

Old Portfolio		New Portfolio	
10% of L's $600,000 equity income	$60,000	10% of U's $900,000 equity income	$90,000
		Less 7.5% interest on $400,000 loan	(30,000)
		Plus 7.5% interest on extra $100,000	7,500
Total income	$60,000	Total income	$67,500

Thus, your net income from common stock would be exactly the same as before, $60,000, but you would have $100,000 left over for investment in riskless debt and this would increase your income by $7,500. Therefore, the total return on your $600,000 net worth would rise to $67,500. And your risk, according to MM, would be the same as before, because you would have simply substituted $400,000 of "homemade" leverage for your 10% share of Firm L's $4 million of corporate leverage. Thus, neither your "effective" debt nor your risk would have changed. Therefore, you would have increased your income without raising your risk, which is obviously desirable.

Modigliani and Miller argued that this arbitrage process would actually occur, with sales of L's stock driving its price down and purchases of U's stock driving its price up, until the market values of the two firms were equal. Until this equality was established, gains could be obtained by switching from one stock to the other; hence the profit motive would force equality to be reached. When equilibrium is established, the values of Firms L and U must be equal, which is what Proposition I states. If their values are equal, then Equation 16-1 implies that WACC = r_{sU}. Because there are no taxes, we have

$$\text{WACC} = [D/(D+S)]r_d + [S/(D+S)]r_{sL}$$

and a little algebra then yields

$$r_{sL} = r_{sU} + (r_{sU} - r_d)(D/S)$$

which is what Proposition II states. Thus, according to MM, both a firm's value and its WACC must be independent of capital structure.

Note that each of the assumptions listed at the beginning of this section is necessary for the arbitrage proof to work exactly. For example, if the companies did not have identical business risk or if transaction costs were significant, then the arbitrage process could not be invoked. We discuss other implications of the assumptions later in the chapter.

16.1d Arbitrage with Short Sales

Even if you did not own any stock in L, you still could reap benefits if U and L did not have the same total market value. Your first step would be to sell short $600,000 of stock in L. To do this, your broker would let you borrow stock in L from another client. Your broker would then sell the stock for you and give you the proceeds, or $600,000 in cash. You would supplement this $600,000 by borrowing $400,000. With the $1 million total, you would buy 10% of the stock in U for $900,000 and have $100,000 remaining.

Your position would then consist of $100,000 in cash and two portfolios. The first portfolio would contain $900,000 of stock in U, which would generate $90,000 of income. Because you would own the stock, we'll call it the "long" portfolio. The other portfolio would consist of $600,000 of stock in L and $400,000 of debt. The value of this portfolio is $1 million, and it would generate $60,000 of dividends and $30,000 of interest. However, you would not own this second portfolio—you would "owe" it. Since you borrowed the $400,000, you would owe the $30,000 in interest. And since you borrowed the stock in L, you would "owe the stock" to the client from whom it was borrowed. Therefore, you would have to pay your broker the $60,000 of dividends paid by L, which the broker would then pass on to the client from whom the stock was borrowed. Thus your net cash flow from the second portfolio would be a negative $90,000. Because you would "owe" this portfolio, we'll call it the "short" portfolio.

Where would you get the $90,000 that you must pay on the short portfolio? The good news is that this is exactly the amount of cash flow generated by your long portfolio. Because the cash flows generated by each portfolio are the same, the short portfolio "replicates" the long portfolio.

Here is the bottom line. You started out with no money of your own. By selling L short, borrowing $400,000, and purchasing stock in U, you ended up with $100,000 in cash plus the two portfolios. The portfolios mirror one another, so their net cash flow is zero. This is perfect arbitrage: You invest none of your own money, you have no risk, you have no future negative cash flows, but you end up with cash in your pocket.

Not surprisingly, many traders would want to do this. The selling pressure on L would cause its price to fall, and the buying pressure on U would cause its price to rise, until the two companies' values were equal. To put it another way, *if the long and short replicating portfolios have the same cash flows, then arbitrage will force them to have the same value.*

This is one of the most important ideas in modern finance. Not only does it give us insights into capital structure, but it is the fundamental building block underlying the valuation of real and financial options and derivatives as discussed in Chapters 6 and 24. Without the concept of arbitrage, the options and derivatives markets we have today simply would not exist.

16.1e MM with Corporate Taxes

Modigliani and Miller's original work, published in 1958, assumed zero taxes. In 1963, they published a second article that incorporated corporate taxes. With corporate income taxes, they concluded that leverage will increase a firm's value. This occurs because interest is a tax-deductible expense; hence more of a levered firm's operating income flows through to investors.

Later in this chapter we present a proof of the MM propositions when personal taxes as well as corporate taxes are allowed. The situation when there are corporate taxes but no personal taxes is a special instance of the situation with both personal and corporate taxes, so we only present results in this case.

Proposition I

The value of a levered firm is equal to the value of an unlevered firm in the same risk class (V_U) *plus* the value of the tax shield ($V_{Tax \ shield}$) due to the tax deductibility of interest expenses. The value of the tax shield, which is often called *the gain from leverage,* is the present value of the annual tax savings. The annual tax saving is equal to the interest payment multiplied by the tax rate, T:

$$\text{Annual tax saving} = r_d D(T)$$

Modigliani and Miller assume a no-growth firm, so the present value of the annual tax saving is the present value of a perpetuity. They assume that the appropriate discount rate for the tax shield is the interest rate on debt, so the value of the tax shield is

$$V_{Tax \ shield} = \frac{r_d D(T)}{r_d} = TD$$

Therefore, the value of a levered firm is

$$(16\text{-}4) \qquad \begin{aligned} V_L &= V_U + V_{Tax \ shield} \\ &= V_U + TD \end{aligned}$$

The important point here is that, when corporate taxes are introduced, the value of the levered firm exceeds that of the unlevered firm by the amount TD. Since the gain from leverage increases as debt increases, this implies that a firm's value is maximized at 100% debt financing.

Because all cash flows are assumed to be perpetuities, the value of the unlevered firm can be found by using Equation 16-3 and incorporating taxes. With zero debt (D = $0), the value of the firm is its equity value:

$$V_U = S = \frac{\text{EBIT }(1-T)}{r_{sU}}$$

(16–5)

Note that the discount rate, r_{sU}, is not necessarily equal to the discount rate in Equation 16-1. The r_{sU} from Equation 16-1 is the required discount rate in a world with no taxes, whereas the r_{sU} in Equation 16-5 is the required discount rate in a world with taxes.

Proposition II

The cost of equity to a levered firm is equal to (1) the cost of equity to an unlevered firm in the same risk class plus (2) a risk premium whose size depends on (a) the difference between the costs of equity and debt to an unlevered firm, (b) the amount of financial leverage used, and (c) the corporate tax rate:

$$r_{sL} = r_{sU} + (r_{sU} - r_d)(1-T)(D/S)$$

(16–6)

Observe that Equation 16-6 is identical to the corresponding without-tax Equation 16-2 except for the term (1 – T), which appears only in Equation 16-6. Because (1 – T) is less than 1, corporate taxes cause the cost of equity to rise less rapidly with leverage than it would in the absence of taxes. Proposition II, coupled with the reduction (due to taxes) in the effective cost of debt, is what produces the Proposition I result— namely, that the firm's value increases as its leverage increases.

As shown in Chapter 15, Professor Robert Hamada extended the MM analysis to define the relationship between a firm's beta, b, and the amount of leverage it has. The beta of an unlevered firm is denoted by b_U, and Hamada's equation is

$$b = b_U[1 + (1 - T)(D/S)]$$

(16–7)

Note that beta, like the cost of stock shown in Equation 16-6, increases with leverage.

16.1f Illustration of the MM Models

To illustrate the MM models, assume that the following data and conditions hold for Fredrickson Water Company, an established firm that supplies water to residential customers in several no-growth upstate New York communities.

WEB

See **Ch16 Tool Kit.xls** on the textbook's Web site for all calculations.

1. Fredrickson currently has no debt; it is an all-equity company.
2. Expected EBIT = $2,400,000. This value is not expected to increase over time, so Fredrickson is in a no-growth situation.
3. Because it does not need new capital, Fredrickson pays out all of its income as dividends.

4. If Fredrickson begins to use debt, it can borrow at a rate $r_d = 8\%$. This borrowing rate is constant—it does not increase regardless of the amount of debt used. Any money raised by selling debt would be used to repurchase common stock, so *Fredrickson's assets would remain constant.*

5. The business risk inherent in Fredrickson's assets, and thus in its EBIT, is such that its beta is 0.80; this is called the unlevered beta, b_U, because Fredrickson has no debt. The risk-free rate is 8%, and the market risk premium (RP_M) is 5%. Using the Capital Asset Pricing Model (CAPM), Fredrickson's required rate of return on stock, r_{sU}, is 12% if no debt is used:

$$r_{sU} = r_{RF} + b_U(RP_M) = 8\% + 0.80(5\%) = 12\%$$

With Zero Taxes

To begin, assume that there are no taxes and so $T = 0\%$. At any level of debt, Proposition I (Equation 16-1) can be used to find Fredrickson's value in an MM world, $20 million:

$$V_L = V_U = \frac{\text{EBIT}}{r_{sU}} = \frac{\$2.4 \text{ million}}{0.12} = \$20.0 \text{ million}$$

If Fredrickson uses $10 million of debt, then the value of its stock must be $10 million:

$$S = V - D = \$20 \text{ million} - \$10 \text{ million} = \$10 \text{ million}$$

We can also find Fredrickson's cost of equity, r_{sL}, and its WACC at a debt level of $10 million. First, we use Proposition II (Equation 16-2) to find r_{sL}, Fredrickson's levered cost of equity:

$$\begin{aligned} r_{sL} &= r_{sU} + (r_{sU} - r_d)(D/S) \\ &= 12\% + (12\% - 8\%)(\$10 \text{ million}/\$10 \text{ million}) \\ &= 12\% + 4.0\% = 16.0\% \end{aligned}$$

Now we can find the company's weighted average cost of capital:

$$\begin{aligned} \text{WACC} &= (D/V)(r_d)(1 - T) + (S/V)r_{sL} \\ &= (\$10/\$20)(8\%)(1.0) + (\$10/\$20)(16.0\%) = 12.0\% \end{aligned}$$

Fredrickson's value and cost of capital based on the MM model without taxes at various debt levels are shown in Panel a on the left side of Figure 16-1. Here we see that, in an MM world without taxes, financial leverage simply does not matter: *The value of the firm and its overall cost of capital are both independent of the amount of debt.*

With Corporate Taxes

To illustrate the MM model with corporate taxes, assume that all of the previous conditions hold except for the following changes:

Figure 16-1	Effects of Leverage: MM Models (Millions of Dollars)

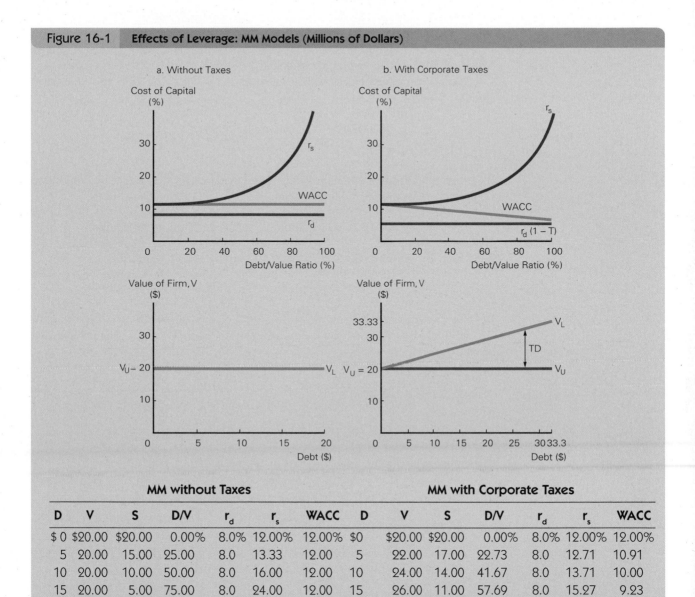

MM without Taxes

D	V	S	D/V	r_d	r_s	WACC
$ 0	$20.00	$20.00	0.00%	8.0%	12.00%	12.00%
5	20.00	15.00	25.00	8.0	13.33	12.00
10	20.00	10.00	50.00	8.0	16.00	12.00
15	20.00	5.00	75.00	8.0	24.00	12.00
20	20.00	0.00	100.00	12.0	—	12.00

MM with Corporate Taxes

D	V	S	D/V	r_d	r_s	WACC
$0	$20.00	$20.00	0.00%	8.0%	12.00%	12.00%
5	22.00	17.00	22.73	8.0	12.71	10.91
10	24.00	14.00	41.67	8.0	13.71	10.00
15	26.00	11.00	57.69	8.0	15.27	9.23
20	28.00	8.00	71.43	8.0	18.00	8.57
25	30.00	5.00	83.33	8.0	24.00	8.00
30	32.00	2.00	93.75	8.0	48.00	7.50
33.33	33.33	0.00	100.00	12.0		12.00

1. Expected EBIT = $4,000,000.[4]
2. Fredrickson has a 40% federal-plus-state tax rate, so T = 40%.

---

4. If we had left Fredrickson's EBIT at $2.4 million, then introducing corporate taxes would have reduced the firm's value from $20 million to $12 million:

$$V_L = \frac{\text{EBIT}(1 - T)}{r_{sU}} = \frac{\$2.4 \text{ million}(0.6)}{0.12} = \$12.0 \text{ million}$$

Corporate taxes reduce the amount of operating income available to investors in an unlevered firm by the factor $(1 - T)$, so the value of the firm would be reduced by the same amount, holding r_{sU} constant.

Other things held constant, the introduction of corporate taxes would lower Fredrickson's net income and hence its value, so we increased EBIT from $2.4 million to $4 million to facilitate comparisons between the two models.

When Fredrickson has zero debt but pays taxes, Equation 16-5 can be used to find its value:

$$V_U = \frac{EBIT(1 - T)}{r_{sU}} = \frac{\$4 \text{ million}(0.6)}{0.12} = \$2.0 \text{ million}$$

If Fredrickson now uses $10 million of debt in a world with taxes, we see by Proposition I (Equation 16-4) that its total market value rises from $20 to $24 million:

$$V_L = V_U + TD = \$20 \text{ million} + 0.4(\$10 \text{ million}) = \$24 \text{ million}$$

Therefore, the implied value of Fredrickson's equity is $14 million:

$$S = V - D = \$24 \text{ million} - \$10 \text{ million} = \$14 \text{ million}$$

We can also find Fredrickson's cost of equity, r_{sL}, and its WACC at a debt level of $10 million. First, we use Proposition II (Equation 16-6) to find r_{sL}, the levered cost of equity:

$$\begin{aligned}
r_{sL} &= r_{sU} + (r_{sU} - r_d)(1 - T)(D/S) \\
&= 12\% + (12\% - 8\%)(0.6)(\$10 \text{ million}/\$14 \text{ million}) \\
&= 12\% + 1.71\% = 13.71\%
\end{aligned}$$

The company's weighted average cost of capital is then

$$\begin{aligned}
WACC &= (D/V)(r_d)(1 - T) + (S/V)r_{sL} \\
&= (\$10/\$24)(8\%)(0.6) + (\$14/\$24)(13.71\%) = 10.0\%
\end{aligned}$$

Note that we can also find the levered beta and then the levered cost of equity. First, we apply Hamada's equation to find the levered beta:

$$\begin{aligned}
b &= b_U[1 + (1 - T)(D/S)] \\
&= 0.80[1 + (1 - 0.4)(\$10 \text{ million}/\$14 \text{ million})] \\
&= 1.1429
\end{aligned}$$

Applying the CAPM then yields the levered cost of equity as

$$r_{sL} = r_{RF} + b(RP_M) = 8\% + 1.1429(5\%) = 0.1371 = 13.71\%$$

Observe that this is the same levered cost of equity that we obtained directly using Equation 16-6.

Fredrickson's value and cost of capital at various debt levels with corporate taxes are shown in Panel b on the right side of Figure 16-1. In an MM world with corporate taxes, financial leverage does matter: The value of the firm is maximized—and its overall cost of capital is minimized—if it uses almost 100% debt financing. The increase in value is due solely to the tax deductibility of interest payments, which lowers both the cost of debt and the equity risk premium by $(1 - T)$.[5]

To conclude this section, compare the "Without Taxes" and "With Corporate Taxes" sections of Figure 16-1. Without taxes, both WACC and the firm's value (V) are constant. With corporate taxes, WACC declines and V rises as more and more debt is used; thus, under MM with corporate taxes, the optimal capital structure is 100% debt.

Is there an optimal capital structure under the MM zero-tax model?

What is the optimal capital structure under the MM model with corporate taxes?

How does the Proposition I equation differ between the two models?

How does the Proposition II equation differ between the two models?

Why do taxes result in a "gain from leverage" in the MM model with corporate taxes?

An unlevered firm has a value of $100 million. An otherwise identical but levered firm has $30 million in debt. Under the MM zero-tax model, what is the value of the levered firm? **($100 million)** Under the MM corporate tax model, what is the value of a levered firm if the corporate tax rate is 40%? **($112 million)**

16.2 Introducing Personal Taxes: The Miller Model

Although MM included *corporate taxes* in the second version of their model, they did not extend the model to include *personal taxes*. However, in his presidential address to the American Finance Association, Merton Miller presented a model to show how leverage affects firms' values when both personal and corporate taxes are taken into account.[6] To explain Miller's model, we begin by defining T_c as the

---

5. In the limit case where the firm used 100% debt financing, the bondholders would own the entire company and so would bear all the business risk. (Up until this point, MM assume that stockholders bear all the risk.) If the bondholders bear all the risk, then the capitalization rate on the debt should be equal to the equity capitalization rate at zero debt, $r_d = r_{sU} = 12\%$.

   The income stream to the stockholders in the all-equity case was $\$4,000,000(1 - T) = \$2,400,000$, and the value of the firm was

   $$V_U = \frac{\$2,400,000}{0.12} = \$20,000,000$$

   With all debt, the entire $4,000,000 of EBIT would be used to pay interest charges: r_d would be 12%, so $I = 0.12(\text{Debt}) = \$4,000,000$. Taxes would be zero, so the investors (bondholders) would get the entire $4,000,000 of operating income (they would not have to share it with the government). Thus, the value of the firm at 100% debt would be

   $$V_L = \frac{\$4,000,000}{0.12} = \$33,333,333 = D$$

   There is, of course, a transition problem in all this. Modigliani and Miller assume that $r_d = 8\%$ regardless of how much debt the firm has until debt reaches 100%, at which point r_d jumps to 12%, the cost of equity. As we shall see later in the chapter, r_d actually rises as the risk of financial distress increases.

6. See Merton H. Miller, "Debt and Taxes," *Journal of Finance*, May 1977, pp. 261–275.

corporate tax rate, T_s as the personal tax rate on income from stocks, and T_d as the personal tax rate on income from debt. Note that stock returns are expected to come partly as dividends and partly as capital gains, so T_s is a weighted average of the effective tax rates on dividends and capital gains. However, essentially all debt income comes from interest, which is effectively taxed at investors' top rates; thus T_d is higher than T_s.

With personal taxes included and under the same set of assumptions used in the earlier MM models, the value of an unlevered firm is found as follows:

(16–8)

$$V_U = \frac{EBIT(1-T_c)}{r_{sU}}$$
$$= \frac{EBIT(1-T_c)(1-T_s)}{r_{sU}(1-T_s)}$$

The $(1 - T_s)$ term takes account of personal taxes. Note that, in order to find the value of the unlevered firm, we can either discount pre-personal-tax cash flows at the pre-personal-tax rate of r_{sU} or discount after-personal-tax cash flows at the after-personal-tax rate of $r_{sU}(1 - T_s)$. Therefore, the numerator in the second line of Equation 16-8 shows how much of the firm's operating income is left after the unlevered firm pays corporate income taxes and its stockholders subsequently pay personal taxes on their equity income. Note also that the discount rate, r_{sU}, in Equation 16-8 is not necessarily equal to the discount rate in Equation 16-5. The r_{sU} from Equation 16-5 is the required discount rate in a world with corporate taxes but no personal taxes; the r_{sU} in Equation 16-8 is the required discount rate in a world with both corporate and personal taxes.

Miller's formula can be proved by an arbitrage proof similar to the one we presented earlier. However, the alternative proof shown below is easier to follow. To begin, we partition the levered firm's annual cash flows, CF_L, into those going to stockholders and those going to bondholders *after* corporate and personal taxes:

(16–9)

$$CF_L = \text{Net CF to stockholders} + \text{Net CF to bondholders}$$
$$= (EBIT - I)(1 - T_c)(1 - T_s) + I(1 - T_d)$$

where I is the annual interest payment. Equation 16-9 can be rearranged as follows:

(16–9a)

$$CF_L = [EBIT(1 - T_c)(1 - T_s)] - [I(1 - T_c)(1 - T_s)] + [I(1 - T_d)]$$

The first term in Equation 16-9a is identical to the after-personal-tax cash flow of an unlevered firm as shown in the numerator of Equation 16-8, and its present value is found by discounting the perpetual cash flow by $r_{sU}(1 - T_s)$.

The second and third terms reflect leverage and result from the cash flows associated with debt financing, which under the MM assumptions are riskless (because the firm's debt is riskless under those assumptions). We can either discount pre-personal-tax interest payments at the pre-personal-tax rate of r_d or discount after-personal-tax interest payments at the after-personal-tax rate of $r_d(1 - T_d)$.

Because they are after-personal-tax cash flows to debtholders, the present value of the last two right-hand terms in Equation 16-9a can be obtained by discounting at the after-personal-tax cost of debt, $r_d(1 - T_d)$. Combining the present values of the three terms, we obtain this value for the levered firm:

$$V_L = \frac{\text{EBIT}(1 - T_c)(1 - T_s)}{r_{sU}(1 - T_s)} - \frac{I(1 - T_c)(1 - T_s)}{r_d(1 - T_d)} + \frac{I(1 - T_d)}{r_d(1 - T_d)} \qquad (16\text{--}10)$$

The first right-hand term in Equation 16-10 is identical to V_U in Equation 16-8. Recognizing this and consolidating the second two terms, we obtain

$$V_L = V_U + \left[1 - \frac{(1 - T_c)(1 - T_s)}{(1 - T_d)}\right]\left[\frac{I(1 - T_d)}{r_d(1 - T_d)}\right] \qquad (16\text{--}10a)$$

Now recognize that the after-tax perpetual interest payment divided by the after-tax required rate of return on debt, $I(1 - T_d)/r_d(1 - T_d)$, is equal to the market value of the perpetual debt, D:

$$D = \frac{I}{r_d} = \frac{I(1 - T_d)}{r_d(1 - T_d)} \qquad (16\text{--}11)$$

Substituting D into Equation 16-10a and rearranging, we obtain the following expression, which is called the **Miller model**:

$$\text{Miller model: } V_L = V_U + \left[1 - \frac{(1 - T_c)(1 - T_s)}{(1 - T_d)}\right]D \qquad (16\text{--}12)$$

The Miller model provides an estimate of the value of a levered firm in a world with both corporate and personal taxes.

The Miller model has several important implications, as follows.

1. The term in brackets,

$$\left[1 - \frac{(1 - T_c)(1 - T_s)}{(1 - T_d)}\right]$$

when multiplied by D, represents the gain from leverage. The bracketed term thus replaces the corporate tax rate, T, in the earlier MM model with corporate taxes ($V_L = V_U + TD$).

2. If we ignore all taxes (i.e., if $T_c = T_s = T_d = 0$) then the bracketed term is zero, so in this case Equation 16-12 is the same as the original MM model without taxes.

3. If we ignore personal taxes (i.e., if $T_s = T_d = 0$) then the bracketed term reduces to $[1 - (1 - T_c)] = T_c$, so in this case Equation 16-12 is the same as the MM model with corporate taxes.

4. If the effective personal tax rates on stock and bond incomes were equal (i.e., if $T_s = T_d$), then $(1 - T_s)$ and $(1 - T_d)$ would cancel and so the bracketed term would again reduce to T_c.

5. If $(1 - T_c)(1 - T_s) = (1 - T_d)$, then the bracketed term would be zero and so the value of using leverage would also be zero. This implies that the tax advantage of debt to the firm would be exactly offset by the personal tax advantage of equity. Under this condition, capital structure would have no effect on a firm's value or its cost of capital, so we would be back to MM's original zero-tax proposition.

6. Because taxes on capital gains are lower than on ordinary income and can be deferred, the effective tax rate on stock income is normally less than that on bond income. This being the case, what would the Miller model predict as the gain from leverage? To answer this question, assume the tax rate on corporate income is $T_c = 34\%$, the effective rate on bond income is $T_d = 28\%$, and the effective rate on stock income is $T_s = 15\%$. Using these values in the Miller model, we find that a levered firm's value exceeds that of an unlevered firm by 22% of the market value of corporate debt:

$$
\begin{aligned}
\text{Gain from leverage} &= \left[1 - \frac{(1 - T_c)(1 - T_s)}{(1 - T_d)} \right] D \\
&= \left[1 - \frac{(1 - 0.34)(1 - 0.15)}{(1 - 0.28)} \right] D \\
&= (1 - 0.78) D \\
&= 0.22 D
\end{aligned}
$$

Note that the MM model with corporate taxes would indicate a gain from leverage of $T_c(D) = 0.34D$, or 34% of the amount of corporate debt. Thus, with these assumed tax rates, adding personal taxes to the model lowers but does not eliminate the benefit from corporate debt. In general, whenever the effective tax rate on income from stock is less than the effective rate on income from bonds, the Miller model produces a lower gain from leverage than is produced by the MM model with taxes.

In his paper, Miller argued that firms in the aggregate would issue a mix of debt and equity securities such that the before-tax yields on corporate securities and the personal tax rates of the investors who bought these securities would adjust until equilibrium was reached. At equilibrium, $(1 - T_d)$ would equal $(1 - T_c)(1 - T_s)$ and so, as we noted in item 5 above, the tax advantage of debt to the firm would be exactly offset by personal taxation and thus capital structure would have no effect on a firm's value or its cost of capital. Hence, according to Miller, the conclusions derived from the original MM zero-tax model are correct!

Others have extended and tested Miller's analysis. Generally, these extensions question Miller's conclusion that there is no advantage to the use of corporate debt. In fact, Equation 16-12 shows that both T_c and T_s must be less than T_d if there is to be zero gain from leverage. For most U.S. corporations and investors, the effective tax rate on income from stock is less than the rate on income from bonds; that is, $T_s < T_d$. However, many corporate bonds are held by tax-exempt institutions, and in those cases T_c is generally greater than T_d. Also, for those high-tax-bracket individuals with $T_d > T_c$, T_s may be large enough that $(1 - T_c)(1 - T_s)$ is less than $(1 - T_d)$; in this case, there would be an advantage to using corporate debt. Still, Miller's work does show that personal taxes offset some of the benefits of corporate debt. This means that the tax advantages of corporate debt are less than were implied by the earlier MM model, where only corporate taxes were considered.

As we discuss in the next section, both the MM and the Miller models are based on strong and unrealistic assumptions, so we should regard our examples as indicating the general effects of leverage on a firm's value and not a precise relationship.

Self Test

How does the Miller model differ from the MM model with corporate taxes?

What are the implications of the Miller model if $T_c = T_s = T_d = 0$? If $T_s = T_d = 0$?

Considering the current tax structure in the United States, what is the primary implication of the Miller model?

An unlevered firm has a value of $100 million. An otherwise identical but levered firm has $30 million in debt. Use the Miller model to calculate the value of a levered firm if the corporate tax rate is 40%, the personal tax rate on equity is 15%, and the personal tax rate on debt is 35%. **($106.46 million)**

16.3 Criticisms of the MM and Miller Models

The conclusions of the MM and Miller models follow logically from their initial assumptions. However, both academicians and executives have voiced concerns over the validity of the MM and Miller models, and virtually no one believes they hold precisely. The MM zero-tax model leads to the conclusion that capital structure doesn't matter, yet we observe systematic capital structure patterns within industries. Further, when used with "reasonable" tax rates, both the MM model with corporate taxes and the Miller model lead to the conclusion that firms should use 100% debt financing, but real-life firms do not (deliberately) go to that extreme.

People who disagree with the MM and Miller theories generally attack them on the grounds that their assumptions are invalid. Here are the main objections.

1. Both MM and Miller assume that personal and corporate leverage are perfect substitutes. However, an individual investing in a levered firm has less loss exposure as a result of corporate *limited liability* than if she used "homemade" leverage. For example, in our earlier illustration of the MM arbitrage argument, it should be noted that only the $600,000 our investor had in Firm L would be lost if that firm went bankrupt. However, if the investor engaged in arbitrage transactions and employed "homemade" leverage to invest in Firm U, then she could lose $900,000—the original $600,000 investment plus the $400,000 loan less the $100,000 investment in riskless bonds. This increased personal risk exposure would tend to restrain investors from engaging in arbitrage, and that could cause the equilibrium values of V_L, V_U, r_{sL}, and r_{sU} to be different from those specified by MM. Restrictions on institutional investors, who dominate capital markets today, may also hinder the arbitrage process, because many institutional investors cannot legally borrow to buy stocks and hence are prohibited from engaging in homemade leverage.

   However, even though limited liability may present a problem to individuals, it does *not* present a problem to corporations that are set up to undertake **leveraged buyouts (LBOs)**. Thus, after MM's work became widely known, literally hundreds of LBO firms were established whose founders made billions by recapitalizing underleveraged firms. "Junk bonds" were created to aid in the process, and the managers of underleveraged firms who did not want their firms to be taken over increased debt usage on their own. Thus, MM's work raised the level of debt in corporate America, which probably raised the level of economic efficiency.

2. If a levered firm's operating income declined, then it would sell assets and take other measures to raise the cash necessary to meet its interest obligations and thus avoid bankruptcy. If our illustrative unlevered firm experienced the same decline in operating income, it would probably take the less drastic measure of cutting dividends rather than selling assets. But if dividends were cut then investors who employed homemade leverage would not receive cash to pay the interest on their debt. Thus, homemade leverage puts stockholders in greater danger of bankruptcy than does corporate leverage.

3. Brokerage costs were assumed away by MM and Miller, which makes the switch from L to U costless. However, brokerage and other transaction costs do exist, and they also impede the arbitrage process.

4. Modigliani and Miller initially assumed that corporations and investors could borrow at the risk-free rate. Although risky debt has been introduced into the analysis by others, to reach the MM and Miller conclusions it is still necessary to assume that both corporations and investors can borrow at the same rate. Although major institutional investors probably can borrow at the corporate rate, many institutions are not allowed to borrow to buy securities. Furthermore, most individual investors must borrow at higher rates than those paid by large corporations.

5. In his article, Miller concluded that equilibrium would be reached, but to reach his equilibrium the tax benefit from corporate debt must be the same for all firms and must also be constant for an individual firm regardless of the amount of leverage used. However, we know that tax benefits vary from firm to firm: Highly profitable companies gain the maximum tax benefit from leverage, whereas the benefits to firms that are struggling are much smaller. Moreover, some firms have other tax shields (e.g., high depreciation, pension plan contributions, operating loss carryforwards), and these shields reduce the tax savings from interest payments.[7] It also is simplistic to assume that the expected tax shield is unaffected by the amount of debt used. Higher leverage increases the probability that the firm will not be able to use the full tax shield in the future, because higher leverage increases the probability of future unprofitability and consequently lower tax rates. Note also that large, diversified corporations can use losses in one division to offset profits in another. Thus, the tax shelter benefit is more certain in such firms than in smaller, single-product companies. All things considered, it appears likely that the interest tax shield from corporate debt is more valuable to some firms than to others.

6. MM and Miller assume that there are no costs associated with financial distress, and they also ignore agency costs. Further, they assume that all market participants have identical information about firms' prospects, which is clearly an oversimplification.

These six points all suggest that the MM and Miller models lead to questionable conclusions and that the models would be better if certain of their assumptions could be relaxed. We discuss an extension of the models in the next section.

---

7. For a discussion of the impact of tax shields, see Harry DeAngelo and Ronald W. Masulis, "Optimal Capital Structure under Corporate and Personal Taxation," *Journal of Financial Economics,* March 1980, pp. 3–30; Thomas W. Downs, "Corporate Leverage and Nondebt Tax Shields: Evidence on Crowding-Out," *The Financial Review,* November 1993, pp. 549–583; John R. Graham, "Taxes and Corporate Finance: A Review," *Review of Financial Studies,* Winter 2003, pp. 1075–1129; and Jeffrey K. Mackie-Mason, "Do Taxes Affect Corporate Financing Decisions?" *Journal of Finance,* December 1990, pp. 1471–1493.

Should we accept that one of the models presented thus far (MM with zero taxes, MM with corporate taxes, or Miller) is correct? Why or why not?

Are any of the assumptions used in the models worrisome to you, and what does "worrisome" mean in this context?

16.4 An Extension of the MM Model: Nonzero Growth and a Risky Tax Shield

In this section, we discuss an extension of the MM model that incorporates growth and different discount rates for the debt tax shield.[8]

Modigliani and Miller assumed that firms pay out all of their earnings as dividends and therefore do not grow. However, most firms do grow, and growth affects the MM and Hamada results (as found in the first part of this chapter). Recall that, for an unlevered firm, the WACC is just the unlevered cost of equity: WACC = r_{sU}. If g is the constant growth rate and FCF is the expected free cash flow, then the corporate value model from Chapter 11 shows that

$$V_U = \frac{FCF}{r_{sU} - g} \tag{16-13}$$

As shown by Equation 16-4, the value of the levered firm is equal to the value of the unlevered firm plus gain from leverage, which is the value of the tax shield:

$$V_L = V_U + V_{\text{Tax shield}} \tag{16-4a}$$

However, when there is growth, the value of the tax shield is not equal to TD as it is in the MM model with corporate taxes. If the firm uses debt and if g is positive then, as the firm grows, the amount of debt will increase over time; hence the size of the annual tax shield will also increase at the rate g, provided the debt ratio remains constant. Moreover, the value of this growing tax shield is greater than the value of the constant tax shield in the MM analysis.

Modigliani and Miller assumed that corporate debt was riskless and that the firm would always be able to use its tax savings. Therefore, they discounted the tax savings at the cost of debt, r_d, which is the risk-free rate. However, corporate debt is not risk free—firms do occasionally default on their loans. Also, a firm may not be able to use tax savings from debt in the current year if it already has a pre-tax loss from operations. Therefore, the flow of tax savings to the firm is not risk-free and hence it should be discounted at a higher rate than the risk-free rate. In addition, since debt is safer than equity to an investor because it has a higher priority claim on the firm's cash flows, its discount rate should be no greater than the unlevered cost of equity. For now, assume that the appropriate discount rate for the tax savings

8. See Michael C. Ehrhardt and Phillip R. Daves, "Corporate Valuation: The Combined Impact of Growth and the Tax Shield of Debt on the Cost of Capital and Systematic Risk," *Journal of Applied Finance*, Fall/Winter 2002, pp. 31–38.

is r_{TS}, which is greater than or equal to the cost of debt, r_d, and less than or equal to the unlevered cost of equity, r_{sU}.

If r_{TS} is the appropriate discount rate for the tax shield, r_d is the interest rate on the debt, T is the corporate tax rate, and D is the current amount of debt, then the present value of this growing tax shield is

$$ (16\text{--}14) \qquad V_{\text{Tax shield}} = \frac{r_d TD}{r_{TS} - g} $$

This formula is similar to the dividend growth formula from Chapter 5, except it has $r_d TD$ as the growing cash flow generated by the tax savings and r_{TS} as the discount rate. Substituting Equation 16-14 into Equation 16-4a yields a valuation expression that incorporates constant growth:

$$ (16\text{--}15) \qquad V_L = V_U + \left(\frac{r_d}{r_{TS} - g} \right) TD $$

The difference between Equation 16-15 for the value of the levered firm and the expression given in Equation 16-4 is the $r_d/(r_{TS} - g)$ term in large parentheses, which reflects the added value of the tax shield due to growth. In the MM model, $r_{TS} = r_d = r_{RF}$ and $g = 0$, so the term in parentheses is equal to 1.0.

If $r_{TS} < r_{sU}$, then growth can actually cause the levered cost of equity to be *less* than the unlevered cost of equity.[9] This happens because the combination of rapid growth and a low discount rate for the tax shield causes the value of the tax shield to dominate the unlevered value of the firm. If this were true, then high-growth firms would tend to have larger amounts of debt than low-growth firms. However, this is not consistent with either intuition or what we observe in the market: High-growth firms actually tend to have lower levels of debt. Regardless of the growth rate, firms with more debt should have a higher cost of equity than firms with no debt. These inconsistencies can be resolved if $r_{TS} = r_{sU}$. Given this equality, the value of the levered firm becomes[10]

$$ (16\text{--}16) \qquad V_L = V_U + \left(\frac{r_d TD}{r_{sU} - g} \right) $$

In view of this valuation equation, expressions for the levered cost of equity and the levered beta (corresponding to Equations 16-6 and 16-7) become

$$ (16\text{--}17) \qquad r_{sL} = r_{sU} + (r_{sU} - r_d)\frac{D}{S} $$

---

9. See the paper by Ehrhardt and Daves cited in footnote 8.
10. For a discussion of the *compressed APV* valuation method, which assumes that $r_{TS} = r_{sU}$, see Steven N. Kaplan and Richard S. Ruback, "The Valuation of Cash Flow Forecasts: An Empirical Analysis," *Journal of Finance*, September 1995, pp. 1059–1093.

and

$$b = b_U + (b_U - b_D)\frac{D}{S}$$

(16–18)

As in Chapter 15, b_U is the beta of an unlevered firm and b is the beta of a levered firm. Because debt is not riskless, it has a beta (b_D).

Although the derivations of Equations 16-17 and 16-18 reflect corporate taxes and growth, neither of these expressions includes the corporate tax rate or the growth rate. This means that the expression for the levered required rate of return, Equation 16-17, is exactly the same as MM's expression for the levered required rate of return *without taxes,* Equation 16-2. And the expression for the levered beta, Equation 16-18, is exactly the same as Hamada's equation (with risky debt) but *without taxes.* The reason the tax rate and the growth rate drop out of these two expressions is that the growing tax shield is discounted at the unlevered cost of equity, r_{sU}, not at the cost of debt as in the MM model. The tax rate drops out because no matter how high the level of T, the total risk of the firm will not be changed: The unlevered cash flows and the tax shield are discounted at the same rate. The growth rate drops out for the same reason: An increasing debt level will not change the riskiness of the entire firm no matter what rate of growth prevails.[11]

Observe that Equation 16-18 includes the term b_D. Since MM and Hamada assumed that corporate debt is riskless, its beta should be zero. However, if corporate debt is not riskless then its beta, b_D, may not be zero. If we assume that bonds lie on the Security Market Line, then a bond's required return, r_d, can be expressed as $r_d = r_{RF} + b_D RP_M$. Solving for b_D then gives $b_D = (r_d - r_{RF})/RP_M$.

16.4a Illustration of the MM Extension with Growth

Earlier in this chapter we examined Fredrickson Water Company, a zero-growth firm with unlevered value of $20 million. To see how growth affects the levered value of the firm and the levered cost of equity, let's look at Peterson Power Inc., which is similar to Fredrickson except that it is growing. Peterson's expected free cash flow is $1 million, which is expected to grow at a rate of 7%. Like Fredrickson, Peterson has an unlevered cost of equity of 12% and faces a 40% tax rate. Peterson's unlevered value is $V_U = (\$1 \text{ million})/(0.12 - 0.07) = \$20$ million, the same as Fredrickson's.

Suppose now that Peterson, like Fredrickson, uses $10 million of debt with a cost of 8%. We see from Equation 16-16 that

$$V_L = \$20 \text{ million} + \left(\frac{0.08 \times 0.40 \times \$10\,\text{million}}{0.12 - 0.07}\right) = \$26.4 \text{ million}$$

---

11. Of course, Equations 16-14, 16-15, and 16-16 also apply to firms that don't happen to be growing. In this special case, the difference between the Ehrhardt and Daves extension and the MM with taxes treatment is that MM assume that the tax shield should be discounted at the risk-free rate, whereas this extension of their model shows it is more reasonable for the tax shield to be discounted at the unlevered cost of equity, r_{sU}. Because r_{sU} is greater than the risk-free rate, the value of a nongrowing tax shield will be lower when discounted at this higher rate, giving a lower value of the levered firm than what MM would predict.

and that the implied value of equity is

$$S = V_L - D = \$26.4 \text{ million} - \$10 \text{ million} = \$16.4 \text{ million}$$

The increase in value due to leverage when there is 7% growth is $6.4 million, compared with the increase in value of only $4 million for Fredrickson. The reason for this difference is that even though the debt tax shield is currently (0.08)(0.40)(10 million) = $0.32 million for each company, this tax shield will grow at an annual rate of 7% for Peterson but will remain fixed over time for Fredrickson. And even though Peterson and Fredrickson have the same initial dollar value of debt, their debt weights, w_d, are not the same. Peterson's w_d is $D/V_L = \$10/\$26.4 = 37.88\%$, whereas Fredrickson's w_d is $\$10/\$24 = 41.67\%$.

With $10 million in debt, Peterson's new cost of equity is given by Equation 16-17:

$$r_{sL} = 12\% + (12\% - 8\%)\frac{0.3788}{0.6212} = 14.44\%$$

This is higher than Fredrickson's levered cost of equity of 13.71%. Finally, Peterson's new WACC is (1.0 − 0.3788)14.44% + 0.3788(1 − 0.40)8% = 10.78% versus Fredrickson's WACC of 10.0%.

In sum, using the MM and Hamada models to calculate the value of a levered firm and its cost of capital when there is growth will: (1) underestimate the value of the levered firm, because these models underestimate the value of the growing tax shield; and (2) underestimate the levered WACC and levered cost of capital because, for a given initial amount of debt, these models overestimate the firm's w_d.

Self Test

Why is the value of the tax shield different when a firm grows?

Why would it be inappropriate to discount tax shield cash flows at the risk-free rate as MM do?

How will your estimates of the levered cost of equity be biased if you use the MM or Hamada models when growth is present? Why does this matter?

An unlevered firm has a value of $100 million. An otherwise identical but levered firm has $30 million in debt. Suppose both firms are growing at a constant rate of 5%, the corporate tax rate is 40%, the cost of debt is 6%, and the unlevered cost of equity is 8% (assume r_{sU} is the appropriate discount rate for the tax shield). What is the value of the levered firm? (**$124 million**) What is the value of the stock? (**$94 million**) What is the levered cost of equity? (**8.64%**)

16.5 Risky Debt and Equity as an Option

In the previous sections, we evaluated equity and debt using the standard discounted cash flow techniques. However, we learned in Chapter 13 that if there is an opportunity for management to make a change as a result of new information after a project or investment has been started, then there might be an option component to the project or investment being evaluated. This is the case with equity. To see why, consider Kunkel Inc., a small manufacturer of electronic wiring harnesses and instrumentation located in Minot, North Dakota. Kunkel's current value (debt plus equity) is $20 million, and its debt consists of $10 million face value of 5-year zero coupon bonds. What decision does management make when the debt comes due? In most cases, it would pay the $10 million that is due. But what if the company has done poorly and the firm is worth only $9 million? In that case, the firm is technically bankrupt, since its value is less than the amount of debt due. Management will choose to default on the loan; in this case, the firm will be liquidated or sold for $9 million, the debtholders will get all $9 million, and the stockholders will get nothing. Of course, if the firm is worth $10 million or more then management will choose to repay the loan. The ability to make this decision—to pay or not to pay—looks very much like an option, and the techniques we developed in Chapter 6 can be used to value it.

16.5a Using the Black-Scholes Option Pricing Model to Value Equity

WEB

See *Ch16 Tool Kit.xls* on the textbook's Web site for all calculations.

To put this decision into an option context, suppose P is Kunkel's total value when the debt matures. Then, if the debt is paid off, Kunkel's stockholders will receive the equivalent of P − $10 million if P > $10 million.[12] They will receive nothing if P ≤ $10 million because management will default on the bond and the bondholders will take over the company. These facts can be summarized as follows:

$$\text{Payoff to stockholders} = \text{MAX}(P - \$10 \text{ million}, 0)$$

This is exactly the same payoff as a European call option on the total value (P) of the firm with a strike price equal to the face value of the debt, $10 million. We can use the Black-Scholes option pricing model from Chapter 6 to determine the value of this asset.

Recall from Chapter 6 that the value of a call option depends on five things: the price of the underlying asset, the strike price, the risk-free rate, the time to expiration, and the volatility of the market value of the underlying asset. Here the underlying asset is the total value of the firm. If we assume that volatility is 40% and that the risk-free rate is 6%, then the inputs for the Black-Scholes model are as follows:

$$
\begin{aligned}
P &= \$20 \text{ million} \\
X &= \$10 \text{ million} \\
t &= 5 \text{ years} \\
r_{RF} &= 6\% \\
\sigma &= 40\%
\end{aligned}
$$

The value of a European call option, as shown in Chapter 6, is

$$V = P[(N(d_1)] - Xe^{-r_{RF}t}[N(d_2)] \tag{16-19}$$

where

$$d_1 = \frac{\ln(P / X) + (r_{RF} + \sigma^2/2)t}{\sigma\sqrt{t}} \tag{16-20}$$

---

12. Actually, rather than receive cash of P − $10 million, the stockholders will keep the company (which is worth P − $10 million) rather than turn it over to the bondholders.

and

(16-21)

$$d_2 = d_1 - \sigma\sqrt{t}$$

For Kunkel Inc.,

$$d_1 = \frac{\ln(20/10) + (0.06 + 0.40^2/2)5}{0.40\sqrt{5}} = 1.5576$$

$$d_2 = 1.5576 - 0.40\sqrt{5} = 0.6632$$

Using the *Excel* NORMSDIST function gives $N(d_1) = N(1.5576) = 0.9403$, $N(d_2) = N(0.6632) = 0.7464$, and $V = \$20(0.9403) - \$10e^{-0.06(5)}(0.7464) = \$13.28$ million. So Kunkel's equity is worth $13.28 million, and its debt must be worth what is left over: $20 − $13.28 = $6.72 million. Since this is 5-year, zero coupon debt, its yield must be

$$\text{Yield on debt} = \left(\frac{10}{6.72}\right)^{1/5} - 1 = 0.0827 = 8.27\%$$

Thus, when Kunkel issued the debt, it received $6.72 million and the yield on the debt was 8.27%. Notice that the yield on the debt, 8.27%, is greater than the 6% risk-free rate. This is because the firm might default if its value falls enough, so the bonds are risky. Note also that the yield on the debt depends on the value of the option and hence on the riskiness of the firm. The debt will have a lower value—and a higher yield—the more the option is worth.

16.5b Managerial Incentives

The only decision an investor in a stock option can make, once the option is purchased, is whether and when to exercise it. However, this restriction does not apply to equity when it is viewed as an option on the total value of the firm. Management has some leeway to affect the riskiness of the firm through its capital budgeting and investment decisions, and it can affect the amount of capital invested in the firm through its dividend policy.

16.5c Capital Budgeting Decisions

When Kunkel issued the $10 million face value debt discussed previously, the yield was determined in part by Kunkel's riskiness, which in turn was determined in part by what management intended to do with the $6.72 million it raised. We know from our analysis in Chapter 6 that options are worth more when volatility is higher. This means that if Kunkel's management can find a way to increase its riskiness without decreasing the total value of the firm, then doing so will increase the equity's value while decreasing the debt's value. Management can accomplish this by selecting risky rather than safe investment projects. Table 16-1 shows the value of equity, the value of debt, and the yield on debt for a range of possible volatilities. See *Ch16 Tool Kit.xls* for the calculations.

Kunkel's current volatility is 40%, so its equity is worth $13.28 million and its debt is worth $6.72 million. But if, after incurring the debt, management undertakes projects that increase its riskiness from a volatility of 40% to a volatility of 80%, then the value of Kunkel's equity will increase by $2.53 million to $15.81 million and the value of its debt will decrease by the same amount. This 19% increase in the

TABLE 16-1	The Value of Kunkel's Debt and Equity for Various Levels of Volatility (Millions of Dollars)		
Standard Deviation	**Equity**	**Proceeds from Debt**	**Debt Yield**
20%	$12.62	$7.38	6.25%
30	12.83	7.17	6.89
40	**13.28**	**6.72**	**8.27**
50	13.86	6.14	10.25
60	14.51	5.49	12.74
70	15.17	4.83	15.66
80	15.81	4.19	18.99
90	16.41	3.59	22.74
100	16.96	3.04	26.92
110	17.46	2.54	31.56
120	17.90	2.10	36.68

© Cengage Learning 2013

value of the equity represents a transfer of wealth from bondholders to stockholders. A corresponding transfer of wealth from stockholders to bondholders would occur if Kunkel undertook projects that were safer than originally planned. Table 16-1 shows that if management undertakes safe projects and drives the volatility down to 30%, then stockholders will lose (and bondholders will gain) $0.45 million.

WEB

See **Ch16 Tool Kit.xls** on the textbook's Web site for all calculations.

Such a strategy of investing borrowed funds in risky assets is called **bait and switch** because the firm obtains the money by promising one investment policy and then switching to another policy. The bait-and-switch problem is more severe when a firm's value is low relative to its level of debt. If Kunkel's total value is $20 million, then doubling its volatility from 40% to 80% increases its equity value by 19%. But if Kunkel had done poorly in recent years and its total value were only $10 million, then the impact of increasing volatility would be much greater. Table 16-2 shows that if Kunkel's total value were only $10 million and it issued $10 million face value of 5-year, zero coupon debt, then its equity would be worth $4.46 million at a volatility of 40%. Doubling the volatility to 80% would increase the value of the equity to $6.83 million, or by 53%. The incentive for management to "roll the dice" with borrowed funds can be enormous, and if management owns many stock options then their payoff from rolling the dice is even greater than the payoff to stockholders!

Bondholders are aware of these incentives and write covenants into debt issues that restrict management's ability to invest in riskier projects than originally promised. However, their attempts to protect themselves are not always successful, as the failures of Enron, Lehman Brothers, and AIG demonstrate. The combination of a risky industry, high levels of debt, and option-based compensation has proven to be very dangerous.

16.5d Equity with Risky Coupon Debt

We have analyzed the simple case when a firm has zero coupon debt outstanding. The analysis becomes much more complicated when a firm has debt that requires periodic interest payments, because then management can decide whether or not to default on each interest payment date. For example, suppose Kunkel's $10 million of debt is a 1-year, 8% loan with semiannual payments. The scheduled payments are $400,000 in 6 months, and then $10.4 million at the end of the year. If management makes the

TABLE 16-2   Debt and Equity Values for Various Levels of Volatility When the Firm's Total Value is $10 Million (Millions of Dollars)

Standard Deviation	Equity	Value of Debt	Debt Yield
20%	$3.16	$6.84	7.90%
30	3.80	6.20	10.02
40	**4.46**	**5.54**	**12.52**
50	5.10	4.90	15.35
60	5.72	4.28	18.49
70	6.30	3.70	21.98
80	6.83	3.17	25.81
90	7.31	2.69	30.04
100	7.74	2.26	34.68
110	8.13	1.87	39.77
120	8.46	1.54	45.36

scheduled $400,000 interest payment, then the stockholders will acquire the right to make the next payment of $10.4 million. If it does not make the $400,000 payment, then by defaulting the stockholders lose the right to make that next payment and hence lose the firm.[13] In other words, at the beginning of the year the stockholders have an option to purchase an option. The option they own has an exercise price of $400,000 and it expires in 6 months, and if they exercise it, they will acquire an option to purchase the entire firm for $10.4 million in another 6 months.

If the debt were 2-year debt, then there would be four decision points for management and the stockholders' position would be like an option on an option on an option on an option! These types of options are called **compound options,** and techniques for valuing them are beyond the scope of this book. However, the incentives discussed previously for the case when a firm has risky zero coupon debt still apply when the firm has periodic interest payments to make.[14]

Self Test	Discuss how equity can be viewed as an option. Who has the option and what decision can they make?
	Why would management want to increase the riskiness of the firm? Why would this make bondholders unhappy?
	What can bondholders do to limit management's ability to bait and switch?

13. Actually, bankruptcy is far more complicated than our example suggests. As a firm approaches default it can take a number of actions, and even after filing for bankruptcy the stockholders can substantially delay a takeover by bondholders, during which time the value of the firm can deteriorate further. As a result, stockholders can often extract concessions from bondholders in situations where it would seem that the bondholders should get all of the firm's value. Bankruptcy is discussed in more detail in Chapter 25.

14. For more on viewing equity as an option, see D. Galai and R. Masulis, "The Option Pricing Model and the Risk Factor of Stock," *Journal of Financial Economics*, Vol. 3, 1976, pp. 53–81. For a discussion on compound options, see Robert Geske, "The Valuation of Corporate Liabilities as Compound Options," *Journal of Financial and Quantitative Analysis*, June 1984, pp. 541–552.

16.6 Capital Structure Theory: Our View

The great contribution of the capital structure models developed by MM, Miller, and their followers is that these models identified the specific benefits and costs of using debt: the tax benefits, financial distress costs, and so on. Prior to MM, no capital structure theory existed and so we had no systematic way of analyzing the effects of debt financing.

The trade-off model discussed in Chapter 15 is summarized graphically in Figure 16-2. The top graph shows the relationships between the debt ratio and the cost of debt, the cost of equity, and the WACC. Both r_s and $r_d(1 - T_c)$ rise steadily with increases in leverage, but the rate of increase accelerates at higher debt levels; this reflects agency costs and the increased probability of financial distress. Under increasing leverage the WACC first declines, then hits a minimum at D/V*, and then begins to rise. Note that the value of D in D/V* in the upper graph is D*, the level of debt in the lower graph that maximizes the firm's value. Thus, a firm's WACC is minimized and its value is maximized at the same capital structure. Note also that the general shapes of the curves apply regardless of whether we are using the modified MM with corporate taxes model, the Miller model, or a variant of these models.

Unfortunately, it is impossible to quantify accurately the costs and benefits of debt financing, so it is impossible to pinpoint D/V*, the capital structure that maximizes a firm's value. Most experts believe that such a structure exists for every firm but that it changes over time as a firm's operations and investor preferences change. Most experts also believe that, as shown in Figure 16-2, the relationship between value and leverage is relatively flat over a fairly broad range, so large deviations from the optimal capital structure can occur without materially affecting the stock price.

Now consider signaling theory, which we discussed in Chapter 15. Because of asymmetric information, investors know less about a firm's prospects than its managers know. Furthermore, managers try to maximize value for *current* stockholders, not new ones. Hence, if the firm has excellent prospects then management will not want to issue new shares, but if things look bleak then a new stock offering would benefit current stockholders. Investors therefore view a stock offering as a signal of bad news, so stock prices tend to decline when new issues are announced. As a result, new equity financings are relatively expensive. The net effect of signaling is to motivate firms to maintain a reserve borrowing capacity so that future investment opportunities can be financed by debt if internal funds are not available.

By combining the trade-off and asymmetric information theories, we obtain the following explanation for firms' behavior.

1. Debt financing provides benefits because of the tax deductibility of interest, so firms should have some debt in their capital structures.
2. However, financial distress and agency costs place limits on debt usage—beyond some point, these costs offset the tax advantage of debt. The costs of financial distress are especially harmful to firms whose values consist primarily of intangible growth options, such as research and development. Such firms should have lower levels of debt than firms whose asset bases consist mostly of tangible assets.
3. Because of problems resulting from asymmetric information and flotation costs, low-growth firms should follow a pecking order by raising capital first from internal sources, then by borrowing, and finally by issuing new stock. In fact, such low-growth firms rarely need to issue external equity. High-growth firms whose growth occurs primarily through increases in tangible assets should follow the same pecking order, but usually they will need to issue new stock as well as

Figure 16-2   Effects of Leverage: The Trade-off Models

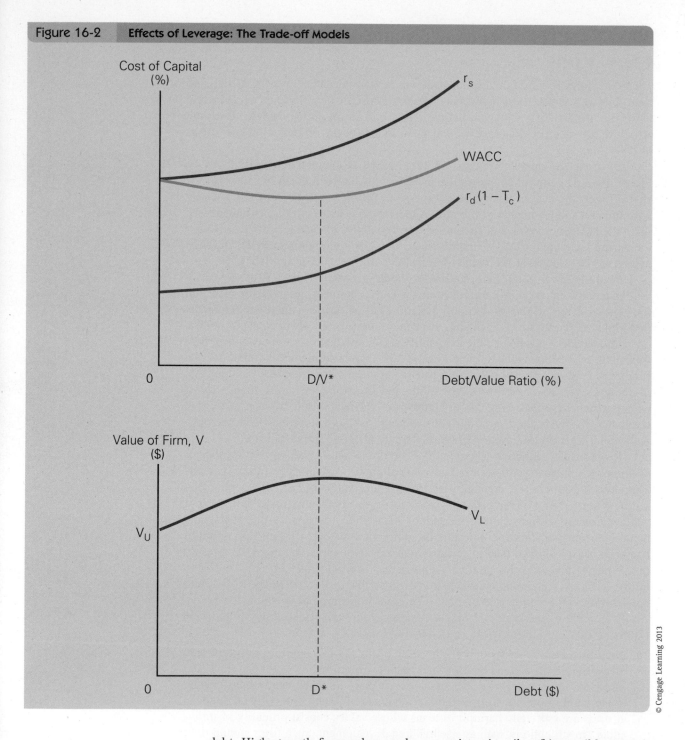

debt. High-growth firms whose values consist primarily of intangible growth
options may run out of internally generated cash, but they should emphasize
stock rather than debt because of the severe problems that financial distress
imposes on such firms.

4. Managers have better information than investors about a firm's prospects. This
informational asymmetry causes investors to view a stock issue as a negative signal, which leads to a decline in stock price. To prevent this, firms should maintain

a reserve of borrowing capacity so they can take advantage of investment opportunities without having to issue stock at low prices. This reserve will cause the actual debt ratio to be lower than that suggested by the trade-off models.

There is some evidence that managers do attempt to behave in ways that are consistent with this view of capital structure. In a survey of CFOs, about two-thirds said they follow a "hierarchy in which the most advantageous sources of funds are exhausted before other sources are used." The hierarchy usually followed the pecking order of first internally generated cash flow, then debt, and finally external equity, which is consistent with the predicted behavior of most low-growth firms. But there were occasions in which external equity was the first source of financing, which would be consistent with the theory for either high-growth firms or firms whose agency costs and level of financial distress have exceeded the benefit of tax savings.[15]

Self Test

Summarize the trade-off and signaling theories of capital structure.

Are the trade-off and signaling theories mutually exclusive or might *both* be correct?

Does capital structure theory provide managers with a model that can be used to set a precise optimal capital structure?

Summary

In this chapter we discussed a variety of topics related to capital structure decisions. The key concepts covered are listed below.

- In 1958, **Franco Modigliani and Merton Miller** (MM) proved, under a restrictive set of assumptions including zero taxes, that capital structure is irrelevant; thus, according to the original MM article, a firm's value is not affected by its financing mix.
- Modigliani and Miller later added **corporate taxes** to their model and reached the conclusion that capital structure does matter. Indeed, their model led to the conclusion that firms should use 100% debt financing.
- MM's model with corporate taxes demonstrated that the primary benefit of debt stems from the **tax deductibility of interest payments**.
- Later, Miller extended the theory to include **personal taxes**. The introduction of personal taxes reduces, but does not eliminate, the benefits of debt financing. Thus, the **Miller model** also leads to 100% debt financing.

---

15. For more on capital budgeting issues, see Ravindra R. Kamath, "Long-Term Financing Decisions: Views and Practices of Financial Managers of NYSE Firms," *The Financial Review,* May 1997, pp. 350–356; Michael T. Dugan and Keith A. Shriver, "An Empirical Comparison of Alternative Methods for Estimating the Degree of Operating Leverage," *The Financial Review,* May 1992, pp. 309–321; and Dilip K. Ghosh, "Optimum Capital Structure Redefined," *The Financial Review,* August 1992, pp. 411–429.

- The introduction of growth changes the MM and Hamada results for the levered cost of equity and the levered beta.
- If the firm is growing at a constant rate, the debt tax shield is discounted at r_{sU}, and debt remains a constant proportion of the capital structure, then

$$r_{sL} = r_{sU} + (r_{sU} - r_d)\frac{D}{S}$$

and

$$b = b_U + (b_U - b_D)\frac{D}{S}$$

- When debt is risky, management may choose to default. If the debt is zero coupon debt, then this makes equity like an option on the value of the firm with a strike price equal to the face value of the debt. If the debt has periodic interest payments then the equity is like an option on an option, or a **compound option**.
- When a firm has risky debt and equity is like an option, management has an incentive to increase the firm's risk in order to increase the equity value at the expense of the debt value. This is called **bait and switch**.

Questions

16-1 Define each of the following terms:
    a. MM Proposition I without taxes and with corporate taxes
    b. MM Proposition II without taxes and with corporate taxes
    c. Miller model
    d. Financial distress costs
    e. Agency costs
    f. Trade-off model
    g. Value of debt tax shield
    h. Equity as an option

16-2 Explain, in words, how MM use the arbitrage process to prove the validity of Proposition I. Also, list the major MM assumptions and explain why each of these assumptions is necessary in the arbitrage proof.

16-3 A utility company is allowed to charge prices high enough to cover all costs, including its cost of capital. Public service commissions are supposed to take actions that stimulate companies to operate as efficiently as possible in order to keep costs, and hence prices, as low as possible. Some time ago, AT&T's debt ratio was about 33%. Some individuals (Myron J. Gordon, in particular) argued that a higher debt ratio would lower AT&T's cost of capital and permit it to charge lower rates for telephone service. Gordon thought an optimal debt ratio for AT&T was about 50%. Do the theories presented in the chapter support or refute Gordon's position?

16-4 Modigliani and Miller assumed that firms do not grow. How does positive growth change their conclusions about the value of the levered firm and its cost of capital?

16-5 Your firm's CEO has just learned about options and how your firm's equity can be viewed as an option. Why might he want to increase the riskiness of the firm, and why might the bondholders be unhappy about this?

Problems   Answers Appear in Appendix B

Easy Problems 1–3

16-1 **MM Model with Zero Taxes** An unlevered firm has a value of $500 million. An otherwise identical but levered firm has $50 million in debt. Under the MM zero-tax model, what is the value of the levered firm?

16-2 **MM Model with Corporate Taxes** An unlevered firm has a value of $800 million. An otherwise identical but levered firm has $60 million in debt. Assuming the corporate tax rate is 35%, use the MM model with corporate taxes to determine the value of the levered firm.

16-3 **Miller Model with Corporate and Personal Taxes** An unlevered firm has a value of $600 million. An otherwise identical but levered firm has $240 million in debt. Under the Miller model, what is the value of the levered firm if the corporate tax rate is 34%, the personal tax rate on equity is 10%, and the personal tax rate on debt is 35%?

Intermediate Problems 4–7

16-4 **Business and Financial Risk—MM Model** Air Tampa has just been incorporated, and its board of directors is currently grappling with the question of optimal capital structure. The company plans to offer commuter air services between Tampa and smaller surrounding cities. Jaxair has been around for a few years, and it has about the same basic business risk as Air Tampa would have. Jaxair's market-determined beta is 1.8, and it has a current market value debt ratio (total debt to total assets) of 50% and a federal-plus-state tax rate of 40%. Air Tampa expects to be only marginally profitable at start-up; hence its tax rate would only be 25%. Air Tampa's owners expect that the total book and market value of the firm's stock, if it uses zero debt, would be $10 million. Air Tampa's CFO believes that the MM and Hamada formulas for the value of a levered firm and the levered firm's cost of capital should be used. (These are given in Equations 16-4, 16-6, and 16-7.)

   a. Estimate the beta of an unlevered firm in the commuter airline business based on Jaxair's market-determined beta. (*Hint:* This is a levered beta; use Equation 16-7 and solve for b_U.)

   b. Now assume that $r_d = r_{RF} = 10\%$ and that the market risk premium $RP_M = 5\%$. Find the required rate of return on equity for an unlevered commuter airline.

   c. Air Tampa is considering three capital structures: (1) $2 million debt, (2) $4 million debt, and (3) $6 million debt. Estimate Air Tampa's r_s for these debt levels.

   d. Calculate Air Tampa's r_s at $6 million debt while assuming its federal-plus-state tax rate is now 40%. Compare this with your corresponding answer to part c. (*Hint:* The increase in the tax rate causes V_U to drop to $8 million.)

16-5 **MM without Taxes** Companies U and L are identical in every respect except that U is unlevered while L has $10 million of 5% bonds outstanding. Assume that (1) there are no corporate or personal taxes, (2) all of the other MM assumptions are met, (3) EBIT is $2 million, and (4) the cost of equity to Company U is 10%.

   a. What value would MM estimate for each firm?

   b. What is r_s for Firm U? For Firm L?

c. Find S_L, and then show that $S_L + D = V_L = \$20$ million.

d. What is the WACC for Firm U? For Firm L?

e. Suppose $V_U = \$20$ million and $V_L = \$22$ million. According to MM, are these values consistent with equilibrium? If not, explain the process by which equilibrium would be restored.

16-6 MM with Corporate Taxes Companies U and L are identical in every respect except that U is unlevered while L has $10 million of 5% bonds outstanding. Assume that (1) all of the MM assumptions are met, (2) both firms are subject to a 40% federal-plus-state corporate tax rate, (3) EBIT is $2 million, and (4) the unlevered cost of equity is 10%.

a. What value would MM now estimate for each firm? (*Hint:* Use Proposition I.)

b. What is r_s for Firm U? For Firm L?

c. Find S_L, and then show that $S_L + D = V_L$ results in the same value as obtained in part a.

d. What is the WACC for Firm U? For Firm L?

16-7 Miller Model Companies U and L are identical in every respect except that U is unlevered while L has $10 million of 5% bonds outstanding. Assume that (1) all of the MM assumptions are met, (2) both firms are subject to a 40% federal-plus-state corporate tax rate, (3) EBIT is $2 million, (4) investors in both firms face a tax rate of $T_d = 28\%$ on debt income and $T_s = 20\%$ (on average) on stock income, and (5) the appropriate required pre-personal-tax rate r_{sU} is 10%.

a. What is the value V_U of the unlevered firm? (Note that V_U is now reduced by the personal tax on stock income, so $V_U = \$12$ million as in Problem 16-6.)

b. What is the value of V_L?

c. What is the gain from leverage in this situation? Compare this with the gain from leverage in Problem 16-6.

d. Set $T_c = T_s = T_d = 0$. What is the value of the levered firm? The gain from leverage?

e. Now suppose $T_s = T_d = 0$ and $T_c = 40\%$. What are the value of the levered firm and the gain from leverage?

f. Assume that $T_d = 28\%$, $T_s = 28\%$, and $T_c = 40\%$. Now what are the value of the levered firm and the gain from leverage?

Challenging Problems 8–10

16-8 MM Extension with Growth Schwarzentraub Industries' expected free cash flow for the year is $500,000; in the future, free cash flow is expected to grow at a rate of 9%. The company currently has no debt, and its cost of equity is 13%. Its tax rate is 40%. (*Hint:* Use Equations 16-16 and 16-17.)

a. Find V_U.

b. Find V_L and r_{sL} if Schwarzentraub uses $5 million in debt with a cost of 7%. Use the extension of the MM model that allows for growth.

c. Based on V_U from part a, find V_L and r_{sL} using the MM model (with taxes) if Schwarzentraub uses $5 million in 7% debt.

d. Explain the difference between your answers to parts b and c.

16-9 MM with and without Taxes International Associates (IA) is about to commence operations as an international trading company. The firm will have book assets of $10 million, and it expects to earn a 16% return on these assets before taxes. However, because of certain tax arrangements with foreign governments, IA will not pay any taxes; that is, its tax rate will be zero. Management is trying to decide how to raise the required $10 million. It is known that the capitalization rate r_U for an all-equity firm in this business is 11%, and IA can borrow at a rate $r_d = 6\%$. Assume that the MM assumptions apply.

a. According to MM, what will be the value of IA if it uses no debt? If it uses $6 million of 6% debt?

b. What are the values of the WACC and r_s at debt levels of D = $0, D = $6 million, and D = $10 million? What effect does leverage have on firm value? Why?

c. Assume the initial facts of the problem ($r_d = 6\%$, EBIT = $1.6 million, $r_{sU} = 11\%$), but now assume that a 40% federal-plus-state corporate tax rate exists. Use the MM formulas to find the new market values for IA with zero debt and with $6 million of debt.

d. What are the values of the WACC and r_s at debt levels of D = $0, D = $6 million, and D = $10 million if we assume a 40% corporate tax rate? Plot the relationship between the value of the firm and the debt ratio as well as that between capital costs and the debt ratio.

e. What is the maximum dollar amount of debt financing that can be used? What is the value of the firm at this debt level? What is the cost of this debt?

f. How would each of the following factors tend to change the values you plotted in your graph?

(1) The interest rate on debt increases as the debt ratio rises.

(2) At higher levels of debt, the probability of financial distress rises.

16-10 **Equity Viewed as an Option** A. Fethe Inc. is a custom manufacturer of guitars, mandolins, and other stringed instruments that is located near Knoxville, Tennessee. Fethe's current value of operations, which is also its value of debt plus equity, is estimated to be $5 million. Fethe has $2 million face value, zero coupon debt that is due in 2 years. The risk-free rate is 6%, and the standard deviation of returns for companies similar to Fethe is 50%. Fethe's owners view their equity investment as an option and would like to know the value of their investment.

a. Using the Black-Scholes option pricing model, how much is Fethe's equity worth?

b. How much is the debt worth today? What is its yield?

c. How would the equity value and the yield on the debt change if Fethe's managers could use risk management techniques to reduce its volatility to 30%? Can you explain this?

Spreadsheet Problem

16-11 **Build a Model: Equity Viewed as an Option** Start with the partial model in the file *Ch16 P11 Build a Model.xls* on the textbook's Web site. Rework Problem 16-10 using a spreadsheet model. After completing the problem as it appears, answer the following related questions.

a. Graph the cost of debt versus the face value of debt for values of the face value from $0.5 to $8 million.

b. Graph the values of debt and equity for volatilities from 0.10 to 0.90 when the face value of the debt is $2 million.

c. Repeat part b, but instead using a face value of debt of $5 million. What can you say about the difference between the graphs in part b and part c?

David Lyons, CEO of Lyons Solar Technologies, is concerned about his firm's level of debt financing. The company uses short-term debt to finance its temporary working capital needs, but it does not use any permanent (long-term) debt. Other solar technology companies average about 30% debt, and Mr. Lyons wonders why they use so much more debt and how it affects stock prices. To gain some insights into the matter, he poses the following questions to you, his recently hired assistant.

a. *BusinessWeek* recently ran an article on companies' debt policies, and the names Modigliani and Miller (MM) were mentioned several times as leading researchers on the theory of capital structure. Briefly, who are MM, and what assumptions are embedded in the MM and Miller models?

b. Assume that Firms U and L are in the same risk class and that both have EBIT = $500,000. Firm U uses no debt financing, and its cost of equity is $r_{sU} = 14\%$. Firm L has $1 million of debt outstanding at a cost of $r_d = 8\%$. There are no taxes. Assume that the MM assumptions hold.

   (1) Find V, S, r_s, and WACC for Firms U and L.
   (2) Graph (a) the relationships between capital costs and leverage as measured by D/V and (b) the relationship between V and D.

c. Now assume that Firms L and U are both subject to a 40% corporate tax rate. Using the data given in part b, repeat the analysis called for in b(1) and b(2) under the MM model with taxes.

d. Suppose investors are subject to the following tax rates: $T_d = 30\%$ and $T_s = 12\%$.

   (1) According to the Miller model, what is the gain from leverage?
   (2) How does this gain compare with the gain in the MM model with corporate taxes?
   (3) What does the Miller model imply about the effect of corporate debt on the value of the firm; that is, how do personal taxes affect the situation?

e. What capital structure policy recommendations do the three theories (MM without taxes, MM with corporate taxes, and Miller) suggest to financial managers? Empirically, do firms appear to follow any one of these guidelines?

f. How is the analysis in part c different if Firms U and L are growing? Assume both firms are growing at a rate of 7% and that the investment in net operating assets required to support this growth is 10% of EBIT.

g. What if L's debt is risky? For the purpose of this example, assume that the value of L's operations is $4 million (the value of its debt plus equity). Assume also that its debt consists of 1-year, zero coupon bonds with a face value of $2 million. Finally, assume that L's volatility, σ, is 0.60 and that the risk-free rate, r_{RF}, is 6%.

h. What is the value of L's stock for volatilities between 0.20 and 0.95? What incentives might the manager of L have if she understands this relationship? What might debtholders do in response?

Selected Additional Cases

The following cases from TextChoice, *Cengage Learning's online case library, cover many of the concepts discussed in this chapter and are available at* **www.textchoice2.com/casenet.**

Klein-Brigham Series:

Case 7, "Seattle Steel Products," Case 9, "Kleen Kar, Inc.," Case 10, "Aspeon Sparkling Water," Case 43, "Mountain Springs," Case 57, "Greta Cosmetics," Case 74, "The Western Company," Case 83, "Armstrong Production Company," and Case 99, "Moore Plumbing Supply Company," focus on capital structure theory. Case 8, "Johnson Window Company," and Case 56, "Isle Marine Boat Company," cover operating and financial leverage.

Brigham-Buzzard Series:

Case 8, "Powerline Network Corporation," covers operating leverage, financial leverage, and the optimal capital structure.

Chapter 21

Working Capital Management

Working capital management involves two basic questions: (1) What is the appropriate amount of working capital, both in total and for each specific account, and (2) how should working capital be financed? Note that sound working capital management goes beyond finance. Indeed, improving the firm's working capital position generally comes from improvements in the operating divisions. For example, experts in logistics, operations management, and information technology often work with engineers and production specialists to develop ways to speed up the manufacturing process and thus reduce the goods-in-process inventory. Similarly, marketing managers and logistics experts cooperate to develop better ways to deliver the firm's products to its customers. Finance comes into play in evaluating how effective the firm's operating departments are relative to other firms in its industry and also in evaluating the profitability of alternative proposals for improving working capital management. In addition, financial managers decide how much cash their companies should keep on hand and how much short-term financing should be used to finance their working capital.

Here are some basic definitions and concepts.

1. **Working capital,** sometimes called *gross working capital*, simply refers to current assets used in operations.[1]
2. **Net working capital** is defined as current assets minus all current liabilities.
3. **Net operating working capital (NOWC)** is defined as operating current assets minus operating current liabilities. Generally, NOWC is equal to cash required in operations, accounts receivable, and inventories, less accounts payable and accruals. Marketable securities not used in operations, cash in excess of operating needs, and other short-term investments are generally not considered to be operating current assets, so they are typically excluded when NOWC is calculated. The firm itself determines how much of its cash is required for operations, but all of the cash of most firms is used in operations.

---

1. The term "working capital" originated with the old Yankee peddler, who would load his wagon with pots and pans and then take off to peddle his wares. His horse and wagon were his fixed assets, while his merchandise was sold, or turned over at a profit, and thus was called his *working capital.*

Beginning of Chapter Questions

As you read this chapter, consider how you would answer the following questions. You *should not* necessarily be able to answer the questions before you read the chapter. Rather, you should use them to get a sense of the issues covered in the chapter. After reading the chapter, you should be able to give at least partial answers to the questions, and you should be able to give better answers after the chapter has been discussed in class. Note, too, that it is often useful, when answering conceptual questions, to use hypothetical data to illustrate your answer. We illustrate the answers with an *Excel* model that is available on the textbook's Web site. Accessing the model and working through it is a useful exercise, and it provides insights that are useful when answering the questions.

1. What is the **cash conversion cycle (CCC)?** Why is it better, other things held constant, to have a shorter rather than a longer CCC? Suppose you know a company's annual sales, average inventories, average accounts receivable, average accounts payable, and annual cost of goods sold. How could you use that information to determine the company's CCC? If you also knew its cost of capital, how could you determine its annual cost of carrying working capital? How could you determine how much the company would save if it could reduce the CCC by, say, 5 days? What are some actions it might take to reduce the CCC?

2. What is a **cash budget,** and how is this statement used by a business? How is the cash budget affected by the CCC? By credit policy?

3. Differentiate between **free** and **costly trade credit.** What is the formula for determining the **nominal annual cost rate** associated with a credit policy? What is the formula for the **effective annual cost rate?** How would these cost rates be affected if a firm buying on credit could "stretch" either the discount days or the net payment days— that is, take discounts on payments made after the discount period or else pay later than the stated payment date?

4. What are some advantages of **matching the maturities** of claims against assets with the lives of the assets financed by those claims? Is it feasible for a firm to match perfectly the maturities of all assets and claims against assets? Why might a firm deliberately mismatch some asset and claim maturities?

5. Define the terms **aggressive** and **conservative** when applied to financing, give examples of each, and then discuss the pros and cons of each approach. Would you expect to find entrenched firms in monopolistic (or oligopolistic) industries leaning more toward the aggressive or the conservative approach?

21.1 Current Asset Holdings

Current assets can be divided into two categories, operating and nonoperating. Operating current assets consist of cash plus marketable securities held as a substitute for operating cash, inventories, and accounts receivable. These are assets that are necessary to operate the business. Nonoperating current assets consist of any other current assets, principally short-term securities in excess of what is required in operations, funds held in case a good merger opportunity arises, cash from the sale of a stock or bond issue before the funds can be invested in fixed assets, or funds held in case the firm loses a lawsuit and is required to compensate the winning party. *Our focus in this section is strictly on operating current assets.*

The amount of operating current assets held is a policy decision, and one that affects profitability. Figure 21-1 shows three alternative policies regarding the size of the firm's operating current assets. The top line has the steepest slope, which indicates that the firm holds a lot of cash, marketable securities, receivables, and inventories relative to its sales. If receivables are high, the firm has a liberal credit

CORPORATE VALUATION AND WORKING CAPITAL MANAGEMENT

Superior working capital management can dramatically reduce required investments in operating capital, which can lead in turn to larger free cash flows and greater firm value.

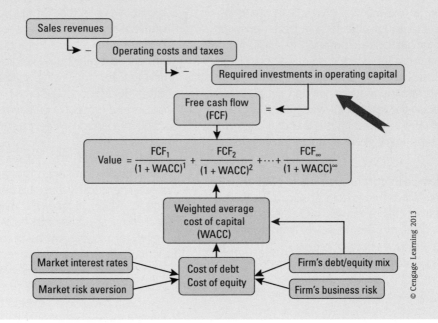

policy that results in a high level of accounts receivable. This is a **relaxed policy**. On the other hand, if a firm has a **restricted policy,** holdings of current assets are minimized and we say that the firm's policy is *tight* or *"lean-and-mean."* A **moderate policy** lies between the two extremes.

We can use the Du Pont equation to demonstrate how working capital management affects the return on equity:

$$\text{ROE} = \text{Profit margin} \times \text{Total assets turnover} \times \text{Equity multiplier}$$

$$= \frac{\text{Net income}}{\text{Sales}} \times \frac{\text{Sales}}{\text{Assets}} \times \frac{\text{Assets}}{\text{Equity}}$$

A relaxed policy means a high level of assets and hence a low total assets turnover ratio; this results in a low ROE, other things held constant. Conversely, a restricted policy results in low current assets, a high turnover, and hence a relatively high ROE. However, the restricted policy exposes the firm to risk, because shortages can lead to work stoppages, unhappy customers, and serious long-run problems. The moderate policy falls between the two extremes. The optimal strategy is the one that management believes will maximize the firm's long-run free cash flow and thus the stock's intrinsic value.

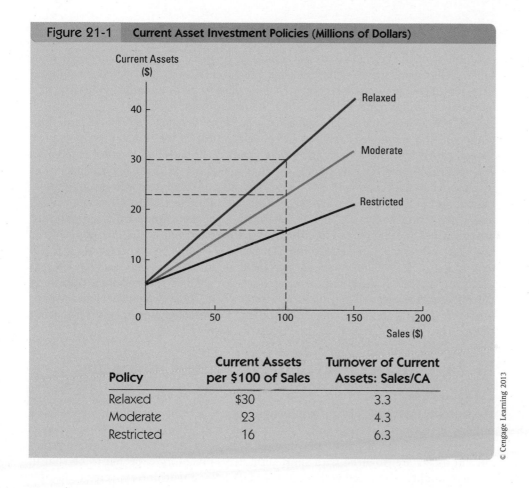

Figure 21-1   Current Asset Investment Policies (Millions of Dollars)

Policy	Current Assets per $100 of Sales	Turnover of Current Assets: Sales/CA
Relaxed	$30	3.3
Moderate	23	4.3
Restricted	16	6.3

© Cengage Learning 2013

Note that changing technologies can lead to changes in the optimal policy. For example, if a new technology makes it possible for a manufacturer to produce a given product in 5 rather than 10 days, then work-in-progress inventories can be cut in half. Similarly, retailers such as Wal-Mart and Home Depot have inventory management systems that use bar codes on all merchandise. These codes are read at the cash register; this information is transmitted electronically to a computer that adjusts the remaining stock of the item; and the computer automatically places an order with the supplier's computer when the stock falls to a specified level. This process lowers the "safety stocks" that would otherwise be necessary to avoid running out of stock. Such systems have dramatically lowered inventories and thus boosted profits.

Self Test

Identify and explain three alternative current asset investment policies.

Use the Du Pont equation to show how working capital policy can affect a firm's expected ROE.

What are the reasons for not wanting to hold too little working capital? For not wanting to hold too much?

21.2 Current Assets Financing Policies

Investments in operating current assets must be financed, and the primary sources of funds include bank loans, credit from suppliers (accounts payable), accrued liabilities, long-term debt, and common equity. Each of those sources has advantages and disadvantages, so a firm must decide which sources are best for it.

To begin, note that most businesses experience seasonal and/or cyclical fluctuations. For example, construction firms tend to peak in the summer, retailers peak around Christmas, and the manufacturers who supply both construction companies and retailers follow related patterns. Similarly, the sales of virtually all businesses increase when the economy is strong, so they increase operating current assets during booms but let inventories and receivables fall during recessions. However, current assets rarely drop to zero—companies maintain some **permanent operating current assets**, which are the operating current assets needed even at the low point of the business cycle. For a growing firm in a growing economy, permanent current assets tend to increase over time. Also, as sales increase during a cyclical upswing, current assets are increased; these extra current assets are defined as **temporary operating current assets** as opposed to permanent current assets. The way permanent and temporary current assets are financed is called the firm's **operating current assets financing policy**. Three alternative policies are discussed next.

21.2a Maturity Matching, or "Self-Liquidating," Approach

The **maturity matching**, or **"self-liquidating," approach** calls for matching asset and liability maturities as shown in Panel a of Figure 21-2. All of the fixed assets plus the permanent current assets are financed with long-term capital, but temporary current assets are financed with short-term debt. Inventory expected to be sold in 30 days would be financed with a 30-day bank loan; a machine expected to last for 5 years would be financed with a 5-year loan; a 20-year building would be financed with a 20-year mortgage bond; and so on. Actually, two factors prevent an exact maturity matching: (1) The lives of assets are uncertain. For example, a firm might finance inventories with a 30-day bank loan, expecting to sell the inventories and use the cash to retire the loan. But if sales are slow, then the cash would not be forthcoming and the firm might not be able to pay off the loan when it matures. (2) Some common equity must be used, and common equity has no maturity. Still, if a firm attempts to match or come close to matching asset and liability maturities, this is defined as a *moderate current asset financing policy*.

21.2b Aggressive Approach

Panel b of Figure 21-2 illustrates the situation for a more aggressive firm that finances some of its permanent assets with short-term debt. Note that we used the term "relatively" in the title for Panel b because there can be different *degrees* of aggressiveness. For example, the dashed line in Panel b could have been drawn *below* the line designating fixed assets, indicating that all of the current assets—both permanent and temporary—and part of the fixed assets were financed with short-term credit. This policy would be a highly aggressive, extremely nonconservative position, and the firm would be subject to dangers from loan renewal as well as rising interest rate problems. However, short-term interest rates are generally lower than long-term rates, and some firms are willing to gamble by using a large amount of low-cost, short-term debt in hopes of earning higher profits.

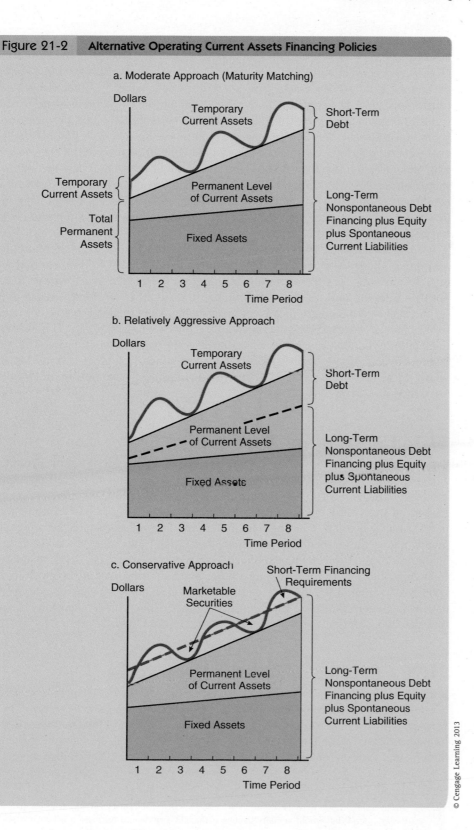

Figure 21-2   **Alternative Operating Current Assets Financing Policies**

a. Moderate Approach (Maturity Matching)

b. Relatively Aggressive Approach

c. Conservative Approach

A possible reason for adopting the aggressive policy is to take advantage of an upward sloping yield curve, for which short-term rates are lower than long-term rates. However, as many firms learned during the financial crisis of 2009, a strategy of financing long-term assets with short-term debt is really quite risky. As an illustration, suppose a company borrowed $1 million on a 1-year basis and used the funds to buy machinery that would lower labor costs by $200,000 per year for 10 years.[2] Cash flows from the equipment would not be sufficient to pay off the loan at the end of only one year, so the loan would have to be renewed. If the economy were in a recession like that of 2009, the lender might refuse to renew the loan, and that could lead to bankruptcy. Had the firm matched maturities and financed the equipment with a 10-year loan, then the annual loan payments would have been lower and better matched with the cash flows, and the loan renewal problem would not have arisen.

Under some circumstances, even maturity matching can be risky, as many firms that thought they were conservatively financed learned in 2009. If a firm borrowed on a 30-day bank loan to finance inventories that it expected to sell within 30 days but then sales dropped, as they did for many firms in 2009, the funds needed to pay off the maturing bank loan might not be available. Then the bank might not extend the loan, and if it did not then the firm could be forced into bankruptcy. This happened to many firms in 2009, and it was exacerbated by the banks' own problems. The banks had lost billions on mortgages, mortgage-backed bonds, and other bad investments, which led banks to restrict credit to their normal business customers in order to conserve their own cash.

21.2c Conservative Approach

Panel c of the figure shows the dashed line *above* the line designating permanent current assets, indicating that long-term capital is used to finance all permanent assets and also to meet some seasonal needs. In this situation, the firm uses a small amount of short-term credit to meet its peak requirements, but it also meets a part of its seasonal needs by "storing liquidity" in the form of marketable securities. The humps above the dashed line represent short-term financings, while the troughs below the dashed line represent short-term security holdings. This conservative financing policy is fairly safe, and the wisdom of using it was demonstrated in 2009: When credit dried up, firms with adequate cash holdings were able to operate more effectively than those that were forced to cut back their operations because they couldn't order new inventories or pay their normal workforce.

21.2d Choosing among the Approaches

Because the yield curve is normally upward sloping, *the cost of short-term debt is generally lower than that of long-term debt.* However, *short-term debt is riskier to the borrowing firm* for two reasons: (1) If a firm borrows on a long-term basis then its interest costs will be relatively stable over time, but if it uses short-term credit then its interest expense can fluctuate widely—perhaps reaching such high levels that

---

2. We are oversimplifying here. Few lenders would explicitly lend money for 1 year to finance a 10-year asset. What would actually happen is that the firm would borrow on a 1-year basis for "general corporate purposes" and then actually use the money to purchase the 10-year machinery.

profits are extinguished.[3] (2) If a firm borrows heavily on a short-term basis, then a temporary recession may adversely affect its financial ratios and render it unable to repay its debt. Recognizing this fact, the lender may not renew the loan if the borrower's financial position is weak, which could force the borrower into bankruptcy.

Note also that *short-term loans can generally be negotiated much faster* than long-term loans. Lenders need to make a thorough financial examination before extending long-term credit, and the loan agreement must be spelled out in great detail because a lot can happen during the life of a 10- to 20-year loan.

Finally, *short-term debt generally offers greater flexibility.* If the firm thinks that interest rates are abnormally high and due for a decline, it may prefer short-term credit because prepayment penalties are often attached to long-term debt. Also, if its needs for funds are seasonal or cyclical, then the firm may not want to commit itself to long-term debt because of its underwriting costs and possible prepayment penalties. Finally, long-term loan agreements generally contain provisions, or *cove-nants,* that constrain the firm's future actions in order to protect the lender, whereas short-term credit agreements generally have fewer restrictions.

All things considered, it is not possible to state that either long-term or short-term financing is generally better. The firm's specific conditions will affect its decision, as will the risk preferences of managers. Optimistic and/or aggressive managers will lean more toward short-term credit to gain an interest cost advantage, whereas more con-servative managers will lean toward long-term financing to avoid potential renewal problems. The factors discussed here should be considered, but the final decision will reflect managers' personal preferences and subjective judgments.

Self Test

Differentiate between permanent operating current assets and temporary operating current assets.

What does maturity matching mean, and what is the logic behind this policy?

What are some advantages and disadvantages of short-term versus long-term debt?

21.3 The Cash Conversion Cycle

All firms follow a "working capital cycle" in which they purchase or produce inventory, hold it for a time, and then sell it and receive cash. This process is known as the **cash conversion cycle (CCC)**.

21.3a Calculating the Target CCC

Assume that Great Basin Medical Equipment (GBM) is just starting in business, buying orthopedic devices from a manufacturer in China and selling them through distributors in the United States, Canada, and Mexico. Its business plan calls for it to purchase $10,000,000 of merchandise at the start of each month and have

---

3. The prime interest rate—the rate banks charge very good customers—hit 21% in the early 1980s. This produced a level of business bankruptcies that was not seen again until 2009. The primary reason for the very high interest rate was that the inflation rate was up to 13%, and high inflation must be compensated by high interest rates. Also, the Federal Reserve was tightening credit in order to hold down inflation, and it was encouraging banks to restrict their lending.

it sold within 50 days. The company will have 40 days to pay its suppliers, and it will give its customers 60 days to pay for their purchases. GBM expects to just break even during its first few years and so its monthly sales will be $10,000,000, the same as its purchases (or cost of goods sold). For simplicity, assume that there are no administrative costs. Also, any funds required to support operations will be obtained from the bank, and those loans must be repaid as soon as cash becomes available.

This information can be used to calculate GBM's target, or theoretical, cash conversion cycle, which "nets out" the three time periods described below.[4]

1. **Inventory conversion period.** For GBM, this is the 50 days it expects to take to sell the equipment, converting it from equipment to accounts receivable.[5]
2. **Average collection period (ACP).** This is the length of time customers are given to pay for goods following a sale. The ACP is also called the *days sales outstanding* (DSO). GBM's business plan calls for an ACP of 60 days based on its 60-day credit terms. This is also called the *receivables conversion period,* as it is supposed to take 60 days to collect and thus convert receivables to cash.
3. **Payables deferral period.** This is the length of time GBM's suppliers give it to pay for its purchases, which in our example is 40 days.

On Day 1, GBM expects to buy merchandise, and it expects to sell the goods and thus convert them to accounts receivable within 50 days. It should then take 60 days to collect the receivables, making a total of 110 days between receiving merchandise and collecting cash. However, GBM is able to defer its own payments for only 40 days.

We can combine these three periods to find the theoretical, or target, cash conversion cycle, shown below as an equation and diagrammed in Figure 21-3.

(21-1)

$$\begin{matrix} \text{Inventory} & & \text{Average} & & \text{Payables} & & \text{Cash} \\ \text{conversion} & + & \text{collection} & - & \text{deferral} & = & \text{conversion} \\ \text{period} & & \text{period} & & \text{period} & & \text{cycle} \end{matrix}$$

$$50 \quad + \quad 60 \quad - \quad 40 \quad = \quad 70 \text{ days}$$

Although GBM is supposed to pay its suppliers $10,000,000 after 40 days, it does not expect to receive any cash until $50 + 60 = 110$ days into the cycle. Therefore, it will have to borrow the $10,000,000 cost of the merchandise from its bank on Day 40, and it does not expect to be able to repay the loan until it collects on Day 110. Thus, for $110 - 40 = 70$ days—which is the theoretical cash conversion cycle (CCC)—it will owe the bank $10,000,000 and it will be paying interest on this debt. The shorter the cash conversion cycle the better, because a shorter CCC means lower interest charges.

Observe that if GBM could sell goods faster, collect receivables faster, or defer its payables longer without hurting sales or increasing operating costs, then its CCC would decline, its expected interest charges would be reduced, and its expected profits and stock price would be improved.

---

4. See Verlyn D. Richards and Eugene J. Laughlin, "A Cash Conversion Cycle Approach to Liquidity Analysis," *Financial Management,* Spring 1980, pp. 32–38.
5. If GBM were a manufacturer, the inventory conversion period would be the time required to convert raw materials into finished goods and then to sell those goods.

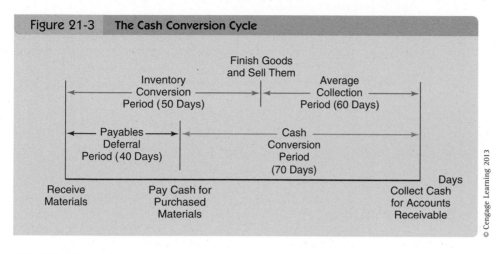

Figure 21-3 The Cash Conversion Cycle

© Cengage Learning 2013

21.3b Calculating the Actual CCC from Financial Statements

So far we have illustrated the CCC from a theoretical standpoint. However, in practice we would generally calculate the CCC based on the firm's financial statements, and the actual CCC would almost certainly differ from the theoretical value because of real-world complexities such as shipping delays, sales slowdowns, and slow-paying customers. Moreover, a firm such as GBM would be continually starting new cycles before the earlier ones ended, and this too would muddy the waters.

To see how the CCC is calculated in practice, assume that GBM has been in business for several years and is in a stable position, placing orders, making sales, receiving payments, and making its own payments on a recurring basis. The following data were taken from its latest financial statements, in millions:

Annual sales	$1,216.7
Cost of goods sold	1,013.9
Inventories	140.0
Accounts receivable	445.0
Accounts payable	115.0

Thus, its net operating working capital due to inventory, receivables, and payables is $140 + $445 − $115 = $470 million, and that amount must be financed—in GBM's case, through bank loans at a 10% interest rate. Therefore, its interest expense is $47 million per year.

We can analyze the situation more closely. First, consider the inventory conversion period:[6]

$$\text{Inventory conversion period} = \frac{\text{Inventory}}{\text{Cost of goods sold per day}} \quad (21\text{--}2)$$

$$= \frac{\$140.0}{\$1,013.9/365} = 50.4 \text{ days}$$

---

6. In past editions of this book we divided inventories by daily sales to be consistent with many reported data sources. We believe that dividing by daily cost of goods sold provides a more meaningful cash conversion period, so we changed the formula in this edition.

Thus, it takes GBM an average of 50.4 days to sell its merchandise, which is very close to the 50 days called for in the business plan. Note also that inventory is carried at cost, which explains why the denominator in Equation 21-2 is the cost of goods sold per day, not daily sales.

The average collection period (or days sales outstanding) is calculated next:

(21–3)
$$\text{Average collection period} = \text{ACP (or DSO)} = \frac{\text{Receivables}}{\text{Sales}/365}$$

$$= \frac{\$445.0}{\$1,216.7/365} = 133.5 \text{ days}$$

Thus, it takes GBM 133.5 days after a sale to receive cash, not the 60 days called for in its business plan. Because receivables are recorded at the sales price, we use daily sales (rather than the cost of goods sold per day) in the denominator for the ACP.

The payables deferral period is found as follows, again using daily cost of goods sold in the denominator because payables are recorded at cost:

(21–4)
$$\frac{\text{Payables}}{\text{deferral period}} = \frac{\text{Payables}}{\text{Purchases per day}} = \frac{\text{Payables}}{\text{Cost of goods sold}/365}$$

$$= \frac{\$115.0}{\$1,013.9/365} = 41.4 \text{ days}$$

GBM is supposed to pay its suppliers after 40 days, but it actually pays on average just after Day 41. This slight delay is normal, since mail delays and time for checks to be cashed generally slow payments down a bit.

We can now combine the three periods to calculate GBM's actual cash conversion cycle:

Cash conversion cycle (CCC) = 50.4 days + 133.5 days − 41.4 days = 142.5 days

WEB

See *Ch21 Tool Kit.xls* on the textbook's Web site for details.

Figure 21-4 summarizes all of these calculations and then analyzes why the actual CCC exceeds the theoretical CCC by such a large amount. It is clear from the figure that the firm's inventory control is working as expected in that sales match the inflow of new inventory items quite well. Also, its own payments match reasonably well the terms under which it buys. However, its accounts receivable are much higher than they should be, indicating that its customers are not paying on time. In fact, they are paying 73.5 days late, which is increasing GBM's working capital. Because working capital must be financed, the collections delay is lowering the firm's profits and presumably hurting its stock price.

When the CFO reviewed the situation, she discovered that GBM's customers—doctors, hospitals, and clinics—were themselves reimbursed by insurance companies and government units, and those organizations were paying late. The credit manager was doing everything he could to collect faster, but the customers said that they just could not make their own payments until they themselves were paid. If GBM wanted to keep making sales, it seemed that it would have to accept late-paying

Figure 21-4   **Summary of the Cash Conversion Cycle (Millions of Dollars)**

	A	B	C	D	E	F	G
9	Panel a. Target CCC: Based on Planned Conditions						
10	Cash Conversion Cycle (CCC)	=	Planned Inventory Conversion Period (ICP)	+	Credit Terms Offered to Our Customers	-	Credit Terms Our Supplier Offers Us
11		=	50.0	+	60.0	-	40.0
12							
13	Target CCC	=	70.0				
14							
15	Panel b. Actual CCC: Based on Financial Statements						
16							
17	Sales	$1,216.7					
18	COGS	$1,013.9					
19	Inventories	$140.0					
20	Receivables	$445.0					
21	Payables	$115.0					
22	Days/year	365					
23	Actual CCC	=	Inventory ÷ COGS/365	+	Receivables ÷ Sales/365	-	Payables ÷ COGS/365
24		=	$140 ÷ ($1,013.9/365)	+	$445 ÷ ($1,216.7/365)	-	$115 ÷ ($1,013.9/365)
25		=	50.4	+	133.5	-	41.4
26							
27	Actual CCC	=	142.5				
28							
29	Panel c. Actual versus Target Components						
30			ICP		ACP		PDP
31	Actual - Target	=	50.4 - 50.0		133.5 - 60.0		41.4 - 40.0
32		=	0.4	+	73.5	-	1.4
33	% Difference	=	0.8%		122.5%		3.5%
34			OK		VERY BAD		OK

Note: GBM's inventories are in line with its plans, and it's paying its suppliers nearly on time. However, some of its customers are paying quite late, so its average collection period (or DSO) is 133.5 days even though all customers are supposed to pay by Day 60.

© Cengage Learning 2013

customers. However, the CFO wondered if collections might come in faster if GBM offered substantial discounts for early payments. We will take up this issue later in the chapter.

21.3c Benefits of Reducing the CCC

As we have seen, GBM currently has a CCC of 142.5 days, which results in $470 million being tied up in net operating working capital. Assuming that its cost of debt to carry working capital is 10%, this means that the firm is incurring interest charges of $47 million per year to carry its working capital. Now suppose the company can speed up its sales enough to reduce the inventory conversion period from 50.4 to 35.0 days. In addition, it begins to offer discounts for early payment and thereby reduces its average collection period to 40 days. Finally, assume that it could negotiate a change in its own payment terms from 40 to 50 days. The "New" column of Figure 21-5 shows the net effects of these improvements: a 117.5-day reduction in the cash conversion cycle and a reduction in net operating working capital from $470.0 to $91.7 million, which saves $37.8 million of interest.

Recall also that free cash flow (FCF) is equal to NOPAT minus the net new investment in operating capital. Therefore, if working capital *decreases* by a given amount while other things remain constant, then FCF *increases* by that same amount—$378.3 million in the GBM example. If sales remained constant in the following years, then this reduction in working capital would simply be a one-time cash inflow. However, suppose sales grow in future years. When a company improves its working capital management, the components (inventory conversion period, collection period, and payments period) usually remain at their improved levels, which means the NOWC-to-Sales ratio remains at its new level. With an improved NOWC-to-Sales ratio, less working capital will be required to support future sales, leading to higher annual FCFs than would have otherwise existed.

Thus, an improvement in working capital management creates a large one-time increase in FCF at the time of the improvement as well as higher FCF in future years. Therefore, an improvement in working capital management is a gift that keeps on giving.

These benefits can add substantial value to the company. Professors Hyun-Han Shin and Luc Soenen studied more than 2,900 companies over a 20-year period, finding a strong relationship between a company's cash conversion cycle and its stock performance.[7] For an average company, a 10-day improvement in its CCC

Figure 21-5   Benefits from Reducing the Cash Conversion Cycle (Millions of Dollars)

	A	B	C	D	E	F	G
44					Old (Actual)		New (Target)
45	Inventory conversion period (ICP, days)				50.4		35.0
46	Average collection period (ACP, days)				133.5		40.0
47	Payable deferral period (PDP, days)				-41.4		-50.0
48	Cash Collection Cycle (CCC, days)				142.5		25.0
49							
50	Reduction in CCC					117.5	
51							
52	Effects of the CCC Reduction						
53	Annual sales				$1,216.7		$1,216.7
54	Costs of goods sold (COGS)				$1,013.9		$1,013.9
55	Inventory = Actual Old, New = new ICP(COGS/365)				$140.0		$97.2
56	Receivables = Actual Old, New = new ACP(Sales/365)				445.0		133.3
57	Payables = Actual Old, New = new PDP(COGS/365)				-115.0		-138.9
58	Net operating WC = Inv + Receivables − Payables				$470.0		$91.7
59							
60	Reduction in NOWC					$378.3	
61	Reduction in interest expense @ 10%					$37.8	

© Cengage Learning 2013

---

7. Hyun-Han Shin and Luc Soenen, "Efficiency of Working Capital Management and Corporate Profitability," *Financial Practice and Education,* Fall/Winter 1998, pp. 37–45.

SOME FIRMS OPERATE WITH NEGATIVE WORKING CAPITAL!

Some firms are able to operate with zero or even negative net working capital. Dell Computer and Amazon.com are examples. When customers order computers from Dell's Web site or books from Amazon, they must provide a credit card number. Dell and Amazon then receive next-day cash, even before the product is shipped and even before they have paid their own suppliers. This results in a negative CCC, which means that working capital *provides* cash rather than using it.

In order to grow, companies normally need cash for working capital. However, if the CCC is negative then growth in sales *provides* cash rather than *uses* it. This cash can be invested in plant and equipment, research and development, or for any other corporate purpose. Analysts recognize this point when they value Dell and Amazon, and it certainly helps their stock prices.

was associated with an increase in pre-tax operating profit margin from 12.76% to 13.02%. Moreover, companies with cash conversion cycles 10 days shorter than the average for their industry had annual stock returns that were 1.7 percentage points higher than the average company. Given results like these, it's no wonder firms place so much emphasis on working capital management![8]

Define the following terms: inventory conversion period, average collection period, and payables deferral period. Give the equation for each term.

What is the cash conversion cycle? What is its equation?

What should a firm's goal be regarding the cash conversion cycle, holding other things constant? Explain your answer.

What are some actions a firm can take to shorten its cash conversion cycle?

A company has $20 million of inventory, $5 million of receivables, and $4 million of payables. Its annual sales revenue is $80 million, and its cost of goods sold is $60 million. What is its CCC? (**120.15**)

21.4 The Cash Budget

Firms must forecast their cash flows. If they are likely to need additional cash then they should line up funds well in advance, yet if they are likely to generate surplus cash then they should plan for its productive use. The primary forecasting tool is the cash budget, illustrated in Figure 21-6, which is a screenshot from the chapter's *Excel Tool Kit* model. The illustrative company is Educational Products Corporation (EPC), which supplies educational materials to schools and retailers in the Midwest. Sales are cyclical, peaking in September and then declining for the balance of the year.

WEB

See *Ch21 Tool Kit.xls* on the textbook's Web site for details.

---

8. For more on the CCC, see James A. Gentry, R. Vaidyanathan, and Hei Wai Lee, "A Weighted Cash Conversion Cycle," *Financial Management,* Spring 1990, pp. 90–99.

Figure 21-6   EPC's Cash Budget, July–December 2013 (Millions of Dollars)

	A	B	C	D	E	F	G	H	I	J	K	L	M	N
73	Base Case					May	June	July	August	Sept	Oct	Nov	Dec	Jan
74	*Forecasted gross sales (manual inputs):*					$200.0	$250.0	$300.0	$400.0	$500.0	$350.0	$250.0	$200.0	$200.0
75	Adjustment: % deviation from forecast					0%	0%	0%	0%	0%	0%	0%	0%	0%
76	Adjusted gross sales forecast					$200.0	$250.0	$300.0	$400.0	$500.0	$350.0	$250.0	$200.0	$200.0
77														
78	*Collections on sales:*													
79	During sales' month:	0.2 (Sales)(1 – discount %)						$58.8	$78.4	$98.0	$68.6	$49.0	$39.2	
80	During 2nd month:	0.7 (prior month's sales)						175.0	210.0	280.0	350.0	245.0	175.0	
81	Due in 3rd month:	0.1 (sales 2 months ago)						20.0	25.0	30.0	40.0	50.0	35.0	
82	Less bad debts (BD% × Sales 2 months ago)							0.0	0.0	0.0	0.0	0.0	0.0	
83	Total collections							$253.8	$313.4	$408.0	$458.6	$344.0	$249.2	
84														
85	*Purchases: 60% of next month's sales*					$180.0	$240.0	$300.0	$210.0	$150.0	$120.0	$120.0		
86	*Payments*													
87	Pmt for last month's purchases (30 days of credit)						$180.0	$240.0	$300.0	$210.0	$150.0	$120.0		
88	Wages and salaries							30.0	40.0	50.0	40.0	30.0	30.0	
89	Lease payments							30.0	30.0	30.0	30.0	30.0	30.0	
90	Other payments (interest on LT bonds, dividends, etc.)							30.0	30.0	30.0	30.0	30.0	30.0	
91	Taxes									30.0			30.0	
92	Payment for plant construction									150.0				
93	Total payments							$270.0	$340.0	$590.0	$310.0	$240.0	$240.0	
94														
95	*Net cash flows:*													
96	Assumed <u>excess</u> cash on hand at start of forecast period							$0.0						
97	Net cash flow (NCF): Total collections – Total pmts							-16.2	-26.6	-182.0	148.6	104.0	9.2	
98	Cumulative NCF: Prior month cum plus this month's NCF							-$16.2	-$42.8	-$224.8	-$76.2	$27.8	$37.0	
99														
100	*Cash surplus (or loan requirement)*													
101	Target cash balance							$10.0	$10.0	$10.0	$10.0	$10.0	$10.0	
102	Surplus cash or loan needed: Cum NCF – Target cash							-$26.2	-$52.8	-$234.8	-$86.2	$17.8	$27.0	
103														
104	Max required loan (most <u>negative</u> on Row 102)						$234.8							
105	Max investable funds (most <u>positive</u> on Row 102)						$27.0							

Notes:

1. Although the budget period is July through December, sales and purchases data for May and June are needed to determine collections and payments during July and August.

2. Firms can both borrow and pay off commercial loans on a daily basis, so the $26.2 million loan needed for July would likely be gradually borrowed as needed on a daily basis, and during October the $234.8 million loan that presumably existed at the beginning of the month would be reduced daily to the $86.2 million ending balance—which, in turn, would be completely paid off sometime during November.

3. The data in the figure are for EPC's base-case forecast. Data for alternative scenarios are shown in the chapter's *Excel Tool Kit* model.

21.4a Monthly Cash Budgets

Cash budgets can be of any length, but EPC and most companies use a monthly cash budget such as the one in Figure 21-6, but set up for 12 months. We used only 6 months for the purpose of illustration. The monthly budget is used for longer-range planning, but a daily cash budget is also prepared at the start of each month to provide a more precise picture of the daily cash flows for use in scheduling actual payments on a day-by-day basis.

The cash budget focuses on cash flows, but it also includes information on forecasted sales, credit policy, and inventory management. Since the statement is a forecast and not a report on historical results, actual results could vary from the figures given. Therefore, the cash budget is generally set up as an expected, or base-case, forecast, but it is created with a model that makes it easy to generate alternative forecasts to see what would happen under different conditions.

Figure 21-6 begins with a forecast of sales for each month on Row 74. Then, on Row 75, it shows possible percentage deviations from the forecasted sales. Since we are showing the base-case forecast, no adjustments are made, but the model is set up to show the effects if sales increase or decrease and so result in "adjusted sales" that are above or below the forecasted levels.

The company sells on terms of "2/10, net 60." This means that a 2% discount is given if payment is made within 10 days; otherwise, the full amount is due in 60 days. However, like most companies, EPC finds that some customers pay late. Experience shows that 20% of customers pay during the month of the sale and take the discount. Another 70% pay during the month immediately following the sale, and 10% are late, paying in the second month after the sale.[9]

The statement (Line 85) next shows forecasted materials purchases, which equal 60% of the following month's sales. EPC buys on terms of net 30, meaning that it receives no discounts and is required to pay for its purchases within 30 days of the purchase date. The purchases information is followed by forecasted payments for materials, labor, leases, other payments such as dividends and interest on long-term bonds, taxes (due in September and December), and a payment of $150 million in September for a new plant that is being constructed.

When the total forecasted payments are subtracted from the forecasted collections, the result is the expected net cash gain or loss for each month. This gain or loss is added to or subtracted from the excess cash on hand at the start of the forecast (which we assume was zero), and the result—the *cumulative net cash flow*—is the amount of cash the firm would have on hand at the end of the month if it neither borrowed nor invested.

EPC's target cash balance is $10 million, and it plans either to borrow to meet this target or to invest surplus funds if it generates more cash than it needs. How the target cash balance is determined is discussed later in the chapter, but EPC believes that it needs $10 million.

By subtracting the target cash balance from the cumulative cash flow, we calculate the *loan needed or surplus cash,* as shown on Row 102. A negative number indicates that we need a loan, whereas a positive number indicates that we forecast surplus cash that is available for investment or other uses.

If we total the net cash flows on Row 97 then the sum is $37 million, the cumulative NCF as shown in Cell M98. Because this number is positive, it indicates that EPC's cash flow is positive. Also, note that EPC borrows on a basis that allows it to borrow or repay loans on a daily basis. Thus, it would borrow a total of $26.2 million in July, increasing the loan daily, and would continue to build up the loan through September. Then, when its cash flows turn positive in October, it would start repaying

---

9. A negligible percentage of sales results in bad debts. The low bad-debt losses evident here result from EPC's careful screening of customers and its generally tight credit policies. However, the cash budget model is able to show the effects of bad debts, so EPC's CFO could show top management how cash flows would be affected if the firm relaxed its credit policy in order to stimulate sales or if the recession worsened and more customers were forced to delay payments.

the loan on a daily basis and completely pay it off sometime in November, assuming that everything works out as forecasted.

Note that our cash budget is incomplete in that it shows neither interest paid on the working capital loans nor interest earned on the positive cash balances. These amounts could be added to the budget simply by adding rows and including them. Similarly, if the firm makes quarterly dividend payments, principal payments on its long-term bonds, or any other payments, or if it has investment income, then those cash flows also could be added to the statement. In our simplified statement, we just lumped all such payments into "other payments."

Under the base-case forecast, the CFO will need to arrange a line of credit so that the firm can borrow up to $234.8 million, increasing the loan over time as funds are needed and repaying it later when cash flows become positive. The treasurer would show the cash budget to the bankers when negotiating for the line of credit. Lenders would want to know how much the firm expects to need, when the funds will be needed, and when the loan will be repaid. The lenders—and EPC's top executives—would question the treasurer about the budget, and they would want to know how the forecasts would be affected if sales were higher or lower than those projected, how changes in customers' payment times would affect the forecasts, and the like. The focus would be on these two questions: *How accurate is the forecast likely to be? What would be the effects of significant errors?* The first question could best be answered by examining historical forecasts, and the second by running different scenarios as we do in the *Excel Tool Kit* model.

WEB

See *Ch21 Tool Kit.xls* on the textbook's Web site for details.

No matter how hard we try, no forecast will ever be exactly correct, and this includes cash budgets. You can imagine the bank's reaction if the company negotiated a loan of $235 million and then came back a few months later saying that it had underestimated its requirements and needed to boost the loan to say $260 million. The banker might well refuse, thinking the company was not very well managed. Therefore, EPC's treasurer would undoubtedly want to build a cushion into the line of credit—say, a maximum commitment of $260 million rather than the forecasted requirement of $234.8 million. However, as we discuss later in the chapter, banks charge commitment fees for guaranteed lines of credit; thus, the higher the cushion built into the line of credit, the more costly the credit will be. This is another reason why it is important to develop accurate forecasts.

21.4b Cash Budgets versus Income Statements and Free Cash Flows

If you look at the cash budget, it looks similar to an income statement. However, the two statements are quite different. Here are some key differences: (1) In an income statement, the focus would be on sales, not collections. (2) An income statement would show accrued taxes, wages, and so forth, not the actual payments. (3) An income statement would show depreciation as an expense, but it would not show expenditures on new fixed assets. (4) An income statement would show a cost for goods purchased when those goods were sold, not for when they were ordered or paid.

These are obviously large differences, so it would be a big mistake to confuse a cash budget with an income statement. Also, the cash flows shown on the cash budget are different from the firm's free cash flows, because FCF reflects after-tax operating income and the investments required to maintain future operations whereas the cash budget reflects only the actual cash inflows and outflows during a particular period.

The bottom line is that cash budgets, income statements, and free cash flows are all important and are related to one another, but they are also quite different.

Each is designed for a specific purpose, and the main purpose of the cash budget is to forecast the firm's liquidity position, not its profitability.

21.4c Daily Cash Budgets

Note that if cash inflows and outflows do not occur uniformly during each month, then the actual funds needed might be quite different from the indicated amounts. The data in Figure 21-6 show the situation on the last day of each month, and we see that the maximum projected loan during the forecast period is $234.8 million. Yet if all payments had to be made on the 1st of the month but most collections came on the 30th, then EPC would have to make $270 million of payments in July before it received the $253.8 million from collections. In that case, the firm would need to borrow about $270 million in July, not the $26.2 million shown in Figure 21-6. This would make the bank unhappy—perhaps so unhappy that it would not extend the requested credit. A daily cash budget would have revealed this situation.

Figure 21-6 was prepared using *Excel,* which makes it easy to change the assumptions. In the *Tool Kit* model we examine the cash flow effects of changes in sales, in customers' payment patterns, and so forth. Also, the effects of changes in credit policy and inventory management could be examined through the cash budget.

WEB

See *Ch21 Tool Kit.xls* on the textbook's Web site for details.

Self Test

How could the cash budget be used when negotiating the terms of a bank loan?

How would a shift from a tight credit policy to a relaxed policy be likely to affect a firm's cash budget?

How would the cash budget be affected if our firm's suppliers offered us terms of "2/10, net 30," rather than "net 30," and we decided to take the discount?

Suppose a firm's cash flows do not occur uniformly throughout the month. What effect would this have on the accuracy of the forecasted borrowing requirements based on a monthly cash budget? How could the firm deal with this problem?

21.5 Cash Management and the Target Cash Balance

Cash is needed to pay for labor and raw materials, to purchase fixed assets, to pay taxes, to service debt, to pay dividends, and so on, but cash itself (and the money in most commercial checking accounts) earns no interest. Thus, the goal of the cash manager is to minimize the cash amount the firm must hold for conducting its normal business activities while continuing to maintain a sufficient cash reserve to (1) take trade discounts, (2) pay promptly and thus maintain its credit rating, and (3) meet any unexpected cash needs. We begin our analysis with a discussion of the traditional reasons for holding cash.

21.5a Reasons for Holding Cash

Firms hold cash for two primary reasons:

1. *Transactions, both routine and precautionary.* Cash balances are necessary in business operations. Payments must be made in cash, and receipts are deposited in

THE *CFO* CASH MANAGEMENT SCORECARD

Each year, *CFO Magazine* publishes a cash management scorecard, prepared by REL Consultancy Group, based on the 1,000 largest publicly traded U.S. companies. On the one hand, if a company holds more cash than needed to support its operations, its return on invested capital (ROIC) will be dragged down because cash earns a low rate of return. On the other hand, if a company doesn't have enough cash, then it might experience financial distress if there is an unexpected downturn in business. How much cash is enough?

Although the optimum level of cash depends on a company's unique set of circumstances, REL defines industry benchmarks as that quartile of firms in an industry that have the lowest cash/sales ratios—on the theory that these firms have the best cash management procedures. A recent average benchmark cash/sales ratio was 5.6%, whereas the average firm had a ratio of 10.4%. This suggests that many firms had a lot more cash than they actually needed.

It's one thing to talk about reducing cash, but how can a company do it? A good relationship with its banks is one key to keeping low cash levels. Jim Hopwood, treasurer of Wickes, says, "We have a credit revolver if we ever need it." The same is true at Havertys Furniture, where CFO Dennis Fink says that if you have solid bank commitments, "You don't have to worry about predicting short-term fluctuations in cash flow."

Sources: Randy Myers, "Tight Makes Right," *CFO*, December 2008, pp. 64–70; D. M. Katz, "Cash Scorecard: Unleash the Hoards," *CFO.com*, October 17, 2006, **www.cfo.com/article.cfm/8048654?f=search**; Randy Myers, "Stuck on Yellow," *CFO*, October 2005, pp. 81–90; and S. L. Mintz, "Lean Green Machine," *CFO*, July 2000, pp. 76–94. For updates, go to **www.cfo.com** and search for "cash management."

---

the cash account. Cash balances associated with routine payments and collections are known as **transactions balances**. Cash inflows and outflows are unpredictable, and the degree of predictability varies among firms and industries. Therefore, firms need to hold some cash to meet random, unforeseen fluctuations in inflows and outflows. These "safety stocks" are called **precautionary balances**, and the less predictable the firm's cash flows, the larger such balances should be.

2. *Compensation to banks for providing loans and services.* A bank makes money by lending out funds that have been deposited with it, so the larger its deposits, the better the bank's profit position. If a bank is providing services to a customer, then it may require that customer to leave a minimum balance on deposit to help offset the costs of providing those services. Also, banks may require borrowers to hold their transactions deposits at the bank. Both types of deposits are called **compensating balances**. In a 1979 survey, 84.7% of responding companies reported they were required to maintain compensating balances to help pay for bank services; only 13.3% reported paying direct fees for banking services.[10] By 1996, those findings were reversed: Only 28% paid for bank services with compensating balances, while 83% paid direct fees.[11] Although the use of compensating balances to pay for services has declined,

---

10. See Lawrence J. Gitman, E. A. Moses, and I. T. White, "An Assessment of Corporate Cash Management Practices," *Financial Management*, Spring 1979, pp. 32–41.
11. See Charles E. Maxwell, Lawrence J. Gitman, and Stephanie A. M. Smith, "Working Capital Management and Financial-Service Consumption Preferences of US and Foreign Firms: A Comparison of 1979 and 1996 Preferences," *Financial Practice and Education*, Fall/Winter 1998, pp. 46–52.

these balances improve a firm's relationship with its bank and are still a reason why some companies hold additional cash.

In addition to holding cash for transactions, precautionary, and compensating balances, it is essential that the firm have sufficient cash to take **trade discounts**. Suppliers frequently offer customers discounts for early payment of bills. As we will see later in this chapter, the cost of not taking discounts is sometimes very high, so firms should have enough cash to permit payment of bills in time to take discounts.

Finally, for a number of reasons firms often hold short-term investments in excess of the cash needed to support operations. We discuss short-term investments later in the chapter.

Self Test

Why is cash management important?

What are the primary motives for holding cash?

21.6 Cash Management Techniques

In terms of dollar volume, most business is conducted by large firms, many of which operate nationally or globally. They collect cash from many sources and make payments from a number of different cities or even countries. For example, companies such as IBM, General Electric, and Hewlett-Packard have manufacturing plants all around the world, even more sales offices, and bank accounts in virtually every city where they do business. Their collection centers follow sales patterns. However, while some disbursements are made from local offices, most are made in the cities where manufacturing occurs or else from the home office. Thus, a major corporation might have hundreds or even thousands of bank accounts located in cities all over the globe, but there is no reason to think that inflows and outflows will balance in each account. Therefore, a system must be in place to transfer funds from where they come in to where they are needed, to arrange loans to cover net corporate shortfalls, and to invest net corporate surpluses without delay. Some commonly used techniques for accomplishing these tasks are discussed next.[12]

21.6a Synchronizing Cash Flow

If you as an individual were to receive income once a year, then you would probably put it in the bank, draw down your account periodically, and have an average balance for the year equal to about half of your annual income. If instead you received income weekly and paid rent, tuition, and other charges on a daily basis, then your average bank balance would still be about half of your periodic receipts and thus only 1/52 as large as if you received income only once annually.

Exactly the same situation holds for businesses: By timing their cash receipts to coincide with their cash outlays, firms can hold their transactions balances to a minimum. Recognizing this fact, firms such as utilities, oil companies, and credit card companies arrange to bill customers—and to pay their own bills—on regular "billing cycles" throughout the month. This **synchronization of cash flows** provides cash when it is needed and thus enables firms to reduce their average cash balances.

---

12. For more information on cash management, see Bruce J. Summers, "Clearing and Payment Systems: The Role of the Central Bank," *Federal Reserve Bulletin*, February 1991, pp. 81–91.

21.6b Speeding Up the Check-Clearing Process

When a customer writes and mails a check, the funds are not available to the receiving firm until the **check-clearing process** has been completed. First, the check must be delivered through the mail. Checks received from customers in distant cities are especially subject to mail delays.

When a customer's check is written on one bank and a company deposits the check in another bank, the company's bank must verify that the check is valid before the payee can use those funds. Checks are generally cleared through the Federal Reserve System or through a clearinghouse set up by the banks in a particular city.[13] Before 2004, this process sometimes took 2 to 5 days. But with the passage of a federal law in 2004 known as "Check 21," banks can exchange digital images of checks. This means that most checks now clear in a single day.

21.6c Using Float

Float is defined as the difference between the balance shown in a firm's (or individual's) checkbook and the balance on the bank's records. Suppose a firm writes, on average, checks in the amount of $5,000 each day, and suppose it takes 6 days for these checks to clear and be deducted from the firm's bank account. This will cause the firm's own checkbook to show a balance that is $30,000 smaller than the balance on the bank's records; this difference is called **disbursement float**. Now suppose the firm also receives checks in the amount of $5,000 daily but that it loses 4 days while those checks are being deposited and cleared. This will result in $20,000 of **collections float**. In total, the firm's **net float**—the difference between the $30,000 positive disbursement float and the $20,000 negative collections float—will be $10,000. In sum, collections float is bad, disbursement float is good, and positive net float is even better.

Delays that cause float will occur because it takes time for checks to (1) travel through the mail (mail float), (2) be processed by the receiving firm (processing float), and (3) clear through the banking system (clearing, or availability, float). Basically, the size of a firm's net float is a function of its ability to speed up collections on checks it receives and to slow down collections on checks it writes. Efficient firms go to great lengths to speed up the processing of incoming checks, thus putting the funds to work faster, and they try to stretch their own payments out as long as possible, sometimes by disbursing checks from banks in remote locations.

21.6d Speeding Up Collections

Two major techniques are used to speed collections and to get funds where they are needed: lockboxes and electronic transfers.

Lockboxes

A **lockbox system** is one of the oldest cash management tools. In a lockbox system, incoming checks are sent to post office boxes rather than to the firm's corporate headquarters. For example, a firm headquartered in New York City might have its

---

13. For example, suppose a check for $100 is written on Bank A and deposited at Bank B. Bank B will usually contact either the Federal Reserve System or a clearinghouse to which both banks belong. The Fed or the clearinghouse will then verify with Bank A that the check is valid and that the account has sufficient funds to cover the check. Bank A's account with the Fed or the clearinghouse is then reduced by $100, and Bank B's account is increased by $100. Of course, if the check is deposited in the same bank on which it was drawn, that bank merely transfers funds by bookkeeping entries from one depositor to another.

West Coast customers send their payments to a post office box in San Francisco, its customers in the Southwest send their checks to Dallas, and so on, rather than having all checks sent to New York City. Several times a day, a local bank will empty the lockbox and deposit the checks into the company's local account. The bank then provides the firm with a daily record of the receipts collected, usually via an electronic data transmission system in a format that permits online updating of the firm's accounts receivable records.

A lockbox system reduces the time required to receive incoming checks, to deposit them, and to get them cleared through the banking system and available for use. Lockbox services can make funds available as many as 2 to 5 days faster than via the "regular" system.

Payment by Wire or Automatic Debit

Firms are increasingly demanding payments of larger bills by wire or by automatic electronic debits. Under an electronic debit system, funds are automatically deducted from one account and added to another. This is, of course, the ultimate in a speeded-up collection process, and computer technology is making such a process increasingly feasible and efficient, even for retail transactions.

Self Test

What is float? How do firms use float to increase cash management efficiency?

What are some methods firms can use to accelerate receipts?

YOUR CHECK ISN'T IN THE MAIL

Issuing payroll checks to thousands of employees is expensive—in both the time and resources it takes the company to print, process, and deliver the checks, and in the time it takes the employee to deposit or cash the check. Paper checks cost a company between $1 and $2 each, and multiply that by thousands of employees, some of whom are paid weekly or biweekly, it adds up to a lot of money every year! Direct deposit of payroll checks into the employee's checking account reduces these costs, but there are still many employees, especially seasonal, temporary, part-time, or young employees, who don't have a checking account.

A growing solution to high check costs and the needs of these "unbanked" employees is the payroll debit card. Companies, in partnership with a bank, issue the employee a debit card that is automatically filled each payday. The employee either uses the debit card to make purchases or withdraws cash at an ATM. The cost to load a debit card is around $0.20, and so saves the companies 80% to 90% of the cost to print a check, and saves the unbanked employee from paying the frequently usurious check cashing fees that can be 10% or more. In fact, because debit card transactions that are processed as a credit card result in fees to the merchant, there is a small amount of money available to provide a rebate to the employer. For example, Premier Pay Cards offers a 0.1% rebate to the employer on certain purchases the employee makes with the debit card.

Although the use of a debit card for payroll eliminates the float that would occur with check-based pay, for many companies the reduced processing costs and increased employee satisfaction more than outweigh the reduction in float.

Sources: "The End of the Paycheck," *Fortune Small Business Magazine*, December 5, 2006, and **www.premierpaycards .com**.

21.7 Inventory Management

Inventory management techniques are covered in depth in production management courses. Still, financial managers have a responsibility for raising the capital needed to carry inventory and for overseeing the firm's overall profitability, so it is appropriate that we cover the financial aspects of inventory management here.

The twin goals of inventory management are (1) to ensure that the inventories needed to sustain operations are available, but (2) to hold the costs of ordering and carrying inventories to the lowest possible level. While analyzing improvements in the cash conversion cycle, we identified some of the cash flows associated with a reduction in inventory. In addition to the points made earlier, lower inventory levels reduce costs due to storage and handling, insurance, property taxes, spoilage, and obsolescence.

Before the computer age, companies used such simple inventory control techniques as the "red line" system, where a red line was drawn around the inside of a bin holding inventory items; when the actual stock declined to the level where the red line showed, inventory would be reordered. But now computers have taken over, and supply chains have been established that provide inventory items just before

SUPPLY CHAIN MANAGEMENT

Herman Miller Inc. manufactures a wide variety of office furniture, and a typical order from a single customer might require work at five different plants. Each plant uses components from different suppliers, and each plant works on orders for many customers. Imagine all the coordination that is required. The sales force generates the order, the purchasing department orders components from suppliers, and the suppliers must order materials from their own suppliers. The suppliers make and then ship the components to Herman Miller, the factory builds the products, the different products are gathered together to complete the order, and then the order is shipped to the customer. If one part of that process malfunctions, then the order will be delayed, inventory will pile up, extra costs to expedite the order will be incurred, and the customer's goodwill will be damaged, hurting future growth.

To prevent such consequences, many companies employ supply chain management (SCM). The key element in SCM is sharing information all the way back from the retailer where the product is sold, to the company's own plant, then back to the firm's suppliers, and even back to the suppliers' suppliers. SCM requires special computer software, but even more important is that it requires cooperation among the different companies and departments in the supply chain. This culture of open communication is often difficult for many companies, which can be reluctant to divulge operating information. For example, EMC Corp., a manufacturer of data storage systems, has become deeply involved in the design processes and financial controls of its key suppliers. Many of EMC's suppliers were initially wary of these new relationships. However, SCM has been a win–win proposition, with higher profits for both EMC and its suppliers.

The same is true at many other companies. After implementing SCM, Herman Miller was able to reduce its days of inventory on hand by a week and to cut 2 weeks off of delivery times to customers. It was also able to operate its plants at a 20% higher volume without additional capital expenditures, because downtime due to inventory shortages was virtually eliminated. As another example, Heineken USA can now get beer from its Dutch breweries to its customers' shelves in less than 6 weeks, compared with 10 to 12 weeks before implementing SCM. As these and other companies have found, SCM increases free cash flows, and that leads to more profits and higher stock prices.

Sources: Elaine L. Appleton, "Supply Chain Brain," *CFO*, July 1997, pp. 51–54; and Kris Frieswick, "Up Close and Virtual," *CFO*, April 1998, pp. 87–91.

they are needed—the *just-in-time* system. For example, consider Trane Corporation, which makes air conditioners and currently uses just-in-time procedures. In the past, Trane produced parts on a steady basis, stored them as inventory, and had them ready whenever the company received an order for a batch of air conditioners. However, the company's inventory eventually covered an area equal to three football fields, and it still could take as long as 15 days to fill an order. To make matters worse, occasionally some of the necessary components simply could not be located; in other instances, the components were located but found to have been damaged from long storage.

Then Trane adopted a new inventory policy—it began producing components only after receiving an order and then sending the parts directly from the machines that make them to the final assembly line. The net effect: Inventories fell nearly 40% even as sales were increasing by 30%.

Such improvements in inventory management can free up considerable amounts of cash. For example, suppose a company has sales of $120 million and an inventory turnover ratio of 3. This means the company has an inventory level of

$$\text{Inventory} = \text{Sales/(Inventory turnover ratio)}$$
$$= \$120/3 = \$40 \text{ million}$$

If the company can improve its inventory turnover ratio to 4, then its inventory will fall to

$$\text{Inventory} = \$120/4 = \$30 \text{ million}$$

This $10 million reduction in inventory boosts free cash flow by $10 million.

However, there are costs associated with holding too little inventory, and these costs can be severe. If a business lowers its inventories then it must reorder frequently, which increases ordering costs. Even worse, if stocks become depleted then firms can miss out on profitable sales and also suffer lost goodwill, which may lead to lower future sales. Therefore, it is important to have enough inventory on hand to meet customer demands but not so much as to incur the costs we discussed previously. Inventory optimization models have been developed, but the best approach—and the one most firms today are following—is to use supply chain management and monitor the system closely.[14]

What are some costs associated with high inventories? With low inventories?

What is a "supply chain," and how are supply chains related to just-in-time inventory procedures?

A company has $20 million in sales and an inventory turnover ratio of 2.0. If it can reduce its inventory and improve its inventory turnover ratio to 2.5 with no loss in sales, by how much will FCF increase? **($2 million)**

14. For additional insights into the problems of inventory management, see Richard A. Followill, Michael Schellenger, and Patrick H. Marchard, "Economic Order Quantities, Volume Discounts, and Wealth Maximization," *The Financial Review,* February 1990, pp. 143–152.

21.8 Receivables Management

Firms would, in general, rather sell for cash than on credit, but competitive pressures force most firms to offer credit for substantial purchases, especially to other businesses. Thus, goods are shipped, inventories are reduced, and an **account receivable** is created.[15] Eventually, the customer will pay the account, at which time (1) the firm will receive cash and (2) its receivables will decline. Carrying receivables has both direct and indirect costs, but selling on credit also has an important benefit: increased sales.

Receivables management begins with the firm's credit policy, but a monitoring system is also important to keep tabs on whether the terms of credit are being observed. Corrective action is often needed, and the only way to know whether the situation is getting out of hand is with a good receivables control system.[16]

21.8a Credit Policy

The success or failure of a business depends primarily on the demand for its products—as a rule, high sales lead to larger profits and a higher stock price. Sales, in turn, depend on a number of factors: Some, like the state of the economy, are exogenous, but others are under the firm's control. The major controllable factors are sales prices, product quality, advertising, and the firm's **credit policy**. Credit policy, in turn, consists of the following four variables.

1. *Credit period.* A firm might sell on terms of "net 30," which means that the customer must pay within 30 days.
2. *Discounts.* If the credit terms are stated as "2/10, net 30," then buyers may deduct 2% of the purchase price if payment is made within 10 days; otherwise, the full amount must be paid within 30 days. Thus, these terms allow a discount to be taken.
3. *Credit standards.* How much financial strength must a customer show to qualify for credit? Lower credit standards boost sales, but they also increase bad debts.
4. *Collection policy.* How tough or lax is a company in attempting to collect slow-paying accounts? A tough policy may speed up collections, but it might also anger customers and cause them to take their business elsewhere.

The credit manager is responsible for administering the firm's credit policy. However, because of the pervasive importance of credit, the credit policy itself is normally established by the executive committee, which usually consists of the president plus the vice presidents of finance, marketing, and production.

---

15. Whenever goods are sold on credit, two accounts are created—an asset item entitled *accounts receivable* appears on the books of the selling firm, and a liability item called *accounts payable* appears on the books of the purchaser. At this point, we are analyzing the transaction from the viewpoint of the seller, so we are concentrating on the variables under its control (i.e., the receivables). We examine the transaction from the viewpoint of the purchaser later in this chapter, where we discuss accounts payable as a source of funds and consider their cost.

16. For more on credit policy and receivables management, see Shehzad L. Mian and Clifford W. Smith, "Extending Trade Credit and Financing Receivables," *Journal of Applied Corporate Finance,* Spring 1994, pp. 75–84; and Paul D. Adams, Steve B. Wyatt, and Yong H. Kim, "A Contingent Claims Analysis of Trade Credit," *Financial Management,* Autumn 1992, pp. 104–112.

21.8b The Accumulation of Receivables

The total amount of accounts receivable outstanding at any given time is determined by two factors: (1) the credit sales per day and (2) the average length of time it takes to collect cash on accounts receivable:

$$\frac{\text{Accounts}}{\text{receivable}} = \frac{\text{Credit sales}}{\text{per day}} \times \frac{\text{Length of}}{\text{collection period}}$$

(21–5)

For example, suppose Boston Lumber Company (BLC), a wholesale distributor of lumber products, opens a warehouse on January 1 and, starting the first day, makes sales of $1,000 each day. For simplicity, we assume that all sales are on credit and that customers are given 10 days to pay. At the end of the first day, accounts receivable will be $1,000; they will rise to $2,000 by the end of the second day; and by January 10, they will have risen to 10($1,000) = $10,000. On January 11, another $1,000 will be added to receivables, but payments for sales made on January 1 will be collected and thus will reduce receivables by $1,000, so total accounts receivable will remain constant at $10,000. Once the firm's operations have stabilized, the following situation will exist:

$$\frac{\text{Accounts}}{\text{receivable}} = \frac{\text{Credit sales}}{\text{per day}} \times \frac{\text{Length of}}{\text{collection period}}$$
$$= \quad \$1,000 \quad \times \quad 10 \text{ days} \quad = \$10,000$$

If either credit sales or the collection period changes, these changes will be reflected in the accounts receivable balance.

21.8c Monitoring the Receivables Position

Both investors and bank loan officers should pay close attention to accounts receivable, because what you see on a financial statement is not necessarily what you end up getting. To see why, consider how the accounting system operates. When a credit sale is made, these events occur: (1) inventories are reduced by the cost of goods sold; (2) accounts receivable are increased by the sales price; and (3) the difference is reported as a profit, which is adjusted for taxes and then added to the previous retained earnings balance. If the sale is for cash, then the cash from the sale has actually been received by the firm and the scenario just described is completely valid. If the sale is on credit, however, then the firm will not receive the cash from the sale unless and until the account is collected. Firms have been known to encourage "sales" to weak customers in order to report high current profits. This could boost the firm's stock price–but only for a short time. Eventually, credit losses will lower earnings, at which time the stock price will fall. This is another example of how differences between a firm's stock price and its intrinsic value can arise, and it is something that security analysts must keep in mind.

An analysis along the lines suggested in the following sections will detect any such questionable practice, and it will also help a firm's management learn of problems that might be arising. Such early detection helps both investors and bankers avoid losses, and it also helps a firm's management maximize intrinsic values.

SUPPLY CHAIN FINANCE

In our global economy, companies purchase parts and materials from suppliers located all over the world. For small and mid-size suppliers, especially those in less developed economies, selling to international customers can lead to cash flow problems. First, many suppliers have no way of knowing when their invoices have been approved by their customers. Second, they have no way of knowing when they will actually receive payment from their customers. With a 4–5-month lag between the time an order is received and the time the payment occurs, many suppliers resort to expensive local financing that can add as much as 4% to their costs. Even worse, some suppliers go out of business, which reduces competition and ultimately leads to higher prices.

Although most companies now work very hard with their suppliers to improve their supply chain operations, which is at the heart of supply management, a recent poll shows that only 13% actively use supply chain finance (SCF) techniques. However, that figure is likely to rise in the near future.

For example, Big Lots joined a Web-based service operated by Prime-Revenue that works like this: First, invoices received by Big Lots are posted to the system as soon as they are approved. The supplier doesn't need specialized software but can check its invoices using a Web browser. Second, the supplier has the option of selling the approved invoices at a discount to financial institutions and banks that have access to the PrimeRevenue network. A further advantage to the supplier is that it receives cash within a day of the invoices' approval. In addition, the effective interest rate built into the discounted price is based on the credit rating of Big Lots, not that of the supplier.

As Big Lots treasurer Jared Poff puts it, this allows vendors to "compete on their ability to make the product and not on their ability to access financing."

Source: Kate O'Sullivan, "Financing the Chain," *CFO,* February 2007, pp. 46–53.

Days Sales Outstanding (DSO)

Suppose Super Sets Inc., a television manufacturer, sells 200,000 television sets a year at a price of $198 each. Assume that all sales are on credit under the terms 2/10, net 30. Finally, assume that 70% of the customers take the discount and pay on Day 10 and that the other 30% pay on Day 30.[17]

Super Sets's **days sales outstanding (DSO)**, sometimes called the *average collection period (ACP),* is 16 days:

$$\text{DSO} = \text{ACP} = 0.7(10 \text{ days}) + 0.3(30 \text{ days}) = 16 \text{ days}$$

Super Sets's *average daily sales (ADS)* is $108,493:

(21–6)
$$\text{ADS} = \frac{\text{Annual sales}}{365} = \frac{(\text{Units sold})(\text{Sales price})}{365}$$

$$= \frac{200,000(\$198)}{365} = \frac{\$39,600,000}{365} = \$108,493$$

---

17. Unless otherwise noted, we assume throughout that payments are made either on the *last day* for taking discounts or on the *last day* of the credit period. It would be foolish to pay on (say) the 5th day or on the 20th day if the credit terms were 2/10, net 30.

Super Sets's accounts receivable—assuming a constant, uniform rate of sales throughout the year—will at any point in time be $1,735,888:

$$\text{Receivables} = (\text{DSO})(\text{ADS}) \qquad (21\text{–}7)$$

$$= (\$108,493)(16) = \$1,735,888$$

Note that DSO, or average collection period, is a measure of the average length of time it takes the firm's customers to pay off their credit purchases. Super Sets's DSO is 16 days versus an industry average of 25 days, so either Super Sets has a higher percentage of discount customers or else its credit department is exceptionally good at ensuring prompt payment.

Finally, note that you can derive both the annual sales and the receivables balance from the firm's financial statements, so you can calculate DSO as follows:

$$\text{DSO} = \frac{\text{Receivables}}{\text{Sales per day}} = \frac{\$1,735,888}{\$108,493} = 16 \text{ days}$$

The DSO can also be compared with the firm's own credit terms. For example, suppose Super Sets's DSO had been averaging 35 days. With a 35-day DSO, some customers obviously are taking more than 30 days to pay their bills. In fact, if many customers are paying by Day 10 to take advantage of the discount, then the others must be taking, on average, *much* longer than 35 days. A way to check this possibility is to use an aging schedule, as described next.

Aging Schedules

An **aging schedule** breaks down a firm's receivables by age of account. Table 21-1 shows the December 31, 2012, aging schedules of two television manufacturers, Super Sets and Wonder Vision. Both firms offer the same credit terms, and they have the same total receivables. Super Sets's aging schedule indicates that all of its customers pay on time: 70% pay by Day 10 and 30% pay by Day 30. In contrast, Wonder Vision's schedule, which is more typical, shows that many of its customers are not paying on time: 27% of its receivables are more than 30 days old, even though Wonder Vision's credit terms call for full payment by Day 30.

TABLE 21-1 Aging Schedules

Age of Account (Days)	Super Sets Value of Account	Super Sets Percentage of Total Value	Wonder Vision Value of Account	Wonder Vision Percentage of Total Value
0–10	$1,215,122	70%	$ 815,867	47%
11–30	520,766	30	451,331	26
31–45	0	0	260,383	15
46–60	0	0	173,589	10
Over 60	0	0	34,718	2
Total receivables	$1,735,888	100%	$1,735,888	100%

Aging schedules cannot be constructed from the type of summary data reported in financial statements; rather, they must be developed from the firm's accounts receivable ledger. However, well-run firms have computerized their accounts receivable records, so it is easy to determine the age of each invoice, to sort electronically by age categories, and thus to generate an aging schedule.

Management should constantly monitor both the DSO and the aging schedule to detect any trends, to see how the firm's collections experience compares with its credit terms, and to see how effectively the credit department is operating in comparison with other firms in the industry. If the DSO starts to lengthen or the aging schedule begins to show an increasing percentage of past-due accounts, then the credit manager should examine why these changes are occurring.

Although increases in the DSO and the aging schedule are warning signs, this does not necessarily indicate the firm's credit policy has weakened. If a firm experiences sharp seasonal variations or if it is growing rapidly, then both the aging schedule and the DSO may be distorted. To see this point, note that the DSO is calculated as follows:

$$\text{DSO} = \frac{\text{Accounts receivable}}{\text{Annual sales}/365}$$

Receivables at any point in time reflect sales in the past 1 or 2 months, but sales as shown in the denominator are for the past 12 months. Therefore, a seasonal increase in sales will increase the numerator more than the denominator and hence will raise the DSO, even if customers continue to pay just as quickly as before. Similar problems arise with the aging schedule, because if sales are rising then the percentage in the 0–10-day category will be high, and the reverse will occur if sales are falling. Therefore, a change in either the DSO or the aging schedule should be taken as a signal to investigate further; it is not necessarily a sign that the firm's credit policy has weakened.

Self Test

Explain how a new firm's receivables balance is built up over time.

Define days sales outstanding (DSO). What can be learned from it? How is it affected by sales fluctuations?

What is an aging schedule? What can be learned from it? How is it affected by sales fluctuations?

A company has annual sales of $730 million. If its DSO is 35, what is its average accounts receivables balance? **($70 million)**.

21.9 Accruals and Accounts Payable (Trade Credit)

Recall that net operating working capital is equal to operating current assets minus operating current liabilities. The previous sections discussed the management of operating current assets (cash, inventory, and accounts receivable), and the following sections discuss the two major types of operating current liabilities: accruals and accounts payable.[18]

---

18. For more on accounts payable management, see James A. Gentry and Jesus M. De La Garza, "Monitoring Accounts Payables," *Financial Review,* November 1990, pp. 559–576.

21.9a Accruals

Firms generally pay employees on a weekly, biweekly, or monthly basis, so the balance sheet will typically show some accrued wages. Similarly, the firm's own estimated income taxes, employment and income taxes withheld from employees, and sales taxes collected are generally paid on a weekly, monthly, or quarterly basis. Therefore, the balance sheet will typically show some accrued taxes along with accrued wages.

These **accruals** can be thought of as short-term, interest-free loans from employees and taxing authorities, and they increase automatically (that is, *spontaneously*) as a firm's operations expand. However, a firm cannot ordinarily control its accruals: The timing of wage payments is set by economic forces and industry norms, and tax payment dates are established by law. Thus, firms generally use all the accruals they can, but they have little control over the levels of these accounts.

21.9b Accounts Payable (Trade Credit)

Firms generally make purchases from other firms on credit, recording the debt as an *account payable*. Accounts payable, or **trade credit**, is the largest single operating current liability, representing about 40% of the current liabilities for an average non-financial corporation. The percentage is somewhat larger for smaller firms: Because small companies often have difficulty obtaining financinsg from other sources, they rely especially heavily on trade credit.

Trade credit is a spontaneous source of financing in the sense that it arises from ordinary business transactions. For example, suppose a firm makes average purchases of $2,000 a day on terms of net 30, meaning that it must pay for goods

A WAG OF THE FINGER OR TIP OF THE HAT? THE COLBERT REPORT AND SMALL BUSINESS PAYMENT TERMS

On February 17, 2011, The Colbert Report featured an interview with Jeffrey Leonard. During a spirited exchange with Stephen Colbert, Leonard accused many large businesses of imposing onerous payment terms on their small suppliers. According to Leonard, when Cisco Systems sells to the U.S. government, Cisco receives its payment in 30 days, the standard credit terms used by the federal government. Yet Cisco changed its own credit policy in 2010 to "net 60," meaning that Cisco's suppliers don't get paid for 60 days. In other words, many small companies essentially are helping Cisco finance its working capital, even though Cisco has over $39 billion in cash. Cisco isn't alone in delaying its payments: Dell, Wal-Mart, and AB InBev (the owner of Anheuser-Busch) also pay slower than 30 days.

Colbert and Leonard agreed on the facts, but interpreted them differently. Leonard suggested that the government help small businesses by requiring its own supplier companies to offer their vendors the same terms as the government does. Colbert, however, suggested (perhaps with tongue-in-cheek) that this was just the natural result of free markets and that no government interference was warranted.

You be the judge. When big companies legally take what they can from smaller companies, should they receive a wag of the finger or a tip of the hat?

Sources: **www.washingtonmonthly.com/features/2011/1101.leonard.html,www.colbertnation.com/the-colbert-report-videos/374633/february-17-2011/jeffrey-leonard**, and **www.allbusiness.com/company-activities-management/management-benchmarking/15472247-1.html**.

30 days after the invoice date. On average, it will owe 30 times $2,000, or $60,000, to its suppliers. If its sales, and consequently its purchases, were to double, then its accounts payable would also double, to $120,000. So simply by growing, the firm would spontaneously generate an additional $60,000 of financing. Similarly, if the terms under which the firm buys were extended from 30 to 40 days, then its accounts payable would expand from $60,000 to $80,000 even with no growth in sales. Thus, both expanding sales and lengthening the credit period generate additional amounts of financing via trade credit.

21.9c The Cost of Trade Credit

Firms that sell on credit have a *credit policy* that includes their *terms of credit*. For example, Microchip Electronics sells on terms of 2/10, net 30: It gives customers a 2% discount if they pay within 10 days of the invoice date, but the full invoice amount is due and payable within 30 days if the discount is not taken.

The "true price" of Microchip's products is the net price, or 0.98 times the list price, because any customer can purchase an item at that price as long as payment is made within 10 days. Now consider Personal Computer Company (PCC), which buys its memory chips from Microchip. One chip is listed at $100, so its "true" price to PCC is $98. Now if PCC wants an additional 20 days of credit beyond the 10-day discount period, it must incur a finance charge of $2 per chip for that credit. Thus, the $100 list price consists of two components:

$$\text{List price} = \$98 \text{ true price} + \$2 \text{ finance charge}$$

The question PCC must ask before it turns down the discount to obtain the additional 20 days of credit is this: Could credit be obtained at a lower cost from a bank or some other lender?

Now assume that PCC buys $11,923,333 of memory chips from Microchip each year at the net, or true, price. This amounts to $11,923,333/365 = $32,666.67 per day. For simplicity, assume that Microchip is PCC's only supplier. If PCC decides not to take the additional 20 days of trade credit—that is, if it pays on the 10th day and takes the discount—then its payables will average 10($32,666.67) = $326,667. Thus, PCC will be receiving $326,667 of credit from Microchip.

Now suppose PCC decides to take the additional 20 days credit and so must pay the full list price. Since PCC will now pay on the 30th day, its accounts payable will increase to 30($32,666.67) = $980,000.[19] Microchip will now be supplying PCC with an additional $980,000 − $326,667 = $653,333 of credit, which PCC could use to build up its cash account, to pay off debt, to expand inventories, or even to extend credit to its own customers, hence increasing its own accounts receivable.

Thus the additional trade credit offered by Microchip has a cost: PCC must pay a finance charge equal to the 2% discount it is forgoing. PCC buys $11,923,333 of chips at the true price, so the added finance charge would increase the total cost to $11,923,333/0.98 = $12,166,666. Therefore, the annual financing cost is $12,166,666 − $11,923,333 = $243,333. Dividing the $243,333 financing cost by

---

19. A question arises here: Should accounts payable reflect gross purchases or purchases net of discounts? Generally accepted accounting principles permit either treatment if the difference is not material, but if the discount is material then the transaction must be recorded net of discounts, or at "true" prices. Then, the higher payment that results from not taking discounts is reported as an expense called "discounts lost." Therefore, *we show accounts payable net of discounts even if the company does not expect to take discounts.*

the $653,333 of additional credit, we calculate the nominal annual cost rate of the additional trade credit to be 37.2%:

$$\text{Nominal annual costs} = \frac{\$243,333}{\$653,333} = 37.2\%$$

If PCC can borrow from its bank (or some other source) at an interest rate less than 37.2%, then it should take the 2% discount and forgo the additional trade credit.

The following equation can be used to calculate the nominal cost (on an annual basis) of not taking discounts, illustrated with terms of 2/10, net 30:

$$\begin{matrix} \text{Nominal cost} \\ \text{of trade credit} \end{matrix} = \text{Cost per period} \times \text{Number of periods per year}$$

$$\begin{matrix} \text{Nominal cost} \\ \text{of trade credit} \end{matrix} = \frac{\text{Discount percentage}}{100 - \begin{matrix}\text{Discount}\\\text{percentage}\end{matrix}} \times \frac{365}{\begin{matrix}\text{Days credit is}\\\text{outstanding}\end{matrix} - \begin{matrix}\text{Discount}\\\text{period}\end{matrix}} \qquad (21\text{--}8)$$

$$= \frac{2}{98} \times \frac{365}{20} = 2.04\% \times 18.25 = 37.2\%$$

The numerator of the first term, Discount percentage, is the cost per dollar of credit, while the denominator, 100 – Discount percentage, represents the funds made available by not taking the discount. Thus, the first term, 2.04%, is the cost per period for the trade credit. The denominator of the second term is the number of days of extra credit obtained by not taking the discount, so the entire second term shows how many times each year the cost is incurred—18.25 times in this example.

This nominal annual cost formula does not consider the compounding of interest. In terms of effective annual interest, the cost of trade credit is even higher:

$$\text{Effective annual rate} = (1.0204)^{18.25} - 1.0 = 1.4459 - 1.0 = 44.6\%$$

Thus, the 37.2% nominal cost calculated with Equation 21-8 actually understates the true cost.

Note, however, that the calculated cost of trade credit can be reduced by paying late. Thus, if PCC could get away with paying in 60 days rather than the specified 30 days, then the effective credit period would become 60 – 10 = 50 days, the number of times the discount would be lost would fall to 365/50 = 7.3, and the nominal cost would drop from 37.2% to 2.04% × 7.3 = 14.9%. Then the effective annual rate would drop from 44.6% to 15.9%:

$$\text{Effective annual rate} = (1.0204)^{7.3} - 1.0 = 1.1589 - 1.0 = 15.9\%$$

In periods of excess capacity, firms may be able to get away with deliberately paying late, or **stretching accounts payable**. However, they will also suffer a variety of problems associated with being a "slow payer." These problems are discussed later in the chapter.

The costs of the additional trade credit from forgoing discounts under some other purchase terms are taken from the chapter's *Excel Tool Kit* model and shown here as Figure 21-7. As these numbers indicate, the cost of not taking discounts can be substantial.

WEB

See *Ch21 Tool Kit.xls* on the textbook's Web site for details.

Figure 21-7	Varying Credit Terms and Their Associated Costs

	A	B	C	D	E	F
32		Days in year:	365		Cost of additional	
33					credit	
34	Credit terms	Discount	Discount period	Net period	Nominal	Effective
35	1/10, net 20	1%	10	20	36.87%	44.32%
36	1/10, net 30	1%	10	30	18.43%	20.13%
37	1/10, net 90	1%	10	90	4.61%	4.69%
38	2/10, net 20	2%	10	20	74.49%	109.05%
39	2/10, net 30	2%	10	30	37.24%	44.59%
40	3/15, net 45	3%	15	45	37.63%	44.86%

© Cengage Learning 2013

On the basis of the preceding discussion, trade credit can be divided into two components: (1) **free trade credit**, which involves credit received during the discount period, and (2) **costly trade credit**, which involves credit in excess of the free trade credit and whose cost is an implicit one based on the forgone discounts. *Firms should always use the free component, but they should use the costly component only after analyzing the cost of this capital to make sure it is less than the cost of funds that could be obtained from other sources.* Under the terms of trade found in most industries, the costly component is relatively expensive, so stronger firms generally avoid using it.

Note, though, that firms sometimes offer favorable credit terms in order to stimulate sales. For example, suppose a firm has been selling on terms of 2/10, net 30, with a nominal cost of 37.24%, but a recession has reduced sales and the firm now has excess capacity. It wants to boost the sales of its product without cutting the list price, so it might offer terms of 1/10, net 90, which implies a nominal cost of additional credit of only 4.61%. In this situation, its customers would probably be wise to take the additional credit and reduce their reliance on banks and other lenders. So, turning down discounts is not always a bad decision.

Self Test

What are accruals? How much control do managers have over accruals?

What is trade credit?

What's the difference between free trade credit and costly trade credit?

How does the cost of costly trade credit generally compare with the cost of short-term bank loans?

A company buys on terms of 2/12, net 28. What is its nominal cost of trade credit? (**46.6%**) The effective cost? (**58.5%**)

21.10 Short-Term Marketable Securities

Short-term marketable securities are held for two separate and distinct purposes: (1) to provide liquidity, as a substitute for cash; and (2) as a nonoperating investment, generally on a temporary basis while awaiting deployment for long-term, permanent investments. Of course, it is difficult to separate these two purposes, because securities held while awaiting reinvestment are available for liquidity purposes.

With regard to operating funds, companies typically lump liquid marketable securities in with currency and bank demand deposits and call the total "cash and cash equivalents." These are the current assets that the firm needs to carry in its operations on an uninterrupted basis. If the company needs to write checks in amounts greater than its demand deposits, it simply makes a phone call to a broker and places a market sell order; the broker in turn will sell the securities, and almost immediately the sale proceeds will be deposited in the firm's bank account. Because cash and most commercial checking accounts yield nothing whereas marketable securities provide at least a modest return, firms choose to hold part of their liquid assets as marketable securities rather than pure cash balances.

Note also that firms' cash and equivalents holdings can be reduced by having unused credit lines with banks. A firm can negotiate a line of credit under which it can borrow immediately if it needs cash for transactions. It can simply call the bank, ask to "take down" a portion of its line, and the bank will immediately deposit funds in its account that can then be used for writing checks. This ready source of funds proved to be not quite so reliable for some firms during the financial crisis of 2008 and 2009 and the credit crunch that led up to it as banks refused to renew or extend lines of credit. Even today (mid-year 2011) banks are stricter in their lending practices than they were before the financial crisis. As a result, some companies are holding higher cash and marketable securities balances rather than relying as much on lines of credit.

There are both benefits and costs associated with holding marketable securities. The benefits are twofold: (1) the firm reduces risk and transaction costs, because it won't have to issue securities or borrow as frequently to raise cash; and (2) it will have ready cash to take advantage of bargain purchases or growth opportunities. Funds held for the second reason are called **speculative balances**. The primary disadvantage is that the after-tax return on short-term securities is very low. Thus, firms face a trade-off between benefits and costs.

Recent research supports this trade-off hypothesis as an explanation for firms' cash holdings.[20] Firms with high growth opportunities suffer the most if they don't have ready cash to quickly take advantage of an opportunity, and the data show that these firms do hold relatively high levels of marketable securities. Firms with volatile cash flows are the ones most likely to run low on cash, so they tend to hold high levels of cash. In contrast, cash holdings are less important to large firms with high credit ratings, because they have quick and inexpensive access to capital markets. As expected, such firms hold relatively low levels of cash. Of course, there will always be outliers such as Microsoft, which is large, strong, and cash-rich, but volatile firms with good growth opportunities are still the ones that hold the most marketable securities, on average.

Self Test

Why might a company hold low-yielding marketable securities when it could earn a much higher return on operating assets?

---

20. See Tim Opler, Lee Pinkowitz, René Stulz, and Rohan Williamson, "The Determinants and Implications of Corporate Cash Holdings," *Journal of Financial Economics*, 1999, pp. 3–46. For additional insights into maturity choice, see Karlyn Mitchell, "The Debt Maturity Choice: An Empirical Investigation," *Journal of Financial Research*, Winter 1993, pp. 309–320.

21.11 Short-Term Financing

The three possible short-term financing policies described earlier in the chapter were distinguished by the relative amounts of short-term debt used under each policy. The aggressive policy called for the greatest use of short-term debt, and the conservative policy called for using the least; maturity matching fell in between. Although short-term credit is generally riskier than long-term credit, using short-term funds does have some significant advantages. The pros and cons of short-term financing are considered in this section.

21.11a Advantages of Short-Term Financing

First, a short-term loan can be obtained much faster than long-term credit. Lenders will insist on a more thorough financial examination before extending long-term credit, and the loan agreement will have to be spelled out in considerable detail because a lot can happen during the life of a 10- to 20-year loan. Therefore, if funds are needed in a hurry, the firm should look to the short-term markets.

Second, if its needs for funds are seasonal or cyclical, then a firm may not want to commit itself to long-term debt. There are three reasons for this: (1) Flotation costs are higher for long-term debt than for short-term credit. (2) Although long-term debt can be repaid early (provided the loan agreement includes a prepayment provision), prepayment penalties can be expensive. Accordingly, if a firm thinks its need for funds will diminish in the near future, it should choose short-term debt. (3) Long-term loan agreements always contain provisions, or covenants, that constrain the firm's future actions. Short-term credit agreements are generally less restrictive.

The third advantage is that, because the yield curve is normally upward sloping, interest rates are generally lower on short-term debt. Thus, under normal conditions, interest costs at the time the funds are obtained will be lower if the firm borrows on a short-term rather than a long-term basis.

21.11b Disadvantages of Short-Term Debt

Even though short-term rates are often lower than long-term rates, using short-term credit is riskier for two reasons: (1) If a firm borrows on a long-term basis then its interest costs will be relatively stable over time, but if it uses short-term credit then its interest expense will fluctuate widely, at times going quite high. For example, the rate banks charged large corporations for short-term debt more than tripled over a 2-year period in the 1980s, rising from 6.25% to 21%. Many firms that had borrowed heavily on a short-term basis simply could not meet their rising interest costs; as a result, bankruptcies hit record levels during that period. (2) If a firm borrows heavily on a short-term basis, a temporary recession may render it unable to repay this debt. If the borrower is in a weak financial position then the lender may not extend the loan, which could force the firm into bankruptcy.

Self Test

What are the advantages and disadvantages of short-term debt compared with long-term debt?

21.12 Short-Term Bank Loans

Loans from commercial banks generally appear on balance sheets as notes payable. A bank's importance is actually greater than it appears from the dollar amounts shown on balance sheets because banks provide *nonspontaneous* funds. As a firm's financing needs increase, it requests additional funds from its bank. If the request is denied, the firm may be forced to abandon attractive growth opportunities. The key features of bank loans are discussed in the following paragraphs.

21.12a Maturity

Although banks do make longer-term loans, *the bulk of their lending is on a short-term basis*—about two-thirds of all bank loans mature in a year or less. Bank loans to businesses are frequently written as 90-day notes, so the loan must be repaid or renewed at the end of 90 days. Of course, if a borrower's financial position has deteriorated then the bank may refuse to renew the loan. This can mean serious trouble for the borrower.

21.12b Promissory Notes

When a bank loan is approved, the agreement is executed by signing a **promissory note**. The note specifies (1) the amount borrowed, (2) the interest rate, (3) the repayment schedule, which can call for either a lump sum or a series of installments, (4) any collateral that might have to be put up as security for the loan, and (5) any other terms and conditions to which the bank and the borrower have agreed. When the note is signed, the bank credits the borrower's checking account with the funds; hence both cash and notes payable increase on the borrower's balance sheet.

21.12c Compensating Balances

Banks sometimes require borrowers to maintain an average demand deposit (checking account) balance of 10% to 20% of the loan's face amount. This is called a compensating balance, and such balances raise the effective interest rate on the loans. For example, if a firm needs $80,000 to pay off outstanding obligations but it must maintain a 20% compensating balance, then it must borrow $100,000 to obtain a usable $80,000. If the stated annual interest rate is 8%, the effective cost is actually 10%: $8,000 interest divided by $80,000 of usable funds equals 10%.[21]

As we noted earlier in the chapter, recent surveys indicate that compensating balances are much less common now than earlier. In fact, compensating balances are now illegal in many states. Despite this trend, some small banks in states where compensating balances are legal still require their customers to maintain them.

21.12d Informal Line of Credit

A **line of credit** is an informal agreement between a bank and a borrower indicating the maximum credit the bank will extend to the borrower. For example, on December 31, a bank loan officer might indicate to a financial manager that the bank regards the firm as being "good" for up to $80,000 during the forthcoming year, provided the borrower's financial condition does not deteriorate. If on January 10 the financial manager signs a 90-day promissory note for $15,000, this would be called

---

21. Note, however, that the compensating balance may be set as a minimum monthly *average,* and if the firm would maintain this average anyway then the compensating balance requirement would not raise the effective interest rate. Also, note that these loan compensating balances are *added to* any compensating balances that the firm's bank may require for services performed, such as clearing checks.

"taking down" $15,000 of the total line of credit. This amount would be credited to the firm's checking account at the bank, and the firm could borrow additional amounts up to a total of $80,000 outstanding at any one time.

21.12e Revolving Credit Agreement

A **revolving credit agreement** is a formal line of credit often used by large firms. To illustrate, suppose in 2012 Texas Petroleum Company negotiated a revolving credit agreement for $100 million with a group of banks. The banks were formally committed for 4 years to lend the firm up to $100 million if the funds were needed. Texas Petroleum, in turn, paid an annual commitment fee of 0.25% on the unused balance of the commitment to compensate the banks for making the commitment. Thus, if Texas Petroleum did not take down any of the $100 million commitment during a year, it would still be required to pay a $250,000 annual fee, normally in monthly installments of $20,833.33. If it borrowed $50 million on the first day of the agreement, then the unused portion of the line of credit would fall to $50 million and the annual fee would fall to $125,000. Of course, interest would also have to be paid on the money Texas Petroleum actually borrowed. As a general rule, the interest rate on "revolvers" is pegged to the London Interbank Offered Rate (LIBOR), the T-bill rate, or some other market rate, so the cost of the loan varies over time as interest rates change. The interest that Texas Petroleum must pay was set at the prime lending rate plus 1.0%.

Observe that a revolving credit agreement is similar to an informal line of credit but has an important difference: The bank has a *legal obligation* to honor a revolving credit agreement, and it receives a commitment fee. Neither the legal obligation nor the fee exists under the informal line of credit.

Often a line of credit will have a **cleanup clause** that requires the borrower to reduce the loan balance to zero at least once a year. Keep in mind that a line of credit typically is designed to help finance seasonal or cyclical peaks in operations, not as a source of permanent capital. For example, our cash budget for Educational Products Corporation showed negative flows from July through September but positive flows from October through December. Also, the cumulative net cash flow goes positive in November, indicating that the firm could pay off its loan at that time. If the cumulative flows were always negative, this would indicate that the firm was using its credit lines as a permanent source of financing.

21.12f Costs of Bank Loans

The costs of bank loans vary for different types of borrowers at any given point in time and for all borrowers over time. Interest rates are higher for riskier borrowers, and rates are also higher on smaller loans because of the fixed costs involved in making and servicing loans. If a firm can qualify as a "prime credit" because of its size and financial strength, it can borrow at the **prime rate,** which at one time was the lowest rate banks charged. Rates on other loans are generally scaled up from the prime rate. Loans to large, strong customers are made at rates tied to LIBOR; and the costs of such loans are generally well below prime:

Rates on March 3, 2011	
Prime	3.25%
1-Year LIBOR	0.79%

The rate to smaller, riskier borrowers is generally stated something like "prime plus 1.0%"; but for a larger borrower it is generally stated as something like "LIBOR plus 1.5%."

Bank rates vary widely over time depending on economic conditions and Federal Reserve policy. When the economy is weak, loan demand is usually slack, inflation is low, and the Fed makes plenty of money available to the system. As a result, rates on all types of loans are relatively low. Conversely, when the economy is booming, loan demand is typically strong, the Fed restricts the money supply to fight inflation, and the result is high interest rates. As an indication of the kinds of fluctuations that can occur, the prime rate during 1980 rose from 11% to 21% in just 4 months; during 1994, it rose from 6% to 9%.

Calculating Banks' Interest Charges: Regular (or "Simple") Interest

Banks calculate interest in several different ways. In this section, we explain the procedure used for most business loans. For illustration purposes, we assume a loan of $10,000 at the prime rate, currently 3.25%, with a 360-day year. Interest must be paid monthly, and the principal is payable "on demand" if and when the bank wants to end the loan. Such a loan is called a **regular interest** loan; it is also called a **simple interest** loan.

We begin by dividing the nominal interest rate (3.25% in this case) by 360 to obtain the rate per day. This rate is expressed as a *decimal fraction*, not as a percentage:

$$\text{Simple interest rate per day} = \frac{\text{Nominal rate}}{\text{Days in year}}$$

$$= 0.0325/360 = 0.000090278$$

To find the monthly interest payment, the daily rate is multiplied by the amount of the loan, then by the number of days during the payment period. For our illustrative loan, the daily interest charge would be $0.902777778, and the total for a 30-day month would be $27.08:

$$\text{Interest charge for month} = (\text{Rate per day})(\text{Amount of loan})(\text{Days in month})$$

$$= (0.000090278)(\$10,000)(30 \text{ days}) = \$27.08$$

The *effective interest rate* on a loan depends on how frequently interest must be paid—the more frequently interest is paid, the higher the effective rate. If interest is paid once per year, then the nominal rate is also the effective rate. However, if interest must be paid monthly, then the effective rate is $(1 + 0.0325/12)^{12} - 1 = 3.2989\%$.

Calculating Banks' Interest Charges: Add-on Interest

Banks and other lenders typically use **add-on interest** for automobiles and other types of installment loans. The term *add-on* means that the interest is calculated and then added to the amount borrowed to determine the loan's face value. To illustrate, suppose you borrow $10,000 on an add-on basis at a nominal rate of 7.25% to buy a car, with the loan to be repaid in 12 monthly installments. At a 7.25% add-on rate, you would make total interest payments of $10,000(0.0725) = $725. However, since the loan is paid off in monthly installments, you would have the use of the full $10,000 for only the first month; then the outstanding balance would decline until, during the last month, only 1/12 of the original loan was still outstanding. Thus, you would be paying $725 for the use of only about half the loan's face amount, since the average usable funds would be only about $5,000. Therefore, we can calculate the approximate annual rate as 14.5%:

(21–9)

$$\text{Approximate annual rate}_{\text{Add-on}} = \frac{\text{Interest paid}}{(\text{Amount received})/2}$$

$$= \frac{\$725}{\$10,000/2} = 14.5\%.$$

The annual percentage rate (APR) the bank would provide to the borrower would be 13.12%, and the true effective annual rate would be 13.94%.[22] Both of these rates are much higher than the nominal 7.25%.

Self Test

What is a promissory note, and what are some terms that are normally included in promissory notes?

What is a line of credit? A revolving credit agreement?

What's the difference between simple interest and add-on interest?

Explain how a firm that expects to need funds during the coming year might make sure that the needed funds will be available.

How does the cost of costly trade credit generally compare with the cost of short-term bank loans?

If a firm borrowed $500,000 at a rate of 10% simple interest with monthly interest payments and a 365-day year, what would be the required interest payment for a 30-day month? **($4,109.59)** If interest must be paid monthly, what would be the effective annual rate? **(10.47%)**

If this loan had been made on a 10% add-on basis, payable in 12 end-of-month installments, what would be the monthly payment amount? **($45,833.33)** What is the annual percentage rate? **(17.97%)** The effective annual rate? **(19.53%)**

www

For updates on the outstanding balances of commercial paper, go to **www.federalreserve.gov/ econresdata/releases/ statisticsdata.htm** and check out the volume statistics for Commercial Paper and the weekly releases for Assets and Liabilities of Commercial Banks in the United States.

21.13 Commercial Paper

Commercial paper is a type of unsecured promissory note issued by large, strong firms and sold primarily to other business firms, to insurance companies, to pension funds, to money market mutual funds, and to banks. In July 2011, there was approximately $1.1 trillion of commercial paper outstanding, versus nearly $1.3 trillion of commercial and industrial bank loans. Most, but not all, commercial paper outstanding is issued by financial institutions.

---

22. To find the annual percentage rate and the effective rate on an add-on loan, we first find the payment per month, $10,725/12 = $893.75. With a financial calculator, enter N = 12, PV = 10000, PMT = −893.75, and FV = 0; then press I/YR to obtain 1.093585%. This is a monthly rate, so multiply by 12 to get 13.12%, which is the APR the bank would report to the borrower. The effective annual rate would then be $(1.010936)^{12} − 1 = 13.94\%$, quite a bit above the APR.

21.13a Maturity and Cost

Maturities of commercial paper generally vary from 1 day to 9 months, with an average of about 5 months.[23] The interest rate on commercial paper fluctuates with supply and demand conditions—it is determined in the marketplace, varying daily as conditions change. Recently, commercial paper rates have ranged from 1.5 to 3.5 percentage points below the stated prime rate and up to half of a percentage point above the T-bill rate. For example, in March 2011, the average rate on 3-month commercial paper was 0.25%, the prime rate was 3.25%, and the 3-month T-bill rate was 0.13%.

www

For current rates, see **www.federalreserve.gov/ econresdata/releases/ statisticsdata.htm** and look at the Daily Releases for Selected Interest Rates.

21.13b Use of Commercial Paper

The use of commercial paper is restricted to a comparatively small number of very large concerns that are exceptionally good credit risks. Dealers prefer to handle the paper of firms whose net worth is $100 million or more and whose annual borrowing exceeds $10 million. One potential problem with commercial paper is that a debtor who is in temporary financial difficulty may receive little help because commercial paper dealings are generally less personal than are bank relationships. Thus, banks are generally more able and willing to help a good customer weather a temporary storm than is a commercial paper dealer. On the other hand, using commercial paper permits a corporation to tap a wide range of credit sources, including financial institutions outside its own area and industrial corporations across the country, and this can reduce interest costs.

Self Test

What is commercial paper?

What types of companies can use commercial paper to meet their short-term financing needs?

How does the cost of commercial paper compare with the cost of short-term bank loans? With the cost of Treasury bills?

21.14 Use of Security in Short-Term Financing

Thus far, we have not addressed the question of whether or not short-term loans should be secured. Commercial paper is never secured, but other types of loans can be secured if this is deemed necessary or desirable. Other things held constant, it is better to borrow on an unsecured basis, since the bookkeeping costs of **secured loans** are often high. However, firms often find that they can borrow only if they put up some type of collateral to protect the lender or that, by using security, they can borrow at a much lower rate.

Several different kinds of collateral can be employed, including marketable stocks or bonds, land or buildings, equipment, inventory, and accounts receivable. Marketable securities make excellent collateral, but few firms that need loans also

---

23. The maximum maturity without SEC registration is 270 days. Also, commercial paper can be sold only to "sophisticated" investors; otherwise, SEC registration would be required even for maturities of 270 days or less.

WEB

For a more detailed discussion of secured financing, see **Web Extension 21A** on the textbook's Web site.

hold portfolios of stocks and bonds. Similarly, real property (land and buildings) and equipment are good forms of collateral, but they are generally used as security for long-term loans rather than for working capital loans. Therefore, most secured short-term business borrowing involves the use of accounts receivable and inventories as collateral.

To understand the use of security, consider the case of a Chicago hardware dealer who wanted to modernize and expand his store. He requested a $200,000 bank loan. After examining the business's financial statements, his bank indicated that it would lend him a maximum of $100,000 and that the effective interest rate would be 9%. The owner had a substantial personal portfolio of stocks, and he offered to put up $300,000 of high-quality stocks to support the $200,000 loan. The bank then granted the full $200,000 loan at the prime rate of 3.25%. The store owner might also have used his inventories or receivables as security for the loan, but processing costs would have been high.[24]

Self Test

What is a secured loan?

What are some types of current assets that are pledged as security for short-term loans?

Summary

This chapter discussed working capital management and short-term financing. The key concepts covered are listed below.

- **Working capital** refers to current assets used in operations, and **net working capital** is defined as current assets minus all current liabilities. **Net operating working capital** is defined as operating current assets minus operating current liabilities.

- Under a **relaxed working capital policy,** a firm would hold relatively large amounts of each type of current asset. Under a **restricted working capital policy,** the firm would hold minimal amounts of these items.

- A **moderate** approach to short-term financing involves matching, to the extent possible, the maturities of assets and liabilities, so that temporary operating current assets are financed with short-term debt and permanent operating current assets and fixed assets are financed with long-term debt or equity. Under an **aggressive** approach, some permanent operating current assets, and perhaps even some fixed assets, are financed with short-term debt. A **conservative** approach would be to use long-term sources to finance all permanent operating capital and some of the temporary operating current assets.

---

24. The term "asset-based financing" is often used as a synonym for "secured financing." In recent years, accounts receivable have been used as security for long-term bonds, permitting corporations to borrow from lenders such as pension funds rather than just from banks and other traditional short-term lenders.

- **Permanent operating current assets** are the operating current assets the firm holds even during slack times, whereas **temporary operating current assets** are the additional operating current assets needed during seasonal or cyclical peaks. The methods used to finance permanent and temporary operating current assets define the firm's **short-term financing policy.**

- The **inventory conversion period** is the average time required to convert materials into finished goods and then to sell those goods:

$$\text{Inventory conversion period} = \text{Inventory} \div \text{Cost of goods sold per day}$$

- The **average collection period** is the average length of time required to convert the firm's receivables into cash—that is, to collect cash following a sale:

$$\text{Average collection period} = \text{DSO} = \text{Receivables} \div (\text{Sales}/365)$$

- The **payables deferral period** is the average length of time between the purchase of materials and labor and the payment of cash for them:

$$\text{Payables deferral period} = \text{Payables} \div \text{Cost of goods sold per day}$$

- The **cash conversion cycle (CCC)** is the length of time between the firm's actual cash expenditures to pay for productive resources (materials and labor) and its own cash receipts from the sale of products (that is, the length of time between paying for labor and materials and collecting on receivables):

$$\begin{matrix} \text{Cash} & & \text{Inventory} & & \text{Average} & & \text{Payables} \\ \text{conversion} & = & \text{conversion} & + & \text{collection} & - & \text{deferral} \\ \text{cycle} & & \text{period} & & \text{period} & & \text{period} \end{matrix}$$

- A **cash budget** is a schedule showing projected cash inflows and outflows over some period. The cash budget is used to predict cash surpluses and deficits, and it is the primary cash management planning tool.

- The **primary goal of cash management** is to minimize the amount of cash the firm must hold for conducting its normal business activities while at the same time maintaining a sufficient cash reserve to take discounts, pay bills promptly, and meet any unexpected cash needs.

- The **transactions balance** is the cash necessary to conduct routine day-to-day business; **precautionary balances** are cash reserves held to meet random, unforeseen needs. A **compensating balance** is a minimum checking account balance that a bank requires as compensation either for services provided or as part of a loan agreement.

- The twin goals of **inventory management** are (1) to ensure that the inventories needed to sustain operations are available, but (2) to hold the costs of ordering and carrying inventories to the lowest possible level.

- When a firm sells goods to a customer on credit, an **account receivable** is created.

- A firm can use an **aging schedule** and the **days sales outstanding (DSO)** to monitor its receivables balance and to help avoid an increase in bad debts.

- A firm's **credit policy** consists of four elements: (1) credit period, (2) discounts given for early payment, (3) credit standards, and (4) collection policy.

- **Accounts payable**, or **trade credit**, arises spontaneously as a result of credit purchases. Firms should use all the **free trade credit** they can obtain, but they should use **costly trade credit** only if it is less expensive than other forms of short-term debt. Suppliers often offer discounts to customers who pay within a stated period. The following equation may be used to calculate the nominal cost, on an annual basis, of not taking such discounts:

$$\begin{array}{c}\text{Nominal}\\\text{annual cost of}\\\text{trade credit}\end{array} = \frac{\text{Discount percentage}}{100 - \begin{array}{c}\text{Discount}\\\text{percentage}\end{array}} \times \frac{365}{\begin{array}{c}\text{Days credit is}\\\text{outstanding}\end{array} - \begin{array}{c}\text{Discount}\\\text{period}\end{array}}$$

- The advantages of short-term credit are (1) the **speed** with which short-term loans can be arranged, (2) increased **flexibility**, and (3) generally **lower interest rates** than with long-term credit. The principal disadvantage of short-term credit is the **extra risk** the borrower must bear because (1) the lender can demand payment on short notice, and (2) the cost of the loan will increase if interest rates rise.
- **Bank loans** are an important source of short-term credit. When a bank loan is approved, a **promissory note** is signed. It specifies: (1) the amount borrowed, (2) the percentage interest rate, (3) the repayment schedule, (4) the collateral, and (5) any other conditions to which the parties have agreed.
- Banks sometimes require borrowers to maintain **compensating balances**, which are deposit requirements set at between 10% and 20% of the loan amount. Compensating balances raise the effective interest rate on bank loans.
- A **line of credit** is an informal agreement between the bank and the borrower indicating the maximum amount of credit the bank will extend to the borrower.
- A **revolving credit agreement** is a formal line of credit often used by large firms; it involves a **commitment fee**.
- A **simple interest** loan is one in which interest must be paid monthly and the principal is payable "on demand" if and when the bank wants to end the loan.
- An **add-on interest loan** is one in which interest is calculated and added to the funds received to determine the face amount of the installment loan.
- **Commercial paper** is unsecured short-term debt issued by large, financially strong corporations. Although the cost of commercial paper is lower than the cost of bank loans, it can be used only by large firms with exceptionally strong credit ratings.
- Sometimes a borrower will find it is necessary to borrow on a **secured basis**, in which case the borrower pledges assets such as real estate, securities, equipment, inventories, or accounts receivable as collateral for the loan. For a more detailed discussion of secured financing, see *Web Extension 21A.*

Questions

21-1 Define each of the following terms:
  a. Working capital; net working capital; net operating working capital
  b. Relaxed policy; restricted policy; moderate policy
  c. Permanent operating current assets; temporary operating current assets
  d. Moderate (maturity matching) financing policy; aggressive financing policy; conservative financing policy
  e. Inventory conversion period; average collection period; payables deferral period; cash conversion cycle

    f. Cash budget; target cash balance

    g. Transactions balances; compensating balances; precautionary balances

    h. Trade discounts

    i. Credit policy; credit period; credit standards; collection policy; cash discounts

    j. Account receivable; days sales outstanding; aging schedule

    k. Accruals; trade credit

    l. Stretching accounts payable; free trade credit; costly trade credit

    m. Promissory note; line of credit; revolving credit agreement

    n. Commercial paper; secured loan

21-2 What are the two principal reasons for holding cash? Can a firm estimate its target cash balance by summing the cash held to satisfy each of the two reasons?

21-3 Is it true that, when one firm sells to another on credit, the seller records the transaction as an account receivable while the buyer records it as an account payable and that, disregarding discounts, the receivable typically exceeds the payable by the amount of profit on the sale?

21-4 What are the four elements of a firm's credit policy? To what extent can firms set their own credit policies as opposed to accepting policies that are dictated by its competitors?

21-5 What are the advantages of matching the maturities of assets and liabilities? What are the disadvantages?

21-6 From the standpoint of the borrower, is long-term or short-term credit riskier? Explain. Would it ever make sense to borrow on a short-term basis if short-term rates were above long-term rates?

21-7 Discuss this statement: "Firms can control their accruals within fairly wide limits."

21-8 Is it true that most firms are able to obtain some free trade credit and that additional trade credit is often available, but at a cost? Explain.

21-9 What kinds of firms use commercial paper?

Problems   Answers Appear in Appendix B

Easy Problems 1–5

21-1 **Cash Management** Williams & Sons last year reported sales of $10 million and an inventory turnover ratio of 2. The company is now adopting a new inventory system. If the new system is able to reduce the firm's inventory level and increase the firm's inventory turnover ratio to 5 while maintaining the same level of sales, how much cash will be freed up?

21-2 **Receivables Investment** Medwig Corporation has a DSO of 17 days. The company averages $3,500 in credit sales each day. What is the company's average accounts receivable?

21-3 **Cost of Trade Credit** What is the nominal and effective cost of trade credit under the credit terms of 3/15, net 30?

21-4 **Cost of Trade Credit** A large retailer obtains merchandise under the credit terms of 1/15, net 45, but routinely takes 60 days to pay its bills. (Because the retailer is an important customer, suppliers allow the firm to stretch its credit terms.) What is the retailer's effective cost of trade credit?

21-5 **Accounts Payable** A chain of appliance stores, APP Corporation, purchases inventory with a net price of $500,000 each day. The company purchases the inventory under the credit terms of 2/15, net 40. APP always takes the discount but takes the full 15 days to pay its bills. What is the average accounts payable for APP?

Intermediate Problems 6–12

21-6 **Receivables Investment** Snider Industries sells on terms of 2/10, net 45. Total sales for the year are $1,500,000. Thirty percent of customers pay on the 10th day and take discounts; the other 70% pay, on average, 50 days after their purchases.
   a. What is the days sales outstanding?
   b. What is the average amount of receivables?
   c. What would happen to average receivables if Snider toughened its collection policy with the result that all nondiscount customers paid on the 45th day?

21-7 **Cost of Trade Credit** Calculate the nominal annual cost of nonfree trade credit under each of the following terms. Assume that payment is made either on the discount date or on the due date.
   a. 1/15, net 20
   b. 2/10, net 60
   c. 3/10, net 45
   d. 2/10, net 45
   e. 2/15, net 40

21-8 **Cost of Trade Credit**
   a. If a firm buys under terms of 3/15, net 45, but actually pays on the 20th day and *still takes the discount,* what is the nominal cost of its nonfree trade credit?
   b. Does it receive more or less credit than it would if it paid within 15 days?

21-9 **Cost of Trade Credit** Grunewald Industries sells on terms of 2/10, net 40. Gross sales last year were $4,562,500 and accounts receivable averaged $437,500. Half of Grunewald's customers paid on the 10th day and took discounts. What are the nominal and effective costs of trade credit to Grunewald's nondiscount customers? (*Hint:* Calculate daily sales based on a 365-day year, then calculate average receivables of discount customers, and then find the DSO for the nondiscount customers.)

21-10 **Effective Cost of Trade Credit** The D.J. Masson Corporation needs to raise $500,000 for 1 year to supply working capital to a new store. Masson buys from its suppliers on terms of 3/10, net 90, and it currently pays on the 10th day and takes discounts. However, it could forgo the discounts, pay on the 90th day, and thereby obtain the needed $500,000 in the form of costly trade credit. What is the effective annual interest rate of this trade credit?

21-11 **Cash Conversion Cycle** Negus Enterprises has an inventory conversion period of 50 days, an average collection period of 35 days, and a payables deferral period of 25 days. Assume that cost of goods sold is 80% of sales.
   a. What is the length of the firm's cash conversion cycle?
   b. If Negus's annual sales are $4,380,000 and all sales are on credit, what is the firm's investment in accounts receivable?
   c. How many times per year does Negus Enterprises turn over its inventory?

21-12 **Working Capital Cash Flow Cycle** Strickler Technology is considering changes in its working capital policies to improve its cash flow cycle. Strickler's sales last year were $3,250,000 (all on credit), and its net profit margin was 7%. Its inventory turnover was 9.0 times during the year, and its DSO was 41 days. Its annual cost of goods sold was $1,895,000. The firm had fixed assets totaling $535,000. Strickler's payables deferral period is 45 days.
   a. Calculate Strickler's cash conversion cycle.
   b. Assuming Strickler holds negligible amounts of cash and marketable securities, calculate its total assets turnover and ROA.
   c. Suppose Strickler's managers believe the annual inventory turnover can be raised to 12 times without affecting sales. What would Strickler's cash conversion cycle, total assets turnover, and ROA have been if the inventory turnover had been 12 for the year?

Challenging Problems 13–17

21-13 **Working Capital Policy** Payne Products's sales last year were an anemic $1.6 million, but with an improved product mix it expects sales growth to be 25% this year, and Payne would like to determine the effect of various current assets policies on its financial performance. Payne has $1 million of fixed assets and intends to keep its debt ratio at its historical level of 60%. Payne's debt interest rate is currently 8%. You are to evaluate three different current asset policies: (1) a tight policy in which current assets are 45% of projected sales, (2) a moderate policy with 50% of sales tied up in current assets, and (3) a relaxed policy requiring current assets of 60% of sales. Earnings before interest and taxes is expected to be 12% of sales. Payne's tax rate is 40%.
   a. What is the expected return on equity under each current asset level?
   b. In this problem, we have assumed that the level of expected sales is independent of current asset policy. Is this a valid assumption?
   c. How would the overall riskiness of the firm vary under each policy?

21-14 **Cash Budgeting** Dorothy Koehl recently leased space in the Southside Mall and opened a new business, Koehl's Doll Shop. Business has been good, but Koehl has frequently run out of cash. This has necessitated late payment on certain orders, which is beginning to cause a problem with suppliers. Koehl plans to borrow from the bank to have cash ready as needed, but first she needs a forecast of just how much she should borrow. Accordingly, she has asked you to prepare a cash budget for the critical period around Christmas, when needs will be especially high.

Sales are made on a cash basis only. Koehl's purchases must be paid for during the following month. Koehl pays herself a salary of $4,800 per month, and the rent is $2,000 per month. In addition, she must make a tax payment of $12,000 in December. The current cash on hand (on December 1) is $400, but Koehl has agreed to maintain an average bank balance of $6,000— this is her target cash balance. (Disregard the amount in the cash register, which is insignificant because Koehl keeps only a small amount on hand in order to lessen the chances of robbery.)

The estimated sales and purchases for December, January, and February are shown below. Purchases during November amounted to $140,000.

	Sales	Purchases
December	$160,000	$40,000
January	40,000	40,000
February	60,000	40,000

a. Prepare a cash budget for December, January, and February.
b. Now suppose that Koehl starts selling on a credit basis on December 1, giving customers 30 days to pay. All customers accept these terms, and all other facts in the problem are unchanged. What would the company's loan requirements be at the end of December in this case? (*Hint:* The calculations required to answer this part are minimal.)

21-15 Cash Discounts Suppose a firm makes purchases of $3.65 million per year under terms of 2/10, net 30, and takes discounts.
a. What is the average amount of accounts payable net of discounts? (Assume the $3.65 million of purchases is net of discounts—that is, gross purchases are $3,724,489.80, discounts are $74,489.80, and net purchases are $3.65 million.)
b. Is there a cost of the trade credit the firm uses?
c. If the firm did not take discounts but did pay on the due date, what would be its average payables and the cost of this nonfree trade credit?
d. What would be the firm's cost of not taking discounts if it could stretch its payments to 40 days?

21-16 Trade Credit The Thompson Corporation projects an increase in sales from $1.5 million to $2 million, but it needs an additional $300,000 of current assets to support this expansion. Thompson can finance the expansion by no longer taking discounts, thus increasing accounts payable. Thompson purchases under terms of 2/10, net 30, but it can delay payment for an additional 35 days—paying in 65 days and thus becoming 35 days past due— without a penalty because its suppliers currently have excess capacity. What is the effective, or equivalent, annual cost of the trade credit?

21-17 Bank Financing The Raattama Corporation had sales of $3.5 million last year, and it earned a 5% return (after taxes) on sales. Recently, the company has fallen behind in its accounts payable. Although its terms of purchase are net 30 days, its accounts payable represents 60 days' purchases. The company's treasurer is seeking to increase bank borrowings in order to become current in meeting its trade obligations (that is, to have 30 days' payables outstanding). The company's balance sheet is as follows (in thousands of dollars):

Cash	$ 100	Accounts payable	$ 600
Accounts receivable	300	Bank loans	700
Inventory	1,400	Accruals	200
Current assets	$1,800	Current liabilities	$1,500
Land and buildings	600	Mortgage on real estate	700
Equipment	600	Common stock, $0.10 par	300
		Retained earnings	500
Total assets	$3,000	Total liabilities and equity	$3,000

a. How much bank financing is needed to eliminate the past-due accounts payable?

b. Assume that the bank will lend the firm the amount calculated in part a. The terms of the loan offered are 8%, simple interest, and the bank uses a 360-day year for the interest calculation. What is the interest charge for 1 month? (Assume there are 30 days in a month.)

c. Now ignore part b and assume that the bank will lend the firm the amount calculated in part a. The terms of the loan are 7.5%, add-on interest, to be repaid in 12 monthly installments.
   1. What is the total loan amount?
   2. What are the monthly installments?
   3. What is the APR of the loan?
   4. What is the effective rate of the loan?

d. Would you, as a bank loan officer, make this loan? Why or why not?

Spreadsheet Problem

21-18 **Build a Model: Cash Budgeting** Start with the partial model in the file *Ch21 P18 Build a Model.xls* on the textbook's Web site. Rusty Spears, CEO of Rusty's Renovations, a custom building and repair company, is preparing documentation for a line of credit request from his commercial banker. Among the required documents is a detailed sales forecast for parts of 2013 and 2014:

	Sales	Labor and Raw Materials
May 2013	$60,000	$ 75,000
June	100,000	90,000
July	130,000	95,000
August	120,000	70,000
September	100,000	60,000
October	80,000	50,000
November	60,000	20,000
December	40,000	20,000
January 2014	30,000	NA

Estimates obtained from the credit and collection department are as follows: collections within the month of sale, 15%; collections during the month following the sale, 65%; collections the second month following the sale, 20%. Payments for labor and raw materials are typically made during the month following the one in which these costs were incurred. Total costs for labor and raw materials are estimated for each month as shown in the table.

General and administrative salaries will amount to approximately $15,000 a month; lease payments under long-term lease contracts will be $5,000 a month; depreciation charges will be $7,500 a month; miscellaneous expenses will be $2,000 a month; income tax payments of $25,000 will be due in both September and December; and a progress payment of $80,000 on a new office suite must be paid in October. Cash on hand on July 1 will amount to $60,000, and a minimum cash balance of $40,000 will be maintained throughout the cash budget period.

a. Prepare a monthly cash budget for the last 6 months of 2013.

b. Prepare an estimate of the required financing (or excess funds)—that is, the amount of money Rusty's Renovations will need to borrow (or will have available to invest)—for each month during that period.

c. Assume that receipts from sales come in uniformly during the month (i.e., cash receipts come in at the rate of 1/30 each day) but that all outflows are paid on the 5th of the month. Will this have an effect on the cash budget—in other words, would the cash budget you have prepared be valid under these assumptions? If not, what can be done to make a valid estimate of peak financing requirements? No calculations are required, although calculations can be used to illustrate the effects.

d. Rusty's Renovations produces on a seasonal basis, just ahead of sales. Without making any calculations, discuss how the company's current ratio and debt ratio would vary during the year assuming all financial requirements were met by short-term bank loans. Could changes in these ratios affect the firm's ability to obtain bank credit?

e. If its customers began to pay late, this would slow down collections and thus increase the required loan amount. Also, if sales dropped off, this would have an effect on the required loan amount. Perform a sensitivity analysis that shows the effects of these two factors on the maximum loan requirement.

MINI CASE

Karen Johnson, CFO for Raucous Roasters (RR), a specialty coffee manufacturer, is rethinking her company's working capital policy in light of a recent scare she faced when RR's corporate banker, citing a nationwide credit crunch, balked at renewing RR's line of credit. Had the line of credit not been renewed, RR would not have been able to make payroll, potentially forcing the company out of business. Although the line of credit was ultimately renewed, the scare has forced Johnson to examine carefully each component of RR's working capital to make sure it is needed, with the goal of determining whether the line of credit can be eliminated entirely. In addition to (possibly) freeing RR from the need for a line of credit, Johnson is well aware that reducing working capital can also add value to a company by improving its EVA (Economic Value Added). In her corporate finance course Johnson learned that EVA is calculated by taking net operating profit after taxes (NOPAT) and then subtracting the dollar cost of all the capital the firm uses:

$$EVA = NOPAT - \text{Capital costs}$$

$$= EBIT(1 - T) - WACC(\text{Total capital employed})$$

If EVA is positive then the firm's management is creating value. On the other hand, if EVA is negative, then the firm is not covering its cost of capital and stockholders' value is being eroded. If RR could generate its current level of sales with fewer assets, it would need less capital. This would, other things held constant, lower capital costs and increase its EVA.

Historically, RR has done little to examine working capital, mainly because of poor communication among business functions. In the past, the production manager resisted Johnson's efforts to question his holdings of raw materials, the marketing manager resisted questions about finished goods, the sales staff resisted questions about credit policy (which affects accounts receivable), and the treasurer did not want to talk about the cash and securities balances. However, with the recent credit scare, this resistance became unacceptable and Johnson has undertaken a company-wide examination of cash, marketable securities, inventory, and accounts receivable levels.

Johnson also knows that decisions about working capital cannot be made in a vacuum. For example, if inventories could be lowered without adversely affecting operations, then less capital would be required, the dollar cost of capital would decline, and EVA would increase. However, lower raw materials inventories might lead to production slowdowns and higher costs, and lower finished goods inventories might lead to stock-outs and loss of sales. So, before inventories are changed, it will be necessary to study operating as well as financial effects. The situation is the same with regard to cash and receivables. Johnson has begun her investigation by collecting the ratios shown below. (The partial cash budget shown after the ratios is used later in this mini case.)

a. Johnson plans to use the preceding ratios as the starting point for discussions with RR's operating team. She wants everyone to think about the pros and cons of changing each type of current asset and how changes would interact to affect profits and EVA. Based on the data, does RR seem to be following a relaxed, moderate, or restricted working capital policy?

b. How can one distinguish between a relaxed but rational working capital policy and a situation in which a firm simply has excessive current assets because it is inefficient? Does RR's working capital policy seem appropriate?

c. Calculate the firm's cash conversion cycle given that annual sales are $660,000 and cost of goods sold represents 90% of sales. Assume a 365-day year.

d. What might RR do to reduce its cash without harming operations?

In an attempt to better understand RR's cash position, Johnson developed a cash budget. Data for the first 2 months of the year are shown above. (Note that Johnson's preliminary cash budget does not account for interest income or interest expense.) She has the figures for the other months, but they are not shown.

e. Should depreciation expense be explicitly included in the cash budget? Why or why not?

f. In her preliminary cash budget, Johnson has assumed that all sales are collected and thus that RR has no bad debts. Is this realistic? If not, how would bad debts be dealt with in a cash budgeting sense? (*Hint:* Bad debts will affect collections but not purchases.)

	RR	Industry
Current	1.75	2.25
Quick	0.92	1.16
Total liabilities/assets	58.76%	50.00%
Turnover of cash and securities	16.67	22.22
Days sales outstanding (365-day basis)	45.63	32.00
Inventory turnover	12.00	20.00
Fixed assets turnover	7.75	13.22
Total assets turnover	2.08	3.00
Profit margin on sales	2.07%	3.50%
Return on equity (ROE)	10.45%	21.00%
Payables deferral period	30.00	33.00

Cash Budget
(Thousands of Dollars)

	Nov	Dec	Jan	Feb	Mar	Apr
Sales Forecast						
(1) Sales (gross)	$71,218.00	$68,212.00	$65,213.00	$52,475.00	$42,909.00	$30,524.00
Collections						
(2) During month of sale: (0.2)(0.98)(month's sales)			12,781.75	10,285.10		
(3) During first month after sale: (0.7)(previous month's sales)			47,748.40	45,649.10		
(4) During second month after sale: (0.1)(sales 2 months ago)			7,121.80	6,821.20		
(5) Total collections (Lines 2 + 3 + 4)			$67,651.95	$62,755.40		
Purchases						
(6) (0.85)(forecasted sales 2 months from now)		$44,603.75	$36,472.65	$25,945.40		
Payments						
(7) Payments (1-month lag)			44,603.75	36,472.65		
(8) Wages and salaries			6,690.56	5,470.90		
(9) Rent			2,500.00	2,500.00		
(10) Taxes						
(11) Total payments			$53,794.31	$44,443.55		
NCFs						
(12) Cash on hand at start of forecast			$3,000.00			
(13) NCF: Coll. − Pmts. = Line 5 − Line 11			$13,857.64	$18,311.85		
(14) Cum NCF: Prior + this mos. NCF			$16,857.64	$35,169.49		
Cash Surplus (or Loan Requirement)						
(15) Target cash balance			1,500.00	1,500.00		
(16) Surplus cash or loan needed			$15,357.64	$33,669.49		

g. Johnson's cash budget for the entire year, although not given here, is based heavily on her forecast for monthly sales. Sales are expected to be extremely low between May and September but then to increase dramatically in the fall and winter. November is typically the firm's best month, when RR ships its holiday blend of coffee. Johnson's forecasted cash budget indicates that the company's cash holdings will exceed the targeted cash balance every month except for October and November, when shipments will be high but collections will not be coming in until later. Based on the ratios shown earlier, does it appear that RR's target cash balance is appropriate? In addition to possibly lowering the target cash balance, what actions might RR take to better improve its cash management policies, and how might that affect its EVA?

h. What reasons might RR have for maintaining a relatively high amount of cash?

i. Is there any reason to think that RR may be holding too much inventory? If so, how would that affect EVA and ROE?

j. If the company reduces its inventory without adversely affecting sales, what effect should this have on the company's cash position (1) in the short run and (2) in the long run? Explain in terms of the cash budget and the balance sheet.

k. Johnson knows that RR sells on the same credit terms as other firms in its industry. Use the ratios presented earlier to explain whether RR's customers pay more or less promptly than those of its competitors. If there are differences, does that suggest RR should tighten or loosen its credit policy? What four variables make up a firm's credit policy, and in what direction should each be changed by RR?

l. Does RR face any risks if it tightens its credit policy?

m. If the company reduces its DSO without seriously affecting sales, what effect would this have on its cash position (1) in the short run and (2) in the long run? Answer in terms of the cash budget and the balance sheet. What effect should this have on EVA in the long run?

    In addition to improving the management of its current assets, RR is also reviewing the ways in which it finances its current assets. With this concern in mind, Johnson is also trying to answer the following questions.

n. Is it likely that RR could make significantly greater use of accruals?

o. Assume that RR purchases $200,000 (net of discounts) of materials on terms of 1/10, net 30, but that it can get away with paying on the 40th day if it chooses not to take discounts. How much free trade credit can the company get from its equipment supplier, how much costly trade credit can it get, and what is the nominal annual interest rate of the costly credit? Should RR take discounts?

p. RR tries to match the maturity of its assets and liabilities. Describe how RR could adopt either a more aggressive or a more conservative financing policy.

q. What are the advantages and disadvantages of using short-term debt as a source of financing?

r. Would it be feasible for RR to finance with commercial paper?

Selected Additional Cases

The following cases from TextChoice, Cengage Learning's online case library, cover many of the concepts discussed in this chapter and are available at **www.textchoice2.com/casenet.**

Klein-Brigham Series:
Case 29, "Office Mates, Inc.," which illustrates how changes in current asset policy affect expected profitability and risk; Case 32, "Alpine Wear, Inc.," which illustrates the mechanics of the cash budget and the rationale behind its use; Case 33, "Upscale Toddlers, Inc.," which deals with credit policy changes; Case 34, "Texas Rose Company," which focuses on receivables management; Case 50, "Toy World, Inc.," and Case 66, "Sorenson Stove Company," which deal with cash budgeting.

Brigham-Buzzard Series:
Case 11, "Powerline Network Corporation (Working Capital Management)."

Chapter 22

Providing and Obtaining Credit

WEB

The textbook's Web site contains an *Excel* file that will guide you through the chapter's calculations. The file for this chapter is **Ch22 Tool Kit.xls**, and we encourage you to open the file and follow along as you read the chapter.

Chapter 21 covered the basics of working capital management, including a brief discussion of trade credit from the standpoint of firms that grant credit and report it as accounts receivable and also from the standpoint of firms that use credit and report it as accounts payable. In this chapter, we expand the discussion of this important topic and also discuss the cost of the other major source of short-term financing, bank loans.

Beginning of Chapter Questions

As you read the chapter, consider how you would answer the following questions. You *should not* necessarily be able to answer the questions before you read the chapter. Rather, you should use them to get a sense of the issues covered in the chapter. After reading the chapter, you should be able to give at least partial answers to the questions, and you should be able to give better answers after the chapter has been discussed in class. Note, too, that it is often useful, when answering conceptual questions, to use hypothetical data to illustrate your answer. We illustrate the answers with an *Excel* model that is available on the textbook's Web site. Accessing the model and working through it is a useful exercise, and it provides insights that are useful when answering the questions.

1. How do each of the items in a firm's **credit policy**—defined to include the credit period, the discount and discount period, the credit standards used, and the collection policy—affect its sales, the level of its accounts receivable, and its profitability?
2. Does its management typically have complete control over a firm's credit policy? As a general rule, is it more likely that a company would increase its profitability if it tightened or loosened its credit policy?

3. How does credit policy affect the cash conversion cycle as discussed in the last chapter?
4. Suppose a company's current credit terms are 1/10, net 30, but management is considering changing its terms to 2/10, net 40, relaxing its credit standards, and putting less pressure on slow-paying customers. How would you expect these changes to affect (a) sales, (b) the percentage of customers who take discounts, (c) the percentage of customers who pay late, and (d) the percentage of customers who end up as bad debts?
5. How would you decide whether or not to make the change described in question 4? Assume you also have information on the company's cost of capital, tax rate, and variable costs. How would the company's capacity utilization affect the decision?
6. What are some ways banks can state their charges, and how should the cost of bank debt be analyzed? In the early 1970s, Congress debated the need for new legislation, and it ended up passing a "Truth in Lending" law. One part of the law was the requirement that banks disclose their **APR**. How is the APR calculated? Do you think the Truth in Lending law was really necessary?

22.1 Credit Policy

As we stated in Chapter 21, the success or failure of a business depends primarily on the demand for its products: As a rule, the higher its sales, the larger its profits and the higher its stock price. Sales, in turn, depend on a number of factors, some exogenous but others under the firm's control. The major controllable determinants of demand are sales price, product quality, advertising, and the firm's **credit policy**. Credit policy, in turn, consists of these four variables:

1. *Credit period,* which is the length of time buyers are given to pay for their purchases.
2. *Discounts* given for early payment, including the discount percentage and how rapidly payment must be made to qualify for the discount.
3. *Credit standards,* which refer to the required financial strength of acceptable credit customers.
4. *Collection policy,* which is measured by the firm's toughness or laxity in attempting to collect on slow-paying accounts.

The credit manager is responsible for administering the firm's credit policy. However, because of the pervasive importance of credit, the credit policy itself is normally established by the executive committee, which usually consists of the president plus the vice presidents of finance, marketing, and production.

22.2 Setting the Credit Period and Standards

A firm's regular **credit terms**, which include the **credit period** and **discount**, might call for sales on a 2/10, net 30 basis to all "acceptable" customers. Here customers are required to pay within 30 days, but they are given a 2% discount if they pay by the 10th day. The firm's *credit standards* would be applied to determine which customers qualify for the regular credit terms and the amount of credit available to each customer.

22.2a Credit Standards

Credit standards refer to the financial strength and creditworthiness a customer must exhibit in order to qualify for credit. A customer that does not qualify for the regular credit terms can still purchase from the firm but only under more restrictive terms. For example, a firm's "regular" credit terms might call for payment within 30 days, and these terms might be offered to all qualified customers; the firm's credit standards are applied when determining which customers qualify. The major factors considered when setting credit standards concern the likelihood that a given customer will pay slowly or perhaps end up as a bad-debt loss.

Setting credit standards requires a measurement of *credit quality,* which is defined in terms of the probability of a customer's default. The probability estimate for a given customer is, for the most part, a subjective judgment. Nevertheless, credit evaluation is a well-established practice, and a good credit manager can make reasonably accurate judgments of the probability of default by different classes of customers.

Managing a credit department requires fast, accurate, and up-to-date information. To help get such information, the National Association of Credit Management (a group with 43,000 member firms) persuaded TRW, a large credit-reporting agency, to develop a computer-based telecommunications network for the collection, storage, retrieval, and distribution of credit information. A typical business credit report would include the following pieces of information:

1. A summary balance sheet and income statement.
2. A number of key ratios, including trend information.
3. Information obtained from the firm's suppliers telling whether it pays promptly or slowly and whether it has recently failed to make any payments.
4. A verbal description of the physical condition of the firm's operations.
5. A verbal description of the backgrounds of the firm's owners, including any previous bankruptcies, lawsuits, divorce settlement problems, and the like.
6. A summary rating, ranging from A for the best credit risks down to F for those deemed likely to default.

Consumer credit is appraised similarly, using income, years of employment, ownership of home, and past credit history (pays on time or has defaulted) as criteria.

Although a great deal of credit information is available, it must still be processed in a judgmental manner. Computerized information systems can assist in making better credit decisions, but, in the final analysis, most credit decisions are really exercises in informed judgment.[1]

What are credit terms?

What is credit quality, and how is it assessed?

22.3 Setting the Collection Policy

Collection policy refers to the procedures the firm follows to collect past-due accounts. For example, a letter might be sent to customers when a bill is 10 days past due; a more severe letter, followed by a telephone call, would be sent if payment is not received within 30 days; and the account would be turned over to a collection agency after 90 days.

The collection process can be expensive in terms of both out-of-pocket expenditures and lost goodwill—customers dislike being turned over to a collection agency. However, at least some firmness is needed to prevent an undue lengthening of the collection period and to minimize outright losses. A balance must be struck between the costs and benefits of different collection policies.

Changes in collection policy influence sales, the collection period, and the bad-debt loss percentage. All of this should be taken into account when setting the credit policy.

How does collection policy influence sales, the collection period, and the bad-debt loss percentage?

22.4 Cash Discounts

The last element in the credit policy decision, the use of **cash discounts** for early payment, is analyzed by balancing the costs and benefits of different cash discounts. For example, a firm might decide to change its credit terms from "net 30," which means that customers must pay within 30 days, to "2/10, net 30," in which a 2% discount is given if payment is made within 10 days. This change should produce two benefits: (1) it should attract new customers who consider the discount to be a price reduction; and (2) it should lead to a reduction in the days sales outstanding (DSO), because some existing customers will pay more promptly in order to get the discount. Offsetting these benefits is the dollar cost of the discounts. The optimal discount percentage is established at the point at which the marginal costs and benefits are exactly offsetting.

---

1. Credit analysts use procedures ranging from highly sophisticated, computerized "credit-scoring" systems, which actually calculate the statistical probability that a given customer will default, to informal procedures, which involve going through a checklist of factors that should be considered when processing a credit application. The credit-scoring systems use various financial ratios such as the current ratio and the debt ratio (for businesses) and income, years with the same employer, and the like (for individuals) to determine the statistical probability of default. Credit is then granted to those with low default probabilities. The informal procedures often involve examining the "5 C's of Credit": character, capacity, capital, collateral, and conditions. Character is obvious; capacity is a subjective estimate of ability to repay; capital means how much net worth the borrower has; collateral means assets pledged to secure the loan; and conditions refers to business conditions that affect ability to repay.

If sales are seasonal, a firm may use **seasonal dating** on discounts. For example, Slimware Inc., a swimsuit manufacturer, sells on terms of 2/10, net 30, May 1 dating. This means that the effective invoice date is May 1, even if the sale was made back in January. The discount may be taken up to May 10; otherwise, the full amount must be paid by May 30. Slimware produces throughout the year, but retail sales of bathing suits are concentrated in the spring and early summer. By offering seasonal dating, the company induces some of its customers to stock up early, saving Slimware some storage costs and also "nailing down sales."

Self Test	How can cash discounts be used to influence sales volume and the DSO?
	What is seasonal dating?

22.5 Other Factors Influencing Credit Policy

In addition to the factors discussed in previous sections, two other points should be made regarding credit policy: the potential for profit and the legal considerations.

22.5a Profit Potential

We have emphasized the costs of granting credit. However, *if it is possible to sell on credit and also to impose a carrying charge on receivables that are outstanding, then credit sales can actually be more profitable than cash sales.* This is especially true for consumer durables (autos, appliances, and so on), but it is also true for certain types of industrial equipment.[2]

The carrying charges on outstanding credit are generally about 18% on a nominal basis: 1.5% per month, so $1.5\% \times 12 = 18\%$. This is equivalent to an effective annual rate of $(1.015)^{12} - 1.0 = 19.6\%$. Having receivables outstanding that earn more than 18% is highly profitable unless there are too many bad-debt losses.

22.5b Legal Considerations

It is illegal, under the Robinson-Patman Act, for a firm to charge prices that discriminate between customers unless these differential prices are cost-justified. The same holds true for credit—it is illegal to offer more favorable credit terms to one customer or class of customers than to another unless the differences are cost-justified.

Self Test	How do profit potential and legal considerations affect a firm's credit policy?

22.6 The Payments Pattern Approach to Monitoring Receivables

In Chapter 21, we discussed two methods for monitoring a firm's receivables position: days sales outstanding and aging schedules. These procedures are useful, particularly

---

2. Companies that do a large volume of sales financing typically set up subsidiary companies called *captive finance companies* to do the actual financing.

for monitoring an individual customer's account, but neither is totally suitable for monitoring the aggregate payment performance of all credit customers, especially for a firm that experiences fluctuating credit sales. In this section, we present another way to monitor receivables, the **payments pattern approach.**

The primary point in analyzing the aggregate accounts receivable situation is to see if customers, on average, are paying more slowly. If so, then accounts receivable will build up, as will the cost of carrying receivables. Furthermore, the payment slowdown may signal a decrease in the quality of the receivables and hence an increase in bad-debt losses down the road. The DSO and aging schedules are useful in monitoring credit operations, but both are affected by increases and decreases in the level of sales. Thus, changes in sales levels, including normal seasonal or cyclical changes, can change a firm's DSO and aging schedule even though its customers' payment behavior has not changed at all. For this reason, a procedure called the *payments pattern approach* has been developed to measure any changes that might be occurring in customers' payment behavior. To illustrate the payments pattern approach, consider the Hanover Company, a small manufacturer of hand tools that commenced operations in January 2012. Table 22-1 contains Hanover's credit sales and receivables data for 2012. Column 2 shows that Hanover's credit sales are seasonal, with the lowest sales in the fall and winter months and the highest during the summer.

Now assume that 10% of Hanover's customers pay in the month the sale is made, 30% pay in the first month following the sale, 40% pay in the second month, and the remaining 20% pay in the third month. Further, assume that Hanover's customers have the same payment behavior throughout the year; that is, they always take the same length of time to pay. Column 3 of Table 22-1 contains Hanover's receivables

TABLE 22-1   Hanover Company: Receivables Data for 2012 (Thousands of Dollars)

Month (1)	Credit Sales for Month (2)	Receivables at End of Month (3)	Based on Quarterly Sales Data		Based on Year-to-Date Sales Data	
			ADS[a] (4)	DSO[b] (5)	ADS[c] (6)	DSO[c] (7)
January	$ 60	$ 54				
February	60	90				
March	60	102	$1.98	52 days	$1.98	52 days
April	60	102				
May	90	129				
June	120	174	2.97	59	2.47	70
July	120	198				
August	90	177				
September	60	132	2.97	44	2.64	50
October	60	108				
November	60	102				
December	60	102	1.98	52	2.47	41

[a]ADS = Average daily sales.
[b]DSO = Days sales outstanding.
[c]We assume that each quarter is 91 days long.

© Cengage Learning 2013

balance at the end of each month. For example, during January Hanover had $60,000 in sales. Because 10% of the customers paid during the month of sale, the receivables balance at the end of January was $60,000 − 0.1($60,000) = (1.0 − 0.1)($60,000) = 0.9($60,000) = $54,000. By the end of February, 10% + 30% = 40% of the customers had paid for January's sales and 10% had paid for February's sales. Thus, the receivables balance at the end of February was 0.6($60,000) + 0.9($60,000) = $90,000. By the end of March, 80% of January's sales had been collected, 40% of February's sales had been collected, and 10% of March's sales had been collected, so the receivables balance was 0.2($60,000) + 0.6($60,000) + 0.9($60,000) = $102,000, and so on.

Columns 4 and 5 give Hanover's average daily sales (ADS) and days sales outstanding (DSO), respectively, as these measures would be calculated from quarterly financial statements. For example, in the April–June quarter, ADS = ($60,000 + $90,000 + $120,000)/91 = $2,967, and the end-of-quarter (June 30) DSO = $174,000/$2,967 = 58.6 days. Columns 6 and 7 also show ADS and DSO, but here they are calculated on the basis of accumulated sales throughout the year. For example, at the end of June ADS = $450,000/182 = $2,473 and DSO = $174,000/$2,473 = 70 days. (For the entire year, sales are $900,000; ADS = $2,466 and DSO at year-end = 41 days. These last two figures are shown at the bottom of the last two columns.)

The data in Table 22-1 illustrate two major points. First, fluctuating sales lead to changes in the DSO, which suggests that customers are paying faster or slower even though we know that customers' payment patterns are not changing at all. The rising monthly sales trend causes the calculated DSO to rise, whereas declining sales (as in the third quarter) cause the calculated DSO to fall, even though nothing is changing with regard to when customers actually pay. Second, we see that the DSO depends on an averaging procedure; however, regardless of whether quarterly, semiannual, or annual data are used, the DSO is unstable even when payment patterns are *not* changing. Therefore, it is inadvisable to use the DSO as a monitoring device if the firm's sales exhibit seasonal or cyclical patterns.

Seasonal or cyclical variations also make it difficult to interpret aging schedules. Table 22-2 contains Hanover's aging schedules at the end of each quarter. At the end of June, Table 22-2 shows that Hanover's receivables balance was $174,000: 0.2($60,000) + 0.6($90,000) + 0.9($120,000) = $174,000. Note again that Hanover's customers had not changed their payment patterns. However, rising sales during the second quarter created the impression of faster payments when judged by the percentage aging schedule, and declining sales after July created the opposite appearance. Thus, neither the DSO nor the aging schedule provides an accurate picture of customers' payment patterns if sales fluctuate during the year or are trending up or down.

With this background, we can now examine another basic tool, the *uncollected balances schedule,* as shown in Table 22-3. At the end of each quarter, the dollar amount of receivables remaining from each of the 3 month's sales is divided by that

TABLE 22-2   Hanover Company: Quarterly Aging Schedules for 2012 (Thousands of Dollars)

Ages of Accounts (Days)	Value and Percentage of Total Accounts Receivable at the End of Each Quarter							
	March 31		June 30		September 30		December 31	
0–30	$ 54	53%	$108	62%	$ 54	41%	$ 54	53%
31–60	36	35	54	31	54	41	36	35
61–90	12	12	12	7	24	18	12	12
	$102	100%	$174	100%	$132	100%	$102	100%

TABLE 22-3	Hanover Company: Quarterly Uncollected Balances Schedules for 2012 (Thousands of Dollars)		

Quarter	Monthly Sales	Remaining Receivables at End of Quarter	Remaining Receivables as a Percentage of Month's Sales at End of Quarter
Quarter 1:			
January	$ 60	$ 12	20%
February	60	36	60
March	60	54	90
		$102	170%
Quarter 2:			
April	$ 60	$ 12	20%
May	90	54	60
June	120	108	90
		$174	170%
Quarter 3:			
July	$120	$ 24	20%
August	90	54	60
September	60	54	90
		$132	170%
Quarter 4:			
October	$ 60	$ 12	20%
November	60	36	60
December	60	54	90
		$102	170%

month's sales to obtain three receivables-to-sales ratios. For example, at the end of the first quarter, $12,000 of the $60,000 January sales, or 20%, are still outstanding, 60% of February sales are still out, and 90% of March sales are uncollected. Exactly the same situation is revealed at the end of each of the next three quarters. Thus, Table 22-3 shows that Hanover's customers' payment behavior has remained constant.

Recall that, at the beginning of the example, we assumed the existence of a constant payments pattern. In a normal situation, the firm's customers' payments pattern would probably vary somewhat over time. Such variations would be shown in the last column of the uncollected balances schedule. For example, suppose customers began to pay their accounts more slowly in the second quarter. That might cause the second-quarter uncollected balances schedule to look like this (in thousands of dollars):

Quarter 2, 2012	Sales	New Remaining Receivables	New Receivables/Sales
April	$ 60	$ 16	27%
May	90	70	78
June	120	110	92
		$196	197%

We see that the receivables-to-sales ratios are now higher than in the corresponding months of the first quarter. This causes the total uncollected balances percentage to rise from 170% to 197%, which should alert Hanover's managers that customers are paying more slowly than they did earlier in the year.

The uncollected balances schedule permits a firm to monitor its receivables better, and it can also be used to forecast future receivables balances. When Hanover's projected 2013 quarterly balance sheets are constructed, management can use the historical receivables-to-sales ratios, coupled with 2013 sales estimates, to project each quarter's receivables balance. For example, with projected sales as given below and using the same payments pattern as in 2012, Hanover's projected end-of-June 2013 receivables balance would be as follows:

Quarter 2, 2013	Projected Sales	Receivables/Sales	Projected Receivables
April	$ 70	20%	$ 14
May	100	60	60
June	140	90	126

Total projected receivables = $200

The payments pattern approach permits us to remove the effects of seasonal and/or cyclical sales variation and to construct a more accurate measure of customers' payments patterns. Thus, it provides financial managers with better aggregate information than the days sales outstanding or the aging schedule. Managers should use the payments pattern approach to monitor collection performance as well as to project future receivables requirements.

Except possibly in the inventory and cash management areas, nowhere in the typical firm have computers had more of an effect than in accounts receivable management. A well-run business will use a computer system to record sales, to send out bills, to keep track of when payments are made, to alert the credit manager when an account becomes past due, and to take action automatically to collect past-due accounts (for example, to prepare form letters requesting payment). Additionally, the payment history of each customer can be summarized and used to help establish credit limits for customers and classes of customers, and the data on each account can be aggregated and used for the firm's accounts receivable monitoring system. Finally, historical data can be stored in the firm's database and used to develop inputs for studies related to credit policy changes, as we discuss in the next section.

Self Test

Define days sales outstanding. What can be learned from it? Does it have any deficiencies when used to monitor collections over time?

What is an aging schedule? What can be learned from it? Does it have any deficiencies when used to monitor collections over time?

What is the uncollected balances schedule? What advantages does it have over the DSO and the aging schedule for monitoring receivables? How can it be used to forecast a firm's receivables balance?

22.7 Analyzing Proposed Changes in Credit Policy

In Chapter 21, our discussion of credit policy included setting the credit period, credit standards, collection policy, and discount percentage as well as the factors that influence credit policy. A firm's credit policy is reviewed periodically, and policy changes may be proposed. However, before a new policy is adopted, it should be analyzed to determine whether it is indeed preferable to the existing policy. In this section, we discuss procedures for analyzing proposed changes in credit policy.

If a firm's credit policy is *eased* by such actions as lengthening the credit period, relaxing credit standards, following a less tough collection policy, or offering cash discounts, then sales should increase: *Easing the credit policy stimulates sales.* Of course, if credit policy is eased and sales rise, then costs will also rise because more labor, materials, and other inputs will be required to produce the additional goods. Additionally, receivables outstanding will also increase, which will increase carrying costs. Moreover, bad debts and/or discount expenses may also rise. Thus, the key question when deciding on a proposed credit policy change is this: Will sales revenues increase more than costs, including credit-related costs, or will the increase in sales revenues be more than offset by higher costs?

Table 22-4 illustrates the general idea behind the analysis of credit policy changes. Column 1 shows the projected income statement for Monroe Manufacturing under the assumption that the firm's current credit policy is maintained throughout the upcoming year. Column 2 shows the expected effects of easing the credit policy by extending the credit period, offering larger discounts, relaxing

TABLE 22-4	Monroe Manufacturing Company: Analysis of Changing Credit Policy (Millions of Dollars)		
	Projected 2013 Net Income under Current Credit Policy (1)	Effect of Credit Policy Change (2)	Projected 2013 Net Income under New Credit Policy (3)
Gross sales	$400	+ $130	$530
Less discounts	2	+ 4	6
Net sales	$398	+ $126	$524
Production costs, including overhead	280	+ 91	371
Profit before credit costs and taxes	$118	+ $ 35	$153
Credit-related costs:			
Cost of carrying receivables	3	+ 2	5
Credit analysis and collection expenses	5	− 3	2
Bad-debt losses	10	+ 22	32
Profit before taxes	$100	+ 14	$114
State-plus-federal taxes (50%)	50	+ 7	57
Net income	$ 50	+ $ 7	$ 57

Note: The table reports only those cash flows that are related to the credit policy decision.

© Cengage Learning 2013

credit standards, and easing collection efforts. Specifically, Monroe is analyzing the effects of changing its credit terms from 1/10, net 30, to 2/10, net 40, relaxing its credit standards, and putting less pressure on slow-paying customers. Column 3 shows the projected 2013 income statement incorporating the expected effects of easing the credit policy. The generally looser policy is expected to increase sales and lower collection costs, but discounts and several other types of costs would rise. The overall, bottom-line effect is a $7 million increase in projected net income. In the following paragraphs, we explain how the numbers in the table were calculated.

Monroe's annual sales are $400 million. Under its current credit policy, 50% of those customers who pay do so on Day 10 and take the discount, 40% pay on Day 30, and 10% pay late, on Day 40. Thus, Monroe's days sales outstanding is (0.5)(10) + (0.4)(30) + (0.1)(40) = 21 days, and discounts total (0.01)($400,000,000)(0.5) = $2,000,000.

The cost of carrying receivables is equal to the average receivables balance multiplied by the variable cost ratio times the cost of money used to carry receivables. The firm's variable cost ratio is 70%, and its pre-tax cost of capital invested in receivables is 20%. Thus, its annual cost of carrying receivables is $3 million:

$$(DSO)\left(\frac{\text{Sales}}{\text{per day}}\right)\left(\frac{\text{Variable}}{\text{cost ratio}}\right)\left(\frac{\text{Cost of}}{\text{funds}}\right) = \text{Cost of carrying receivables}$$

$$(21)(\$400,000,000/365)(0.70)(0.20) = \$3,221,918 \approx \$3 \text{ million}$$

Only variable costs enter this calculation, because this is the only cost element in receivables that must be financed. We are seeking the cost of carrying receivables, and variable costs represent the firm's investment in the cost of goods sold.

Even though Monroe spends $5 million annually to analyze accounts and to collect bad debts, 2.5% of sales will never be collected. Bad-debt losses therefore amount to (0.025)($400,000,000) = $10,000,000.

Monroe's new credit policy would be 2/10, net 40 versus the old policy of 1/10, net 30, so it would call for a larger discount and a longer payment period in addition to a relaxed collection effort and lower credit standards. The company believes these changes will lead to a $130 million increase in sales to $530 million per year. Under the new terms, management believes that 60% of the customers who pay will take the 2% discount, so discounts will increase to (0.02)($530,000,000)(0.60) = $6,360,000 ≈ $6 million. Half of the nondiscount customers will pay on Day 40 and the remainder on Day 50. The new DSO is thus estimated to be 24 days:

$$(0.6)(10) + (0.2)(40) + (0.2)(50) = 24 \text{ days}$$

Also, the cost of carrying receivables will increase to $5 million[3]:

$$(24)(\$530,000,000/365)(0.70)(0.20) = \$4,878,904 \approx \$5 \text{ million}$$

---

3. Since the credit policy change will result in a longer DSO, the firm will have to wait longer to receive its profit on the goods it sells. Therefore, the firm will incur an opportunity cost due to not having the cash from these profits available for investment. The dollar amount of this opportunity cost is equal to the old sales per day multiplied by the change in DSO times the contribution margin (1 – Variable cost ratio) times the firm's cost of carrying receivables, or

Opportunity cost = (Old sales/365)(ΔDSO)(1 – V)(r)
= ($400/365)(3)(0.3)(0.20)
= $0.197 = $197,000

For simplicity, we have ignored this opportunity cost in our analysis. However, we consider opportunity costs in the next section, where we discuss incremental analysis.

The company plans to reduce its annual credit analysis and collection expenditures to $2 million. The reduced credit standards and the relaxed collection effort are expected to raise bad-debt losses to about 6% of sales, or to (0.06)($530,000,000) = $31,800,000 ≈ $32,000,000, which is an increase of $22 million from the previous level.

The combined effect of all the changes in credit policy is a projected $7 million annual increase in net income. There would, of course, be corresponding changes on the projected balance sheet—the higher sales would necessitate somewhat larger cash balances, inventories, and (depending on the capacity situation) perhaps more fixed assets. Accounts receivable would, of course, also increase. Because these asset increases would have to be financed, certain liabilities and/or equity would have to be increased.

The $7 million expected increase in net income is, of course, an estimate, and the actual effects of the change could be quite different. In the first place, there is uncertainty—perhaps quite a lot—about the projected $130 million increase in sales. Indeed, if the firm's competitors matched its changes then sales might not rise at all. Similar uncertainties must be attached to the number of customers who would take discounts, to production costs at higher or lower sales levels, to the costs of carrying additional receivables, and to bad-debt losses. In the final analysis, the decision will be based on judgment, especially concerning the risks involved, but the type of quantitative analysis set forth in this section is essential to the process.

Self Test

Describe the procedure for evaluating a change in credit policy using the income statement approach.

Do you think that credit policy decisions are made more on the basis of numerical analyses or on judgmental factors?

22.8 Analyzing Proposed Changes in Credit Policy: Incremental Analysis

To evaluate a proposed change in credit policy, one could compare alternative projected income statements, as we did in Table 22-4. Alternatively, one could develop the data in Column 2, which shows the incremental effect of the proposed change, without first developing the projected financial statements. This second approach is often preferable: Given that firms usually change their credit policies in specific divisions or on specific products, and not across the board, it may not be feasible to develop complete corporate income statements. Of course, the two approaches are based on exactly the same data, so they should produce identical results.

In an incremental analysis, we attempt to determine the increase or decrease in both sales and costs associated with a given easing or tightening of credit policy. The difference between incremental sales and incremental costs is defined as **incremental profit**. If the expected incremental profit is positive and if it is sufficiently large to compensate for the risks involved, then the proposed credit policy change should be accepted.

22.8a The Basic Equations

In order to ensure that all relevant factors are considered, it is useful to set up some equations for analyzing changes in credit policy. We begin by defining the following terms and symbols:

S_0 = Current gross sales.

S_N = New gross sales after the change in credit policy; note that S_N can be greater or less than S_0.

$S_N - S_0$ = Incremental (change in) gross sales.

V = Variable costs as a percentage of gross sales; V includes production costs, inventory carrying costs, the cost of administering the credit department, and all other variable costs *except* bad-debt losses, financing costs associated with carrying the investment in receivables, and costs of giving discounts.

$1 - V$ = Contribution margin, or the percentage of each gross sales dollar that goes toward covering overhead and increasing profits; the contribution margin is sometimes called the *gross profit* margin.

r = Cost of financing the investment in receivables.

DSO_0 = Days sales outstanding prior to the change in credit policy.

DSO_N = New days sales outstanding after the credit policy change.

B_0 = Average bad-debt loss at the current sales level as a percentage of current gross sales.

B_N = Average bad-debt loss at the new sales level as a percentage of new gross sales.

P_0 = Percentage of total customers (by dollar amount) who take discounts under the current credit policy; in other words, the percentage of gross sales that is discount sales.

P_N = Percentage of total customers (by dollar amount) that will take discounts under the new credit policy.

D_0 = Discount percentage offered at the present time.

D_N = Discount percentage offered under the new credit policy.

With these definitions in mind, we can calculate values for the incremental change in the level of the firm's investment in receivables, ΔI, and the incremental change in pre-tax profits, ΔP. The formula for calculating ΔI differs depending on whether the change in credit policy results in an increase or decrease in sales. Here we simply present the equations; we discuss and explain them shortly, through use of examples, once all the equations have been set forth.

If the change is expected to *increase* sales—either additional sales to old customers or sales to newly attracted customers, or both—then we have the following situation.

Formula for ΔI if Sales Increase:

$$\Delta I = \begin{pmatrix} \text{Increased investment in} \\ \text{receivables associated} \\ \text{with original sales} \end{pmatrix} + \begin{pmatrix} \text{Increased investment in} \\ \text{receivables associated} \\ \text{with incremental sales} \end{pmatrix}$$

$$= \begin{pmatrix} \text{Change in} \\ \text{days sales} \\ \text{outstanding} \end{pmatrix} \begin{pmatrix} \text{Old} \\ \text{sales} \\ \text{per day} \end{pmatrix} + V \begin{pmatrix} DSO_N \begin{pmatrix} \text{Incremental} \\ \text{sales} \\ \text{per day} \end{pmatrix} \end{pmatrix}$$

$$= [(DSO_N - DSO_0)(S_0/365)] + V[(DSO_N)(S_N - S_0)/365]$$

(22-1)

However, if the change in credit policy is expected to *decrease* sales, then the change in the level of investment in receivables is calculated as follows.

Formula for ΔI if Sales Decrease:

$$\Delta I = \begin{pmatrix} \text{Decreased investment in} \\ \text{receivables associated with} \\ \text{remaining original customers} \end{pmatrix} + \begin{pmatrix} \text{Decreased investment in} \\ \text{receivables associated} \\ \text{with customers who left} \end{pmatrix}$$

$$= \begin{pmatrix} \text{Change in} \\ \text{days sales} \\ \text{outstanding} \end{pmatrix} \begin{pmatrix} \text{Remaining} \\ \text{sales} \\ \text{per day} \end{pmatrix} + V \begin{pmatrix} DSO_0 \begin{pmatrix} \text{Incremental} \\ \text{sales} \\ \text{per day} \end{pmatrix} \end{pmatrix}$$

$$= [(DSO_N - DSO_0)(S_N/365)] + V[(DSO_0)(S_N - S_0)/365]$$

(22-2)

Having calculated the change in receivables investment, we can now analyze the pre-tax profitability of the proposed change.

Formula for ΔP:

$$\Delta P = \begin{pmatrix} \text{Change in} \\ \text{gross} \\ \text{profit} \end{pmatrix} - \begin{pmatrix} \text{Change in cost} \\ \text{of carrying} \\ \text{receivables} \end{pmatrix} - \begin{pmatrix} \text{Change in} \\ \text{bad-debt} \\ \text{losses} \end{pmatrix} - \begin{pmatrix} \text{Change in} \\ \text{cost of} \\ \text{discounts} \end{pmatrix}$$

$$= (S_N - S_0)(1 - V) - r(\Delta I) - (B_N S_N - B_0 S_0) - (D_N S_N P_N - D_0 S_0 P_0)$$

(22-3)

Thus, changes in credit policy are analyzed by using either Equation 22-1 or 22-2, depending on whether the proposed change is expected to increase or decrease sales, together with Equation 22-3. The rationale behind these equations will become clear as we work through several illustrations. Note that all the terms in Equation 22-3 need not be used in a particular analysis. For example, a change in credit policy might not affect discount sales or bad-debt losses, in which case the last two terms of the equation would both be zero. Note also that the form of the equations depends on the way in which the variables are first defined.[4]

---

4. For example, P_0 and P_N are defined as the percentage of *total* customers who take discounts. If P_0 and P_N were defined as the percentage of *paying* customers (excluding bad debts) who take discounts, then Equation 22-3 would become

$$\Delta P = (S_N - S_0)(1 - V) - r(\Delta I) - (B_N S_N - B_0 S_0) - [D_N S_N P_N(1 - B_N) - D_0 S_0 P_0(1 - B_0)]$$

Similarly, changing the definitions of B_0 and B_N would affect the third term of Equation 22-3, as we discuss later.

28.8b Changing the Credit Period

In this section, we examine the effects of changing the credit period, and in the subsequent sections we consider changes in credit standards, collection policy, and cash discounts. Throughout, we illustrate the situation with data on Stylish Fashions Inc.

Lengthening the Credit Period

Stylish Fashions currently sells on a cash-only basis. Since it extends no credit, the company has no funds tied up in receivables, no bad-debt losses, and no credit expenses of any kind. On the other hand, its sales volume is lower than it would be if credit terms were offered. Stylish is now considering offering credit on 30-day terms. Current sales are $100,000 per year, variable costs are 60% of sales, excess production capacity exists (so no new fixed costs would be incurred as a result of expanded sales), and the cost of capital invested in receivables is 10%. Stylish estimates sales would increase to $150,000 per year if credit were extended and that bad-debt losses would be 2% of total sales. Thus, we have the following:

S_0 = $100,000
S_N = $150,000
V = 60% = 0.6
$1 - V$ = $1 - 0.6$ = 0.4
r = 10% = 0.10
DSO_0 = 0 days
DSO_N = 30 days. Here we assume that all customers will pay on time, so DSO = specified credit period. Generally, some customers pay late, so in most cases DSO is greater than the specified credit period.
B_0 = 0% = 0.00. There are currently no bad-debt losses.
B_N = 2% = 0.02. These losses apply to the entire $150,000 new level of sales.
$D_0 = D_N$ = 0%. No discounts are given under either the current or the proposed credit policies.

Because sales are expected to increase, Equation 22-1 is used to determine the change in the investment in receivables:

$$\Delta I = [(DSO_N - DSO_0)(S_0/365)] + V[(DSO_N)(S_N - S_0)/365]$$
$$= [(30 - 0)(\$100,000/365)] + 0.6[30(\$150,000 - \$100,000)/365]$$
$$= \$8,219 + \$2,466 = \$10,685$$

Note that the first term, the increased investment in accounts receivable associated with *old sales,* is based on the full amount of the receivables, whereas the second term, the investment associated with *incremental sales,* consists of incremental receivables multiplied by V, the variable cost percentage. This difference reflects that (1) the firm invests only its variable cost in incremental receivables, but (2) it would have collected the full sales price on the old sales earlier had it not made the credit policy change. There is an *opportunity cost* on the profit and a *direct financing cost* associated with the $8,219 additional investment in receivables from old sales, but only a direct financing cost associated with the $2,466 investment in receivables from incremental sales.

Looking at this another way, incremental sales will generate an actual increase in receivables of $(DSO_N)(S_N - S_0)/365 = 30(\$50,000/365) = \$4,110$. However, the only part of that increase that must be financed (by bank borrowing or from other sources) and reported as a liability on the right-hand side of the balance sheet is the cash outflow required to support the incremental sales—that is, the variable costs $V(\$4,110) = 0.6(\$4,110) = \$2,466$. The remainder of the receivables increase, $\$1,644$ of accrued before-tax profit, is reflected on the balance sheet not as some type of credit used to finance receivables but rather as an increase in retained earnings generated by the sales. On the other hand, the old receivables level was zero, meaning that the original sales produced cash of $\$100,000/365 = \$273.97$ per day, which was immediately available for investing in assets or for reducing capital from other sources. The change in credit policy will cause a delay in the collection of these funds and hence will require the firm (1) to borrow to cover the variable costs of the sales and (2) to forgo a return on the retained earnings portion, which would have been available immediately had the credit policy change not been made.

Given ΔI, we may now use Equation 22-3 to determine the incremental profit, ΔP, associated with the proposed credit period change:

$$\Delta P = (S_N - S_0)(1 - V) - r(\Delta I) - (B_N S_N - B_0 S_0) - (D_N S_N P_N - D_0 S_0 P_0)$$
$$= (\$50,000)(0.4) - 0.10(\$10,685) - [0.02(\$150,000) - 0.00(\$100,000)] - \$0$$
$$= \$20,000 - \$1,069 - \$3,000 = \$15,931$$

Since pre-tax profits are expected to increase by $\$15,931$, the credit policy change appears to be desirable.

Two simplifying assumptions that were made in our analysis should be noted: We assumed (1) that all customers paid on time (DSO = credit period) and (2) that there were no current bad-debt losses. The assumption of prompt payment can be relaxed quite easily—we can simply use the actual days sales outstanding (say, 40 days), rather than the 30-day credit period, to calculate the investment in receivables and then use this new (higher) value of ΔI in Equation 22-3 to calculate ΔP. Thus, if DSO_N were 40 days then the increased investment in receivables would be

$$\Delta I = [(40 - 0)(\$100,000/365)] + 0.6[40(\$50,000/365)]$$
$$= \$10,959 + \$3,288 = \$14,247$$

and the change in pre-tax profits would be

$$\Delta P = \$50,000(0.4) - 0.10(\$14,247) - 0.02(\$150,000)$$
$$= \$20,000 - \$1,425 - \$3,000 = \$15,575$$

The longer collection period causes incremental profits to fall slightly, but they are still positive and so the credit policy should probably be relaxed.

If the company had been selling on credit initially and therefore incurring some bad-debt losses, then this information would need to be included in Equation 22-3. In our example, $B_0 S_0$ was equal to zero because Stylish Fashions did not previously sell on credit; therefore, the change in bad-debt losses was equal to $B_N S_N$.

Note that B_N is defined as the average credit loss as a percentage of total sales, not of incremental sales. Bad debts might be higher for new customers attracted by the credit terms than for old customers who take advantage of them, but B_N is an average of these two groups. However, if one wanted to keep the two groups separate, it would be easy enough to define B_N as the bad-debt percentage of the incremental sales only.

Other factors could also be introduced into the analysis. For example, the company could consider a further easing of credit by extending the credit period to 60 days, or it could analyze the effects of a sales expansion so great that fixed assets, and hence fixed costs, had to be added. Or the variable cost ratio might change as sales increased, falling if economies of scale were present or rising if diseconomies were present. Adding such factors complicates the analysis, but the basic principles are the same; just bear in mind that we are seeking to determine the *incremental sales revenues,* the *incremental costs,* and consequently the *incremental before-tax profit* associated with a given change in credit policy.

Shortening the Credit Period

Suppose that a year after Stylish Fashions began offering 30-day credit terms its management decided to consider the possibility of shortening the credit period from 30 to 20 days. It was believed that sales would decline by $20,000 per year from the current level of $150,000, so $S_N = \$130,000$. It was also believed that the bad-debt percentage on these lost sales would be 2%, the same as on other sales, and that all other values would remain as given in the previous section.

We first calculate the incremental investment in receivables. Because the change in credit policy is expected to decrease sales, Equation 22-2 is used:

$$\Delta I = [(DSO_N - DSO_0)(S_N/365)] + V[(DSO_0)(S_N - S_0)/365]$$
$$= [(20 - 30)(\$130,000/365)] + 0.6[30(\$130,000 - \$150,000)/365]$$
$$= (-10)(\$356.16) + 0.6[(30)(-\$54.79)]$$
$$= -\$3,562 - \$986 = -\$4,548$$

With a shorter credit period, there is a shorter collection period, so sales are collected sooner. There is also a smaller volume of business, and hence a smaller investment in receivables. The first term captures the speedup in collections, while the second reflects the reduced sales and hence the lower receivables investment (at variable cost).

Note that V is included in the second term but not in the first. The logic here is similar to the logic underlying Equation 22-1: V is included in the second term because, by shortening the credit period, Stylish Fashions will drive off some customers and forgo sales of $20,000 per year, or $54.79 per day. The firm's investment in those sales was only 60% of the average receivables outstanding, or 0.6(30)($54.79) = $986. However, the situation is different for the remaining customers. They would have paid their full purchase price—variable cost plus profit—after 30 days. Now, however, they will have to pay this amount 10 days sooner, so those funds will be available to meet operating costs or for investment. Therefore, the first term should not be reduced by the variable cost factor. In total, then, reducing the credit period would result in a $4,548 reduction in the investment in receivables, consisting of a $3,562 decline in receivables associated with continuing customers and a further $986 decline in investment as a result of the reduced sales volume.

Having calculated the change in investment, we can now use Equation 22-3 to analyze the profitability of the proposed change:

$$\Delta P = (S_N - S_0)(1 - V) - r(\Delta I) - (B_N S_N - B_0 S_0) - (D_N S_N P_N - D_0 S_0 P_0)$$
$$= (\$130,000 - \$150,000)(0.4) - 0.10(-\$4,548)$$
$$\quad - [(0.02)(\$130,000) - (0.02)(\$150,000)] - \$0$$
$$= -\$8,000 + \$455 + \$400 = -\$7,145$$

Because the expected incremental pre-tax profits are negative, the firm should not reduce its credit period from 30 to 20 days.

28.8c Changes in Other Credit Policy Variables

In the preceding section, we examined the effects of changes in the credit period. Changes in other credit policy variables may be analyzed similarly. In general, we would follow these steps.

Step 1 Estimate the effect of the policy change on sales, on DSO, on bad-debt losses, and so on.

Step 2 Determine the change in the firm's investment in receivables. If the change will increase sales, use Equation 22-1 to calculate ΔI. Conversely, if the change will decrease sales then use Equation 22-2.

Step 3 Use Equation 22-3, or one of its variations, to calculate the effect of the change on pre-tax profits. If profits are expected to increase, the policy change should be made—unless it is judged to increase the firm's risk by a disproportionate amount.

28.8d Simultaneous Changes in Policy Variables

In the preceding discussion, we considered the effects of changes in only one credit policy variable. The firm could, of course, change several or even all policy variables simultaneously. An almost endless variety of equations could be developed, depending on which policy variables are manipulated and on the assumed effects on sales, discounts taken, the collection period, bad-debt losses, the existence of excess capacity, changes in credit department costs, changes in the variable cost percentage, and so on. The analysis would get "messy" and the incremental profit equation would be complex, but the principles we have developed could be used to handle any type of policy change.

Describe the incremental analysis approach for evaluating a proposed credit policy change.

How can risk be incorporated into the analysis?

Self Test

22.9 The Cost of Bank Loans

In Chapter 21, we discussed the various short-term bank loans that are typically available: promissory notes, informal lines of credit, and revolving credit agreements. We provide a more in-depth and comprehensive discussion here.

The terms on a short-term bank loan to a business are spelled out in the promissory note. Here are the key elements contained in most promissory notes.

1. *Interest-only versus amortized.* Loans are either *interest-only,* meaning that only interest is paid during the life of the loan and the principal is repaid when the loan matures, or *amortized,* meaning that some of the principal is repaid on each payment date. Amortized loans are called *installment loans.* Note, too, that loans can be fully or partially amortized. For example, a loan may mature after 10 years, but payments may be based on 20 years, so an unpaid balance will still exist at the end of the 10th year. Such a loan is called a "balloon" loan.

2. *Collateral.* If a short-term loan is secured by some specific collateral, generally accounts receivable or inventories, then this fact is indicated in the note. If the collateral is to be kept on the premises of the borrower, then a form called a

UCC-1 (Uniform Commercial Code-1) is filed with the Secretary of State for the state in which the collateral resides, along with a *Security Agreement* (also part of the Uniform Commercial Code) that describes the nature of the agreement. These filings prevent the borrower from using the same collateral to secure loans from different lenders, and they spell out conditions under which the lender can seize the collateral.

3. *Loan guarantees.* If the borrower is a small corporation, its bank will probably insist that the larger stockholders *personally guarantee* the loan. Banks have often seen a troubled company's owner divert assets from the company to some other entity he or she owned, so banks protect themselves by insisting on personal guarantees. However, stockholder guarantees are virtually impossible to secure in the case of larger corporations that have many stockholders. Also, guarantees are unnecessary for proprietorships or partnerships because in those cases the owners are already personally liable for the businesses' debts.

4. *Nominal, or stated, interest rate.* The interest rate can be either *fixed* or *floating.* If it floats, then it is generally indexed to LIBOR. Most loans of any size ($25,000 and up) have floating rates if their maturities are greater than 90 days. The note will also indicate whether the bank uses a *360- or 365-day year* for purposes of calculating interest.

5. *Frequency of interest payments.* If the note is on an interest-only basis, it will indicate *how frequently interest must be paid.* Interest is typically calculated on a daily basis but paid monthly.

6. *Maturity.* Long-term loans always have specific maturity dates. A short-term loan may or may not have a specified maturity. For example, a loan may mature in 30 days, 90 days, 6 months, or 1 year; or it may call for "payment on demand," in which case the loan can remain outstanding as long as the borrower wants to continue using the funds and the bank agrees. Banks virtually never call demand notes unless the borrower's creditworthiness deteriorates, so some "short-term loans" remain outstanding for years, with the interest rate floating with rates in the economy.

7. *Calculation and payment of interest.* For most loans, interest is paid after it is earned. But not all loans follow this convention, and the method by which interest is calculated and paid affects the overall cost of credit. One alternate method is *discount interest.* A *discount loan* requires that interest be paid in advance. If the loan is on a discount basis, the borrower actually receives less than the face amount of the loan, and this increases the loan's effective cost. We discuss discount loans in a later section. Another method is used in an *add-on basis installment loan.* Auto loans and other types of consumer installment loans are generally set up on an "add-on basis," which means that interest over the life of the loan is calculated and then added to the face amount of the loan. Thus, the borrower signs a note for the funds received plus the interest. The add-on feature also raises the effective cost of a loan, as we demonstrate in a later section.

8. *Other cost elements.* Some commercial loans require the borrower to keep a percentage of the borrowed funds in an account at the lending bank. These held funds are called *compensating balances.* In addition, revolving credit agreements often require *commitment fees* in which the borrower pays interest on the amount actually drawn plus a separate fee based either on the total size of the line of credit or on the unused credit. Both of these conditions will be spelled out in the loan agreement, and both raise the effective cost of a loan above its stated nominal rate.

9. The **annual percentage rate (APR)**. The various fees and methods of calculating interest mean that the nominal, or stated, interest rate may not reflect the true cost of the loan. The APR calculation incorporates all of the costs of borrowing and reports a single nominal rate that reflects all of these costs. However, this rate is required to be reported only for consumer loans.

10. *Key-person insurance.* Often the success of a small company is linked to its owner or to a few important managers. It's a sad fact, but many small companies fail when one of these key individuals dies. Therefore, banks often require small companies to take out *key-person insurance* on their most important managers as part of the loan agreement. Usually the loan becomes due and payable should there be an untimely demise, with the insurance benefits being used to repay the loan. This makes the best of a bad situation—the bank gets its money, and the company reduces its debt burden without having to use any of its operating cash.

In the following sections, we explain how to calculate the effective cost of different bank loans. For illustrative purposes, we assume a loan of $10,000 at a nominal interest rate of 12% and with a 365-day year.

22.9a Regular, or Simple, Interest

In Chapter 21, we explained **simple interest**, which is also called **regular interest**. We review that discussion here. Most short-term business lending is with interest-only loans. The first step is to divide the nominal interest rate, 12% in this case, by 365 (or 360 in some cases) to obtain the rate per day:

$$\frac{\text{Interest rate}}{\text{per day}} = \frac{\text{Nominal rate}}{\text{Days in year}} \qquad \text{(22-4)}$$

$$= 0.12/365 = 0.00032876712$$

This rate is then multiplied by the number of days during the specific payment period and then by the amount of the loan. For example, if the loan is interest-only with monthly payments, then the interest payment for January would be $101.92:

$$\frac{\text{Interest charge}}{\text{for period}} = (\text{Days in period})(\text{Rate per day})(\text{Amount of loan}) \qquad \text{(22-5)}$$

$$= (31 \text{ days})(0.00032876712)(\$10,000) = \$101.92$$

If interest were payable quarterly and if there were 91 days in the quarter, then the interest payment would be $299.18. The annual interest would be 365 × 0.00032876712 × $10,000 = $1,200.00. Note that if the bank had based the interest calculation on a 360-day year, as most banks do, then the interest charges would have been slightly higher and the annual charge would have been $1,216.67. Obviously, banks use a 360-day year to boost their earnings.

The effective interest rate on a loan depends on how frequently interest must be paid—the more frequently, the higher the effective rate. We demonstrate this point with two time lines, one for interest paid once a year and one for quarterly payments:

Interest Paid Annually:

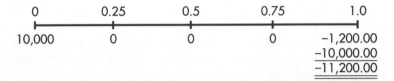

	0	0.25	0.5	0.75	1.0
	10,000	0	0	0	−1,200.00
					−10,000.00
					−11,200.00

The borrower gets $10,000 at t = 0 and pays $11,200 at t = 1. On a financial calculator, enter N = 1, PV = 10000, PMT = 0, and FV = −11200; then press I/YR to get the effective cost of the loan, 12%.

Interest Paid Quarterly:

	0	0.25	0.5	0.75	1.0
	10,000	−299.18	−299.18	−302.47	−299.18
					−10,000.00
					−10,299.18

Note that the third quarter has 92 days. After entering the data in the cash flow register of a financial calculator (being sure to use the +/− key to enter −299.18), we find the periodic rate to be 2.9999%. The effective annual rate is 12.55%:

$$\text{Effective annual rate, quarterly} = (1 + 0.029999)^4 - 1 = 12.55\%$$

Had the loan called for interest to be paid monthly then the effective rate would have been 12.68%, and if interest had been paid daily then the rate would have been 12.75%. These rates would be higher if the bank used a 360-day year.

In these examples, we assumed that the loan matured in 1 year but that interest was paid at various times during the year. The rates we calculated would have been exactly the same even if the loan had matured on each interest payment date. In other words, the effective rate on a monthly payment loan would be 12.68% regardless of whether it matured after 1 month, 6 months, 1 year, or 10 years, providing the stated rate remained at 12%.

22.9b Discount Interest

In a **discount interest** loan, the bank deducts the interest in advance (*discounts the loan*). Thus, the borrower receives less than the face value of the loan. On a 1-year, $10,000 loan with a 12% (nominal) rate and discount basis, the interest is $10,000(0.12) = $1,200. Therefore, the borrower obtains the use of only $10,000 − $1,200 = $8,800. If the loan were for less than a year then the interest charge (the discount) would be lower; in our example, it would be $600 if the loan were for 6 months and so the amount received would be $9,400.

The effective rate on a discount loan is always higher than the rate on an otherwise similar simple interest loan. To illustrate, consider the situation for a discounted 12% loan for 1 year, as follows.

Discount Interest, Paid Annually:

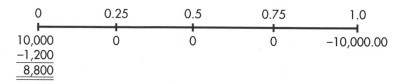

On a financial calculator, enter N = 1, PV = 8800, PMT = 0, and FV = −10000; then press I/YR to get the effective cost of the loan, 13.64%.[5]
If a discount loan matures in less than a year—say, after 1 quarter—then we have the following situation.

Discount Interest, One Quarter:

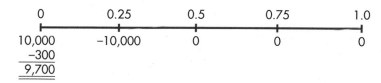

Enter N = 1, PV = 9700, PMT = 0, and FV = −10000, and then press I/YR to find the periodic rate, 3.092784% per quarter, that corresponds to an effective annual rate of 12.96%. Thus, shortening the period of a discount loan lowers the effective rate of interest.

22.9c Effects of Compensating Balances

If the bank requires a compensating balance and if the amount of the required balance exceeds the amount the firm would normally hold on deposit, then the excess must be deducted at t = 0 and then added back when the loan matures. This has the effect of raising the effective rate on the loan. To illustrate, here is the setup for a 1-year discount loan requiring a 20% compensating balance that the firm would not otherwise hold on deposit.

---

5. Note that the firm actually receives less than the face amount of the loan:

   Funds received = (Face amount of loan)(1.0 − Nominal interest rate)

   We can solve for the face amount as follows:

   $$\text{Face amount of loan} = \frac{\text{Funds received}}{1.0 - \text{Nominal interest rate}}$$

   Therefore, if the borrowing firm actually requires $10,000 of cash, it must borrow $11,363.64:

   $$\text{Face value} = \frac{\$10,000}{1.0 - 0.12} = \frac{\$10,000}{0.88} = \$11,363.64$$

   Now the borrower will receive $11,363.64 − 0.12($11,363.64) = $10,000. Increasing the face value of the loan does not change the effective rate of 13.64% on the $10,000 of usable funds.

Discount Interest, Paid Annually, with 20% Compensating Balance:

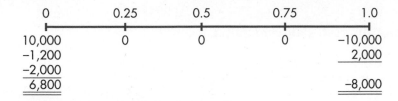

0	0.25	0.5	0.75	1.0
10,000	0	0	0	−10,000
−1,200				2,000
−2,000				
6,800				−8,000

Note that the bank initially gives, and the borrower gets, $10,000 at time 0. However, the bank takes out the $1,200 of interest in advance, and the company must leave $2,000 in the bank as a compensating balance; hence the borrower's effective net cash flow at t = 0 is $6,800. At t = 1, the borrower must repay the $10,000, but $2,000 is already in the bank (the compensating balance), so the company must repay a net amount of $8,000.

On a financial calculator, enter N = 1, PV = 6800, PMT = 0, and FV = −8000; then press I/YR to get the effective cost of the discount loan with a compensating balance, 17.65%.

Note that banks recently have moved away from requiring compensating balances for fear of violating anti-trust regulations. Tying deposit services to lending services can be viewed as anti-competitive.

29.9d Installment Loans: Add-on Interest

Lenders typically charge **add-on interest** on automobile and other types of installment loans. The term "add-on" means the interest is calculated and then added to the amount received to determine the loan's face value. To illustrate, suppose you borrow $10,000 on an add-on basis at a nominal rate of 12% to buy a car, with the loan to be repaid in 12 monthly installments. At a 12% add-on rate, you will pay a total interest charge of $10,000(0.12) = $1,200. However, since the loan is paid off in monthly installments, you have the use of the full $10,000 for only the first month; then the outstanding balance declines until, during the last month, only one-twelfth of the original loan is still outstanding. Thus, you are paying $1,200 for the use of only about half the loan's face amount, as the average usable funds are only about $5,000. Therefore, we can calculate the approximate annual rate as follows:

(22–6)
$$\text{Approximate annual rate}_{\text{Add-on}} = \frac{\text{Interest paid}}{(\text{Amount received})/2}$$

$$= \frac{\$1,200}{\$10,000/2} = 24.0\%$$

To determine the effective rate of an add-on loan, we proceed as follows.

1. The total amount to be repaid is $10,000 of principal, plus $1,200 of interest, or $11,200.
2. The monthly payment is $11,200/12 = $933.33.

3. You are, in effect, paying off a 12-period annuity of $933.33 in order to receive $10,000 today, so $10,000 is the present value of the annuity. Here is the time line:

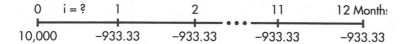

4. On a financial calculator, enter N = 12, PV = 10000, PMT = −933.33, and FV = 0; then press I/YR to obtain 1.7880%. However, this is a monthly rate.
5. The effective annual rate is found as follows:[6]

$$\text{Effective annual rate}_{\text{Add-on}} = (1 + r_d)^n - 1.0 \qquad (22\text{–}7)$$

$$= (1.01788)^{12} - 1.0$$
$$= 1.2370 - 1.0 \doteq 23.7\%$$

29.9e Annual Percentage Rate

The various ways of calculating interest (simple, discount, add-on), together with the various costs that are also frequently associated with smaller loans (e.g., credit report, loan processing and origination fees), cause the effective annual rate to differ even for loans that have identical stated interest rates. For example, although the add-on interest rate in our example above is 12%, its effective rate is 23.7%. If the loan used discount interest paid quarterly then the effective rate would be 12.96%, and if the loan used monthly simple interest the effective rate would be $(1.01)^{12} - 1.0 = 12.68\%$. In order to attempt to bring some consistency to reporting the cost of credit across various loan types, Congress passed the Truth in Lending Act in 1968. This legislation required that the **annual percentage rate (APR)** for all "consumer loans" be stated in bold print on the loan agreement.

The APR is the annual nominal effective cost of the credit, taking into account fees and the timing of payments:

$$\text{APR} = (\text{Periods per year})(\text{Rate per period})$$

So for a loan with 1% monthly simple interest, the APR would be 12(1%) = 12%. For the 12% add-on loan with monthly payments, the APR would be 12(1.788%) = 21.46%. For the 12% discount loan with quarterly payments, the APR would be 4(3.093%) = 12.37%. In most cases, this means that the effective annual rate can easily be calculated from the APR by compounding:

$$\text{Effective annual rate} = (1 + \text{APR}/n)^n - 1$$

where n is the number of periods per year.

The truth-in-lending laws apply primarily to consumer (not business) loans, so the APR does not necessarily appear on a business loan. In these cases the all-in borrowing cost must be calculated by the borrower.

---

6. Note that if an installment loan is paid off ahead of schedule, additional complications arise. For the classic discussion of this point, see Dick Bonker, "The Rule of 78," *Journal of Finance*, June 1976, pp. 877–888.

Name four different ways that banks can calculate interest on loans.

What is a compensating balance? What effect does a compensating balance requirement have on the effective interest rate on a loan?

22.10 Choosing a Bank

Individuals whose only contact with their bank is through the use of its checking services generally choose a bank for the convenience of its location and the competitive cost of its services. However, a business that borrows from banks must look at other criteria and recognize that important differences exist among banks. Some of these differences are considered next.

22.10a Willingness to Assume Risks

Banks have different basic policies toward risk. Some follow relatively conservative lending practices, while others engage in what are properly termed "creative banking practices." These policies reflect partly the personalities of bank officers and partly the characteristics of the bank's deposit liabilities. Thus, a bank with fluctuating deposit liabilities in a static community will tend to be a conservative lender, whereas a bank whose deposits are growing with little interruption may follow more liberal credit policies. Similarly, a large bank with broad diversification over geographic regions and across industries can obtain the benefit of combining and averaging risks. Thus, marginal credit risks that might be unacceptable to a small or specialized bank can be pooled by a branch banking system to reduce the overall risk of a group of marginal accounts.[7]

22.10b Advice and Counsel

Some bank loan officers are active in providing counsel and in granting loans to firms in their early and formative years. Certain banks have specialized departments that make loans to firms that are expected to grow and thus to become more important customers. The personnel of these departments can provide valuable counseling to customers: The bankers' experience with other firms in growth situations may enable them to spot, and then to warn their customers about, developing problems.

22.10c Loyalty to Customers

Banks differ in their support of borrowers in bad times. This characteristic is referred to as the degree of *loyalty* of the bank. Some banks may put great pressure on a business to liquidate its loans when the firm's outlook becomes clouded, whereas others will stand by the firm and work diligently to help it get back on its feet.

---

7. Bank deposits are insured by a federal agency, and banks are required to pay premiums toward the cost of this insurance. Logically, riskier banks should pay higher premiums, but to date political forces have limited the use of risk-based insurance premiums. As an alternative, banks with riskier loan portfolios are required to have more equity capital per dollar of deposits than less risky banks. Until the 1980s, the savings and loan industry had federal insurance, no differential capital requirements, and lax regulations. As a result, some S&L operators wrote risky loans at high interest rates using low-cost, insured deposits. If the loans paid off, the S&L owners would get rich. If they went into default, the taxpayers would have to pay off the deposits. Those government policies ended up costing taxpayers more than $100 billion.

An especially dramatic illustration of this point was Bank of America's bailout of Memorex Corporation. The bank could have forced Memorex into bankruptcy, but instead it loaned the company additional capital and helped it survive a bad period. Memorex's stock price subsequently rose from $1.50 to $68, so Bank of America's help was indeed beneficial.

22.10d Specialization

Banks differ greatly in their degrees of loan specialization. Larger banks have separate departments that specialize in different kinds of loans—for example, real estate loans, farm loans, and commercial loans. Within these broad categories there may be a specialization by line of business, such as steel, machinery, cattle, or textiles. The strengths of banks are also likely to reflect the nature of the businesses and the economic environment in the areas in which they operate. For example, some California banks have become specialists in lending to electronics companies, while many Midwestern banks are agricultural specialists. A sound firm can obtain more creative cooperation and more active support by going to a bank that has experience and familiarity with its particular type of business. Therefore, a bank that is excellent for one firm may be unsatisfactory for another.

22.10e Maximum Loan Size

The size of a bank can be an important factor. Since the maximum loan a bank can make to any one customer is limited to 15% of the bank's capital accounts (capital stock plus retained earnings), it is generally not appropriate for large firms to develop borrowing relationships with small banks.

22.10f Other Services

Banks also provide cash management services, assist with electronic funds transfers, help firms obtain foreign exchange, and the like; and the availability of such services should be taken into account when selecting a bank. Also, if the firm is a small business whose manager owns most of its stock, the bank's willingness and ability to provide trust and estate services should be considered.

What are some factors that should be considered when choosing a bank?	**Self Test**

Summary

This chapter discussed granting credit and the conventions for interest rates on bank loans. It is important to monitor the results of credit policy by monitoring accounts receivable. A firm can affect its level of accounts receivable by changing its credit and collections policy, but doing so also affects sales. Therefore, a complete analysis of the effects of changes in credit policy is necessary. The key concepts covered in this chapter are listed below.

- A firm's credit policy consists of four elements: (1) **credit period**, (2) **discounts** given for early payment, (3) **credit standards**, and (4) **collection policy**. The first two, when combined, are called the **credit terms**.
- Additional factors that influence a firm's overall credit policy are **profit potential** and **legal considerations**.
- The basic objective of the credit manager is to increase profitable sales by extending credit to worthy customers and therefore adding value to the firm.
- Firms can use **days sales outstanding (DSO)** and **aging schedules** to help monitor their receivables position, but the best way to monitor aggregate receivables is the **payments pattern approach**. The primary tool in this approach is the **uncollected balances schedule**.
- If a firm **eases its credit policy** by lengthening the credit period, relaxing its credit standards and collection policy, and offering (or raising) its cash discount, then its sales should increase; however, its costs will also increase. A firm should ease its credit policy only if the costs of doing so will be offset by higher expected revenues. In general, credit policy changes should be evaluated on the basis of incremental profits.
- Changes in credit policy can be analyzed in two ways. First, **projected income statements** can be constructed for both the current and the proposed policies. Second, equations can be used to estimate the **incremental change** in profits resulting from a proposed new credit policy.
- With a **regular**, or **simple, interest loan**, interest is not compounded; that is, interest is not earned on interest.
- In a **discount interest loan**, the bank deducts the interest in advance. Interest is calculated on the face amount of the loan but it is paid in advance.
- Installment loans are typically **add-on interest loans**. Interest is calculated and added to the funds received to determine the face amount of the loan.
- The **annual percentage rate (APR)** is a rate reported by banks and other lenders on consumer loans that reflects all of the various loan fees and the timing of interest and principal payments.

Questions

22-1 Define each of the following terms:
   a. Cash discounts
   b. Seasonal dating
   c. Aging schedule; days sales outstanding (DSO)
   d. Payments pattern approach; uncollected balances schedule
   e. Simple interest; discount interest; add-on interest

22-2 Suppose a firm makes a purchase and receives the shipment on February 1. The terms of trade as stated on the invoice read "2/10, net 40, May 1 dating." What is the latest date on which payment can be made and the discount still be taken? What is the date on which payment must be made if the discount is not taken?

22-3 Is it true that, if a firm calculates its days sales outstanding, it has no need for an aging schedule?

22-4 Firm A had no credit losses last year, but 1% of Firm B's accounts receivable proved to be uncollectible and resulted in losses. Should Firm B fire its credit manager and hire A's?

22-5 Indicate by a (+), (–), or (0) whether each of the following events would probably cause accounts receivable (AR), sales, and profits to increase, decrease, or be affected in an indeterminate manner:

	AR	Sales	Profits
The firm tightens its credit standards.	_____	_____	_____
The terms of trade are changed from 2/10, net 30, to 3/10, net 30.	_____	_____	_____
The terms are changed from 2/10, net 30, to 3/10, net 40.	_____	_____	_____
The credit manager gets tough with past-due accounts.	_____	_____	_____

Problems   Answers Appear in Appendix B

Easy Problems 1–4

22-1 **Cost of Bank Loan** On March 1, Minnerly Motors obtains a business loan from a local bank. The loan is a $25,000 interest-only loan with a nominal rate of 11%. Interest is calculated on a simple interest basis with a 365-day year. What is Minnerly's interest charge for the first month (assuming 31 days in the month)?

22-2 **Cost of Bank Loan** Mary Jones recently obtained an equipment loan from a local bank. The loan is for $15,000 with a nominal interest rate of 11%. However, this is an installment loan, so the bank also charges add-on interest. Mary must make monthly payments on the loan, and the loan is to be repaid in 1 year. What is the effective annual rate on the loan (assuming a 365-day year)?

22-3 **Cost of Bank Loans** Del Hawley, owner of Hawley's Hardware, is negotiating with First City Bank for a 1-year loan of $50,000. First City has offered Hawley the alternatives listed below. Calculate the effective annual interest rate for each alternative. Which alternative has the lowest effective annual interest rate?

  a. A 12% annual rate on a simple interest loan, with no compensating balance required and interest due at the end of the year

  b. A 9% annual rate on a simple interest loan, with a 20% compensating balance required and interest due at the end of the year

  c. An 8.75% annual rate on a discounted loan, with a 15% compensating balance

  d. Interest figured as 8% of the $50,000 amount, *payable at the end of the year*, but with the loan amount repayable in monthly installments during the year

22-4 **Cost of Bank Loans** Gifts Galore Inc. borrowed $1.5 million from National City Bank. The loan was made at a simple annual interest rate of 9% a year for 3 months. A 20% compensating balance requirement raised the effective interest rate.

  a. The nominal annual rate on the loan was 11.25%. What is the true effective rate?

b. What would be the effective cost of the loan if the note required discount interest?

c. What would be the nominal annual interest rate on the loan if the bank did not require a compensating balance but required repayment in three equal monthly installments?

Intermediate Problems 5–7

22-5 **Relaxing Collection Efforts** The Boyd Corporation has annual credit sales of $1.6 million. Current expenses for the collection department are $35,000, bad-debt losses are 1.5%, and the days sales outstanding is 30 days. The firm is considering easing its collection efforts such that collection expenses will be reduced to $22,000 per year. The change is expected to increase bad-debt losses to 2.5% and to increase the days sales outstanding to 45 days. In addition, sales are expected to increase to $1,625,000 per year.

   Should the firm relax collection efforts if the opportunity cost of funds is 16%, the variable cost ratio is 75%, and taxes are 40%?

22-6 **Tightening Credit Terms** Kim Mitchell, the new credit manager of the Vinson Corporation, was alarmed to find that Vinson sells on credit terms of net 90 days while industry-wide credit terms have recently been lowered to net 30 days. On annual credit sales of $2.5 million, Vinson currently averages 95 days of sales in accounts receivable. Mitchell estimates that tightening the credit terms to 30 days would reduce annual sales to $2,375,000, but accounts receivable would drop to 35 days of sales and the savings on investment in them should more than overcome any loss in profit.

   Vinson's variable cost ratio is 85%, and taxes are 40%. If the interest rate on funds invested in receivables is 18%, should the change in credit terms be made?

22-7 **Effective Cost of Short-Term Credit** Yonge Corporation must arrange financing for its working capital requirements for the coming year. Yonge can: (a) borrow from its bank on a simple interest basis (interest payable at the end of the loan) for 1 year at a 12% nominal rate; (b) borrow on a 3-month, but renewable, loan basis at an 11.5% nominal rate; (c) borrow on an installment loan basis at a 6% add-on rate with 12 end-of-month payments; or (d) obtain the needed funds by no longer taking discounts and thus increasing its accounts payable. Yonge buys on terms of 1/15, net 60. What is the effective annual cost (*not* the nominal cost) of the *least expensive* type of credit, assuming 360 days per year?

Challenging Problems 8–10

22-8 **Monitoring of Receivables** The Russ Fogler Company, a small manufacturer of cordless telephones, began operations on January 1. Its credit sales for the first 6 months of operations were as follows:

Month	Credit Sales
January	$ 50,000
February	100,000
March	120,000
April	105,000
May	140,000
June	160,000

Throughout this entire period, the firm's credit customers maintained a constant payments pattern: 20% paid in the month of sale, 30% paid in the first month following the sale, and 50% paid in the second month following the sale.

a. What was Fogler's receivables balance at the end of March and at the end of June?

b. Assume 90 days per calendar quarter. What were the average daily sales (ADS) and days sales outstanding (DSO) for the first quarter and for the second quarter? What were the cumulative ADS and DSO for the first half-year?

c. Construct an aging schedule as of June 30. Use account ages of 0–30, 31–60, and 61–90 days.

d. Construct the uncollected balances schedule for the second quarter as of June 30.

22-9 **Short-Term Financing Analysis** Malone Feed and Supply Company buys on terms of 1/10, net 30, but it has not been taking discounts and has actually been paying in 60 rather than 30 days. Assume that the accounts payable are recorded at full cost, not net of discounts. Malone's balance sheet follows (thousands of dollars):

Cash	$ 50	Accounts payable	$ 500
Accounts receivable	450	Notes payable	50
Inventory	750	Accruals	50
Current assets	$1,250	Current liabilities	$ 600
		Long-term debt	150
Fixed assets	750	Common equity	1,250
Total assets	$2,000	Total liabilities and equity	$2,000

Malone's suppliers are threatening to stop shipments unless the company begins making prompt payments (that is, paying within 30). The firm can borrow on a 1-year note (call this a current liability) from its bank at a rate of 15% discount interest with a 20% compensating balance required. (Malone's $50,000 of cash is needed for transactions; it cannot be used as part of the compensating balance.)

a. How large would the accounts payable balance be if Malone takes discounts? If it does not take discounts and pays in 30 days?

b. How large must the bank loan be if Malone takes discounts? If Malone doesn't take discounts?

c. What are the nominal and effective costs of costly trade credit? What is the effective cost of the bank loan? Based on these costs, what should Malone do?

d. Assume Malone forgoes the discount and borrows the amount needed to become current on its payables. Construct a projected balance sheet based on this decision. (*Hint:* You will need to include an account called "prepaid interest" under current assets.)

e. Now assume that the $500,000 shown on the balance sheet is recorded net of discounts. How much would Malone have to pay its suppliers in order to reduce its accounts payable to $250,000? If Malone's tax rate is 40%, then what is the effect on its net income due to the lost discount when it reduces its accounts payable to $250,000? How much would Malone have to borrow? (*Hint:* Malone will receive a tax deduction due to the lost discount, which will affect the amount it must borrow.) Construct a projected balance sheet based on this scenario. (*Hint:* You will need to include an account called "prepaid interest" under current assets and then adjust retained earnings by the after-tax amount of the lost discount.)

22-10 **Alternative Financing Arrangements** Suncoast Boats Inc. estimates that, because of the seasonal nature of its business, it will require an additional $2 million of cash for the month of July. Suncoast Boats has the following four options available for raising the needed funds.

(1) Establish a 1-year line of credit for $2 million with a commercial bank. The commitment fee will be 0.5% per year on the unused portion, and the interest charge on the used funds will be 11% per annum. Assume the funds are needed only in July and that there are 30 days in July and 360 days in the year.

(2) Forgo the trade discount of 2/10, net 40, on $2 million of purchases during July.

(3) Issue $2 million of 30-day commercial paper at a 9.5% annual interest rate. The total transaction fee (including the cost of a backup credit line) for using commercial paper is 0.5% of the amount of the issue.

(4) Issue $2 million of 60-day commercial paper at a 9% annual interest rate plus a transaction fee of 0.5%. Since the funds are required for only 30 days, the excess funds ($2 million) can be invested in 9.4% per annum marketable securities for the month of August. The total transaction costs of purchasing and selling the marketable securities is 0.4% of the amount of the issue.

a. What is the dollar cost of each financing arrangement?

b. Is the source with the lowest expected cost necessarily the one to select? Why or why not?

Spreadsheet Problem

22-11 **Build a Model: Short-Term Financing Analysis** Start with the partial model in the file *Ch22 P11 Build a Model.xls* on the textbook's Web site. Rework parts a through d of Problem 22-9 using a spreadsheet model. Then answer the following related question.

f. Using interest rates in the range of 5% to 25% and compensating balances in the range of 0% to 30%, perform a sensitivity analysis that shows how the size of the bank loan would vary with changes in the interest rate and the compensating balance percentage.

MINI CASE

Rich Jackson, a recent finance graduate, is planning to go into the wholesale building supply business with his brother, Jim, who majored in building construction. The firm would sell primarily to general contractors, and it would start operating next January. Sales would be slow during the cold months, rise during the spring, and then fall off again in the summer, when new construction in the area slows. Sales estimates for the first 6 months are as follows (in thousands of dollars):

January	$100	March	$300	May	$200
February	200	April	300	June	100

The terms of sale are net 30 but, because of special incentives, the brothers expect 30% of the customers (by dollar value) to pay on the 10th day following the sale, 50% to pay on the 40th day, and the remaining 20% to pay on the 70th day. No bad-debt losses are expected because Jim, the building construction expert, knows which contractors are having financial problems.

a. Discuss, in general, what it means for the brothers to set a credit and collections policy.

b. Assume that, on average, the brothers expect annual sales of 18,000 items at an average price of $100 per item. (Use a 365-day year.)

   (1) What is the firm's expected days sales outstanding (DSO)?

   (2) What is its expected average daily sales (ADS)?

   (3) What is its expected average accounts receivable (AR) level?

   (4) Assume the firm's profit margin is 25%. How much of the receivables balance must be financed? What would the firm's balance sheet figures be for accounts receivable, notes payable, and retained earnings at the end of 1 year if notes payable are used to finance the investment in receivables? Assume that the cost of carrying receivables had been deducted when the 25% profit margin was calculated.

   (5) If bank loans have a cost of 12%, what is the annual dollar cost of carrying the receivables?

c. What are some factors that influence (1) a firm's receivables level and (2) the dollar cost of carrying receivables?

d. Assuming the monthly sales forecasts given previously are accurate and that customers pay exactly as predicted, what would the receivables level be at the end of each month? To reduce calculations, assume that 30% of the firm's customers pay in the month of sale, 50% pay in the month following the sale, and the remaining 20% pay in the second month following the sale. (*Note:* This is a different assumption than was made earlier.) Also assume there are 91 days in each quarter. Use the following format to answer parts d and e:

Month	Sales	End-of-Month Receivables	Quarterly Sales	ADS	DSO = (AR) ÷ (ADS)
January	$100	$ 70			
February	200	160			
March	300	250	$600	$6.59	37.9
April	300				
May	200				
June	100				

e. What is the firm's forecasted average daily sales for the first 3 months? For the entire half-year? The days sales outstanding is commonly used to measure receivables performance. What DSO is expected at the end of March? At the end of June? What does the DSO indicate about customers' payments? Is DSO a good management tool in this situation? If not, why not?

f. Construct aging schedules for the end of March and the end of June (use the format given below). Do these schedules properly measure customers' payment patterns? If not, why not?

	March		June	
Age of Account (Days)	AR	%	AR	%
0–30	$210	84%		
31–60	40	16		
61–90	0	0	___	___
	$250	100%		

g. Construct the uncollected balances schedules for the end of March and the end of June. Use the format given below. Do these schedules properly measure customers' payment patterns?

	March				June		
Month	Sales	Contribution to AR	AR-to-Sales Ratio	Month	Sales	Contribution to AR	AR-to-Sales Ratio
January	$100	$ 0	0%	April			
February	200	40	20	May			
March	300	210	70	June		___	___

h. Assume that it is now July of Year 1 and that the brothers are developing projected financial statements for the following year. Further, assume that sales and collections in the first half-year matched the predicted levels. Use the Year-2 sales forecasts shown below to estimate next year's receivables levels for the end of March and for the end of June.

Month	Predicted Sales	Predicted AR-to-Sales Ratio	Predicted Contribution to Receivables
January	$150	0%	$ 0
February	300	20	60
March	500	70	350
		Projected March 31 AR balance =	$410
April	$400		
May	300		
June	200		
		Projected June 30 AR balance =	_____

i. Now assume that it is several years later. The brothers are concerned about the firm's current credit terms of net 30, which means that contractors buying building products from the firm are not offered a discount and are supposed to pay the full amount in 30 days. Gross sales are now running $1,000,000 a year, and 80% (by dollar volume) of the firm's *paying* customers generally pay the full amount on Day 30; the other 20% pay, on average, on Day 40. Of the firm's gross sales, 2% ends up as bad-debt losses.

The brothers are now considering a change in the firm's credit policy. The change would entail (1) changing the credit terms to 2/10, net 20, (2) employing stricter credit standards before granting credit, and (3) enforcing collections with greater vigor than in the past. Thus, cash customers and those paying within 10 days would receive a 2% discount, but all others would have to pay the full amount after only 20 days. The brothers believe the discount would both attract additional customers and encourage some existing customers to purchase more from the firm—after all, the discount amounts to a price reduction. Of course, these customers would take the discount and hence would pay in only 10 days. The net expected result is for sales to increase to $1,100,000; for 60% of the paying customers to take the discount and pay on the 10th day; for 30% to pay the full amount on Day 20; for

10% to pay late on Day 30; and for bad-debt losses to fall from 2% to 1% of gross sales. The firm's operating cost ratio will remain unchanged at 75%, and its cost of carrying receivables will remain unchanged at 12%.

To begin the analysis, describe the four variables that make up a firm's credit policy and explain how each of them affects sales and collections. Then use the information given in part h to answer parts j through q.

j. Under the current credit policy, what is the firm's days sales outstanding? What would the expected DSO be if the credit policy change were made?

k. What is the dollar amount of the firm's current bad-debt losses? What losses would be expected under the new policy?

l. What would be the firm's expected dollar cost of granting discounts under the new policy?

m. What is the firm's current dollar cost of carrying receivables? What would it be after the proposed change?

n. What is the incremental after-tax profit associated with the change in credit terms? Should the company make the change? (Assume a tax rate of 40%.)

o. Suppose the firm makes the change but its competitors react by making similar changes to their own credit terms, with the net result being that gross sales remain at the current $1,000,000 level. What would be the impact on the firm's after-tax profitability?

	New	Old	Difference
Gross sales		$1,000,000	
Less discounts	_____	0	_____
Net sales		$1,000,000	
Production costs	_____	750,000	_____
Profit before credit costs and taxes		$ 250,000	
Credit-related costs:			
Carrying costs		8,000	
Bad-debt losses	_____	20,000	_____
Profit before taxes		$ 222,000	
Taxes (40%)	_____	88,800	_____
Net income		$ 133,200	

p. The brothers need $100,000 and are considering a 1-year bank loan with a quoted annual rate of 8%. The bank is offering the following alternatives: (1) simple interest, (2) discount interest, (3) discount interest with a 10% compensating balance, and (4) add-on interest on a 12-month installment loan. What is the

effective annual cost rate for each alternative? For the first three of these assumptions, what is the effective rate if the loan is for 90 days but renewable? How large must the face value of the loan amount actually be in each of the four alternatives to provide $100,000 in usable funds at the time the loan is originated?

Selected Additional Cases

The following cases from TextChoice, *Cengage Learning's online case library, cover many of the concepts discussed in this chapter and are available at* **www.textchoice2.com/casenet.**

Klein-Brigham Series:
Case 33, "Upscale Toddlers, Inc.," which deals with credit policy changes; Case 34, "Texas Rose Company," and Case 67, "Bridgewater Pool Company," which focus on receivables management; Case 79, "Mitchell Lumber Company," which deals with credit policy; Case 88, "Chef's Selection," which deals with short-term financing; and Case 96, "Lifeline Health Products," which deals with credit policy.

Values of the Areas under the Standard Normal Distribution Function

TABLE A-1	Values of the Areas under the Standard Normal Distribution Function								
Z	0.00	0.01	0.02	0.03	0.04	0.05	0.06	0.07	0.08	0.09
0.0	.0000	.0040	.0080	.0120	.0160	.0199	.0239	.0279	.0319	.0359
0.1	.0398	.0438	.0478	.0517	.0557	.0596	.0636	.0675	.0714	.0753
0.2	.0793	.0832	.0871	.0910	.0948	.0987	.1026	.1064	.1103	.1141
0.3	.1179	.1217	.1255	.1293	.1331	.1368	.1406	.1443	.1480	.1517
0.4	.1554	.1591	.1628	.1664	.1700	.1736	.1772	.1808	.1844	.1879
0.5	.1915	.1950	.1985	.2019	.2054	.2088	.2123	.2157	.2190	.2224
0.6	.2257	.2291	.2324	.2357	.2389	.2422	.2454	.2486	.2517	.2549
0.7	.2580	.2611	.2642	.2673	.2704	.2734	.2764	.2794	.2823	.2852
0.8	.2881	.2910	.2939	.2967	.2995	.3023	.3051	.3078	.3106	.3133
0.9	.3159	.3186	.3212	.3238	.3264	.3289	.3315	.3340	.3365	.3389
1.0	.3413	.3438	.3461	.3485	.3508	.3531	.3554	.3577	.3599	.3621
1.1	.3643	.3665	.3686	.3708	.3729	.3749	.3770	.3790	.3810	.3830
1.2	.3849	.3869	.3888	.3907	.3925	.3944	.3962	.3980	.3997	.4015
1.3	.4032	.4049	.4066	.4082	.4099	.4115	.4131	.4147	.4162	.4177
1.4	.4192	.4207	.4222	.4236	.4251	.4265	.4279	.4292	.4306	.4319
1.5	.4332	.4345	.4357	.4370	.4382	.4394	.4406	.4418	.4429	.4441
1.6	.4452	.4463	.4474	.4484	.4495	.4505	.4515	.4525	.4535	.4545
1.7	.4554	.4564	.4573	.4582	.4591	.4599	.4608	.4616	.4625	.4633
1.8	.4641	.4649	.4656	.4664	.4671	.4678	.4686	.4693	.4699	.4706
1.9	.4713	.4719	.4726	.4732	.4738	.4744	.4750	.4756	.4761	.4767
2.0	.4773	.4778	.4783	.4788	.4793	.4798	.4803	.4808	.4812	.4817
2.1	.4821	.4826	.4830	.4834	.4838	.4842	.4846	.4850	.4854	.4857
2.2	.4861	.4864	.4868	.4871	.4875	.4878	.4881	.4884	.4887	.4890
2.3	.4893	.4896	.4898	.4901	.4904	.4906	.4909	.4911	.4913	.4916
2.4	.4918	.4920	.4922	.4925	.4927	.4929	.4931	.4932	.4934	.4936
2.5	.4938	.4940	.4941	.4943	.4945	.4946	.4948	.4949	.4951	.4952
2.6	.4953	.4955	.4956	.4957	.4959	.4960	.4961	.4962	.4963	.4964
2.7	.4965	.4966	.4967	.4968	.4969	.4970	.4971	.4972	.4973	.4974
2.8	.4974	.4975	.4976	.4977	.4977	.4978	.4979	.4979	.4980	.4981
2.9	.4981	.4982	.4982	.4982	.4984	.4984	.4985	.4985	.4986	.4986
3.0	.4987	.4987	.4987	.4988	.4988	.4989	.4989	.4989	.4990	.4990

Answers to End-of-Chapter Problems

We present here some intermediate steps and final answers to selected end-of-chapter problems. Please note that your answer may differ slightly from ours because of rounding differences. Also, although we hope not, some of the problems may have more than one correct solution, depending on what assumptions are made when working the problem. Finally, many of the problems involve some verbal discussion as well as numerical calculations; this verbal material is not presented here.

2-1 $b = 1.08$.

2-2 $r_s = 10.40\%$.

2-3 $r_M = 12\%$; $r_{sB} = 16.9\%$.

2-4 $\hat{r} = 11.40\%$; $\sigma = 26.69\%$; $CV = 2.34$.

2-5 a. $\hat{r}_M = 13.5\%$; $\hat{r}_j = 11.6\%$.
   b. $\sigma_M = 3.85\%$; $\sigma_j = 6.22\%$.
   c. $CV_M = 0.29$; $CV_j = 0.54$.

2-6 a. $b_A = 1.40$.
   b. $r_A = 15\%$.

2-7 a. $r_i = 14.8\%$.
   b. (1) $r_M = 13\%$; $r_i = 15.8\%$.
      (2) $r_M = 11\%$; $r_i = 13.8\%$.
   c. (1) $r_i = 17.6\%$.
      (2) $r_i = 13.4\%$.

2-8 $b_N = 1.25$.

2-9 $b_p = 0.7625$; $r_p = 12.1\%$.

2-10 $b_N = 1.1250$.

2-11 4.5%.

2-12 a. $\bar{r}_A = 11.80\%$; $\bar{r}_B = 11.80\%$.
   b. $\bar{r}_p = 11.80\%$.
   c. $\sigma_A = 25.3\%$; $\sigma_B = 24.3\%$; $\sigma_p = 16.3\%$.

   d. $CV_A = 2.14$; $CV_B = 2.06$; $CV_p = 1.38$.

2-13 a. $b_X = 1.3471$; $b_Y = 0.6508$.
   b. $r_X = 12.7355\%$; $r_Y = 9.254\%$.
   c. $r_p = 12.04\%$.

3-1 1.4.

3-2 12%.

3-3 15.96%.

3-4 16.2%; 45.9%.

3-5 a. $r_i = r_{RF} + (r_M - r_{RF})\dfrac{\rho_{iM}\sigma_i}{\sigma_M}$

3-6 a. 14.15%.
   b. 16.45%.

3-7 a. $b = 0.56$.
   b. X: 10.6%; 13.1%.
      M: 12.1%; 22.6%.
   c. 8.6%.

3-8 a. $b = 0.62$.

4-1 $\$928.39$.

4-2 12.48%.

4-3 8.55%.

4-4 7%; 7.33%.

4-5 2.5%.

4-6 0.3%.

4-7 $\$1,085.80$.

4-8 YTM $= 6.62\%$; YTC $= 6.49\%$.

4-9 a. 5%: $V_L = \$1,518.98$; $V_S = \$1,047.62$.

8%: $V_L = \$1,171.19$;
       $V_S = \$1,018.52$.

12%: $V_L = \$863.78$;
        $V_S = \$982.14$.

4-10   a. YTM at $829 = 13.98\%$;
           YTM at $1,104 = 6.50\%$.

4-11   14.82%.

4-12   a. 10.37%.
       b. 10.91%.
       c. −0.54%.
       d. 10.15%.

4-13   8.65%.

4-14   10.78%.

4-15   YTC = 6.47%.

4-16   a. 10-year, 10% coupon = 6.75%;
           10-year zero = 9.75%;
           5-year zero = 4.76%;
           30-year zero = 32.19%;
           $100 perpetuity = 14.29%.

4-17 $C_0 = \$1,012.79$; $Z_0 = \$693.04$;
       $C_1 = \$1,010.02$; $Z_1 = \$759.57$;
       $C_2 = \$1,006.98$; $Z_2 = \$832.49$;
       $C_3 = \$1,003.65$; $Z_3 = \$912.41$;
       $C_4 = \$1,000.00$; $Z_4 = \$1,000.00$.

4-18   5.8%.

4-19   1.5%.

4-20   6.0%.

4-21   a. $1,251.22.
       b. $898.94.

4-22   a. 8.02%.
       b. 7.59%.

4-23   a. $r_1 = 9.20\%$; $r_5 = 7.20\%$.

5-1 $D_1 = \$1.5750$; $D_3 = \$1.7364$;
       $D_5 = \$2.1011$.

5-2 $\hat{P}_0 = \$21.43$.

5-3 $\hat{P}_1 = \$24.20$; $\hat{r}s = 16.00\%$.

5-4 $r_{ps} = 10\%$.

5-5 $50.50.

5-6 $g = 9\%$.

5-7 $\hat{P}_3 = \$43.08$.

5-8   a. 11.67%.
       b. 8.75%.
       c. 7.00%.
       d. 5.00%.

5-9 $32.00.

5-10   a. $r_C = 10.6\%$; $r_D = 7\%$.

5-11 $25.03.

5-12 $\hat{P}_0 = \$10.76$.

5-13   a. $125.
       b. $83.33.

5-14   a. 7%.
       b. 5%.
       c. 12%.

5-15   a. (1) $15.83.
           (2) $23.08.
       b. (1) Undefined.

5-16   a. $\hat{P}_0 = \$21.43$.
       b. $\hat{P}_0 = \$26.47$.
       c. $\hat{P}_0 = \$32.14$.
       d. $\hat{P}_0 = \$40.54$.

5-17   b. PV = $3.97.
       d. $22.71.

5-18   a. $D_5 = \$3.52$.
       b. $\hat{P}_0 = \$39.42$.
       c. $D_1/P_0 = 5.10\%$;
           $D_6/P_5 = 7.00\%$.

5-19 $\hat{P}_0 = \$78.35$.

6-1 $5; $2.

6-2 $27.00; $37.00.

6-3 $1.67.

6-4 $3.70.

6-5 $1.90.

6-6 $2.39.

6-7 $1.91.

7-1   5.8%.

7-2   25%.

7-3 $3,000,000.

7-4 $2,000,000.

7-5 $3,600,000.

7-6 $25,000,000.

7-7   Tax = $107,855;

   NI = $222,145;

   Marginal tax rate = 39%;

   Average tax rate = 33.8%.

7-8   a. Tax = $3,575,000.

   b. Tax = $350,000.

   c. Tax = $105,000.

7-9   AT&T bond = 4.875%;

   AT&T preferred stock = 5.37%;

   Florida bond = 5%.

7-10   NI = $450,000;

   NCF = $650,000.

7-11   a. $2,400,000.

   b. NI = $0;

   NCF = $3,000,000.

   c. NI = $1,350,000;

   NCF = $2,100,000.

7-12   a. NOPAT = $756 million.

   b. $NOWC_{11}$ = $3.0 billion;

   $NOWC_{12}$ = $3.3 billion.

   c. Op. capital$_{11}$ = $6.5 billion;

   Op. capital$_{12}$ = $7.15 billion.

   d. FCF = $106 million.

   e. ROIC = 10.57%.

   f. Answers in millions:

   A-T int. = $72.

   Inc. in debt = −$284.

   Div. = $220.

   Rep. stock = $88.

   Purch. ST inv. = $10.

7-13   Refund = $120,000.

   Future taxes = $0; $0; $40,000; $60,000;
                 $60,000.

8-1   AR = $400,000.

8-2   D/A = 60%.

8-3   M/B = 10.

8-4   P/E = 16.0.

8-5   ROE = 12%.

8-6   S/TA = 2.4; TA/E = 1.67.

8-7   CL = $2,000,000;

   Inv = $1,000,000.

8-8   Net profit margin = 3.33%;

   D/A = 42.9%.

8-9 $262,500; 1.19.

8-10   TIE = 4.13.

8-11   AP = $110,000;

   Inv. = $120,000;

   FA = $192,000.

8-12   Sales = $2,592,000;

   DSO = 36.33 days.

8-13   a. Current ratio = 2.01;

   DSO = 77 days;

   TA turnover = 1.75;

   Debt ratio = 59.0%.

8-14   a. Quick ratio = 0.8;

   DSO = 37 days;

   ROE = 13.1%;

   Debt ratio = 54.8%.

9-1   AFN = $283,800.

9-2   AFN = $583,800.

9-3   AFN = $63,000.

9-4   ΔS = $202,312.

9-5   a. $590,000; $1,150,000.

   b. $238,563.

9-6   AFN = $360.

9-7   a. $13.44 million.

   b. 6.38%.

   c. Notes payable = $31.44 million.

9-8   a. Total assets = $33,534;

   AFN = $2,128.

   b. Notes payable = $4,228.

9-9   a. AFN = $128,783.

   b. Notes payable = $284,783.

10-1 a. 13%.

     b. 10.4%.

     c. 8.45%.

10-2 5.2%.

10-3 9%.

10-4 5.41%.

10-5 13.33%.

10-6 10.4%.

10-7 9.17%.

10-8 13%.

10-9 7.2%.

10-10 a. 16.3%.

      b. 15.4%.

      c. 16%.

10-11 a. 8%.

      b. $2.81.

      c. 15.81%.

10-12 a. $g = 3\%$.

      b. $EPS_1 = \$5.562$.

10-13 16.1%.

10-14 $(1 - T)r_d = 5.57\%$.

10-15 a. $15,000,000.

      b. 8.4%.

10-16 Short-term debt = 11.14%;

      Long-term debt = 22.03%;

      Common equity = 66.83%.

10-17 $w_{d(Short)} = 0\%$; $w_{d(Long)} = 20\%$;

      $w_{ps} = 4\%$; $w_s = 76\%$;

      r_d(After-tax) = 7.2%;

      $r_{ps} = 11.6\%$; $r_s \approx 17.5\%$.

11-1 FCF = $37.0.

11-2 $V_{op} = \$6,000,000$.

11-3 V_{op} at 2014 = $15,000.

11-4 $V_{op} = \$160,000,000$;

     MVA = –$40,000,000.

11-5 $259,375,000.

11-6 a. $HV_2 = \$2,700,000$.

     b. $2,303,571.43.

11-7 a. $713.33.

     b. $527.89.

     c. $43.79.

11-8 $416 million.

11-9 $46.90.

11-10 a. $34.96 million.

      b. $741.152 million.

      c. $699.20 million.

      d. $749.10 million.

      e. $50.34.

12-1 NPV = $2,409.77.

12-2 IRR = 12.84%.

12-3 MIRR = 11.93%.

12-4 PI = 1.06.

12-5 4.44 years.

12-6 6.44 years.

12-7 5%: $NPV_A = \$16,108,952$;

              $NPV_B = \$18,300,939$.

      10%: $NPV_A = \$12,836,213$;

              $NPV_B = \$15,954,170$.

      15%: $NPV_A = \$10,059,587$;

              $NPV_B = \$13,897,838$.

12-8 $NPV_T = \$409$; $IRR_T = 15\%$;

      $MIRR_T = 14.54\%$; Accept.

      $NPV_P = \$3,318$; $IRR_P = 20\%$;

      $MIRR_P = 17.19\%$; Accept.

12-9 $NPV_E = \$3,861$; $IRR_E = 18\%$;

      $NPV_G = \$3,057$; $IRR_G = 18\%$;

      Purchase electric-powered forklift

      because it has a higher NPV.

12-10 $NPV_S = \$814.33$; $NPV_L = \$1,675.34$;

       $IRR_S = 15.24\%$; $IRR_L = 14.67\%$;

       $MIRR_S = 13.77\%$; $MIRR_L = 13.46\%$;

       $PI_S = 1.081$; $PI_L = 1.067$.

12-11 $MIRR_X = 17.49\%$;

       $MIRR_Y = 18.39\%$.

12-12 a. NPV = $136,578;

         IRR = 19.22%.

12-13 b. $IRR_A = 20.7\%$;
          $IRR_B = 27.9\%$.
       c. 10%: $NPV_A = \$478.83$;
                 $NPV_B = \$373.49$.
          17%: $NPV_A = \$133.76$;
                 $NPV_B = \$193.46$.
       d. (1) $MIRR_A = 14.91\%$;
               $MIRR_B = 17.37\%$.
          (2) $MIRR_A = 18.65\%$;
               $MIRR_B = 22.19\%$.
       e. Crossover rate = 14.07%.

12-14 a. $0; –$10,250,000; $1,750,000.
       b. 16.07%.

12-15 a. $NPV_A = \$18,108,510$;
          $NPV_B = \$13,946,117$;
          $IRR_A = 15.03\%$; $IRR_B = 22.26\%$.
       b. $NPV_\Delta = \$4,162,393$;
          $IRR_\Delta = 11.71\%$.

12-16 Extended $NPV_A = \$12.76$ million;
       Extended $NPV_B = \$9.26$ million.
       $EAA_A = \$2.26$ million;
       $EAA_B = \$1.64$ million.

12-17 Extended $NPV_A = \$4.51$ million.
       $EAA_A = \$0.85$ million;
       $EAA_B = \$0.69$ million.

12-18 NPV of 360-6 = $22,256.
       Extended NPV of 190-3 = $20,070.
       EAA of 360-6 = $5,723.30;
       EAA of 190-3 = $5,161.02.

12-19 d. 7.61%; 15.58%.

12-20 a. Undefined.
       b. $NPV_C = –\$911,067$;
          $NPV_F = –\$838,834$.

12-21 a. A = 2.67 years;
          B = 1.5 years.
       b. A = 3.07 years;
          B = 1.825 years.
       c. $NPV_A = \$12,739,908$;
          Choose both.

       d. $NPV_A = \$18,243,813$;
          Choose A.
       e. $NPV_B = \$8,643,390$;
          Choose B.
       f. 13.53%.
       g. $MIRR_A = 21.93\%$;
          $MIRR_B = 20.96\%$.

12-22 a. 3 years.
       b. No.

13-1   a. $22,000,000.
       b. No.
       c. Charge it against project and add $1.5 million to initial investment outlay.

13-2 $7,000,000.

13-3 $3,600,000.

13-4   NPV = $6,746.78

13-5   a. Straight line: $425,000 per year.
          MACRS: $566,610; $755,650; $251,770; $125,970.
       b. MACRS; $27,043.62 higher.

13-6   a. –$1,118,000.
       b. $375,612; $418,521; $304,148.
       c. $437,343.
       d. NPV = $78,790; Purchase.

13-7   a. –$89,000.
       b. $26,332; $30,113; $20,035.
       c. $24,519.
       d. NPV = –$6,700; Don't purchase.

13-8   a. NPV = $106,520.

13-9   NPV of replace = $2,377.21.

13-10 NPV of replace = $11,468.48.

13-11 E(NPV) = $3 million;
       s_{NPV} = $23.622 million;
       CV_{NPV} = 7.874.

13-12 a. NPV = $15,732; IRR = 11.64%;
          MIRR = 10.88%; Payback = 3.75 years.
       b. $65,770; –$34,307.
       c. E(NPV) = $13,042; σ_{NPV} = $43,289;
          CV = 3.32.

13-13　a. −$87,625.

　　　b. $31,574; $36,244; $23,795; $20,687; $4,575.

　　　c. NPV = −$4,623.

13-14　a. −$529,750.

　　　b. New depreciation: $155,000; $248,000; $148,000; $89,280; $89,280.

　　　c. Net incremental cash flows: $143,000; $175,550; $140,830; $119,998; $203,872.

　　　d. NPV = $30,059.

13-15　a. Expected CF_A = $6,750;

　　　　 Expected CF_B = $7,650;

　　　　 CV_A = 0.0703.

　　　b. NPV_A = $10,036;

　　　　 NPV_B = $11,624.

13-16　a. E(IRR) ≈ 15.3%.

　　　b. NPV = $38,589.

13-17　a. E(NPV) = $117,779.

　　　b. σ_{NPV} = $445,060;

　　　　 CV_{NPV} = 3.78.

14-1　a. $1.074 million.

　　　b. $2.96 million.

14-2　a. $4.6795 million.

　　　b. $3.208 million.

14-3　a. −$19 million.

　　　b. $9.0981 million.

14-4　a. −$2.113 million.

　　　b. $1.973 million.

　　　c. −$70,222.

　　　d. $565,090.

　　　e. $1.116 million.

14-5　a. $2,562.

　　　b. E[NPV] = $9,786; Value of growth option = $7,224.

14-6　P = $18.646 million; X = $20 million; t = 1; r_{RF} = 0.08; σ^2 = 0.0687; V = $2.028 million.

14-7　P = $10.479 million; X = $9 million; t = 2; r_{RF} = 0.06; σ^2 = 0.0111; V = $2.514 million.

14-8　P = $18,646; X = $20,000; t = 2; V = $5,009.

15-1　20,000.

15-2　1.0.

15-3　3.6%.

15-4　$300 million.

15-5　$30.

15-6　40 million.

15-7　a. ΔProfit = $850,000;

　　　　 Return = 21.25% > r_s = 15%.

　　　b. $Q_{BE,Old}$ = 40; $Q_{BE,New}$ = 45.45.

15-8　a. V = $3,348,214.

　　　b. $16.74.

　　　c. $1.84.

　　　d. 10%.

15-9　30% debt:

　　　　 WACC = 11.14%;

　　　　 V = $101.023 million.

　　　50% debt:

　　　　 WACC = 11.25%;

　　　　 V = $100 million.

　　　70% debt:

　　　　 WACC = 11.94%;

　　　　 V = $94.255 million.

15-10　a. 0.870.

　　　b. b = 1.218; r_s = 10.872%.

　　　c. WACC = 8.683%;

　　　　 V = $103.188 million.

15-11　WACC at optimal debt level: 8.89%.

16-1　$500 million.

16-2　$821 million.

16-3　$620.68 million.

16-4　a. b_U = 1.13.

　　　b. r_{sU} = 15.625%.

　　　c. 16.62%; 18.04%; 20.23%.

　　　d. 20.23%.

16-5　a. V_U = V_L = $20 million.

　　　b. r_{sU} = 10%; r_{sL} = 15%.

　　　c. S_L = $10 million.

　　　d. $WACC_U$ = 10%; $WACC_L$ = 10%.

16-6 a. V_U = $12 million; V_L = $16 million.

b. r_{sU} = 10%; r_{sL} = 15%.

c. S_L = $6 million.

d. $WACC_U$ = 10%; $WACC_L$ = 7.5%.

16-7 a. V_U = $12 million.

b. V_L = $15.33 million.

c. $3.33 million versus $4 million.

d. V_L = $20 million; $0.

e. V_L = $16 million; $4 million.

f. V_L = $16 million; $4 million.

16-8 a. V_U = $12.5 million.

b. V_L = $16 million; r_{sL} = 15.7%.

c. V_L = $14.5 million; r_{sL} = 14.9%.

16-9 a. V_U = V_L = $14,545,455.

b. At D = $6 million: r_{sL} = 14.51%; WACC = 11.0%.

c. V_U = $8,727,273; V_L = $11,127,273.

d. At D = $6 million: r_{sL} = 14.51%; WACC = 8.63%.

e. D = V = $14,545,455.

16-10 a. V = $3.29 million.

b. D = $1.71 million; Yield = 8.1%.

c. V = $3.23 million; D = $1.77 million; Yield = 6.3%.

17-1 Payout = 33.33%.

17-2 Payout = 20%.

17-3 Payout = 52%.

17-4 V_{op} = $175 million; n = 8.75 million.

17-5 P_0 = $80.

17-6 $6,900,000.

17-7 n = 4,000; EPS = $5.00; DPS = $1.50; P = $40.00.

17-8 D_0 = $4.25.

17-9 Payout = 17.89%.

17-10 a. (1) $2,808,000.

(2) $3,342,857.

(3) $7,855,000.

(4) Regular = $2,808,000; Extra = $5,047,000.

17-11 a. $10,500,000.

b. DPS = $0.50; Payout = 4.55%.

c. $9,000,000.

d. No.

e. 40%.

f. $1,500,000.

g. $12,875,143.

17-12 a. $848 million.

b. $450 million.

c. $30.

d. 1 million; 14 million.

e. $420 million; $30.

18-1 a. $700,000.

b. $3,700,000.

c. −$2,300,000.

18-2 964,115 shares.

18-3 a. $18,545,783; $18,545.78 per share.

b. Abercrombie: D/A 30.43%; P/E 15.91; M/B 2.19; P/FCF 22.73; ROE 13.8%

c. No.

d. Price based on: Abercrombie P/E $21,199; Gunter P/E $16,701.

Price based on: Abercrombie M/B $16,406; Gunter M/B $16,768.

18-4 a. After-tax call cost = $2,640,000.

b. Flotation cost = $1,600,000.

c. $1,920,000; $768,000.

d. $3,472,000.

e. New tax savings = $16,000; Lost tax savings = $19,200.

f. $360,000.

g. PV = $9,109,413.

h. $5,637,413.

18-5 a. NPV = $2,717,128.

19-1 a. (1) 50%.

(2) 60%.

(3) 50%.

19-2 Cost of owning = −$127; Cost of leasing = −$128.

19-3 a. Energen: Debt/TA = 50%;
         Hastings: Debt/TA = 33%.
      b. TA = $200.
19-4 a. NAL = $108,147.
19-5 a. Cost of leasing = $637,702;
         Cost of owning = $713,300.

20-1 $182.16.
20-2 20 shares.
20-3 a. (1) $0.
         (2) $0.
         (3) $5.
         (4) $75.
      b. 10%; $100.
20-4 Premium = 10%: $46.20;
      Premium = 30%: $54.60.
20-5 a. 14.1%.
      b. $12 million before tax.
      c. $331.89.
      d. Value as a straight bond = $699.25;
         Value in conversion = $521.91.
      f. Value as a straight bond = $1,000.00;
         Value in conversion = $521.91.
20-6 b. Plan 1: 49%; Plan 2: 53%; Plan 3: 53%.
      c. Plan 1: $0.59; Plan 2: $0.64; Plan 3: $0.88.
      d. Plan 1: 19%; Plan 2: 19%; Plan 3: 50%.
20-7 a. Year = 7;
         CV_7 = $1,210.422;
         CF_7 = $1,290.422.
      b. 10.2%.

21-1 $3,000,000.
21-2 AR = $59,500.
21-3 r_{NOM} = 75.26%; EAR = 109.84%.
21-4 EAR = 8.49%.
21-5 $7,500,000.
21-6 a. DSO = 38 days.
      b. AR = $156,164.
      c. AR = $141,781.

21-7 a. 73.74%.
      b. 14.90%.
      c. 32.25%.
      d. 21.28%.
      e. 29.80%.
21-8 a. 45.15%.
21-9 Nominal cost = 14.90%;
      Effective cost = 15.89%.
21-10 14.91%.
21-11 a. 60 days.
      b. $420,000.
      c. 9.1.
21-12 a. 65.6 days.
      b. (1) 2.577.
         (2) 18.04%.
      c. (1) 48.2 days.
         (2) 2.78.
         (3) 19.4%.
21-13 a. ROE_T = 11.75%;
         ROE_M = 10.80%;
         ROE_R = 9.16%.
21-14 a. Feb. surplus = $2,000.
      b. $164,400.
21-15 a. $100,000.
      c. (1) $300,000.
         (2) Nominal cost = 37.24%;
             Effective cost = 44.59%.
      d. Nominal cost = 24.83%;
         Effective cost = 27.86%.
21-16 a. 14.35%.
21-17 a. $300,000.
      b. $2,000.
      c. (1) $322,500.
         (2) $26,875.
         (3) 13.57%.
         (4) 14.44%.

22-1 $233.56.
22-2 EAR = 21.60%.

22-3 a. 12%.

b. 11.25%.

c. 11.48%.

d. 14.47%; Alternative b has the lowest interest rate.

22-4 a. 11.73%.

b. 12.09%.

c. 13.45%.

22-5 $\Delta NI = -\$3,381$.

22-6 $\Delta NI = +\$27,577$.

22-7 d. 8.3723%.

22-8 a. March: $146,000; June: $198,000.

b. Q1: ADS = $3,000; DSO = 48.7 days.

Q2: ADS = $4,500; DSO = 44.0 days.

Cumulative: ADS = $3,750; DSO = 52.8 days.

c. 0–30 days: 65%; 31–60 days: 35%.

d. Receivables/Sales = 130%.

22-9 a. With discount = $83.33;

Without discount = $250.

b. With discount = $641.03;

Without discount = $384.62.

c. Nominal cost of trade credit = 18.18%.

Effective cost of trade credit = 19.83%.

Bank cost = 23.08%.

d. Cash = $126.90; NP = $434.60.

22-10 a. (1) $27,500.

(3) $25,833.

23-1 a. 3,000 bags.

b. 4,000 bags.

c. 2,500 bags.

d. Every 12 days.

23-2 b. $22,500.

c. 100 transfers per year.

24-1 Net payment = LIBOR + 0.2%.

24-2 $r_d = 7.01\%$.

24-3 $r_d = 5.96\%$.

24-4 Net to Carter = 9.95% fixed;

Net to Brence = LIBOR + 3.05% floating.

24-5 a. Sell 105 contracts.

b. Bond = –$1,414,552.69;

Futures = $1,951,497.45;

Net = +$536,944.76.

25-1 AP = $375,000; NP = $750,000;

SD = $750,000; Stockholders = $343,750.

25-2 a. Total assets: $327 million.

b. Income: $7 million.

c. Before: $15.6 million;

After: $13.0 million.

d. Before: 35.7%;

After: 64.2%.

25-3 a. $0.

b. First mortgage holders: $300,000; Second mortgage holders: $100,000 plus $12,700 as a general claimant.

c. Trustee's expenses: $50,000;

Wages due: $30,000;

Taxes due: $40,000.

d. *Before subordination:*

Accounts payable = $6,350;

Notes payable = $22,860;

Second mortgage = $12,700 + $100,000;

Debentures = $25,400;

Sub. debentures = $12,700.

After subordination:

Notes payable = $35,560;

Sub. debentures = $0.

25-4 a. $0 for stockholders.

b. AP = 24%; NP = 100%; WP = 100%;

TP = 100%; Mortgage = 85%; Subordinated debentures = 9%; Trustee = 100%.

26-1 $P_0 = \$25.26$.

26-2 $P_0 = \$41.54$.

26-3 $25.26 to $41.54.

26-4 Value of equity = $46.30 million.

26-5 a. $V_{\text{op Unlevered}}$ = $32.02 million;

$V_{\text{Tax shields}}$ = $11.50 million.

b. V_{op} = $43.52 million;

max = $33.52 million.

26-6 a. 10.96%.

b. (All in millions) FCF_1 = $23.12,
TS_1 = $14.00; FCF_3 = $12.26,
TS_3 = $16.45; FCF_5 = $23.83,
TS_5 = $18.90.

c. HV_{TS} = $510.68 million;

HV_{UL} = $643.89 million.

d. Value of equity = $508.57 million.

27-1 12.358 yen per peso.

27-2 f_t = $0.00907.

27-3 1 euro = $0.9091 or $1 = 1.1 euros.

27-4 0.6667 euros per dollar.

27-5 1.5152 SFr.

27-6 2.4 Swiss francs per pound.

27-7 $r_{\text{NOM–U.S.}}$ = 4.6%.

27-8 117 pesos.

27-9 +$500,000.

27-10 b. $24,500.

27-11 a. $1,659,000.

b. $1,646,000.

c. $2,000,000.

27-12 b. f_t = $1.3990.

27-13 $327,731,092.

27-14 a. $89,357; 20%.

b. 1,039.9 won per U.S. dollar and 1030.0 won per U.S. dollar.

c. 78,150,661 won; 18.85%.

Selected Equations

Chapter 1

$$\text{Value} = \frac{FCF_1}{(1 + WACC)^1} + \frac{FCF_2}{(1 + WACC)^2} + \frac{FCF_3}{(1 + WACC)^3} + \cdots + \frac{FCF_\infty}{(1 + WACC)^\infty}$$

Chapter 2

$$\text{Expected rate of return} = \hat{r} = \sum_{i=1}^{n} P_i r_i$$

$$\text{Historical average, } \overline{r}_{Avg} = \frac{\sum_{t=1}^{n} \overline{r}_t}{n}$$

$$\text{Variance} = \sigma^2 = \sum_{i=1}^{n} (r_i - \hat{r})^2 P_i$$

$$\text{Standard deviation} = \sigma = \sqrt{\sum_{i=1}^{n} (r_i - \hat{r})^2 P_i}$$

$$\text{Historical estimated } \sigma = S = \sqrt{\frac{\sum_{t=1}^{n} (\overline{r}_t - \overline{r}_{Avg})^2}{n - 1}}$$

$$CV = \frac{\sigma}{\hat{r}}$$

$$\hat{r}_p = \sum_{i=1}^{n} w_i \hat{r}_i$$

$$\sigma_p = \sqrt{\sum_{i=1}^{n} (r_{pi} - \hat{r}_p)^2 P_i}$$

$$\text{Estimated } \rho = R = \frac{\sum\limits_{t=1}^{n}(\bar{r}_{i,t} - \bar{r}_{i,Avg})(\bar{r}_{j,t} - \bar{r}_{j,Avg})}{\sqrt{\sum\limits_{t=1}^{n}(\bar{r}_{i,t} - \bar{r}_{i,Avg})^2 \sum\limits_{t=1}^{n}(\bar{r}_{j,t} - \bar{r}_{j,Avg})^2}}$$

$$COV_{iM} = \rho_{iM}\sigma_i\sigma_M$$

$$b_i = \left(\frac{\sigma_i}{\sigma_M}\right)\rho_{iM} = \frac{COV_{iM}}{\sigma_M^2}$$

$$b_p = \sum_{i=1}^{n} w_i b_i$$

Required return on stock market $= r_M$

Market risk premium $= RP_M = r_M - r_{RF}$

$$RP_i = (r_M - r_{RF})b_i = (RP_M)b_i$$

$$SML = r_i = r_{RF} + (r_M - r_{RF})b_i = r_{RF} + RP_M b_i$$

Chapter 3

$$\hat{r}_p = w_A\hat{r}_A + (1 - w_A)\hat{r}_B$$

$$\text{Portfolio SD} = \sigma_p = \sqrt{w_A^2\sigma_A^2 + (1 - w_A)^2\sigma_B^2 + 2w_A(1 - w_A)\rho_{AB}\sigma_A\sigma_B}$$

$$\text{Minimum-risk portfolio: } w_A = \frac{\sigma_B(\sigma_B - \rho_{AB}\sigma_A)}{\sigma_A^2 + \sigma_B^2 - 2\rho_{AB}\sigma_A\sigma_B}$$

$$\hat{r}_p = \sum_{i=1}^{N}(w_i\hat{r}_i)$$

$$\sigma_p^2 = \sum_{i=1}^{N}\sum_{j=1}^{N}(w_iw_j\sigma_i\sigma_j\rho_{ij})$$

$$\sigma_p^2 = \sum_{i=1}^{N}w_i^2\sigma_i^2 + \sum_{i=1}^{N}\sum_{\substack{j=1\\j\neq i}}^{N}w_i\sigma_i\,w_j\sigma_j\rho_{ij}$$

$$\sigma_p = \sqrt{(1 - w_{RF})^2\sigma_M^2} = (1 - w_{RF})\sigma_M$$

$$\text{CML: } \hat{r}_p = r_{RF} + \left(\frac{\hat{r}_M - r_{RF}}{\sigma_M}\right)\sigma_p$$

$$r_i = r_{RF} + \frac{(r_M - r_{RF})}{\sigma_M}\left(\frac{Cov(r_i, r_M)}{\sigma_M}\right) = r_{RF} + (r_M - r_{RF})\left(\frac{Cov(r_i, r_M)}{\sigma_M^2}\right)$$

$$b_i = \frac{\text{Covariance between Stock i and the market}}{\text{Variance of market returns}} = \frac{\text{Cov}(r_i, r_M)}{\sigma_M^2} = \frac{\rho_{iM}\sigma_i\sigma_M}{\sigma_M^2} = \rho_{iM}\left(\frac{\sigma_i}{\sigma_M}\right)$$

$$\text{SML} = r_i = r_{RF} + (r_M - r_{RF})b_i = r_{RF} + (RP_M)b_i$$

$$\sigma_i^2 = b_i^2\sigma_M^2 + \sigma_{e_i}^2$$

$$\text{APT: } r_i = r_{RF} + (r_1 - r_{RF})b_{i1} + \cdots + (r_j - r_{RF})b_{ij}$$

$$\text{Fama-French: } r_i = r_{RF} + a_i + b_i(r_M - r_{RF}) + c_i(r_{SMB}) + d_i(r_{HML})$$

Chapter 4

$$V_B = \sum_{t=1}^{N}\frac{\text{INT}}{(1+r_d)^t} + \frac{M}{(1+r_d)^N}$$

$$\text{Semiannual payments: } V_B = \sum_{t=1}^{2N}\frac{\text{INT}/2}{(1+r_d/2)^t} + \frac{M}{(1+r_d/2)^{2N}}$$

$$\text{Yield to maturity: Bond price} = \sum_{t=1}^{N}\frac{\text{INT}}{(1+\text{YTM})^t} + \frac{M}{(1+\text{YTM})^N}$$

$$\text{Price of callable bond (if called at N)} = \sum_{t=1}^{N}\frac{\text{INT}}{(1+r_d)^t} + \frac{\text{Call price}}{(1+r_d)^N}$$

$$\text{Current yield} = \frac{\text{Annual interest}}{\text{Bond's current price}}$$

$$\text{Current yield} + \text{Capital gains yield} = \text{Yield to maturity}$$

$$i_d = r^* + IP + DRP + LP + MRP$$

$$r_{RF} = r^* + IP$$

$$r_d = r_{RF} + DRP + LP + MRP$$

$$IP_N = \frac{I_1 + I_2 + \cdots + I_N}{N}$$

Chapter 5

$$\hat{P}_0 = \text{PV of expected future dividends} = \sum_{t=1}^{\infty}\frac{D_t}{(1+r_s)^t}$$

$$\text{Constant growth: } \hat{P}_0 = \frac{D_0(1+g)}{r_s - g} = \frac{D_1}{r_s - g}$$

$$\hat{r}_s = \frac{D_1}{P_0} + g$$

$$\text{Capital gains yield} = \frac{\hat{P}_1 - P_0}{P_0}$$

$$\text{Dividend yield} = \frac{D_1}{P_0}$$

$$\text{For a zero growth stock, } \hat{P}_0 = \frac{D}{r_s}$$

$$\text{Horizon value} = \text{Terminal value} = \hat{P}_N = \frac{D_{N+1}}{r_s - g} = \frac{D_N(1+g)}{r_s - g}$$

$$V_{ps} = \frac{D_{ps}}{r_{ps}}$$

$$\hat{r}_{ps} = \frac{D_{ps}}{V_{ps}}$$

$$\bar{r}_s = \text{Actual dividend yield} + \text{Actual capital gains yield}$$

Chapter 6

$$\text{Exercise value} = \text{MAX}[\text{Current price of stock} - \text{Strike price, 0}]$$

$$\text{Number of stock shares in hedged portfolio} = N = \frac{C_u - C_d}{P_u - P_d}$$

$$V_C = P[N(d_1)] - Xe^{-r_{RF}t}[N(d_2)]$$

$$d_1 = \frac{\ln(P/X) + [r_{RF} + (\sigma^2/2)]t}{\sigma\sqrt{t}}$$

$$d_2 = d_1 - \sigma\sqrt{t}$$

$$\text{Put–call parity: Put option} = V_C - P + Xe^{-r_{RF}t}$$

$$\text{V of put} = P[N(d_1) - 1] - Xe^{-r_{RF}t}[N(d_2) - 1]$$

Chapter 7

$$\text{EBIT} = \text{Earnings before interest and taxes} = \text{Sales revenues} - \text{Operating costs}$$

$$\text{EBITDA} = \text{Earnings before interest, taxes, depreciation and amortization}$$

$$= \text{EBIT} + \text{Depreciation} + \text{Amortization}$$

$$\text{Net cash flow} = \text{Net income} + \text{Depreciation and amortization}$$

$$\text{NOWC} = \text{Net operating working capital}$$

$$= \text{Operating current assets} - \text{Operating current liabilities}$$

$$= \begin{pmatrix} \text{Cash} + \text{Accounts receivable} \\ + \text{Inventories} \end{pmatrix} - \begin{pmatrix} \text{Accounts payable} \\ + \text{Accruals} \end{pmatrix}$$

Total net operating capital = Net operating working capital + Operating long-term assets

NOPAT = Net operating profit after taxes = EBIT(1 − Tax rate)

Free cash flow (FCF) = NOPAT − Net investment in operating capital

$$= \text{NOPAT} - \left(\begin{array}{cc} \text{Current year's total} & \text{Previous year's total} \\ \text{net operating capital} & - \quad \text{net operating capital} \end{array} \right)$$

Operating cash flow = NOPAT + Depreciation and amortization

$$\begin{array}{c} \text{Gross investment in} \\ \text{operating capital} \end{array} = \begin{array}{c} \text{Net investment in} \\ \text{operating capital} \end{array} + \text{Depreciation}$$

$$\text{FCF} = \text{Operating cash flow} - \begin{array}{c} \text{Gross investment} \\ \text{in operating capital} \end{array}$$

$$\text{Return on invested capital (ROIC)} = \frac{\text{NOPAT}}{\text{Total net operating capital}}$$

MVA = Market value of stock − Equity capital supplied by shareholders

= (Shares outstanding)(Stock price) − Total common equity

MVA = Total market value − Total investor-supplied capital

$$= \left(\begin{array}{c} \text{Market value of stock} \\ + \text{Market value of debt} \end{array} \right) - \text{Total investor-supplied capital}$$

$$\text{EVA} = \left(\begin{array}{c} \text{Net operating profit} \\ \text{after taxes (NOPAT)} \end{array} \right) - \left(\begin{array}{c} \text{After-tax dollar cost of capital} \\ \text{used to support operations} \end{array} \right)$$

= EBIT(1 − Tax rate) − (Total net operating capital)(WACC)

EVA = (Total net operating capital)(ROIC − WACC)

Chapter 8

$$\text{Current ratio} = \frac{\text{Current assets}}{\text{Current liabilities}}$$

$$\text{Quick, or acid test, ratio} = \frac{\text{Current assets} - \text{Inventories}}{\text{Current liabilities}}$$

$$\text{Inventory turnover ratio} = \frac{\text{Sales}}{\text{Inventories}}$$

$$\text{DSO} = \text{Days sales outstanding} = \frac{\text{Receivables}}{\text{Average sales per day}} = \frac{\text{Receivables}}{\text{Annual sales}/365}$$

$$\text{Fixed assets turnover ratio} = \frac{\text{Sales}}{\text{Net fixed assets}}$$

$$\text{Total assets turnover ratio} = \frac{\text{Sales}}{\text{Total assets}}$$

$$\text{Debt ratio} = \frac{\text{Total liabilities}}{\text{Total assets}}$$

$$\text{Market debt ratio} = \frac{\text{Total liabilities}}{\text{Total liabilities} + \text{Market value of equity}}$$

$$\text{Debt-to-equity ratio} = \frac{\text{Total liabilities}}{\text{Total assets} - \text{Total liabilities}}$$

$$\text{Debt-to-equity} = \frac{\text{Debt ratio}}{1 - \text{Debt ratio}} \text{ and Debt ratio} = \frac{\text{Debt-to-equity}}{1 + \text{Debt-to-equity}}$$

$$\text{Equity multiplier} = \frac{\text{Total assets}}{\text{Common equity}}$$

$$\text{Debt ratio} = 1 - \frac{1}{\text{Equity multiplier}}$$

$$\text{Times-interest-earned (TIE) ratio} = \frac{\text{EBIT}}{\text{Interest charges}}$$

$$\text{EBITDA coverage ratio} = \frac{\text{EBITDA} + \text{Lease payments}}{\text{Interest} + \text{Principal payments} + \text{Lease payments}}$$

$$\text{Net profit margin} = \frac{\text{Net income available to common stockholders}}{\text{Sales}}$$

$$\text{Operating profit margin} = \frac{\text{EBIT}}{\text{Sales}}$$

$$\text{Gross profit margin} = \frac{\text{Sales} - \text{Cost of goods sold}}{\text{Sales}}$$

$$\text{Return on total assets (ROA)} = \frac{\text{Net income available to common stockholders}}{\text{Total assets}}$$

$$\text{Basic earning power (BEP) ratio} = \frac{\text{EBIT}}{\text{Total assets}}$$

$$\text{ROA} = \text{Profit margin} \times \text{Total assets turnover} = \frac{\text{Net income}}{\text{Sales}} \times \frac{\text{Sales}}{\text{Total assets}}$$

$$\text{Return on common equity (ROE)} = \frac{\text{Net income available to common stockholders}}{\text{Common equity}}$$

$$\text{ROE} = \text{ROA} \times \text{Equity multiplier}$$

$$= \text{Profit margin} \times \text{Total assets turnover} \times \text{Equity multiplier}$$

$$= \frac{\text{Net income}}{\text{Sales}} \times \frac{\text{Sales}}{\text{Total assets}} \times \frac{\text{Total assets}}{\text{Common equity}}$$

$$\text{Price/earnings (P/E) ratio} = \frac{\text{Price per share}}{\text{Earnings per share}}$$

$$\text{Price/cash flow ratio} = \frac{\text{Price per share}}{\text{Cash flow per share}}$$

$$\text{Book value per share} = \frac{\text{Common equity}}{\text{Shares outstanding}}$$

$$\text{Market/book (M/B) ratio} = \frac{\text{Market price per share}}{\text{Book value per share}}$$

Chapter 9

$$\begin{matrix} \text{Additional} \\ \text{funds} \\ \text{needed} \end{matrix} = \begin{matrix} \text{Required} \\ \text{asset} \\ \text{increase} \end{matrix} - \begin{matrix} \text{Spontaneous} \\ \text{liability} \\ \text{increase} \end{matrix} - \begin{matrix} \text{Increase in} \\ \text{retained} \\ \text{earnings} \end{matrix}$$

$$\text{AFN} = (A^*/S_0)\Delta S - (L^*/S_0)\Delta S - MS_1(1 - \text{Payout ratio})$$

$$\begin{matrix} \text{Full} \\ \text{capacity} \\ \text{sales} \end{matrix} = \frac{\text{Actual sales}}{\begin{matrix} \text{Percentage of capacity} \\ \text{at which fixed assets} \\ \text{were operated} \end{matrix}}$$

$$\text{Target fixed assets/Sales} = \frac{\text{Actual fixed assets}}{\text{Full capacity sales}}$$

$$\begin{matrix} \text{Required level} \\ \text{of fixed assets} \end{matrix} = (\text{Target fixed assets/Sales})(\text{Projected sales})$$

Chapter 10

$$\text{After-tax component cost of debt} = r_d(1 - T)$$

$$M(1 - F) = \sum_{t=1}^{N} \frac{INT(1 - T)}{[1 + r_d(1 - T)]^t} + \frac{M}{[1 + r_d(1 - T)]^N}$$

$$r_{ps} = \frac{D_{ps}}{P_{ps}(1 - F)}$$

$$\text{Market equilibrium: } \begin{matrix} \text{Expected rate} \\ \text{of return} \end{matrix} = \hat{r}_M = \frac{D_1}{P_0} + g = r_{RF} + RP_M = r_M = \begin{matrix} \text{Required} \\ \text{rate of return} \end{matrix}$$

Note: D_1, P_0, and g are for the market, not an individual company.

$\text{Rep/Div} = $ ratio of payouts via repurchases to payouts via dividends

$$r_M = \hat{r}_M = (1 + \text{Rep/Div})\frac{D_1}{P_0} + g$$

Note: g is long-term growth rate in total payouts for the market, and D_1 and P_0 are for the market, not an individual company

CAPM: $r_s = r_{RF} + b_i(RP_M)$

DCF: $r_s = \hat{r}_s = \dfrac{D_1}{P_0} + \text{Expected g in dividends per share}$

Own-bond yield-plus-judgmental-risk-premium: $r_s = \begin{array}{c}\text{Company's own}\\\text{bond yield}\end{array} + \begin{array}{c}\text{Judgmental risk}\\\text{premium}\end{array}$

$g = (\text{Retention rate})(\text{ROE}) = (1.0 - \text{Payout rate})(\text{ROE})$

$r_e = \hat{r}_e = \dfrac{D_1}{P_0(1-F)} + g$

$\text{WACC} = w_d r_d(1 - T) + w_{ps} r_{ps} + w_s r_s$

Chapter 11

$V_{op} = \text{Value of operations}$

$\qquad = \text{PV of expected future free cash flows}$

$$= \sum_{t=1}^{\infty} \frac{FCF_1}{(1 + \text{WACC})^t}$$

Horizon value: $V_{op(\text{at time N})} = \dfrac{FCF_{N+1}}{\text{WACC} - g} = \dfrac{FCF_N(1+g)}{\text{WACC} - g}$

Total value $= V_{op} + \text{Value of nonoperating assets}$

Value of equity $= \text{Total value} - \text{Preferred stock} - \text{Debt}$

Operating profitability (OP) $= \text{NOPAT/Sales}$

Capital requirements (CR) $= \text{Operating capital/Sales}$

$EROIC_N = \text{Expected return on invested capital}$

$\qquad = NOPAT_{N+1}/Capital_N$

$\qquad = NOPAT_N(1 + g)/Capital_N$

$\qquad = OP_{N+1}/CR_N$

For constant growth:

$$V_{op(\text{at time N})} = Capital_N + \left\{ \left[\frac{Sales_N(1+g)}{\text{WACC} - g} \right] \left[OP - \text{WACC}\left(\frac{CR}{1+g} \right) \right] \right\}$$

$$= Capital_N + \frac{Capital_N(EROIC_N - \text{WACC})}{\text{WACC} - g}$$

$$= Capital_N + \frac{Capital_N \left(\dfrac{OP_{N+1}}{CR_N} - WACC \right)}{WACC - g}$$

Chapter 12

$$NPV = CF_0 + \frac{CF_1}{(1+r)^1} + \frac{CF_2}{(1+r)^2} + \cdots + \frac{CF_N}{(1+r)^N}$$

$$= \sum_{t=0}^{N} \frac{CF_t}{(1+r)^t}$$

$$IRR: CF_0 + \frac{CF_1}{(1+IRR)^1} + \frac{CF_2}{(1+IRR)^2} + \cdots + \frac{CF_N}{(1+IRR)^N} = 0$$

$$NPV = \sum_{t=0}^{N} \frac{CF_t}{(1+IRR)^t} = 0$$

MIRR: PV of costs = PV of terminal value

$$\sum_{t=0}^{N} \frac{COF_t}{(1+r)^t} = \frac{\displaystyle\sum_{t=0}^{N} CIF_t (1+r)^{N-t}}{(1+MIRR)^N}$$

$$PV \text{ of costs} = \frac{Terminal \text{ value}}{(1+MIRR)^N}$$

$$PI = \frac{PV \text{ of future cash flows}}{Initial \text{ cost}} = \frac{\displaystyle\sum_{t=1}^{N} \frac{CF_t}{(1+r)^t}}{CF_0}$$

$$Payback = \begin{array}{c} \text{Number of} \\ \text{years prior to} \\ \text{full recovery} \end{array} + \frac{\begin{array}{c}\text{Unrecovered cost} \\ \text{at start of year}\end{array}}{\begin{array}{c}\text{Cash flow durirg} \\ \text{full recovery year}\end{array}}$$

Chapter 13

$$Project \text{ cash flow} = FCF = \begin{array}{c}\text{Investment outlay} \\ \text{cash flow}\end{array} + \begin{array}{c}\text{Operating} \\ \text{cash flow}\end{array} + \begin{array}{c}\text{NOWC} \\ \text{cash flow}\end{array} + \begin{array}{c}\text{Salvage} \\ \text{cash flow}\end{array}$$

$$Expected \text{ } NPV = \sum_{i=1}^{n} P_i (NPV_i)$$

$$\sigma_{NPV} = \sqrt{\sum_{i=1}^{n} P_i (NPV_i - Expected \text{ } NPV)^2}$$

$$CV_{NPV} = \frac{\sigma_{NPV}}{E(NPV)}$$

Chapter 14

$$CV = \frac{\sigma(\text{PV of future CF})}{E(\text{PV of future CF})}$$

Variance of project's rate of return: $\sigma^2 = \frac{\ln(CV^2 + 1)}{t}$

Chapter 15

$$V_{op} = \sum_{t=1}^{\infty} \frac{FCF_t}{(1+WACC)^t}$$

$$WACC = w_d(1-T)r_d + w_s r_s$$

$$ROIC = \frac{NOPAT}{Capital} = \frac{EBIT(1-T)}{Capital}$$

$$EBIT = PQ - VQ - F$$

$$Q_{BE} = \frac{F}{P-V}$$

$$V_L = S_L + D$$

MM, no taxes: $V_L = V_U$

MM, corporate taxes: $V_L = V_U + TD$

Miller, corporate and personal taxes: $V_L = V_U + \left[1 - \frac{(1-T_c)(1-T_s)}{(1-T_d)}\right]D$

$$b = b_U[1 + (1-T)(D/S)] = b_U[1 + (1-T)(w_d/w_s)]$$

$$b_U = b/[1 + (1-T)(D/S)] = b/[1 + (1-T)(w_d/w_s)]$$

$$r_s = r_{RF} + RP_M(b)$$

$r_s = r_{RF} + $ Premium for business risk + Premium for financial risk

If $g = 0$: $V_{op} = \frac{FCF}{WACC} = \frac{NOPAT}{WACC} = \frac{EBIT(1-T)}{WACC}$

Total corporate value = V_{op} + Value of short-term investments

S = Total corporate value − Value of all debt

$$D = w_d V_{op}$$

$$S = (1 - w_d)V_{op}$$

Cash raised by issuing debt = $D - D_0$

$$P_{Prior} = S_{Prior}/n_{Prior}$$

$P_{Post} = P_{Prior}$

$$n_{Post} = n_{Prior} \left[\frac{V_{opNew} - D_{New}}{V_{opNew} - D_{Old}} \right]$$

$$n_{Post} = n_{Prior} - (D_{New} - D_{Old})/P_{Prior}$$

$$P_{Post} = \frac{V_{opNew} - D_{Old}}{n_{Prior}}$$

$NI = (EBIT - r_d D)(1 - T)$

$EPS = NI/n$

Chapter 16

MM, no taxes:

$$V_L = V_U = \frac{EBIT}{WACC} = \frac{EBIT}{r_{sU}}$$

$$r_{sL} = r_{sU} + \text{Risk premium} = r_{sU} + (r_{sU} - r_d)(D/S)$$

MM, corporate taxes:

$$V_L = V_U + TD$$

$$V_U = S = \frac{EBIT(1 - T)}{r_{sU}}$$

$$r_{sL} = r_{sU} + (r_{sU} - r_d)(1 - T)(D/S)$$

Miller, personal taxes:

$$V_U = \frac{EBIT(1 - T_c)}{r_{sU}} = \frac{EBIT(1 - T_c)(1 - T_s)}{r_{sU}(1 - T_s)}$$

$$CF_L = (EBIT - I)(1 - T_c)(1 - T_s) + I(1 - T_d)$$

$$V_L = V_U + \left[1 - \frac{(1 - T_c)(1 - T_s)}{(1 - T_d)} \right] D$$

Ehrhardt & Daves, impact of growth:

$$V_U = \frac{FCF}{r_{sU} - g}$$

General case:

$$V_L = V_U + V_{\text{Tax shield}}$$

$$V_{\text{Tax shield}} = \frac{r_d TD}{r_{TS} - g}$$

$$V_L = V_U + \left(\frac{r_d}{r_{TS} - g}\right)TD$$

Case for $r_{TS} = r_{sU}$:

$$V_L = V_U + \left(\frac{r_d TD}{r_{sU} - g}\right)$$

$$r_{sL} = r_{sU} + (r_{sU} - r_d)\frac{D}{S}$$

$$b = b_U + (b_U - b_D)\frac{D}{S}$$

Chapter 17

Residual distribution = Net income − [(Target equity ratio)(Total capital budget)]

$$\text{Number of shares repurchased} = n_{Prior} - n_{Post} = \frac{\text{Cash}_{Rep}}{P_{Prior}}$$

$$n_{Post} = n_{Prior} - \frac{\text{Cash}_{Rep}}{P_{Prior}} = n_{Prior} - \frac{\text{Cash}_{Rep}}{S_{Prior}/n_{Prior}} = n_{Prior}\left(1 - \frac{\text{Cash}_{Rep}}{S_{Prior}}\right)$$

Chapter 18

Amount left on table = (Closing price − Offer price)(Number of shares)

Chapter 19

NAL = PV cost of owning − PV cost of leasing

Chapter 20

$$\frac{\text{Price paid for}}{\text{bond with warrants}} = \frac{\text{Straight-debt}}{\text{value of bond}} + \frac{\text{Value of}}{\text{warrants}}$$

$$\text{Conversion price} = P_c = \frac{\text{Par value of bond given up}}{\text{Shares received}}$$

$$= \frac{\text{Par value of bond given up}}{\text{CR}}$$

$$\text{Conversion ratio} = CR = \frac{\text{Par value of bond given up}}{P_c}$$

Chapter 21

$$\text{Inventory conversion period} = \frac{\text{Inventory}}{\text{Cost of goods sold}/365}$$

$$\text{Receivables collection period} = \text{DSO} = \frac{\text{Receivables}}{\text{Sales}/365}$$

$$\text{Payables deferral period} = \frac{\text{Payables}}{\text{Cost of goods sold}/365}$$

$$\begin{matrix}\text{Cash} \\ \text{conversion} \\ \text{cycle}\end{matrix} = \begin{matrix}\text{Inventory} \\ \text{conversion} \\ \text{period}\end{matrix} + \begin{matrix}\text{Average} \\ \text{collection} \\ \text{period}\end{matrix} - \begin{matrix}\text{Payables} \\ \text{deferral} \\ \text{period}\end{matrix}$$

$$\begin{matrix}\text{Accounts} \\ \text{receivable}\end{matrix} = \begin{matrix}\text{Credit sales} \\ \text{per day}\end{matrix} \times \begin{matrix}\text{Length of} \\ \text{collection period}\end{matrix}$$

$$\text{ADS} = \frac{(\text{Units sold})(\text{Sales price})}{365} = \frac{\text{Annual sales}}{365}$$

$$\text{Receivables} = (\text{ADS})(\text{DSO})$$

$$\begin{matrix}\text{Nominal annual cost} \\ \text{of trade credit}\end{matrix} = \frac{\text{Discount percentage}}{100 - \begin{matrix}\text{Discount} \\ \text{percentage}\end{matrix}} \times \frac{365}{\begin{matrix}\text{Days credit is} \\ \text{outstanding}\end{matrix} - \begin{matrix}\text{Discount} \\ \text{period}\end{matrix}}$$

Chapter 22

$$\Delta I \text{ for increase in sales} = [(\text{DSO}_N - \text{DSO}_0)(S_0/365)] + V[(\text{DSO}_N)(S_N - S_0)/365]$$

$$\Delta I \text{ for decrease in sales} = [(\text{DSO}_N - \text{DSO}_0)(S_N/365)] + V[(\text{DSO}_0)(S_N - S_0)/365]$$

$$\Delta P = (S_N - S_0)(1 - V) - r(\Delta I) - (B_N S_N - B_0 S_0) - (D_N S_N P_N - D_0 S_0 P_0)$$

$$\text{Cost of carrying receivables} = (\text{DSO})\left(\frac{\text{Sales}}{\text{per day}}\right)\left(\begin{matrix}\text{Variable} \\ \text{cost ratio}\end{matrix}\right)\left(\begin{matrix}\text{Cost of} \\ \text{funds}\end{matrix}\right)$$

$$\text{Simple interest rate per day} = \frac{\text{Nominal rate}}{\text{Days in year}}$$

$$\text{Simple interest charge for period} = (\text{Days in period})(\text{Rate per day})(\text{Amount of loan})$$

$$\text{Face value}_{\text{Discount}} = \frac{\text{Funds received}}{1.0 - \text{Nominal rate (decimal)}}$$

$$\text{APR rate} = (\text{Periods per year})(\text{Rate per period})$$

Chapter 23

Total costs = Holding costs + Transactions costs

$$= \frac{C}{2}(r) + \frac{T}{C}(F)$$

$$C^* = \sqrt{\frac{2(F)(T)}{r}}$$

$$A = \frac{\text{Units per order}}{2} = \frac{S/N}{2}$$

$$TCC = (C)(P)(A)$$

$$TOC = (F)(N)$$

$$TIC = TCC + TOC$$

$$= (C)(P)(A) + F\left(\frac{S}{2A}\right)$$

$$= (C)(P)(Q/2) + (F)(S/Q)$$

$$EOQ = \sqrt{\frac{2(F)(S)}{(C)(P)}}$$

Chapter 26

$$r_{sL} = r_{sU} + (r_{sU} - r_d)(D/S)$$

$$r_{sU} = w_s r_{sL} + w_d r_d$$

Tax savings = (Interest expense)(Tax rate)

Horizon value of unlevered firm = $HV_{U,N} = \dfrac{FCF_{N+1}}{r_{sU} - g} = \dfrac{FCF_N(1+g)}{r_{sU} - g}$

Horizon value of tax shield = $HV_{TS,N} = \dfrac{TS_{N+1}}{r_{sU} - g} = \dfrac{TS_N(1+g)}{r_{sU} - g}$

$$V_{Unlevered} = \sum_{t=1}^{N} \frac{FCF_t}{(1+r_{sU})^t} + \frac{HV_{U,N}}{(1+r_{sU})^N}$$

$$V_{Tax\ shield} = \sum_{t=1}^{N} \frac{TS_t}{(1+r_{sU})^t} + \frac{HV_{TS,N}}{(1+r_{sU})^N}$$

Value of operations = $V_{op} = V_{Unlevered} + V_{Tax\ shield}$

$$FCFE = \begin{matrix} \text{Free} \\ \text{cash flow} \end{matrix} - \begin{matrix} \text{After-tax} \\ \text{interest expense} \end{matrix} - \begin{matrix} \text{Principal} \\ \text{payments} \end{matrix} + \begin{matrix} \text{Newly issued} \\ \text{debt} \end{matrix}$$

$$= \begin{matrix} \text{Free} \\ \text{cash flow} \end{matrix} - \begin{matrix} \text{Interest} \\ \text{expense} \end{matrix} + \begin{matrix} \text{Interest} \\ \text{tax shield} \end{matrix} + \begin{matrix} \text{Net change} \\ \text{in debt} \end{matrix}$$

$$FCFE = \text{Net income} - \frac{\text{Net investment in}}{\text{operating capital}} + \frac{\text{Net change}}{\text{in debt}}$$

$$HV_{FCFE,N} = \frac{FCFE_{N+1}}{r_{sL} - g} = \frac{FCFE_N(1+g)}{r_{sL} - g}$$

$$V_{FCFE} = \sum_{t=i}^{N} \frac{FCFE_t}{(1+r_{sL})^t} + \frac{HV_{FCFE,N}}{(1+r_{sL})^N}$$

$$S = V_{FCFE} + \text{Nonoperating assets}$$

$$\frac{\text{Total value of shares to target shareholders}}{\text{Total post-merger value of equity}} = \frac{\text{Percent required by}}{\text{target stockholders}} = \frac{n_{New}}{n_{New} + n_{Old}}$$

Chapter 27

$$\frac{\text{Single-period interest}}{\text{rate parity}} : \frac{\text{Forward exchange rate}}{\text{Spot exchange rate}} = \frac{1+r_h}{1+r_f}$$

$$\frac{\text{Expected t-year}}{\text{forward exchange rate}} = (\text{Spot rate})\left(\frac{1+r_h}{1+r_f}\right)^t$$

$$P_h = (P_f)(\text{Spot rate})$$

$$\text{Spot rate} = \frac{P_h}{P_f}$$

Glossary

501(c)(3) corporation A charitable organization that meets the IRS requirements for tax-exempt status under the tax code section 501(c)(3).

abandonment option Allows a company to reduce the capacity of its output in response to changing market conditions. This includes the option to contract production or abandon a project if market conditions deteriorate too much.

absolute priority doctrine States that claims must be paid in strict accordance with the priority of each claim, regardless of the consequence to other claimants.

account receivable Created when a good is shipped or a service is performed and payment for that good is made on a credit basis, not on a cash basis.

accounting income Income as defined by Generally Accepted Accounting Principles (GAAP).

accounting profit A firm's net income as reported on its income statement.

acquiring company A company that seeks to acquire another firm.

actual, or realized, rate of return, $\bar{r}_s$ The rate of return that was actually realized at the end of some holding period.

actuarial rate of return The discount rate used to determine the present value of future benefits under a defined benefits pension plan.

additional funds needed (AFN) Those funds required from external sources to increase the firm's assets to support a sales increase. A sales increase will normally require an increase in assets. However, some of this increase is usually offset by a spontaneous increase in liabilities as well as by earnings retained in the firm. Those funds that are required but not generated internally must be obtained from external sources.

add-on basis installment loan Interest is calculated over the life of the loan and then added on to the loan amount. This total amount is paid in equal installments. This raises the effective cost of the loan.

agency cost or problem An expense, either direct or indirect, that is borne by a principal as a result of having delegated authority to an agent. An example is the costs borne by shareholders to encourage managers to maximize a firm's stock price rather than act in their own self-interests. These costs may also arise from lost efficiency and the expense of monitoring management to ensure that debtholders' rights are protected.

agency debt Debt issued by federal agencies. Agency debt is not officially backed by the full faith and credit of the U.S. government, but investors assume that the government implicitly guarantees this debt, so these bonds carry interest rates only slightly higher than Treasury bonds.

aggressive short-term financing policy Refers to a policy in which a firm finances all of its fixed assets with long-term capital but part of its permanent current assets with short-term, nonspontaneous credit.

aging schedule Breaks down accounts receivable according to how long they have been outstanding. This gives the firm a more complete picture of the structure of accounts receivable than that provided by days sales outstanding.

alternative minimum tax (AMT) A provision of the U.S. Tax Code that requires profitable firms to pay at least some taxes if such taxes are greater than the amount due under standard tax accounting.

amortization A noncash charge against intangible assets, such as goodwill.

amortization schedule A table that breaks down the periodic fixed payment of an installment loan into its principal and interest components.

amortized loan A loan that is repaid in equal periodic amounts (or "killed off") over time.

anchoring bias Occurs when predictions of future events are influenced too heavily by recent events.

animal spirits John Maynard Keynes, writing during the 1920s and 1930s, suggested that—after a period of rising prosperity and stock prices—investors begin to think that the good times will last forever, a feeling that is driven by happy talk and high spirits rather than cool reasoning.

annual report A report issued annually by a corporation to its stockholders. It contains basic financial statements as well as management's opinion of the past year's operations and the firm's future prospects.

annual vesting A certain percentage of the options in a grant vest each year. For example, one-third of the options in the grant might vest each year.

annuity A series of payments of a fixed amount for a specified number of periods.

annuity due An annuity with payments occurring at the beginning of each period.

APR The nominal annual interest rate is also called the annual percentage rate, or APR.

arbitrage The simultaneous buying and selling of the same commodity or security in two different markets at different prices, thus yielding a risk-free return.

Arbitrage Pricing Theory (APT) An approach to measuring the equilibrium risk–return relationship for a given stock as a function of multiple factors, rather than the single factor (the market return) used by the CAPM. The APT is based on complex mathematical and statistical theory, and it can account for several factors (such as GNP and the level of inflation) in determining the required return for a particular stock.

arrearages Preferred dividends that have not been paid and hence are "in arrears."

asset allocation models Used by pension fund managers to make funding and investment decisions; these models use computer simulations to examine the risk/return characteristics of portfolios with various mixes of assets.

asset management ratios A set of ratios that measure how effectively a firm is managing its assets.

assets-in-place Refers to the land, buildings, machines, and inventory that the firm uses in its operations to produce its products and services. Also known as operating assets.

assignment An informal procedure for liquidating debts that transfers title to a debtor's assets to a third person, known as an assignee or trustee.

asymmetric information theory Assumes managers have more complete information than investors and leads to a preferred "pecking order" of financing: (1) retained earnings, followed by (2) debt, and then (3) new common stock. Also known as signaling theory.

average stock's beta, $b_A = b_M$ The beta coefficient (b) is a measure of a stock's market risk. It measures the stock's volatility relative to an average stock, which has a beta of 1.0.

average tax rate Calculated by taking the total amount of tax paid divided by taxable income.

balance sheet A statement of the firm's financial position at a specific point in time. The firm's assets are listed on the left-hand side of the balance sheet; the right-hand side shows its liabilities and equity, or the claims against these assets.

banker's acceptance Created when an importer's bank promises to accept a postdated check written to an exporter even if there are insufficient funds in the importer's account. If the bank is strong, then this financial instrument virtually eliminates credit risk.

Bankruptcy Reform Act of 1978 Enacted to speed up and streamline bankruptcy proceedings. This law represented a shift to a relative priority doctrine of creditors' claims.

basic earning power (BEP) ratio Calculated by dividing earnings before interest and taxes by total assets. This ratio shows the raw earning power of the firm's assets before the influence of taxes and leverage.

Baumol model A model for establishing the firm's target cash balance that closely resembles the economic ordering quantity model used for inventory. The model assumes (1) that the firm uses cash at a steady, predictable rate, (2) that the firm's cash inflows from operations also occur at a steady, predictable rate, and (3) that its net cash outflows therefore also occur at a steady rate. The model balances the opportunity cost of holding cash against the transactions costs associated with replenishing the cash account.

behavioral finance A field of study that analyzes investor behavior as a result of psychological traits. It does not assume that investors necessarily behave rationally.

benchmarking When a firm compares its ratios to other leading companies in the same industry.

best efforts arrangement A type of contract with an investment banker when issuing stock. In a best efforts sale, the investment banker is only committed to making every effort to sell the stock at the offering price. In this case, the issuing firm bears the risk that the new issue will not be fully subscribed.

beta coefficient, b A measure of a stock's market risk, or the extent to which the returns on a given stock move with the stock market.

bird-in-the-hand theory Assumes that investors value a dollar of dividends more highly than a dollar of expected capital gains, because a certain dividend is less risky than a possible capital gain. This theory implies that a high-dividend stock has a higher price and lower required return, all else held equal.

Black-Scholes option pricing model A model to estimate the value of a call option. It is widely used by options traders.

board of trustees Group of community leaders who control a tax-exempt, charitable organization. Members of the board of trustees must have no direct economic interest in the organization.

bond A promissory note issued by a business or a governmental unit.

bond insurance Protects investors against default by the issuer and provides credit enhancement to the bond issue.

book value per share Common equity divided by the number of shares outstanding.

break-even point The level of unit sales at which costs equal revenues.

breakup value A firm's value if its assets are sold off in pieces.

business risk The risk inherent in the operations of the firm, prior to the financing decision. Thus, business risk is the uncertainty inherent in future operating income or earnings before interest and taxes. Business risk is caused by many factors; two of the most important are sales variability and operating leverage.

call option An option that allows the holder to buy the asset at some predetermined price within a specified period of time.

call provision Gives the issuing corporation the right to call the bonds for redemption. The call provision generally states that if the bonds are called then the company must pay the bondholders an amount greater than the par value, or a call premium. Most bonds contain a call provision.

capacity option Allows a company to change the capacity of its output in response to changing market conditions. This includes the option to contract or expand production. It also includes the option to abandon a project if market conditions deteriorate too much.

Capital Asset Pricing Model (CAPM) A model based on the proposition that any stock's required rate of return is equal to the risk-free rate of return plus a risk premium reflecting only the risk remaining after diversification. The CAPM equation is $r_i = r_{RF} + b_i(r_M - r_{RF})$.

capital budget Outlines the planned expenditures on fixed assets.

capital budgeting The whole process of analyzing projects and deciding whether they should be included in the capital budget.

capital gain (loss) The profit (loss) from the sale of a capital asset for more (less) than its purchase price.

capital gains yield Results from changing prices and is calculated as $(P_1 - P_0)/P_0$, where P_0 is the beginning-of-period price and P_1 is the end-of-period price.

capital intensity ratio The dollar amount of assets required to produce a dollar of sales. The capital intensity ratio is the reciprocal of the total assets turnover ratio.

capital market Capital markets are the financial markets for long-term debt and corporate stocks. The New York Stock Exchange is an example of a capital market.

capital rationing Occurs when management places a constraint on the size of the firm's capital budget during a particular period.

capital structure The manner in which a firm's assets are financed; that is, the right side of the balance sheet. Capital structure is normally expressed as the percentage of each type of capital used by the firm such as debt, preferred stock, and common equity.

capitalizing Incorporating the lease provisions into the balance sheet by reporting the leased asset under fixed assets and reporting the present value of future lease payments as debt.

cash balance plan A type of defined benefits plan in which benefits are defined in terms of the cash balance in the employee's account rather than monthly salary.

cash budget A schedule showing cash flows (receipts, disbursements, and cash balances) for a firm over a specified period.

cash conversion cycle The length of time between the firm's actual cash expenditures on productive resources (materials and labor) and its own cash receipts from the sale of products (that is, the length of time between paying for labor and materials and collecting on receivables). Thus, the cash conversion cycle equals the length of time the firm has funds tied up in current assets.

cash discounts The amount by which a seller is willing to reduce the invoice price in order to be paid immediately, rather than in the future. A cash discount might be 2/10, net 30, which means a 2% discount if the bill is paid within 10 days and otherwise the entire amount is due within 30 days.

CDO, collateralized debt obligation Created when large numbers of mortgages are bundled into pools to create new securities that are then sliced into tranches; the tranches are re-combined and re-divided into securities called CDOs.

CDS, credit default swap Derivative in which a counterparty pays if a specified debt instrument goes into default; similar to insurance on a bond.

Chapter 7 The chapter of the Bankruptcy Reform Act that provides for the liquidation of a firm to repay creditors.

Chapter 11 The business reorganization chapter of the Bankruptcy Reform Act. The chapter provides for the reorganization, rather than the liquidation, of a business.

characteristic line Obtained by regressing the historical returns on a particular stock against the historical returns on the general stock market. The slope of the characteristic line is the stock's beta, which measures the amount by which the stock's expected return increases for a given increase in the expected return on the market.

charitable contributions One way that not-for-profit businesses raise equity capital. Individuals and firms make these contributions for a variety of reasons including concern for the well-being of others, the recognition that accompanies large donations, and tax deductibility.

charter The legal document that is filed with the state to incorporate a company.

check-clearing process When a customer's check is written upon one bank and a company deposits the check in its own bank, the company's bank must verify that the check is valid before the company can use those funds. Checks are generally cleared through the Federal Reserve System or through a clearinghouse set up by the banks in a particular city.

classified boards A board of directors with staggered terms. For example, a board with one-third of the seats filled each year and directors serving three-year terms.

classified stock Sometimes created by a firm to meet special needs and circumstances. Generally, when special classifications of stock are used, one type is designated "Class A," another as "Class B," and so on. For example, Class A might be entitled to receive dividends before dividends can be paid on Class B stock. Class B might have the exclusive right to vote.

cleanup clause A clause in a line of credit that requires the borrower to reduce the loan balance to zero at least once a year.

clientele effect The attraction of companies with specific dividend policies to those investors whose needs are best served by those policies. Thus, companies with high dividends will have a clientele of investors with low marginal tax rates and strong desires for current income. Conversely, companies with low dividends will have a clientele of investors with high marginal tax rates and little need for current income.

cliff vesting All the options in a grant vest on the same date.

closely held corporation Refers to companies that are so small that their common stocks are not actively traded; they are owned by only a few people, usually the companies' managers.

coefficient of variation, CV Equal to the standard deviation divided by the expected return; it is a standardized risk measure that allows comparisons between investments having different expected returns and standard deviations.

collection policy The procedure for collecting accounts receivable. A change in collection policy will affect sales, days sales outstanding, bad debt losses, and the percentage of customers taking discounts.

collections float Float created while funds from customers' checks are being deposited and cleared through the check collection process.

combination lease Combines some aspects of both operating and financial leases. For example, a financial lease that contains a cancellation clause—normally associated with operating leases—is a combination lease.

commercial paper Unsecured, short-term promissory notes of large firms, usually issued in denominations of $100,000 or more and having an interest rate somewhat below the prime rate.

commodity futures Futures contracts that involve the sale or purchase of various commodities, including grains, oilseeds, livestock, meats, fiber, metals, and wood.

common stockholders' equity (net worth) The capital supplied by common stockholders— capital stock, paid-in capital, retained earnings, and (occasionally) certain reserves. Paid-in capital is the difference between the stock's par value and what stockholders paid when they bought newly issued shares.

comparative ratio analysis Compares a firm's own ratios to other leading companies in the same industry. This technique is also known as benchmarking.

compensating balance (CB) A minimum checking account balance that a firm must maintain with a bank to compensate the bank for services rendered or for making a loan; generally equal to 10%–20% of the loans outstanding.

composition Creditors voluntarily reduce their fixed claims on the debtor by accepting a lower principal amount, reducing the interest rate on the debt, accepting equity in place of debt, or some combination of these changes.

compounding The process of finding the future value of a single payment or series of payments.

computer/telephone network A computer/telephone network, such as Nasdaq, consists of all the facilities that provide for security transactions not conducted at a physical location exchange. These facilities are, basically, the communications networks that link buyers and sellers.

congeneric merger Involves firms that are interrelated but do not have identical lines of business. One example is Prudential's acquisition of Bache & Company.

conglomerate merger Occurs when unrelated enterprises combine, such as Mobil Oil and Montgomery Ward.

conservative short-term financing policy Refers to using permanent capital to finance all permanent asset requirements as well as to meet some or all of the seasonal demands.

consol A type of perpetuity. Consols were originally bonds issued by England in the mid-1700s to consolidate past debt.

continuous probability distribution Contains an infinite number of outcomes and is graphed from $-\infty$ and $+\infty$.

conversion price The effective price per share of stock if conversion occurs; the par value of the convertible security divided by the conversion ratio.

conversion ratio The number of shares of common stock received upon conversion of one convertible security.

conversion value The value of the stock that the investor would receive if conversion occurred; the market price per share times the conversion ratio.

convertible bond Security that is convertible into shares of common stock, at a fixed price, at the option of the bondholder.

convertible currency A currency that can be traded in the currency markets and can be redeemed at current market rates.

convertible security Bonds or preferred stocks that can be exchanged for (converted into) common stock, under specific terms, at the option of the holder. Unlike the exercise of warrants, conversion of a convertible security does not provide additional capital to the issuer.

corporate alliance A cooperative deal that stops short of a merger; also called a strategic alliance.

corporate beta (b) The quantitative measure of corporate risk of a project; the slope of the corporate characteristic line.

corporate bond Debt issued by corporations and exposed to default risk. Different corporate bonds have different levels of default risk, depending on the issuing company's characteristics and on the terms of the specific bond.

corporate characteristic line The regression line that results when the project's returns are plotted on the Y axis and the returns on the firm's total operations are plotted on the X axis.

corporate governance The set of rules that control a company's behavior toward its directors, managers, employees, shareholders, creditors, customers, competitors, and community.

corporate risk management Managing unpredictable events that have adverse consequences for the firm. This effort involves reducing the consequences of risk to the point where there would be no significant adverse impact on the firm's financial position.

corporate valuation model Defines the total value of a company as the value of operations plus the value of nonoperating assets plus the value of growth options.

corporation A corporation is a legal entity created by a state. The corporation is separate and distinct from its owners and managers.

correlation The tendency of two variables to move together.

correlation coefficient, ρ (rho) A standardized measure of how two random variables covary. A correlation coefficient (ρ) of +1.0 means that the two variables move up and down in perfect synchronization, whereas a coefficient of −1.0 means the variables always move in opposite directions. A correlation coefficient of zero suggests that the two variables are not related to one another; that is, they are independent.

cost of common stock, r_s The return required by the firm's common stockholders. It is usually calculated using Capital Asset Pricing Model or the dividend growth model.

cost of new external common equity, r_e A project financed with external equity must earn a higher rate of return because it must cover the flotation costs. Thus, the cost of new common equity is higher than that of common equity raised internally by reinvesting earnings.

cost of preferred stock, r_{ps} The return required by the firm's preferred stockholders. The cost of preferred stock, r_{ps}, is the cost to the firm of issuing new preferred stock. For perpetual preferred, it is the preferred dividend, D_{ps}, divided by the net issuing price, P_n.

costly trade credit Credit taken (in excess of free trade credit) whose cost is equal to the discount lost.

coupon interest rate Stated rate of interest on a bond; defined as the coupon payment divided by the par value.

coupon payment Dollar amount of interest paid to each bondholder on the interest payment dates.

coverage ratio Similar to the times-interest-earned ratio, but it recognizes that many firms lease assets and also must make sinking fund payments. It is found by adding earnings before interest, taxes, depreciation, amortization (EBITDA), and lease payments and then dividing this total by interest charges, lease payments, and sinking fund payments over 1 − T (where T is the tax rate).

cramdown Reorganization plans that are mandated by the bankruptcy court and binding on all parties.

credit enhancement Enables a bond's rating to be upgraded to AAA when the issuer purchases bond insurance. The bond insurance company guarantees that bondholders will receive the promised interest and principal payments. Therefore, the bond carries the credit rating of the insurance company rather than that of the issuer.

credit period The length of time for which credit is extended. If the credit period is lengthened then sales will generally increase, as will accounts receivable. This will increase the firm's financing needs and possibly increase bad debt losses. A shortening of the credit period will have the opposite effect.

credit policy The firm's policy on granting and collecting credit. There are four elements of credit policy, or credit policy variables: credit period, credit standards, collection policy, and discounts.

credit standards The financial strength and creditworthiness that qualifies a customer for a firm's regular credit terms.

credit terms Statements of the credit period and any discounts offered—for example, 2/10, net 30.

cross rate The exchange rate between two non-U.S. currencies.

crossover rate The cost of capital at which the NPV profiles for two projects intersect.

cumulative preferred dividends A protective feature on preferred stock that requires all past preferred dividends to be paid before any common dividends can be paid.

currency appreciation Occurs when a particular currency is worth more than it previously was.

currency depreciation Occurs when a particular currency is worth less than it previously was.

current ratio Indicates the extent to which current liabilities are covered by those assets expected to be converted to cash in the near future; it is found by dividing current assets by current liabilities.

current yield (on a bond) The annual coupon payment divided by the current market price.

days sales outstanding (DSO) Used to appraise accounts receivable and indicates the length of time the firm must wait after making a sale before receiving cash. It is found by dividing receivables by average sales per day.

DCF (discounted cash flow) techniques The net present value (NPV) and internal rate of return (IRR) techniques are discounted cash flow (DCF) evaluation techniques. These are called DCF methods because they explicitly recognize the time value of money.

dealer market In a dealer market, a dealer holds an inventory of the security and makes a market by offering to buy or sell. Others who wish to buy or sell can see the offers made by the dealers and can contact the dealer of their choice to arrange a transaction.

debenture An unsecured bond; as such, it provides no lien against specific property as security for the obligation. Debenture holders are therefore general creditors whose claims are protected by property not otherwise pledged.

debt ratio The ratio of total liabilities to total assets; it measures the percentage of funds provided by creditors.

debt service requirements The total amount of principal and interest that must be paid on a bond issue.

debt-to-equity ratio Ratio of debt divided by equity.

decision trees A form of scenario analysis in which different actions are taken in different scenarios.

declaration date The date on which a firm's directors issue a statement declaring a dividend.

default risk The risk that a borrower may not pay the interest and/or principal on a loan when it becomes due. If the issuer defaults, investors receive less than the promised return on the bond. Default risk is influenced by the financial strength of the issuer and also by the terms of the bond contract, especially whether collateral has been pledged to secure the bond. The greater the default risk, the higher the bond's yield to maturity.

default risk premium (DRP) The premium added to the real risk-free rate to compensate investors for the risk that a borrower may fail to pay the interest and/or principal on a loan when they become due.

defensive merger Occurs when one company acquires another to help ward off a hostile merger attempt.

defined benefit plan Under this type of pension plan, employers agree to give retirees a specifically defined benefit.

defined contribution plan Under this type of pension plan, employers agree to make specific payments into a retirement fund and retirees receive benefits that depend on the plan's investment success.

depreciation A noncash charge against tangible assets, such as buildings or machines. It is taken for the purpose of showing an asset's estimated dollar cost of the capital equipment used up in the production process.

derivatives Claims whose value depends on what happens to the value of some other asset. Futures and options are two important types of derivatives, and their values depend on what happens

to the prices of other assets. Therefore, the value of a derivative security is derived from the value of an underlying real asset or other security.

detachable warrant A warrant that can be detached and traded separately from the underlying security. Most warrants are detachable.

devaluation The lowering, by governmental action, of the price of its currency relative to another currency. For example, in 1967 the British pound was devalued from $2.80 per pound to $2.50 per pound.

development bond A tax-exempt bond sold by state and local governments whose proceeds are made available to corporations for specific uses deemed (by Congress) to be in the public interest.

direct quotation When discussing exchange rates, the number of U.S. dollars required to purchase one unit of a foreign currency.

disbursement float Float created before checks written by a firm have cleared and been deducted from the firm's account; disbursement float causes the firm's own checkbook balance to be smaller than the balance on the bank's records.

discount bond Bond prices and interest rates are inversely related; that is, they tend to move in the opposite direction from one another. A fixed-rate bond will sell at par when its coupon interest rate is equal to the going rate of interest, r_d. When the going rate of interest is above the coupon rate, a fixed-rate bond will sell at a "discount" below its par value. If current interest rates are below the coupon rate, a fixed-rate bond will sell at a "premium" above its par value.

discount interest Interest that is calculated on the face amount of a loan but is paid in advance.

discount on forward rate Occurs when the forward exchange rate differs from the spot rate. When the forward rate is below the spot rate, the forward rate is said to be at a discount.

discounted cash flow (DCF) method A method of valuing a business that involves the application of capital budgeting procedures to an entire firm rather than to a single project.

discounted payback period The number of years it takes a firm to recover its project investment based on discounted cash flows.

discounting The process of finding the present value of a single payment or series of payments.

distribution policy The policy that sets the level of distributions and the form of the distributions (dividends and stock repurchases).

diversifiable risk Refers to that part of a security's total risk associated with random events not affecting the market as a whole. This risk can be eliminated by proper diversification. Also known as company-specific risk.

divestiture The opposite of an acquisition. That is, a company sells a portion of its assets—often a whole division—to another firm or individual.

dividend irrelevance theory Holds that dividend policy has no effect on either the price of a firm's stock or its cost of capital.

dividend reinvestment plan (DRIP) Allows stockholders to automatically purchase shares of common stock of the paying corporation in lieu of receiving cash dividends. There are two types of plans: One involves only stock that is already outstanding; the other involves newly issued stock. In the first type, the dividends of all participants are pooled and the stock is purchased on the open market. Participants benefit from lower transaction costs. In the second type, the company issues new shares to the participants. Thus, the company issues stock in lieu of the cash dividend.

dividend yield Defined as either the end-of-period dividend divided by the beginning-of-period price or as the ratio of the current dividend to the current price. Valuation formulas use the former definition.

Du Pont chart A chart designed to show the relationships among return on investment, asset turnover, the profit margin, and leverage.

Du Pont equation A formula showing that the rate of return on equity can be found as the profit margin multiplied by the product of total assets turnover and the equity multiplier.

EBITDA Earnings before interest, taxes, depreciation, and amortization.

ECN In an ECN (electronic communications network), orders from potential buyers and sellers are automatically matched and the transaction is automatically completed.

economic life The number of years a project should be operated to maximize its net present value; often less than the maximum potential life.

economic ordering quantity (EOQ) The order quantity that minimizes the costs of ordering and carrying inventories.

Economic Value Added (EVA) A method used to measure a firm's true profitability. EVA is found by taking the firm's after-tax operating profit and subtracting the annual cost of all the capital a firm uses. If the firm generates a positive EVA, its management has created value for its shareholders. If the EVA is negative, management has destroyed shareholder value.

effective (or equivalent) annual rate (EAR or EFF%) The effective annual rate is the rate that, under annual compounding, would have produced the same future value at the end of 1 year as was produced by more frequent compounding, say quarterly. If the compounding occurs annually, then the effective annual rate and the nominal rate are the same. If compounding occurs more frequently, then the effective annual rate is greater than the nominal rate.

efficient frontier The set of efficient portfolios out of the full set of potential portfolios. On a graph, the efficient frontier constitutes the boundary line of the set of potential portfolios.

Efficient Markets Hypothesis (EMH) States (1) that stocks are always in equilibrium and (2) that it is impossible for an investor to consistently "beat the market." The EMH assumes that all important information regarding a stock is reflected in the price of that stock.

efficient portfolio Provides the highest expected return for any degree of risk. The efficient portfolio also provides the lowest degree of risk for any expected return.

embedded options Options that are a part of another project. Also called real options, managerial options, and strategic options.

Employee Retirement Income Security Act (ERISA) The basic federal law governing the structure and administration of corporate pension plans.

entrenchment Occurs when a company has such a weak board of directors and has such strong anti-takeover provisions in its corporate charter that senior managers feel there is little chance of being removed.

EOQ model The equation used to find the economic ordering quantity.

EOQ range The range around the optimal ordering quantity that may be ordered without significantly affecting total inventory costs.

equilibrium The condition under which the intrinsic value of a security is equal to its price; also, when a security's expected return is equal to its required return.

equity premium, RP_M Expected market return minus the risk-free rate; also called market risk premium or equity risk premium.

equity risk premium, RP$_M$ Expected market return minus the risk-free rate; also called market risk premium or equity premium.

EROIC Expected return on invested capital (EROIC) is equal to expected NOPAT divided by the amount of capital that is available at the beginning of the year.

ESOP (employee stock ownership plan) A type of retirement plan in which employees own stock in the company.

euro The currency used by nations in the European Monetary Union.

Eurobond Any bond sold in some country other than the one in whose currency the bond is denominated. Thus, a U.S. firm selling dollar bonds in Switzerland is selling Eurobonds.

Eurodollar A U.S. dollar on deposit in a foreign bank or a foreign branch of a U.S. bank. Eurodollars are used to conduct transactions throughout Europe and the rest of the world.

exchange rate Specifies the number of units of a given currency that can be purchased for one unit of another currency.

exchange rate risk Refers to the fluctuation in exchange rates between currencies over time.

ex-dividend date The date when the right to the dividend leaves the stock. This date was established by stockbrokers to avoid confusion, and it is four business days prior to the holder-of-record date. If the stock sale is made prior to the ex-dividend date, then the dividend is paid to the buyer; if the stock is bought on or after the ex-dividend date, the dividend is paid to the seller.

exercise price The price stated in the option contract at which the security can be bought (or sold). Also called the strike price.

exercise value Equal to the current price of the stock (underlying the option) minus the strike price of the option.

expectations theory States that the slope of the yield curve depends on expectations about future inflation rates and interest rates. Thus, if the annual rate of inflation and future interest rates are expected to increase, then the yield curve will be upward sloping; the curve will be downward sloping if the annual rates are expected to decrease.

expected rate of return, $\hat{r}_s$ The rate of return expected on a stock given its current price and expected future cash flows. If the stock is in equilibrium, the required rate of return will equal the expected rate of return.

extension A form of debt restructuring in which creditors postpone the dates of required interest or principal payments, or both.

extra dividend A dividend paid, in addition to the regular dividend, when earnings permit. Firms with volatile earnings may have a low regular dividend that can be maintained even in years of low profit (or high capital investment) but is supplemented by an extra dividend when excess funds are available.

fairness The standard of fairness states that claims must be recognized in the order of their legal and contractual priority. In simpler terms, the reorganization must be fair to all parties.

Fama-French three-factor model Includes one factor for the excess market return (the market return minus the risk-free rate), a second factor for size (defined as the return on a portfolio of small firms minus the return on a portfolio of big firms), and a third factor for the book-to-market effect (defined as the return on a portfolio of firms with a high book-to-market ratio minus the return on a portfolio of firms with a low book-to-market ratio).

FASB Financial Accounting Standards Board Promulgates standards for issues pertaining to private organizations.

FASB Statement 13 The Financial Accounting Standards Board statement that spells out the conditions under which a lease must be capitalized and the specific procedures to follow.

feasibility The standard of feasibility states that there must be a reasonably high probability of successful rehabilitation and profitable future operations.

feasible set Represents all portfolios that can be constructed from a given set of stocks; also known as the attainable set.

financial distress costs Incurred when a leveraged firm facing a decline in earnings is forced to take actions to avoid bankruptcy. These costs may be the result of delays in the liquidation of assets, legal fees, the effects on product quality from cutting costs, and evasive actions by suppliers and customers.

financial futures Provide for the purchase or sale of a financial asset at some time in the future, but at a price that is established today. Financial futures exist for Treasury bills, Treasury notes and bonds, certificates of deposit, Eurodollar deposits, foreign currencies, and stock indexes.

financial intermediary Intermediary that buys securities with funds that it obtains by issuing its own securities. An example is a common stock mutual fund that buys common stocks with funds obtained by issuing shares in the mutual fund.

financial lease Covers the entire expected life of the equipment; does not provide for maintenance service, is not cancellable and is fully amortized.

financial leverage The extent to which fixed-income securities (debt and preferred stock) are used in a firm's capital structure. If a high percentage of a firm's capital structure is in the form of debt and preferred stock, then the firm is said to have a high degree of financial leverage.

financial merger A merger in which the companies will not be operated as a single unit and for which no operating economies are expected.

financial risk The risk added by the use of debt financing. Debt financing increases the variability of earnings before taxes (but after interest); thus, along with business risk, it contributes to the uncertainty of net income and earnings per share. Business risk plus financial risk equals total corporate risk.

financial service corporation A corporation that offers a wide range of financial services such as brokerage operations, insurance, and commercial banking.

financing feedback Circularity created when additional debt causes additional interest expense, which reduces the addition to retained earnings, which in turn requires a higher level of debt, which causes still more interest expense, causing the cycle to be repeated.

fixed assets turnover ratio The ratio of sales to net fixed assets; it measures how effectively the firm uses its plant and equipment.

fixed exchange rate system The system in effect from the end of World War II until August 1971. Under the system, the U.S. dollar was linked to gold at the rate of $35 per ounce, and other currencies were then tied to the dollar.

floating exchange rates The system currently in effect, where the forces of supply and demand are allowed to determine currency prices with little government intervention.

floating-rate bond A bond whose coupon payment may vary over time. The coupon rate is usually linked to the rate on some other security, such as a Treasury security, or to some other rate, such as the prime rate or LIBOR.

flotation cost, F Those costs occurring when a company issues a new security, including fees to an investment banker and legal fees.

forecasted financial statements approach A method of forecasting financial statements to determine the additional funds needed. Many items on the income statement and balance sheets are assumed to increase proportionally with sales. As sales increase, these items that are tied to sales also increase, and the values of these items for a particular year are estimated as percentages of the forecasted sales for that year. The first step in forecasting financial statements is to forecast the future sales growth rate.

foreign bond A bond sold by a foreign borrower but denominated in the currency of the country in which the issue is sold. Thus, a U.S. firm selling bonds denominated in Swiss francs in Switzerland is selling foreign bonds.

foreign trade deficit A deficit that occurs when businesses and individuals in the United States import more goods from foreign countries than are exported.

forward contract A contract to buy or sell some item at some time in the future at a price established when the contract is entered into.

forward exchange rate The prevailing exchange rate for exchange (delivery) at some agreed-upon future date, which is usually 30, 90, or 180 days from the day the transaction is negotiated.

founders' shares Stock owned by the firm's founders that have sole voting rights but restricted dividends for a specified number of years.

free cash flow (FCF) The cash flow actually available for distribution to all investors after the company has made all investments in fixed assets and working capital necessary to sustain ongoing operations.

free trade credit Credit received during the discount period.

friendly merger Occurs when the target company's management agrees to the merger and recommends that shareholders approve the deal.

fully funded pension plan The present value of all expected retirement benefits is equal to assets on hand.

fund capital Not-for-profit business equivalent of equity capital. It consists of retained profits and charitable contributions.

funding strategy Necessary for a defined benefit plan and involves two decisions: how fast should any unfunded liability be reduced and what rate of return should be assumed in the actuarial calculations.

FVA_N The future value of a stream of annuity payments, where N is the number of payments of the annuity.

$FVIFA_{I,N}$ The future value interest factor for an ordinary annuity of N periodic payments paying I percent interest per period.

$FVIF_{I,N}$ The future value interest factor for a lump sum left in an account for N periods paying I percent interest per period.

FV_N The future value of an initial single cash flow, where N is the number of periods the initial cash flow is compounded.

GAAP, Generally Accepted Accounting Principles A set of standards for financial reporting established by the accounting profession.

GASB, Government Accounting Standards Board Promulgates standards for issues pertaining to governmental entities.

general obligation bonds Type of municipal bonds which are secured by the full faith and credit of a government unit; that is, backed by the full taxing authority of the issuer.

going public The act of selling stock to the public at large by a closely held corporation or its principal stockholders.

golden parachute A payment made to executives who are forced out when a merger takes place.

greenmail Targeted share repurchases that occur when a company buys back stock from a potential acquirer at a higher than fair-market price. In return, the potential acquirer agrees not to attempt to take over the company.

gross profit margin Ratio of gross profit (sales minus cost of goods sold) divided by sales.

growth option Occurs if an investment creates the opportunity to make other potentially profitable investments that would not otherwise be possible, including options to expand output, to enter a new geographical market, and to introduce complementary products or successive generations of products.

GSE (government-sponsored entity) debt Debt issued by government-sponsored entities (GSEs) such as the Tennessee Valley Authority or the Small Business Administration; not officially backed by the full faith and credit of the U.S. government.

guideline lease Meets all of the Internal Revenue Service (IRS) requirements for a genuine lease.

If a lease meets the IRS guidelines, the IRS allows the lessor to deduct the asset's depreciation and allows the lessee to deduct the lease payments. Also called a tax-oriented lease.

hard currencies Currencies considered to be convertible because the nation that issues them allows them to be traded in the currency markets and is willing to redeem them at market rates.

hedging A transaction that lowers a firm's risk of damage due to fluctuating commodity prices, interest rates, and exchange rates.

herding instinct When one group of investors does well, other investors begin to emulate them, acting like a herd of sheep.

holder-of-record date If a company lists the stockholder as an owner on the holder-of-record date, then the stockholder receives the dividend.

holding company A corporation formed for the sole purpose of owning stocks in other companies. A holding company differs from a stock mutual fund in that holding companies own sufficient stock in their operating companies to exercise effective working control.

holdout A problematic characteristic of informal reorganizations whereby all of the involved parties do not agree to the voluntary plan. Holdouts are usually made by creditors in an effort to receive full payment on claims.

horizon value The value of operations at the end of the explicit forecast period. It is equal to the present value of all free cash flows beyond the forecast period, discounted back to the end of the forecast period at the weighted average cost of capital.

horizontal merger A merger between two companies in the same line of business.

hostile merger Occurs when the management of the target company resists the offer.

hurdle rate The project cost of capital, or discount rate. It is the rate used to discount future cash flows in the net present value method or to compare with the internal rate of return.

improper accumulation The retention of earnings by a business for the purpose of enabling stockholders to avoid personal income taxes on dividends.

income bond Pays interest only if the interest is earned. These securities cannot bankrupt a company, but from an investor's standpoint, they are riskier than "regular" bonds.

income statement Summarizes the firm's revenues and expenses over an accounting period. Net sales are shown at the top of each statement, after which various costs, including income taxes, are subtracted to obtain the net income available to common stockholders. The bottom of the statement reports earnings and dividends per share.

incremental cash flow Those cash flows that arise solely from the asset that is being evaluated.

indentures A legal document that spells out the rights of both bondholders and the issuing corporation.

independent projects Projects that can be accepted or rejected individually.

indexed, or purchasing power, bond The interest rate of such a bond is based on an inflation index such as the consumer price index (CPI), so the interest paid rises automatically when the inflation rate rises, thus protecting the bondholders against inflation.

indifference curve The risk–return trade-off function for a particular investor; reflects that investor's attitude toward risk. An investor would be indifferent between any pair of assets on the same indifference curve. In risk–return space, the greater the slope of the indifference curve, the greater is the investor's risk aversion.

indirect quotation When discussing exchange rates, the number of units of foreign currency that can be purchased for one U.S. dollar.

inflation premium (IP) The premium added to the real risk-free rate of interest to compensate for the expected loss of purchasing power. The inflation premium is the average rate of inflation expected over the life of the security.

informal debt restructuring An agreement between a troubled firm and its creditors to change existing debt terms. An extension postpones the required payment date; a composition is a reduction in creditor claims.

information content, or signaling, hypothesis A theory that holds that investors regard dividend changes as "signals" of management forecasts. Thus, when dividends are raised, this is viewed by investors as recognition by management of future earnings increases. Therefore, if a firm's stock price increases with a dividend increase, the reason may not be investor preference for dividends but rather expectations of higher future earnings. Conversely, a dividend reduction may signal that management is forecasting poor earnings in the future.

initial public offering (IPO) Occurs when a closely held corporation or its principal stockholders sell stock to the public at large.

initial public offering (IPO) market Going public is the act of selling stock to the public at large by a closely held corporation or its principal stockholders, and this market is often termed the initial public offering market.

I_{NOM} The nominal, or quoted, interest rate.

insiders The officers, directors, and major stockholders of a firm.

interest coverage ratio Also called the times-interest-earned (TIE) ratio; determined by dividing earnings before interest and taxes by the interest expense.

interest rate parity Holds that investors should expect to earn the same return in all countries after adjusting for risk.

interest rate risk Arises from the fact that bond prices decline when interest rates rise. Under these circumstances, selling a bond prior to maturity will result in a capital loss; the longer the term to maturity, the larger the loss.

interlocking boards of directors Occur when the CEO of Company A sits on the board of Company B while B's CEO sits on A's board.

internal rate of return (IRR) method The discount rate that equates the present value of the expected future cash inflows and outflows. IRR measures the rate of return on a project, but it assumes that all cash flows can be reinvested at the IRR rate.

international bond Any bond sold outside of the country of the borrower. There are two types of international bonds: Eurobonds and foreign bonds.

intrinsic (or fundamental) value, P_0 The present value of a firm's expected future free cash flows.

inventory conversion period The average length of time to convert materials into finished goods and then to sell them; calculated by dividing total inventory by sales per day.

inventory turnover ratio Sales divided by inventories.

inverted (abnormal) yield curve A downward-sloping yield curve.

investment bank A firm that assists in the design of an issuing firm's corporate securities and in the sale of the new securities to investors in the primary market.

investment grade bond Securities with ratings of Baa/BBB or above.

investment strategy Deals with the question of how the pension assets portfolio should be structured given the assumed actuarial rate of return.

investment timing option Gives companies the option to delay a project rather than implement it immediately. This option to wait allows a company to reduce the uncertainty of market conditions before it decides to implement the project.

Jensen's alpha Measures the vertical distance of a portfolio's return above or below the Security Market Line; first suggested by Professor Michael Jensen, it became popular because of its ease of calculation.

joint venture Involves the joining together of parts of companies to accomplish specific, limited objectives. Joint ventures are controlled by the combined management of the two (or more) parent companies.

junk bond High-risk, high-yield bond issued to finance leveraged buyouts, mergers, or troubled companies.

lessee The party leasing the property.

lessee's analysis Involves determining whether leasing an asset is less costly than buying the asset. The lessee will compare the present value cost of leasing the asset with the present value cost of purchasing the asset (assuming the funds to purchase the asset are obtained through a loan). If the present value cost of the lease is less than the present value cost of purchasing, then the asset should be leased. The lessee can also analyze the lease using the IRR approach or the equivalent loan method.

lessor The party receiving the payments from the lease (that is, the owner of the property).

lessor's analysis Involves determining the rate of return on the proposed lease. If the internal rate of return of the lease cash flows exceeds the lessor's opportunity cost of capital, then the lease is a good investment. This is equivalent to analyzing whether the net present value of the lease is positive.

leveraged buyout (LBO) A transaction in which a firm's publicly owned stock is acquired in a mostly debt-financed tender offer, resulting in a privately owned, highly leveraged firm. Often, the firm's own management initiates the LBO.

leveraged lease The lessor borrows a portion of the funds needed to buy the equipment to be leased.

LIBOR (London Interbank Offered Rate) The rate that U.K. banks charge one another.

limited liability partnership A limited liability partnership (LLP), sometimes called a limited liability company (LLC), combines the limited liability advantage of a corporation with the tax advantages of a partnership.

limited partnership A partnership in which limited partners' liabilities, investment returns, and control are limited; general partners have unlimited liability and control.

line of credit An arrangement in which a bank agrees to lend up to a specified maximum amount of funds during a designated period.

liquidation in bankruptcy The sale of the assets of a firm and the distribution of the proceeds to the creditors and owners in a specific priority.

liquidity Liquidity refers to a firm's cash and marketable securities position and to its ability to meet maturing obligations. A liquid asset is any asset that can be quickly sold and converted to cash at its "fair" value. Active markets provide liquidity.

liquidity premium (LP) A liquidity premium is added to the real risk-free rate of interest, in addition to other premiums, if a security is not liquid.

liquidity ratio A ratio that shows the relationship of a firm's cash and other current assets to its current liabilities.

lockbox plan A cash management tool in which incoming checks for a firm are sent to post office boxes rather than to corporate headquarters. Several times a day, a local bank will collect the contents of the lockbox and deposit the checks into the company's local account.

long hedges Occur when futures contracts are bought in anticipation of (or to guard against) price increases.

low-regular-dividend-plus-extras policy Dividend policy in which a company announces a low regular dividend that it is sure can be maintained; if extra funds are available, the company pays a specially designated extra dividend or repurchases shares of stock.

lumpy assets Those assets that cannot be acquired smoothly and instead require large, discrete additions. For example, an electric utility that is operating at full capacity cannot add a small amount of generating capacity, at least not economically.

managerial options Options that give opportunities to managers to respond to changing market conditions. Also called real options.

margin requirement The margin is the percentage of a stock's price that an investor has borrowed in order to purchase the stock. The Securities and Exchange Commission sets margin requirements, which is the maximum percentage of debt that can be used to purchase a stock.

marginal tax rate The tax rate on the last unit of income.

market multiple method Multiplies a market-determined ratio (called a multiple) by some value of the target firm to estimate the target's value. The market multiple can be based on net income, earnings per share, sales, book value, or number of subscribers.

market portfolio A portfolio consisting of all stocks.

market risk That part of a security's total risk that cannot be eliminated by diversification; measured by the beta coefficient.

market risk premium, RP$_M$ The difference between the expected return on the market and the risk-free rate.

Market Value Added (MVA) The difference between the market value of the firm (that is, the sum of the market value of common equity, the market value of debt, and the market value of preferred stock) and the book value of the firm's common equity, debt, and preferred stock. If the book values of debt and preferred stock are equal to their market values, then MVA is also equal to the difference between the market value of equity and the amount of equity capital that investors supplied.

market value ratios Relate the firm's stock price to its earnings and book value per share.

marketable securities Can be converted to cash on very short notice and provide at least a modest return.

maturity date The date when the bond's par value is repaid to the bondholder. Maturity dates generally range from 10 to 40 years from the time of issue.

maturity matching short-term financing policy A policy that matches asset and liability maturities. It is also referred to as the moderate, or self-liquidating, approach.

maturity risk premium (MRP) The premium that must be added to the real risk-free rate of interest to compensate for interest rate risk, which depends on a bond's maturity. Interest rate risk arises from the fact that bond prices decline when interest rates rise. Under these circumstances, selling a

bond prior to maturity will result in a capital loss; the longer the term to maturity, the larger the loss.

merger The joining of two firms to form a single firm.

Miller model Introduces the effect of personal taxes into the valuation of a levered firm, which reduces the advantage of corporate debt financing.

MM Proposition I with corporate taxes $V_L = V_U + TD$. Thus, firm value increases with leverage and the optimal capital structure is virtually all debt.

MM Proposition I without taxes $V_L = V_U = EBIT/r_{sU}$. Since both EBIT and r_{sU} are constant, firm value is also constant and capital structure is irrelevant.

MM Proposition II with corporate taxes $r_{sL} = r_{sU} + (r_{sU} - r_d)(1 - T)(D/S)$. Here the increase in equity costs is less than the zero-tax case, and the increasing use of lower-cost debt causes the firm's cost of capital to decrease. In this case, the optimal capital structure is virtually all debt.

MM Proposition II without taxes $r_{sL} = r_{sU} - (r_{sU} - r_d)(D/S)$. Thus, r_s increases in a precise way as leverage increases. In fact, this increase is just sufficient to offset the increased use of lower-cost debt.

moderate net operating working capital policy A policy that matches asset and liability maturities. It is also referred to as maturity matching or the self-liquidating approach.

Modified Internal Rate of Return (MIRR) method Assumes that cash flows from all projects are reinvested at the cost of capital, not at the project's own IRR. This makes the modified internal rate of return a better indicator of a project's true profitability.

money market A financial market for debt securities with maturities of less than 1 year (short-term). The New York money market is the world's largest.

money market fund A mutual fund that invests in short-term debt instruments and offers investors check-writing privileges; thus, it amounts to an interest-bearing checking account.

Monte Carlo simulation analysis A risk analysis technique in which a computer is used to simulate probable future events and thus to estimate the likely profitability and risk of a project.

mortgage bond A bond for which a corporation pledges certain assets as security. All such bonds are written subject to an indenture.

multinational (or global) corporation A corporation that operates in two or more countries.

municipal bond Issued by state and local governments. The interest earned on most municipal bonds is exempt from federal taxes and also from state taxes if the holder is a resident of the issuing state.

municipal bond insurance An insurance company guarantees to pay the coupon and principal payments should the issuer of the bond (the municipality) default. This reduces the risk to investors who are willing to accept a lower coupon rate for an insured bond issue compared to an uninsured issue.

mutual fund A corporation that sells shares in the fund and uses the proceeds to buy stocks, long-term bonds, or short-term debt instruments. The resulting dividends, interest, and capital gains are distributed to the fund's shareholders after the deduction of operating expenses. Some funds specialize in certain types of securities, such as growth stocks, international stocks, or municipal bonds.

mutually exclusive projects Projects that cannot be performed at the same time. A company could choose either Project 1 or Project 2, or it can reject both, but it cannot accept both projects.

National Association of Securities Dealers (NASD) An industry group primarily concerned with the operation of the over-the-counter (OTC) market.

natural hedge A transaction between two counterparties where both parties' risks are reduced.

net advantage to leasing (NAL) The dollar value of the lease to the lessee. It is, in a sense, the net present value of leasing versus owning.

net cash flow The sum of net income plus noncash adjustments.

net float The difference between a firm's disbursement float and collections float.

net operating working capital (NOWC) Operating current assets minus operating current liabilities. Operating current assets are the current assets used to support operations, such as cash, accounts receivable, and inventory. They do not include short-term investments. Operating current liabilities are the current liabilities that are a natural consequence of the firm's operations, such as accounts payable and accruals. They do not include notes payable or any other short-term debt that charges interest.

net present value (NPV) method Used to assess the present value of the project's expected future cash flows, discounted at the appropriate cost of capital. NPV is a direct measure of the value of the project to shareholders.

net working capital Current assets minus current liabilities.

new issue market The market for stock of companies that go public.

nominal (quoted) interest rate, I_{NOM} The rate of interest stated in a contract. If the compounding occurs annually, the effective annual rate and the nominal rate are the same. If compounding occurs more frequently, the effective annual rate is greater than the nominal rate. The nominal annual interest rate is also called the annual percentage rate, or APR.

nominal rate of return, r_n Includes an inflation adjustment (premium). Thus, if nominal rates of return are used in the capital budgeting process, then the net cash flows must also be nominal.

nominal risk-free rate of interest, r_{RF} The real risk-free rate plus a premium for expected inflation. The short-term nominal risk-free rate is usually approximated by the U.S. Treasury bill rate, and the long-term nominal risk-free rate is approximated by the rate on U.S. Treasury bonds.

nonnormal cash flow projects Projects with a large cash outflow either sometime during or at the end of their lives. A common problem encountered when evaluating projects with nonnormal cash flows is multiple internal rates of return.

nonoperating assets Include investments in marketable securities and noncontrolling interests in the stock of other companies.

nonpecuniary benefits Perks that are not actual cash payments, such as lavish offices, memberships at country clubs, corporate jets, and excessively large staffs.

NOPAT (net operating profit after taxes) The amount of profit a company would generate if it had no debt and no financial assets.

normal cash flow project A project with one or more cash outflows (costs) followed by a series of cash inflows.

normal yield curve When the yield curve slopes upward it is said to be "normal," because it is like this most of the time.

not-for-profit corporation A tax-exempt charitable organization. The tax code defines a charitable organization as any corporation, community chest, fund, or foundation that is organized and operated exclusively for religious, charitable, scientific, public safety, literary, or educational purposes. This standard may be expanded to include an organization that provides health care services provided other requirements are met.

off–balance sheet financing A financing technique in which a firm uses partnerships and other arrangements to (in effect) borrow money while not reporting the liability on its balance sheet. For example, for many years neither leased assets nor the liabilities under lease contracts appeared on the lessees' balance sheets. To correct this problem, the Financial Accounting Standards Board issued FASB Statement 13.

official statement Contains information about municipal bond issues. It is prepared before the issue is brought to market.

open outcry auction A method of matching buyers and sellers in which the buyers and sellers are face-to-face, all stating a price at which they will buy or sell.

operating capital The sum of net operating working capital and operating long-term assets, such as net plant and equipment. Operating capital also is equal to the net amount of capital raised from investors. This is the amount of interest-bearing debt plus preferred stock plus common equity minus short-term investments. Also called total net operating capital, net operating capital, or net operating assets.

operating company A company controlled by a holding company.

operating current assets The current assets used to support operations, such as cash, accounts receivable, and inventory. It does not include short-term investments.

operating current liabilities The current liabilities that are a natural consequence of the firm's operations, such as accounts payable and accruals. It does not include notes payable or any other short-term debt that charges interest.

operating lease Provides for both financing and maintenance. Generally, the operating lease contract is written for a period considerably shorter than the expected life of the leased equipment and contains a cancellation clause; sometimes called a service lease.

operating leverage The extent to which fixed costs are used in a firm's operations. If a high percentage of a firm's total costs are fixed costs, then the firm is said to have a high degree of operating leverage. Operating leverage is a measure of one element of business risk but

does not include the second major element, sales variability.

operating merger Occurs when the operations of two companies are integrated with the expectation of obtaining synergistic gains. These may occur in response to economies of scale, management efficiency, or a host of other factors.

operating profit margin Ratio of earnings before interest and taxes divided by sales.

opportunity cost A cash flow that a firm must forgo in order to accept a project. For example, if the project requires the use of a building that could otherwise be sold, then the market value of the building is an opportunity cost of the project.

opportunity cost rate The rate of return available on the best alternative investment of similar risk.

optimal distribution policy The distribution policy that maximizes the value of the firm by choosing the optimal level and form of distributions (dividends and stock repurchases).

optimal dividend policy The dividend policy that strikes a balance between current dividends and future growth and maximizes the firm's stock price.

optimal portfolio The point at which the efficient set of portfolios—the efficient frontier—is just tangent to the investor's indifference curve. This point marks the highest level of satisfaction an investor can attain given the set of potential portfolios.

option A contract that gives its holder the right to buy or sell an asset at some predetermined price within a specified period of time.

ordinary (deferred) annuity An annuity with a fixed number of equal payments occurring at the end of each period.

original issue discount (OID) bond In general, any bond originally offered at a price that is significantly below its par value.

overfunded pension plan The assets on hand exceed the present value of all expected retirement benefits.

par value The nominal or face value of a stock or bond. The par value of a bond generally represents the amount of money that the firm borrows and promises to repay at some future date. The par value of a bond is often $1,000, but it can be $5,000 or more.

parent company Another name for a holding company. A parent company will often have control over many subsidiaries.

partnership A partnership exists when two or more persons associate to conduct a business.

payables deferral period The average length of time between a firm's purchase of materials and labor and the payment of cash for them. It is calculated by dividing accounts payable by credit purchases per day (i.e., cost of goods sold ÷ 365).

payback period The number of years it takes a firm to recover its project investment. Payback does not capture a project's entire cash flow stream and is thus not the preferred evaluation method. Note, however, that the payback does measure a project's liquidity, so many firms use it as a risk measure.

payment date The date on which a firm actually mails dividend checks.

payment, PMT Equal to the dollar amount of an equal or constant cash flow (an annuity).

payments pattern approach A method of monitoring accounts receivable that looks for changes in a customers' payment pattern. This takes into account the seasonal nature of customer orders.

pegged exchange rates Rates that are fixed against a major currency such as the U.S. dollar. Consequently, the values of the pegged currencies move together over time.

Pension Benefit Guarantee Corporation Established by ERISA to insure corporate defined benefits plans; PBGC steps in and takes over payments to retirees of bankrupt companies with underfunded pension plans.

perfect hedge A hedge in which the gain or loss on the hedged transaction exactly offsets the loss or gain on the unhedged position.

periodic rate, I_{PER} The rate charged by a lender or paid by a borrower each period. It can be a rate per year, per 6-month period, per quarter, per month, per day, or per any other time interval (usually 1 year or less).

permanent net operating working capital The NOWC required when the economy is weak and seasonal sales are at their low point. Thus, this level of NOWC always requires financing and can be regarded as permanent.

perpetuity A series of payments of a fixed amount that continue indefinitely.

physical location exchanges Exchanges, such as the New York Stock Exchange, that facilitate trading of securities at a particular location.

plug technique Technique used in financial forecasting to "plug" in enough new liabilities or assets to make the balance sheets balance.

poison pills Shareholder rights provisions that allow existing shareholders in a company to purchase additional shares of stock at a lower-than-market value if a potential acquirer purchases a controlling stake in the company.

political risk Refers to the possibility of expropriation and the unanticipated restriction of cash flows to the parent by a foreign government.

pooling of interests A method of accounting for a merger in which the consolidated balance sheet is constructed by simply adding together the balance sheets of the merged companies. This is no longer allowed.

portability A portable pension plan is one that the employee can carry from one employer to another.

portfolio A group of individual assets held in combination. An asset that would be relatively risky if held in isolation may have little or no risk if held in a well-diversified portfolio.

post-audit The final aspect of the capital budgeting process. The post-audit is a feedback process in which the actual results are compared with those predicted in the original capital budgeting analysis. The post-audit has several purposes, of which the most important are to improve forecasts and operations.

precautionary balance A cash balance held in reserve for random, unforeseen fluctuations in cash inflows and outflows.

preemptive right Gives the current shareholders the right to purchase any new shares issued in proportion to their current holdings. The preemptive right enables current owners to maintain their proportionate share of ownership and control of the business.

preferred stock A hybrid security that is similar to bonds in some respects and to common stock in other respects. Preferred dividends are similar to interest payments on bonds in that they are fixed in amount and generally must be paid before common stock dividends can be paid. If the preferred dividend is not earned, the directors can omit it without throwing the company into bankruptcy.

premium bond Bond prices and interest rates are inversely related; that is, they tend to move in the opposite direction from one another. A fixed-rate bond will sell at par when its coupon interest rate is equal to the going rate of interest, r_d. When the going rate of interest is above the coupon rate, a fixed-rate bond will sell at a "discount" below its par value. If current interest rates are below the coupon rate, a fixed-rate bond will sell at a "premium" above its par value.

premium on forward rate Occurs when the forward exchange rate differs from the spot rate. When the forward rate is above the spot rate, it is said to be at a premium.

prepackaged bankruptcy (or pre-pack) A type of reorganization that combines the advantages of informal workouts and formal Chapter 11 reorganization.

price/cash flow ratio Calculated by dividing price per share by cash flow per share. This shows how much investors are willing to pay per dollar of cash flow.

price/earnings (P/E) ratio Calculated by dividing price per share by earnings per share. This shows how much investors are willing to pay per dollar of reported profits.

price/EBITDA ratio The ratio of price per share divided by per share earnings before interest, depreciation, and amortization.

primary market Markets in which newly issued securities are sold for the first time.

priority of claims in liquidation Established in Chapter 7 of the Bankruptcy Act. It specifies the order in which the debtor's assets are distributed among the creditors.

private markets Markets in which transactions are worked out directly between two parties and structured in any manner that appeals to them. Bank loans and private placements of debt with insurance companies are examples of private market transactions.

private placement The sale of stock to only one or a few investors, usually institutional investors. The advantages of private placements are lower flotation costs and greater speed, since the shares issued are not subject to Securities and Exchange Commission registration.

probability distribution A listing, chart, or graph of all possible outcomes, such as expected rates of return, with a probability assigned to each outcome.

professional corporation (PC) Has most of the benefits of incorporation but the participants are not relieved of professional (malpractice) liability; known in some states as a professional association (PA).

profit margin on sales Calculated by dividing net income by sales; gives the profit per dollar of sales.

profit sharing plan Under this type of pension plan, employers make payments into the retirement fund but the payments to retirees vary with the level of corporate profits.

profitability index Found by dividing the project's present value of future cash flows by its initial cost. A profitability index greater than 1 is equivalent to a project's having positive net present value.

profitability ratios Ratios that show the combined effects of liquidity, asset management, and debt on operations.

progressive tax A tax system in which the higher one's income, the larger the percentage paid in taxes.

project cash flows The incremental cash flows of a proposed project.

project cost of capital The risk-adjusted discount rate for that project.

project financing Financing method in which the project's creditors do not have full recourse against the borrowers; the lenders and lessors must be paid from the project's cash flows and equity.

projected (pro forma) financial statement Shows how an actual statement would look if certain assumptions are realized.

promissory note A document specifying the terms and conditions of a loan, including the amount, interest rate, and repayment schedule.

proprietorship A business owned by one individual.

prospectus Summarizes information about a new security issue and the issuing company.

proxy A document giving one person the authority to act for another, typically the power to vote shares of common stock.

proxy fight An attempt to take over a company in which an outside group solicits existing shareholders' proxies, which are authorizations to vote shares in a shareholders' meeting, in an effort to overthrow management and take control of the business.

public markets Markets in which standardized contracts are traded on organized exchanges. Securities that are issued in public markets, such as common stock and corporate bonds, are ultimately held by a large number of individuals.

public offering An offer of new common stock to the general public.

publicly owned corporation Corporation in which the stock is owned by a large number of investors, most of whom are not active in management.

purchase accounting A method of accounting for a merger in which the merger is handled as a purchase. In this method, the acquiring firm is assumed to have "bought" the acquired company in much the same way it would buy any capital asset.

purchasing power parity Implies that the level of exchange rates adjusts so that identical goods cost the same in different countries. Sometimes referred to as the "law of one price."

put option Allows the holder to sell the asset at some predetermined price within a specified period of time.

PV The value today of a future payment, or stream of payments, discounted at the appropriate rate of interest. PV is also the beginning amount that will grow to some future value.

PVA_N The value today of a future stream of N equal payments at the end of each period (an ordinary annuity).

$PVIFA_{I,N}$ The present value interest factor for an ordinary annuity of N periodic payments discounted at I percent interest per period.

$PVIF_{I,N}$ The present value interest factor for a lump sum received N periods in the future discounted at I percent per period.

quick, or acid test, ratio Found by taking current assets less inventories and then dividing by current liabilities.

real options Occur when managers can influence the size and risk of a project's cash flows by taking different actions during the project's life. They are referred to as real options because they deal with real as opposed to financial assets. They are also called managerial options because they give opportunities to managers to respond to changing market conditions. Sometimes they are called strategic options because they often deal with strategic issues. Finally, they are also called embedded options because they are a part of another project.

real rate of return, r_r Contains no adjustment for expected inflation. If net cash flows from a project do not include inflation adjustments, then the cash flows should be discounted at the real cost of capital. In a similar manner, the internal rate of return resulting from real net cash flows should be compared with the real cost of capital.

real risk-free rate of interest, r* The interest rate on a risk-free security in an economy with zero inflation. The real risk-free rate could also be called the pure rate of interest since it is the rate of interest that would exist on very short-term, default-free U.S. Treasury securities if the expected rate of inflation were zero.

realized rate of return, $\bar{r}$ The actual return an investor receives on his or her investment. It can be quite different than the expected return.

receivables collection period The average length of time required to convert a firm's receivables into cash. It is calculated by dividing accounts receivable by sales per day.

red herring (preliminary) prospectus A preliminary prospectus that may be distributed to potential buyers prior to approval of the registration statement by the Securities and Exchange Commission. After the registration has become effective, the securities—accompanied by the prospectus—may be offered for sale.

redeemable bond Gives investors the right to sell the bonds back to the corporation at a price that is usually close to the par value. If interest rates rise, then investors can redeem the bonds and reinvest at the higher rates.

refunding Occurs when a company issues debt at current low rates and uses the proceeds to repurchase one of its existing high–coupon rate debt issues. Often these are callable issues, which means the company can purchase the debt at a call price lower than the market price.

registration statement Required by the Securities and Exchange Commission before a company's securities can be offered to the public. This statement is used to summarize various pieces of financial and legal information about the company.

reinvestment rate risk Occurs when a short-term debt security must be "rolled over." If interest rates have fallen, then the reinvestment of principal will be at a lower rate with correspondingly lower interest payments and ending value.

relative priority doctrine More flexible than absolute priority. Gives a more balanced consideration to all claimants in a bankruptcy reorganization than does the absolute priority doctrine.

relaxed net operating working capital policy A policy under which relatively large amounts of cash, marketable securities, and inventories are carried and under which sales are stimulated by a liberal credit policy, resulting in a high level of receivables.

reorder point The inventory level at which a new order is placed.

reorganization in bankruptcy A court-approved attempt to keep a company alive by changing its capital structure in lieu of liquidation. A reorganization must adhere to the standards of fairness and feasibility.

repatriation of earnings The cash flow, usually in the form of dividends or royalties, from the foreign branch or subsidiary to the parent company. These cash flows must be converted to the currency of the parent and thus are subject to future exchange rate changes. A foreign government may restrict the amount of cash that may be repatriated.

replacement chain (common life) approach A method of comparing mutually exclusive projects that have unequal lives. Each project is replicated so that they will both terminate in a common year. If projects with lives of 3 years and 5 years are being evaluated, then the 3-year project would be replicated 5 times and the 5-year project replicated 3 times; thus, both projects would terminate in 15 years.

required rate of return, r_s The minimum acceptable rate of return, considering both its risk and the returns available on other investments.

reserve borrowing capacity Exists when a firm uses less debt under "normal" conditions than called for by the trade-off theory. This allows the firm some flexibility to use debt in the future when additional capital is needed.

residual distribution model In this model, firms should pay dividends only when more earnings are available than needed to support the optimal capital budget.

residual value The market value of the leased property at the expiration of the lease. The estimate of the residual value is one of the key elements in lease analysis.

restricted charitable contributions Donations that can be used only for designated purposes.

restricted net operating working capital policy A policy under which holdings of cash, securities, inventories, and receivables are minimized.

restricted voting rights A provision that automatically deprives a shareholder of voting rights if the shareholder owns more than a specified amount of stock.

retained earnings The portion of the firm's earnings that have been saved rather than paid out as dividends.

retiree health benefits A major issue for employers because of the escalating costs of health care and a recent FASB ruling forcing companies to accrue the retiree health care liability rather than expensing the cash flows as they occur.

return on common equity (ROE) Found by dividing net income by common equity.

return on invested capital (ROIC) Net operating profit after taxes divided by the operating capital.

return on total assets (ROA) The ratio of net income to total assets.

revaluation Occurs when the relative price of a currency is increased. It is the opposite of devaluation.

revenue bonds Type of municipal bonds which are secured by the revenues derived from projects such as roads and bridges, airports, water and sewage systems, and not-for-profit health care facilities.

reverse split Situation in which shareholders exchange a particular number of shares of stock for a smaller number of new shares.

revolving credit agreement A formal, committed line of credit extended by a bank or other lending institution.

rights offering Occurs when a corporation sells a new issue of common stock to its existing stockholders. Each stockholder receives a certificate, called a stock purchase right, giving the stockholder the option to purchase a specified number of the new shares. The rights are issued in proportion to the amount of stock that each shareholder currently owns.

risk arbitrage The practice of purchasing stock in companies (in the context of mergers) that may become takeover targets.

risk aversion A risk-averse investor dislikes risk and requires a higher rate of return as an inducement to buy riskier securities.

risk premium for Stock i, RP_i The extra return that an investor requires to hold risky Stock i instead of a risk-free asset.

risk-adjusted discount rate Incorporates the risk of the project's cash flows. The cost of capital to the firm reflects the average risk of the firm's existing projects. Thus, new projects that are riskier than existing projects should have a higher risk-adjusted discount rate. Conversely, projects with less risk should have a lower risk-adjusted discount rate.

roadshow Before an IPO, the senior management team and the investment banker make presentations to potential investors. They make three to five presentations daily over a 2-week period in 10 to 20 cities.

S corporation A small corporation that, under Subchapter S of the Internal Revenue Code, elects to be taxed as a proprietorship or a partnership yet retains limited liability and other benefits of the corporate form of organization.

safety stock Inventory held to guard against larger-than-normal sales and/or shipping delays.

sale-and-leaseback A type of financial lease in which the firm owning the property sells it to another firm, often a financial institution, while simultaneously entering into an agreement to lease the property back from the firm.

salvage value The market value of an asset after its useful life.

scenario analysis A shorter version of simulation analysis that uses only a few outcomes. Often the outcomes are for three scenarios: optimistic, pessimistic, and most likely.

seasonal effects on ratios Seasonal factors can distort ratio analysis. At certain times of the year, a firm may have excessive inventories in preparation of a "season" of high demand. Therefore, an inventory turnover ratio taken at this time will be radically different than one taken after the season.

secondary market Markets in which securities are resold after initial issue in the primary market. The New York Stock Exchange is an example.

secured loan A loan backed by collateral, which is often in the form of inventories or receivables.

Securities and Exchange Commission (SEC) A government agency which regulates the sales of new securities and the operations of securities exchanges. The SEC, along with other government agencies and self-regulation, helps ensure stable markets, sound brokerage firms, and the absence of stock manipulation.

securitization The process whereby financial instruments that were previously thinly traded are converted to a form that creates greater liquidity. Securitization also applies to the situation where specific assets are pledged as collateral for securities, thus creating asset-backed securities. One example of the former is junk bonds; an example of the latter is mortgage-backed securities.

Security Market Line (SML) Represents, in a graphical form, the relationship between the risk of an asset as measured by its beta and the required rates of return for individual securities. The SML equation is one of the key results of the CAPM: $r_i = r_{RF} + b_i(r_M - r_{RF})$.

semistrong form of market efficiency States that current market prices reflect all publicly available information. Therefore, the only way to gain abnormal returns on a stock is to possess inside information about the company's stock.

sensitivity analysis Indicates exactly how much net present value will change in response to a given change in an input variable, other things held constant. Sensitivity analysis is sometimes called "what if" analysis because it answers this type of question.

shareholder rights provision Also known as a poison pill, it allows existing shareholders to purchase additional shares of stock at a price that is lower than the market value if a potential acquirer purchases a controlling stake in the company.

shelf registration Frequently, companies will file a master registration statement and then update it with a short-form statement just before an offering. This procedure is termed shelf registration because companies put new securities "on the shelf" and then later sell them when the market is right.

short hedges Occur when futures contracts are sold to guard against price declines.

simple interest The situation when interest is not compounded; that is, interest is not earned on interest. Also called regular interest. Divide the nominal interest rate by 365 and multiply by the number of days the funds are borrowed to find the interest for the term borrowed.

sinking fund Facilitates the orderly retirement of a bond issue. This can be achieved in one of two ways: (1) the company can call in for redemption (at par value) a certain percentage of bonds each year; or (2) the company may buy the required amount of bonds on the open market.

social value Projects of not-for-profit businesses are expected to provide a social value in addition to an economic value.

soft currencies Currencies of countries that set the exchange rate but do not allow their currencies to be traded on world markets.

special tax bonds Type of municipal bonds which are secured by a specified tax, such as a tax on utility services.

speculative balances Funds held by a firm in order to have cash for taking advantage of bargain purchases or growth opportunities.

spin-off Occurs when a holding company distributes the stock of one of the operating companies to its shareholders, thus passing control from the holding company to the shareholders directly.

spontaneously generated funds Funds generated if a liability account increases spontaneously (automatically) as sales increase. An increase in a liability account is a source of funds, thus funds have been generated. Two examples of spontaneous liability accounts are accounts payable and accrued wages. Notes payable, although a current liability account, is not a spontaneous source of funds because an increase in notes payable requires a specific action between the firm and a creditor.

spot rate The exchange rate that applies to "on the spot" trades or, more precisely, to exchanges that occur two days following the day of trade (in other words, current exchanges).

spread The difference between the price at which an underwriter sells the stock in an initial public offering and the proceeds that the underwriter passes on to the issuing firm; the fee collected by the underwriter. It is often about 7% of the offering price.

stakeholders All parties that have an interest, financial or otherwise, in a not-for-profit business.

stand-alone risk The risk an investor takes by holding only one asset.

standard deviation, σ A statistical measure of the variability of a set of observations. It is the square root of the variance.

statement of cash flows Reports the impact of a firm's operating, investing, and financing activities on cash flows over an accounting period.

statement of stockholders' equity Statement showing the beginning stockholders' equity, any changes due to stock issues/repurchases, the amount of net income that is retained, and the ending stockholders' equity.

stepped-up strike (or exercise) price A provision in a warrant that increases the strike price over

time. This provision is included to encourage owners to exercise their warrants.

stock dividend Increases the number of shares outstanding but at a slower rate than splits. Current shareholders receive additional shares on some proportional basis. Thus, a holder of 100 shares would receive 5 additional shares at no cost if a 5% stock dividend were declared.

stock option Allows its owner to purchase a share of stock at a fixed price, called the strike price or the exercise price, no matter what the actual price of the stock is. Stock options always have an expiration date, after which they cannot be exercised.

stock repurchase Occurs when a firm repurchases its own stock. These shares of stock are then referred to as treasury stock.

stock split Current shareholders are given some number (or fraction) of shares for each stock share owned. Thus, in a 3-for-1 split, each shareholder would receive three new shares in exchange for each old share, thereby tripling the number of shares outstanding. Stock splits usually occur when the stock price is outside of the optimal trading range.

strategic options Options that often deal with strategic issues. Also called real options, embedded options, and managerial options.

stretching accounts payable The practice of deliberately paying accounts late.

strike (or exercise) price The price stated in the option contract at which the security can be bought (or sold).

strong form of market efficiency Assumes that all information pertaining to a stock, whether public or inside information, is reflected in current market prices. Thus, no investors would be able to earn abnormal returns in the stock market.

structured note A debt obligation derived from another debt obligation. Permits a partitioning of risks to give investors what they want.

subordinated debenture Debentures that have claims on assets, in the event of bankruptcy, only after senior debt (as named in the subordinated debt's indenture) has been paid off. Subordinated debentures may be subordinated to designated notes payable or to all other debt.

sunk cost A cost that has already occurred and is not affected by the capital project decision. Sunk costs are not relevant to capital budgeting decisions.

swap An exchange of cash payment obligations. Usually occurs because the parties involved prefer someone else's payment pattern or type.

sweetener A feature that makes a security more attractive to some investors, thereby inducing them to accept a lower current yield. Convertible features and warrants are examples of sweeteners.

synchronization of cash flows Occurs when firms are able to time cash receipts to coincide with cash requirements.

synergy Occurs when the whole is greater than the sum of its parts. When applied to mergers, a synergistic merger occurs when the post-merger earnings exceed the sum of the separate companies' pre-merger earnings.

takeover An action whereby a person or group succeeds in ousting a firm's management and taking control of the company.

tapping fund assets Deals with the issue of allowing a corporation to invest its pension fund assets to the corporation's own advantage.

target capital structure The relative amount of debt, preferred stock, and common equity that the firm desires. The weighted average cost of capital should be based on these target weights.

target cash balance The desired cash balance that a firm plans to maintain in order to conduct business.

target company A firm that another company seeks to acquire.

target distribution ratio Percentage of net income distributed to shareholders through cash dividends or stock repurchases.

target payout ratio Percentage of net income paid as a cash dividend.

targeted share repurchases Also known as greenmail, occurs when a company buys back stock from a potential acquirer at a price that is higher than the market price. In return, the potential acquirer agrees not to attempt to take over the company.

tax loss carryback and carryforward Ordinary corporate operating losses can be carried backward for 2 years or forward for 20 years to offset taxable income in a given year.

tax preference theory Proposes that investors prefer capital gains over dividends, because capital gains taxes can be deferred into the future but taxes on dividends must be paid as the dividends are received.

taxable income Gross income less a set of exemptions and deductions that are spelled out in the instructions to the tax forms that individuals must file.

technical analysts Stock analysts who believe that past trends or patterns in stock prices can be used to predict future stock prices.

temporary net operating working capital The NOWC required above the permanent level when the economy is strong and/or seasonal sales are high.

tender offer The offer of one firm to buy the stock of another by going directly to the stockholders, frequently over the opposition of the target company's management.

term structure of interest rates The relationship between yield to maturity and term to maturity for bonds of a single risk class.

terminal value Value of operations at the end of the explicit forecast period; equal to the present value of all free cash flows beyond the forecast period, discounted back to the end of the forecast period at the weighted average cost of capital.

time line A graphical representation used to show the timing of cash flows.

times-interest-earned (TIE) ratio Determined by dividing earnings before interest and taxes by the interest charges. This ratio measures the extent to which operating income can decline before the firm is unable to meet its annual interest costs.

total assets turnover ratio Measures the turnover of all the firm's assets; it is calculated by dividing sales by total assets.

total carrying cost The costs of carrying inventory.

total inventory costs The sum of ordering and carrying costs.

total net present value (TNPV) Equal to net present value plus net present social value in a not-for-profit business.

total ordering cost The costs of ordering inventory.

trade credit Debt arising from credit sales and recorded as an account receivable by the seller and as an account payable by the buyer.

trade deficit Occurs when a country imports more goods from abroad than it exports.

trade discounts Price reductions that suppliers offer customers for early payment of bills.

trade-off model The addition of financial distress and agency costs to either the MM tax model or the Miller model. In this model, the optimal capital structure can be visualized as a trade-off between the benefit of debt (the interest tax shelter) and the costs of debt (financial distress and agency costs).

transactions balance The cash balance associated with payments and collections; the balance necessary for day-to-day operations.

Treasury bond Bonds issued by the federal government; sometimes called T-bonds or government bonds. Treasury bonds have no default risk.

trend analysis An analysis of a firm's financial ratios over time. It is used to estimate the likelihood of improvement or deterioration in its financial situation.

uncollected balances schedule Helps a firm monitor its receivables better and also forecast future receivables balances; an integral part of the payments pattern approach.

underfunded pension plan The present value of expected retirement benefits exceeds the assets on hand.

underinvestment problem A type of agency problem in which high debt can cause managers to forgo positive NPV projects unless they are extremely safe.

underwritten arrangement Contract between a firm and an investment banker when stock is issued. An investment banker agrees to buy the entire issue at a set price and then resells the stock at the offering price. Thus, the risk of selling the issue rests with the investment banker.

value drivers The four value drivers are the growth rate in sales (g), operating profitability (OP = NOPAT/Sales), capital requirements (CR= Capital/Sales), and the weighted average cost of capital (WACC).

value of operations (V_{op}) The present value of all expected future free cash flows when discounted at the weighted average cost of capital.

value-based management Managing a firm with shareholder value in mind. It typically involves use of a model of shareholder value, such as the corporate value model.

variance, σ^2 A measure of the distribution's variability. It is the sum of the squared deviations about the expected value.

venture capitalist The manager of a venture capital fund. The fund raises most of its capital from institutional investors and invests in start-up companies in exchange for equity.

vertical merger Occurs when a company acquires another firm that is "upstream" or "downstream"; for example, an automobile manufacturer acquires a steel producer.

vesting If an employee has the right to receive pension benefits even if they leave the company prior to retirement, their rights are said to be vested.

vesting period Period during which employee stock options cannot be exercised.

warrant A call option, issued by a company, that allows the holder to buy a stated number of shares of stock from the company at a specified price. Warrants are generally distributed with debt, or preferred stock, to induce investors to buy those securities at lower cost.

weak form of market efficiency Assumes that all information contained in past price movements is fully reflected in current market prices. Thus, information about recent trends in a stock's price is of no use in selecting a stock.

weighted average cost of capital (WACC) The weighted average of the after-tax component costs of capital—debt, preferred stock, and common equity. Each weighting factor is the proportion of that type of capital in the optimal, or target, capital structure.

white knight A friendly competing bidder that a target management likes better than the company making a hostile offer; the target solicits a merger with the white knight as a preferable alternative.

window dressing Techniques employed by firms to make their financial statements look better than they really are.

working capital A firm's investment in short-term assets—cash, marketable securities, inventory, and accounts receivable.

workout Voluntary reorganization plans arranged between creditors and generally sound companies experiencing temporary financial difficulties. Workouts typically require some restructuring of the firm's debt.

Yankee bonds Bond issued by a foreign borrower denominated in dollars and sold in the United States under SEC regulations.

yield curve The curve that results when yield to maturity is plotted on the y-axis with term to maturity on the x-axis.

yield to call (YTC) The rate of interest earned on a bond if it is called. If current interest rates are well below an outstanding callable bond's coupon rate, then the YTC may be a more relevant estimate of expected return than the YTM because the bond is likely to be called.

yield to maturity (YTM) The rate of interest earned on a bond if it is held to maturity.

zero coupon bond Pays no coupons at all but is offered at a substantial discount below its par value and hence provides capital appreciation rather than interest income.

Name Index

Subject Index